Pelican Books
Iran: Dictatorship and Development

Fred Halliday was born in Dublin in 1946 and studied at Queen's College, Oxford, and the School of Oriental and African Studies, London. He has edited Isaac Deutscher's *Russia, China and the West 1953–1965* (Penguin, 1969); translated Karl Korsch's *Marxism and Philosophy* (1971); and is the author of *Arabia without Sultans* (Penguin, 1974). He is on the editorial board of *New Left Review* and a Fellow of the Transnational Institute.

Fred Halliday

IRAN:
Dictatorship and Development

Penguin Books

Penguin Books Ltd, Harmondsworth,
Middlesex, England
Penguin Books, 625 Madison Avenue,
New York, New York 10022, U.S.A.
Penguin Books Australia Ltd, Ringwood,
Victoria, Australia
Penguin Books Canada Ltd, 2801 John Street,
Markham, Ontario, Canada L3R 1B4
Penguin Books (N.Z.) Ltd, 182–190 Wairau Road,
Auckland 10, New Zealand

First published 1979

Made and printed in Great Britain by
Richard Clay (The Chaucer Press) Ltd, Bungay, Suffolk
Set in Linotype Times

Contents

Author's Preface

This book is intended to give a general introduction to contemporary Iran, and in particular to political and economic developments since the early 1960s.

The first chapter provides a summary account of Iranian society in the twentieth century, and the next three discuss at greater length specific aspects of the state – its historical origins, its main contemporary characteristics, and the instruments of repression that are so central to it. There follow two chapters on the state's economic policies, the first dealing with developments in the rural sector, and the second with industrialization. The final three chapters analyse political questions: the opposition, the Shah's foreign policy, and the future of the present régime in the light of the 1978 crisis.

While the stance of this book is antagonistic to that of the present Iranian government and its international allies, and is written in solidarity with those opposed to it, the analysis is that of one independent and necessarily isolated observer. It does not represent the views of any one section of the Iranian opposition, and it is probable that all of the Shah's Iranian opponents will find something in this work with which they disagree.

Of the many people who have helped me to write this book there are two to whom I owe a special debt: to Maxine Molyneux, who at every stage advised and encouraged me, and whose scrupulous reading did much to improve the original manuscript; and to Eqbal Ahmad, who first proposed to me that I write this study, and who provided me with generous moral and financial support through the Third World Project of the Transnational Institute. I would also like to thank Perry Anderson, Anthony Barnett and Jon Halliday, all of whom read the manuscript in part or in whole and made many fruitful suggestions. Nikki Keddie kindly read the text at the request of the publishers. Finally, I would like to thank all those Iranian friends who over the past decade and more, in Iran and in exile, discussed their country with me, from a variety of perspectives. It only remains to say that the responsibility for whatever errors of fact and judgement this book contains is mine alone.

Fred Halliday
London, September 1978

1 Iranian Society: An Overview

At the start of the twentieth century Iran was an overwhelmingly rural society, with a very weak central government. While not a formal colony of any imperial power, it was in many ways vulnerable to the pressures exerted on it by Russia and Britain. It was in no adequate sense independent. Today Iran is in the midst of a comprehensive economic and social upheaval, a process directed if not controlled by a strong state; and even though foreign influences still affect Iran in many ways, and its ruling class is inextricably tied to the capitalist west, there is no doubt that the country enjoys a degree of political independence unthinkable three quarters of a century ago. Moreover, Iran has been able to arrogate to itself a substantial role in the affairs of the Gulf region and beyond, and has become a significant second-ranking power in international relations – on a par with such states as India, Saudi Arabia and Brazil. Before going into the more detailed analyses of this transformation and its limits contained in later sections, this chapter will provide some initial data on the changing character of Iranian society since 1900, and in particular on changes in demography, class and the position of women.[1]

Iran is a country of 627,000 square miles, i.e. over five times the size of Britain or Italy, and equal to the combined areas of Texas, New Mexico, Arizona and California. Its largest borders are with Russia on the north and Iraq on the west, but it also shares frontiers with Turkey in the north-west, and Afghanistan and Pakistan in the east and south-east respectively. Iran's southern border runs along the coast of the Persian Gulf.

At least 50 per cent of the total land area is desert, much of it in the centre of the country. The settled population lives in about 15 per cent of the total area and the concentrations are distributed around the western, southern and northern edges of the country. The desert, and the harsh mountain ranges that cross the country, have in the past divided the population centres from each other, and it is only in recent decades that a unified communications system, and a unified administration, have been imposed on the country.

The population has risen from an estimated 9·9 millions in 1900 to 14·6 millions in 1940, to 20·4 millions in the first census of 1956, 27·1 millions in 1966 and 33·6 millions in 1976. In population terms this makes Iran one of the major states of the region – surpassed, in 1976 figures, only by Pakistan, Turkey and Egypt (74·2, 41·0 and 37·2 millions respectively). Iran has by far the largest population of any of the Middle East oil states, though both Algeria and Iraq (17·3 and 11·5 millions in 1976) share comparable problems, those of developing a predominantly agricultural country through the deployment of temporary oil revenues. The other major producers such as Saudi Arabia, Libya and Kuwait are, in socio-economic terms, entities of a quite different kind having populations of five, five and one millions respectively and sharing neither the difficulties nor the potentialities of these larger more populated countries.

Until the 1930s the balance of rural and urban population remained relatively stable, with around 21 per cent of the total in the urban sector; by 1956 this had risen to 31 per cent, by 1966 to 39 per cent and by 1976 to 47 per cent. In 1976, out of the total 33·6 millions, 15·7 millions were living in urban areas and 17·9 millions in the rural; official estimates are that by 1992, when the total population will have risen to 53·5 millions, 57 per cent of the population will be in the urban sector and only 43 per cent in the rural.

There are three further demographic features that help to illuminate the structure of Iranian society. The first, a result of the geographic character of the country, is the extreme unevenness of population density. The greatest concentration is in the Central Province, which includes Tehran; in 1976 this accounted for 6·9 millions, or over a fifth of the total population. No second city remotely rivals Tehran in population or importance (it is over seven times larger than any other), and the gap between it and the other cities has been widening.

Table 1: Cities of Over a Quarter of a Million Inhabitants, 1976

Tehran	4,496,159
Isfahan	671,825
Mashad	670,180
Tabriz	598,576
Shiraz	414,408
Ahvaz	329,006
Abadan	296,081
Kermanshah	290,861

Source: *The Middle East and North Africa 1977–1978*, p. 349.

Apart from the Central Province, the most populated provinces are those in the north, where a plentiful rainfall supports the richest agriculture in the country, and in Khuzestan, the oil-producing province in the south. On the other hand, half of the country has a population density of less than five persons per square mile (see map, pp 334–5). The consequence is that, while in comparison with other even more arid Middle Eastern countries Iran has a relatively populated surface, it is sparsely covered in comparison with many other Asian countries. India, for example, supports a population eighteen times as large in an area that is only twice as extensive (622 millions, 1·26 million sq. miles).

A second feature, one of declining but continuing importance, is the presence in Iran of a nomadic population, all of it drawn from tribes speaking languages other than Persian and most of whom have entered what is now Iran in the time since the advent of Islam in the seventh century A.D. In 1800 up to 50 per cent of the population may have been nomadic, and in 1900 between a third and a quarter – perhaps 2·5 millions out of a total of 9·9 millions – was unsettled. Since the 1930s the government has been restricting the migration of nomads and has tried to make them sedentary, whilst economic pressures have attracted nomadic men away from herding and into construction and other non-agricultural branches of employment. According to the 1976 census 2 million people, or 6 per cent of the total population, are still classified as 'unsettled', although this covers both groups that are constantly nomadic and those who move between two, relatively constant, winter and summer grazing areas. While there is reason to believe that the government may be understating the figure for nomads, there is every indication that the tendency for their proportion in the population to decline will continue.

A third very important feature is the linguistic and ethnic diversity of Iran (see map, p. 338). The most important language in Iran is undoubtedly Persian, an Indo-European language, close to Kurdish, Urdu and the Pushtu language of Afghanistan. But, despite official attempts to picture Iran as a linguistically homogeneous country, only about half of the total population have Persian as their first tongue, and the Persian speakers may even be less than half, being thereby a minority, though certainly the largest of the minorities, in Iran.

Authoritative figures are not available, and the following percentage breakdown is probably as close as current conditions permit:

Table 2: Linguistic Groupings in Iranian Society

Language	*Percentage*
Persian	50·2
Azerbaijani	20·6
Gilani	6·1
Luri-Bakhtiari	5·7
Kurdish	5·6
Mazanderani	4·9
Baluchi	2·3
Arabic	2·0
Turkomeni	1·7
Armenian	0·6
Assyrian	0·4

Source: Marvin Zonis, *The Political Élite of Iran*, p. 179.

It is a matter of debate how far these separate linguistic groups also constitute separate 'nationalities'. Probably the Gilani and Mazanderani groups, whose languages are very close to Persian, cannot be regarded as separate ethnic groups, but the Kurds, the Baluchis, the Arabs and those speaking Turkic languages (Azerbaijani, Luri-Bakhtiari, Turkomeni) are ethnically distinct from the dominant Persian-speaking category.[2]

The economic development of Iran has been accompanied by definite, if still uneven, improvements in health and education. The biggest problem has been that the half of the population living outside the urban areas have been affected by these changes to a much smaller extent than those in the towns and cities (see p. 120). In response to improved economic and health conditions, population growth has risen from 0·75 per cent per annum in 1900–1920 to an estimated 3·2 per cent in the early 1970s, a high rate which the government now wishes to reduce. The 1976 census revealed that 53 per cent of all Iranians are under the age of 20, and 45 per cent under 16. But despite substantial injections of oil revenues into the economy and some expansion in health services, Iran's health situation is not substantially different from that of other countries in Asia which might be expected to be worse off. In the early 1970s life expectancy at 50 years was one year less than that in India, and infant mortality at 139 per thousand was the same as India's.[3]

Similar problems can be identified in the field of education. While there has been undoubted expansion in Iran's school and university system, literacy is still restricted to a minority of the adult population – rising from 5 per cent in 1900, to 15 per cent in 1956 and between 30 and 35 per cent in the 1970s, on official estimates. But unofficial estimates dispute the state's figure as being inflated, and the rates of illiteracy in the countryside certainly remain much higher than in the towns. At the higher level, there has been a massive expansion in university education – the number of students rising from 25,000 in 1965 to 170,000 in 1977, with a further 55,000 believed to be studying abroad. Prior to this recent expansion Iran had a much lower proportion of students than other comparable developing countries, such as India, Egypt and Iraq,[4] and the lack of an available stock of qualified personnel has been, and remains, a considerable block to Iran's development.

Beyond these statistics, it is possible in some measure to chart the development of Iranian society in terms of employment pattern and class composition. We have no accurate data on the class character of Iran, but certain general features can be identified. In 1900 the great majority of those economically active outside the home, 90 per cent, were either in agriculture or in the nomadic sector. There was almost no industry, and the remaining 10 per cent were in handicrafts, trade and service. The socially dominant classes were comprised of the tribal leaders, larger landowners, merchants, and aristocrats in the court and civil service. Despite their land ownership, many of the agricultural proprietors lived in the towns.

This pattern changed very little up to the 1940s, even though the actual membership of the landowning class was altered by Reza Shah's acquisitions in the 1920s and 1930s. The state's power remained conditional on the compliance of the pre-existing rural potentates and on the effectiveness of the new central army. Since the 1940s there have been profound changes in Iranian society, which may be summarized as follows:

1. there has been a decline in the position of tribal leaders and of many landowners, as a result of land redistribution and the increased power of the state at village level. Some tribal leaders and landowners have been integrated into the new administrative and economic system, but, while benefiting from this, they have still had to surrender much of their former power.

2. as large estates have been distributed, and previous relations in the countryside dissolved, there has been an expansion in the numbers of farmers with enough land for themselves and their families (3–10 hectares), and in the numbers of landless wage-earning labourers. About thirty-three per cent of those economically active in 1978 still work in agriculture.

3. there has been a shift in the power of the religious leaders, the *ulema* or *mollahs*, who have lost their lands in the reforms, and have become dependent on donations from followers; simultaneously, with the expansion in banks, other state credit institutions and a modern commercial sector, there has been

some decline in the power of the bazaar, although it still controls a third of imports and two-thirds of retail trade.

4. the shift of population from country to town and the expansion in urban employment possibilities has created a massive non-agricultural wage-earning class: in 1977 there were 2·5 million people employed in manufacturing, and another 1 million in construction, out of a total economically active population of 10·4 millions.

5. the state has become the dominant force in the economy and a major employer. Precise figures are not available, but in 1977 around 350,000 people were in the armed forces, and as many as 800,000 in forms of direct civilian state employment, 160,000 of them in education. However, the state was responsible for the employment of a much wider section of the population, in state-run economic enterprises and financial institutions. At least 10 per cent of all those in employment could be said to be government employees, and the number of those indirectly employed, or dependent on state funds for their employment, was probably much higher.

6. the composition of the new Iranian dominant class reflects these recent economic changes. Its three main sections are the upper stratum of the armed forces and of the civil service, the richer capitalist landowners, and the financiers and entrepreneurs benefiting from the oil boom. While no precise data are available to make possible a proper analysis of this new dominant class, its existence is reflected in ownership terms, where a small number of large-scale Iranian capitalists cooperate with the state in industry, commerce and agriculture, and in wealth terms, where the top 10 per cent of the population account for up to 40 per cent of consumption.

7. between the new ruling class and the growing number of wage-labourers in town and country, there exists a new intermediate stratum which is also probably expanding. In the countryside this includes the small but self-sufficient farmers mentioned under section (1); in the urban areas it includes the lower ranks of the civil service, those in the new distributive trade and other services, as well as white-collar workers in factories. In Iran, as in other developing and developed capi-

talist countries, the composition and political orientation of this stratum is and will be of great imporance for the outcome of the overarching conflict between the dominant and wage-earning classes.

The following schematic presentation of changes in employment structure between 1956 and 1972 gives an indication of recent changes and of the relative social weight of different groups:

Table 3: Employment Structure, 1956 and 1972

Category	*1956*	*1972*
Professional, Technical, Related	1·6%	3·5%
Administrative, Management, Clerical	3·1%	4·3%
Sales	5·8%	8·5%
Service	7·7%	6·3%
Agricultural Workers	55·6%	48·5%
Production Workers	22·6%	28·7%
Workers not Classified Elsewhere	3·6%	0·2%

Source: *Iran: Past, Present and Future.*

Such an employment breakdown cannot, of itself, be a guide to the class character of Iranian society, but it does indicate the more general trends, and proportions, within the society as a whole. In subsequent chapters there will be further discussion of these changes in the light of growth of the state, the land reform and industrialization programmes, and of the growth in the size of the Iranian working class.

The final area of consideration is the manner in which recent changes have affected the position of women in Iranian society. In economic terms (see also p. 191) women in Iran were historically present in nomadic activities, in agriculture, and in handicraft workshops. As incomes rise there may have been a slight fall in the rate of rural female economic activity outside the home, since husbands prefer their wives not to work, but there has been a rise in the level of female employment in the towns, which was running at around 11 per cent in the mid-1970s, a low figure for the third world generally, but a high figure for Muslim countries (see p. 192). Women remain, however, in an inferior economic position in many respects. Female illiteracy is about 20 per cent higher than that for men, although the gap is closing, with the result that women work, on average, in the most unskilled and lowest-paid jobs.

Marriage patterns have gradually changed in response to legislation and to economic pressures, but, as with other aspects of social activity, the official figure is too rosy a one, and the countryside lags far behind the towns. The Muslim system of polygamy, under which a man can have four wives, is still legal, although a wife must give her written consent prior to her own marriage that the husband can take a further wife. One way around this has been for the husband to trick the (often illiterate) wife. There has however been an undoubted decline in the numbers of polygamous marriages if only for economic reasons, and the great majority of Iranian marriages are now monogamous. A specifically Iranian institution was *sighe*, a form of temporary marriage, in which a man took a woman as his wife for a limited period. This was, in practice, a form of legalized prostitution and has been banned by the 1967 Family Protection Act, although *mollahs* are believed to be still sanctioning it in some of the more traditional towns. The 1967 Act also imposed minimum ages for marriage – 15 years for girls, and 18 for boys – but here too there is believed to be considerable circumvention in the rural areas.

Beyond these specific institutional changes, it is much less certain how much alteration has occurred in the ways in which men relate to and regard women. Women have been allowed to imitate western consumption patterns – when they can afford this – but whilst young Iranian males have tried to adopt the sexually freer practices of the west, Iranian women have been prevented from doing so and women are still tightly controlled by the menfolk around them, their fathers, brothers, uncles and husbands. Virginity in women is still highly valued, and those women who disregard prevailing norms are usually severely punished. A dual standard therefore operates, not only as between men and women, but between which aspects of western behaviour are, and are not, permissible.[5]

The government itself has put itself forward as the champion of women, but, as with land reform and official trades unions, such a move is designed both to introduce changes in Iranian society necessary to its smoother functioning, and to pre-empt the emergence of movements independent of the state and making radical demands upon it. As in these other cases, it would be just as erroneous to regard the 1967 Family Protection Act, and other legislative and executive actions relating to women, as mere token reforms, as it would be to believe that the underlying inequalities facing Iranian women (or peasants or workers) had been confronted and were being solved. The 1967 Act made illegal the worst abuses of the pre-existing system, but it still left men and women unequal in the family and in economic terms. The predominant posture of Iranian men towards their women is one of control and of superiority – an attitude by no means specific to Iran, but one which wider changes in social and economic life have, so far, done little to erode.

The government has introduced a population policy designed to reduce the birth rate from 3·2 to 2·4 per cent and has established a network of family planning clinics. Opposition to contraception comes not so much from religious leaders or sentiment (Islam is in general much less concerned with this matter than Christianity) but from the families and the husbands of women, where traditionally a large family was looked on with favour. The availability and acceptance of contraception is still limited in Iran, particularly among the poorer sections of the urban and rural population, but it can be anticipated that as state intervention and economic pressure combine some reduction in the birth rate will occur.

The development of Iran, especially noticeable since the early 1960s, has consequently produced a new social configuration, in both demographic and class terms, and with it new tensions have emerged. Despite the centralization of the country, and the official promotion of a unified culture and politics, and despite the apparent decline in overt social conflicts, the present socio-economic system is in several ways unstable. It will become more so as the temporary advantages provided by oil begin to recede. Tensions between the new wage-earning class in town and country and their oppressors, between women and men, between the subordinated ethnic groups and the Persian-speakers – all have been shaped by the rapid and often uncontrolled changes of the recent period. The following chapters will investigate in more detail the major aspects of this transformative process, and will examine some of the factors that appear likely to determine the outcome.

2 The State: Historical Background

The following discussion of contemporary Iran is focused on an analysis of the state. In all societies the state is the institution that monopolizes force and thereby enforces order in the interests of those holding power. In nearly all contemporary societies, capitalist as well as socialist, the state has adopted an interventionist role in the economy and directs economic activity in accordance with the priorities of those in power. Within the range of capitalist societies, the economic role of the state is especially pronounced in developing ones, since the weakness of the indigenous bourgeoisie has tended to draw the state even further into an economically executive position than has been the case in the more developed capitalist countries.

This pronounced role of the state under conditions of capitalist development has been particularly noticeable in Iran, for in addition to sharing the general features of developing capitalism (weak bourgeoisie, etc.) Iranian development has been fuelled by oil and it is a peculiarity of oil that the state alone is the recipient of the revenues from it. The state has therefore determined how the revenues have been channelled into the economy, which projects are provided with capital, and which social groups are given privileged access to the increased consumption possibilities oil provides. Discussion of the state and of the class interests represented in it is therefore essential to the analysis of the economic transformation Iran is undergoing.

Secondly, since political power is wielded through the state, it is possible, by studying it, to begin to unravel the seemingly obscure political system in Iran. In one sense there is no problem about how political power is wielded since the country appears to be ruled by one man, the Shah. But it is evident that one man cannot single-handedly rule thirty-four million people, hence there arises the question of what the classes are which sustain the Iranian state and collaborate with it. If there is a dominant class in Iran, in what sense can it be said to dominate if, as it appears, it has no direct means of influencing the policies of the royal dictator? Moreover, what are the broader interests that determine the context in which the state executes its economic and political policies? And why, if the political system is a dictatorial one, has it taken the specific form it has, that of a monarchist dictatorship, distinct in character from that to be seen in any other developing country?

A third consideration is that Iran is a country whose recent development has been to a considerable degree shaped by the international ties which it has had with the more advanced capitalist economies – in economic terms, through the sale of oil and through foreign investment in Iran, and in political and military terms through the alliance built since the Second World War with the U S A. In both the politico-military and economic spheres that intervention is mediated through the Iranian state, not through other private or sectoral elements in Iranian society. The question of the role of foreign influences in Iran is one that has traditionally lent itself to imprecision – to both exaggeration and undue minimization. In fact, the Shah has been neither as independent as he himself claims nor as reliant on foreign assistance as most of his enemies allege. But it is only possible to establish the nature of external influences in Iran and their changing pattern more precisely once the institution through which they operate has been investigated more closely. This chapter will therefore discuss the historical formation of the Iranian state; the following one will analyse its main contemporary characteristics.

The Five Crises

The contemporary Iranian state is the product of five major crises through which the Iranian political system has passed in the twentieth century. Each of these crises was an occasion on which the state had to face a challenge that was capable of removing the personnel actually in power and of enforcing substantial changes in its class character; in some cases the challenge was resisted, in others not. Each has, however, contributed to determining the specific way that the capitalist state has been constituted in Iran, and it is therefore necessary to look at them and to describe, in outline at least, how each has affected this state's formation.

1. The first of these crises was what is known as the Constitutional Revolution of 1905–11. It was an attempt by merchants and intellectuals to reform the monarchy and establish a constitution and a parliament; as an attempt to do this, it was a failure. Iran was, at that time, ruled by the Qajar dynasty of Shahs, who had held power since the late eighteenth century; but although the Qajars held all formal political power, and although these Shahs were not directly challenged from outside by any colonial force, their position was gradually weakened by their incapacity to administer the provinces outside Tehran and by the spread of foreign goods and commercial influence on the country. In 1891 a major national movement developed in protest against the granting of a tobacco monopoly to a British entrepreneur, and opposition amongst both merchants and *ulema* remained strong until it broke out again in 1906. The precise causes and course of the Constitutional Revolution are still a matter of dispute and do not concern us here: but it is important to register this event as the first in Iranian history in which an attempt was made to limit the power of the monarch and allot power to an elected assembly, the Majlis. The Constitutional Revolution was accompanied by considerable mobilizations of the population in at least two towns, Tehran and Tabriz, and in its later stages there emerged an armed force, the Mojahidin, who fought to defend the gains of the revolution against those opposed to it – the Shah, the Russians and some tribal leaders. In the end, in the period after 1908, it was the latter who triumphed: although the Majlis and the Constitution remained formally in existence, the Shahs were able to regain the position they had previously held. In the final analysis no revolution occurred, and the state was not fundamentally altered by these events.

2. The Qajars were saved above all by the relatively weak character of the forces against them (the latter were confined to the towns) and by the intervention of an outside agency, Tsarist Russia, to support it. The dynasty's end therefore came when this situation was reversed and when outside forces intervened to disrupt the Iranian situation during the First World War. Both British and Russian, as well as Turkish, forces invaded the country and the Russian Revolution removed the Qajars' main patron. By 1919 there was no central government of any adequate kind: separatist movements were in power in the provinces of Khuzistan, Gilan and Khorasan and in this context the only coherent Iranian force at the centre was the military unit established by Russian Cossack officers in 1879. With British encouragement to its leader this force of 3,000 men staged a bloodless coup on 21 February 1921. Within a short time the leader in question, Reza Khan, had established himself as the dominant political personality in the country, and in 1925 he deposed the Qajars. But, unlike Ataturk in Turkey, he did not establish a republic. A year later he made himself king, founding a new dynasty, the Pahlavis (named after an ancient Persian language). Between then and his deposition in 1941 Reza Shah, as he then became known, established the first centralized state in modern Iran. He built a modern army, which he used to enforce government control over the whole country. All separatist movements were crushed. He established the first ministerial system, developed educational, health and transport systems and, after 1934, began to encourage a small industrialization programme. Despite the many differences, the state established by Reza Shah in Iran also bore many similarities to that being built on the ruins of the Ottoman Empire by Turkey's new leader Ataturk. On the other hand, Reza Shah's endeavours were seriously limited: he made no attempt to alter agrarian relations in Iran and his capacity to develop the economy was thereby reduced by the low internal revenues available to him; the revenues from oil were also meagre and made up at most 25 per cent of his government's income. The state he created provided the context for the later capitalist development of Iran but it was incapable itself of

initiating the major changes required in this direction.[1]

3. Reza Khan's rule was, like that of his Qajar predecessors, terminated by outside military intervention. Following the German invasion of Russia in June 1941, the Allies wanted to send supplies to the Russian front through Iran and, since Reza Shah allegedly opposed this, he was ousted by an Anglo-Russian invasion in August 1941. He went into exile, and his son, then aged twenty-two, became Shah. This Allied invasion almost destroyed the Pahlavi state: it was politically discredited by the failure to resist the foreign armies and was undermined by the political freedoms allowed to the opposition by the occupying forces. Liberties not enjoyed since the days of the Constitutional Revolution were restored: trades unions, a free press, rival political parties all thrived. On top of this, the occupation provoked serious economic problems, and at the end of the war two autonomous administrations were set up – in Kurdistan and Azerbaijan – with the support of the Red Army which occupied these areas. The Pahlavi régime was only able to re-establish its control because of a fortuitous international situation. On the one hand, the U S A, which had had military missions in the country since 1942, provided the régime with military and economic aid, as well as with political backing; Iran became, with Turkey and Greece, a country where the U S A declared it would assist anti-communist forces. On the other hand, the Soviet Union was, despite western claims to the contrary, prepared to placate the U S A, and in March 1946 it pulled its troops out, thereby abandoning the Azerbaijani and Kurdish republics to destruction by the Shah's army. By early 1947 the Shah's control extended once again over the whole country, and the strong Tudeh or communist party which had grown during the war years had been pushed onto the defensive. Meanwhile the economic crisis lessened. While it was too early to say that the Pahlavi dynasty's position had been fully restored, it had survived a most serious crisis and was gradually restoring political control.

4. In 1951 a new crisis developed over the issue of oil nationalization. Since the end of the world war, nationalist feeling in Iran had been directed against the continued ownership of the

country's oil by the British-owned Anglo-Iranian Oil Company; when in 1944 the Soviet Union had also tried to acquire an oil concession in the north, it too had become the object of similar antagonism. The leader of the oil protest movement, Mohammad Mossadeq, became prime minister in 1951: he led a coalition of Majlis deputies who formed a group called the National Front, and although this Front was never a coherent political organization it enjoyed a wide following in Tehran and other towns. The oil industry was nationalized soon after Mossadeq became premier and within a few months his government was in direct conflict with the Shah and through the Shah with the U S A, despite Mossadeq's initial attempts to win the latter over. In the end Mossadeq was ousted in August 1953 by a coalition of forces within and outside Iran – just as the Constitutional Revolution had been.

While Mossadeq had tried to gain U S support, he had met with little success, in particular because the 1952 U S Presidential elections had brought to power the more aggressively anti-communist administration of Eisenhower and Dulles. Although Mossadeq himself was not a communist, he was seen as opening the door to communist influence, and given Iran's geographic position on the borders of the Soviet Union, and the strained international climate at that time, the U S A was unwilling to take risks in that country. Had Mossadeq been able to consolidate his position, the U S A might have accepted him – especially since it was only in the last year of his government that the Tudeh Party supported Mossadeq openly. But Mossadeq was not able to stabilize the situation, and in the end he was overthrown by a coalition of internal and external foes.

There is now no doubt that the U S government, and specifically the C I A, played an active part in organizing the coup of 19 August 1953 that ousted Mossadeq, and that this intervention was the fruit of a build-up of the U S presence in Iran that had been under way since the war.[2] But it is misleading to attribute everything to this factor alone: Iranian nationalists tend to do so – and so, on occasion, does the C I A, keen to claim credit for a successful operation. The reality is not so simple since the C I A intervention was only possible because of the internal balance of forces in Iran, the existence of elements within the dominant class that were interested in acting against the Mossadeq régime and the weaknesses of Mossadeq's own position. Without the latter it would have been impossible for the U S A to act as it did; had Mossadeq had a following that was organized, and based on the oppressed in town and country, the resistance to the coup would have been much more substantial than it was. Moreover, there is no doubt that as the oil conflict continued and as the economic situation deteriorated following the end of oil revenues, so Mossadeq's popular support also declined. His attempt to challenge the monarch and the army was not based on any comparable alternative social base and the attempt which he led to alter the pattern of Iran's internal and international political alignments therefore failed. As a consequence the Pahlavi state emerged stronger than it had been prior to the oil crisis.

5. Since 1953 the Shah has been able to strengthen the state's power throughout Iran. All legal and constitutional freedoms were abrogated and within a few months the main centres of opposition had been crushed. For seven years after 1953 the régime concentrated on restoring its position. Then in the period 1960–63 a new crisis developed, one through which the state finally broke free of the constraints operating on it till then, and which enabled it to launch the full-scale capitalist development of Iran. Once again, the constituents of the crisis were both domestic and external.

The Iranian economy had been in recession since 1958, the budget was in deficit, and the Shah was in conflict with a number of civilian and military officials. In January 1961 the Kennedy Administration came to office in Washington and let it be known that it would only continue to support the Shah on condition that he put through a programme of reforms. A $35 millions U S loan was made dependent on certain policies being implemented. The U S position in Iran was similar to its position in Latin America where a reform programme, under the rubric of the Alliance for Progress, was launched to preempt the impact of the Cuban Revolution.[3] In both cases the Kennedy Administration believed that for political reasons the only way to preserve the pro-western (i.e. capitalist) states in the third world was to put through a reform programme, within which land reform held a special place.

This thinking accorded in some degree with that of elements inside Iran who were critical of the Shah. The latter's response was to adopt the slogans of his opponents and to push ahead vigorously with some of the reforms propounded by Washington. He announced a land reform programme, and expansion in social services and education, the whole package being presented in characteristically exaggerated terms as a 'White Revolution'. He also prosecuted some state employees for corruption and pretended to cut back on military expenditure. But he was less consistent in implementing other reforms that went against his logic of consolidating state power. Although he allowed elections in 1960 he never allowed the Majlis to work independently and in July 1962 dismissed the pro-American premier, Ali Amini, who had acted as one of the main advocates of the reforms but was regarded as too independent of the Shah himself. Popular opposition broke out most violently in June 1963 when the army had to be brought in to crush mass demonstrations led by *ulema* in Tehran and other cities, and when several thousand people are believed to have lost their lives.[4]

It is therefore evident that the period 1960–63 did mark a turning point in the development of the Iranian state. On the one hand it marked the time from which the state's promotion of rapid capitalist development can be dated. On the other hand it forced onto the defensive the different political forces that had resisted the Shah's consolidation of power, and the general strengthening of the Pahlavi state: landowners, tribal leaders, *ulema* from the traditional sector of the opposition, and the National Front, the Tudeh, the students and teachers on the other. It marked the end of any hope that the forces released during the 1941–53 period could soon reverse the verdict of the 1953 coup. Until the late 1970s the initiative lay with the régime, and the rises in oil revenue from 1971 onwards, by multiplying government revenues, gave an additional dynamism to the state's policies. The régime then had complete control of all public activities within Iran's boundaries. All independent political activity was banned. The state then became the major economic force and government development plans dictated the pace of the country's economic life. Independent economic agents – whether in agriculture or industry – operated with funds derived from the state. The cultural and ideological life of Iran was also under state domination. This lasted until 1978 when a popular upsurge opened the sixth crisis of the Iranian state.

The Relevance of the Past

This historical overview can help to answer one of the most important issues in discussion of Iran today, namely the relevance of the past to the present. The contemporary Iranian state is, obviously, a product of Iran's recent history, but what is not so obvious is *how* this history has affected it. There is, on one side, a considerable body of literature that analyses the Iranian state or political system in terms of an underlying *continuity*. Such analyses argue, for example, that Iran has always been ruled by Shahs, or that Iran is an Asiatic or oriental country, in which despotism is an inevitable feature of political life. If, as is sometimes conceded, these features are on the decline, they are, it is argued, still influential, and hence the Iranian political system can be characterized as a transitional one.[5]

An analogous approach is to draw attention to the indisputable fact that most Iranians (98 per cent) are Muslim, and to conclude that the Iranian state or Iranian 'political behaviour' is therefore in some sense 'Islamic', that there is perhaps something which can legitimately be called an 'Islamic social structure.'[6] Both historians and political scientists have produced analyses of this kind, seeking to explain the present monarchical régime in Iran by alluding to persistent influences of the Iranian past.

There are, however, strong grounds for arguing a different case: namely that there is a profound discontinuity between Iran prior to the First World War and Iran since then. The Iranian state today is a product of history, but in the sense of being a recent creation, not in the sense of being in any fundamental respect characterized by traditional features of Iranian society. These longer-term historical elements can explain only a certain amount and the onus is on those who stress continuity to prove precisely how features of the Iranian state and of Iranian politics discernible in the past are still operative in the present.

It is to some extent true that Iran has had Shahs over the past two and a half thousand years. There were in fact no monarchs ruling a unified Iran between 633 (the Arab invasion) and 1502 (the emergence of the Safavi state). But, leaving this aside, there is certainly a long history of monarchical rule in the country. This means that the institution of monarchy in the twentieth century must at least have benefited, to some degree, from the ideological heritage which this earlier history has provided. But this explains very little: values have to be re-created or reproduced with each generation, and there are plenty of monarchies that existed continuously as dynasties for centuries prior to this one and were swept away – the Hapsburgs in Austria after five centuries and the Wittelsbachs in Bavaria after ten, both at the end of the First World War. The question remains: why has monarchy continued in Iran? On closer examination, it becomes clear that the continuity is a superficial one. The two Shahs of the Pahlavi dynasty have ruled in a manner quite distinct from that of those who went before them, and the social classes associated with the régime today are quite different from those associated with the monarchy in the nineteenth century. (There are further differences between Reza Shah and his son.) Moreover, whereas the monarchy had very little power over the rest of the country a century ago, it now commands a unified and highly centralized country. There is no substantive continuity between the monarchy of today and that of previous centuries; indeed, in the 1920s the institution essentially disappeared only to be reconstituted on a quite new basis by the military dictator Reza Khan.

This state is therefore quite different from that which existed one hundred years ago. It is capitalist, whereas the other was pre-capitalist. It controls the whole of its national territory, whereas the other's writ did not run outside the main cities. It promotes economic development, whereas the other neglected it. It has a large standing army, whereas the other had virtually no armed force at all. It has to a considerable extent transformed socio-economic relations in the Iranian countryside, whereas the other left the countryside alone. These are the most striking differences between the Pahlavi state and its Qajar predecessor: they are the product of the way in which the state has come through the five crises of the twentieth century and mark out the gulf between the two states, a gulf that is far more significant than the fact that both states have been presided over by men calling themselves 'Shah'.

Similar problems attach to explanations of Iran in terms of its having an Islamic 'state' or 'society'. Since most Iranians are Muslims it is true that, in the past, political protests were often phrased in Islamic terminology and that the social group associted with conducting prayers in the mosque, the *ulema* or *mollahs*, played an active and distinctive role. Today a substantial opposition to the Shah's policies certainly exists amongst people of a religious orientation, and, as in Turkey, Pakistan and Egypt, much of this protest is formulated in Islamic terms.

But there are theoretical and empirical reasons for doubting the use of categories based on the influence of Islam as such. First, the principles of Islam can be read to justify both rebellion and submission to authority: there are strands which urge believers to accept the existing powers, and ones which reject temporal authority as a form of usurpation. Both can be detected in the doctrines of Shi'a Islam, the tendency dominant in Iran. The actual choice of political position is given not by religion as such, but by other forces in society that condition the impact of religion. In empirical terms, moreover, the role of Islamic ideology in Iranian society has until recently been less than in other Muslim countries. Compared with its Arab neighbours in the Middle East, or with Pakistan and Turkey, Iranian political life has in recent decades been influenced to a smaller degree by Islam. Mossadeq, for example, couched his nationalist appeals in secular terms, and those political groups that have been explicitly Islamic have, in the past, had no mass followings. Moreover, as we shall discuss below (p. 60), Islam is a rather insignificant part of the régime's official ideology. The emergence in the 1970s of a widespread opposition movement of an Islamic kind in protest at the régime's policies therefore represents a departure from the pattern of recent decades.

Even less helpful than Islam is explanation of Iran in terms of its supposedly 'Asiatic' character: there is no such thing as a specifically 'Asian' political system, nor is it of any value to invoke concepts of 'Asiatic despotism' to illumine Iranian history. The whole model of a specifically Asiatic economic, social or political system is unfounded, and has done more to obscure than to clarify the study of social formations in the third world.

Causes of Dictatorship

It is by invoking other historically located categories that it becomes possible to identify certain ways in which the past *has* shaped the contemporary character of Iran. In particular, attention can be focused on Iran's relation to imperialism and the growth of class forces. The country has had a relation to the outside world at once less and more involved than other third-world countries. Iran was never colonized in the sense of being formally ruled from abroad, or of having white emigrants settle in it, or of having a substantial part of its economy transformed to meet the economic requirements of the more developed capitalist countries. The very problem with the oil industry was that it was not like mining or plantations which do employ considerable numbers of people and thereby affect the whole economy to some degree: oil failed to do this to any extent. Therefore, despite the scale of oil operations and the role of oil in the international economy, the pre-capitalist class structure survived much longer than elsewhere and capitalism developed in the Iranian economy as a whole much later than in many other third-world countries. After 1921, Reza Shah's state provided some of the pre-conditions for the transformation of Iran by capitalism, but until after the Second World War the majority of the Iranian population lived in a countryside where pre-capitalist relations prevailed (see p. 105). It was only state intervention, via land reform, that turned Iran into a predominantly capitalist country.

The result of this history was that the state established by Reza Shah was not, as is that in many other Asian and African countries, a post-colonial state, in the sense of one that owed its very existence to the links between local bureaucrats and imperialist states outside.[5] Rather, the Iranian state was created in a comparatively independent manner and only afterwards was a close relationship with a stronger outside power built. Another feature often associated with the post-colonial state is the close relationship existing between bureaucrats and landowners: this too has been absent in Iran. While relying on the passive support of the landowners the early Pahlavi state remained to a considerable extent separate from the Iranian landowning class; when the opportunity came to transform agrarian relations in the 1960s the state was able to impose its own policies on the landowners who resisted change.

What has given outside powers such a special interest in Iran has been its strategic situation between Russia and the Gulf. This was important in the nineteenth century when the British were concerned about the approaches to India (and when oil was not even discovered) and has remained the main reason to this day: the advanced capitalist world could survive the loss of Iranian oil. It did so in 1951 and could do so again. But it would feel mortally threatened by an anti-capitalist state in Iran that would affect the oil-producing Gulf area as a whole. Since the Second World War it is because of the global conflict between the Soviet Union and the U S A that the latter has intervened directly in Iranian politics and society and has, since the mid-1960s, come to allocate such a major role to Iran. The Pahlavi state has therefore belatedly found a force to patronize it. It is this patron that has preserved the Iranian state in the three crises since the Second World War and has enabled it to play a new and dynamic international role.

Another equally important feature of recent Iranian history has been the absence till now of any force able to challenge the dictatorial and monarchical character of the state, whether under the Qajars or the Pahlavis. Every attempt, from the Constitutional Revolution through the oppositions of 1946, 1951–3 and 1960–63, has been defeated. Why did no bourgeois democracy emerge in Iran? And why, given that bourgeois democracy has failed, has the bourgeois dictatorship taken the specific form it has, that of monarchy? It is a mistake to imagine that the form of bourgeois rule, that of dictatorship, is an unnatural form of capitalist state: the number of developing capitalist states which have experienced any durable form of bourgeois democracy is very few. Moreover those capitalist countries that were left behind in the process of economic development have tended to undergo at least periods of dictatorial rule – most noticeably fascism in Germany, Italy and Japan.[6] This points to the underlying question of what the conditions are under which bourgeois democracy becomes possible and how they come about. Once one has asked this question it becomes possible to indicate reasons why the ruling class has not come to rule Iran in a democratic manner, but has ruled through a dictatorial form of state which is relatively independent of the bourgeoisie itself.

In the first place, the restricted development of capitalism in Iran until the 1960s meant that the bourgeoisie itself was very weak. The failure of imperialism to subjugate Iran as it had subjugated other third-world countries held back the development of capitalist class forces and allowed the pre-capitalist structure to survive. Moreover, even had the bourgeoisie developed earlier than it did, it could only with great difficulty have ruled through democratic means since the power of the landowners would have remained intact and would probably have ensured that power was wielded in an essentially undemocratic form – the pattern in the fascist countries. On the other hand, the intermittent intervention of foreign powers disrupted the development in Iran of any social or political forces that could have successfully challenged the Qajars and Pahlavis. Iran's misfortune has been to be too far from the mainstream of capitalist economic development, and too near the path of strategic rivalry between the great powers. In addition there is a third factor that has strengthened the state: one already noted. Because oil revenues are paid to the state and because these revenues are the main source of the economic surplus, the state has been able to acquire and retain the dominant position in the overall process of capitalist development, and this economic weight has combined with the pre-existing socio-political weight of the monarchy, backed by U S intervention.

The bourgeoisie that has developed in Iran has done so as a subsidiary of the state, one that by the very nature of the form of capitalist development in Iran has yielded political and economic power to the state itself. Had Iran's recent economic growth been a result of an expansion in privately owned manufacturing, or even in state-owned manufacturing where a class of privileged managers was emerging, then a more overt political life, involving identifiable factions and debate, could have emerged. This is what has happened in two of Iran's neighbours – Turkey and Pakistan – despite the repeated interventions of the army in these two countries. Iran, a country which has been able to acquire far greater amounts of finance through the sale of oil, has by contrast seen uninterrupted dictatorial rule since 1953 (with the brief interlude after 1960) in part because these revenues have helped to strengthen the system of dictatorship. The bourgeoisie has remained in the political shadows and unable to challenge the dictatorial character of the régime.

If no force has been able to challenge the state successfully, there have been occasions when the strength of the popular movements in Iran has itself posed a threat to the Pahlavi state and to its foreign patrons and encouraged a violent reaction. It was the success of the Constitutional Revolution that provoked Russian intervention after 1908; it was the threat of a communist-led movement in the Gilan mountains near the Caspian that, combined with the overall disintegration of the country, encouraged the British to urge Reza Khan to stage his coup in 1921; it was the wide popular support of the Tudeh Party and the existence of autonomous and pro-Soviet republics in Azerbaijan and Kurdistan, and later the threat posed by Mossadeq, that encouraged the U S A to become the major supporter of the Pahlavi state after the Second World War. Similarly the combination of stronger repression and of economic change that began after 1960 was a response to the instability of a régime that faced the threat of internal resistance. By contrast, the military build-up of the 1970s has been a response, not so much to the revival of internal armed resistance (although this accounts for some of the arms purchases), but above all to the development of nationalist and class forces in the countries *around* Iran.

It appears that so far only a dictatorial régime of this kind could, and can, guarantee the interests of the Iranian ruling class and its international allies. The most fundamental reasons for the state taking the dictatorial form lie *within* Iranian society and in the incapacity of the state to permit any less repressive system. In the sense the emphasis laid by so many Iranians on *foreign* influence is one-sided. But the state's very ability to enforce this repression has certainly been premised on the aid it has received from outside. This is not, however, to claim that there has existed a widespread and sustained opposition movement since the establishment of the Pahlavi state. Nationalist and left-wing opponents of the Shah tend to imply that this is so, but the organizations and movements of opposition have been intermittent, and accounts that obscure this fact make it impossible to trace the real history of the Iranian popular resistance in this century, its vicissitudes, the different tendencies within it and the *limits* of its following. Perhaps the most striking weakness of all has been the almost complete lack of resistance by the largest single social group in Iranian society, the peasantry. Tribal resistance has been recurrent but, of its nature, local. The urban opposition has at different times consisted of merchants, intellectuals, workers and students but until the late 1970s these have been led by organizations with substantial mass following only in the period 1941–53.

Of the five earlier crises in this century, it was the third, that at the end of the Second World War, which presented the most serious threat. For in the 1940s the Pahlavi state was at its weakest and the popular movement was at its strongest. Some U S observers believed that the Tudeh would win in a free election.[7] It had a mass following and – uniquely for a Persian political organization – a nation-wide organization, even if this did not include the peasantry. In Kurdistan and Azerbaijan there existed distinct regional state structures that could have assisted the opposition in the rest of the country. This, above all, was the time when the Pahlavi state could have been challenged. The defeat paved the way for the re-establishment of the monarchical dictatorship: the later, more famous, conflict during Mossadeq's premiership was fought out in a context that was already much less favourable, internally and internationally, to the popular resistance and where the counter-revolutionary forces had regained some of their former positions of strength.

Part of the responsibility for the defeat of 1941–7 lies with the Tudeh Party and its allied parties in Kurdistan and Azerbaijan, as well as with the Soviet Union; the latter guided its Iranian client parties in such a disastrous manner and helped to strengthen the position of the Shah by demanding an oil concession similar to that obtained by the British. As was occurring in Greece, France, Italy and China, the Soviet Union was urging communist parties to make peace with bourgeois forces and it was only in China and Vietnam that the party was strong enough to defy this advice. The very position of Iran on the borders of the Soviet Union – a factor that especially alarmed the west – also gave the Tudeh much less room for manoeuvre vis-à-vis the Soviet Union.

When Mossadeq came to challenge the Shah the situation had changed from that in 1946. First, Mossadeq himself took up a position far to the right of the earlier opposition – he was a landowner, an anti-communist, who did nothing to help the workers' movement, women or the nationalities, and who indeed tried to secure an alliance with the U S A. He had no political organization worthy of the name, even in Tehran. Most importantly, the period between 1946 and 1951 had given the Pahlavi state and the U S A the chance to reorganize the counter-revolutionary forces in Iran, and in particular the army. They were consequently in a much stronger position to attack Mossadeq; his government fell almost without a fight. In the perspective of the period since the start of the third crisis in

1941 it was 1946 which paved the way for the defeats of 1953 and 1963. For a decade and a half after 1963 the Pahlavi state, aided by the U S A, continued to consolidate itself, only to face renewed mass opposition once again in 1977 and 1978. The state that was created between 1963 and 1978, in the lull separating the fifth and sixth crises, is the subject of the following chapter.

3 The State: General Characteristics

What are the defining features of the contemporary Iranian state, and how does the régime enforce its control? The following analysis is presented in terms of five general categories that apply to the Iranian state. While all are, to a greater or lesser extent, found in other third-world countries the specific forms that each takes in Iran combine to constitute the Iranian state of the 1970s.

The most fundamental point about the Iranian state is that it is a *capitalist* one, i.e. one that guarantees the conditions for the reproduction and expansion of capitalist ownership and production. In the broadest terms, capitalism is a system in which the factors of production – land, goods, labour – are privately owned and are commodities, i.e. can be bought and sold on the market. In a capitalist society private ownership and commodity production, that is production for exchange, are generalized through the society. It is this which distinguishes capitalism from other modes of production, such as feudalism and communism.

The establishment of capitalism, of a system of commodity production, has two further consequences. First, by creating a market throughout a specific national economy and internationally, it breaks down pre-existing barriers to exchange and provides the context for an expansion in demand and output. It has, historically, been accompanied by a growth of production on a world scale, a process coupled with the destruction of pre-capitalist societies and productive forces. Secondly, there has developed, by the very nature of capitalism's private ownership, a class that benefits by its position in the production process from this system. Where the state also plays an active role in capitalist production, it defends the interests of this class. At the same time, because of the special role played by the state, there is also created a bureaucratic stratum; its members are not direct owners of capital but benefit from their position in the upper sections of the state apparatus from the economic surplus extracted. This stratum participates with the private owners in the management of the economy and forms a component of the dominant class in such a society.

The development of capitalism in Iran has been accompanied by both of these features: on the one hand, substantial expansion in the productive forces of the country, evident in output and income terms, a process linked to the destruction of pre-existing productive forces; on the other hand, the accelerated growth of an Iranian capitalist class, a bourgeoisie that has developed through the economic expansion of the period since the mid-1950s.[1] These definitions and points may appear obvious enough but they need to be made explicit since there is considerable dispute about the relevance, or accuracy, of calling Iran 'capitalist' at all. Non-Marxist writers often abstract from the specific character of the Iranian social system and provide an economic and social analysis, or a political analysis, that treats individual indicators in isolation from the capitalist development of Iran. Those who write about economic and social development without reference to the specifically capitalist character of these processes use generic concepts of 'modernization' and 'development'; the problem is that they do not identify in whose interests these processes are occurring, or what the class content of the proposed goal 'developed' and 'modern' is. This abstractness is noticeable in the work of a number of non-Marxist political scientists who have discussed Iranian political processes in terms of behavioural and élite analysis, or in terms of specific techniques used by the Shah to consolidate his position.[2] Some try to identify groupings within the Iranian 'élite' without making an adequate attempt, even on the basis of existing information, to determine how this élite relates to the distribution of income and property in Iran. Others devote considerable space to stating the behavioural features of the Shah's system of domination, while neglecting the socio-economic context in which this is located. These works contain a considerable amount of descriptive material; but they are precluded, by theoretical choice, from trying to answer the broader questions raised by the Iranian state and the relationship between this state, the development of capitalism and the growth of an Iranian bourgeoisie.

On the other hand Marxist writers too have devoted little attention to the development of capitalism in Iran and to the specific ways this has affected the state. One of the bases of the Leninist and Marxist analysis of the development of capitalism is that this development is in some respects a *progressive* feature, one that socialists should welcome as an improvement over pre-capitalist systems and as paving the way for socialism.[3] Much of the critique of the growth of capitalism by Iranian Marxists has, by contrast, tried to contest the reality of capitalist development or lament it, almost as if the previous impoverished condition of Iran was something that should have been preserved. Others deny capitalist development has occurred at all. A specific version of this is to be found in those who apply to Iran the analysis of China developed by Mao Tse-tung, according to which Iran is still 'semi-feudal' and 'semi-colonial': this is, in the 1970s, untenable since, while pre-capitalist elements remain, Iran has not been feudal in any significant sense since the land reform of the early 1960s.[4] Alternatively, those who admit the capitalist character of Iran tend to content themselves with general moral denunciations of the régime or with characterizations of the régime as 'fascist' or as 'dependent' on western capitalism; they less often go beyond these formulae to provide a more specific and analytic investigation of the Iranian state.

Under capitalism the state's monopoly of violence and its guaranteeing of the prevailing forms of property involve a defence of the interests of a capitalist ruling class and of its international allies. This is true for all capitalist societies, whilst in developing capitalist countries the state plays a further, economically interventionist, role; here it does not merely guarantee the conditions under which capital is reproduced, but it actively promotes capitalist development and accumulation. In Iran, where oil revenues are paid directly to the state, it has become the dominant force in the economy while its aim remains the promotion of *capitalist* development.

The political functions of the capitalist state can be exercised in different ways. While it always guarantees the position of the ruling class, it need not act, in fact it rarely acts, as the simple *instrument* of that class. A bourgeoisie with its internal divisions may or may not be capable of exercising power in a democratic manner, through some kind of parliamentary system. Whether this occurs depends on the form development has taken in that society and whether the pre-conditions for bourgeois democracy have been met. Even here classes act through elected representatives. If as in Iran the conditions for democracy have not been met, then the state acts in a more indirect way as the guarantor of the dominant class's position; in terms of specific policies it may be independent of, or even in conflict with, the express wishes of large sections of that class. Such states are just as common a form of capitalist rule as bourgeois democratic forms of régime. Such a relation to the bourgeoisie does not mean that the state is not, in its overall character, a capitalist state.

The Iranian state is such an institution – one that guarantees the reproduction and development of capitalism without being directly responsive to the influences of the Iranian bourgeoisie. It does, however, reflect the existence of such a class, since the latter (a) provides the social basis of the state, the sector on whose cooperation it rests and without which it could not remain in existence, (b) organizes the distribution of wealth in such a way that this class benefits disproportionately from it and (c) manages accumulation and investment in accordance with the interests of this class. The latter has three main components: the upper stratum of state employees, capitalist landowners, and those engaged in finance, trade and industry. Together these three components form the Iranian bourgeoisie, the class that has expanded with the growth of capitalism in Iran and whose interests are defended by the Pahlavi state. Each indeed owes its present character to the intervention of the state. The state employees are obviously in this position, having grown from a small administrative nucleus in the 1920s. The upper sections of the civil service, and of the armed forces, have served as means of recruiting new personnel to the bourgeoisie, and they depend for employment and privileges entirely on state policy; the availability of oil revenues has greatly increased the numbers and incomes of such people. The landowners too, in town and country, reflect the state's policy of transforming the countryside along capitalist lines: those who agreed to cooperate with this capitalist transformation retained ownership of land, whilst those who lost their land were compensated and encouraged to participate in industry and urban trade (see p. 133). Finally, those active in trade and industry have benefited enormously from the régime's policies since the 1950s: prior to that a significant section of this sector was opposed to the Shah, favouring a more nationalist economic policy that would have reduced foreign competition. The Shah, however, by instituting some protectionist measures and, more importantly, by generous credit and low taxation (made possible by oil), has for the time being at least won the grudging support of this section of the bourgeoisie. As a result of recent policies it has, in the subsequent two decades, greatly expanded its numbers and wealth.

There are objections to treating these three groups as a single class and to arguing that the state reflects their support. The difficulty about treating them as a class is that this class is still in the process of being formed; but there is no case where the composition of a social group is ever static, and the constituents have been in existence long enough for them to be clearly identifiable – the capitalist landowners since the early 1960s, the bourgeoisie in trade and industry since the 1940s, and the upper stratum of state employees since the 1920s, prior to the launching of capitalist growth. The problem of how this class relates to the state is a more difficult one, at least as far as its private capitalist component is concerned. There is a considerable degree of hostility between the régime and Iranian industrialists and businessmen; in the words of one report: 'The attitude of the Iranian bourgeoisie is ambivalent, "schizophrenic" according to one sociologist. It is favourable to the socio-economic system installed by the Shah's "White Revolution", which still allows it, despite everything, to prosper; but it is at the same time greatly indisposed by a political system founded on personal power which excludes it from centres of decision while favouring arbitrary judgement.'[5] This apparent dislocation points to the overall problem of the Iranian bourgeoisie: unable, for the reasons given, to assume a direct role in state policy it has had to concede power to the monarchy; few doubt that a repressive state of this kind is essential for the bourgeoisie to retain its position or that the 'White Revolution' has benefited it. The bourgeoisie has had to submit to the régime's policies, and yet this support for the state is conditional on the latter continuing to benefit the bourgeoisie. Once the state is unable to do this there could be a profound political crisis in Iran.

The benefits which accrue to the bourgeoisie from capitalist development can be stated in the most general terms: the top 10 per cent of the population account for 40 per cent of consumption, and the oil boom of the 1970s has widened the gap between rich and poor in Iran (see p. 166). No régime can rest on coercion alone, and without the support of this class, whose interests it fosters, the Pahlavi state will founder. No doubt, were it to do so, the Iranian bourgeoisie would be forced by its own incapacities to accept another form of state that represented it indirectly, this time one run by the armed forces. It too would be a capitalist state, and would in a similarly indirect way seek to represent the interests of this bourgeoisie and guarantee the reproduction of capital.

The White Revolution

The second major feature of the Iranian state is that it is located not merely in a capitalist country, but also in a *developing* capitalist one. This means that the state is promoting the growth of capitalist social relations, and the expansion of the productive forces, along capitalist lines. This is the import of the Shah's White Revolution, launched in 1962, which led to a number of reforms the basic purpose of which was to pave the way for such a development process. The first six tenets of the White Revolution were: land reform; nationalization of forest lands; sale of state-owned industrial enterprises to private interests; profit-sharing in industry; votes for women; the establishment of an Education Corps to go into the villages. By September 1977 a further thirteen points had been added, including the establishment of a Health Corps, administrative reform, and a workers' shares programme.

Although these points are laid out by the Shah in terms of specific tenets, they are not really comparable in significance. The most important has been the land reform programme, but many of the others are of a less specific character, being vague exhortations to administrative and economic efficiency. Workers' shares and profit-sharing are standard reformist measures, of far less significance than the régime itself pretends, whilst the granting of votes to women and the establishment of local village councils have limited practical consequences in a country where the state manipulates political life. The programme is not in any sense original, in that most of the measures are ones that any process of capitalist development would have had to take. On the other hand, the 'Revolution' avoids any reform of the most important feature of Iranian life, the distribution of political power and the position of the monarchy itself. The White Revolution, now renamed the Shah–People Revolution, is not, of course, a revolution at all: it is rather a reform programme put into effect in order to *prevent* a revolution, and to strengthen the position of the monarch and the state.

One factor that is systematically underestimated by most western and official commentaries on this programme is the international context in which it took place. Politically, the early 1960s were ones in which the Kennedy Administration was urging its allies in the third world to carry out necessary reforms in order to stave off popular unrest – as we have seen, this is the background to both the White Revolution in Iran, and the Alliance for Progress in Latin America. In economic terms, a noticeable shift occurred from the late 1950s onwards in the relations between the advanced and less advanced capitalist countries: whereas up till then the stronger economies had discouraged industrialization in the third world, this ceased to be the case for all less developed countries. A degree of promotion of industry in the less advanced countries began. This was not true for the third world as a whole, but it was true for a number of countries, among them Iran. The U S government, international financial agencies and internationally active capitalist firms, many of them based in the U S A, encouraged this process. The capitalist development of Iran would have been impossible without these two international conditions – political and economic – and the changes they reflected in the policies of the advanced capitalist countries.[6] The same is true of the later developments in the Iranian economy: the rise in the price of Iranian oil exports from 1971 onwards would have been impossible had it not been for the actions of the major oil producers united in O P E C and for the favourable state of the world market which made the price rises feasible.

The whole of Iranian capitalist development since the early 1960s has therefore been premised on changes in the policies of the major capitalist countries and in changes in the economic relations between advanced and less advanced capitalist states.

Mechanisms of Control

The third major feature of the Iranian state is that the form of government associated with it is that of *dictatorship*. While in all societies the state rests on a combination of coercion and consent, the relative weight of these two forms of influence determines whether this rule is dictatorial or democratic. Many capitalist states have been, or are, dictatorships and there is no doubt that since 1953 Iran has been one of them. The historical factors that have made this the inevitable form of bourgeois rule – the weakness of the bourgeoisie, the threat of popular forces – have already been described. Only through such a régime could private property and the interests of international capital be defended; and, given the division and weakness of the bourgeoisie, it is only a state of this kind that could have put through the land reform programme against the opposition of a part of the landowning class. Moreover, a repressive state and one that crushes any independent popular movements is often suited to attracting foreign capital: the praise by foreign businessmen for the 'stability' of Iran is an accurate reflection of how necessary such a policy is, and how succesful it has been. While economic factors dominate in investment decisions, an uncertain system of democracy, with attendant popular protests, strikes and disputes as well as a weak government, would certainly have been less attractive to foreign capital than the oppressed and relatively tranquil country that the Shah ruled after 1953.

The Pahlavi state has continuously increased its control over Iranian society and politics since the 1920s, and this has become especially so since 1953. In the words of one American observer: 'The entire reign of the Shah, with temporary setbacks, can be characterized as a quarter century in which the civil and military bureaucracies have continually expanded their control over the activities of the population at large, while the Shah has even more relentlessly expanded his power over the bureaucracies.'[7] A leading feature of this system is that no independent political activity of any kind is allowed in Iran despite the fact that a formal party system has existed since 1957. From that year until 1975 the Shah allowed two political parties to operate: the 'government' Melliyun, later Iran Novin Party, and the 'opposition' Mardom Party. Each proposed candidates for the Majlis. But these parties were not allowed to suggest any candidates without these first being approved by SAVAK, and the limits of criticism were laid down. The Majlis to which they were elected was powerless, and the Prime Minister was and is an appointee of the Shah.

No one really believed that this system represented something like a two-party system,[8] yet the Shah himself claimed to take it seriously and declared: 'If I were a dictator rather than a constitutional monarch, then I might be tempted to sponsor a single dominant party such as Hitler organized or such as you find today in communist countries.'[9] In practice these organizations were without substance and both wholly under the Shah's domination. On a couple of occasions when the leaders of the Mardom Party did step out of line and voiced serious criticisms, they were dismissed: in 1972 Ali Naqi Kani was sacked, and in 1974 his successor Nasser Ameri met the same fate.[10]

By 1975, however, the Shah had decided to finish this charade, to undertake a more active policy designed to mobilize support for the régime and to strengthen the state's political role, not merely in a passive but in an active way within Iranian society. In an unanticipated initiative he announced the establishment of a new single party, called the Rastakhiz or National Resurgence Party. All Iranians were pressured to join it, and whereas the two earlier entities had had little real organization outside the Majlis this was to become a mass party. By 1977 it was claimed that five million Iranians had joined and local cells were established throughout the country.

The thinking behind the establishment of Rastakhiz was probably that the régime needed a more positive means of winning support and of forcing people, especially those in state employment or state-run organizations like the unions, to declare their loyalty publicly. The anouncement came towards the end of the post-1973 boom, when the first signs of economic trouble were becoming evident and when the Shah was beginning to emphasize the need for discipline in administration and in industry. The Shah's own words on the matter were blunt enough:

> We must straighten out Iranians' ranks. To do so, we divide them into two categories: those who believe in Monarchy, the Constitution, and the Sixth Bahman Revolution [i.e. the date on which the White Revolution was announced in 1963]; and those who don't ... A person who does not enter the new political party and does not believe in the three cardinal principles which I referred to, will have only two choices. He is either an individual who belongs to an illegal organization, or is related to the outlawed Tudeh Party, or in other words is a traitor. Such an individual belongs in an Iranian prison, or if he desires he can leave the country tomorrow, without even paying exit fees; he can go any-

where he likes, because he is not an Iranian, he has no nation, and his activities are illegal and punishable according to the law. An individual who is neither an element of the Tudeh Party and/or a stateless traitor, but who does not believe in the three principles, is free on condition that he openly expresses his disapproval and if he is not anti-nationalist, we will leave him free. But if he applies double standards, or hides to cover up an incident, or plays around as we have seen some do, this is not acceptable. Everyone must be man enough to clarify his position in this country. He either approves of the conditions or he does not. As I said before, if his disapproval has treacherous overtones, his fate is clear. If it has ideological roots, he is free in Iran, but he should not have any expectations. At the same time, he will be totally protected by Iran's laws as an individual in the society. We expect everyone, any individual who has come of age, to vote, either to enter this new political structure or to clarify his position as of tomorrow or as soon as possible.[11]

The pressure was therefore on, for everyone to be seen to join the new entity: the ominous phrase 'he should not have any expectations' takes on a special meaning in a country where the state is the dominant patron and source of advancement. It would be a mistake to see Rastakhiz as simply designed to further the pretence that there exists in Iran a form of democracy that is in reality absent. These organizations have an additional and important purpose, namely to generate support for the régime and to provide a means of forcing people to compromise themselves by declarations of loyalty. Promotion, security, contacts – much can depend on whether someone is a party member or not.

The state's control extends into all areas of Iranian public life. The Shah may claim that he upholds the Constitution (that of 1906), but he has in fact long since abolished it, and the freedoms it guarantees. No other political organizations can operate: SAVAK ensures that individuals and organizations critical of the régime are crushed. Emigration is also controlled: while the apolitical middle class are allowed to stream abroad, several thousand people suspected of political dissidence are believed to be denied passports. The legal profession is virtually prevented from operating in the case of political offences, since these are reserved for military tribunals. The press is also under state control, even though the two main dailies, *Kayhan* and *Etela'at*, are owned by individual entrepreneurs. These papers are sycophantic products, which give tedious prominence to the latest official statements and respect the censorship guidelines sent around each month by S A V A K. In 1975 the government went further and closed down 95 per cent of all publications in Iran by decreeing that they all had to have a circulation of 3,000 or more. Book publishers face an additional hurdle, in that the censorship authorities only pass books once they have been printed. This means that publishers run the risk of not being able to market a book after they have incurred the costs of printing: an extremely cautious publishing policy is the inevitable result. Nor does state control of the media remain confined to prohibitions: the state-run Pars News Agency isues its own material and many of the state-run organizations, like the trades unions or the Rastakhiz, have their own journals.

State control pervades other institutions. All trades unions are government-run and operate to enforce labour discipline and mobilize support for the régime. The religious leaders were for a long time restricted if not totally controlled by forms of state supervision, their sermons monitored by government agents in the mosque. In the tribal areas, the government has tried to recruit chiefs into the government machinery, giving them offices and funds to enforce government programmes. A similar process has occurred in the villages where since the land reform headmen and other richer peasants have been coopted by the state-run rural agencies: indeed the major political effect of the land reform has been to replace the power of the landowners by that of the state official within the village.[12] The intelligentsia has also been encouraged to follow the government's line: since all educational appointments are state ones, employment in this sector is granted on condition of cooperation; the state, through the universities or S A V A K, has even subsidized magazines that are run by collaborating writers.

The degree of state political control in Iran has gone far beyond that in other capitalist states in the third world which have superficially similar repressive régimes. Brazil in the decade after 1964 is a comparable case. The régime was a military dictatorship under which thousands were killed and tortured and all power held in the hands of the military rulers. But the press in Brazil enjoyed a margin of criticism and satire unthinkable in Iran, and books of a Marxist orientation, provided they were not about armed resistance, were quite widely available. The Catholic Church was also able to act as an independent organization, and to denounce torture and the state's economic policies. Even the rather feeble opposition party, the Brazilian Democratic Movement (MDB), was on occasion able to put up its own election candidates and to denounce the régime in quite forthright terms in parliament. Other groups of critical intellectuals were allowed to research and publish on the social and political character of the régime in a way impossible in Iran. All this is not to deny the brutal and repressive character of the Brazilian junta; but it does show up the extent of the repression in Iran, even by the standards of such régimes.[13]

Why, one can ask, was it necessary for the Shah's régime to control Iranian political life and public expression to quite this extent? Part of the answer lies in the strength of the forces opposed to the Shah. But in itself this is not an adequate answer, since the repression continued long after 1953 and 1963, when it might have been thought to be most needed to crush opposition. A further reason would seem to be the uncertain base of the Pahlavi monarchy itself, the uneasy link to the Iranian bourgeoisie and the weak ideological support which the latter provided. The fragile implantation of the Pahlavi state even half a century after it was founded is probably the fundamental reason why it has to suppress discussion and criticism, even when no coherent opposition movement was presenting a challenge to it.

Forms of Dictatorship

It is insufficient, however, just to state that a capitalist dictatorship exists in Iran, since such a dictatorship can take a number of forms. Moreover, it is also mistaken to use the term 'fascist', as many writers do, indiscriminately about repressive capitalist governments, since fascism is merely one form such régimes can take. There does not exist an adequate typology of such régimes, and so far Marxist discussion has tended to confine itself to three categories: fascism, Bonapartism, and military dictatorship. Yet, while each of these has certain features in common with the Iranian régime, none is an adequate characterization because the specific form the dictatorship takes is that of *monarchy*. One can show this by discussing the ways in which the Iranian régime does, and does not, conform to these three types.[14]

In a military dictatorship the mainstay of the régime is the armed forces; this has been and remains the case in Iran. Even though the army did not intervene on the streets between 1963 and 1978, it remained ready to do so, and SAVAK, a component of the military system, was responsible for everyday repression. No one doubts too that the armed forces have a specially privileged position in terms of the distribution of oil revenues. But there is a further feature of the military dictatorship, evident in recent military régimes in Greece, Chile and Indonesia, namely that the centre of decision lies with the commanders of the armed forces or with an individual dictator who has risen from the armed forces and could, in theory at least, be replaced by another officer. The main personnel of government are drawn predominantly, if not exclusively, from the ranks of the military, and in ideological terms the armed forces present themselves as the guardians of the nation's destiny. In Iran this is not so: so far, it is the Shah who controls the armed forces, symbolically and actually, and not the other way round. Although his father, Reza Khan, was in origin a colonel, he created distance between himself and the armed forces by becoming monarch, and by becoming the undisputed dictator. His son has increased this distance, and made it much more difficult for any armed forces commander to dispute his position without challenging the whole structure of the régime. Here, the monarch rests upon the armed forces, without the régime being in any straightforward sense a military dictatorship.

The second form of bourgeois dictatorship, Bonapartism, was theorized by Marx and Engels in their discussion of France after 1848.[15] The defining feature of Bonapartism was the relative autonomy of the state, the fact that, in Marx's words, 'Bonapartist semi-dictatorship ... upholds the big material interests of the bourgeoisie (even against the will of the bourgeoisie) but allows the bourgeoisie no part in the power of government.'[16] Engels writes of Bonaparte in terms that are, to a certain degree, applicable to Iran under the Shah: 'Only under the second Bonaparte does the state seem to have made itself completely independent. As against civil society, the state machine has consolidated its position so thoroughly.'[17] Because the bourgeoisie is incapable of assuming power directly, the Bonapartist régime, resting on the army, has replaced a parliamentary régime. But if Bonapartist France in the 1860s and Pahlavi Iran in the 1970s share these features, and in particular a state that is autonomous of the class whose interests it defends, there are also substantial differences. The Bonapartist state arose in a situation where a militant working class already menaced the state, at least in Paris: but the working class in Iran is in political terms somewhat weaker than it was in France a century ago, and has not yet posed a threat comparable to that posed in France in 1848. Secondly, the Bonapartist state rested on the social support of the conservative peasantry, whose lack of class consciousness, reflecting a fragmented tenure system, allowed the dictatorial state to survive. But in Iran there is no peasantry of the kind that existed in France, and the rural differentiation attendant upon capitalist development has gone a good deal further. Despite the similarities, therefore, the Iranian dictatorship cannot be classified as Bonapartist.

The third form of bourgeois dictatorship is fascist, and it is very common to hear critics of the Shah's régime call it by this name. But this is usually meant to mean simply that the régime is a repressive capitalist one, relying on torture, the secret police and imprisonment to crush its opponents. Applied to Iran, as when it is applied to repressive régimes in Latin America, it avoids the question of what the *particular form* of repressive capitalist state is. Here, too, there are definite similarities with fascism. Repression of an analogous kind occurs. Since the late 1950s, the secret police has, as under fascism, come to play a central role in ensuring the régime's political stability. Moreover, the Pahlavi régime, like those in Nazi Germany and Fascist Italy, propounds a vigorous nationalist ideology based on chauvinism, imperial nostalgia and the cult of a leader. A point of peculiar similarity is that the Shah himself has made a point of re-emphasizing his belief in the racist theory of Iran being an 'Aryan' country, and has adopted as one of his official titles *Aryamehr* (Light of the Aryans).[18] There are also more fundamental parallels in the conditions that led to the emergence of the state. In Iran this dictatorial state is the product of a counter-attack by a weak capitalist class against a revolutionary movement, in a country that has slipped behind in the process of capitalist development. This class could only then redress this position by repression and state-directed economic growth. This was also the case in Italy, Germany, Japan and Spain.[19]

However, Iran cannot be classified as a fascist state in any precise sense of the term. In the first place, the countries where fascism arose were capitalist countries that were, it is true, retarded in comparison with the most developed ones, but were still advanced when compared with the colonial and semi-colonial world. They were ones where a previous period of capitalist development had already produced a bourgeoisie, both industrial and financial, and where a substantial working class had emerged. Iran has not reached any comparable stage and its bourgeoisie is far less developed. Moreover, the fascist states of the 1930s had reached the point where they had become rivals to the most advanced capitalist countries and in the end went to war with them; whereas the Iranian state has come to take the form it has precisely through the patronage of the U S A. Despite its substantial oil revenues there is no sense in which Iran could rival the major imperialist countries in the way that Germany did in the Second World War: the international context for the formation of the contemporary Iranian state is therefore quite different.

There are substantial further differences in the political composition of the two régimes. The central instrument of a fascist movement is the party: it uses the party to seize power, and as the main instrument of political consolidation after it has seized power. There did exist a small fascist party modelled on the Nazi Party prior to the 1953 coup: but this organization, the Sumka (National Socialist Workers Party of Iran), played no significant role in the coup or in the post-coup régime and has long since disappeared. Other groups with extreme nationalist ideologies were equally marginal. Since the coup, there has been no party worthy of the name under the Pahlavi dictatorship and the state-run entities created have been of far less importance than the parties under fascism. There is a further difference between fascism and the Pahlavi régime, namely that no fascist régime has carried out a land reform. Although not in any simple sense an expression of the landed oligarchy, the Nazi state was careful not to antagonize it and in its ideology there was a mystical evocation of the land and its values, a rural component of which there is no counterpart in Iran. Of course, such a tolerance was only possible because the countryside had already become capitalist, albeit in a conservative mould; in Iran, on the other hand, the régime has had to impose reforms on the landowning class in order to further the process of capitalist development.

Each of these three classic models of bourgeois dictatorship does therefore tell us something about Iran, yet each is, in its own way, inappropriate. There is an irreducible particularity about the form that bourgeois dictatorship has taken in Iran, which is inseparable from the role played by the monarch. The first thing that strikes one about Iran is that it is the Shah who holds full executive power in a rapidly developing capitalist state, and that he has been able to increase his strength as this development has unfolded. It is therefore a simplification, but not totally misleading, to concentrate on the actions and position of the monarch when analysing Iranian politics. The originality of this phenomenon should not be overlooked, even though the Shah does not operate in a vacuum and relies on the régime's passive social base and the international political and economic conditions for his retention of power.

The concentration of political power in the hands of one man is not by any means specific to Iran; it is something that has been seen in a wide variety of countries during the twentieth century. Such power can be built up through the elimination of rivals, the division of the opposition, the establishment of a client following, the growth of a leadership cult. Both techniques for establishing and those for maintaining such a system are well known, and there is little specific to the Iranian monarchy in the way the Shah has consolidated his reign. Like all monarchs he has benefited from the fact that it is more difficult to challenge a king than a civilian dictator, since the only legitimate challengers are those from within the royal family, and the Shah has had no such rivals.

The most striking feature of the Iranian monarchy is that it has been able to strengthen its position as capitalist development has continued, and in this respect it is almost unique in the twentieth century. In some western European countries, the monarch has survived – but only as a force of ideological diversion, symbolizing national unity. This is the case in Holland, Britain, Sweden and Denmark. In some other capitalist countries the monarchs have continued to play a more active role, but this has been in competition, or collaboration, with other forces within the state: Emperor Hirohito of Japan shared executive power with the military in the 1930s and 1940s, and the King of Thailand has retained some power through cooperation with his armed forces. But in many other less developed countries the process of capitalist development has produced a situation in which the monarchs have been, sooner or later, overthrown. Haile Selassie of Ethiopia was ousted in 1974 after almost six decades in power. In the immediate vicinity of Iran the fate of monarchs has been little better. Every single monarchy in a country bordering Iran has been swept away in this century: in Russia (1917), Turkey (1923), Iraq (1958) and Afghanistan (1973). The coups in Egypt (1952) and Libya (1969) also produced republics. The only countries where monarchs retain similar powers are Nepal, some Pacific islands and some Arab states: Morocco, Jordan, Saudi Arabia, Oman and the smaller Gulf entities. Yet none of these states, with the possible exception of Morocco, has undergone social, political and economic upheavals of the kind Iran has been through. Iran is probably the only country in the world where the state has combined the vigorous promotion of capitalist development with a fully constituted monarchist régime.

How important is the specifically monarchist element in this dictatorship? Would it not be possible to see Mohammad Reza Pahlavi as a successful dictator, operating as many have done under republican systems, with the difference only that here he is surrounded by imperial symbols? It is true that the monarchical system differs from systems of republican dictatorship much less than the defenders of either would claim. But there are nonetheless differences that go beyond the realm of formality. This is evident from the fact that in some third-world countries attempts have been made by republican dictators to convert their régimes into monarchical ones, and that these attempts have failed in one way or another. In China Yuan Shi-kai tried to declare himself monarch in 1916 and in so doing provoked his own downfall; in such countries as Haiti (Duvalier) and the Central African Republic (Bokassa) dictators have succeeded in declaring themselves emperors, but in such a manner that no one has accorded them legitimacy as monarchs. The ideological mythology which the Iranian régime has fostered may well be artificial, but there is no doubt that the Pahlavi monarchs have been able to establish a much more stable imperial system than one which an individual dictator could have done. This is because they have been accepted as their representatives by the dominant classes and because of their use of the monarchical tradition in Iran for quite novel purposes.

This monarchical dictatorship dates only from the early 1960s, for it was then that the Shah achieved effective domination over the other groups within the state, the civilian politicians and the army, with whom he had on occasion had to share power since the 1953 coup. The armed forces are now under his full control. Most civilian politicians act on his orders and dare not criticize. The Majlis and the press are docile instruments. The Shah has made sure that any members of the state apparatus who are winning popularity for their actions are dismissed: this was the case with Hassan Arsanjani, Minister of Agriculture ousted in 1963, with the mayor of Tehran, Ahmad Nafici, sacked and imprisoned in 1963, and with the leaders of the Mardom Party in the early 1970s. Obviously one person cannot run a country single-handedly, and there must therefore be an element of delegation of power. But the Shah has ensured that those beneath him have, to the greatest degree possible, to cooperate through him and he fosters rivalry between different groups who spy on and rival each other. This has been successful insofar as most leading government officials accept the Shah's dominance, but it has had the negative effect of making the system a highly inflexible one, where all initiatives come from the top and where rivalries between sections of the administration take up a large amount of effort. In the words of one observer: 'Beset by personal insecurities, mistrustful of themselves and their fellows, and cynical about the motives of all persons and the outcome of all programmes, the élite respond by coping with the system, not by attempting to alter it in fundamental ways. And the process of coping consists, basically, of learning to operate within its norms while maximizing the benefits that can be derived from it.'[20]

The Shah himself has given every indication that he believes in his own right to rule in this way. In his own words: 'When there's no monarchy, there's anarchy, or an oligarchy or a dictatorship. Besides, a monarchy is the only possible means to govern Iran. If I have been able to do something, a lot, in fact, for Iran it is owing to the detail, slight as it may seem, that I'm its king. To get things done, one needs power, and to hold on to power one mustn't ask anyone's permission or advice. One mustn't discuss decisions with anyone.'[21] Reports of cabinet meetings or of other government discussions between the Shah and his subordinates suggest that these are stilted affairs, in which little adequate or open discussion takes place.[22] And it may be this as much as deliberate exaggeration on his part which accounts for the Shah's ability to make wholly unreasonable predictions about Iran's future capacities in the economic and military field.

For if the Shah has a personal failing that affects policy it is his incapacity to grasp the complexity of economic problems, and his reliance on orders and moral exhortation alone to solve the difficulties which Iran faces. This failing, combined with the subservient conduct of those around him, was not so important when Iran's oil revenues were multiplying; but in the worsening economic situation of the later years it has become a factor of much greater significance. Those critics, whether in the CIA or the opposition, who consider the Shah to be a megalomaniac and who ascribe government policies to this, are probably wide of the mark. The Shah has a streak of grandiose irrationality, but overall, his policies on oil, military purchases and economic development have been rational ones for someone in this position to take, and there is no real evidence that he is mad, or particularly unstable. In the long run of course such factors have a limited importance. The causes of Iran's political and economic problems lie not in the psychology of its ruler so much as in the character of Iranian society.

National Mythology

An important component of the monarchical system is the ideology purveyed by the régime. No state rests on repression alone, and the Iranian state, like many other third-world states, engages in a comprehensive ideological campaign to mobilize support, both among its immediate social base, and among the population as a whole. A leading component of this ideology is a vigorous nationalism, which evokes the greatness of the Iranian past, and stresses the fact that it was monarchs who brought this about. The fabrication of a specifically Iranian 'national mythology' began among intellectuals in the nineteenth century and was greatly encouraged under Reza

Khan. He had Iranian history rewritten to play down the Islamic period that began in the seventh century when the Arabs conquered Iran. Instead he glorified the pre-Islamic past stretching from the fifth century B.C. The state promoted archaeological work to excavate the remains of this period. This propagandistic history was what children were taught in schools, and Iranian magazines today contain chauvinistic stories about how such and such a king invented military strategy or about how Iranian culture outshone all others. Monarchism and nationalism are carefully used to reinforce each other here, since the constant theme is that Iran is only strong when it has a strong Shah. The celebration of 2,500 years of monarchy in 1971 was designed to underline this connection.

The rejection of the Islamic period involves propagating a chauvinist idea about Arabs whose 'barbarism' (*vahshigari arab*) is blamed for the subsequent ills of Iran. It is a considerable irony that, on the available evidence, the Arabs conquered Iran so easily because they were welcomed by the mass of the Iranian population. The latter saw the Arab invasion as a means of throwing off their oppressive Shahs and embraced Islam because, at least in part, is was a more democratic religion than the hierarchical Zoroastrian creed that had prevailed till then. A further distortion by the régime, begun by Reza Khan in 1936, has been the attempt to purge the Persian language of foreign words – especially Arab and Turkish ones – and to introduce new 'pure Persian' (*farsi-ye ser'e*) substitutes. Official documents in the army are supposed to be written in this neologistic style but the policy has overall been a failure: the Shah himself never speaks in this 'pure Persian', and the régime has always baulked at introducing the most needed reform of all, viz. the replacing of the highly inefficient Arabic script by one in which vowels as well as consonants are recorded. Ataturk carried out this reform in 1928 for the Turks. However, as part of the attempt to foster official ideology the state has also laid down guidelines for the teaching not only of history but also of literature: pupils are instructed to read poetry, the main literary form in Iran, so as to emphasize special virtues, such as obedience to authority and acceptance of fate. This form of ideological reading is known as *nasihat*; it finds its parallel in the military field, where the *Shahname*, the epic poem of the tenth-century writer Firdausi, is used as the basis for patriotic songs by the army.

The régime makes an attempt, as far as possible, to adopt the more acceptable slogans of the opposition. The Shah himself purports to yield to no one in proclaiming nationalist sentiments, and his defence of Iranian interests. The régime's reply to critics abroad, whether the U S Congress, Amnesty International or political exiles, is to claim that this is an interference in Iran's internal affairs and the work of the enemies of the Iranian nation. The régime also includes a populist element in its rhetoric; the Shah often criticizes businessmen for making excessive profits and not treating their workers properly. In 1975 over 8,000 businessmen were fined or imprisoned in an anti-inflation drive. Similarly the Shah has introduced a number of welfare schemes for workers which, although confined to a few workers, are presented in the media as indications of the Shah's concern for the people. All the talk about the Shah's 'revolution' is part of this policy, and although much of it is bombast that few take seriously, it would be premature to assume that it has no effect at all. So long as the régime can provide some of the material benefits desired by the population, a significant number of Iranians may go along with the régime's ideology, whatever they may think in private. Since the spread of education and the mass media to the villages is something which the régime itself has organized in the past ten years, it would not be surprising if a vague pro-Shah sentiment was present in the countryside, as a result of the high monarchist content in the material to which the rural population is exposed, and the improvement in living conditions that part of the rural population has experienced.

A curious absence from official ideology is any substantial emphasis on Islam. The nationalist movement in the late nineteenth century was explicitly Islamic in content and was led by *ulema*, but in the twentieth century the groups which espoused an outspoken Islamic policy have not been as important, and both Shahs have clashed with religious leaders by secularizing education and the law. There was not, until the late 1970s, the kind of overtly Islamic backlash against secularization that has been seen in Turkey since the end of the Second World War despite a diffuse religious hostility to the Shah's programme. Yet, if Islam is comparatively less important, it is still used in certain ways. The state remains officially Islamic, and the régime has tried half-heartedly to win over the religious leaders. The Pahlavi monarchs have also made concessions to Islamic sensibilities, and it cannot be an accident that the Shah's personal names are Mohammad Reza – Mohammad being the prophet of God in Islam, and Reza being a leading figure in the Shi'a brand of Islam to which most Iranians belong. Moreover, the régime played on Shi'a sentiments in the clashes with Iraq that persisted up to 1975: during the propaganda war between the two countries in the early 1970s the régime's policy was to identify the Iraqi government with Yazid, the ruler of Iraq who in the seventh century killed Hossein, one of the founders of Shi'a Islam. The distinctive feature of this use of Islam is of course that it is a reflection of a conflict *within* Islam, and part of Iranian anti-Arab ideology; by contrast, Islamic nationalist ideology in Pakistan, Turkey, Indonesia and the Arab world is directed against non-Muslims and predominantly against western colonialist or imperialist powers.

Iran's 'national mythology' is therefore an integral part of the régime's means of reinforcing itself, and the monarch occupies a special place within this system. The fact that this ideological concoction is both historically inaccurate and based on the fostering of illusions is beside the point: it is probably no more so than comparable national mythologies found in other countries, and it is an important reflection of the specific form of dictatorial capitalist state, monarchist dictatorship, which has been formed in Iran.

The fifth and final feature of the Iranian state can be dealt with more briefly. This is that the state has been, to a considerable degree, *dependent* on the support it receives from the USA and the advanced capitalist world generally. The very concept of 'dependency' has been the subject of controversy, and it is used here in the most general sense. Since 1946 Iran has been closely tied at the political and military levels to the U S A. Had it not been for the U S military and political support in the decade after the Second World War, the Iranian monarch and possibly a capitalist state of any kind might have been overthrown. Since the early 1960s it is U S pressure and support that has made possible both the 'White Revolution' and the development by the Shah of the military arsenal needed to dominate the Gulf region. In more general terms, Iran's capitalist development has come about through the cooperation between the Iranian state and foreign interests, both at the state and private enterprise level. Iran's acquisition of skilled personnel, technology and training assistance from the advanced capitalist countries indicates the continued need for such cooperation if capitalist development is to continue. But, insofar as Iran does develop along capitalist lines, it may lessen this degree of dependence, at least in the political sphere. Iran has, for example, clashed with the U S A over the price of oil since it has been in Iran's interest to have the price as high as possible. However, even though the relationship between Iran and the advanced capitalist countries has certainly altered in many respects since the end of the Second World War, Iran remains a weaker partner in the international capitalist system and will depend on outside support for many years to come in the economic and military fields. Provided one is precise about what is meant by the term, and provided one identifies the changes taking place, it will remain accurate to call the Iranian state 'dependent'.

This analysis has yielded five characteristics that define the Iranian state: it is *capitalist*, it is *developing* capitalism, it is *dictatorial*, it is a *monarchist* form of dictatorship, and it is in a certain sense *dependent* on the advanced capitalist countries. These categories tell us more about contemporary Iran than invocations of an Islamic, Asiatic or despotic tradition. It is against this general background that it now becomes possible to examine some of the recent changes in Iranian society and politics in more detail. The current policies of the régime reflect Iran's capitalist development and are designed to promote those transformations that will guarantee the long-run stability of capitalism in Iran. So long as the state could meet its economic and social requirements, the political challenges it faced were to a great extent controllable. But, as now seems evident, the régime's policies will meet with only partial success, and the political conflicts, within the régime itself as well as between the régime and its opponents, must inevitably take a more acute form; this may, in the long run, undermine the willingness of the régime's international allies to support it. It is to these specific questions about contemporary Iran that we now turn.

4 The Armed Forces and S A V A K

The Iranian armed forces and related security units constitute, by any standards, an exceptional set of institutions. In the mid-1970s the military apparatus attracted special attention as for a while the largest single purchaser of U S arms in the world, and through these acquisitions Iran in a short space of time became a major power in western Asia. This military build-up will inevitably affect the balance of power there, and that region's international relations, for some decades at least. Yet there is another reason for paying attention to Iran's military apparatus, one that predates the current arms purchases and which in part determines the uses to which the new arms are being put. This is that Iran is a society where, since the 1920s, the régime has been based on the army, and where repression is the main means of ensuring the government's political control. Iran is probably the state where rule based on the military has been the norm for longer than anywhere else in Asia or Africa. What has changed in recent years is that Iran has acquired large sums of money from oil which have enabled it to purchase enormous quantities of weapons, and that it has at the same time been encouraged by the U S A to become a regional power. Hence the present military expansion of Iran, and the effects both external and internal of this, are the consequences of the combination of a repressive régime backed by the army on the one side, with a changed international political and economic situation on the other. It is an ominous combination, unique in the contemporary world.

Monarchy and the Armed Forces

As we have seen, Iran is in several ways an outright military dictatorship. No independent political activity has been allowed by the government; many opponents are jailed, tortured and killed. There can, consequently, be no doubt that Iran is a *dictatorship.* There are also persuasive reasons for thinking this dictatorship is a *military* one. First, the repressive apparatus in general (i.e. the armed forces and the security units) is the main institution sustaining the régime internally. Secondly, this apparatus, in particular the army, plays a major role in social and economic life. Moreover the régime is historically one that owes its existence to military coups (1921, 1953). Both Pahlavi Shahs were brought to power by the army and both have relied on it to rule Iran. Both have also seen it as their prime duty to strengthen and to retain the loyalty of the armed forces.

Iran is *not*, however, a military dictatorship for one overriding reason, namely the position of the monarch. As we have seen in Chapter Three the two Pahlavi Shahs have been able to dominate the military and to develop a monarchical system of government quite distinct in practice and in ideology from that found in military dictatorships. The Shah's father may have been a colonel, but he was one who put a crown on his own head. He was then able to establish a position of personal dominance that took the form of monarchy and which his son, after initial hesitations up to 1953, has been able to develop further.

Among the factors contributing to the growth of this system where a monarch controls the army has been the fact that Iran has had an exceptionally weak military institution. Its present army is a twentieth-century creation with no strong predetermined social character or historical role. Some Shahs did raise large armies in the past: the monarchs of Ancient Persia, the Safavis in the sixteenth century, Nadir Shah who invaded the Arabian Peninsula and in 1739 conquered Delhi with, it is said, 160,000 mounted troops. But there were long gaps between these periods of strength and from the middle of the nineteenth century Iran had no significant standing army at all. In 1914 the government had a ramshackle force of 5,000 men. Those better-armed units that did exist were disunited and under foreign influence: in 1879 Russian Cossack officers had set up a unit in the north of the country; in 1911 Swedish officers established a gendarmerie for controlling the rural areas; and in 1915 the British, in the south of Iran, established the South Persia Rifles, a force commanded by Indian officers. By 1920, these three forces contained 22,000 men in all: 8,000 in the Cossack Brigade, 8,400 in the gendarmerie, and 6,000 in the South Persia Rifles. The other main armed forces in the country were under the control of regional chiefs, in greater or lesser dispute with the central government.[1]

After the 1917 Revolution the British replaced the Russians as patrons of the Cossack Brigade which they wanted to use as an instrument of stabilization. It was they who encouraged Colonel Reza Khan to march on Tehran and seize power in February 1921. Yet although Reza Khan acted with British support in his coup, he was not a British client – indeed he later showed excessive sympathies for Nazi Germany. Rather, he worked to make Iran as independent as was possible in the constricted economic and strategic conditions of the time; his first and abiding concern was to build a strong army as the foundation of his state. In 1922 military appropriations accounted for 47 per cent of the total budget, and by 1925 a unified army of 40,000 had come into existence. In 1926 the first general conscription law was introduced; by 1930 the army stood at 80,000 men, rising to 125,000 in 1941. Reza Khan set up two military schools in Tehran, and sent officers to France, Germany and Russia for training. In 1924 a small air force was established and in 1932 a navy. He used the army to crush opposition both in the towns and in the countryside and through it he forged a centralized state for the first time in two centuries of Iranian history.

There does not therefore exist a significant hereditary officer corps in Iran of the kind found in certain European countries – most noticeably in the case of the German army – and in many former colonial countries where the armed forces were built on a selective basis by the colonial powers. Since Iran was never a colonized country in the proper sense of the word the army is not an ex-colonial one. Nor is the officer corps drawn from the same origins as those with economic power: in the 1920s and 1930s the sons of the rich landowners and urban merchants did not go into the army, and there was therefore no close socio-political link between the repressive apparatus and the ruling class. The Shah's father was the son of an officer, but there was little hereditary continuity; many of those who went into the officer corps in the 1920s and 1930s were of modest origins, sons of small landowners and civil servants. We do not have any information on the current class origins of the officer corps, but it is probable that recent recruitment has been from similar backgrounds. The irony is indeed that today the Iranian régime tries to foster a sense of continuous military strength through the ages. But, apart from the obviously chauvinist and dangerous nature of this kind of propaganda, it is also an ideological construct, one designed to obscure the predominant *discontinuity* in Iran's military history. The present Iranian army is a product of the last half century: it has no more connexion with the armies of Xerxes and Nadir Shah than did the army of Mussolini with the legions of the Roman Empire.

The dominant position of the monarch combined with his special reliance on the military is evident in Iran today. In formal terms the Shah is, in accordance with the Constitution, Commander-in-Chief. He frequently appears in military uniform and attends many officer passing-out parades. For their part all members of the armed forces swear loyalty to three entities – *Khoda, Shah, Mihan* (God, Shah, Country), and are constantly reminded in their training of their loyalty to the Shah and of the need to re-create the past greatness of Iran, a greatness inextricably linked in current mythology with the institution of monarchy. But this is not just a formality, and is in no way comparable with, for example, the role of the monarch in the British or Dutch armed forces. The Shah may rely on the army, but he also controls it, and has been increasingly able to depoliticize it. In the 1940s and early 1950s, when the monarch was in a weak position, the army was divided into visible political factions and some generals had followings of their own. But this has changed since 1953. A substantial pro-communist organization with several hundred members in the officer corps was destroyed in 1954. The only attempted coup that is known of since then was in 1958 when General Gharani, the head of Military Intelligence, was accused of plotting to overthrow the Shah. The first head of SAVAK, General Bakhtiar, was accused of opposing the Shah in 1961, but he was dismissed without difficulty and the degree of support he had has probably been exaggerated by the régime. The Shah devotes two mornings a week to meeting service chiefs, but the three services are allowed to communicate only via the Supreme Commander's (i.e. the Shah's) own staff.

The mechanisms of the Shah's control are pervasive. No general can visit Tehran or meet with another general without the Shah's specific permission. He is believed to check promotions above the rank of major, and in the air force (his favourite service) all entrants to training school are vetted by him. Moreover, whilst the Shah accords a privileged position to the officer corps in material terms, he is careful to ensure that they do not forget their dependence on him. He frequently shuffles top commanders to ensure that they do not form power bases or enduring alliances. He uses a personal secret police, the Imperial Organization, as well as the conventional Military Intelligence unit, to carry out surveillance of the officer corps. Perhaps the most striking case of the Shah's power over the military came in 1961 when at one stroke he dismissed General Bakhtiar, head of SAVAK, General Abdullah Hedayat, chief of the supreme commander's staff and the most powerful military man after the Shah, and General Alavi Kia, the head of Military Intelligence. This illustrates the *exceptional dominance* of monarch over the armed forces. On several occasions since he has purged officers suspected of disloyalty under the guise of waging anti-corruption campaigns. No one seriously believes that the Shah can eliminate, or even wants to eliminate, corruption. But what these fitful campaigns illustrate is the Shah's capacity to strike down any officer at will. As one writer has put it: 'Frequently, members of the elite will be charged with corruption and removed from office, exiled, or imprisoned when their offence was, in fact, entirely political. Such charges are advanced in order to mask the existence of the political turmoil that endures beneath the placid façade of Iranian unity and stability.'[2] In 1974 three generals and two colonels, all from the Ground Forces Transportation Corps, were tried for corruption. In February 1976 the former head of the navy, Rear-Admiral Ramzi Abbas Attaie, and his deputy, Rear-Admiral Hassan Rafaie, were sentenced to five years' imprisonment for bribery, in a trial in which fourteen people, twelve of them naval officers, were sentenced. Previously, in the early 1960s, the Shah had sacked several hundred officers, including five generals, for corruption; in 1963 alone 300 colonels were dismissed. There can be no doubt that the Shah's personal control over the officer corps is even stronger today than it was then.

In recent years the Shah's power has become evident in a further dimension – that of weapons procurement. The details of this are discussed later in this chapter but it is worth noting here that all major arms purchases are decided upon by the Shah, and by him alone. It is for this very reason, the dependence of arms procurement on the knowledge and impulses of one person who does not always have a realistic picture of his country's capacities, that Iran is now committed to buying weapons that it will only be able to use by bringing in tens of thousands of U S personnel.

The most stable members of the officer corps are those who have over the years demonstrated loyalty to him: i.e. whereas in a conventional military dictatorship it would be the officers who had built the strongest power bases of their own who could retain positions, the opposite is the case in Iran. Four of those who fell in such a category in the early 1970s exemplify this kind of officer:

1. General Hussein Fardust: born in 1919, the son of an army lieutenant, Fardust was sent with the Shah to be educated in Switzerland and has been a personal servant ever since. He has been trained in the U S A, has worked in S A V A K and to-

day heads the Imperial Inspectorate Organization, the Shah's personal secret police.

2. General Hassan Toufanian: Deputy Minister of War, and the officer charged below the Shah with overseeing arms purchases from abroad. One of the most powerful officers, he is reputed to be a close friend of the Shah's.

3. General Mohammad Khatami: born in 1920, Khatami was from 1946 to 1958 the Shah's personal pilot, who flew him to safety in 1953 when the Shah fled the country. Khatami later married the Shah's sister Fatimah and was commander of the air force from 1958 till his death in a gliding accident in 1975.

4. General Nematollah Nassiri: born in 1907, Nassiri was the 'monitor' of the Shah's class at the Tehran Officers' Training School. From 1950 he was commander of the Imperial Guard in Tehran and was the man sent by the Shah in August 1953 to arrest Mossadeq. He was appointed head of SAVAK in 1965, a post he held till becoming Ambassador to Pakistan in 1978.

These four generals were among the handful of most influential military men in Iran; the ambiguous nature of their power is a result of the peculiar position which the monarch has won for himself. However, even if the monarch appears to have complete control, this does not mean that there is no room for political manoeuvre by the military. A leading US expert on Iran, questioned by a Congressional committee in 1973 on the 'probability' of a coup in Iran, gave the following answer: 'What I believe exists in Iran, as I think in most military dictatorships, is the omnipresence of military cabals which are plotting to take over. I think you can be absolutely confident that that is occurring but I have no ability to estimate who they are or how strong they are, and for that reason I would not dare say probably.'[3] At the moment the most likely issues of dispute concern matters internal to the army – pay, promotions, weapons systems, budget allocations, divisions of responsibility. Politics is likely to play a less central role than it did between 1941 and the early 1960s. But the Shah knows that the army could, if united against him, or even if seriously split between pro- and anti-Shah factions, put an end to his reign. He knows that all four monarchies bordering Iran in this century have been overthrown by coups – and has voiced his anxiety about a possible republican coup in Saudi Arabia.[4] His capacity to control the army is not however merely a matter of keeping it materially happy and its top leadership insecure; it is above all a function of the general economic and political stability of Iran. As long as the state has the money to meet the army's demands and to ensure prosperity for the Iranian bourgeoisie, the Shah's capacity to control the repressive apparatus will be considerable; if these conditions cease to apply, the threat of a coup will increase. In such a situation Generals Nassiri, Toufanian and Fardust, or other men at the moment in the imperial shadow, could well step forward to wield more overt political power.

An Economic and Social Power

In addition to its role as the instrument of political repression the Iranian military apparatus plays a major economic and social role. The economic weight of the military is evident in at least five ways:

1. Since the 1920s the armed forces have taken a large part of government revenues and hence of the monies paid to the Iranian state by the oil companies. Under Reza Khan the military budget constituted on average a third of all expenditure; despite the enormous rise in government revenues in recent years military expenditure has continued to absorb a significant portion of them.

Between 1953 and 1970 defence expenditure rose from $67 millions to $844 millions, a rise of over 12 times; between 1970 and 1977 it rose by almost the same proportion again to $9,400 millions. In 1974, the year in which oil price rises were reflected in a 141 per cent increase on the previous year's expenditure, defence spending was 32 per cent of total budget allocations, and whilst this percentage declined somewhat after that, it was estimated that in the 1973–8 Plan defence would amount to

31 per cent of total planned expenditure, or over 9 per cent of G N P.[5] Iran in 1976 spent as much on defence as the People's Republic of China, but had only one tenth the number of men in the armed forces; *per capita* defence expenditure was *26 times higher* in Iran ($314) than in China ($12) and overall expenditure was estimated to be eight times higher than in neighbouring Iraq where the numbers in the armed forces were just over half the numbers in Iran (158,000 to 300,000).

2. Since the 1920s the armed forces have been an important source of employment. In 1976 the 300,000 men under arms represented 3 per cent of all those in employment, and 5 per cent of those in non-agricultural employment. The numbers servicing the armed forces indirectly must include tens of thousands more. But the oil boom has altered the relation of the military to the labour market: whereas previously it was a relatively privileged branch of employment, competition from the private sector for technicians has altered the comparative advantages of each branch and put the armed forces at a disadvantage. Like the private sector, the armed forces are experiencing a growing lack of skilled personnel and the two are in competition. In 1974 wages of a rank-and-file soldier were 500–600 rials a month, those of a captain around 30,000 rials a month, those of a colonel 60,000 and those of a general 70,000 to 100,000 (68 rials=U S $1). In the lower ranks these compared unfavourably with the wages of skilled workers in the private sector, although in volume and regularity they were better than those of the mass of urban and rural poor.

3. The Iranian military plays an important role in production. Reza Khan began producing ammunition and army uniforms, and today Iran has a number of plants assembling transport vehicles, and producing armour plating and ordnance. These plants are under the control of the Iranian Military Industries Organizations: its factories are run by generals and are organized along military lines.

4. The armed forces also have their own service units. The Bank Sepah (Army Bank) founded in 1925, and today owned by the army pension fund, specializes in providing cheap loans to officers. The Cooperative Organization of the Forces of

Order, founded in 1941, provides cheap food, clothing and other goods: its imports are exempted from customs duty, the railways are bound by law to carry its good free of charge, and since land reform it has acquired direct control of the produce of some villages.

5. Finally, the armed forces play a role in current development programmes. The military – both the army and SAVAK – have organized the Literacy and Health Corps sent out to the villages under the land reform programme. The expansion in base facilities, especially in the southern part of the country, in the 1960s and 1970s has also had profound economic effects: the population of Bandar Abbas, the Gulf port chosen as the new naval HQ, has risen from 18,000 in 1960 to 200,000 in the early 1970s and is expected to reach 400,000 by 1980. The road and railway developments have also been part of the military expansion.

Whilst military development has in this way determined the character of much current expenditure, the priority given to the military budget has diverted resources from other projects and constituted a distortion of Iran's overall development. Iran, despite its oil revenues, is still short of capital relative to its needs and the monies spent on arms are thereby lost to forms of productive investment. The same applies to skilled labour, and to infrastructural growth. There is, no doubt, some positive contribution to economic development to be gained from this military expenditure, but this is extremely small and the overall balance is a negative one, a vast subtraction from the resources available to Iran in its attempt to develop the economy.

The military also plays a marked social role, evident in at least four respects:

1. The armed forces are a vehicle of social mobility. While we lack details of the social origins of the Iranian officer corps, it appears that since many are of relatively unprivileged backgrounds (lower civil servants, farmers) the rise of the officer corps as a force in Iranian society under the Pahlavi régime has introduced a new component into the ruling class. This

social composition may, among other factors, explain why the army supported land reform and did not protect the big landowners. Lower down in the ranks, conscription has also acted as a means of social mobility: although conscription for a 24-month period is general, most of those eligible (they have to present themselves aged nineteen on 21 March, the Persian New Year) are rejected because of physical ailments. But for those peasants who do join, the army provides a way out of the poverty of the villages, even though it also leads to problems of readjustment when such young men return to their families.

2. The army has been used as an instrument of national integration by both Shahs. In the 1920s and 1930s Reza Khan used the army as a coercive instrument for crushing tribal resistance. The last substantial tribal revolt was in Fars province in 1963, but, although this kind of campaign is no longer fought, the army is used for the same ends in a different way: sons of tribal leaders are encouraged to become army officers and the régime has tried to promote the enlistment of men from the oppressed minorities. We do not know the ethnic balance in the armed forces, but a comprehensive recruitment policy certainly operates. This contrasts with the situation in other Middle Eastern states such as Jordan and Saudi Arabia where ethnically and regionally selective recruitment policies operate.

3. The armed forces act as an instrument for diffusing the régime's ideology, and in particular loyalty to the monarch. First of all, army training includes a large component of imperial history, chauvinist songs, and monarchist values. As the régime is trying to rid Persian of Arabic and Turkish words, official military documents are supposed to be written in a fabricated 'pure Persian': recruits have to study special vocabulary lists to rid themselves of 'impure' words. But this function extends beyond the armed forces, for the paramilitary corps created in the 1960s themselves teach these values in the villages, and the Shah himself uses his position as Commander-in-Chief as part of his public image. The strength of the Iranian armed forces is presented as being dependent upon the existence of a strong Shah.

4. The armed forces also provide personnel for running other

government activities, as is the case in many overt military dictatorships. Generals have run the land reform programmes and factories, as well as those branches of the repressive apparatus that in other societies might be run by policemen or even civilians (S A V A K, the gendarmerie). The officer corps therefore provides a reserve of personnel on which the régime can draw to administer wider sections of the economy.

Political Repression

The most important function which the repressive apparatus performs is however still that of guarantor of the régime's survival. But having said this it is essential to see *how* the apparatus is used, and in what manner its different branches are deployed. As we have seen, direct intervention by the army is how both Shahs came to have effective power – in the 1921 and 1953 coups. Both monarchs have also used the army to crush resistance in town and country. The present Shah used the army to crush the autonomous movements in Azerbaijan and Kurdistan in 1946–7, and to defeat the communists and National Front after 1953. Both actions have been given a special place in the régime's official mythology. The former is of special ideological importance since it has served to obscure the humiliating defeat of 1941 in which Anglo-Russian forces occupied the country against token resistance. The latter ended the elimination of opposition that had begun in 1946. Since then, 12 December (21 Azar) commemorating the occupation of Azerbaijan, and 19 August (28 Mordad) have been celebrated as national holidays. Subsequently, throughout the 1950s it was no secret that the main, indeed only, function of the Iranian army was to maintain the internal position of the régime; although the provision of U S arms was justified on the grounds that Iran needed them to ward off a Soviet attack, this was only a pretence. As U S Senator Hubert Humphrey put it in 1960: 'Do you know what the head of the Iranian army told one of our people? He said the army was in good shape, thanks to U S aid – it was now capable of coping with the civilian population.'[6]

However, the political role of the army has altered since that time from being in the front line of repression. Before the army was sent to confront demonstrators in 1978, the last occasion on which the army was used in a major urban operation was in crushing the mass uprising of June 1963 in Tehran and a number of other towns, in which over 1,000 people were killed. From 1963 to 1978 the army remained garrisoned near towns, occupied universities and was sent into tribal areas on a number of small-scale campaigns. Political trials were held before military tribunals. But it was not the army that played the most active repressive role in Iran: this was shared out among the other sections of the repressive apparatus, behind whom the army stood in reserve. The nature and scope of these other sections is to some extent a matter of conjecture, and the Shah, like other autocrats, is careful to promote rivalry and mutual surveillance among them. This is especially so since the two main challenges to his rule from within the repressive apparatus have come from the intelligence services – from General Gharani, head of Military Intelligence, in 1958, and from General Bakhtiar, head of SAVAK, in 1961.

Apart from or within the three main branches of the armed forces, it is possible to identify at least eight distinct repressive units, four of which are in some way overt police units, and the other four which perform various intelligence and secret police functions.[7]

A. Police Units:

1. Military Police
2. Town and City Police (*Shahrbani*)
3. Imperial Guard
4. Imperial Iranian Gendarmerie

B. Intelligence Units:

5. SAVAK
6. Military Intelligence (known as *Rokn-i Do*, or Department Two, i.e. G-2)
7. Imperial Iranian Inspectorate
8. Special Bureau (*Daftar-i Vizhe*)

Military Intelligence, the Military Police, and the Town and

City Police appear to perform the roles conventionally associated with these institutions, whilst the Town and City Police has its own intelligence subdivision. The other five have a more special position within the overall structure of the repressive apparatus. The Imperial Guard is a unit of about 2,000 men: all are officers and have been so since 1965 when a soldier in the unit tried to kill the Shah. They are stationed in Tehran, guarding the Shah, and are part of an élite corps of 70,000 men, including the parachutists and counter-insurgency rangers, deployed in and around the capital. The Inspectorate, set up in 1958, after the attempted coup by General Gharani, and in response to a welter of U S accusations about corruption, is the Shah's personal instrument for watching the armed forces and ensuring that no further conspiracies are hatched. The Special Bureau has wider powers: it is the most secretive of all units, and, among other functions, has responsibility for keeping an eye on S A V A K.

The Imperial Iranian Gendarmerie is, by contrast, a highly visible para-military force. Founded in 1911 with the aid of Swedish officers, it was advised from 1942 until 1976 by a team of U S specialists, and has for some decades been the main instrument for rural control – i.e. in those areas not covered by the regular police: this means all communities of 5,000 people and under, still half of the population and over 80 per cent of the country's area. The army is only brought in when the I I G has been unable to cope with events. I I G stations, of which there are over 2,000, are located in villages and at the crossings of rural roads, but whereas its main function in the past was controlling the tribes and peasants, it is now above all a counter-insurgency force. For this reason, it has been greatly expanded and modernized in recent years, just as the initial reason for its establishment has become less relevant. In the mid-1960s it had a force of 35,000 men and this has now been doubled to 70,000. Since 1970 all I I G stations have been linked by direct radio to H Q in Tehran. The I I G is also a highly mechanized unit: it has its own aircraft, helicopters, cars, jeeps and patrol craft. Its officers are trained in the army, and here too the Shah approves all promotions above a certain rank. This means that the Iranian countryside does not afford conditions favourable to building up a guerrilla force or indeed any opposition activities such as are found in some other third-world countries: through the IIG the state has extended its control in an extremely efficient way across the whole of the rural areas.

SAVAK

The most pervasive of all the security instruments is, of course, SAVAK. Reza Khan had his own intelligence system in the 1920s and 1930s, but SAVAK is a product of the repression following 1953 and of the US role in the latter. It was already noticeable during the early 1950s that some of the most active opponents of Mossadeq within the armed forces were in Military Intelligence; Mossadeq tried to win over, and then to purge, the armed forces but he did not have the power base to do this and was in the end overthrown by the military. In this respect there are many striking analogies with the fate of President Allende's Popular Unity government in Chile, exactly twenty years later, where US intervention via the army also overthrew a constitutionally elected government.

Following the coup, the main instrument of repression was the Military Governorate of Tehran, headed by General Teimour Bakhtiar, and under Bakhtiar were two specialized intelligence units: one, the Military Intelligence, had as its main responsibility the removal of opponents from within the armed forces; the other, Police Intelligence (*Agahi Kar*) was used for dealing with opposition parties, trades unions, and publications. At this time Bakhtiar was helped by US advisers, and when, in 1957, a new intelligence unit was set up, these became a permanent secret US mission attached to it. This new unit was SAVAK – *Sazman-i Etelaat va Amjniat-i Keshvar*, or the National Information and Security Organization. The law establishing SAVAK contained three main articles stipulating that:

1. SAVAK is part of the Prime Minister's office; its head

is appointed by the Shah and has the rank of Deputy Prime Minister.

2. SAVAK concerns itself with obtaining information 'required for the maintenance of national security'; with uncovering espionage; and with those suspected of violating laws relating to anti-monarchical activity, armed opposition, military crimes and attempts on the life of the King and Crown Prince. The most frequently used of these laws is the Treason Act of 1931 (22 Khordad 1310) which makes it a crime to advocate 'collectivist' (i.e. socialist or communist) ideas.

3. SAVAK officials act as the military magistrates in judging crimes falling within their jurisdiction, in accordance with the military tribunal system set up to try political crimes.[8]

SAVAK has only acquired its special position since 1963. It was established *after* the main opposition of the early 1950s had been crushed, and it proved incapable of containing the political situation and preventing riots in the early 1960s: it was for this reason that the army was called into action again in June 1963. The Shah also clashed with the two first heads of the organization. General Bakhtiar, who headed SAVAK till 1961, was dismissed after failing to stage-manage some elections efficiently and for building a power base within the armed forces: he subsequently went into exile where he organized some opposition before being shot dead by a SAVAK assassin in Iraq in 1970. The second head of SAVAK, General Hassan Pakravan, had been formerly head of Military Intelligence and then Bakhtiar's deputy in SAVAK; but he proved too lenient for the Shah's liking, and fell from grace after the June 1963 rising. He was finally sacked in 1965 after an attempt on the Shah's life by a soldier; his place was taken by General Nassiri, the man appointed as Military Governor of Tehran in June 1963, and therefore *de facto* chief of security from that date.

Nassiri's tenure of office lasted until 1978 and his period marked the end of the internal and executive uncertainties of the first eight years. Nassiri proved to be as ruthless as Bakhtiar, without, it seems, having Bakhtiar's personal ambitions.

What we know about SAVAK gives us at least a glimpse of its range of activities. The official budget for 1972–3 was $255 millions, for 1973–4 $310 millions; but this could well be an understatement and other allocations hidden in other sections of the security budget. Estimates of those who work for SAVAK vary from 3,120 (the Shah, 1976) to 30,000–60,000 (*Newsweek*, 1974);[9] but whilst there is uncertainty about the number of full-time employees, no one denies that SAVAK has a far larger army of part-time informers spread throughout Iran and Iranian communities abroad. *Newsweek* claimed in 1974 that up to 3 million Iranians acted in one way or another as SAVAK informers, and in a rare public statement a SAVAK official in 1971 confirmed that this latter category included 'workers, farmers, students, professors, teachers, guild members, political parties and other associations'.[10] Such is the power of SAVAK that it has recruited quite a number of former members of the opposition; some are ex-communists, and one at least is a former member of the student opposition, a vocal exponent of Guevarism who was imprisoned for a time in the mid-1960s.

SAVAK's responsibilities cover a much wider range than those often allocated to a single security agency – espionage and counter-espionage, political and military intelligence. It appears that the organization is divided into nine separate units: one is concerned with personnel, one with prisons, one with liaison with foreign espionage services, one with co-operation with the police and Military Intelligence, one with spying on Iranians abroad. The most important section is known as 'Internal Security and Action': this is the one responsible for domestic repression and is accordingly subdivided into different regional sections, and into sections with specific responsibilities for individual political groups. This 'Internal Security and Action' branch was initially headed by General Nasser Moqaddem, who held the post for fifteen years before becoming head of Military Intelligence and in 1978 head of SAVAK. The present head of this section is Parviz Sabeti. Born in 1936 and the brother of a prominent businessman Sabeti is believed to have been trained in Israel. He is officially described as 'Deputy Director of SAVAK', and Chairman of the joint Committee of the National Police Force and SAVAK. Sabeti's office is in the main building of the police and SAVAK in central Tehran, the notorious *Comité* building where political detainees are usually first taken to be tortured.

The main task of SAVAK is the identification and destruction of all those who in any way oppose the Shah's dictatorship; but in the execution of this task, it goes beyond the narrow limits of what could be termed secret police work. In the first place, SAVAK is a *secret* organization with a public face. It is part of the régime's policy to let it be known that such an entity exists; on occasion officials justify SAVAK's existence by pointing to threats facing Iran, and to the fact that other countries also have security agencies. In Iran itself, officials like Sabeti occasionally give interviews, and Iranians are encouraged to bear in mind that this pervasive institution is there: inhabitants of towns like Tehran or Tabriz can tell visitors which buildings are known to be used by SAVAK. Students at Tehran University know that since the riots of 1962 two houses near by – in 21 Azar Street and Anatole France Street – have been occupied by SAVAK agents and ordinary police whose job it is to quell student dissent. It is through the balance of the secret and the overt that fear and suspicion are most effectively maintained.

SAVAK's internal role goes far beyond that of mere repression. In any such society where free expression is banned the régime has to promote the appearance of at least some freedom and has to gather information on popular sentiments through the secret police. Thus, SAVAK is the agent of censorship in Iran: but it also publishes books and magazines, and even uses some of its ex-opposition members to promote certain kinds of confusionist 'opposition' thinking. SAVAK also runs the 600-odd government trades unions and SAVAK officials have offices in some factories; again, they do not just repress strikes, but also mediate between workers and owners, and try to mobilize support among the workers for the régime and for increased output. Such is the suspicion of Iranians about SAVAK and so multifarious are its forms of activity that almost anyone who does voice protest about the government runs the risk of being suspected of being a SAVAK agent. Conversely, at home and abroad, the régime encourages a climate of hostility among dissidents in which each and every one is suspicious of the other working with SAVAK. It is a very effective and insidious way of demoralizing any opposition.

SAVAK's activities extend beyond Iran's frontiers in at least four respects – espionage, covert actions abroad, liaison with foreign intelligence services, and surveillance of Iranian dissidents. Iranian agents certainly operate in those countries of western Asia about which Iran is concerned and in which it claims to have a strategic interest. According to one source: 'Western spy chiefs give them exceptionally high marks for their intelligence-gathering operations in the Middle East, particularly in the Persian Gulf, Egypt and Lebanon.'[11] There is no known case of an Iranian spy being caught in any of these countries, but the extent of Iranian undercover activity in Iraq is illustrative. In July 1969 Iranian agents conspired with Iraqi army officers in an unsuccesful coup. In 1970 a SAVAK agent assassinated General Bakhtiar whilst the latter was out hunting. Between 1972 and 1975 SAVAK agents worked with the forces of Kurdish leader Barzani in revolt against the Baghdad government: SAVAK agents openly assisted foreign journalists visiting the Kurdish areas via Iran, and SAVAK personnel set up a client security network in the Kurdish mountains; this unit, known as *Parastin*, was responsible only to the Barzani himself and was used to quell dissent within the Kurdish population.

The two foreign agencies with which SAVAK has co-operated the longest have been those of the USA and Israel. The establishment of SAVAK was, as already noted, carried out under US supervision, and it is significant that it was not just the CIA, i.e. the *foreign* spy agency, but also the FBI, the *domestic* agency that provided aid. (In the USA, the FBI is used both for crime-busting and tracking political enemies.) As Iran has developed its foreign espionage activities one can assume that a further U S agency, the electronic surveillance National Security Agency, has developed its links with S A V A K. Since 1973 Tehran has been the H Q of the C I A in the Middle East (this was previously in Nicosia). The appointment as U S Ambassador of former C I A chief Richard Helms between 1973 and 1976 is also indicative in this respect. No one indeed denies this link: a State Department official confirmed to me in October 1976 that there was 'no secret about cooperation between S A V A K and the C I A.' Iran's cooperation with Mossad, the Israeli intelligence service, goes back to the early 1950s, when Iran and Israel shared a common hostility to Arab nationalism. In the past few years, S A V A K has developed ties with other intelligence services: in Pakistan, Jordan, Egypt and until the left-wing coup of April 1978 in Afghanistan. Information is exchanged and common enemies are kept under observation.

The area of overseas S A V A K action that has received most attention is its pursuit of Iranian dissidents. Documents taken from the Iranian Embassy in Geneva in 1975 indicated that this was the H Q of S A V A K activity in Europe: instructions from Sabeti in Tehran included one to the London Embassy urging them to get information on two Labour Members of Parliament known for voicing criticisms of the Shah. These documents testify to phone tapping, installing microphones, photographing dissidents and break-ins by S A V A K agents abroad. Such agents act under diplomatic cover. In August 1976, following the publication of these documents, the Swiss government expelled a First Secretary, Ahmed Malek Mahdavi, whom it alleged was a senior S A V A K official with overall responsibility for western Europe. The Geneva documents also confirmed that in the Paris Embassy an official named as Homayun Keikabusi was in fact a S A V A K agent. In October 1976 the *Washington Post*, quoting U S intelligence sources, named Mansur Rafizadeh, an official at Iran's U N Mission, as head of S A V A K in the U S A.[12] Although Rafizadeh himself denied having anything to do with S A V A K, both the Shah and Sabeti in interviews with U S journalists admitted that S A V A K carried out observation on Iranian dissidents abroad.[13] In Britain too SAVAK has been identified in action: in 1974 the *Sunday Times* (12 May) recorded the SAVAK director for the UK working in the Embassy, Ali Abdol Jahanbin, trying to persuade an Iranian student to gather information on dissident exiles.

SAVAK bears many similarities to other security organizations in repressive capitalist third-world states in recent years. It is most similar to those organizations founded, like itself, in third-world countries where a popular resistance exists and which the régime is trying, with US backing, to crush. In both Brazil after the coup of 1964 and in Chile after 1973 SAVAK-type units came into existence as SAVAK had done: they were detached from the main body of the army and police and reorganized with US assistance. In the former case the DOPS (Department for Political and Social Order) and in the latter the DINA (Directorate of National Intelligence) were formed to make repression a permanent feature of the new régime, something in addition to the already crushing weight of the army, riot squads and the rest. Another point of comparison is, tragically, in the systematic incidence of torture, found in all three countries, as well as in many others. SAVAK used torture in the 1950s, but this was of a comparatively crude kind. In the 1970s torture of a sophisticated kind became for several years a normal part of SAVAK's interrogation routine for political prisoners, as it became in Chile and Brazil. The methods used, as well as the instruments, in all three countries bear striking similarities. No one has been able to prove that US advisers have taught or participated in torture in these countries; but the diffusion of techniques, and the common sponsorship of all three organizations, indicates that their common patron the US government bears a heavy responsibility for what has occurred, as it has for other client secret police forces such as the Korean CIA and, up to 1975, the secret police of the Saigon dictatorship.

The Violation of Human Rights

The facts of SAVAK brutality have been known for a

number of years and had become a byword for the systematic application of cruelty by a government agency. In the words of the Secretary General of Amnesty International in 1975, 'No country in the world has a worse record in human rights than Iran.'[14] Using reports by Amnesty International and the International Commission of Jurists, the record up to the end of 1976 can be summarized as follows:[15]

1. Arrest and Detention: S A V A K arrests and detains any person at will. There is no legal preliminary to searches and arrests, no time limit on detention, no right of the detainee to independent access to lawyers. S A V A K's power is arbitrary and absolute.

2. Trials: all political trials are held before military tribunals. The judges are either army officers or S A V A K officials. They are held in secret. No defence witnesses are allowed. Amnesty report that no foreign observers were allowed to attend such trials after March 1972 and that it 'knows of no case of a defendant being acquitted'.

3. Prison Conditions: there are three kinds of prison in Iran – police detention centres, which are mainly for short-term sentences; court prisons, usually for criminal offences; and long-term penitentiaries, where S A V A K victims are sent. The best-known political prisons are in or around Tehran – Qasr, Evin and Qezel Qale. Others include those in Tabriz, Shiraz, Rezaie, Rasht, Arak, Bandar Abbas, Mashad, Mahabad, Borazjan, Booshehr, Zahedan, Semnan and Kermanshah. A Colonel M. A. Kasrai, Deputy Director of the General Prison Department, told a British visitor in May 1975 that there were in all 6,000 prisons in Iran: this may well have been an exaggeration unless every police station was included, and the political prisoner population is probably concentrated in a dozen or so centres. No independent observers have even been allowed to visit these prisons, but there have been many reports of sub-human conditions. In the words of the Amnesty report, pre-trial prisoners are 'locked up in small damp cells with only a straw mattress on which to sleep ... Lack of heating in the winter or cooling in the summer create extra hardship frequently remarked upon by prisoners. Washing faci-

lities are inadequate and opportunities for washing are infrequent. Food rations are small and inadequate and no opportunities are provided for exercise.' Analogous conditions prevail after sentencing and in addition: 'Medical treatment is practically non-existent and prisoners are hardly ever seen by a doctor, sent to hospital or allowed to receive medicines. Discipline is severe and in cases of indiscipline prisoners may be put into solitary confinement for anything up to three or four months.'[16]

4. Release: political prisoners who recant in court, or who agree to make public statements renouncing their previous views, are given lighter sentences. SAVAK makes a special point of putting such prisoners on national television, and there getting them to make confessions and denounce their companions. But prisoners who do not recant may well remain in prison after their terms have officially expired. Amnesty reports that a special section of Qasr prison is reserved for those who are not to be released but have served their terms.

There is no accurate information on the numbers arrested, sentenced or in prison for political offences. Since all political crimes are classed as 'criminal' under the 1931 law the authorities often deny there are any political prisoners. The Shah himself on one occasion in 1977 admitted to 3,200 prisoners;[17] foreign observers have spoken of between 25,000 and 100,000.[18] Given conditions in Iran it is impossible to estimate the number, let alone discern such matters as how many are short-term and how many long-term detainees. In any case, the absolute numbers are not the main point at issue: the most serious question concerns the continued violation of human rights by the Shah's régime. On top of the issues already discussed concerning arrest and imprisonment, there is the even more serious question of torture.

SAVAK has used torture before trials, to get information and confessions from detainees, and after trials, to intimidate and pressure prisoners so that they will make public confessions. Torture is no longer an exceptional part of Iranian police procedure: since the late 1960s it has become a normal part of the interrogation and detention system. Amnesty summarizes what it has been told: 'Alleged methods of torture include whipping and beating, electric shocks, the extraction of nails and teeth, boiling water pumped into the rectum, heavy weights hung on the testicles, tying the prisoner to a metal table heated to a white heat, inserting a broken bottle into the anus, and rape.'[19] The following four specific cases are, whilst only a fraction of the misery imposed in the Shah's jails, illustrative of what occurs:

1. In 1972 a French lawyer, Nuri Albala, attended the trial in Tehran of Masoud Ahmadzadeh, an engineer later executed by the régime. At one point Ahmadzadeh pulled up his pullover to reveal the marks of torture on himself. In Albala's words: 'The whole of the middle of his chest and his stomach was a mass of twisted scars from very deep burns. They looked appalling ... His back was even worse. There was a perfect oblong etched into it, formed by a continuous line of scar tissue. Inside the oblong, the skin was again covered in shiny scars from burning. I would estimate that the width of the table marks on his back was at least nine inches.' Further investigations by Albala revealed that Ahmadzadeh and other prisoners had been toasted on a special hot table – 'an iron frame, rather like a bed-frame, covered with wire mesh which was electrically heated like a toaster'.[20]

2. Ashraf Dehqani, a woman guerrilla who later escaped from prison, recounts in her memoirs how during her interrogation by S A V A K she was raped by her torturers and had live snakes placed on her. In particular she named Captain Bijan Niktab, a S A V A K officer mentioned by other prisoners as having worked in the *Comité* prison in central Tehran.[21]

3. An Iranian student whom I interviewed in 1976 described how he was arrested in 1973 and take to the *Comité* prison. During interrogation he was tied to a bed, and the soles of his feet were beaten with a wire rope (*feleke*, a traditional form of brutality in the Middle East). Then, when he refused to give information, his trousers were pulled down and a baton with an electric charge on the end was applied to his genitals: this baton, known to Iranian prisoners as the 'electric stick' (*asa barqi*), is a modified cattle prod, also commonly used by

torturers in Latin America. In this case, the three interrogators (who referred to each other as 'Doctor') used this on him for some hours, shouting abuse at him all the time. According to this student, the main torture rooms are on the third floor of the *Comité*, and at night the shouts of SAVAK's victims can be heard throughout the building.

4. Reza Baraheni, a writer held in *Comité* prison for 102 days in 1973, describes a similar experience:

The torture on the second day of my arrest consisted of 75 blows with a plaited wire whip at the soles of my feet. I was whipped on my hands as well, and the head torturer took the small finger of my left hand and broke it, saying that he was going to break my fingers one by one, one each day. Then I was told that, if I didn't confess, my wife and thirteen-year-old daughter would be raped in front of my eyes. All this time I was being beaten from head to toe. Then a pistol was held at my temple by the head torturer, Dr Azudi, and he prepared to shoot. In fact, the sound of shooting came, and I fainted. When I opened my eyes, I was being interrogated by someone who called himself Dr Rezvan. The interrogation, combined with psychological torture and sometimes additional beatings, went on for 102 days until I was let out.[22]

The initial reason for such torture is to obtain information and to break prisoners *before* the trial. There are in fact two forms of preliminary interrogation: one, *bazjui*, is carried out by SAVAK and is really designed to extract as much information as possible before legal proceedings begin; the other, *bazporsi*, is carried out by interrogators attached to the military tribunals, and is specifically related to preparing the prosecution case. Torture usually accompanies *bazjui* rather than *bazporsi*. But harsh treatment does not end at the trials: numerous cases of torture after trial have been reported, and an unknown number of people have been killed while serving their sentences. In 1974 two members of the Tudeh Party died of brutal treatment in prison. In April 1975 it emerged that nine men, all members of an opposition group imprisoned in 1967, had been shot. Although they were nearing the end of their sentences, the régime claimed they were 'shot while trying to escape'. Their relatives were never allowed to see their bodies, and many people suspect they were killed after refusing to make public recantations.

S A V A K kills in at least three distinguishable ways. First, an unknown number of people have been shot outright – in clashes with police, or 'resisting arrest'. Since guerrilla resistance began in 1971, dozens of young people have been officially reported killed in this way, although the real figure may be higher still. S A V A K has it seems sometimes deliberately killed opponents rather than arrest them. Secondly, a considerable number of people have been shot after trial by military tribunals. In the 1950s before S A V A K itself was created the former Foreign Minister in Mossadeq's government and at least thirty-six army officers were shot in this way. From 1971 to 1976 over 300 people were officially executed after being sentenced by military tribunals.[23] Thirdly, an unknown number of people have died of maltreatment and torture under interrogation, or in jail.

The Iranian government denies these allegations. The Shah denies that physical torture is used, although he admits it was used in the past. Sabeti has stated: 'We never torture.'[24] The press attaché at the Iranian Embassy in Washington, Manoucheir Ardalan, told the author in October 1976 that no torture was used in Iran. Embassy officials elsewhere say the same. Iran's major ally, the U S A, has also tried to deny that torture is used. A State Department official told a Congressional committee in September 1976 that he did not believe there was torture in Iran, although he accepted there was 'harsh treatment'.[25] Iran has, however, not allowed independent investigation of these matters: there is, obviously, no independent press, judiciary or legal profession in Iran which could check them. Iran is certainly not the only country in the world to violate human rights in this way. But this in no way lessens the horrors of what is, and has been, happening in Iran.

In 1977 the régime introduced a number of modifications in the policies it had pursued up to that time. The Red Cross was permitted to visit certain prisons, as were a few foreign journalists. The first foreign observers to be allowed to attend a trial sat in on the court where eleven members of the opposition were being prosecuted. Legislation was introduced making political trials public, unless there were strong reasons against this, and allowing those undergoing trial to have civilian lawyers. It was rumoured that the incidence of torture had declined. However, these reports should be treated with circumspection. In the first place, such changes have occurred in the past and have proved only temporary. This was the case in the early 1960s. Secondly, the only adequate guarantee against such practices is the existence of a legal profession and a press able to monitor them. The pressure from abroad was such that the régime may have felt obliged to introduce certain changes: only time will tell how far these changes go, or how long they last. For the main factors behind this abuse, the political conditions and state institutions using torture, have remained intact, and personnel running them are the same. What has been modified one year can easily be changed back in the next.

The Role of the U S A

The contemporary character of the repressive apparatus in Iran has been shaped by the relationship with the U S A, from the Phantom jets of the air force to the investigation practices of S A V A K learnt from the F B I. As we have seen, the armed forces acquired a dominant position in Iran in the 1920s *before* the U S A played any significant role. But it is above all the relationship with the U S A that has since 1941 consolidated the role of the military and enabled it to acquire quite new dimensions, abroad as well as at home. The U S A has sold weapons to many other countries in the world, but in no case, not even Israel or Brazil, has the client relationship with the U S A enabled a third-world country to become a major regional power in the manner and to the extent that Iran has.

The military relationship with the U S A has gone through four distinct phases, in each of which new economic and strategic factors have taken the alliance on to a grander scale:

1. *1942–7*: When Britain and Russia occupied Iran in 1941,

they paved the way for 30,000 U S troops of the Persian Gulf Command to enter Iran to work on transporting supplies to Russia. The Iranian armed forces had been shattered by 1941, and in 1942 the U S A brought two small missions to help rebuild these forces. A Military Mission was assigned to the army in an advisory role, and another more operational mission, GENMISH, worked with the Gendarmerie. GENMISH was at this time the most important link between the U S A and the Iranian security apparatus: it was through GENMISH, and its head Colonel Norman Schwartzkopf, a former F B I official and chief of the New Jersey State Police, that the U S A played an active part in crushing popular resistance in Azerbaijan and Kurdistan after they were reoccupied in 1946–7.

2. *1947–64*: from this initially limited beginning, the U S A consolidated its relations with Iran as the cold war began. Iran was a front-line state and the U S A, having got its foot in the door, was determined to turn Iran into a stronghold in the anti-Russian offensive. In 1947 the previously advisory Military Mission became an operational one – ARMISH – and the U S A began to bring in surplus war material to boost the Iranian armed forces. The limit was first set at $10 millions but this was raised to $60 millions in 1948, and in 1950 a Mutual Defence Assistance Agreement was signed. This provided the basis for much subsequent reinforcement. In overall terms, between 1946 and 1970 Iran received $1,365·6 millions in military aid from the U S A; of this aid to Iran $830·4 millions came in the form of military assistance, and amounted to 7 per cent of all the U S aid under its Military Assistance Programme in this period; the remaining $504·1 millions came in the form of credit. In the period from the end of the war until 1975, a total of over 11,000 Iranian military personnel were trained at installations in the U S A.

From 1947 until the early 1960s the Iranian military's main, indeed sole, aim was internal repression, and it was U S aid and advice that made possible both the coup of 1953 and the subsequent consolidation of the Shah's régime. Sherman tanks, provided in 1951, were used to crush popular resistance in

Tehran; a convenient supply of US military and economic credits in the months after the coup gave the régime the funds it needed to stabilize its position. Throughout this period the USA maintained at least four separate military missions in Iran: GENMISH, which handled the IIG, the two armed forces missions, ARMISH and MAAG, and a secret mission with SAVAK. In the late 1950s as many as 900 US personnel were working with the Iranian armed forces.

No one pretended that this was necessary to meet Iran's border defence needs: the Soviet Union had nothing to fear from the Iranian army, and the foes against which the Shah was being armed were those inside and not outside the country. Yet by the early 1960s US criticism of the Iranian government had increased, and it was realized in Washington that such a régime was not in its existing form a long-term guarantor of stability in Iran. The Kennedy administration therefore urged social reforms on the Shah. But the US criticism was also in part directed at the armed forces themselves. In the words of Kennedy's personal adviser, Theodore Sorensen: 'In Iran the Shah insisted on our supporting an expensive army too large for border incidents and internal security and of no use in an all-out war. His army ... resembled the proverbial man who was too heavy to do any light work and too light to do any heavy work.'[26] In response the Shah made certain changes: hundreds of officers were sacked in anti-corruption campaigns, and the formal size of the army was reduced from 125,000 to 100,000. But whilst the Shah pushed ahead with his reforms he also reminded Iranians of the army's place in maintaining order: its role in quelling the urban risings of June 1963 and the tribal resistance in Fars should have removed any doubts on this score.

3. *1964–72*: the critical climate of the early 1960s soon dispersed, and Iran was then able to increase the flow of US arms. This was facilitated by two further developments. First, Iran began to develop a regional foreign policy for the first time; the Shah could argue that it was defending western interests in the face of radical Arab régimes such as that of Nasser's Egypt and of republican Iraq, on Iran's borders.

Secondly, U S arms policy shifted away from the direct provision of aid towards the sale of arms on credit. Iran qualified for such credit, both in the sense that it was an ally and in the sense that with rising oil revenues it could afford to borrow on a considerable scale. Three dates stand out in this period:

(i) June 1964: the Shah on a visit to Washington persuaded a previously reluctant President Johnson to provide Iran with military sales credit. This credit rose from an initial $48 millions in 1965 to $300 millions in 1973. These credits marked a strategic shift in U S policy to a new level of arms supplies. The U S Military Assistance Programme ended in 1969, whilst government-to-government sales rose by an even greater amount. Between 1950 and 1964 these had come to only $1·3 millions but orders then rose to $208 millions in 1966 alone.

(ii) January 1968: the British announced they would pull their forces out of the Persian Gulf by the end of 1971 and Iran let it be known that it was determined to take Britain's place as the dominant military power. The Gulf and northern Indian Ocean then became the major concern in Iranian defence planning: troops were moved from the borders with Russia to the western border with Iraq and to the southern provinces of Iran, bordering the Gulf. The three main army corps had their H Qs in positions corresponding to this new posture: the 1st Army Corps was based at Kermanshah, the 2nd at Tehran and the 3rd at Shiraz.

(iii) July 1969: U S President Nixon stated on the island of Guam that the U S A was now concerned to encourage third-world states to assume greater responsibility for their own defence and that the U S A would encourage this process. Although most immediately related to Vietnam, this new doctrine had implications for Iran, and the Shah had the money, and occupied the strategic position, to take advantage of the opportunity. It came three years later.

4. *1972 onwards*: Iran was able to enter a quite new dimension of army purchases as a result of two further events:

(i) In May 1972 President Nixon visited Tehran, and in a secret agreement, unparalleled in the U S A's relations with any other non-industrialized country, agreed to sell Iran any conventional weapons it required. In particular he agreed to provide Iran with F-14 and F-15 combat aircraft, the most advanced then in existence.

(ii) In late 1973 the OPEC states raised the price of oil by five times. Iran's oil revenues thereby multiplied, and with them its capacity to purchase weapons. These two events together unleashed the largest arms sales boom in history.

The Arms Boom

The dimensions of the arms flow released by this conjuncture can be stated in a summary form. First, Iran's outlay on defence has escalated in the past two decades: from $78 millions in 1954 to $241 millions in 1964 to $3,680 millions in 1974. Under the 1973–8 Five Year Plan, revised after the 1973 OPEC price rises, Iran will spend 31 per cent of all its monies on military expenditure.

Table 4: Iran's Defence Budget 1970–77
In US $ millions at current prices

Year	*Defence Budget*	*Percentage Increase on Previous Year*
1970	880	–
1971	1,065	17
1972	1,375	29
1973	1,525	11
1974	3,680	141
1975	6,325	72
1976	8,925	41
1977	9,400	5

Source: *US Military Sales to Iran,* Staff Report to the Subcommittee on Foreign Assistance of the Senate Foreign Relation Committee, Washington, 1976, p. 13.

Secondly, between 50 and 80 per cent of this expenditure is going on foreign purchases, and in particular on purchases from the USA. Iran is in the mid-1970s the largest single purchaser of US arms in the world, and total sales in the years 1972–6 came to $10·4 billions. The 1970–83 total is estimated at $18·5 billions.

Table 5: U S Military Sales to Iran 1950–77
In U S $ millions at current prices

Year	
1950–69	757·0
1970	113·2
1971	396·8
1972	519·1
1973	2,157·4
1974	4,373·2
1975	3,021·0
1976	1,458.7
1977*	4,213·0
1950–77	17,009·4

*estimate

Source: Michael Klare, based on U S Department of Defense publications.

The arms purchased in these years did not all arrive in the same period – some will not arrive till the early 1980s, but by then new forward purchases will presumably also have been made. As a result of the arms inflow there has been a great expansion in the size, fire-power and deployment of the Iranian forces. The numbers of men under arms in all services has risen from 161,000 in 1970 to 413,000 in 1978; of these 250,000 are in the army. But the increase in armaments has been even more spectacular:

1. By 1976 the Iranian army had ordered or acquired nearly 3,000 modern tanks, and by the early 1980s may have as many as 6,000. Between 1975 and 1977 it acquired over 9,000 T O W anti-tank missiles. The army is also developing a large army aviation unit, a counter-insurgency force which by 1978 is expected to have 14,000 personnel and over 890 modern helicopters. In the same year it is reckoned that Iran will have twice the number of soldiers, arms and armament of the British army.

2. The Iranian navy has acquired the largest hovercraft

fleet in the world, and has on order 4 U S-built Spruance destroyers, to be delivered in 1980–81. These ships, which will be deployed in the Indian Ocean, can be used for anti-submarine and anti-shipping operations, as well as for coastal bombardment. The cost of each rose from $120 millions in 1974 to $339 millions in 1976. The navy has also ordered 3 Tang class submarines for use in the Indian Ocean.

3. The largest purchases have been of aircraft – $11·8 billions' worth up to the end of 1976. Iran placed F-4 Phantoms on order in 1965 and the first ones arrived in 1968. Iran now has on order 290 Phantom bombers, 33 F-5 light interceptor planes, 80 F-14s and 160 F-16s, all for delivery by the end of 1978. Iran's air force will then be numerically the fourth largest in the world, and in armaments at least the third most sophisticated. This arms boom has been accompanied by a vast infrastructural expansion. The air force has seven major bases, with three more operational bases in the east. Current work includes the construction of fifty smaller airfields where Hawk anti-aircraft missiles will be stationed. The navy had in 1976 six naval bases along the coast of the Gulf, but plans exist for the construction of a new, larger, base at Chah Bahar on the Indian Ocean. This will serve as the base for the Spruances and the Tangs. Most base expansion has taken place in the south of the country and there are plans to invest up to $30 billions in the Gulf provinces between 1975 and 1982, much of it in defence-related expenditure. It may be too early to determine what the effects of these developments are; but it is already obvious that a whole number of problems and dangers have arisen. These fall into two main categories: first, problems internal to the arms flow itself, and secondly the political implications, inside and outside Iran, of this military growth.

Problems of the Arms Flow

Following Nixon's 1972 agreement with the Shah, and especially after the rise in the price of oil, an army of U S arms salesmen descended on Iran, as did, in smaller numbers, their counterparts from Britain and France. It soon became clear, however, that even in terms of what the Iranian government and its foreign suppliers were trying to do, i.e. leaving aside the political implications, serious difficulties had arisen:

1. The arms flow was out of control: no U S agency was overseeing what Iran was ordering and no Iranian government agency was either. Sole responsibility for major purchases lay with the Shah, and he did not take care to investigate the details of what Iran was acquiring. By 1976 relations between the U S and Iranian officials involved had deteriorated: the Shah was accusing U S firms of dumping useless equipment onto Iran, and of unjustifiably hiking prices, whilst U S Congressional investigators were questioning Iran's capacity to use the weapons it was getting. Even the Chairman of the Joint Chiefs of Staff, General George Brown, was heard to remark: 'The military programmes the Shah has coming, it just makes you wonder whether he doesn't some day have visions of the Persian Empire', and the U S Ambassador in Tehran, Richard Helms, declared that he had 'washed his hands' of parts of the U S military sales programme.[27]

2. The most serious on-the-ground problem was the shortage of Iranians with the skills to maintain and use the new equipment. According to a Congressional report, technical manpower requirements in the Iranian air force are likely to rise from 20,000 in 1976 to 40,000 in 1981. The 1976 shortfall was 7,000 and could rise to 10,000 by 1981. The navy too was experiencing difficulties in getting trainees for its submarine crews, because of the demand for such personnel for the Spruance programme. The same report indicated that most training and equipment programmes were running considerably behind schedule.[28] The great shortage of skilled personnel in the Iranian economy as a whole (700,000 in the 1973–8 Plan period) will only increase the pressure on the military.

3. No proper estimates exist of how efficient the Iranian military machine is, but because of its lack of serious combat experience it is not comparable in practical terms with other Asian forces – those of India, Pakistan, Jordan or Israel, for example. U S officials estimate that the 40 per cent wastage found in the economy as a whole will probably also apply to

the armed forces. The campaign fought by the Shah's army in Dhofar between 1973 and 1976 was a low-level one, and not therefore indicative of how the military machine could cope with a large-scale conflict. But the Shah used this occasion to train many men in combat conditions: the 3,000-man expeditionary force was rotated every four months to provide the maximum spread of experience. Non-Iranian observers have noted that Iranians in Dhofar were reluctant to engage directly with the guerrillas, but relied on their heavy fire-power instead. U S pilots at the aviation training school in Isfahan have also been critical, often dismissive, of their charges: after a strike by U S personnel in 1975 these complained they were being made to pass pilots who were not properly qualified. As for the navy, one can only point out that it is a very recently expanded force with little experience in handling its new equipment. In the words of the British Naval Attaché in Tehran in 1975 it is 'inefficient and understaffed'.

4. The flow of U S arms has brought with it the need to import more and more U S military personnel. In 1976 there were 2,941 former members of the U S armed forces working for U S firms and another 1,435 directly under the U S Department of Defense. By 1980 it is reckoned by U S Senate investigations there may be 50,000–60,000 U S personnel and their families in Iran, most on defence-related contracts. Iran will not be able to fight a war of any duration without the active collaboration of U S experts. Although more and more Iranians will be trained to service and use these weapons, there will be a substantial U S military community in Iran right through the 1980s – hostages to the policies of the Shah, and to the anger of his enemies. Between 1973 and 1976 six Americans working in Iran on security activities were assassinated by Iranian guerrillas, and the incidence of this could well increase. A further dangerous indication is the fact that there is already evidence that U S personnel have participated in active military operations with Iranian forces. U S air personnel flew operational missions during the war in Iraqi Kurdistan, and surveillance planes in the war in Dhofar; a small group of U S experts was also involved on the ground in

Dhofar, and some of the surveillance of the Gulf and northern Indian Ocean by Iranian F-14 planes is being done by U S personnel.[29]

5. Iran is also critically reliant on the U S A for continued supplies. It is now engaged in trying to build up a military production industry. Iran is building an $800 millions ordnance factory at Isfahan with British help, and in 1976 assembly of Bell A H–1 J helicopters began at Shiraz; but this assembly programme is one that in no way lessens Iran's dependence on imported supplies and technology. Iran has also purchased a fleet of arms transport planes and converted Boeing 707 in-flight refuelling tankers in order to enable it to fly in its own supplies from the U S A during a possible conflict. But Iran will only be able to get the supplies in the first place if its patron and ally agrees.

6. The Iranian arms boom has, not unexpectedly, been accompanied by considerable corruption, in particular the taking of bribes or commissions by middlemen acting for U S and other arms firms. The Shah has tried to focus attention on members of the armed forces involved in this – like the heads of the navy and gendarmerie who were prosecuted in 1976 and 1974 respectively. But U S Congressional investigations in 1976 revealed that far more important people were involved: among them were the Shah's nephew Prince Sharam and the head of the air force, General Khatami, both agents for Northrop. Three Iranian brothers now resident in the U S A, the Lavi brothers, received $6 millions from Grumman for their services.[30] The Shah has also realized that not only does Iran have to pay for the bribes (the U S firms add them to the cost) but that in some cases the equipment acquired in this way is ill-suited to Iran's needs, even in the manner in which these are conceived of by the Shah.

The Political Consequences

The technical difficulties attending the arms programme, and the acrimonious disputes within the U S business and defence communities about the Iranian programme, are in the end of only secondary importance. Indeed the greed and short-sightedness illustrated by the post-1972 developments are most reprehensible, not because of the inefficient use of weaponry but because they demonstrate once again how much the monies that Iran so needs for its development are being wasted. But, despite the internal problems involved, the military reinforcement of the Shah's régime over the past decade is a development that is having enormous implications, which we can, briefly, survey.

In terms of the internal context, there can be no doubt that the arms purchases have further strengthened the position of the military. In the most direct sense, its repressive capacities have been reinforced; although Spruance and F-14s are of no use in fighting guerrillas, there has been a comparable expansion in counter-insurgency equipment. The 890 helicopters, and the computerized information system for the police being installed, are all designed for this purpose and the new tanks have been used on the streets of Tehran. Secondly, by acquiring such enormous amounts of weapons the armed forces have strengthened their economic position: more and more people depend on them for employment and for supplying their needs, and given the immense continuous investment required the military of all three services will continue to make a substantial claim on the budget. There can be no doubt that were the Shah to be assassinated or his prestige seriously weakened then the armed forces would be willing and able to intervene.

The military build-up also has ominous implications for Iranian foreign policy. Iran has in the past decade carried out a number of aggressive foreign actions, some overt and some covert. It has dispatched troops to Oman, Iraq and the United Arab Emirates (see pp. 270–71), and has loaned or supplied arms to a range of other governments – South Vietnam, Somalia, Jordan, Morocco and North Yemen. As Iran becomes stronger, the temptation to intervene abroad will certainly become greater and while there is nothing inevitable about this development, there are a number of factors which taken together will make Iranian attacks on its neighbours more likely (see p. 269).

In all these economic and strategic changes Iran is, of course, closely tied to the U S A. The present arms boom has benefited the U S A in a number of ways. U S arms firms, and the U S armed services, have seen the costs of research and production of new weapons substantially lowered by Iranian orders. The aerospace and defence industries in the U S A have benefited outright by the exports to Iran. For Washington, the growth of Iran as a regional power has meant that western interests are defended without the west having to pay for them: indeed, the Nixon doctrine is still working in such a way that the oil revenues being paid to Iran are paying for Iran's military build-up. Moreover, despite Iran's increased independence in many respects, the character of the present arms flow has created new forms of reliance in the economic, military and foreign policy spheres.

Iran is also serving, as it has done since the 1940s, as a forward base for spying on the Soviet Union: the U S A and Iran are together developing a new $500 millions monitoring system, using eleven ground posts and six airborne units for surveillance of the Soviet Union. This project, known as Ibex, will involve several hundred U S monitoring experts working permanently in Iran, and is testimony to the enduring strategic alliance of the two states not only in the Gulf and Indian Ocean but also against Iran's northern neighbour.[31]

The military are today a powerful institution in numerous third-world countries, and in many of these it is evident that this institution has been, and is, supported by the U S A and other advanced capitalist states in order to crush popular and democratic movements. Insofar as these forces also buy weapons, they make a contribution to the profits of the major capitalist economies. It is for this reason that no study of the incidence and durability of military rule in the third world can ignore the international factors that have, since the Second World War, encouraged the spread of the military in poorer societies. The Iranian military's case is in some ways, as we have seen, anomalous. Because of the Shah's position as an effective monarch it is not a military dictatorship of the Greek, Chilean, Brazilian or Indonesian kind. Moreover, in historical terms the army was dominant *before* the U S A intervened, i.e. it does not owe its position to outside support. The most significant regional difference is that the Iranian military apparatus, for reasons of economics and strategy, has gone further than any other in developing a new kind of alliance with the U S A. Not only is the military apparatus holding down the Iranian people in a brutal manner, but it is also acting as the guarantor of the counter-revolutionary régimes in western Asia. Beyond that it is playing an important role in balancing the books of the U S defence establishment and industry. Finally and above all else Iran is developing towards a situation in which the likelihood of its launching aggression against its neighbours is increasing.

5 Agricultural Development

The Iranian land reform programme began in 1962 and officially ended in 1971. In terms of the recent transformation of Iranian society, it has immense importance.[1] In the first place, over half the Iranian population still reside in the countryside and hence live their lives under the impact of this reform. Secondly, the Shah himself has chosen to make the land reform the symbol of his 'revolution' and the main token of his concern for his people. However, there are other reasons why the reform is of central concern to any study of Iran. It has been the chief means through which the state has encouraged the capitalist transformation of the countryside. Although it was carried out under the slogan of 'land to the tiller', and thereby supposed to have an egalitarian character, the implementation of the reform has been such as to create new social divisions in the countryside, in fact to create a capitalist class structure in place of the earlier pre-capitalist one. We do not know what degree of class antagonism there now exists in the rural areas, but it is conceivable, at least, that the immense inequalities created by the reform will yield conflict in the future. One consequence for the future is, however, beyond doubt: this is that whilst the reform itself may have been a political victory for the Shah, the régime's whole agricultural policy has proven to be an economic failure, and the protracted crises of the Iranian countryside in the 1970s and 1980s, i.e. after the reform, will constitute a limitation on Iran's capacity to achieve an overall development of its economy. For this reason, the reform is a part of a much wider process of change in the countryside since 1960.

Most discussion about the Iranian land reform is posed in terms of the specific conditions under which it was launched:

most prominently, the crisis of the early 1960s, and the pressure of the Kennedy administration. This is all perfectly relevant, but it leads to a certain distortion, since judged by the narrow political concerns of that period the reform was a success. The Americans were pleased and the Shah emerged in a stronger position. The reform, and the defeat of the opposition in the 1960–63 period, marked a further step in the state's land reform process of consolidation. On the other hand, these historical factors are of limited help in assessing the import of the land reform, since the land reform was an inevitability if Iran was to attempt capitalist development. No country that has not transformed the rural sector can develop. And it is rather in terms of the latter consideration that the reform should be judged.

In essence, the spread of capitalism defined in a classic account by Lenin can be identified in terms of three processes:[2] (1) The spread of commodity relations, through which the major inputs of agriculture (land and labour) become separated from each other and become objects of exchange to be bought and sold on a market, and through which the agricultural product also becomes a commodity. Where previously custom, law and non-monetary arrangements prevailed, money now regulates the disposition of the inputs and product of agriculture. (2) The growth of a home market, and with it the expansion in the output of the agriculture sector, as well as in the exchanges of commodities between the agrarian and non-agrarian sectors of the economy. (3) The growth of a capitalist class structure: the word 'peasant' no longer indicates membership of a specific class even if it did previously, since it covers both those who own land (rural bourgeois and petty-bourgeois) and those who have only their labour to sell (rural proletarians).

This transformation of the countryside, essential to capitalist development, may be stimulated by private appropriation and market forces alone. It did so in England. But in most capitalist countries the state has intervened, at some stage or other, to bring the rural sector into line with the rest of the economy, and in particular by altering the pattern of land ownership in the countryside. This, strictly speaking, is all that land reform is – the alteration of land ownership by the state in order to encourage the growth of a home market and a capitalist class structure in the countryside. Land reforms under socialism perform different tasks, and are also equally designed to align the rural sector with the requirements of overall development.

Two things cannot be treated as automatic components of land reform and capitalist development in the countryside. First of all, no specific form of land ownership is entailed by capitalist development: there can be large-scale estates, medium-size holdings, cooperatives, or small family plots. It is not, therefore, enough to say that capitalism has been introduced into the Iranian countryside: one has to say what specific property relations have been introduced in this case. Secondly, the mere fact of land reform, and of the permeation of the countryside by capitalist relations, is not in itself enough to ensure that the agrarian sector does meet the requirements of the rest of the economy. The new agrarian bourgeoisie may be indifferent to the demands by the rest of the economy for investment funds and may withhold part of the agricultural output needed by that other sector: this has been the case in India since the reform of the 1960s. In Iran too one encounters a situation where the state has imposed capitalist relations, belatedly and deliberately, on the countryside, but has failed to mobilize rural resources in a manner remotely consonant with the needs of the rest of the economy.

Before the Reform

Iranian agriculture faces a hostile, begrudging environment. Of the country's total land area (165 million hectares) 55 per cent is unusable because it is desert, mountains or swamps, and another 30 per cent or more is forest and pasture. Only an estimated 12 per cent is cultivated, and of this up to half may have to be left fallow at any one time, because of the persistence of traditional farming methods. Only 5 per cent (8 million hectares) is permanently cultivated. Whilst some officials claim that 20 million hectares are cultivable there exists considerable difficulty in using this, above all because of the shortage of water. It is estimated that only about 500,000 hectares enjoy complete irrigation and that only 4·5 million hectares are potentially irrigable.[3] The Shah himself once remarked with justice that Iran would be better off without oil and with an adequate annual rainfall.

There are no precise statistics on land holdings before the reform, and the basic unit used to measure ownership, namely the village and a sixth of a village (*dang*), do not correlate with any fixed area. A village, of which there are estimated to have been 50,000, could have between 20 and 500 inhabitants. There are, nevertheless, data which give some idea of the ownership pattern, and which illustrate the composite character of the Iranian landowning class in this period.

Table 6: Land Ownership Before the Reform

Type of Conversion	*% of all land owned*	*number of villages*	*% of villages*
Large proprietors	56·0	13,569	34·43
(of whom those owning over 100 hectares)	33·8	—	—
Small proprietors	10–12	16,522	41·93
Royal domain	10–13	812	2·06
Religious endowment	1–2	713	1·81
Tribal holdings	13·0	—	—
Public domain	3–4	1,444	3·67
Other holdings	—	6,346	16·10

Source: *The Cambridge History of Iran*, vol. 1, Cambridge, 1968, p. 687.

The membership of the landowning class was an agglomeration of different components that had been assembled over the previous century. It included members of the court who had been given land by the Shah, traditional landowners, tribal leaders who had acquired individual control of lands previously under communal ownership, and merchants who had bought land out of trading profits. Most of the owners resided in towns, and in their personal and family connections they intermixed with the commercial and state bourgeoisie. The most powerful group consisted of 400–450 families, some of whom are reputed to have owned as many as 300 villages. According to one estimate, 37 families alone owned 19,000 villages, i.e. around 38 per cent of the total, whilst another group of medium landlords, owning 1–5 villages each, owned 7,000 villages, or 14 per cent of the total. Reza Khan appropriated 2,100 villages in the 1920s and 1930s and thereby made himself and the Pahlavi family the largest landowners in the country.[4] Many of the smaller units of land were also owned by absentee landowners, and only 5 per cent of peasants are believed to have owned the land they tilled.

The two most important ways in which the product was extracted were through *bigari*, or unpaid labour for the landowner, and through various forms of share-cropping. The latter system involved peasants working on the land for a share of the crop; the share system varied considerably, but the most common pattern was for the crop to be divided into five, according to the five inputs – land, labour, water, animals and seed. Hence, a peasant who provided only labour might get 20 per cent of the crop, whilst the landowner automatically got his 20 per cent. But the Iranian village was not usually a simple combination of owner and labourer, since two further kinds of division operated. Those peasants who were entitled to the share were those who had conventionally been allowed to work on the strip in question (the *nasagh*), while there was an inferior group of casual labourers (the latter sometimes called *khosh-neshin*[5]). The latter received an even smaller recompense than that given to the others. Secondly, between the *nasagh*-holders and the landowners there was often a stratum of those who controlled the other three inputs – seed, water and animals (usually oxen). In many villages oxen were owned by a separate group, who contributed their own labour, and may also have owned some land as well. The result was that prior to the land reform there existed a system of hierarchy in the village: if there was a typical case, this comprised the landowners proper, the animal-owning intermediaries, the *nasagh*-holders, and the labourers. Although pre-capitalist in origin, this pre-existing division provided the context within which the land reform itself took place and to a considerable extent determined the character of the post-reform social structure.[6]

Whilst it shared many problems with other comparable third-world countries, the Iranian countryside also reflected more specific historical characterictics. In the first place, since Iran had never been subjected to colonial domination, the countryside had not been affected by the processes of colonialism: there was no efficient taxation, and little encouragement of the growth of cash crops for export. Before the land reform the only major agricultural export was cotton, 40 per cent of which went abroad. Some dry fruits and nuts were also exported. In no sense was Iran like India, Ceylon, Kenya or Latin America – a country whose rural sector had been to a significant extent transformed by the impact of colonialism and international trade. And this may have been one of the factors making land reform easier for the Shah: there was no strong landowning class with international ties and a clear class-consciousness that could offer a determined resistance to his policies. Those merchants who invested their profits in land did not then transform these lands along commercial lines. They held the land as a form of wealth in itself, as much as a means of realizing further profits.

Another striking peculiarity of the Iranian countryside is the apparent absence of peasant revolts in recent Iranian history. It has been shown that peasant movements rarely take place on a national scale, and that they tend to be local, often spontaneous, outbursts.[7] It is also probable that some localized peasant revolts occur without ever being properly documented, so that the 'absence' of such revolts only reflects the fact that they were not recorded. But even allowing for these factors, it seems that the incidence of peasant revolts and resistance in the nineteenth and twentieth centuries has been very low. Where there have been uprisings in the countryside, these have taken place within a tribal or ethnic context (Kurds, Arabs, Qashqai, etc.) or have been regional movements at a time when the state was weak (the Gilani movement after 1917). Despite the deterioration of conditions in the countryside in the first half of this century, and the relatively low level of migration to the towns, no significant resistance by peasants has been recorded.

A number of factors have been adduced to explain this: the geographical dispersal of villages, the persistent threats of raiding nomads, the absence of a middle peasantry.[8] It may also be that factors within the structure of village life itself have contributed to the peasants' tranquillity: cooperation among villages was strong because of water shortages and hence rebellions by breakaway groups were more difficult. Whatever the reasons, the result was that the régime faced no direct threat from the peasantry, of a kind that in other countries forced governments to introduce a pre-emptive land reform. It may be that the long-term threat of a peasant movement weighed on the Shah and his advisers; but in the immediate situation, it was the need to transform the countryside economically, and the critical turn in relations between the Shah and his opponents, which brought about the land reform programme.[9]

The Reform and Its Phases

The Shah was by no means the first person to call for land reform in Iran; the necessity for such reform was long evident to many observers. The first Majlis set up during the Constitutional Revolution had not called for land reform since it had been dominated by landowners; but under the Gilan Republic of 1917–21 large estates in the areas held by the rebels were distributed to the peasants. A similar reform took place in Azerbaijan during the autonomous republic of 1945–6. Both these cases were, however, ones in which land distribution was decided on by a revolutionary grouping then in power, and they were not in the first instance results of the demands of a peasant movement. Another advocate of land reform from the mid-1940s onwards was Hassan Arsanjani, a radical liberal who was later the first Minister of Agrarian Reform. In a move designed to offset criticism in 1949 the Shah himself distributed 517 of the 2,100 villages seized by Reza Khan, and these went to their cultivators. But in general landlords retained power in the Iranian countryside until the reform, and as late as 1959 they blocked a land reform proposal that had been tabled in the Majlis.

The change came with the crisis of 1961 and the advent of the Amini government; in January 1962 an initial land reform decree was promulgated, with the encouragement and advice of U S officials. This law, subsequently known as the 'first phase', contained four main provisions:

1. Ownership was limited to one village or to six *dangs* in separate villages. Exempted were orchards, tea plantations, homesteads, groves, and land where there was mechanized cultivation using daily wage-labour.

2. Landowners were to be compensated by the state over 10 years (later extended to 15) on the basis of the taxes they had been paying. The peasants who received land were to repay the value plus 10 per cent over a period of 15 years; those who defaulted for three years running were to be dispossessed.

3. Land was to be redistributed to those who were already farming land, with priority going to those who provided more than just labour: i.e. oxen-owners had priority. Then came *nasagh*-holders, and finally labourers. All those receiving land had to become members of cooperatives.

4. Where no distribution took place, that is in villages retained by landlords, there was to be an end to arbitrary dismissal of peasants. Share-cropping rates were raised by 5 per cent of the crop on irrigated land and by 10 per cent on non-irrigated.

This law seems to have aroused considerable enthusiasm in the countryside: it showed that the landlord had lost his total control of the village, and promised prosperity to the rural population. But, if the initial popularity was based on the hope that the peasantry as a whole would get land, this was in error. First of all, official figures for the first phase show that by October 1972, i.e. a decade after implementation began, the law had covered only around 30 per cent of the villages in Iran (14,646), and that of these less than 10 per cent (3,920) had been wholly redistributed. In the rest only some *dangs* had been sold to the peasants. The total number of families receiving land under this phase was 690,466: given the fact that the rural population is around 3·5 million families (17 million people) this means that under a fifth of all peasants appear to have benefited from this first phase of the reform.

Moreover, a considerable number of landowners were able to evade redistribution. The law enabled rich owners to transfer excess lands to their relatives, an escape many are believed to have taken. Other farmers carried out mechanizations that were only token: 850 owners claimed to have mechanized their farms, and some drove the peasants off the land in order to qualify for this. Another 1,500 opted for escape under the 'orchards' provision: this may explain why Iranian pistachio nut and apple output rose by 600 per cent between 1960 and 1968. Nor is there any doubt that some owners were able in one way or another to bend with the wind and bribe the reform officials so that they could retain some of the lands to which they were no longer entitled. Finally, a considerable amount of doubt attaches to how many wholly-owned villages there were: the state's figure in recent statistics has been 3,920, whilst Minister of Agrarian Reform Arsanjani stated in 1962 that there were 15,000 villages owned by people who had more than five in their possession. The drop in the number of villages that should have been totally redistributed is consequently rather suspicious.[10]

A second stage of land reform came into effect in January 1963, but it was considered too radical and was watered down in a number of ways in 1964. It was designed to cover that land which had not been affected by the first stage, and under it landlords were faced with five alternatives on the land they retained. Their options are listed below, with percentages of peasants affected given in brackets:

1. To rent the land to peasants on 30-year leases (80·08 per cent).

2. To sell the land to peasants at a mutually agreed price (3·67 per cent).

3. To divide the land in proportion to the prevailing crop-sharing distribution of the harvest (10·04 per cent).

4. To set up joint stock companies in which landlords and peasants were to be shareholders (5·35 per cent).

5. To purchase the land from peasants (0·86 per cent).

As can be seen, most landlords decided to hold on to their lands, and to reach tenancy agreements with the peasants. A total of 1,246,652 peasant families received leases on their lands. Therefore, whilst the second phase affected more peasant families than the first phase (1,600,000 as compared with 700,000), far fewer peasants actually acquired land: 57,164 families purchased their land, and another 156,279 acquired land through division. In total about 210,000 families acquired land under phase two as opposed to the 700,000 who had received it under phase one. The arrangements so reached under phase two were inadequate; in particular, agricultural productivity was not rising sufficiently and peasants reportedly resisted tenancies, so in 1968 a third phase of reform was introduced, which was designed to convert the tenancy arrangements of phase two into ownership. Land affected by sections one and four of phase two, i.e. tenanted and joint stock company land, was to be sold to the peasants. But after four years of rearrangement under which this land was redistributed, it seems that only 738,119 out of the 1·3 million eligible families had in fact acquired land, i.e. under phase three about 592,000 families *lost* the position they had acquired under phase two.[11] Taken together phases one to three seem to have given land to about 1,638,000 families: 690,000 under phase one, 210,000 under phase two and 738,000 under phase three. Yet this figure of 1·6 million families is, as will be discussed later in this chapter, under half of the total number of rural families in Iran.

However, from the government's point of view, the main problem is not the partiality of its distribution policy, but rather the failure of the reforms to increase agricultural output in a satisfactory way. Many of the peasants who did get plots of land under the reform received it in amounts that were too small to be viable. Sixty-eight per cent received plots of under 5 hectares, whilst the minimum viable outside the north is 7 hectares per family. Hence, from the mid-1960s onwards there has been another trend in government policy, one designed to supersede individual ownership with larger-scale farming. Phase three was, in part, a preparation for this new process which aimed above all to consolidate rural holdings. The new policy either encourages farmers to participate in new state-run farming corporations, or displaces them through the private agricultural firms in which Iranian and foreign business interests are collaborating to apply capital-intensive techniques to the countryside. The farm corporations are modelled on the Israeli *moshavim*, cooperatives of individual producers, and many managers of these units have been trained in Israel[12]; the private capital-intensive farms are modelled on U S agri-business corporations. Legislation on the farm corporations was passed in 1967 and by the spring of 1973 43 had been set up. They are confined to selected areas of the country, with the aim that there should be 140 of them by the end of 1978. The purpose is to introduce modern mechanized farming techniques, and to consolidate uneconomic holdings into units of at least 20 hectares. Under the 1967 Act, corporations are formed, provided 51 per cent of the owners considered eligible for such corporations give their consent. Members receive shares in the corporations, but use of their lands passes to the corporations, and power in effect resides with the state-appointed managers. This measure obviously runs counter to the formal intent of earlier reform measures. Not only does it abolish individual ownership in the areas covered, but it also has effects on the majority of peasants not covered by the corporations; they see that what the state gives it may also take away. The probability is therefore that the corporations, which are designed to increase output, will discourage the new owners elsewhere from increasing their output and from investing their profits, because of the pervasive insecurity which the establishment of the corporations induces. There has certainly been resistance to the setting up of the corporations, as is evidenced by a bill enacted in 1975 which tightens up the original 1967 provisions. Holdings belonging to those farmers who refuse or are unable to join farm corporations being established on their land are to be forcibly expropriated, and all land so taken over is to be placed under the control of a Regional Agricultural Development Organization. One account, paraphrasing government thinking, has put it in these words: 'Iran's small and relatively unproductive farmers are an extravagance that the country can no longer afford.'[13] It is evident that in a decade and a half the Iranian state has come, or has been forced to come, a long way from the elgalitarian land-to-the-tiller slogans of the early 1960s.

A further twist to this latter tendency is 'agri-business', the intervention of foreign and Iranian capitalists into agricultural production.[14] Foreign business interests first entered Iran in the 1950s after the former head of the Tennessee Valley Authority, David Lilienthal, visited Iran to investigate the possibilities of a similar operation there. The result was a large-scale development plan for the province of Khuzistan, where water was to be provided by the newly-built Dez Dam. Initially, despite the successful development of a sugar plantation at Haft Teppeh, the production required did not materialize in the area of the Dez Irrigation Project and in 1968 the state enterprise, Khuzistan Water and Power Authority, decided to dispossess the farmers working on the 250,000 acres. K W P A bought out the farmers in 58 villages affected and handed the land over to six private firms. One, for example, controlling 20,000 acres, was run by Hashim Naraghi, an expatriate Iranian who had been successful in California. He owned 51 per cent of the firm, the First National City Bank of New York 30 per cent, and the rest was divided up amongst smaller Iranian interests. Similar consortia involving U S and Iranian capital were set up in the rest of the Khuzistan project area, and throughout the first half of the 1970s the government went on encouraging more such businesses to interest themselves in the selected growth areas. By the end of 1978, 8 per cent of the irrigated land will, it is claimed, be run by these enterprises.

This policy is one which has several negative consequences and a marked turn away from it became noticeable after 1975. First of all, the introduction of mechanization in farm corporations and even more so in enterprises such as those in Khuzistan is increasing rural unemployment. Not only casual labourers, but even many with a claim to specific pieces of land, are being driven out. In Khuzistan, an estimated 17,000 people had been driven out by 1974; they were being rehoused in five new towns called *shahraks*, where they live in poor conditions and have to work as seasonal labourers on land they previously owned. Their villages have been bulldozed away. Moreover, the interests of private business lie in obtaining a return on their investment, and they will pull out of these enterprises if it is profitable to do so. Hashim Naraghi himself sold his holding to the state in 1975, after being accused of mismanagement, and was sentenced to prison *in absentia* a year later.

A number of U S shareholders in a 10,000-hectare enterprise called Iran-California sold up too, once better investment possibilities had opened up. But even on the strictest criterion of all, namely food output, there is considerable doubt as to how successful this programme can be. A comparison of field crops in California and Khuzistan found that whereas the Californian farmers had their highest yields on units of around 300 hectares, the Iranian units were measured in thousands of hectares. Beyond a certain point economies of scale do not normally hold in agriculture, and large-scale agriculture involves very high overheads, a feature already evident in the Khuzistan enterprises. For this reason, a new policy of encouraging medium-sized farms began to replace the earlier enthusiasm for agri-business.

There can be no doubt at all that, whatever the long-term effects on output, the first and second phases of the reform did encourage a fundamental capitalist transformation of the Iranian countryside in the Leninist sense, i.e. they promoted commodity relations and created some of the elements of a capitalist class structure. Land has become a commodity: landlords were compensated for it in cash or instalments thereof, and the peasants have to pay off their purchases in annual amounts. The advent of capitalist interests from outside the agrarian sector altogether also confirms the commodity character of land after the reform. Labour too has become monetized although a reverse tendency is also seen; the second phase of the reform put an end to the non-monetary relations that had previously tied owner and labourer, turning share-cropping arrangements into tenancies. *Bigari*, forced labour and practices such as the giving of presents (*roshve*) to landlords, i.e. a form of bribing, have also largely disappeared. Former *nasagh*-holders and labourers now work for landlords of corporations on a wage basis. On the other hand, the reform did not end, nor could it, labour on a non-monetary *family* basis, and because of the distribution policy the incidence of this kind of labour has apparently increased since the reform began.

The role of money has also been increased by the expansion in credit institutions of both a state and private kind. Those peasants who received land under the distributions have become indebted and often have to borrow against the next crop to meet their instalments. Moreover, the Agricultural Bank has, via the cooperatives, infused sums of money into the countryside, especially under the increased allocations of the 1973–8 Five Year Plan. Finally, the produce of agriculture has become a commodity; indeed, increasing demand by the non-agrarian sector is putting increasing strains on the productive capacities of the Iranian farmer.

Lenin's second criterion, class formation, highlights both the general character of the process, capitalist development, and the specific form this has taken in Iran. It is evident that the pre-reform landowning families did not, as the German Junkers did, transform themselves automatically into a capitalist class. The state had to intervene to redistribute land and to encourage the capitalist development of agriculture. At the same time many of the old landowners were able to preserve some of their land either by taking various kinds of evasive measures, or by complying with the stipulated exemption conditions. This distinction is important since there is a basic difference between a landowner retaining land through circumventing the reform, and one doing so by meeting requirements such as mechanization. Both limit the degree to which land has been distributed, but the latter also bring about those developments in agriculture which the reform is designed to encourage. They are contrary to an egalitarian principle of land to the tiller, but not to the development of capitalism.

Those landowners who retained some land have been joined by those who acquired land under the three phases. Land was not distributed equally to all peasants: the estimated 47.5 per cent of the rural population who were most deprived before the reform have not benefited from the distribution.[15] This is because land was distributed according to the pre-existing system of village labour, i.e. to those who were more than casual labourers. The beneficiaries were the oxen-owners and the *nasagh*-holders. As one exponent of the reform has said: 'The centre of attention was upon him who, in the text of the law, does not own the land but cultivates it with the help of his family and is in possession of oxen, and who in exchange for the use of the land and landlord's services, renders to the landlord part of the harvest in kind or its equivalent in cash.'[16] The specific character of the Iranian land reform is brought into focus here: the reform was first of all one which was deliberately designed to distribute land unequally, to the richer farmers, and to exclude at least half of the rural population from its scope; and secondly, it was one which used the existing pre-capitalist structure of the village as the basis for this policy. While a degree of capitalist differentiation existed prior to the reform, a rural bourgeoisie and a rural proletariat are being deliberately and more rapidly created by it, through using and transforming the old village system.

As reform has proceeded, there has been a continuous reduction of the number of families possessing land, and an increasing number have been pushed into the ranks of the rural labourers. First of all, the mechanization provisions of phases one and two led some landlords to displace oxen-owners and *nasagh*-holders from their land and hence to deprive them of the possibility of getting some of the redistributed plots. Then, under phase two, a small number of families, 57,000 of them, 'sold' their land to the landlords under the provisions of that stage: over half of these were in an area controlled by the powerful Alam family. Then, in the transition between phases two and three, another 592,000 families seem to have failed to convert their tenancies into ownership; most of these must have been forced into the proletariat. Now a much wider expropriation is taking place as the corporations and the agri-business firms drive peasants off the land and lower the demand even for casual labour. Nor should it be forgotten that an unknown number of those who received land under the first three phases may have defaulted on their payments and have been dispossessed as a result. They too will have been forced from the class of those who own into the class of those who have only their labour to sell.

Reform has consequently created a new rural bourgeoisie and a new proletariat. The bourgeoisie's members include some of the old landowning families who have in one way or another retained land, plus those members of the previously better-off peasantry who have become owners too. Next to them is another section of the village which has greatly expanded since reform, the shopkeepers and moneylenders who have benefited from the development of commodity relations, and from the expansion of demand and of debt. This latter group often overlaps with the former, insofar as a farmer may open a shop, or a shopkeeper may buy land. On the other side is the new rural proletariat. Its majority is made up of the labourers of pre-reform times; to it have been added those families who might have acquired land but were prevented from doing so, or who acquired it and then lost it through the erosion of the distribution policy *nasagh*-holders who did not get land. In general, one can say that the Iranian countryside is now a capitalist one. Pre-capitalist features must certainly survive: old cultivation methods, old attitudes, and old unreformed ownership patterns do not disappear at once. But the predominant relations are commodity ones and the social structure of the village is now becoming capitalist. This is the first main achievement of the reform.

There is, however, one further element in the capitalist Iranian village that has to be analysed: the state. The other main result of the reform is that the state has intervened in the village, and is now in three ways the dominant power there. First of all, like all states, it has guaranteed and where necessary created private property in land. In the tribal areas especially, the state has created private property which did not previously exist in a developed form. Secondly, because of the retarded character of the countryside, the state has redistributed land through the reforms; most of this distribution took place peacefully, but where, as in Fars in late 1963, the landlords put up resistance, the gendarmerie and the army intervened to enforce the government's will. Then, in the middle and late 1960s, it became obvious that the mere distribution of land to richer peasants and the creation of credit cooperatives was not enough, and the state therefore intervened at a third level, at the point of production itself, first through the cooperatives, then via farm corporations and the agri-business enterprises.

The promotion of agri-business at the expense of individual ownership may appear to indicate that Iranian government policy is erratic; but the policy, or rather policies, pursued since 1962 are more consistent if seen in the context of the overall requirements of developing capitalism in Iran and of the inescapable conflicts within this process. What the reform, and later agri-business, underline is the ever-increasing role of the state in the transformation of the Iranian countryside. Not only did the alteration of rural property relations have to be consciously organized, but even after the state had intervened to alter these relations, the hoped-for increase in output did not occur. That is why the state has now taken it upon itself to supervise production, in alliance with the richer peasants and with private capital that is being encouraged to invest in the rural sector.

In all villages in Iran, whether incorporated into farm corporations or not, the state has replaced the landowner as the dominant power. Ultimately, the instruments of state power are the gendarmerie and the army, but these are rarely used actively and in most cases the state intervenes through specific institutions that have been created during reform. In the 1960s two special corps were set up to introduce new ideas into the village: a Literacy Corps, established in 1963, and a Health Corps, established in 1964. Participation in these institutions was a form of national service, and thousands of townspeople were dispatched to the rural areas. Between 1963 and 1971 a total of 62,730 people served in the Literacy Corps; most of these were at first men, but in 1969 a Women's Education Corps was also established. Over this period 13,782 elementary schools in village areas were set up, and the total number of people enrolled in such schools in the rural areas rose from 675,000 to 1,830,000. The Health Corps had a more complex role, but in the first three years of its existence it set up 500 medical units in the countryside, and as these were frequently mobile they allegedly covered a number of villages each.

The success of these corps has, nevertheless, been a small one. A great deal of official bombast has produced meagre results. Only about 10,000 people a year passed through the Literacy Corps, and even if official figures are to be accepted, less than 15 per cent of the rural population was receiving any education in 1971. In 1975 illiteracy rates in the countryside were still very high – 60 per cent for men, and 90 per cent for women. The Health Corps was equally limited, since assuming that each medical unit covered 10 villages each, this would still have meant that 90 per cent of Iranian villages were without medical facilities. A report presented to the government in 1974 provided the following sober evaluation:

> Despite measures and government spending undertaken in recent years, many of Iran's major health and medical problems remain unsolved. Of the 10,000 doctors in Iran, 5,000 are in Tehran, more than 3,000 are in other cities and only 1,500 are in rural areas. There are 40,000 hospital beds in the country and all of them are in Tehran or in other large cities. The majority of the Iranian people have only the services of 1,000 ill-equipped dispensaries. As a result, personnel and facilities are concentrated in Tehran, while in practice 18 million Iranians have no access to any of the services offered by modern advanced medicine.[17]

Beside these corps there are other state bodies related to the land reform itself. The land reform organization has itself distributed land, but in so doing it works most closely with village headmen and with existing landlords. After the reform was carried through, the main day-to-day institutions in villages not covered by the corporations became the Agricultural Bank and the cooperatives. The Bank pays dispossessed landlords their instalments and peasants have to pay them for the land they have received. But the Bank also lends money to peasants through the cooperatives. Membership in cooperatives was a pre-condition for acquiring land under phases one and two, but many of those established existed only on paper. An important reason why they were not encouraged in the middle 1960s was that the state was concerned to prevent the emergence of strong peasant-run organizations, as was originally envisaged by Minister of Agriculture Arsanjani. By the early 1970s there were about 6,700 cooperatives in the country covering about two-thirds of all villages, and the government was trying to centralize and extend the system, reducing the total number to 3,000. Today the cooperatives are run by a government body, the Central Organization of Rural Cooperatives, which is in essence a credit-giving body under the Agricultural Bank run to assist the richer peasants. The latter have special access to the C O R C first of all because a member's share in a cooperative depends on the amount of land owned, the secondly because a member of a cooperative can borrow money according to his shares in the cooperative.

A study of Gilan in the late 1960s, covering 18 cooperatives, found that of 104 officials, 29 were rich peasants, 54 medium and only 11 classified as poor.[18] The same study found that a split-level credit system also operated: whereas cooperative members could borrow at 7·4 per cent interest, poorer peasants had to borrow from private lenders at around 50 per cent. Since most borrowing was from the spring to the end of the harvest, this amounted in effect to a rate of 100 per cent per annum. It was also common for richer peasants to borrow from the banks or the cooperative and then to lend at higher rates to the poorer workers. Hence the overall effect of land reform and the presence of cooperative officials in the villages was that the latter acted in alliance with the richer peasants and shopkeepers, and that the state, by its distribution and credit policies, helped to consolidate the new rural bourgeoisie. In the areas covered by the corporations the situation is even clearer: only the richest peasants can be partners of the state and of the state-appointed farm managers. If one attempts to sum up the specificities of the Iranian land reform, and to go beyond the *general* fact that a capitalist transformation has been taking place, there are three characteristics of the change that are especially striking. First, the previous landowning class was not eliminated, but was either incorporated into the urban bourgeoisie, with which it probably had ties anyway, or was incorporated into the new rural bourgeoisie; where it was forced to lose its land, it was compensated and integrated with the urban bourgeoisie. Secondly, the distribution policy was selective, and the pre-capitalist social structure of the village acted as the basis for creating a new capitalist class system. Thirdly, the state is now the most powerful economic, as well as political, force in the Iranian countryside.

It is important to bear these specific characteristics in mind, especially in the context of the oft-heard assertion that the Iranian land reform succeeded because it was able to eliminate the power of the old landowning class. This is, in one important sense, true. But it is also misleading because the original rhetoric of the land reform period stressed the transfer of land to the peasantry: and the implication was that the power previously held by the landowners would be transferred to the peasantry as well. In practice, land has been transferred only to *some* peasants, while power in the village has been to a great extent appropriated by the state. The Iranian peasantry are as powerless as they were before 1962: their master has, however, changed. The claim that the landowners' power has been broken is also false, insofar as many landlords have retained some of their land, and have been free to retain their best land. Moreover, those landlords who had been dispossessed have received money in compensation which has enabled them to continue to be members of the Iranian ruling class, if not in its agrarian sector. They have been forcibly transferred from agriculture, and like all other sections of the ruling class they have had to surrender executive power to the ever-increasing state. But as a section of Iranian society they have not been forced to surrender their position of relative economic privilege.

This means that despite the great enthusiasm aroused by the first phase of reform, the Iranian state has been able to put through a singularly inegalitarian policy, and one that has become more so as the years have gone by.

At the same time the reform has been erratic in form. There was a noticeable divergence between phase one, emphasizing ownership, and phase two, which created tenancies, and then between the original version of phase two, which placed upper limits on ownership, and the later 1964 revised version which allowed unlimited ownership of mechanized and irrigated land that was unirrigated before. Even more contradictory has been the relation between phase two and phase three, since the latter tried to convert the tenancies of phase two into ownership; in effect, because it was rushed through, 40 per cent of those qualified to get land lost their place. Now, while phase three has encouraged individual ownership, corporations and agri-business are replacing individual control by the power of the state or private consortia. These changes are not as erratic as may at first sight appear, since they are to some extent explained by a factor that is rarely seen in the open but which has played a recurrent role during the whole land reform, namely the class struggle.

In the early 1960s there was no significant peasant movement in Iran, either nationally or locally; the peasantry played a role only in the long-term sense that it was evident from what had happened elsewhere in Asia (in China and Vietnam, for example) that failure to effect reform could produce a peasant explosion. The primary conflict in this period was between the state and landlords, one between different fractions of the ruling class over whether or not capitalist development of the countryside was to occur. Some landlords, and some religious personnel, opposed the reform, the latter because the reform symbolized the Shah's whole endeavour as much as for immediate questions of religious property. They were defeated, both in the villages themselves, through the implementation of phase one, and in the political arena by the defeat of the June 1963 demonstrations. In carrying through this policy, however, the Shah had to ally with a liberal wing of the ruling class, amongst whom was Hassan Arsanjani, the Minister of Agriculture. Moreover, as part of the campaign against the opponents of reform, the Shah and Arsanjani appealed to the peasantry directly and when the first title deeds were handed out, at Maragheh in Azerbaijan, the Shah himself gave the documents to the peasants who received land. This alliance could not last, especially since Arsanjani, who may have had political ambitions of his own, proceeded to mobilize peasant support himself. He is believed to have wanted to build up the cooperatives into active peasant institutions under his guidance and in January 1963 he organized a conference in Tehran at which 4,700 cooperative members attended. This conference was important for several reasons: although the delegates were appointed, not elected, it was the first time in history that any representatives of the Iranian peasantry had met *nationally*, and in the conference resolutions the delegates, under supervision, not only proclaimed their loyalty to the Shah but also called for an (albeit undefined) freedom in Iran. At the same time, in some parts of Iran peasants who had been encouraged by phase one of the reform began to by-pass government officials and to occupy lands they considered were covered by the Act. In an initial way, the Iranian peasantry were being politically mobilized as a national force for the first time, and in Arsanjani they had an organizer with a national position.[19]

Within weeks of the peasant congress, Arsanjani had been dismissed, and as phase two was implemented the original peasant movement was defused. The original struggle within the ruling class had been won; now the Shah could dispense with his liberal allies and with the incipient peasant movement. Phase two with its milder provisions followed and was made milder still by the revisions introduced by the new Minister of Agriculture, General Valian. Had the Shah wanted the peasantry to become an independent political force this would have been the time to encourage the processes brought into play by phase one; this was politically unacceptable and the second phase was used to shift the character of the reform decisively rightwards. Subsequent changes followed from this: phase three and the farm corporations represented a further attempt to strengthen the richer owners and to eliminate smaller proprietors. But a still further conflict has thereby arisen, namely that between the régime's political desire for a secure rural base, and its economic requirement for higher output. The underlying consideration is that the peasants who have received land from the distributions are not producing enough; they may be in favour of the régime in a vague way, because they have received land, but they are either not increasing production enough or are consuming more food and hence allowing less to reach the market. This is why the state has been forced to intervene further and to encourage the corporations and the agri-business consortia. But this policy, which runs counter to the earlier political aims of the reform, has its own negative consequences, too: peasants are now more cautious about the régime than they were since they see that they may lose the land they have acquired; a new, silent but pervasive struggle is taking shape in which the government is increasingly being driven to dispossess those peasants to whom it has given land in order to meet the more long-term requirements of capitalist development.

In talking of class struggle in the Iranian countryside one is therefore talking of a number of separate struggles, each of which has been reflected in a change in government policy. The state won the first round, against those landowners and *ulema* who opposed reform. It won the second round, against the peasant movement that was coming into being. It is now fighting a third round against the smaller proprietors in order to boost production, and it may face a fourth, against the millions of landless workers who have so far remained silent. The government's needs are great, but they are facing a peasantry who, while unlikely in the short run to revolt, can still offer stubborn resistance.

Successes and Failures

The vagaries of government policy draw attention to the most important underlying question about the reform, namely what it has and has not achieved. It has been shown that capitalism has been imposed on the Iranian countryside, and that this took the form of an unequal distribution of land, under increasing state control. It is now possible to examine not merely what kind of reform has taken place, but also how far the Iranian reform has met the requirements generally experienced by any developing country, capitalist or not. This relates back to the need to analyse agriculture in terms broader than those of the reform itself and its origins in 1961–2: the political success was, in the long run, secondary. Far more important is the reform's contribution to the economic development of Iran. The following offers six criteria, four of them primarily economic, and two socio-political, outlining the main ways in which an agrarian transformation can assist overall development.

1. *Supplying the demand for agricultural products*: a developing economy requires increased agricultural output to feed its population, to provide industry with raw materials, and to export in order to finance the import of capital goods. An attempt is usually made to counter the increase in demand and the shift of population away from agriculture by increases in productivity through changes in cultivation methods, and the introduction of fertilizers and new seeds. By far the most pressing part of this demand is the need to feed the population. Not only does demand in most third-world countries rise by 2·5 or 3·0 per cent a year because of population increases far higher than those experienced in earlier industrialization processes; but there is also the increased demand arising from the rise in *per capita* income: in poorer countries the income elasticity of demand for food may be as high as 0·6 to 0.8, so that even were population to remain constant demand for food would have to rise to maintain equilibrium.[20]

Iranian performance in this field has been bad. Iran never was a major exporter of primary agricultural produce, and oil has provided the money to finance capital imports. But oil is also now financing the *import* of food, since reform has failed to increase output. Agricultural production has risen by, at most, 2·5–3·0 per cent annum since the early 1960s, and may even have risen by as little as 1 per cent in some years. This is below the rate of increase in population (3 per cent) and far below the combined rate produced by the rise in population and income. By the mid-1970s demand for agricultural produce was rising by 12·5 per cent per annum and it is scheduled to reach 14 per cent over the following decade as incomes rise over a wider spectrum.[21] The demand for red meat, which is highly income-elastic, has been especially responsive to the rise in income: *per capita* consumption of 8 kilos a year rose to 18 kilos in the mid-1970s and is scheduled to reach 47 kilos a head in 1992. In Tehran, where most foreigners and wealthy Iranians live, consumption of red meat rose by 100 per cent in 1974–5. Such is the rise in food demand that overall consumption is expected to increase from 245 billion rials in 1971 to 1,300 billion rials in 1987.

It is not surprising that there was an initial shortfall in agricultural production since this is common in the immediate aftermath of land reform: in China, for example, available supplies of food fell by 33 per cent in the year following col-

Table 7: Production Indices of Iranian Agriculture 1961–73

Year	*Total Agriculture* (100 = 1961–5)	*Per Capita Agriculture* (100 = 1961–5)
1961–5	100	100
1964	97	94
1965	105	99
1966	110	101
1967	122	109
1968	133	115
1969	128	108
1970	131	107
1971	127	100
1972	133	102
1973*	135	101

*preliminary

Source: US Department of Agriculture, *Iran: Agricultural Production and Trade*, 1974, p. 11.

lectivization. But in Iran this weakness has continued long after the short-term unsettlement of the reform itself has worn off. The state has consequently been faced with a choice: either to curtail supply, and thereby to create dissatisfaction amongst the Iranian middle class, or to import food in order to meet this new demand. The policy pursued has been the latter: food imports have risen considerably since land reform, and the government, mindful of the need to avoid discontent, has implemented a food subsidy programme which in 1974–5 cost it $3 billions. Food imports were running at $2·6 billions in 1977, and may reach $4 billions by the early 1980s, when up to a third of Iran's food requirements may have to be imported.[22]

Oil has of course provided the money to finance these imports, but it has also enabled Iranian agriculture to remain inefficient much longer than would have been possible in a country lacking oil without this provoking any serious political consequences.[23] There are several reasons for this shortfall in output. First of all, there are absolute limits on increasing output: there is the inescapable physical fact that most of Iran is not cultivable. There is also the fact that although ownership patterns changed there was no automatic change for the better in cultivation methods; indeed, one consequence of the breakdown of the old *nasagh* system is that the traditional form of peasants working in work-teams (*boneh*) seems also to have broken down. Oxen-owners no longer use so much labour. On top of this was the failure throughout the 1960s to inject capital into the countryside. In 1969, for example, only 6 per cent of total investment went into agriculture. Under the Fifth Plan funding of agriculture has increased, but this in itself cannot be sufficient: much of the money allocated goes to rich peasants and is for relatively short-term needs, usually to tide a peasant over up to the harvest. In the period 1960–68, for example, over 65 per cent of loans were for a 6–12 month period only, and less than 15 per cent over five years.[24] Underlying all these technical factors is the relative passivity of the peasantry, or, put another way, the absence of a peasant movement and the failure to convert peasant acceptance of the state into an active, mobilized commitment to increase production. The failure to produce enough food emphasizes once again the bureaucratic character of the land reform. Land reform and the rise in the income of the richer peasants has also increased rural consumption: although precise data are not available, some accounts tell of farmers using their new income to carry out the pilgrimage to Mecca and to marry again, rather than boost output. Many are afraid to reinvest because of uncertainty about the government's intentions.

2. *Structuring the labour market*: when it comes to employment, there is a profound divergence between the requirements of earlier and later industrializing countries. In the earlier instances, population growth was lower, and industry was more labour-intensive: one of the requirements of agricultural development and of higher agricultural productivity was to release labour to meet the demands of the urban sector. In most of the third world today the reverse is so: industry is more capital-intensive, at least in its 'modern' sector, and population is growing faster than urban employment generally. Hence land reform, far from being designed to release labour from the countryside, should provide or at least stabilize employment in agriculture. There may well be a relative shift of labour from agricultural to non-agricultural activities as the economy develops, but because of population growth and the limited rise in other employment, the absolute numbers employed in agriculture will not fall till a much later stage. Many developing countries have failed to resolve this problem: the result is migration to the towns without there being the employment there to absorb these migrants, combined with continued under-employment of the rural labour force. In Latin America, for example, this is very clear: 'In seven Latin American countries data for the decade of the 1950s show that 11 million people of a total natural increase in rural areas of 19 million migrated to the cities.'[25] This is a failure which has effects far beyond the shanty-towns themselves: it represents a terrible waste of human resources, and an obvious limitation of internal demand. It may also have long-term political consequences, if the frustrations of these migrants

find some organized expression.

In Iran the percentage employed in agriculture has been falling: from 56 per cent in 1956 to 33 per cent in 1976. But, as mentioned above, this relative decline is consistent with an absolute increase: from 3,326,000 in 1956 to 3,445,000 in 1976. This underscores the fact that population is rising so rapidly in Iran that agriculture has to sustain its absolute level of employment in order to avoiding adding to the already large number of people coming on to the labour market. According to the I L O, it will be necessary to create 1·5 million new jobs elsewhere in the economy during the Fifth Plan merely in order to avoid an increase in unemployment, provided there is no reduction in agricultural employment. But the evidence suggests that current agricultural policy *is* diminishing the demand for labour: mechanization and the spread of orchards, already encouraged by phases one and two of the reform, have reduced the numbers employed, as did the partial concentration brought about by phase three. The agri-business and farm corporation policies are deliberate attempts to reduce the labour content of agriculture. It was reported in 1973 that agri-business and farm corporations cultivated about 15 per cent of the total cultivated area, but employed only 0·3 per cent of the agricultural labour force, i.e. five times less than the national average. Meanwhile under-employment in the countryside is running at around 40 per cent. The conclusion is inevitably that insofar as land reform has not altered production methods traditional under-employment remains; insofar as it has, the use of labour has declined.

3. *Expanding the home market*: while there is no doubt that a home market has been created in Iran in the sense that commodity relations have pervaded the countryside, and that the agricultural surplus is being marketed, there is considerable doubt as to how far reform has led to an *expansion* in the market, and in particular to an increased demand by the rural sector for the products of the rest of the economy. One of the underlying functions of the transformation of the agrarian sector is that there should be an increased demand from it both for products that can be used as agrarian inputs (machinery, chemicals) and for consumer goods which peasants will

now buy with their increased incomes. But there are several obstacles to this occurring, and they are evident in the case of Iran. First of all, peasants may produce more, but, as has been mentioned, they may also consume more or spend their monies on goods other than the products of the industrial sector.

Table 8: *Per Capita* Rural Income and Expenditure 1972
(US $ *per capita*)

Income:		
Category	*Mean Income*	*Percent of Rural Population*
More than 400	1,000	1·2 (farmers with over 50 hectares)
200–400	302	19·2 (animal herders and 11–50 ha.)
100–200	131	32·9 (3–10 ha.)
Less than 100	70	46·7 (less than 3 ha. and landless)
		100·0
Expenditure:		
More than 395		2·2
296–395		2·2
211–316		6·9
123–247		30·3
89–148		33·6
Less than 133		24·8
		100·0

Source: World Bank, *The Economic Development of Iran*, vol. 2, part 1, 1974, p. 20.

Secondly, the unequal distribution of land necessarily leads to inequalities in income, and the 50 per cent or thereabouts of the population in the countryside who have not received land have not seen their incomes rise substantially.[26] Prior to the rise in oil prices, as the figures in Table 8 make clear, 80 per cent of the rural population received around $200 each per year, with the mean income being only $96. At the same time 60 per cent of the rural population had an annual expenditure per head estimated at less than $150. Given the rising gap between urban and rural incomes (see p. 166), it is doubtful if the multiplying of oil prices has had much impact on the majority of the rural population.

Another condition for the expansion of the home market is that there should be a growth in linkages between the agrarian and non-agrarian sectors; here, there seems to have been little progress. The I L O reports that the cooperatives, as well as failing in any degree to market the produce of their members, also fail to provide their members with inputs, remaining predominantly credit-giving organizations. Another analysis based on a 1965 survey showed that the linkages of industry and agriculture are also weak: 'Agricultural purchases from industry were 15 per cent of its input, while industry purchases were about 30 per cent of its requirements from domestic agriculture. The forward linkage with agriculture is very weak; industry does not supply agriculture with the inputs that are essential to its growth.'[27] In the long run the failure to expand this rural market, which involves half the population, must act as a significant brake on the growth of the Iranian economy.

4. *Generating a surplus*: the conventional way for a developing country to industrialize is to squeeze the necessary surplus out of agriculture, through taxation, forced acquisition of food, and other means: Japan, for example, acquired 80 per cent of its government's revenues in the 1880s and 1890s, at the height of its initial industrialization, from the agricultural tax. A similar concern can be seen in both Russia and China, where one of the fiercest issues of political dispute within the respective communist parties has been about how far to squeeze the rural sector. It is a commonplace to say that oil has saved Iran from having to generate its surplus from agriculture, but this does not mean that agriculture has no role to play in providing the surplus for industrialization. Agriculture did provide up to 20 per cent of revenue under Reza Khan, and this helped him to carry out the limited industrialization of the 1930s. Since oil has come to play the leading role, agriculture has been allowed to lag even more,

and agricultural taxation has been reduced since land reform. But oil is a wasting asset, and the failure of agriculture to be efficient has meant both that oil revenues have had to provide more of the surplus than would have been needed if agriculture had been more efficient, and that oil revenues are now being used to finance the import of food. On top of this is the fact that agriculture should be generating a surplus in order to develop agriculture itself: as it is, agriculture has been short of funds in the 1960s and it is only in the 1970s, under the Fifth Plan, that substantial funds have become available. The new flow now is not from the rural to the industrial sectors, but from the government to agriculture: given the availability of oil revenues this is not in itself undesirable, but the volume required and the degree to which these funds are well used are reduced by the present condition of the agricultural sector.

The first four functions of land reform are predominantly economic; the final two are mainly political and social.

5. *Transforming the old landowning class*: the pre-capitalist landowning class has to be eliminated as such since it constitutes an economic and political block to capitalist development and to state control of the countryside. Iran's landowning class has been seen to have conserved some of its land; some landowners have become part of the urban bourgeoisie while those with larger holdings have been integrated into the new, composite, rural bourgeoisie. Some have become state employees of one kind or another; others have gone into private business. The state has indeed encouraged the conversion of landowners into urban capitalists by providing some of the dispossessed landowners with their compensation in the form of shares in government industries. This is a conventional component of reforms carried out in post-war capitalist countries: it occurred in Taiwan and Peru. In Iran, on one estimate, 20 per cent of the total value realized through compensations in phase one was used to buy shares in government-promoted industries, although this may be an exaggeration since the shares were believed to be overpriced and were therefore not attractive.[28] Landowners were encouraged to accept these shares rather than instalment payments, since the latter were only

gaining interest at 6 per cent and the former could yield a higher return. How far this process went is questionable, however, since the shares so given were resaleable, and many were sold to brokers or merchants at a discount in order to realize an immediate cash sum. Whatever the specific class destinations of the old landowners, there is no doubt that whilst their power in the village was broken by the intervention of the state, they themselves were reintegrated into the new Iranian ruling class as capitalist farmers, state employers, merchants or shareholders in industry. There never was any intention of expropriating all land from this class. As one exponent of the reform policies has put it: 'It had always been the hope of His Imperial Majesty the Shahanshah that the private landlords would ... not confuse the land reform policies with unjust expropriation and doctrinaire philosophies of imagined or manifest class struggles.'[29] Given the record of the reform programme, they must surely be content.

6. *Stabilizing the rural areas*: the reform in Iran is one of many land reforms carried out by conservative governments in order not merely to meet the four economic aims mentioned above, but also in order to impose a political solution on the countryside. The function of such a policy is both to eliminate a real or possible revolutionary threat from a discontented peasantry, and to create a new social grouping in the rural areas which will support government policies. It is this political purpose that has often been the immediate propulsion to reform, and which explains why counter-revolutionary capitalist governments have favoured such apparently radical changes. This two-pronged policy also explains why since the Second World War the U S government has encouraged land reform in countries under its influence. The initial thinking on this was developed in relation to Japan, where a group of sociologists including Talcott Parsons saw the need for a stable state to have a contented peasant class. Subsequent to the reforms in Japan, U S advisers helped supervise reforms in China (prior to 1949), Korea, Taiwan, the Philippines, Egypt, Bolivia – and Iran. All of these reforms had an explicitly conservative aim: even where, as in both Japan and Iran, there was no

immediate threat from a peasant movement, the U S advisers realized the need to reorganize the countryside in order to produce long-term stability. In the words of one writer on development: 'No government can hope to satisfy the demands of rioting students. But a government can, if it is so minded, significantly affect the conditions of the countryside so as to reduce the propensity of peasants to revolt. While reforms may be the catalyst of revolutions in the cities, they may be a substitute for revolution in the countryside.'[30] The words of the then premier Ali Amini in 1961 strike a similar note: 'We must not allow the people's anger to rise. It would sweep us all away, the Shah and the Aminirs.'

The other recurring feature of these reforms was that they were unequal reforms, which concentrated on encouraging a rich farming class. In Japan, for example, post-war reforms increased the percentage of owner-operated land from 54 per cent of all cultivated land in 1947 to 90 per cent in 1950; but 43 per cent of all households then owned less than half a hectare and hence they had to rent from others or, more probably, work as labourers. In Egypt, a series of reductions of the upper limit allowed has since 1952 provided land to around 400,000 families, in amounts of five acres and under. But there are 3·2 million rural families in all and the great majority of these have therefore remained homeless.[31] In India the various changes since 1947 and the Green Revolution have produced a strong rich-peasant sector. As one expert has written: 'The kulaks are well on their way to becoming the masters of the Indian countryside. Political and social power has shifted from the old-style landed gentry to the rich peasants, and rich peasants have shown themselves capable of exercising political power ... Poor and middle peasants and landless labourers, however, have gained very little from land reform.'[32] The major difference between India and Iran lies in the fact that the Iranian state is far more effective than the Indian one, and has appropriated power and initiative to itself. But the social consequences of the reform at village level are similar.

The decision to distribute land in this way is often defended by the Iranian government on the grounds that an egalitarian distribution was not feasible. The argument runs as follows: there is too little land to go round, and the best way to boost the rural economy is to give land to those peasants who have some experience of farming techniques, the oxen-owners, rather than to the 'ignorant' and 'illiterate' peasantry. There could be some truth in this – in the absence of a peasant mobilization, such as occurred in China and Vietnam, and as long as the policy remained one of dividing the land up into further individual plots. But neither of these two conditions was economically necessary: they follow from the political choices of the régime, and from the kind of rural social base the state has tried to foster. Moreover, this kind of distribution policy is itself economically unsound: the switch away from individual farming in the 1970s shows that there has been a conflict between the political and economic aims of the reform programme. Far more suitable would have been a really cooperative system of distribution, not in the watered-down sense of a cooperative that has prevailed but in the sense of a shared peasant cooperation at the point of production itself. 'The communal open-field system of agriculture, prevalent in Iran, is by nature more amenable to a cooperative form of production than to a system of production based on individual enterprise. In a cooperative system, the over-fragmentation of lands and the grazing problems can be overcome by introducing production plans for the entire village.'[33] The kind of reform carried out in Iran was not therefore unavoidable: it was a product of the capitalist character of the Iranian state and the particular options it chose.

The most difficult question about the land reform concerns the political impact of the reform on the rural population. There can be little doubt that the removal of landlord power in the villages was very popular, and that those peasants who received land were pleased to do so. At the same time, the initial hopes that everyone would get land have been disappointed, and it is therefore quite plausible that discontent amongst the landless 50 per cent is prevalent. The more recent mechanization and consolidation programmes may also lead to increased resentment amongst the rural population. The régime has certainly gone to great lengths to use its power in the villages to inculcate loyalty to the state and its presiding figure. Protests, whether radical or petty, are usually made by appealing to him. No outspoken hostility to the Iranian state from the peasantry has been heard. 'Based on a general fear, suspicion and relations with the state, peasant initiatives always begin by a profession of loyalty. What has been decided on high is, by definition, just and good. Of that there can be no question.'[34] But beneath these declarations, reminiscent of similar 'loyal' protestations to the Tsar of all the Russias, may lie deeper resentments. We simply do not know what degree of politicization and increased consciousness has resulted from the reform and the subsequent cultural changes. It is possible that this split consciousness does prevail, wherein peasants resent richer landowners and state officials but still revere the Shah; yet this is a precarious situation, and not even the Pahlavi dictatorship may be able to prevent it from exploding.

6 Oil and Industrialization

The Iranian economy has undergone a major transformation since the early 1960s, when the state began to promote capitalist development in a concerted manner. All the conventional indices of growth demonstrate this. In terms of current prices GNP rose by 8 per cent per annum in the 1960s, by 14·2 per cent in 1972–3, by 30·3 per cent in 1973–4 and by 42 per cent in 1974–5. Between 1972 and 1978 GNP grew from $17·3 billions to an estimated $54·6 billions. GNP *per capita* has also risen substantially – from around $450 in 1971 to $2,400 in 1978. There has at the same time been an impressive rise in the output of the manufacturing sector: from 1968 it rose at 14 per cent per annum, rising to 17 per cent in 1973–6: it has come to occupy a growing place in the economy as a whole, employing nearly a quarter of the total labour force and accounting for 16 per cent of GDP by 1977–8. Further examination will show that the Iranian economic record cannot simply be presented in these terms, that many statistics are exaggerated and, in addition, that the rates of the early 1970s are unlikely to continue. But, whatever qualifications are made, there can be no doubt that Iran's record is both a substantial one and, in any comparative sense, exceptional. Iran, now one of the most developed such states, has had one of the highest sustained growth rates of any third-world country, capitalist or communist.

The basis of this expansion has, of course, been oil and it is the peculiar features of this resource that have provided the opportunities and at the same time shaped the limitations of Iranian economic development. One effect of the boom has been that the economy's dependence on oil has in fact increased: from representing 17 per cent of GNP in 1967–8 oil rose to 38 per cent in 1977–8. In 1977 it accounted for 77 per cent of government revenue and 87 per cent of foreign exchange earnings. Iran's growth, past and prospective, would be unthinkable without it. The most eloquent reflection of this is in the growth in government revenues from oil: they rose from $817 millions in 1968 to $2·25 billions in 1972–3 to $19·16 billions in 1975–6. Government development plans have also risen accordingly: the First (1948–56) Plan had a projected expenditure of $350 millions, the Fourth (1968–72) a projected expenditure of $8,284 millions and the Fifth (1972–8) was increased after the oil price rises to $69 billions. Yet if oil has provided the opportunity for growth it has also imposed other limits on the economy, ones that are not insuperable but which revenues alone will not remove. *The flow of oil revenues to the Iranian state has provided a limited historical opportunity for Iran to develop: it remains to be seen whether and, if so, how far this opportunity will be utilized.*

In the simplest terms this issue can be presented in terms of three problems. First, on its own oil has no developmental effects, i.e. it establishes no significant linkages with the rest of the economy. It has no 'backward linkages' in that it employs a tiny labour force, and acquires its capital and technology from abroad; in the first decades of the Iranian oil industry even the food for the oil company was brought in from outside Iran. Nor does oil establish 'forward linkages', in that most of its product is exported: it only builds these interactions in that it provides a source of energy and thereby saves the foreign exchange that would otherwise be used in importing the needed supply. Oil has only one substantial effect: it provides the state with an income, which can, for all intents and purposes, be treated as a form of rent.[1] What further effects oil has depend on what is done with the rent – i.e. on the class character of the state and on the development programmes it initiates. The state's political and social priorities will necessarily find a reflection in these. The question is therefore one which combines economic, political and social issues, of how the state *transforms* income and of the opportunities and obstacles this transformation encounters.

But there is more to the issue than this, since the injection of large sums of capital raises two further problems. Transformation involves not only overcoming blockages present in the economy (e.g. illiteracy or lack of communications), but also removing new obstacles created by the flow of oil monies itself, such as inflation, uncompetitive industry, an explosion in unproductive economic activities, and income inequality. In an underdeveloped oil-producing country such as Iran these two sets of problems compound each other and combine to divert the state's income from investment to consumption, and thereby lessen oil's contribution to developing the economy in the longer term. Finally, there is the fact that oil is a wasting asset: revenues misspent in one year represent a net loss in the country's accumulation process. The transformation of revenue into increased output is therefore a race against time, to use oil so that the economy is as independent of oil and as developed as possible by the time oil runs out.

The following analysis of oil and its contribution to Iranian development will examine three general issues: the development of the oil industry itself and its relation to the state; the extent to which revenues are being used to the best advantage as far as overall development is concerned; and the extent to which Iran is growing fast enough and in the right direction so that it will be able to retain and improve levels of non-oil output and consumption once the wells dry up. A discussion of these three problems will help to place Iran's apparently favourable growth figures in a light which, though not inevitably catastrophic, is certainly far from optimistic.

The Oil Industry

Iranian oil production began, before that in any other Gulf country, in 1908.[2] Its output has risen many times since then and in 1975 Iranian output at 5.4 million barrels per day ranked it second, after Saudi Arabia, amongst Middle East producers. The main producing area is in the southern province of Khuzistan and in 1976 there were 30 major wells, 19 onshore and 11 offshore. Iranian oil reserves are estimated to be sixty billion barrels which at 1975 rates of exploitation would give it thirty-one years of production, i.e. till the year 2006. But given increased demand at home and rising costs of extracting some of this Iran may cease to be a major exporter of oil by 1990 or even before. Its reserves are therefore less substantial than those of some other states, such as Iraq, Kuwait and Saudi Arabia, which can expect to continue exporting for several decades longer than Iran. Iran also differs from states such as Saudi Arabia, Libya and the smaller Gulf entities in that it has a large population (34 millions) and needs to maximize its revenues now in order to push on with its development programmes. This is a problem it shares with some of the other producers – with Iraq, Algeria, Nigeria, Venezuela, Indonesia, Angola – and it places a special pressure on the state to maximize the inflow of revenues in the time available.

The exploitation of Iranian oil was until 1951 in the hands of a British-owned company – first known as the Anglo-Persian Oil Company, then as the Anglo-Iranian Oil Company, and now as British Petroleum. It initially paid a low revenue and even after Reza Shah renegotiated the agreement in 1933 the revenues paid to the state were small: between 1915 and 1950 the company had a profit of \$613 millions, and paid only \$316 millions to the government. Iran therefore suffered in two ways: it received a low inflow of revenue, and its income was determined not by its own policies and needs but by the quite separate needs of the company. It was in response to this that after the Second World War a growing movement in Iran, of which the most prominent spokesman was Mohammad Mossadeq, called for oil nationalization. In 1951 oil was nationalized but B P and the Iranian government failed to agree on the terms of a settlement and B P successfully imposed a world-wide boycott of Iranian oil. In 1954, a year after Mossadeq had been overthrown, the Iranian government signed a new agreement: the oil industry was, formally, still nationalized but this was little more than a legal fiction since effective control over the two main issues, price and output, still lay with the international consortium that replaced the oil company.[3]

The real changes after 1953 lay in three other spheres. First, the Iranian state body, the National Iranian Oil Company, was given a small share in production by taking over what were called 'non-basic operations' (servicing) and it also became the sole distributor of oil inside Iran. Secondly, as the new company remained confined to its area of current production, NIOC invited in other independent companies on terms more favourable to Iran: but although they operated under novel arrangements, these firms did not discover sufficient quantities of oil to present a challenge to the consortium and accounted for only around 4 per cent of output in the mid-1970s. The most important change was that BP lost its monopoly position: a new consortium was established in which US capital now had a share. BP retained 40 per cent, Shell acquired 14 per cent, CFP 6 per cent, and the remaining 40 per cent was divided among the five main US companies (with 7 per cent each) and a group of smaller US firms (sharing the last 5 per cent). It was above all this internationalization of oil operations that distinguished the pre-1951 position from that which followed 1953.

Much more fundamental changes took place two decades later, in the early 1970s. Iran had joined the Organization of Petroleum Exporting Countries when it was established in 1960, but throughout that decade the price of oil had been static. Then, beginning in 1970, the OPEC states were able to reduce excessive production and to raise the price several times over: oil rose from $1.79 a barrel in 1971 to $11.65 in December 1973. Iran, being one of the producer states most in need of oil revenues, supported the moves and in February 1971 the Shah presided over an OPEC meeting in Tehran at which a coordinated breach in the oil company's control of prices was made. In 1973, when the largest price rises occurred, and in the years after that, Iran remained one of the leading hawks within OPEC. Indeed, according to the Algerian negotiator in that organization, there are only two really significant states in OPEC – on the one side, Saudia Arabia, and on the other, Iran. The former, given a much smaller population and much larger reserves, has been cautious on oil price rises in a way

Iran has not, and in December 1976 there occurred an open split between the two camps, led respectively by the Iranians and Saudis, as the former raised the price of oil by 10 per cent and the latter by only 5 per cent.[4] Although this division lasted only six months, it highlighted the varied economic interests within the OPEC coalition.

The result of all these changes is that the revenues paid to the Iranian state have risen spectacularly since the early 1970s. But this rise in price has gone together with another change which has given the Iranian state effective control over the output of the oil industry through a renegotiation of the 1954 agreement. There is a formal difference between these two

Table 9: Iranian Oil Revenues

	US $ m.
1965	522
1966	593
1967	737
1968	817
1969	938
1970	1,093
1971	1,870
1972	2,308
1973	5,600
1974	22,000
1975	20,500
1976	
1977	

Source: *The Middle East and North Africa, 1976–1977*, p. 94.

changes in that the price rises were negotiated *multilaterally* by the oil producers through OPEC, whereas the changes in ownership have come through *bilateral* agreements in each individual case. But this is a misleading distinction, since the conditions of Iran being able to take over *de facto* control of the oil industry in 1973 were just as international as those that made possible the rise in price. Iran could never have renegotiated its agreement with the consortium had the other producer states not been in the process of doing the same thing.

It was because Mossadeq *was* isolated in 1951–3 that he was, in the end, defeated. The new agreement gave the N I O C full control of output throughout the area previously controlled by the consortium; it officially limited the oil companies to the role of being purchasers of Iranian oil and providers of some technical services.

These developments raise two general questions: the relation between the state and the oil companies in the post-1973 situation, and the future capacity of Iran to rely on oil and oil-related activities for development. The official Iranian position is that Iran now operates an 'independent' oil policy; that of the régime's critics is that the 1973 changes are deceptive and that the oil companies still control Iranian oil. Neither of these two positions is accurate, in that the degree of power exerted by Iran over the oil industry has certainly increased, whilst at the same time there are many limits on this power given by the international conditions within which the oil industry operates. The influence which the policies of other producer states exerts has already been mentioned – both in pushing up the price in 1971–4 and in stabilizing it in 1976–7. There is too no doubt that the companies still play an important role, even if not in the same way that they did prior to 1973. Like some other producers, Iran has retained the consortium as a source of technical expertise within the production process. For its part, the consortium has been guaranteed twenty years' supply. But this is a relatively secondary matter as far as the continued power of the companies is concerned. They themselves reap a proportion of the benefit from price rises and their real power, and the real locus of Iran's continuing dependence, lies in the continued control by the companies of distribution in the markets to which Iran exports. Like the producer of any commodity, Iran is limited in what it can produce and earn by what it can sell, and it has no more control of this in the 1970s than it had in the 1950s. While Iran does now control the price and the output of oil, neither it nor any other producer state has been able to make any significant inroads into distribution within the major industralized countries. Hence while *they* rely on the producer states, the reciprocal power of the companies themselves remains and it is here that the limits on Iranian dependence are evident. This was borne out by events in early 1977 when, as a result of the split in OPEC, demand for Iranian oil fell off as purchasers preferred to buy cheaper oil from Saudi Arabia and the Emirates, the states whose price was 5 per cent less than Iran's. Iranian oil exports therefore fell by up to 30 per cent, with serious results for the state's revenues and development programmes. It is consequently misleading to argue that no changes have therefore taken place; but given the workings of the market Iran remains in quite a vulnerable position and would only be able to end this reliance if, in combination with the other main producers, it was able to control the distribution end of the oil industry. This is something that neither the oil companies nor the industralized states are likely to permit.

The other major question concerns the future: in particular, the contribution that oil will continue to make to Iranian growth. Essentially, Iran has three related sources of income from energy exports: oil, petrochemicals and gas. It is estimated that Iran will remain a major exporter of oil until the late 1980s, although an unexpected rise in domestic demand could bring the date of falling off nearer, and new discoveries of reserves could postpone it into the next century. Present information therefore indicates that Iran has only a decade and a half to make itself independent of oil. Iran has tried to increase its export earnings by refining oil rather than exporting it crude, but the benefits of this are limited: the value added on refining is very low, and there already exists a world surplus of refining capacity. Petrochemicals are an obvious area where the value of exports can be boosted, and investment in petrochemical plants forms a major part of the 1973–8 Five Year Plan, with only metals and steel being allocated a higher proportion of the industrial development funds. In 1976 the National Petrochemical Company already had four complexes working, making fertilizers, PVC and other products. But here too there are serious limits. The cost of erecting such a plant is 50–80 per cent higher than in the countries of final demand such as Japan, and given increased petrochemical investment throughout the world the markets for such goods are not without serious competition. Moreover, as Iranian domestic demand grows, so the amount available to earn foreign currency will decline. Hence, even on optimistic bases, Iran's petrochemical output will not substantially reduce its reliance on oil exports.

The prospects for gas exports are more favourable. Iran has estimated reserves of 10,600 billion cubic metres of gas. This is 16 per cent of the world total and more than any other single country except the Soviet Union.[5] At 1975 rates Iran could continue to produce gas for 234 years. This is potentially a major source of income, and since 1970 Iran has exported gas to the Soviet Union via a pipeline. It is estimated that Iran's gas income could rise to between $3,400 millions and $5,600 millions by the late 1980s.[6] Much will depend on how far gas plays a major role in the energy requirements of the advanced capitalist countries in future decades, but even if it does become very important Iran cannot rely on gas to fill the gap left by oil. The highest estimates of gas income amount to only 25 per cent of that being earned from oil. In addition, the marketing of Iranian gas in western Eurape will encounter serious competition from Holland and Algeria, two countries that are in a better geographic position: since the costs of transporting gas are up to ten times those of transporting oil this is a significent factor. According to one estimate, European countries will import between 6·5 and 7·4 trillion cubic feet (T C F) of gas in 1985: Holland will provide 2·1 T C F, Algeria 1·5–1·6 and Iran 1·4–1·8. Iran has indeed already begun to feel the limits of this competitive market, and in October 1976 it cancelled a major agreement signed in 1974 with two Belgian companies and the El Paso Natural Gas Company of the U S A because it could not ensure favourable marketing conditions. The resulting prospect is that, whilst Iran will benefit to a substantial extent from gas exports in the future, these are uncertain in volume and will not adequately offset the loss of income as oil exports fall.

Industrial Development

Iran has therefore to find another branch of economic activity through which to meet domestic demand and to earn the foreign exchange it needs to import goods. If Iran had a long-term comparative advantage in some other branch of activity then development would not inevitably rely on industralization. But there is no such comparative advantage elsewhere: oil and related areas will not be sufficient beyond the early 1990s and agriculture is and will remain in deficit for a long time. Iran must therefore industrialize.

Iran has several advantages in its attempt to industrialize. Unlike most third-world countries it has the investment funds, and so should not need either to borrow abroad or to squeeze the rural sector to generate capital. In Iran there is also a potentially large market of 34 million people, and there is a variety of raw materials, mineral and agricultural, in the country. There is also a strong agent, the state, which professes its desire to put through an industrialization programme. The growth of Iranian industry has been, in the main, a result of state intervention in the period since the 1950s. Neither a native Iranian bourgeoisie, nor foreign capital, was in the past able or willing to industrialize; but, under favourable financial and political conditions forged since 1953, these two private branches of capital have agreed to participate in the industrialization programme.

However, despite these considerable advantages, and in particular despite the ample supply of capital, Iranian industrialization has encountered serious obstacles. Iran lacks the skilled and managerial personnel its industry requires, and despite rapid training of Iranian labour and the import of tens of thousands of foreign workers its industry has remained highly inefficient; the availability of government funds has helped to cushion weak enterprises longer than would otherwise have been the case. Income distribution has been increasingly unequal, with the result that only a small percentage of Iran's population constitute a growing market. The chronic failure of agriculture also acts as a brake on industrialization, in that it requires government funds and fails to meet either the raw material needs or the demand needs of industry: the linkage between industry and agriculture is strikingly low.[7] Above all, given the falling off in oil, Iran must export industrialized goods; and here its failure is immense and growing. Iran may therefore be in a more favourable position to industrialize than many other third-world countries but, despite the expansion in output since the early 1960s, Iranian industrialization is failing to meet the targets which must be met if the post-oil continuity is to be possible.

As occurred elsewhere in Asia (India, Syria), the influx of cheaper manufactured products in the nineteenth century depressed local artisanal production. It was only after a degree of state control, of output and trade, was established by Reza Shah that any industry could develop: between 1934 and 1940 the government's modest industrial promotion campaign brought into existence 200 industrial plants employing 50,000 to 60,000 workers. In the private sector the largest number produced textiles, whilst the state owned an arsenal and factories producing sugar, cement, tobacco and textiles. A second wave of industrialization occurred during the two years of Mossadeq's government when the lack of foreign exchange promoted import substitution by private entrepreneurs.[8] But the main growth in industry has been since the mid-1960s, and in the decade 1965–75 industry grew at an average rate of 15 per cent per annum. By 1977 there were an estimated 2·5 million people employed in industry; and of the estimated 250,000 manufacturing establishments, around 6,000 employed ten or more people and could be classed in the loosest sense as modern industrial establishments. Apart from the petrochemical sector there were other major units – a steel mill at Isfahan, a growing car truck and bus industry, machine-tool factories, and electronic assembly plants. Automobile output rose from 2,300 in 1964 to 73,000 cars, 1,911 buses and 29,365 trucks and vans in 1974–5. The aim is to produce 2 million automobiles of all kinds by the end of the Sixth Plan in 1983. Within this growth there have however been noticeable shifts: the main goal in the 1960s was import substitution and this led to a growth of light industry in and around Tehran; the Fifth Plan (1973–8) has concentrated on steel, metals and petrochemicals, and the Sixth will do the same, while trying to remove specific obstacles that have arisen in the previous fifteen or so years.

Table 10: Industrial Output

	Units	*1969*	*1971*	*1973*	*1975 (1st nine months)*
Glass plates	1,000 tons	17·7	30·6	86·9	59·5
Passenger cars	1,000 units	28·3	38·9	49·8	68·0
Trucks, pick-ups, station wagons	units	5,089·0	12,313·0	23,258·0	33,580·0
Buses & mini-buses	units	3,161·0	3,008·0	5,007·0	3,482·0
Trailers	units	961·0	586·0	1,133·0	978·0
Tractors	units	399·0	3,833·0	7,124·0	6,500·0
Refrigerators	1,000 units	176·8	192·5	324·0	332·8
Electrical outlets, switches, etc.	1,000 units	5,832·0	6,374·0	25,237·0	25,336·0
Television sets	1,000 units	87·3	150·0	218·8	230·4
Coolers	1,000 units	64·1	112·7	139·4	126·3
Water heaters	1,000 units	42·9	55·6	83·7	98·0
Cement	million tons	2.3	2·8	3·3	3·8
Paint	1,000 tons	14·1	16·9	22·4	24·0
Cardboard	1,000 tons	10·0	13·1	12·9	10·5
Beer	million litres	25·8	29·7	39·0	41·2

Source: Bank Markazi

As the recipient of oil revenues the state has been the main instigator of industrial growth and it has carried out this policy in a number of ways. (1) The state has invested directly in industry: under the Third Plan 53·1 per cent of all industrial investment was by the state; under the Fourth 38·8 per cent; under the Fifth 40·0 per cent. The 1973 oil price rises increased this proportion so that in 1975 a full 60 per cent of all industrial investment was directly by the state. This preponderance is especially noticeable outside the light-industry sector – in petrochemicals, steel, car assembly and analogous activities. (2) The state has provided the funds for the private sector to develop. The private banking sector has never been strong and has never therefore been a source of industrial finance. Nor is the Tehran Stock Exchange, founded in 1967, anything more than a shadow of its counterparts in other capitalist countries.[9] In the past loans to traders were made in the bazaar, but the monies available there have been wholly inadequate to the tasks of recent industrialization. Moreover, the bazaar has been in decline since the 1950s as its social, economic and political position has been undermined by the rise of the state's power. The government has therefore provided the funds for industry through a number of special institutions set up for this purpose of which the most important are four: the Industrial Credit Bank, the Industrial and Mining Development Bank of Iran, the Industrial Guarantee Fund, and the Development and Investment Bank of Iran. The Bank Melli, the main bank in the country, also provides large amounts of credit for industrial development. Through these measures the state is to some extent fostering an industrial bourgeoisie, albeit one that is reliant on the state, and as this sector has grown some shares in government industries have been sold off to individual buyers. (3) Fiscal measures have also played a significant role. High rates of duty are levied on imports in an attempt to promote domestic production: these may be as high as 200 or 300 per cent, and the average is about 80 per cent. A state licensing system limits competition in production within Iran. The state also exempts firms from taxation in the initial period and exempts from duty those capital goods that firms have to import to construct their plant. In an attempt to reduce pressure on the Tehran region, the government has given extra exemptions to firms setting up plants at least 120 kilometres from Tehran. This is expected to be a priority in the Sixth Plan. (4) As elsewhere, the state has also undertaken primary responsibility for building the infrastructure which is needed for industrial expansion: the roads, ports, dams, power systems which private interests would not construct themselves. This is especially the case as an attempt is being made to remove the communication and power bottlenecks that became evident in the mid-1970s.

The state plays a major role in all capitalist economies today, even in such developed ones as the U S A (the New Deal) and Britain. In developing countries, the state has intervened further to restrict imports and to promote domestic output more directly, either through state monopolies or through encouragement to private capitalists. In Iran a further stage has been reached, because of the fact that the major source of funds, oil revenues, is paid to the state which must therefore distribute money through its development policies.

The second agent of industrialization is the Iranian bourgeoisie. Historically there was no strong bourgeoisie committed to industrialization in Iran; private capitalist activity was based on trade and centred in the bazaar.[10] It is only the government's promotion of industry and the land reform programme that have brought into existence a significant fraction of the bourgeoisie which is willing to participate in the current industrialization programme. Since its existence remains dependent on state funds and state policies, it would be erroneous to see this bourgeoisie as analogous to those in India and Brazil since the latter have pursued dynamic industrialization policies. Moreover it has concentrated on investment in less demanding sections of the economy – in housing and in light industry – and has left other ventures to the state. Although we do not have accurate data on this group it is clear that an identifiable social group has developed since the late 1950s.

In 1974, 45 families controlled 85 per cent of firms with a turnover of more than 10 million rials. This group has three main origins. First, there are ex-landowners, who received compensation for the lands they lost in whole or in part in the 1960s. It is worth bearing in mind that the ties between landowning and commercial sectors were always close in Iran: up to the 1960s merchants would buy land in the countryside (rather than invest in industry) and landowners often had urban interests too. When land reform came these owners of agricultural land were offered shares in government-run industries which they could either hold or sell. A small percentage retained these and the transition has consequently been only partial, but it would still be true to say that through land reform a sub-section of the industrial bourgeoisie was either created or at least directed towards new areas of economic activity by being provided with more capital.

Another component of the industrial bourgeoisie is made up of civil servants who have amassed funds either through saving or through corruption. The latter is an integral part of the Iranian civil service and the country could not run in its present form without corruption. Details are obviously not available on those government employees, military as well as civilian, who have made money in this way, but there is no doubt that it is a widespread phenomenon. One foreign adviser to the Iranian government argued to me that it was in practice the best way of overcoming traditional reluctance to place money into risky industrial ventures, since the investors were guaranteed their regular income anyway and would be thereby more willing to chance their extra monies in industry. A third component of the industrial bourgeoisie is made up of former bazaar traders. Some prominent Iranian merchants have risen from poor backgrounds through the bazaar. Some traders made a beginning during the speculation and shortages of the Second World War and later moved into industry; others benefited from the import duty exemptions in the 1960s to bring in goods, only some of which they actually used for industrial investment while the rest they were able to market in an unrestricted way.[11]

There is an inevitable simplification in distinguishing these three components in that the structure of economic and family ties in Iran is such that many people with interests in land are traders and have relatives in the civil service. But it is from these three sources, in whatever combination, that those Iranians who do run industry and invest in it are drawn. The most important qualification to make is in another regard, namely in their degree of independence. The state's policy is a thoroughly capitalist one – to promote the growth of an Iranian industrial bourgeoisie. But the latter's policy is rather to use the protection and privileges offered by the state to maximize profits and to keep to those areas of economic activity that are safest. This bourgeoisie is therefore in many respects dependent on the state and has no intention, or interest, in becoming independent of it. The problems will therefore arise when the state is no longer in the financial position to offer that protection.

The third, final, agent in the industrialization drive has been foreign capital. Prior to the 1950s the only significant foreign investment in Iran was in the oil industry. The Iranian state gradually encroached on this foreign position, so that after 1973 the oil companies played no role *within* the Iranian economy, even though their policies continued to have a major effect *on* it. The first moves to encourage foreign capital to invest elsewhere in the economy were taken after the 1953 coup: in 1955 a Centre for the Attraction and Promotion of Foreign Investment (CAPFI) was established,[12] and under CAPFI's supervision a number of guarantees were given to foreign firms. They were given five years' exemption from taxation, the right to repatriate profits in the currency in which they first invested, and exemption from duty on necessary imports. For the first few years, up to 1964, foreign capital was hesitant about investment in Iran, and only thirty-two firms did so. But by 1974, twenty years after CAPFI had been established, 183 foreign firms had invested in Iran, 32 of them in 1974 alone.

Table 11: Private Foreign Investment in Iran 1956–74

Country	*No. of Ventures*	*Capital (m. rials)*
USA	43	5,711
FRG	23	1,669
Japan	23	2,737
UK	20	347
Switzerland	13	1,360
France	12	547
Mixed company	17	1,435
Other*	32	1,423
Total	183	15,227

*Italy and Denmark, 5 each; Sweden and Netherlands, 4 each; Belgium and Luxemburg, 3 each; Israel 2; and Australia, Austria, Greece, India, Kenya, Panama, 1 each

Source: *Iran: Past, Present and Future*, pp. 379, 380.

The aim of CAPFI has been to channel foreign investment into the areas where Iranian expertise is lacking: hence in the 1960s the main areas of foreign investment were rubber, chemicals, building materials and mining; these were extended in the 1970s to include automobile manufacturing, steel production and armaments (as well as agri-business). Because Iran has had plentiful supplies of capital, the main aim has not been, as it has in many other third-world countries, to get investment monies from these firms, and indeed they make up a small part of the total invested: under the 1973–8 Plan foreign capital is scheduled to have invested \$2·8 billions in Iran, whilst the state invested \$46·2 billions, the private sector \$23·4 billions and \$2·7 billions was loaned to the private sector by the state. Moreover, whilst the firms have been guaranteed favourable terms, the Iranian state has also imposed quite strict terms on them in other respects, a strictness made possible by oil revenues. The foreign firms can only operate through joint ventures with an Iranian partner, private or state-owned, and can only have a minority holding in these ventures. Since the workers' share programme was introduced in 1975, the foreign firms have had on average a 25 per cent holding, although it is evident that the managerial and technological monopoly of these foreign firms gives them a power that is in practice much larger than their formal legal holding. The Iranian state, for its part, is heavily reliant on these firms for its industrialization programme since it is only in this way that under capitalist relations it can instal and run the equipment needed for developing the medium and heavy sides of industry. The leading instance is Iran's cooperation with the steel firm Krupp. If Iran is to succeed in meeting its industrial goals, then the key to this expansion lies through the joint ventures.

There are no accurate figures on profits in Iranian industry but both Iranian and foreign investors seem to have benefited substantially from the industrial growth. Iranians ensure that they use the government's facilities to the maximum, and for their part foreign investors have reported rates of return up to 40 or 50 per cent on Iranian ventures. But the relationship between the state and its partners is in many ways an uneasy one, and this unease restricts industrial growth.[13] First of all, private capitalists have to spend a considerable amount of time and energy simply dealing with the state machine – getting permissions, bribing, coping with new and contradictory regulations and so on. The Iranian state machine itself has not been properly converted to the needs of promoting rapid capitalist development, with the result that the flow of information and cooperation between the private sectors is often extremely bad. Even in the early 1970s foreign firms complained a good deal about this problem, but when the Iranian state began to run short of cash in 1976–7 and default on payments the difficulties got much worse. Some firms pulled out of Iran altogether.[14]

The régime is also caught by a conflict between the need to ensure the cooperation of individual capitalists and the wider political need to pose as a popular and nationalist government. A clear instance of this came in the summer and autumn of 1975 when, as the first post-1973 problems began to emerge, the Shah launched three distinct campaigns, one against price profiteering, one against corruption, and one to establish workers' shares in industry (see p. 193). The share programme was in part intended to discourage labour mobility by providing workers with an incentive to remain where they were already employed. The price campaign led to the arrest or fining of over 8,000 Iranian businessmen; the anti-corruption drive led to attacks on a number of foreign firms, including the U S arms firms Grumman, the British sugar firm Tate & Lyle, and the German firm Siemens; and the workers' share project was seen by nearly all businessmen, Iranian and foreign, as a threat to their position since it further reduced their equity shares. As a result private investment fell off, and up to $2 billions of Iranian private money (10 per cent of that year's oil revenues) left the country in a few weeks. Foreign businesses operating in Iran are for their part determined to ensure that they get their money back as quickly as possible, and it is this criterion, not the longer-term interests of Iranian development, that governs their policy. A U S State Department official responsible for Iran, whom I interviewed in

October 1976, pointed out that U S firms in Iran worked on a 'get it while you can' basis; they assumed that an investment was only worth-while if they could get their money back in 4–5 years. Ironically, many Iranian businesses operate at a higher rate, requiring returns of 30 per cent or over from an investment.

It is neither surprising nor novel to point out that private firms, Iranian or foreign, operate on this basis: such is the logic of capitalism and it would be strange if these enterprises behaved differently. They are neither in principle opposed to the industrial development of Iran nor committed to it – their conduct is determined by other factors, and were these factors to be favourable then private firms could and would favour the industrialization of Iran. Part of the cause for the difficulties of Iranian industrialization must lie in the character of the state machine and in its own weaknesses. Decisions are rarely planned and executed in an efficient manner: many of the sums allocated to specific projects are never spent – during the Fourth (1969–73) Plan only 60 per cent of all allocations were disbursed. Nor is there even any proper planning machine: in the words of one expert 'the only kind of planning in Iran is what the Shah wants'. The same expert pointed out that many of the statistics are exaggerated: those for industrial output are less so, but those for price changes are considerably understated whilst those for agricultural output are magnified by over 100 per cent. Moreover, many of the credit facilities allegedly spent on development have been diverted to consumption or to other branches of economic activity such as speculative housing. The G N P growth figures for the 1970s are somewhat misleading in that oil represents a large percentage of G D P and therefore the rise in its price implies a rise in physical output that has not in fact occurred.

Not all the alleged changes in the Iranian economy have been illusory, but there has been a considerable degree of fantasy and deceit even in those areas to which the government chooses to draw attention. The régime proposes targets that are not properly estimated in advance and it often lacks the capacity to meet them. The Iranian media are full of grandiose claims by the monarch or his ministers about some triumph or other; a welter of committees and organizations has been established to oversee economic growth. But a great deal of this *is* rhetoric – in such matters as the boosting of industrial exports, of increases in agricultural productivity, or campaigns against illiteracy. A closer examination of Iranian industry will help to make this clear. What emerges is that whilst oil has enabled a considerable expansion in industrial output and in industrial employment, Iranian industry is still in many ways backward and is heavily reliant on oil revenues to sustain itself. It seems that it will in no way be able to face the challenges presented as oil revenues decline. Oil has therefore both acted as the motor of Iranian development and helped to distort the path of that development in such a way that many opportunities have been lost and a dangerous dependence on oil revenues has been created.

Economic Weaknesses

1. Whilst industrial output has expanded in recent years, an increasing proportion of the oil income has been spent in ways which have not contributed to developing Iran's productive capabilities. The most obvious examples of these are arms expenditure and services. Arms expenditure (see p. 94) has taken up a consistently higher percentage of available funds than industry and, despite some indirect (infrastructural) benefits to the economy, must be seen as a net drain on Iran's economic development. At the same time, whilst industrial output has expanded, the service sector has grown even more: whereas in 1959–60 it accounted for 31·5 per cent of G D P, in 1974–5 it accounted for 39·4 per cent, with industry making up only 16·1 per cent. It is universally the case that rent-based economies encourage the service sector at the expense of the productive sector: this is the area where expansion is easier and where, unless effective counter-measures are taken, expansion in outlay and employment grows fastest. But such growth does not necessarily represent a net gain to the country's long-term economic strength, and in the case of Iran the service

sector expansion has above all reflected the expansion of an inflated state employment and of services catering to the consumption requirements of the better off, the import component of the latter form of demand is, of course, very high. Finally the most important misallocation of monies has been a negative one – the depriving of agriculture of the funds it needed in the 1960s to make the land reform an economic, as distinct from a political, success.

2. The main form of industrial expansion has been in import substitution, and this has taken the form of a growth of small labour-intensive units. In 1976 only 17 per cent of the labour force worked in the 6,000 manufacturing units with ten or more people (see p. 182). Whereas the development of modern industry accompanies the transition from labour-intensive artisanal units to more capital-intensive ones, industrial expansion in Iran has taken the form of a disproportionate expansion in the artisanal sector. While many of these may use their labour well and therefore be efficient, productivity must of necessity be low, given the high contribution of labour to the final product. What information there is suggests, on the contrary, that there is a high degree of wastage in Iranian industry. For example, a U S government report suggested in 1976 that the waste factor in the Iranian economy as a whole was 40 per cent. Even the modern industrial sector suffers from serious drawbacks, for most of the plants producing finished goods are assembling rather than making the components of the goods in question. Iran has no independent technology and relies on foreign firms for this. The Iranian units are much less efficient than those elsewhere: in 1976 it took 45 hours to assemble a G M Chevrolet in Iran, whilst the same process could be done in 25 hours in West Germany. Nor is it possible to advance the argument that Iranian wages are much lower than those elsewhere – a conventional justification for such inefficiencies: wages in skilled jobs rose by up to 50 per cent in 1974 and in 1975 and these rates, plus the production weaknesses, make Iranian industrial goods highly priced compared with their international counterparts.

What has protected this sector are the extremely high tariffs.

But the purpose of these, like the early import substitution phase of industrialization, should be to give domestic industry a breathing space in which it can become competitive on an international scale. If instead the tariffs are used to shield Iranian industry permanently from the effects of foreign competition then the initial justification does not hold. In Iran protection has had this effect: an estimate for 1972 discovered that Iranian-manufactured goods were 25–33 per cent more expensive than average world prices and one can only assume that the post-1973 inflation in Iran has increased this gap.[15] An official West German report, published in 1974, gave the following sober estimate and drew attention to a further problem – the high import component in Iranian industry: 'Iranian industry produces at too high a price and is not internationally competitive. The reasons for this lie in the high dependence on imports, low level of value added, inappropriate plant size and inadequate project planning. Whereas the intention was to replace imports and to save on foreign exchange, the establishment of enterprises that are restricted to the technologically relatively simple final stages of production, such as the assembly of cars, radios and electrical domestic appliances, has led to a disproportionate increase in the need to import the necessary components.'[16]

3. Whilst this inefficiency represents a serious and permanent loss of resources for the Iranian people, it is most immediately dangerous because it undermines any hope Iran may have of increasing industrial exports to meet foreign exchange requirements as oil income falls. This is the most telling weakness of Iranian industry, and it is one that can be meaured not only against what Iran will need by the 1990s but also against what other third-world countries are now able to achieve. The problem is that Iran's imports have risen spectacularly as a result of the oil boom: from $400 millions in 1958–9 to $3·56 billions in 1972–3, to $18·45 billions in 1975–6. By 1983 they may reach $29 billions. Some of this rise can be justified as a temporary measure needed to meet the capital goods requirements of Iranian development; but this is less than a third of the total, and a serious cutback in imports would inevitably have

political consequences in cutting off the flow of consumer goods. Iran has therefore to boost its exports of industrialized goods. But it has, in fact, had a large and growing deficit on the non-oil current account: non-oil exports have declined from around 22 per cent of imports in 1959 to 19 per cent in 1973 and 5 per cent in 1975. The expansion in industrial output has therefore gone together with a growing gap between what Iran imports and what it exports apart from oil.

Table 12: Iran's Balance of Payments

	1972–3 *$ billion*	*1973–4* *$ billion*	*1974–5* *$ billion*	*1975–6* *$ billion*
Current account				
Receipts: from oil	2·25	4·47	18·20	19·1
from other exports, etc.	1·09	1·81	2·95	2·6
total	3·34	6·28	21·15	21·7
Expenditures: on goods	2·99	4·95	10·38	15·3
on services	0·51	0·95	2·26	3·1
total	3·50	5·90	12·64	18·4
Balance	−0·16	+0·38	+8·51	+3·3
Capital account (net)	+0·66	+0·68	−3·26	−4·27
Total balance	+0·50	+1·06	+5·25	−0·97

Source: *The Economist*, 28 August 1976.

Although the government claims it has tried to reverse this tendency, the situation has only deteriorated. In 1975 non-oil exports were only equal to $700 millions whilst imports ran at $19 billions. In the first half of 1976–7 imports rose by 42 per cent and non-oil exports by only 6 per cent. Non-oil exports fell 10 per cent in volume between 1971 and 1976. When one examines the structure of these non-oil exports the situation appears even more alarming since these come overwhelmingly from the traditional sector. In 1974–5 72 per cent of Iran's non-oil exports were from this area, one that is relatively inelastic; only 28 per cent of the non-oil exports came from the 'new industrial' sector, i.e. the one where future expansion will have to take place.

Table 13: Iran's Non-Oil Exports 1974–5
(in percentages)

1. Traditional and agricultural goods	72·0
Carpets	20·5
Cotton	14·7
Fresh and dried fruits	12·3
Skins and leather	4·8
Mineral and metal ores	5.6
Others	14·1
2. New indusrial produces	28·0
Detergents and soap	2·1
Glycerine and chemicals	3·8
Shoes	1·2
Ready-made clothes, knitwear	7·6
and textiles	3·6
Road motor vehicles	9·7
Others	
Total	100·0

Source: Foreign Trade Statistics of Iran.

In this context, Iran's industrial growth can be distinguished from that of several other third-world countries whose recent industrial growth might appear comparable with Iran's. They have comparable growth rates or ones that are lower but this growth is based on more solid foundations since manufactured exports account for a much higher percentage of the total. They can therefore claim they have developed their productive resources in a competitive manner, in a way that Iran cannot. For example, in 1975 manufactured goods made up over 50 per cent of India's exports, 33 per cent of Mexico's, and 60 per cent of Singapore's.

There are two main reasons for Iran's poor performance in

this regard. The first is that the years of protection and subsidizing by the state from the 1960s onwards have created an inefficient industrial sector that cannot compete internationally; the only markets where Iran can sell industrial goods without fearing competition are those of the communist countries where trade is arranged on the basis of state-to-state barter agreements running over several years. While Iran is trying to promote such agreements, there are limits on how far these markets can absorb the exports Iran wants to sell and they would by definition fail to provide foreign currency for other imports. The other reason is that the rise in domestic demand has more than overtaken the rise in output. In the aftermath of the oil price rises, this has meant that even less of the industrial output is available for export. In 1975–6 for example, Iran produced 87,000 saloon cars, an increase of 12,000 on the previous year; but domestic demand was such that a further 65,000 were imported and, despite high duties, were purchased. In no area is this clearer than in steel production. In 1976–7 Iran produced 1 million tons of steel, but demand had risen in only three years from 2·2 million tons to 5·5 million; although output was expected to rise at the end of 1977 to 1·9 million tons, no additional output was expected before the early 1980s. Therefore to meet domestic demand, including the rising demands of the automobile industry, Iran has to import more steel.

The only way to resolve this problem would be to restrict domestic demand: but this is politically difficult for the régime since to do so would undermine the sense of almost unlimited prosperity that sustains the support of the richer Iranians. Some restriction of non-essential imports or of domestic consumption of goods needed for export is in the long run inevitable: but despite the state's promotion of industry these are policies which the class character of the régime dictates should be postponed for as long as possible. There is a conflict within the state itself on this issue.

4. The industrialization drive has also run into a number of major internal obstacles which have prevented the implementation of plans and provoked serious wastage of resources. The

infrastructure available has been quite inadequate to the task of importing the goods ordered and in 1975 ships were waiting over 100 days at the southern ports of Bandar Abbas and Khorramshahr. Once the goods were landed, they often waited for weeks in the docks, and many decayed or corroded as a result. In 1975 alone Iran paid out $1·5 billions in demurrage charges (i.e. over 7 per cent of all its oil income) because of delays in importing goods. Another problem was fire: one fire alone at the Julfa border post on the Irano-Soviet border lasted for three days in August 1976 and resulted in insurance claims of $150 millions.[17] Although some of these bottlenecks were reduced over time and more efficient and capable infrastructural facilities will be available in the future, problems in internal communications will continue to be a serious brake on Iran's race against time.

A second major problem is in the field of management and the labour force. It was estimated that under the 1973–8 development plan Iran would need 2·1 million skilled workers and be able to supply only 1·4 million of them; whatever the precise situation, the level of skills and management is known to be extremely deficient. There is a dispute among economists about how far labour really has constituted a bottleneck and about how long it will last, given increased vocational and on-the-job training. But even where labour has been found it has been able to command a very high price and thereby push up the costs of the final product. Moreover, Iran has an educational system that is woefully inadequate to the needs of an industrializing nation: in the late 1950s it was producing only as many university graduates as Japan a century before and as the output of higher education has increased so the quality has fallen. Lower down the scale Iran still suffers from illiteracy of over 60 per cent – higher than India – and this too must have a major if unmeasurable effect on the overall efficiency of the workforce.

These and other problems reflect the relative unpreparedness of the Iranian economy for the injection of large sums of money. Immediately after the 1973 price rises they were concealed by a flood of official optimism which misled quite a number of commentators, in Iran and elsewhere. In November 1976, however, the seriousness of the situation had become such that the Shah himself announced the need to fight a war against waste: 'It is time to stop dreaming and get down to work,' he declared, without being too precise about what was involved in this. An indication of the régime's thinking was given by the scope of the imperial commission set up at this time to look into waste in the economy. Its areas of investigation included: the spoiling of agricultural products through deficient packing and distribution; a similar investigation into industrial goods, both publicly and privately produced; delays in the ports; failures in the rural and consumer cooperatives; power failures (increasingly common in 1976 and 1977); and drawbacks in education. This move was as unlikely as previous imperial exhortations to deal effectively with the problems, but it showed how serious things had become, and they were to become even more serious within two months when the split in OPEC cut into Iran's 1977 oil income.

5. These problems are ones that are inherited from the past, and that can inevitably be remedied much more slowly than the revenues rise and imports increase. But there are other problems that result to a greater or lesser extent from the very manner in which oil monies have been spent. The class character of the régime has shown itself in the failure to counteract the tendencies which develop if large amounts of money flow into a system in the absence of countervailing measures. One such problem is inflation: although official statistics give moderate rates of inflation in the early and middle 1970s these are known to be incorrect. After the oil rise food rose by as much as 30 per cent per annum, and in 1974–5 rents in Tehran rose by as much as 200 per cent and by another 100 per cent in 1975–6.[18] Another is the import of non-essential goods: between 1972 and 1975 only 29 per cent of Iran's imports were on investment goods. Similarly the enormous rise in food demand and in food imports could certainly have been reduced by state control and rationing; instead $1·5 millions were spent per annum on food subsidies. Control of these constituents of the economy would however entail serious political problems

and weaken the air of optimism generated by the Shah's talk about Iran becoming a 'new Japan' and forging a 'Great Civilization'.

A further indication of this, of the invisible or 'shadow' costs of the régime's policy, is in the realm of taxation. Because it can rely on oil, direct taxation plays only a small part in the state's total revenues – 23 per cent in 1969 – and with the rise in oil prices which raised incomes and state revenues it declined further. Personal income tax is low and evaded; but the record of businesses is even worse. In 1969 corporate taxes made up only 5 per cent of government revenue and in 1975 the Finance Minister revealed that of Iran's 20,000 registered companies only 9,362 were sending in tax records and of these 43 per cent declared losses. The result was that only a quarter of Iran's firms paid any taxes, and taxes represented only 3·5 per cent of G D P as opposed to the 20–25 per cent which the government claimed it wanted.[19] No doubt tax evasion is an effect of the relatively early stages of capitalist development in Iran and of the backwardness of the state machine. The state may be able to levy more taxes in time. But the régime's ability to neglect this sector, like its neglect of agriculture, was made possible by oil, combined with the political reluctance to antagonize the régime's class base. A similar reluctance applies in foreign exchange dealings: part of the prosperity enjoyed by the Iranian rich has been the ability to travel freely abroad. Around the Iranian New Year (21 March) many thousands travel to Europe, and by the end of 1976 20,000 Iranians had bought houses in or near London. There were not yet any restrictions on the export of capital and an Iranian could go to the bank and take out $250,000 in travellers' cheques. It was this which made possible the flight of $2 billions in 1975, and of $300 millions in one devaluation scare in 1977.

The most pernicious reflection of this policy is in the realm of income distribution. It is a conventional argument of development economics that an initial increase in the inequality of income is, or may be, beneficial to the long-term growth of an economy, and that after *per capita* income crosses the $500 mark this inequality should begin to decline. But this argument, even if valid, does not apply to rent-based economies since the corrective forces operating in other economies do not operate. On the contrary, because the distribution of income reflects the social character of the state itself the inequalities are compounded so that the gap between rich and poor continues to widen way past the $500 mark; moreover, the alleged benefits of higher incomes for some – saving and investment – do not occur, since the state itself performs these functions and private incomes are devoted mainly to consumption. An evaluation carried out in 1969 showed that the top 10 per cent of the population accounted for 32·5 per cent of consumption, and that the next 10 per cent accounted for 15·5 per cent, i.e. the top 20 per cent accounted for nearly half, 48 per cent, of consumption. The effects of the oil price rise will have been to widen this gap: whilst the consumption capacities of the very poor have almost certainly risen somewhat the rich have got much richer. One report for 1976 indicated that the top 10 per cent now consumed 40 per cent of the total – up 7·5 per cent on 1969. It would therefore seem that it is the top 10 per cent, perhaps 3·5 million people or under a million families, who are enjoying the fruits of the oil boom.[20]

Another aspect of income distribution is the urban–rural gap. About half of Iran's population still live in the countryside (53 per cent in the 1976 census), and the gap between its income and that of the town and city dwellers is widening: the ratio declined from 2·13 in 1959 to 1·91 in 1965 (reflecting the land reform's benefits), rose to 3·21 in 1972 and may rise to 8·0 or even 12·0 in the 1980s, before it declines.[21] An income distribution pattern of this kind is encouraged by the way in which oil revenues enter the economy, by the absence of any effective taxation system and by the government's promotion of a prosperous bourgeoisie. While this is politically necessary for the régime, it means that the latter is running serious risks in the longer term for in purely economic terms the growth of the home market is being restricted. Politically this policy will pose considerable problems since, even if the income of the mass of the population does rise, the perceived gap between rich and poor will widen.

Obstacles to Development: Internal or External?

The prospects for Iranian development in the decades during and after the export of oil are therefore dependent on whether and how far the régime can reverse the tendencies inherent in the economy in the mid-1970s. Immediately after the rise in oil prices the government expanded its Plan allocations by 90 per cent to $69 billions and proclaimed an optimistic perspective in which Iran would within two decades become a major industrialized power and catch up with the advanced capitalist countries. For two years Iran even had a surplus of foreign exchange and began to invest and to lend abroad. But two years later the situation was quite different and the demands of the economy itself and the fall in world demand for Iranian oil so considerable that Iran was now unable to carry out some of the development projects it had announced. Iran's role as a foreign investor was a transient one, and it faced the prospect of becoming once again a borrower on the international markets. The limits to development, even with large sums of money, have therefore become more evident. As a report by the Hudson Institute in 1975 indicated Iran would, even in the unlikely event of its meeting its growth targets by 1985, have an economy not much more developed than India's and equal to or just behind Mexico's. If these targets are not met then 'Iran, in the final decade of this century, could prove to be no more than a half-completed industrial edifice, with the trappings of power and international influences and none of the substance.'[22]

The difficulties which Iran faces are by no means specific to that country. Many are found in the third world as a whole, and what the Iranian case provides is a clear instance of how other problems remain when the most pressing problem, an acute shortage of capital, is removed. The countries most analogous with Iran are those other oil-producing states which also have substantial populations and land areas and are therefore at least candidates for long-term economic development. Like Iran, Iraq and Algeria suffer from a long-term crisis in agricultural productivity; Venezuela too has become a net importer of food, and suffers from unequal distribution of income and shortages similar to Iran's. Venezuela, like the Middle Eastern states, has a shortage of skilled and managerial personnel.[23] In another sphere, corruption, there are also comparisons: Nigeria and Indonesia both witnessed spectacular cases of corruption following the rise in oil prices – the former in the cement industry, the latter within Pertamina, the state oil company. As the Hudson Institute put it: '... the oil countries, Iran included, are actually fragile economies in the very earliest stages of national development. With their high new oil incomes they have the *opportunity* to make great strides forward in developing their industries and carrying out social reforms. But even if they capitalize on this opportunity – and many, it is probable, will not – they are condemned to remain members of what the United Nations politely describes as the "less developed countries", for many years to come.'[24]

The question is therefore whether Iran will use the opportunity presented to it, and, if not, why not. From the above analysis, it seems that the opportunity will be used only partially, and this raises the question of evaluating the weight to be attached to the different forces involved. In the first place, there is the role of imperialism, of the advanced capitalist countries and their specific elements – imperialist states, international firms, and multilateral agencies under imperialist control. While these do not necessarily work in a coordinated manner, there is a strong convergence between them.

It is a conventional nationalist argument, in Iran as elsewhere, and one to which the left usually lends support, that the domination by imperialism has retarded the development of the third world and that this is a continuing phenomenon. Such a retarding control was certainly true in the first half of this century, but there are numerous indications that, as a result of changes within the advanced capitalist economies since 1945, and especially in the 1960s and 1970s, as well as of changes in relations between developed and developing capitalist countries, the straightforward retardation theory is no longer applicable. In fact, advanced capitalism has, through one or other channel, given considerable encouragement to industrial development in certain countries of the third world.[25] Iran is a case of this. Foreign firms have, as we have seen, been willing to invest in Iran to an increasing extent, and have done so in accordance with the same criteria affecting investment anywhere – security and rate of return on investment. Capital operates internationally and invests on international criteria. Some 'anti-imperialist' analyses point to the very fact of foreign investment as an index of the retarding impact of advanced capitalism: but this is a misleading approach and one which ignores the real question, namely how this investment is being used and how far the state can control its disposal. Moreover, the rush of foreign exporters to sell their goods to Iran since 1973 shows that they are well aware of the expanded market possibilities there. All this has to be seen in the first place as a result of the oil boom, i.e. a rise in the rent paid to the Iranian state, rather than as an expansion in productive capacity itself; but for whatever reasons there can be no doubt that imperialist states, firms and agencies have given some support to the growth of the productive forces in Iran. However, the centrality of oil points to a further aspect of the changes since 1945, namely the growing ability of the Iranian state to impose its terms on economic relations with imperialism. Precisely because these concessions have had to be won by Iran, and its allies in OPEC, it is evident that the advanced capitalist countries have not made these concessions willingly: but there is no doubt that, whilst a real conflict continues and must continue as long as there is an international capitalist system, the Iranian state has made some advances. It has been able to impose quite strict regulations on foreign firms investing in Iran, and through participation in OPEC has been able to multiply its oil revenues in a few years.

The manner in which Iran is still subordinated to imperialism, to the advanced capitalist countries, and in which the unevenness of capitalist development on a world scale still makes Iran a weak constituent of the system, has to be defined quite carefully, taking into account the shifts in international capitalism of which OPEC is the most striking instance. Iran, like the other oil exporters, remains weak because its economic prosperity still rests on the export of a single primary product whose market it does not control. It is therefore vulnerable to shifts in demand and to manipulations of distribution by the oil company cartel. Secondly, Iran has no independent technological capability and has still to import semi-finished goods to meet final industrial output. But under some circumstances technology, like goods, can be bought and here too it depends on state policy how far the acquisition of technology in itself produces dependencies. Thirdly, just as Iran is vulnerable in its exports so it is vulnerable in its imports and in the inflation in price of the goods it purchases abroad. It is not a large enough purchaser to influence the market price on its own. Most importantly, Iran had, with other O P E C states, to *force* concessions from the advanced capitalist countries. Having said this, it is nevertheless important to emphasize that Iran is to a greater extent than in the past an independent actor in the international capitalist system, although the stronger actors in this system, the imperialist states, will encourage its development only in so far as this accords with their own interests. One can expect that as Iran becomes less well placed in the 1980s the conflicts between it and other states will intensify.

The alternative to blaming Iran's problems on imperialism is to argue that the obstacles are endogenous: as Bill Warren has put it 'capitalist industrialization faces serious problems' in the third world, but 'these are now rooted in the internal contradictions of underdeveloped countries'.[26] Now it is certainly true that many of the obstacles to Iranian development are not so much the results of imperialism, but rather of the historical backwardness of Iran, itself a product of the failure of imperialism to transform the Iranian economy and of the slow growth of the productive forces until the 1960s. Illiteracy, backward agriculture, deficient communications, lack of skilled labour, a weak industrial sector, an inappropriate state machine – these are to a certain extent *internal* problems resulting from the failure of Iran to develop in the past and cannot be attributed solely to any contemporary or recent discouragement of Iranian development by the U S A or multinational companies. The latter have, indirectly, reinforced Iran's backwardness, but they did not create it. It is conventional for Iranian nationalists – among them the Shah – and for the Iranian left to locate the cause of Iran's economic problems in the influence of imperialism; but, on its own, such an analysis only serves to distract attention from the problems internal to Iranian society itself. In the Shah's case it is a convenient way of distracting attention from the shortcomings of his own régime.

Yet this too is an inadequate if partially true account since the present endogenous obstacles to growth are themselves, in part, a result of Iran's recent history. On three occasions in this century military invasion from abroad has destroyed an attempt by Iranian political forces to chart an independent path of national development – in 1908 after the Constitutional Revolution, in 1941 and in 1953. Hence the continuance of Iran's underdevelopment is in part attributable to the political and military intervention of outside powers, all of them, with the exception of Russia in 1941, capitalist ones. Each of these disrupted an indigenous process of development. More important, however, is the recent influence of the advanced capitalist countries on Iran: the main contemporary obstacles to developing the Iranian economy and to achieving a successful post-oil normalization include not only exploitation by the advanced capitalist countries or the historical weaknesses of Iranian society, but are also to be found at the point where most western observers see the greatest reason for approval, namely in the state itself. For, if Iran fails to benefit fully from its short-lived assets, if the economy is not developed by the time oil runs out, this will in part be because the régime has misspent the money it received, despite all its 'plans' and propaganda. And the cause of this misspending lies in its political character – in the expansion of arms purchases and services, in the incapacity to implement early enough the unpopular economic measures needed to curb imports, consumption and capital flight.

It is the régime's class character which dictates this policy and the political limits within which it must operate. But this is itself not a purely endogenous factor: for the Iranian state is to some degree a creation of U S imperialism in the post-war epoch and is a result of the interventions of imperialism in 1953 and in the subsequent years of consolidation. Iran may have disputes with the major capitalist countries – most obviously about the price of its imports and its oil exports, but it is tied into the international capitalist system and has benefited in the past from direct political and military support of the major capitalist nations. It is a contradiction in the policy of the latter that, whilst they are willing to encourage economic growth in third-world countries, they also sustain for political and miliary reasons régimes that are in some way unsuited to such an economic endeavour, even while pursuing a policy of industrialization.

7 The Working Class

A major constituent of almost all contemporary economic development is the shift of population from agricultural to non-agricultural activity, and Iran is no exception to this. At the start of this century 90 per cent of the labour force was estimated to be working in agriculture, and as late as 1946 75 per cent of the workforce remained in this sector. But the percentage has fallen with increasing rapidity since then: already by 1966 less than half of the economically active population, 47 per cent, was in agriculture, and in the late 1970s the figure has fallen to probably around 33 per cent.[1] Out of a total labour force of 10·6 millions in 1977, an estimated 6·8 millions worked outside the agricultural sector; of these a full 2·5 millions, or close on a quarter of the total, were employed in manufacturing of some kind.[2]

Since this shift in sectoral distribution has been accompanied by the spread of capitalist relations, the majority of the economically active population are now in one form or another wage-earners, and a substantial new social force has therefore been created. Yet, despite its growing numerical strength, the working class has been prevented, since the coup of 1953, from playing an independent political role or finding an independent expression. This is a situation which is unlikely in the long run to continue, and there are already indications that the working class of Iran, so greatly expanded in size by comparison with that of a generation ago, is starting to play a role, albeit within narrow limits. The care taken by the régime to placate the working class, while repressing independent political initiatives, testifies to *its* awareness of the working class as a force in Iranian life, whilst the increased number of strikes in Iranian industry after 1973 indicates the potentiality for increased worker resistance to employers and to the state. The analysis that follows will try first to identify the main features of the Iranian working class today, and then to describe its political role, both in two previous phases of overt political activity, and in the post-1973 period.

In this chapter I shall analyse three kinds of non-agricultural wage-earners – those employed in the oil, manufacturing, and construction sectors. But while leaving on one side the theoretical problem of boundaries, i.e. who is and is not a member of the working class, it is worth noting the uncertain social and therefore political contours of the working class in all capitalist societies, and the especially ragged edges of the working class in developing capitalist countries,[3] in Iran as elsewhere, because of the varieties of employment. Only a small minority of Iranian workers are employed in modern industrial plants, yet the majority of the economically active population is involved in wage-earning, agricultural or non-agricultural. This poses not only analytic questions, of whether all these wage-earners are members of the working class, but also political ones, of how this heterogeneous body will act politically in the future and whether it will be able to act within a unified political framework.

A further problem involved in analysing the working class follows from the above: it is that of defining the sub-divisions within it, both of a horizontal kind (between workers in different sectors of industry) and of a vertical kind (between skilled and unskilled, men and women, highly and not so highly paid workers). In addition to the differences produced by the varied structure of industry itself, there are also differences imported into the working class by pre-existing differences in society: these include regional, linguistic and ethnic differences, all of which may continue to operate in an urban context. The existence of such differences does not mean that there is no identifiable working class, where such a class is identified by its relation to capital. Such a class exists, but the divisions within it, a product of both industrial and pre-capitalist structures, are such that it is misleading to talk of the working class, either in economic terms or in terms of potential political consciousness, as a homogeneous entity.[4] Those concerned to build a strong and unified workers' movement in Iran will have to take account of these divisions, just as they will have to be aware of the different objective interests of those who are on the margin of the working class in such a developing capitalist society.

The Growth of the Working Class

The expansion of the working class is above all an effect of the pace and character of economic development. To some extent political considerations may also play a role, in that governments faced with a militant working class may encourage capital-intensive industries even more than they otherwise would, and may thereby try to keep down the numerical weight of the proletariat. Such considerations can only, however, play a contributory role within the general pattern of capitalist development: the growth and sectoral allocation of the labour force reflects the overall pattern of national and international economic expansion, within which political attitudes to the working class play a secondary role.

The pattern of economic growth in Iran has already been discussed. Oil was the sole major individual activity prior to the Second World War and significant industrialization began only in the 1950s. Since then, whilst employment in oil (never massive) has stagnated, employment in manufacturing and in construction has increased substantially. In the simplest terms, whilst employment in oil has not gone beyond 1 per cent of the total economically active population, employment in these other two sectors has trebled over the twenty years since 1956. Since the total labour force has grown by only two-thirds, the relative weight of these sections of the working class has correspondingly risen.[5]

Two peculiarities of this picture will emerge in the analysis: first, the enormous and growing disproportion between oil's contribution to the economy generally and its impact on the labour force; secondly, the disequilibrium within the manufacturing sector between those employed in modern industrial plants, and those in artisanal, small-scale, units. But, whilst

Table 14: The Iranian Labour Force 1956–77
Manpower budget: employed population by major economic sector, and labour force, 1956–77
(In thousands)

Sector	*Annual totals*				*Increases*
	1956	*1966*	*1972*	*1977*	*1972–7*
Agriculture	3,326	3,774	3,800	3,800	0
Oil	25	26	40	55	15
Mining and manufacturing (including handicrafts)	816	1,324	1,820	2,500	680
Construction	336	520	710	980	270
Utilities	12	53	60	65	5
Commerce	355	513	650	725	75
Transport & communications	208	224	255	280	25
Government services	248	474	640	780	140
Banking, other services and n.a.d.	582	650	900	1,040	140
Total fully or seasonally employed	5,908	7,558	8,875	10,225	1,350
Wholly unemployed	158	284	320	375	55
Total labour force	6,066	7,842	9,195	10,600	1,405

n.a.d. = not adequately described.

Source: *Employment and Income Policies for Iran*, I L O, 1973, p. 31.

bearing these features in mind, it is also significant to note that Iran has a relatively high percentage of its labour force in manufacturing industry as a proportion of the total labour force. In overall terms at least, Iran has one of the larger manufacturing labour forces in the third world. This force is, however, concentrated in specific industrial centres. We do not know the geographical distribution of those in manufacturing and other wage-earning non-agricultural activities, but we do have figures on the concentration of industrial units: in 1973–4, 48·7 per cent of these were in the Tehran area, i.e. nearly half were around the capital. The other main centres were Isfahan (7·8), Tabriz and environs (6·9) and Khuzistan, the oil-producing area (6·6). As the number of employees per plant is probably higher in Tehran, the majority of the industrial labour force is almost certainly there. The three main areas of productive wage-earning activity are oil, manufacturing and construction. Each is here considered in turn.

(i) Oil

Oil production created the first substantial section of the Iranian proletariat, initially from Iranian migrant workers in the oil-fields and towns of the Caucasus, in southern Russia, and then in the oil-fields of southern Iran, where exploration began in 1901 and production in 1908. Between the early 1890s and 1917, when Iranian migrants ceased going to Russia, several hundred thousand Iranian workers from the northern provinces of Iran went to work in the Caucasian fields and in the other activities that grew up around that early oil boom. In 1905 alone an estimated 300,000 Iranians crossed the frontiers to find work; much of it was probably seasonal, and a small amount of it in the oil-fields themselves. We know that in 1915 there were 13,500 Iranians in the oil workforce of Russian Azerbaijan, yet this, though a fraction of all Iranians in Russia, represented 29 per cent of the total oil labour force.[6] In the quite separate growth of the oil-fields of Khuzistan, employment also grew quickly so that by 1920 20,000 Iranians were employed, and this number grew to reach 55,000 in 1951, with a further 15,000 working for employers who received contract work from the oil company. Khuzistan was one of the least urbanized areas of Iran at that time, and as a result of oil no less than eight separate towns came into existence: the largest, Abadan, site of the refinery, grew from being a fishing village of a few hundreds in 1900 to being a city of 170,000 in the late 1940s, where virtually the whole population depended directly or indirectly on the oil company for employment.[7] This city became known, in a Persian rhyme, as the 'second London' – *Abadan, Landan-i Dovvom.*

The workforce in the oil industry fell into three categories. The majority were unskilled and skilled labourers, and either recruited locally from the Arab tribes of Khuzistan and from the Bakhtiari nomads of the surrounding mountains (see pp. 12–13) or, in the case of skilled workers, from Isfahan and Tehran. At the end of 1949 an estimated 33,000 out of 38,000 employees at Abadan were wage-earners of this kind, whilst in the fields themselves 15,000 out of 17,000 fell into this category. These workers were involved in construction, maintenance, transportation, loading, work on pipelines. It is significant that despite the capital-intensive nature of the industry a large proportion of workers were unskilled; part of the explanation lies in the fact that the production and refining processes were so automated even then that only a small number of skilled workers were strictly required. In the middle was a layer of technical and clerical workers: many of these were in the first years brought from India; but as Iranian nationalist protests increased the company trained a larger number of local personnel, and recruited Iranians for these jobs.[8] On top was an upper level of managerial and engineering staff: these were mainly British employees, but by 1949 a majority were Iranians, even if power lay with the British, and after the nationalization of oil the number of foreign personnel in the oil industry fell substantially. Whereas in the 1920s there were reckoned to be around 7,000 imported personnel as against 20,000 Irans, and there were in 1949 still about 2,440 foreign salaried personnel and another 989 artisans, the number of foreign personnel overall had fallen to 480 by 1956.

The absolute number of people employed in the oil industry has continued declining since the 1950s. The consortium itself began cutting back on labour in 1957. But although there is believed to have been a slight rise of 15 per cent in the period 1972–7 the real changes do not lie in the actual numbers employed so much as in the increasing productivity of the workforce. Whilst the oil labour force has fluctuated between 40,000 and 45,000, the output of the industry, and even more so the revenues it has earned, have multiplied. Value added per employee has therefore risen spectacularly in the two and a half decades since nationalization. Between 1961 and 1966 alone the number of employees required to produce 111 barrels

Table 15: Employment and Productivity in the Iranian Oil Industry

Year	Staff		Manual			Production in	Productivity in
	Iranian	Foreign	Labour	Contractor[a]	Total	Thousands of Cubic Metres	Thousands of Cubic Metres/Employee
1958	8,139	693	48,477	4,724	62,033	47,767	0·77
1961	10,188	847	39,638	1,619	52,292	68,581	1·30
1964	9,888	474	31,564	727	42,653	98,343	2·30
1967	11,659[b]	—	29,426	1,385	42,470	150,681	3·50
1970	12,547[b]	—	26,952	1,917	41,416	222,180	5·40
1972	12,831	497	24,931	2,766	41,812	294,100	7·03

[a]Excluding foreign employees of the contractors.
[b]Including foreign staff.

Source: For employment figures up to 1967, M. Nezam-Mafi, 'Role of Oil in the Iranian Economy', booklet published by N I O C Public Relations Office, 1967. For other data, N I O C's Statistical and Information Office of the Affiliated Companies. As published in Fereidun Fesharaki, *The Development of the Iranian Oil Industry*, London, 1976, p. 145.

of crude fell from 8·5 to 3·5. In 1975 output per worker was 20 times higher than in the 1950s.

Although oil has dominated the Iranian economy it has, from an employment point of view, always been a factor of small importance. This is not just a matter of oil's enclave character since oil differs from other primary products that are also constitutive of enclave economies and are, therefore, comparable with oil in other respects. Agricultural activities such as tea or cotton do employ a large number of people, however low their wages or seasonal their employment. Other forms of mineral extraction also employ substantial labour forces: the South African mines employed over 600,000 African workers in the mid-1970s, 400,000 of them in the gold mines. Chile, Bolivia and Zambia have substantial workforces in the primary export sector dominated by mining. One of the distinguishing features of oil as a primary produce is that it does *not* provide many jobs, either directly or indirectly. It employs very few people in the direct processes of oil production – in exploration, production, refining, loading. Moreover, in underdeveloped countries, it establishes few linkages with the local economy, since it brings in its technology and capital goods from abroad; it therefore fails to create jobs elsewhere in the economy. Of the small number of people it trains some do acquire skills, but in a country like Iran the oil industry has not, and indeed could not, make a major contribution to training the skilled industrial labour force which the country requires. The limited employment and training effect of oil is not primarily a matter of oil company policy: it is a given of the oil industry itself. And that is why the pattern, the disproportion, evident in Iran can be seen in other oil-producing countries. It is evident in other populous producer states such as Venezuela and Algeria: in the former oil provided in 1975 93 per cent of foreign exchange and only 1·6 per cent of employment (5,000); in the latter, similarly, oil employs 16,600 out of a total workforce of 2·5 millions. Even in the less populated states oil employs a very small percentage of the labour force: a mere 20,000 out of 1·5 millions in Saudi Arabia; only 7,000 out of 550,000 in Libya. If oil does create employment, and if it has a significant impact on the formation of a working class, this is in an indirect manner, i.e. through the jobs created by the state in its disposition of the revenues it receives.[9]

(ii) Manufacturing

Table 16 shows how employment in manufacturing has risen several times in the past two decades. The ILO estimate on which this table is based reckons that in the period 1972–7 alone employment in manufacturing will have risen by 680,000, 580,000 of which is accounted for by employment in industrial establishments and the remaining 100,000 by self-employment, in both urban and rural areas. In the euphoria after the 1973 oil price rises official projections put the figure at the end of the Fifth Plan even higher, at 3·77 millions; but given the retrenchment which followed soon afterwards it is unlikely that such a large estimate is valid. Official figures on employment in manufacturing do show a steady increase in employment throughout the 1970s, which follow the lines of the ILO projection:

Table 16: Indices of Wages and Employment in Selected Industries 1969–70 – 1974–5
(100 = 1969–70)

Industries	*Wages 1974–5*	*Employment 1974–5*
Total, selected industries	292·2	140·4
of which:		
Tobacco	221·8	111·5
Spinning and textiles	274·3	121·4
Leather	219·4	98·0
Machine-made shoes	297·4	168·5
Petrochemicals	402·8	242·3
Pharmaceuticals	282·1	173·2
Cement	283·6	148·0
Basic metals	349·8	195·8
Household appliances (electrical and non-electrical)	272·9	136·8
Radio, TV, telephone	377·1	226·8
Electrical tools	352·9	217·0
Motor vehicles	368·8	170·1
Sheet glass	562·5	325·9

Source: *Bank Markazi Annual Report, 1975–6*, pp. 84, 85.

This general picture is, however, misleading in that it does not reveal the enormous differences within the manufacturing labour force. In the first place, between 10 and 20 per cent of those employed are self-employed: they are not wage-earners or workers in any strict sense of these terms. Secondly, as the previous discussion of industry has indicated, the majority of units are small-scale ones, employing less than ten people: in 1972 219,000 out of 225,000 establishments were of this kind. The expansion in large-scale industry has, in Iran, gone together with a multiplication of smaller-scale enterprises, and hence the distribution of the labour force between the two sectors has changed only slightly. Figures for 1968 indicated that units employing more than 50 workers accounted for 11 per cent of employment; units employing between 10 and 50 for another 6 per cent. Hence 83 per cent of all workers were in units of less than ten people. In 1977 it is estimated that of the 2·5 millions in employment, 1·78 millions, or 72 per cent, will still be employed in units of under 10 persons. Indeed, given the overall growth in the manufacturing labour force in this period, the absolute numbers employed in these smaller units will rise and continue to rise. The 'core' industrial labour force in Iran, those employed in industrial units of over ten persons, is therefore around 700,000 or about 7 per cent of the total economically active population. Those in genuinely large enterprises will be even smaller.[10]

There are consequently two kinds of manufacturing labour force in Iran; the gulf between them may in many respects be widening as a result of the kind of economic development strategy being pursued by the government, and by the negligent social and educational policies characteristic of the Pahlavi régime. The majority of the Iranian population are, in the first place, still illiterate; the official estimate was 62 per cent in 1976 but the real figure was almost certainly higher. There is probably a high correlation between literacy and membership of the top sector of the labour force. Secondly, the level of industrial training has been and remains extremely low. In the early 1970s it was discovered that only 1–2 per cent of those who were skilled workers had received any instruction apart from on-the-job training and despite a crash programme in training the supply of skilled labour is far behind that of demand.[11] Thirdly, there are, as will be seen, large and growing disparities in wages between different sectors of manufacturing, with those in 'advanced' sectors related to construction goods, cars and oil receiving wages twice or even more times as high as those in 'traditional' areas such as textiles and shoes (p. 189). It will be evident that the government's profit-sharing and workers' share programmes are aimed uniquely at this upper stratum of the manufacturing working class (p. 193). A minority of those wage-earners employed in manufacturing are therefore benefiting from the development policies of the government, whilst the majority are allocated by the labour market to the less developed and more underprivileged sector.

(iii) Construction

Construction is *par excellence* an area of underprivileged manual wage-earning employment: in the advanced capitalist countries of western Europe it is an area of primary concentration by immigrants (such as the Irish in England, and the Algerians in France), and employment is often of a casual and seasonal nature. The working class in this sector is therefore often of a less stable kind, either in economic or political terms, than in the industrial sector, and in a migratory situation often retains stronger ties with the villages from which the workers come. It is characteristically the first employment a peasant acquires on coming to a town. Construction itself is also a more volatile sector of the economy: in the oil states generally it is the area that has boomed most rapidly as a result of the 1973 changes, both because construction (of plant, communications, housing) is a precondition for the expansion of other sectors, and because it is simply easier to launch a construction programme than to develop industry or agriculture. In states such as Saudi Arabia and Libya, where there are overall labour shortages, hundreds of thousands of workers have been brought in from neighbouring peasant countries to work in construction: in 1976 there were reckoned to be 1·2 million Yemenis in Saudi Arabia, mostly in construction, and 200,000 Egyptians and 40,000 Tunisians in Libya, again in the same sector. In Iran, the construction workers have been brought in from the Iranian countryside itself. Employment in construction has risen from 336,000 in 1956 to over 900,000 in 1977, so that it now represents close on 10 per cent of the labour force. Indeed in the period 1972–7 employment in construction has risen at 6·7 per cent per annum, faster than that of any other sector.

Within the construction labour force it is possible to identify an upper stratum of skilled workers – plumbers, electricians, carpenters – whose wages have risen spectacularly in the mid-1970s boom. In 1975–6 wages for some workers in construction are believed to have risen by as much as 48 per cent.[12] The majority of workers in construction do not, however, fall into this category. Unskilled workers in this sector are probably exposed to a considerable extent to the double oppression of low wages and insecure employment. As early as 1969 skilled construction workers were earning up to fifteen times the rates of the unskilled in this sector. In some areas groups of workers from the most impoverished Iranian provinces, Baluchistan and Sistan, are to be found working in the most degraded conditions. In the Isfahan area, many of those employed on construction are believed to be peasants from villages in the region who come into town for a few months of the year. The wages of these workers, averaged out over a year, may be as low or lower than those in the less favoured sector of manufacturing employment, and the conditions under which they live, given their non-permanent presence in the city, may also be worse.

Characteristics of the Labour Force

(i) Migration

Many of the features of the labour market in Iran are common to other industrializing third-world countries. As would be expected, the majority of those employed in industry are from a peasant background. A survey carried out in 1963 showed that 68·3 per cent of all Tehran factory workers had been born in villages.[13] This peasant origin is bound to be true of most of the urban working class, and, given the continued expansion in numbers employed, it is unlikely that before the 1980s the majority of the working class will itself have been born in the urban areas. What happens when peasants come to cities is a subject of considerable debate, and there is not enough evidence available from Iran to contribute to this discussion. But there are a number of specific characteristics of Iranian migration that can be identified and which help to disaggregate the general figures available.

In the first place, there is one sector, the oil industry, where the working class may well be predominantly second-generation. Until the 1950s the unskilled were peasants and nomads, the skilled being drawn from the cities or the company's training schemes. But the numbers in oil have not risen since, and indeed in the 1960s there was some migration by the children of oil workers from Abadan to other parts of Iran. One can therefore expect that the majority of those today employed in the oil industry are themselves the children of the working class formed in Khuzistan in the 1930s and 1940s.

On the other hand, it is mistaken to identify all manufacturing with urban employment: a distinctive feature of Iranian industry is that a high proportion of textile workers are employed in the rural areas (where 'rural' denotes places of less than 5,000 inhabitants). The rural areas account for around 70 per cent of employment in carpets and cloth weaving; in 1966 1·2 million people, or around 17 per cent of the total labour force, were in non-agricultural rural activities.[14] Artisanal as this sector may be, it is still a significant factor in the whole employment situation.

However, despite these qualifications, the main feature of Iranian working class formation is that it is based on massive and recent migration, and in particular migration to Tehran. In 1956 only 31 per cent of the population was urban; by 1976 this had risen to 47 per cent. Tehran has received a disproportionate amount of this movement; this is in common with the general Middle Eastern pattern whereby in the period 1950–70 cities of over 100,000 have grown twice as fast as those with populations of less than 100,000.[15] In the case of Iran, where population has risen by around 3·5 per cent per annum, Tehran grew in the 1950s and 1960s by around 5·5 per cent per annum, whilst the population of the rural areas rose by only 1·7 per cent. After the 1973 boom, the rate of growth of Tehran rose to 8 per cent. From being a city of under 1 million in the late 1940s it rose to one of 4·5 millions in the mid-1970s, and the population may reach 9 millions by 1990. The pressure on traffic, on housing, on water, on the atmosphere has already reached intolerable proportions; the complaints of the rich have been the most heard, but it is the poor, in the southern part of the city, who suffer the most.

A study of urbanization in Tehran, based on research in the early 1970s, noted 'the massive gulf in life-style between the bulk of north Tehrani residents and the bulk of those in the south', and continued: 'Despite the lack of data on incomes, casual empiricism suggests that in no European city can this gulf be so wide; moreover the evidence suggests that as Iran's economy grows and Tehran grows with it this gulf is actually widening.'[16] Southern Tehran is the Iranian exemplar of unplanned migration to the towns, in the absence of housing and social services to cope with the influx. An additional problem is caused by the fact that Tehran has no modern sewage system, and is partly encircled by mountains; the waste and polluted air are most concentrated in the lower, southern, part.

It is possible to identify further distinctions within the migratory flow. Until the 1960s much migration to Tehran came not from the countryside but from other smaller towns in Iran, whose economic position was undermined by the centralization of the country and by the relatively depressed conditions of the 1940s and 1950s. Since the 1950s cities such as Isfahan and Tabriz have attracted part of the migrant flow, but it appears that migration from some provinces, on a permanent basis at least, is much stronger than from others. Whereas some areas nearer Tehran, Isfahan, Shiraz and Tabriz have seen considerable transfers of population, remoter areas such as Kurdistan and Baluchistan have lost far less of their population.

(ii) Unemployment

It is being increasingly recognized that unemployment constitutes one of the major features of underdevelopment. The World Employment Conference in Geneva in 1976 reckoned that there were 300 millions unemployed and semi-employed in the world in 1970 and the figure would rise to 700 millions within a generation. Iran, of course, exhibits many of the employment problems characteristic of third-world countries generally: a high birth-rate and a rise in urban employment which while larger than in most underdeveloped countries is not large enough to absorb those coming into the labour market, combined with excessive migration to the towns. Part of the negative impact of the land reform is seen in this urban context. Developments in the countryside are such that, even if official expectations are borne out, overall employment will be maintained whilst no additional jobs will be created; but the indications are that the level of employment in the rural areas is actually being reduced.

Iran exhibits an unemployment situation that is at first paradoxical, but is in fact explicable in terms of the pattern of its development. It has both a labour surplus and a labour shortage. The shortage is for skilled and managerial personnel: that is why in 1976 there were an estimated 50,000 foreigners working in Iran in the upper echelons of employment, with the possibility of several times that number coming in by 1980. For those Iranians with the skills – whether in medicine, construction or whatever – there is no significant unemployment and many such people are now brought in from abroad. On the other hand the great majority of Iranians, unskilled and illiterate, do face unemployment of one kind or another.

The one available estimate for unemployment in the absolute sense is low: whereas it was officially 158,000 in 1956 and 320,000 in 1972, it reckons unemployment will rise to 375,000 in 1977, or about 3·5 per cent of the total. On closer examination this figure is evidently inadequate. First, official figures are deficient: since there are no unemployment benefits there is no incentive to register as unemployed, and, as in more developed capitalist societies, women tend not to register when out of a job. Estimates were also based only on those who had looked for work in the previous week. Even in the towns there are really two kinds of unemployed: the relatively educated, who may well register, and the impoverished inhabitants of areas like southern Tehran and the shanty-towns of Isfahan, who are unlikely to do so. This is confirmed by the fact that unemployment in the 15–24 age-bracket in 1972 was 9 per cent of the total, twice the general average for over-15s of 4·6 per cent. Many of these are secondary school graduates. Far more serious is the situation in the countryside. Here there may be no absolute unemployment, since those with no jobs at all will as likely as not go to the towns. But there is chronic under-employment in the countryside, where according to a 1973 survey nearly 14 per cent of the total rural population were working less than 28 hours a week, and where almost 40 per cent were working less than 42 hours a week during the off season. Indeed the *average* number of days worked in the rural areas in the early 1970s was only 108. Just as in the town there may be substantial misallocation of labour and overstaffing in government-run enterprises, so the problem in the countryside is one of the degree of employment rather than of absolute unemployment. In this Iran is not unlike many other Asian countries, with the difference that its overall economic level is higher than that of other countries.[17] A different situation would arise if instead of planting one crop per year, farmers planted two: but this, like other forms of increased rural employment, would require government inputs of funds and facilities on a scale much larger than has been the case so far.

(iii) Wages

Official figures for wage levels in Iran suggest that the oil boom has been accompanied by a considerable rise in some workers' earnings (Table 17). One may or may not accept these, but even if true they leave unanswered two questions: first, how many workers receive these wages and rates of increase, and secondly, how much these wages can buy in real terms and how far they keep pace with inflation.

The official data apply only to the better-paid workers in manufacturing industry; and we know that wage rises there of between 30 and 50 per cent per annum did occur in the boom conditions of the mid-1970s. Wages in mining and manufacturing rose 28 per cent in 1976–7. We do not know what the average wage of workers is, nor how it has changed. There is too an official minimum wage: in the early 1970s it was 50 rials per day, by 1976 it had risen to 90 rials. But there is no indication that this wage has been enforced, and that it does correspond to a minimum, *or even an average wage*, for most workers. Selected data published in 1972 indicate enormous disparities in the average wages in different industries, and here too one can only suspect that these as often under- rather than over-state the real picture.

Table 17: Workers' Wages in Selected Manufacturing Industries 1972

Industry	*Number of workers*	*Average wages*
Textiles	62,183	66,529
Machine-made shoes	5,880	52,721
Petrochemicals	2,073	145,683
Leather	1,591	57,825
Tobacco	4,910	169,450
Automobile tyres	938	106,610
Base metals	3,089	101,975
Automobiles	8,286	89,669

Source: *Central Bank Bulletin*, vol. 12, No. 69, quoted in Fereidun Firoozi, 'Labour and Trades Unions in Iran'.

One survey of the subject, presented in February 1974, and covering 224,000 workers in 2,779 different enterprises, provided the following picture: 'Nine families in ten have only one source of income. The hourly wages of an unskilled worker (13·5 per cent of the sample studied) is 16 rials; that of a skilled worker (78·4 per cent of the sample) is 21 rials; that of a foreman (9·5 per cent) 43 rials; and finally that of a technician

(0·1 per cent) is 69 rials. The figures reveal the existence of a "labour aristocracy": while more than half the families have a weekly income per head of less than 100 rials, 34·5 per cent of them receive more than 501 rials each ... The report concludes that for the working population as a whole 73 per cent receive less than the legal minimum.'[18] The differences within specific enterprises are compounded by regional differences within the country. In general the gap between urban and rural incomes has been widening in recent years; by 1973 it had risen to 3·2, and it has certainly risen still further subsequent to the boom. The high wage rates and high growth rates indicated in official statistics therefore refer to the top of a very wide range.

In terms of real purchasing power there is again a problem of analysis. Officially consumer prices have risen rather slowly during the boom: by 13·1 per cent in 1969–70 and by 20 per cent in 1973–4. But in one area at least, housing, these low rates are certainly not accurate and rents absorb up to 60 per cent of some workers' wages. Rents in Tehran rose by 15 times between 1960 and 1975; they rose by 200 per cent in 1974–5 and by another 100 per cent in 1975–6. Nor, given the domination of private enterprise in this sector, has the expansion in Tehran's housing taken place with the housing of the poor as a priority: the pressure on the already overloaded lower section will therefore have increased, and many urban families are reported to have been spending 60-70 per cent of their income on rent.

The living standards of a section of the working class have certainly improved in recent years. In addition, the régime's subsidy policies, however short-sighted in overall economic terms, have prevented the price of food from rising as high as it would otherwise have done. Yet the majority of wage-earners have been faced with escalating costs in housing and other services, and the gap between well-paid and unskilled workers has expanded. Even those workers whose real wages have gone up will have been affected by the overall inflation in the cities. These are, at least in part, the factors that underlie the strike wave of the mid-1970s, as well as the wider outburst of discontent in 1978.

Women in the Economy

The position of women in Iran's economic system has changed considerably as a result of the recent growth, but these changes have been such as to integrate women into economic life in a predictably subordinate manner so that, with the exception of the professional minority, they are lower-paid and less skilled than men, and often work much longer hours. Official statistics state that in 1972 about 13 per cent of all women over the age of 12, or 1·4 millions, were employed, the comparable figure for men being around 68 per cent. Of these 64 per cent were in industry, 11 per cent in agriculture, and 22 per cent in services. But this is a misleading picture, since it understates the role of women in the rural economy, as a result of the under-recording of women's work, and the fact that the majority of women work as unpaid family labourers. For this reason, it is best to treat the rural and urban sectors separately.[19]

Traditionally, most women have been active participants in the economy. In addition to their role as domestic labourers, where they work alone, women have been active in nomadic and agricultural activities alongside men. This pattern has continued through the land reforms, although where family incomes have risen it has been possible for the farmer to take his wife out of production in the fields and hire a wage-labourer instead: there has therefore probably been a slight diminution of women's participation in this sector as a result of the spread of capitalist relations to the countryside. However, women's work in the rural areas has never been confined to the home and agriculture: for a large proportion of Iran's textile and carpet industry has been and remains in the rural sector (a feature discussed under migration) and here the majority of the workers are women. In 1972 it was estimated that 70 per cent of all cloth-weaving employment and 72 per cent of carpet-weaving employment was in the rural sector, and the majority of those employed were probably women. These women are the most degraded section of the industrial labour force: they receive very low wages, work in appalling conditions, and are at the mercy of the middle-men who employ them or farm work out to them. Illiteracy amongst rural women is very high – 90 per cent in 1975, even by official estimations – and this means that women constitute a vast reserve of unskilled labour on which the lower end of the Iranian industrial structure can draw. At the same time, this industrial labour by women is a very important part of the rural economy: in tribal societies, women rug-weavers provide the goods through which the tribe earns cash, and a similar reliance on this source of income probably operates in more isolated agricultural communities too.

The situation is relatively different in the urban areas. First of all, the literacy rate amongst women is much higher than in the countryside – over 50 per cent by official figures – and the pattern of female employment has changed considerably in the middle 1970s, as the shortage of labour has drawn into employment a wider section of women than was previously the case. In general, female employment in the urban sector is much lower in the Muslim Middle East than in other third-world areas: the average for the developing countries is around 25 per cent, but in the Middle East it is 5 per cent, and as low as 3·1 per cent in Egypt, 2 per cent in Algeria, and under 1 per cent in Saudi Arabia. In Iran, the rate for Tehran (where the rate of female employment is highest) actually fell between 1956 and 1966, probably as a result of rising incomes; but it has subsequently risen, from 9 per cent in the early 1960s, to 11 per cent in 1971. It is anticipated that the rate of urban female employment may rise to 25 per cent by the early 1990s.

Of these urban employed women there is a small upper section in the professional category: of the 200,000 such women in 1971, 45 per cent were in teaching, 44 per cent in clerical and administrative positions, and the remaining 11 per cent in medical and para-medical positions. But most urban women workers were in services – an estimated 53 per cent in 1971; hence Iran has the paradoxical pattern of a substantial female industrial labour force in the *rural* sector, whilst in the urban areas women make up a much lower proportion of those employed in industry.

Government Policies: Profit-sharing and Workers' Shares

The Iranian government confronts a two-fold problem in the execution of its development programme. On the one hand this programme requires consistent political repression, and hence, among other things, the denial of any independent voice to the working class. On the other hand, the régime knows that a sullen or actively hostile workforce can impede the industrialization programme; to meet its goals, the régime has to win the cooperation of at least part of the working class. It has therefore both to control and to elicit the cooperation of the proletariat: the alternative is, in the short term, stagnation and, in the long run, the failure of the régime itself. This is a problem faced before in authoritarian capitalist régimes bent on rapid industrialization: for example, in the 1890s the Kaiser appealed to the German working class for support, and masqueraded as a defender of its interests. Under both German and Italian fascist régimes the government first destroyed existing trades unions and then organized its own unions and often invoked pro-worker themes in its propaganda. Neither the problem encountered nor the solution attempted by the Pahlavi régime is therefore unique.

Iranian industry suffers from a chronic low productivity and it is this, rather than the overt threat of militant political action, which has prompted the régime's policy of providing benefits to the working class. In 1960 a workers' insurance scheme was established, and since then a number of measures have been promulgated in relation to housing and cooperatives. But these, like other schemes, affect only a minority of workers: in 1975 31 per cent of the larger industrial enterprises had set up housing cooperatives, whilst 8 per cent had consumer cooperatives. The insurance schemes may cover a wider spectrum, but as a means of forcing the workers to save they are often resented as a net subtraction from real wages. The two most substantial schemes have been the profit-sharing scheme of 1963 and the workers' share programme of 1975, respectively the sixth and thirteenth principles of the White Revolution. Once one puts aside all the official populist propaganda about these and about how they illustrate the Shah's beneficence, they emerge as two modest and so far rather unsuccessful attempts to get Iranian workers to boost productivity.

The profit-sharing scheme applied to workers in enterprises of ten workers and over, but excluded those in the oil, railway and tobacco industries. Workers were to receive up to 20 per cent of the profits, and these were to be distributed according to seniority and wages: the law called for agreements between workers and management to determine what profits were, in return for increases in productivity. In reality, the measure was less far-reaching than was claimed at the time. Some businessmen felt the measure was a threat to them, and they seem to have made sure that no one, including the state, was therefore able to ascertain what their profits were by not publishing accounts or by faking tax losses. In 1974, as noted, a quarter of Iran's 20,000 companies submitted tax returns, and of these only 53 per cent admitted to any profit. Moreover, as the workers had no independent organizations and had no access to the company's files they had no way of telling what profits were. The law itself expressly stated that 'No worker shall be entitled to construe this decree as authorizing him to participate in the management of the undertaking' (Article 17). The books of the enterprises were therefore closed, and in some cases firms gave an extra month's salary to their employees rather than disclose their true profits.

The other defining feature of the profit-sharing scheme is that it applies to relatively few workers, and that many receive comparatively small amounts of money. By 1972, i.e. after nine years, the scheme covered only 175,000 workers in 3,135 establishments; by 1976 the number had gone up to 295,000, still only 15 per cent of those employed in manufacturing. Information on the amount distributed stated that for the first decade the average share in certain enterprises rose from 1,509 rials to 6,664 rials; but this is almost certainly an exaggeration as far as industry as a whole is concerned. One report published in 1975 estimated that, whilst a third of the workers covered received between 3,000 and 6,000 rials a year, half received 300 rials or less.[20] Since the average wage in industry was around

100,000 rials, the top rate of share was equivalent to about 6 per cent of earnings.

In June 1975 a workers' share scheme was introduced, designed like the first to raise productivity. Whilst the profit-sharing scheme was designed to boost workers' incomes (by in effect adding to their wages), this second measure was designed to increase savings by workers, since it involved the sale to employees of 49 per cent of the shares in their companies. The purpose of the laws was clearly stated by Minister of Economics Ansari: 'We feel this will strengthen relations between all elements involved in manufacturing; it will encourage greater production, a greater sense of belonging and a greater sense of social acceptance,' he said.[21] Conditions were even more stringent than for the profit-sharing scheme. First, in order to discourage the widespread problem of workers moving frequently from one job to another, only those workers who had been with a firm for three years were eligible. Moreover companies only fell under the law if they were profitable, if they had been in production for five years and if they met one of three other criteria: registered capital was over 100 million rials; fixed assets were 200 million rials; or turnover was 250 million rials.

In all 320 companies have been selected to transfer their shares by March 1978. Workers can either buy the shares directly, or purchase them with 4 per cent loans over ten years from a special Financing Organization for Share Participation. But workers could borrow from this source only 20 per cent of the value purchased. To make up for the inevitable shortfall in demand, a new National Investment Company of Iran was established with a capital of 10 billion rials to purchase shares, and, over a period of time, to sell them to the general public, if workers' demand proved insufficient. By August 1976 45,000 workers had received shares in about ninety companies, and by 1978 the scheme was to be extended to the other firms designated in the policy.

This programme is, like the profit-sharing scheme, far less dramatic than at first might appear. Some foreign and domestic businesses did take fright when the law was introduced but the government stressed to them the limits of the law, and the fact that workers would still not control these companies; the intervention of NICI means that some, perhaps the majority, of the shares will go to the general public and not to the workers concerned and this is certainly a relief to the companies. Official statements try to link these schemes to the land reform programme. But there is no real similarity between them, except in the sense that both the extent and originality of both are greatly exaggerated by the régime. Under land reform those who benefited were given individual plots of land, something at least to hold on to as their own. No such division is possible in industry: it is not as if factories were or could have been broken up and divided amongst the workforce. Hence the class difference, between employers and employed, remained, and indeed the conflict between the two was in some ways intensified. The workers were made more aware of their weakness and inability to enforce the schemes. On their side, the managers and owners felt the profit-sharing and workers' share schemes to be encroachments on their position.

From a strictly economic point of view there is no indication that either scheme has solved the problems it set out to confront. Both schemes tried to boost productivity and generally mobilize support amongst workers, but whilst productivity in Iranian industry, or parts of it, may have risen the underlying difficulties have remained and will not be removed by what are predominantly symbolic exercises. On the other hand the attempt to increase the capital available to firms by the workers' share scheme is also a palliative: it is not so much the capital available as the use to which it is put which affects the efficiency of Iranian industry, and the resolution of this too requires changes more far-reaching than the régime has so far contemplated. The combination of worker reluctance and entrepreneurs' fears may turn the workers' share scheme into a general issue of shares to the public, but this only transfers the problem to another realm. For the weakness of the stock market in Iran is no mere accident: it reflects the fact that investors can often find more profitable and rapid forms of investment than industry, especially in the more uncertain conditions following the 1975 retrenchment. It will consequently take more than the sixth and thirteenth principles of the White Revolution to solve the underlying problems of Iranian industry.

Iran also faces a serious shortage of skilled labour. The government has tried to remedy this with training programmes, and aims to have trained 205,000 technicians and 604,000 skilled and semi-skilled workers in the 1972–7 period. But mention should also be made of a third government policy designed to boost output and productivity: the import of foreign labour. Estimates for the Fifth Plan (1974–8) spoke of a 'manpower gap' of 721,000 persons, and by 1976 an estimated 50,000 managerial and skilled personnel and their families from abroad were already working in the country.[22] Whilst many of these were from advanced capitalist countries, government policy for the late 1970s is to import single men and women from poorer Asian countries on government-to-government contracts – medical personnel from India, Pakistan, Bangladesh and the Philippines, and skilled workers in transport and construction from South Korea.[23] It is extremely unlikely that as large a number as the 721,000 'needed' by the plan will enter Iran in the rest of the 1970s; but there may well be an influx of a hundred or two hundred thousand Asian workers under tight control by their own, and the Iranian, governments. Given the short-term and segregated conditions of their employment, and the barriers of language and culture, it is unlikely that they will be able to form any effective links with their Iranian co-workers. The need for them reflects the enormous backwardness of education and industrial training after fifty years of Pahlavi rule in Iran, and well as constituting a net drain on the even more impoverished Asian countries which are forced to lose some of their own scarce, skilled personnel, who are attracted elsewhere by higher wages.

The Growth of Trades Unions

The Iranian working class has, for much of its history, been denied the right to any independent political activity; yet there are three periods in which it is possible to identify a degree of autonomous class action. The first was in the two decades prior to the consolidation of the Reza Khan régime in the late 1920s; the second, and most remarkable, was in the period between 1945 and 1953; and the third has been in the years after the 1973 oil price rise. While there appears to be relatively little continuity between these three phases, since the régime has been able to fracture working-class history, they each illustrate the combative potentiality and political make-up of the working class at different points in its growth.

In the first two decades of the century the wage-earning working class in the towns was extremely small, since modern industry was virtually non-existent. Workers were at this stage represented in two quite different kinds of organization. The first were the guilds, pre-industrial organizations uniting workers and employers, which were on occasion prominent in the political activity of Tehran and Tabriz. During the Constitutional Revolution the guilds were in the forefront of the campaigns and demonstrations against Russian goods and the import of foreign goods. As organizations of the bazaar, they remained influential for decades afterwards. They united employers and workers in a pre-industrial form of organization, one that embodied common problems in the work-place and may have represented a real coincidence of interests between employers and employees in the face of a government dominated by landed and foreign interests. But there was no sense in which they could survive as independent entities under the Pahlavi régime, and they were not the basis for the emergence of a workers' movement. Given the combined presence of employers and workers the guilds could not form the context for any demands involving the conflicting interests of the two. Secondly, as the bazaar declined in importance, so too did the guilds, since an increasing amount of industrial activity was transferred to factories and workshops elsewhere. And this decline was reflected in political matters: a survey carried out in 1949 indicated that few Tehrani workers would vote for their masters in elections.[24]

In a separate development, clearly working-class organizations began to appear around the turn of the century, first amongst the hundreds of thousands of Iranian workers in Russia and then amongst the small industrial working class in Iran itself: by 1914 there were estimated to be 126,300 people employed inside the country in industrial and artisanal activity, half of them in the carpet industry. The first known trade union in Iran was formed by the Tehran printing workers in 1906, and it produced several issues of a socialist magazine, *Ittifaq-i Kargaran*. By 1922 there were reported to be 20,000 people in 12 unions in Tehran, this being 20 per cent of all the workers in the city, whilst another 10,000 workers were organized in other parts of the country.[25]

These workers' organizations were probably influenced by the Iranian Communist Party and in 1921 some of the Tehran unions affiliated to the Profintern, the Trades Union International based in Moscow. Other influences – socialist, anarchist – appear to have been absent. However, the indications available on their programmes suggest that national, political demands (against foreign interference and oligarchic disruption of Majlis elections) were as important as demands over strictly economic matters. Whatever their complexion, they were too weak; the working class was too small to prevent the establishment of the Pahlavi dynasty and in 1928 the abolition of all trades unions. The first comprehensive labour law in Iran, that of 1936, did not discuss the right to strike or to form trades unions, and limited itself to the question of working conditions in industrial establishments. It was only with the invasion of 1941 that unions were able to be active again, and with the worsening economic conditions (600 per cent inflation during the war) popular discontent grew. In these circumstances there emerged the strongest trades unions ever seen in Iranian history.[26]

Early in 1942 the communists were able to establish a Central Council of the Trade Unions in Iran, which in 1944 became the United Central Council of the Unified Trades Unions of Iranian Workers, known in Persian as the *Shoraye Motahhedi Markazi*, or Central Unified Council, and in English by the initials CUCTU. By 1945 it claimed a membership of 200,000 workers, and by 1946 a membership of 400,000 with 186 unions affiliated to it. In 1946 it affiliated to the World Federation of Trades Unions. It published a daily paper, *Zafar*, and in Reza Rusta, an Azari Turk born in Gilan and former blacksmith, it had an energetic and determined leader.[27] Given the size of the Iranian working class at that time, it was not a national movement in any real sense, but it claimed a strong membership in all the main industrial centres. In August 1946, at the height of CUCTU's power, its membership was as follows: in the oilfields of Khuzistan 90,000; in the manufacturing plants of Tehran and Tabriz 50,000 each; in the textile mills of Isfahan, Shiraz and Yazd 65,000; and in the textile mills, coalfields and railways of Gilan and Mazanderan 45,000. Given the size of the working class at that time, it was not a fully national movement, and as with the Tudeh Party itself it had virtually no peasant members. But even if there was exaggeration in the official figures the scale of the movement was such as to constitute a major threat to the régime.

In the first years of activity strike action was restrained because it might have weakened the Soviet Union's war effort. But once the war was over strikes spread: there were 7 in 1942, 14 in 1944, and in 1946 there were 25 major stoppages and five separate regional general strikes. The two main centres were Tehran and the oilfields. In the former the working class and its supporters were most evident in mass demonstrations. Fifty thousand demonstrated on May Day 1946 in Tehran; in October 100,000 turned out. In the oilfields, by contrast, the main form of activity was the strike: here, in the refinery at Abadan and in a half dozen distinct production centres, there were major strikes in the 1945–6 period, the most important being a three-day general strike in July 1946 over pay and conditions. Given the importance of the oil industry, this action in which the workers won most demands was of immense significance and demonstrated how a small but strategically placed working class can play a major role in an economy like Iran's.[28]

Such was the threat posed by this that the government moved to crush the movement. In 1946 the Qavam cabinet set up a rival trades union Federation of Iranian Workers (ESKI): but this was a self-evidently official entity; it split twice in the following years, and although admitted to the U S-run International Confederation of Free Trades Unions in 1951 it had by 1952 a membership of only 3,000. The régime's response did not however consist primarily in winning workers to rival organizations, but rather in trying to crush independent workers' organizations altogether. 1946 was the high-water mark of the trades unions organized in C U C T U. As support for the communists waned following the defeat of the Azerbaijan republic, and as the economic situation eased, the number of strikes declined; there were only five in 1947–8 and the movement was beginning to revive in 1949 when the Tudeh Party and C U C T U were banned following the attempt on the Shah's life in February of that year. When the Mossadeq government came to power in 1951 the communist workers' movement was, in line with the Tudeh Party, at first opposed to it. Indeed there was a major confrontation between the oil workers and the Mossadeq government in March–April 1951 when the local Iranian governor attacked the strikers and arrested their leaders on the grounds that mass action against the company would provoke a British military intervention and thereby undermine the oil nationalization campaign. Later, in 1952, the unions fell in line behind Mossadeq, and whilst he never lifted the ban on C U C T U it was able to re-start its activities in a semi-legal manner. In the period 1951–3 there were over 200 strikes on economic matters. With the coup of August 1953, however, the unions were decisively crushed and the twelve years of organizational activity brought to an almost complete end.

This period of Iranian working-class history is remarkable in a number of ways. However qualified the official statistics should be, there is no doubt, especially given the alarm of the régime and of the U S A, that the working class formed a major mass threat to the Pahlavi dynasty at this time. The combativity and extent of C U C T U's organizations are remarkable in the overall context of trades unions in third-world countries of Asia and Africa (Latin America having a different and more developed tradition). At the same time, the attention which this working-class movement must still attract should not obscure the weaknesses that underlay it. It depended on the conditions of legality created by the allied invasion and its room for manoeuvre was reduced following the defeat of the Azerbaijan revolution. Moreover, the movement suffered from strategic dislocation, in that the centre of *political power* in Tehran was 500 miles distant from the centre of *strike activity* in the oilfields of the south. The workers were able to menace foreign capital, but less able to exert direct pressure on the AIOC and the government in a combined manner. The presence of the militant working class was felt less in the capital than it might otherwise have been. Moreover, the union organizations were too recent in origin and the social base was itself too confined, given the level of development in Iran, for CUCTU to resist the onslaught following the coup of 1953. In that year a long night fell over the Iranian working class, a darkness from which it only began slowly to emerge after the passage of twenty years.

Official Unions and Illegal Strikes

The Iranian régime's policy towards the working class has evolved over the years from one of outright suppression to one that combines suppression and enticement. In the aftermath of the Mossadeq period, the régime suppressed all opposition activity and all unions, even the shadowy official ones, were banned in 1957. This cleared the way for a new régime-directed programme aimed at the working class: the 1959 Labour Law specified that unions could be established if recognized by the Ministry of Labour, and the 1960 special insurance and 1963 profit-sharing laws established the basis for a system of benefits to selected workers. The rationale for this policy is simple: the régime cannot simply crush the workers. It must have their cooperation to industrialize; it needs to have access to workers' opinions in order to know what compensatory measures to take; it needs to expand at least some workers' incomes in order to develop the home market.

This explains why the régime has created its own system of trades unions. While it would be naive to accept the official claims made for these as being representative of the workers' interests, it would be almost equally erroneous to overlook the very real functions that they perform in securing the political and ideological position of the régime. This kind of trade union is not, it should be emphasized, peculiar to Iran although the direct role of the secret police is distinctive. Under German and Italian fascism, as well as in Franco's Spain, state-run workers' organizations existed, whilst these régimes, objectively the guardians of capitalist interests, often used a workerist vocabulary and indulged in anti-capitalist diatribes as a means of winning some working-class support.[29] In the post-war epoch, the phenomenon of 'controlled trades unionism' has been common in Latin America: here as in Iran developing capitalist states of varying hues require not merely the political tranquillity but also the active cooperation of a working class in the process of industrialization. In Mexico under the Institutionalized Revolutionary Party, in Argentina under Peron, and in Peru under the post-1968 military junta, official trades unions of these kinds have been established as part of the régime's overall economic and political programme.

The basis of state-run unions in Iran is the 1959 Labour Law which bears some similarity to the regulations in fascist states. This specifies that all unions have to be recognized by the Ministry of Labour, and it lists the function of unions as being: to conclude collective agreements; to purchase, sell and acquire movable and immovable property, on condition that it is not for commercial purposes or with a view to profit; to defend the occupational rights and interests of their members; to establish cooperative societies to meet the requirements of their members; to establish unemployment funds for the purpose of assisting unemployed workers.[30] No mention is made of the right to strike, and apart from those dealing with profit sharing few collective agreements between workers and managers have been entered into. At the same time an increasing number of these unions has been established: a list of those existing in 1971 named 397 in all. By 1978 there were reported to be 1,023 such entities. A substantial number of Iranian non-agricultural wage-earners are in such organizations. From this list it is evident that these are not industry-wide unions, but that the official system is extremely fragmented, and unions are probably confined to individual factories. For example, the existence of twenty-six unions in the oil industry alone, even if this does include distribution, and of seven separate automobile worker industries, suggests a deliberate attempt to prevent any national workers' organizations from emerging, even under official control.

Table 18: State-Run Trades Unions 1971

Kind of Activity	*Number of Organizations*	
	Workers	*Employers*
Automobile	7	—
Metal-working	13	5
Textile	43	7
Transport	42	64
Water and power	18	3
Leather and intestine	9	2
Oil	26	—
Chemistry	5	1
Printing	4	3
Services	56	30
Food	68	22
Abattoirs	20	—
Construction	24	10
Art, cinema and theatre	6	—
Clothing	13	3
Communication	2	—
Glass and crystal	2	1
Banks	7	—
Paper manufacturing	2	—
Health services	4	9
Carpet weaving	10	2
Miscellaneous	16	6
Total	397	168

Source: *Labour Legislation, Practice and Policy*, ILO Mission Working Paper IX, Geneva, 1973, p. 21.

The Labour Law forbids unions to engage in any political activity; but they are allowed to 'show preferences towards, or cooperate with, political parties'. Since there is now only one, Rastakhiz, and it is controlled by the régime, this is no concession. In fact the unions are highly political and part of the régime's mobilizing drive. The union structure is run directly by SAVAK. In some factories SAVAK officials have their own offices, and some foreign businessmen who have worked in Iran have been heard to complain about these powerful and interfering agents of the Iranian state, to whom they have to pay salaries and from whom they must, on occasion, accept instructions. Precisely because their job is not only to repress but also to induce cooperation these SAVAK agents can, and sometimes do, create difficulties for management. The information is not available, but it would not be inconsistent if some of the wage rises in the mid-1970s had been urged on employers by SAVAK representatives in the trades union structure, aware of worker discontent within the factories where they were stationed.[31]

What are the functions of these unions? First, they incorporate workers into a number of welfare schemes related to insurance, housing, pensions and the like. These are both a means of increasing the workers' sense of security (especially in the difficult housing market) and of encouraging saving. The pages of *Rastakhiz-i Kargaran*, the official workers' paper, contain many reports on welfare schemes of this kind. Secondly, these unions administer the profit-sharing and workers' share programmes. Indeed, the unions can afford to be quite militant on these issues, where the decrees apply, since, as has been suggested by one Iranian writer, it is in the régime's interests to shift the locus of workers' demands away from wage demands as such and onto the forms of benefit scheme set up by the state.[32] Not only does this deflect pressure for wage rises, but it also serves to confer some legitimacy on these schemes. Even where direct wage increases are asked for, there appears to be a deliberate attempt by the régime to channel these: for example, workers justify their claims by reference to wage laws, or whilst on strike chant pro-Shah slogans. Thirdly, these unions play a mobilizing role. On state holidays and for political meetings, SAVAK arranges for employees to be paraded in pro-régime demonstrations. During the political turmoil of the early 1960s some labour leaders, licensed by the régime, were used in pro-Shah actions. Shoya ed-Din Molayeri, for example, organized his 2,000 Tehran bus drivers so that they formed, in the words of one observer, 'a disciplined force of highly mobile, able-bodied male demonstrators'.[33] After June 1963, when order had been reimposed, there was no more use for Molayeri and those of his ilk. Similar pro-Shah workers' mobilizations were organized during the 1978 protests.

The greatest area for mobilization is however within the factory itself, since it is here that the attack on low productivity has to take place. In justifying the welfare programmes, and at the periodic labour congresses held by the government, officials return again and again to the question of increasing output. The corporatist rhetoric of the régime stresses how workers and managers should strive together to meet their goals. At the Third Iranian Labour Congress of May 1976, attended by 2,350 workers' representatives, Labour Minister Moini declared that 'workers would strive to work harder, improve their skills and raise productivity in an effort to repay their debts to the Shahanshah.' In the factories of the Military Industrial Organization production is organized along military lines, with workers wearing military uniforms and parading on special occasions. Union officials are on occasion armed, just as the managers may be generals or ex-generals seconded to this sector. Taken as a whole, these policies represent an attempt to control and at the same time mobilize the working class; it is an essentially contradictory venture that underlines more and more the conflict between the objective power of the Iranian proletariat and the political rights which, individually and as a class, they are permitted to exercise.

This power has found renewed independent expression in the increased incidence of strikes noticeable since the oil boom of 1973. No reliable information on strikes is available, but it is possible from a variety of sources to reconstruct a probable picture of recent developments in this sphere.[34] (1) The numbers of strikes reported has risen from a handful in 1971–3 to as many as 20 or 30 per year in 1975. (2) Most of these take place in individual factories. (3) Most concern economic issues – wages, bonuses, and hours of work. Overtime appears to be a particular source of grievance since employers are under pressure to get as much extra output and hence overtime from workers as possible, whilst the latter are demanding higher rates of payment in return. (4) Many of the strikes reported have been brief in duration – a matter of a few hours, or, at most, a day or two. Management and the authorities intervene rapidly to end strikes in one way or another.

A surprising feature of these strikes is that a considerable number are successful. This underlines the dilemma faced by the régime. There have been reports of several strikes over wages in the oil industry and oilfields (August and October 1973, March 1975) and these seem to have been met by concessions. Similarly in 1974 there was a strike at the Mashin Sazi factory in Tabriz where 800 workers in what is one of the country's largest factories struck about overtime. The police dispersed the strikers and twenty-five of the younger workers were sent off to do military service, whilst a further 100 were sacked. It seems that those in the army had to stay there, but the 100 workers, many of them skilled, were taken back by the company because of the shortage of trained personnel.

Other strikes, probably the majority, are resisted. In 1971, for example, workers at the Shah Jaheet textile factory at Karaj north of Tehran struck, and then marched towards the capital, carrying pictures of the Shah. The police opened fire, killing at least three and possibly as many as thirteen of them. In June 1974 the leader of the Tabriz transport workers, Majid Saleh Jahani, a driver and known organizer, was killed in prison after a strike. In September 1975 workers at a textile factory at Shahi, north of Tehran, occupied their factory after the management had refused to implement the profit-sharing plan. Fighting between police and workers broke out, and after other workers from different shifts and local students became involved the police attacked the factory in the night. Three workers were killed, 70–80 people injured and an estimated 450 people arrested before the factory was cleared of protesters. The political and economic situation in Iran is certainly such that no strike is likely to be allowed to continue for any period of time: either demands are to be met by quick official intervention with the management, or the opposition is put down.

It does appear that a combination of economic pressure by workers, shortage of skilled workers, and government benefit programmes contributed in the aftermath of 1973 to eroding the confidence of business, both Iranian and foreign. The economic pressure of the better-off workers posed a serious problem. The following complaints by the organ of the Tehran business community are illustrative of this:

Wages and salaries are increasing constantly and yet manpower productivity is being neglected. The unreasonable increase in wages and salaries has reached such a stage that a father is ashamed in front of his son, because despite the experience gained from many years of work he receives lower wages than his son who has just started working. Even more important is the fact that employees who lose their jobs because of repeated mistakes or low productivity find much better jobs with much higher wages immediately, and this ridicules the former employer ... The public has been spoilt. Thus the individual who used to live on bread and cheese does not find anything less than chelokebab satisfactory and an unskilled construction worker expects to go to work in a Paykan ... Of course we will thank God the day even the unskilled labourers are able to own cars, and with the wages of these days this may be achieved very soon. But it must be remembered that it is impossible for everyone to own an automobile at once without an increase in efficiency and productivity.[35]

This alarm presents one side of the picture: the Iranian working class has considerable economic power, and although the slowdown after 1975 may lessen the rise in wages the régime's long-term economic programme is so reliant on working-class support that this power will continue to be exerted. Moreover as economic constraints become tighter it may be more difficult to win or maintain the cooperation of workers, and the experiences of the strikes in the mid-1970s, whether these continue or not, may have awakened some lasting militant consciousness in those proletarians directly involved.

On the other hand, the evidence available suggests several

reasons for caution about the future workers' movement in Iran. In the first place the working class has been denied any political tradition, so that the strikes of the 1940s and up to 1953 can only be a memory for a tiny percentage of today's workers, and most of the leading militants of that period must have been removed. The experience of C U C T U was too brief and too far away to leave a permanent mark, quite apart from the inevitable cultural divide that has arisen between workers of the older and younger generations. Nor are there indigenous political traditions within the working class that have in the past contributed and could again contribute to a working-class movement: there is nothing, for example, comparable to anarchism in Iranian working-class politics. The conditions under which workers are forced to live also make it extremely difficult for any workers' movement to grow. The efficiency and ruthlessness of the Pahlavi régime is far greater than that of, for example, the Tsarist state in the 1890s and 1900s, and the repression as well as the officially-induced fragmentation make it extremely difficult for militants in different areas to establish or maintain contact. Whatever workers' organizations may exist must operate in the deepest secrecy, and it is certainly significant that at no stage in recent years has any source, of any political affiliation, claimed that there exists a widespread underground workers' movement or organization in Iran. All protests seem to be at the local level.

There are amongst Iranian socialists two opposing views about what political character the Iranian working class will adopt in the future. On the one hand there are those who expect a working-class movement of growing influence and confidence to emerge in opposition to the dictatorship. There are others who emphasize the divisive policies of the régime, and who argue that the upper section of the working class at least have been won over by the benefits they have acquired. It would, for any observer, be naive to undervalue the limits of the strike movement which has a mainly *economic* as opposed to political character. No workers' movement will be able to emerge under conditions of severe repression such as exist in Iran. On the other hand the material capacity of the régime to satisfy popular demands will necesssarily shrink in the years ahead. The enormous objective power of the Iranian working class may therefore find itself thrown increasingly into conflict with the régime, and the opposition of the working class, fragmented as it must be for a time, may well add to the difficulties which the state encounters. A combination of social weight and political conjuncture may then be created in which the Iranian working class, so long denied its just place in its society, will be able to play a fuller and more independent role. The form and timing of this emergence is one of the most, perhaps *the* most, intriguing questions in Iran's future.

8 The Opposition

Before the re-emergence of a mass opposition movement in 1978 it was extremely difficult to form an accurate picture of the Iranian opposition. Given the suppression of all independent political activity, it is not only outsiders, but also the majority of Iranians, who were unsure of what was happening. An added complication is that SAVAK has a policy of fostering individuals and magazines of an apparently dissident character, in order to induce confusion whilst it tries, on the other hand, to have genuine opposition elements themselves branded as 'SAVAK agents'. It is, moreover, usually impossible to gauge whether claims by a group in exile correspond to what this group is doing inside Iran, nor whether reports that a guerrilla group has carried out a specific action are accurate or not.

To take one kind of problem: in the decade between 1965 and 1975 a number of individuals known to have been critical of the régime died in circumstances that give some cause for suspicion. Some or all of them could have died naturally or in accidents, as is officially claimed; there again, they could all have been murdered. We do not know and probably never shall, given the suspicion and restriction that prevails in Iran.[1] More generally, unverifiable reports of opposition, violent and peaceful, occasionally came out of the country. Since 1971 there have been reports of dozens of clashes between the two main guerrilla groups and security forces. Some are publicized by the government, some by the guerrillas. Other incidents not involving these two groups are also supposed to have occurred. In August 1973 there was a violent clash in the southern city of Abadan, allegedly involving Iranians of Arab origin. In 1974 there were reports that a local doctor, Hushang Azami, was leading a band of guerrilla shepherds in the mountains of Luristan.[2] In June 1975 hundreds of theology students are said to have been arrested in the town of Qom, during a commemoration of the June 1963 uprising.[3] In December 1977 at least six people were reported to have been killed in Qom in a further clash, after which *mollahs* throughout Iran called for a protest strike. There have been reports of other strikes, but these are like the other pieces of information – belated, partial, disconnected, unverifiable. As with so much else in Iran, it is not only that there may be much that we do not hear about; it may also be that what we do hear about as having happened never did so, or at least not in the way it is claimed.

Between the crushing of the 1963 resistance and the beginning of 1977, opposition remained at a low, fragmented and often partially invisible level. But in 1977 and 1978 there was a change of significant proportions, even if it was not possible to say how permanent it was. For the first time a vocal and sustained opposition became evident, with protests by writers, lawyers and politicians about restrictions on freedom, widespread student demonstrations on campuses, and in March 1978 a prolonged hunger strike by political prisoners in Evin jail. Beyond these incidents there unfolded a mass opposition in over thirty towns – especially, Qom, Tabriz, Isfahan and Tehran. Hundreds of thousands of people marched through the streets, and, when martial law was imposed in September, thousands were killed and wounded by the army and police. The motivation of these rioters was diverse, and there was no sustained organization behind them, but the extent and fury of their actions pointed to a deep, underlying frustration with the economic problems and the political system present in Iran, a frustration increased rather than offset by the rapid and chaotic socio-economic changes of the previous decade and a half (see Chapter 10).

The strength and activity of opposition *organizations* in Iran must under existing conditions be rather small, but, as 1978 showed, the grounds for opposition, and hence the opposition *forces* that exist fermenting below the surface, are very large. Under different political conditions the two may draw closer together, and for this reason the present chapter will examine both the social forces in potential opposition to the state, and the actual organizations that can under present circumstances be identified.

Opposition Forces

The largest single group oppressed by the régime is the rural poor. In 1976, 53 per cent of the total population of Iran lived in the countryside, and about half of these were landless labourers.[4] Yet resistance in the countryside, either to the state or to the rural rich, has been slight, both before and after land reform. There was no major peasant movement at any time in the six decades of the century prior to land reform, except where a regional or nationality component also existed (as in Gilan). Since land reform, there are believed to have been cases where peasants have protested at the government's failure to implement the reforms, and some of those who have lost land in the 1970s that they were given in the 1960s have also protested. But the overall picture is of a rural population that has been remarkably quiescent, and has remained outside the mainstream of Iranian political life.[5]

There are a number of additions that can be made to this picture. First, it is an illusion of urban observers that peasant resistance takes an explicit, let alone armed, form. In the absence of any favourable military circumstances, such forms of resistance may be inadvisable; resistance can rather take a passive form – resisting government measures, withholding crops, keeping back information. It would appear that resistance of this kind has been common in Iran, and that it has been the form through which hostility to the inequalities of the land reform programme has been shown. Some cases of overt hostility to agri-business have been reported.[6] Secondly, the state now has a presence throughout the countryside such that there is no comparison between the Iranian villages of today and, say, those in China in the 1920s and 1930s, or those in parts of Latin America in the 1960s. Land reform officials, and the omnipresent rural police force, the Gendarmerie, make any initiatives of an independent kind extremely difficult. On top of this there is the fact that the rural population have remained relatively isolated from other political influences: most are still illiterate, and the villages have, until recently, had little contact with the outside world or with each other. The state has taken care to ensure that the political influences to which the villagers are now subjected are its own, although it is doubtful how deep these influences have penetrated.

The rural resistance that has occurred in Iran has nearly always come from the non-Persian population and often from the nomads, all of whom are non-Persian. In the former case, to be examined later, a desire for political and cultural autonomy has apparently been more important than specifically economic issues. The latter have accounted for some of the most spectacular rural resistance movements of all in this century; the last such uprising was that of the Qashqai in the southern province of Fars who rose in 1963 and were only put down after jets had strafed the flocks of the nomadic population and over one hundred people had been killed. No doubt there have been other cases of tribal resistance, as the nomads have resisted the government's settlement programme and the intrusions of state control into their areas. The armed resistance reported in Luristan in 1974 was, if it really occurred, probably a response of this kind. But the problem with such activities is that by their very nature they are sporadic and limited. The proportion of nomads in Iranian society is also declining (from up to 50 per cent of the population in 1800 to probably only 5 per cent in the late 1970s) and the days when a major tribal uprising could threaten an Iranian government, or at least act as the rural ally of an insurrectionary urban force, are almost certainly now over.

The nationalities (see p. 12) overlap with both the rural and nomadic populations, but pose a distinct political problem. Many villagers are Persians, whilst with large-scale migration to the towns a significant proportion of the urban population is drawn from the nationalities. A town like Tabriz has always been a predominantly Azerbaijani one and Ahvaz an Arab one. The policy of the Pahlavi régime has been to deny any national or cultural rights to these non-Persian groups. Persian is the only language of education, law and government business. As only a little can be published in the minority languages, and as there is no teaching in them, the culture of these peoples is inevitably impoverished. Those wanting to read material in their own languages have to turn to abroad – the Azerbaijanis to Soviet Azerbaijan, the Arabs and the Kurds to Iraq. Obviously, given the denial of elementary cultural rights, there is no question of any regional autonomy.[7]

The top officials of the Iranian state are drawn in a disproportionate degree from the dominant Persian section of society: a survey in the 1960s showed that only 17 per cent of the top officials spoke a local language other than Persian, and of these 23 out of 25 spoke a variant of Turkish.[8] This predominance of Persian culture is reinforced by the fact that all of Iranian life is concentrated in Tehran, an imbalance that is worsening despite government attempts to reverse this trend. Not only are all major political and economic decisions taken there, but the cultural life of the country is also concentrated in the capital, and even such things as interest rates vary between Tehran and the provinces. The régime has tried to integrate sections of the nationalities into the state machine: tribal chiefs have become army officers, and Azerbaijani aristocrats have become high state officials. But this has been done by denying any specific rights to the groups from which these people come, and in such a way as to reinforce the domination of the Persian speakers. Among the latter, prejudices against non-Persians are extremely strong: Turks are frequently referred to as 'donkeys' (*khar*), Arabs as 'mouse-eaters' and so on. Similarly, in the teaching of history in state schools, Persian cultural superiority has a prominent role and serves to confirm the system of national oppression on which the Pahlavi state is built.

In the past, a number of attempts have been made to win some autonomy for the nationalities; but these have not been supported by the dominant section of the nationalist movement. In the 1940s and early 1950s the Tudeh and to a much greater extent the National Front were equivocal on this issue.[9] Those nationalities that have been most active have been the Azerbaijanis and the Kurds: the former played an important role in the Constitutional Revolution, and the latter put up a vigorous opposition to Reza Khan's centralization programme. In 1945, with the support of Soviet forces, both these nationalities set up autonomous republics, but these were, as we have seen, defeated, and no concessions to their rights have subsequently been won by the nationalities. All have been increasingly subjected to the cultural and political domination of the Persian régime at the centre, and the only form of advance for individuals has been through assimilation.

In the urban areas there are three main forces that could act as the bases of an opposition: workers, the bazaar, and intellectuals and students. The growth and strike activity of the working class have already been discussed (see p. 206); here it is relevant only to repeat that so far as is known no organization of any coherent kind exists among the working class. This section of society is of relatively recent origin, and its political complexion will become clear only through time. In the long run, and in the event of changes in the economic fortunes of the Pahlavi state, the working class could play a much more important and even decisive role.

By contrast, the bazaar, the traditional commercial centre dominated by small traders and religious functionaries, has been a long-standing source of opposition, and it played a leading role in the 1978 opposition movement. Since 1963 the leaders of the bazaar have been restricted in their activities, and the most prominent of all, Ayatollah Khomeini, has been exiled. In addition to the ban on overt political activity has come the overall decline of the bazaar's economic role, as alternative financial institutions (the state and banks) and new trading companies have displaced it. But the bazaar, with its cohesive social and ideological milieu, has continued to form a source of opposition, and it has rightly been claimed that the bazaar is the *only* organized national opposition force of any kind in Iran. Khomeini has continued to denounce the Shah for 'tyranny' and 'extravagance' from abroad, whilst it has been claimed that the 'Islamic' guerrilla group, the Mojahidin, have been able to recruit from within the bazaar. Evidently opposition to the régime is strongly felt here, especially since the social and economic displacement of the bazaar from its position of dominance has continued; the bazaar has retained a political influence because of its links with the mosque and thereby with the urban poor, in particular the migrants who have flocked into the cities over the past two decades. Consequently it played an important role in the upsurge of 1978.

The Iranian intelligentsia and student body have provided the leadership of many of the political movements in this century, and most of the personnel of the opposition groups that have been active since June 1963. One account of 2,101 people arrested for political offences between 1963 and 1975 estimated that 90 per cent of these were intellectuals of some kind – either religious leaders, *ulema*, or people with a university education.[10] On the other hand the culture of students and intellectuals is marked by a strong pessimism and individualism, which has led in some cases to the rejection of politics in favour of more personal forms of expression and in others to an adventurist conception of political action.

The place of students and intellectuals in Iranian society is in certain respects an uneasy one and, while not a full explanation, the following factors may help to explain this unease and the attendant pessimism we have noted. In the first place, the official culture of the Pahlavi régime is an extremely philistine one. Few intellectuals can take the régime's fabricated 'national mythology' seriously, with its militaristic and chauvinist overtones, whilst for its part the culture of the growing Tehran bourgeoisie is an equally repugnant one, since it rejects the past of Persian culture, with its rich poetic and artistic legacy, in favour of the more superficial aspects of western society. Iranian intellectuals, whether from rich families or not, are often scornful of the *No-Kisé* (literally, 'new pockets', i.e. nouveaux riches) and the *Bi-farhang* (cultureless) elements who have been enjoying the fruits of the current boom. Many intellectuals feel themselves trapped, on the one hand aware of the limits of Iranian history and culture, and on the other revolted in a nationalist and aesthetic way by the specific form of western culture that is being imported into Iran. A few have opted outright for a return to the past – to Islamic, or pre-Islamic values, the latter option being accompanied by anti-Arab chauvinistic ideas. Others try to vault over the immediate barriers of consumer-based western culture to acquaint themselves with other facets of European and American life and thought; but, given the wide cultural gap between most Iranian students and this culture, this is a difficult thing to accomplish.

A second problem facing the intellectuals is simply that in a dictatorship the room for expression is so small: large areas of exploration – anything touching on history, society, the nationalities – are prohibited. A touring theatre company, for instance, was stopped from performing in 1975. It had staged a play called *The Teachers*, which had been written by one of its members, Said Sultanpur. The play concerned some teachers who try to enlighten their pupils and, after finding this impossible, turn to more explicit political action. The group had also put on the works of Gorky and Brecht, which were taken to be indirect criticisms of the Iranian state itself. The members received 2 to 11 years in prison. Only those forms of cultural activity are permitted which keep away from the areas that the régime regards as sensitive or which phrase resistance in the most indirect ways; and this inevitably includes a large part of the subject matter which such people wish to cover.

A third factor of considerable importance for those leaving secondary school is that Iranian higher education is in an especially critical condition, whilst at the same time a *licence* or degree is an essential condition for access to employment above a certain level. Pressure on university places is consequently enormous. In 1963, 14·7 per cent of those who applied to go to university were accepted; in 1969, this had fallen to 13·3 per cent. In 1977, of the 290,000 who applied for places, only 60,000 were accepted.[11] Indeed, the numbers of students in Iranian higher education is proportionately much lower than in other Middle Eastern countries, and government measures to increase the numbers at university have often resulted in a lowering of standards.[12] For some, the solution is emigration: Iran has a higher number of students abroad than any other country in the world – as many as 80,000 in West Germany, Britain and the U S A. But for those at home the pressure to get in, and once one is in to have access to teaching and books, can be overpowering. Hence on top of the problems of political restriction, there are serious problems of adjustment for those coming out of secondary education, and great psychological pressures on them. At an institution like Tehran University, where the majority of the students come from rural or provincial backgrounds, the students have the additional problems of trying to cope with the chaotic conditions of life in the Iranian capital.

There are many indications of the psychological pressures to which the students and intellectuals of Iran feel they are subjected. For a start, 75 per cent of all suicides in Iran are in the 15–30 age group. Heroin addiction is on the increase, and Iran is believed to have the highest rate of such addiction outside the U S A. Many thousands of Iranian professionals have left the country altogether, despite opportunities and good wages at home, in order to escape the stifling intellectual and cultural atmosphere of their country. A sense of pessimism, reflecting these pressures, runs through much of contemporary Iranian literature. As James Bill has written of a characteristic group of leading modern poets: 'A survey of fifty poems ... reveals an extraordinary emphasis upon such themes as "walls", "loneliness", "darkness", "fatigue", and "nothingness". These poems deplore the situation of the Iranian intellectual and obliquely criticize and condemn the existing sociopolitical system in which the intellectual is chained.'[13] And if anyone wants to savour the taste of this feeling, there is nowhere better to turn than the first paragraph of the most famous modern Persian novel of all, Sadegh Hedayat's *The Blind Owl*. 'There are sores which slowly erode the mind in solitude like a kind of canker,' he writes. 'It is impossible to convey a just idea of the agony which this disease can inflict. In general, people are apt to relegate such inconceivable sufferings to the category of the incredible ... mankind has not yet discovered a cure for this disease. Relief from it is to be found only in the oblivion brought about by wine and in the artificial sleep induced by opium and similar narcotics. Alas, the effects of such medicines are only temporary. After a certain point, instead of alleviating pain, they only intensify it . . .'[14]

Some writers have tried to go along an alternative path, closer to politics. In the period between 1941 and 1953 a number of writers influenced by Marxism attempted to relate their work to the social and political problems of contemporary Iran. Among them was Bozorg Alavi, the son of a merchant, who had been imprisoned under Reza Khan. The coup obviously put an end to this kind of writing in Iran and Alavi has since 1953 lived in exile in East Germany. In the late 1960s during a brief interlude of comparative literary freedom between 1965 and 1970, a number of writers stressing critical social themes emerged into public view; among them were Samad Behrangi and Reza Baraheni, writers of Azerbaijani origin who, while writing of necessity in Persian, raised the problem of the nationalities and portrayed the cultural dilemmas in which they were placed. The writer Gholamhussein Saedi tried in his work *Mourners of Bayial*, which as *The Cow* later became a famous film, to discuss the neglect of the Iranian countryside. The most coherent centre of the opposition was the Writers' Guild (*Kanun-i Nevesandigan*), a group of around eighty intellectuals, which called publicly for a relaxation of the censorship. But in 1970 the Guild was suppressed, and much tighter censorship was imposed. Behrangi and Al-i Ahmad both died in dubious circumstances (see note 1) and Baraheni and Saedi were both imprisoned for a time. In 1974 another prominent intellectual, the scriptwriter Khosrow Golesorkhi, was executed on what was generally held to be a trumped-up charge of plotting to shoot the Shah.

Iranian students have provided the most vocal and consistent opposition to the régime of any section of society since the 1953 coup. The first major act of resistance after the coup was in a clash between Tehran students and the army on 7 December 1953, when three students were killed and a number of others wounded. There were a number of violent clashes in the period 1960–63, and since that time police forces have been stationed near the campuses. Although quiet in the aftermath of June 1963, the students began to voice public opposition again in 1969, when they demonstrated in opposition to a rise in the Tehran bus fares. Since that time there have been several strikes in different faculties, and these have been closed for periods of time by the authorities. In October and November 1977 thousands of students in Tehran and the provinces demonstrated in support of political liberalization, before being attacked by plain-clothes policemen. Even though it is impossible to gauge the precise ideological character of these student protests, there is no doubt that the Tehran campuses have been a continuing source of opposition to the régime, and that in the 1970s the underground guerrilla groups have drawn their main support from this area. The tens of thousands of Iranian students abroad have also, since the early 1960s, formed the basis of a very active, if also very divided, opposition movement. Given the continuation and indeed intensification of pressures on the students, there is no reason to expect that the students will not remain a source of continued resistance to the régime, in whatever form such resistance proves possible.

Organizations 1: The Nationalities

Apart from the *mollahs* and the bazaar, there are three kinds of organization opposed to the Pahlavi state: those based on specific nationalities; the two groups most prominent in the 1941–53 period, the Tudeh Party and the National Front; and the guerrilla groups that began operating in 1971.

There are identifiable political groups among three nationalities – the Kurds, the Arabs and the Baluchis. The Kurdish Democratic Party of Iran (KDPI) was founded in 1945, during the period of the autonomous republic. After the Iranian army reoccupied the Kurdish areas in 1946, the KDPI went underground and it claims that up to 15,000 people were killed in the subsequent repression. Following the defeat, the Kurds in Iran maintained relations with those in Iraq, and after the June 1958 republican coup in Iraq, they had links to the Kurdish Democratic Party of Mostafa Barzani which had formed in Iraqi Kurdistan. But whilst the interests of the Iranian Kurds lay in getting the help of their fellow Kurds in Iraq against the Shah, the aim of Barzani was the reverse: to get the assistance of the Shah in his fight against the Iraqi government, a policy that contradicted resistance to the Shah by Iranian Kurds. For this reason Barzani tried to gain control of the K D P I, which always remained separate from the Iraqi K D P, in order to subordinate it to his interests.

By the middle of the 1960s relations between Barzani and at least some of the Iranian Kurds had deteriorated. In 1964 the K D P I held its Second Congress, at which the pro-Barzani group dominated, but soon afterwards, in February 1965, a breakaway 'revolutionary tendency' in the K D P began to criticize the prevailing line and called for a new 'revolutionary' policy. Then in 1967 a few dozen Iranian Kurds who had been fighting with Barzani's forces in Iraq separated and returned to Iran in order to start their own independent campaign against the Shah.

These Kurds began their guerrilla campaign in the winter of 1967, and they continued fighting for eighteen months in the mountains between Mahabad and the towns of Baneh and Sar-Dasht. The politics of this group are not clear, but an article purportedly representing their view and published in 1968 called for a guerrilla war on the basis of the Cuban or 'foco' theory; it denounced the established K D P for being 'petty bourgeois' and confined to the urban areas.[15] In the end the movement was defeated, and several dozen people killed. Apart from the intervention of the Iranian army, the guerrillas also had to contend with the hostility of Barzani. Barzani's forces are believed to have killed at least one Iranian Kurd, Suleiman Mouini, who was trying to go back to Iran to take part in the fighting.

However, although this guerrilla campaign was defeated, it led to a change of line within the K D P I and at the latter's Third Congress, in September 1973, it broke with the Iraqi K D P. Whilst declaring its general support for the guerrilla movement of 1967–8, it criticized those involved for failing to build an adequate political organization prior to the launching of the guerrilla struggle. This K D P Congress, at which a generally pro-Soviet line was evident, also made clear that it was not calling for the establishment of a separate Kurdish state, but only for 'the right of the oppressed people of Iran to autonomy within the boundaries of the state of Iran'. The Congress slogan was: 'Democracy for Iran and Autonomy for Kurdistan'.[16]

The Arabs in southern Iran have always had an uneasy relationship with the Pahlavi régime: at the time of the establishment of the Pahlavi state, the Arabs of the south enjoyed a considerable degree of autonomy, until in 1924 Reza Khan forcibly reasserted Tehran's control. In 1958, a new political organization emerged, the Front for the Liberation of Ahvaz (*Jabhat Tahrir Ahvaz*) which called for the liberation of the Arab areas of Iran from Iranian rule. In the middle 1960s, and perhaps on some occasions in the 1970s, the Front was also able to launch some armed actions against the Iranian state in the southern areas. But although it enjoyed the support of Iraq in one form or another after 1958, this aid ceased in 1975 when Iran and Iraq settled their differences. Since then the Front, while obtaining some support from Libya, has been in a more precarious situation.

The policies of the Front are not clear and raise a number of difficult issues. In the first place, the Front claims that the Arab area – which it calls Ahvaz, after the main town, or just 'Arabestan' – was independent of Iran before the 'Iranian occupation' of 1924. This is historically inaccurate, since the independence enjoyed by the local ruler, Sheikh Khazal, was a product of the temporary disintegration of the Iranian state during the First World War, and of the protection he enjoyed from the British at that time. Khuzistan had been part of Iran for centuries, despite fluctuations in control from the centre. Secondly, the Front claims that the area it operates in is a predominantly Arab one; in fact, whereas it may have had an Arab majority fifty years ago, this is no longer so, since there has been a considerable migration of non-Arab Iranians into the area. Thirdly, the Front, or at least one section of it, calls for the separation of this 'Arabestan' from Iran, and this cause is commonly taken up by nationalist states and other political organizations in the Arab world. However, there exists no justification for this demand, given the inadequate historical and demographic arguments on which it is based; moreover, since all the Iranian oilfields are located in this area, there is no chance whatsoever of such a demand being granted.

By posing such a goal, the Front is in practice making it more difficult to obtain proper cultural and linguistic rights for the Arabs in Iran, who are as oppressed as the other nationalities.[17] The role of Arab states in encouraging this only adds fuel to the fire of Iranian anti-Arab chauvinism, and makes it more likely that the oppression of the Iranian Arabs will continue.

These issues seem to have found some echo within the Arab underground movement itself, since in the mid-1970s a separate group emerged, entitled the Revolutionary Democratic Movement for the Liberation of Arabestan. This group, which explicitly called itself 'Marxist-Leninist', rejected the policy of the other Front: it called for autonomy, not independence, for the Arabs in Iran and for a common struggle by all the oppressed nationalities in Iran for equality.

The Baluchi people of south-east Iran live mainly from herding animals, and have the lowest standard of living and *per capita* income of any part of the economy. In other parts of Iran, Baluchis are to be found amongst the most impoverished workers – casual labourers on building sites and seasonal migrants. In both the Iranian and Pakistani areas of Baluchistan there exists a long tradition of tribal guerrilla resistance to the central government. In the period after 1958 Baluchi groups from both sides of the border received some help from the Iraqi government, until this was ended by the 1975 Iran–Iraq agreement, and broadcasts to Iranian Baluchistan were made by an organization known as the Baluchistan People's League (*Baluch Ulus Mahaz*). Since the 1975 agreement, the League has lost its main outlet, the Iraqi radio facilities, but just as a low-level resistance to Pakistani rule has continued on the other side of the border, so there is a degree of political, if not military, opposition on the Iranian side.

Whilst it is impossible to estimate how far under current conditions these organizations have a following amongst their own nationalities, in addition to having a presence in exile, there is no doubt that since their activities are directed against a central part of the Pahlavi state, its oppression of the nationalities, they would probably enjoy considerable popularity if control lessened. The greatest problem arises in discussing what long-term solution is possible – autonomy or separation. The Azerbaijanis have not had a separate organization since the Azerbaijan Democratic League merged with the Tudeh in 1960. They are, however, the largest nationality, with a strong cultural identity. They and the Kurds in the KDPI, seem to accept a degree of autonomy within the Iranian state. The same is probably also true of the Baluchis, since the idea of a 'Greater Baluchistan', an independent entity drawn from parts of Iran and Pakistan, seems to have been abandoned on both sides of the border. The demand for separation is still raised by some Arabs, and this is encouraged by some Arab governments; but such a demand by any nationality is, as noted, bound to have the effect of reinforcing Persian determination not to concede to the demands of the nationalities for any rights whatsoever.

Organizations 2: The Traditional Groups

The two main organizations of the 1941–53 period were Mossadeq's National Front and the Tudeh Party. Both experienced a partial revival in the early 1960s, the Front more than the Tudeh; and although it would seem that they have been abandoned by many of their older followers and have failed to attract much support from the younger generations, they have continued in existence in exile. For some of the older generation they still represent an alternative to the régime, and hence whilst their activities within the country have been on a small scale, they must still command some sympathy. On the other hand, two and a half decades have passed since the 1953 coup, and the great majority of Iranians have no memory of this period and its politics. It is therefore unlikely that these two groups will easily be able to regain the position they enjoyed in the 1940s and early 1950s.

The National Front was never a proper political organization, but was rather a coalition of different factions within the parliament. Following the coup Mossadeq himself was sentenced to three years' imprisonment, and after his release he was confined on his estate at Ahmadabad north of Tehran until his death in 1967. He never again played an active role in politics, although he remained a symbol around which others mobilized support. When political controls were relaxed in 1961, it became possible for a new group of politicians to organize meetings, under the title of National Front II. Their main demand was the 'restoration of constitutional government', and an estimated 80,000 people attended their first public meeting.[18] The Front's attacks on the Shah corresponded to a widespread feeling that the years of militarized dictatorship might be coming to an end.

Yet after this interlude, the National Front II adopted a cautious 'wait and see' policy and in the end it was crushed, as its predecessor had been, by repression, in June 1963. This time, however, there was more determined opposition than there had been in 1953. But for this reason perhaps the subsequent disillusion was more total, and in the aftermath of the defeat, a younger generation of dissidents turned to new forms of political activity. Mossadeq's death in 1967 probably also ended another lingering hope. Nevertheless, two further groups did continue in exile, each claiming some connection with the earlier Front: these were the 'National Front in the Middle East', and the self-proclaimed 'National Front III', based in France.

However, there are two senses at least in which the National Front may find it difficult to provide the basis for a future opposition of a progressive kind. First, it was never a political party in the sense of having a party structure, and did not have the organizational capacity to survive under conditions of dictatorship; some of its former leaders have since remained in a silent opposition of some kind, but this may not be enough to rally support under conditions very different from those in which the Front had first appeared. Secondly, some of the Front's support comes from somewhat conservative sections of

Iranian society, religious elements opposed to parts of the Shah's programme. It is doubtful if these forces are, in political and social terms, more radical than the Pahlavi dictatorship itself. None advocate the kind of terror practised by SAVAK, but religious leaders such as Ayatollah Khomeini and his sympathizers in Iran offer an ill-defined, ambiguous, alternative to the Shah.

If, however, the Front has no definite future as an organization in Iran, some of the forces that were formerly represented in it now enjoy a revival. In particular, the currents of opposition that phrase their hostility to the Shah in religious terms still have considerable powers of attraction, and, whilst controlled by the régime in the mid-1970s have developed a more active presence as this control has slackened. In the late 1960s, for example, a group of religious reformers, among them the writer Ali Shariatti, used the Hoseiniye Ershad mosque in Tehran for criticizing the régime; and, although this mosque and others like it were subsequently closed, reports of continued hostility to the régime by circles such as this were reported. The religious school, *madrase*, in the pilgrimage city of Qom is known to be a focus of such opposition, and many younger people, students in such schools, are formulating their opposition in Islamic terms. This kind of movement is far wider than that of the religiously orientated guerrillas that are also in opposition and the events of 1978 showed that there is the basis in Iran for a new popular movement evoking Islamic ideology to emerge, as it has done in Turkey, Pakistan and some of the Arab countries. On the other hand, such a movement, despite its appeals, is the first such tendency in Iran since the 1890s, and is competing with other political movements for the support of the oppressed classes.

The Tudeh Party was, in contrast to the National Front, an organized political party, indeed the most organized political force ever seen in Iranian politics. The earlier Communist Party (founded 1921) had been crushed by Reza Khan, and under a 1931 law it became illegal for any organization to profess communist, or 'collectivist', views. Hence when it became possible to form a party again after the Allied invasion in 1941, it was decided to call the party the Masses (Tudeh) Party; the Tudeh was, however, in practice the orthodox pro-Russian Iranian communist party and remains so to this day.

The Tudeh's following in the 1940s was an enormous one – it had at most 25,000 members, but its trades union affiliates had up to 400,000 members. While its leadership was mostly of professional and aristocratic origins, its membership was mainly from urban workers and its following remained a predominantly urban one. The Tudeh never made any significant inroads into the rural areas. In terms of nationalities, it seems to have been restricted to the Persians, except for Tabriz where the Azerbaijani movement was based. Moreover, the party was unable to retain the initiative it had won during the war and the immediate post-war period and, after the defeat of the republics in Kurdistan and Azerbaijan, it was forced onto the defensive. In 1949 it was banned on a pretext, and during Mossadeq's period in office the Tudeh remained until far too late in a position of opposition. After the coup it was forced underground and in time its members were tracked down: an estimated 3,000 Tudeh militants were arrested, and the network inside the officer corps, numbering over 500, was uncovered in 1954. Tudeh enjoyed a brief revival in the early 1960s when, although unable to act openly, it aligned itself with the National Front opposition to the régime. But, with the imposition of the ban on political activities in 1963, it lost even this room for manoeuvre.

Since that time Tudeh's activities have been in exile. Anti-communist sources give its membership at 2,000 or under,[19] and the last occasion on which it was claimed by the régime or the Tudeh that members of the organization had been on trial was in 1966, when two leading officials, Parviz Hekmatjou and Ali Khavar, and a number of others were sentenced to jail. It is believed that a number of Tudeh members have been kept in jail despite the fact that their sentences have ended, and in 1974 Hekmatjou himself was murdered in captivity. But there have been few or no other signs of its overt existence inside Iran, and all those arrested after the mid-1960s have come from other political tendencies. The U S State Department claims that 90 per cent of those arrested after 1953 are now supporters of the régime,[20] and a number of former members are now in influential positions within the government – in the Plan Organization, in SAVAK and as licensed exponents of a confusionist left ideology. One recent cabinet has contained two ministers who were former members of the Tudeh.

The leadership in exile is drawn from survivors of the pre-1953 period: secretary-general Iraj Iskandari; central committee secretary Nureddin Kianuri; former secretary-general Reza Radmanesh; and Ihsan Tabari, a historian and literary critic. Tudeh publishes a fortnightly paper, *Mardom* (The People), and a theoretical journal, *Donya* (The World). In 1959 it acquired a radio station known as *Peik-i Iran* (Iran Courier) that was closed down in 1976. It was at that time located in Bulgaria, and it appears that it was silenced as a result of a trade agreement between the Bulgarian and Iranian governments.

There have been a number of divisions in Tudeh's history, the product of its policies, and in particular of its unswerving loyalty to the Soviet Union. The first split was in 1948, when a group of members, led by Khalil Maleki, left the party. At that time, Maleki's main public criticism was that the party was too loyal to the Soviet Union; he later founded a group called the Third Force and through it pioneered an attempt to found an independent socialist position in Iran. Colloquially referred to as a 'Titoist', Maleki, who died in 1969, was unable to develop this position in a coherent programmatic form, let alone in any practical manner, and he ended up a victim of the régime's manipulations, alternately licensed and then silenced by it. However, Maleki's break with the Tudeh now seems to have involved other reasons, and in particular a belated recognition on his part of the importance of the national and specifically Azerbaijani questions, a topic on which the Tudeh was at that time unwilling to adopt a clear position.[21]

During Mossadeq's period, a second division occurred within the party, between a group around Kianuri and one around

Radmanesh. The former advocated a less sectarian approach to the National Front, whilst the latter maintained the prevailing hostile attitude until the latter part of 1952. This division did not produce an actual split in the party, but the defeat of 1953 forced it to review its position, as did the general shift in Soviet policy towards alliances with nationalist states in the third world that occurred around that time. In 1957, at the Tudeh's Fourth Plenum, it officially criticized 'the party's failure to understand the nature of bourgeois nationalism and its anti-imperialist potential'.[22] Instead, it called for a broad democratic front of all those opposed to the Shah's dictatorship, and this paved the way for its policies in the early 1960s: first, the reunification with the Azerbaijani Democratic League in 1960, and then the attempt to ally with the National Front in the period up to 1963.

In later versions of its programme, the Tudeh has spread its alliance even wider. An article by Kianuri in 1976 called for an alliance with the intermediate strata, i.e. the petty bourgeoisie and white-collar workers, and also with peasants, the clergy, the national bourgeoisie, and even some of what he regarded as the 'big bourgeoisie', i.e. those working with international capital. Kianuri also referred to 'patriotic and progressive tendencies' in the armed forces and argued that 'though the army is the power base of the régime today, we can count in favourable conditions on part of the armed forces siding with the working class'. In sum, Kianuri argued that 'the revolution in Iran is at its initial, i.e. anti-imperialist and democratic stage', and that Tudeh should include in its alliance 'social forces in Iran which, though far removed from the left, even from anything democratic, are eager to see the present régime done away with'.[23]

This adoption of a less sectarian approach was in part a response to events inside Iran but also corresponded to changes in the policies of many communist parties in the 1960s and 1970s. Parties in quite different countries such as Chile or Spain were adopting similarly broad definitions of the popular alliance they were trying to build. However, these changes were of little practical import since Tudeh had no active presence inside Iran and this led to hostility from the younger militants. Moreover, the party was battered by a further loss of credibility which increased its isolation from the younger generation of militants inside the country. Five distinct episodes contributed to this. First, the policy of supporting the National Front in 1960–63 discredited the Tudeh Party among many young people who criticized it for relying on constitutional methods. Then, after 1962, Iran improved its relations with the Soviet Union and Eastern Europe; the Soviet press gave some qualified support to the Shah's economic reforms, and in 1967 Soviet arms were sold to Iran. This apparent Soviet support for the Shah not only embarrassed the Tudeh Party but led it into a number of further difficulties: it had to praise Soviet assistance, and attribute Iran's progress to this, while at the same time the facilities available to it were reduced.[24] Thirdly, the Sino-Soviet dispute, which broke into public view in 1963, had its impact on the Tudeh: in 1965 three members or alternate members of the Central Committee (Ahmad Ghassemi, Gholamhussein Forutan and Abbas Seghai) launched an attack on Soviet policies and called for a 'violent revolution'. They founded a new Revolutionary Organization (*Sazman-i Inqilabi*) of the Tudeh. Their break was an explicit rejection of the Fourth Plenum resolutions and all that had followed. The group they founded was based in western Europe, and although it itself had no great impact, it marked the beginning of a period in which pro-Chinese policies of one sort or another were dominant within Iranian exile circles; this was especially so in those countries, such as the USA and West Germany, where Maoism was a dominant force within the local left-wing movement. The Revolutionary Organization, and a group that broke from it called Typhoon (*Tufan*), were active in exile; inside Iran two other groups, Red Star (*Setar-i Sorkh*) and Towards the Revolution (*Bisu-yi Inqilab*), formed in the late 1960s and are believed to have been planning guerrilla actions when they were destroyed by SAVAK in 1971.

If a diffuse sympathy for more violent actions whether of a pro-Chinese or more generic Guevarist character were prevalent amongst young militants in the late 1960s, two further actions by Tudeh added to its lack of credibility in Iran. The details of these are by no means clear, but through them SAVAK is supposed to have taken control of the Tehran and Khuzistan branches of the Tudeh Party and in this way discovered the identity of dozens of young militants in the post-1963 period. The head of this branch, Abbas Ali Shahriyari, was, it is now claimed by the guerrillas, a SAVAK agent (he was shot dead by them in 1975); Tudeh's apparent error in allowing SAVAK to penetrate the organization in this way seems to have turned a number of people against them. A second initiative of an analogous kind concerned General Teimur Bakhtiar, the former head of SAVAK who was dismissed by the Shah in 1961 and subsequently went into exile. Bakhtiar had been the Military Governor of Tehran between 1953 and 1957, i.e. the man in charge of persecuting communists; but in spite of this Tudeh made contacts with him, when, in the late 1960s, he began organizing some opposition to the Shah from Lebanon and Iraq. Since Bakhtiar himself was shot (presumably by a SAVAK emissary) in 1970, nothing came of the initiative, but it, and the murky events surrounding Shahriyari, added support to the widespread belief that Tudeh was an unreliable section of the opposition, over and above the formal political positions it espoused.

The Tudeh claims that it has a programme consonant with the objective situation in Iran and with what is sees as the primary political requirement of the situation, i.e. the need to rally as wide a front as possible against the dictatorship. It is critical of the guerrilla groups, whilst it recognizes their sincerity and calls for a united front with them. The latter, for their part, have refused to cooperate with the Tudeh: they consider the Tudeh to be a party of 'traitors', and that the Tudeh Party is a historically discredited party with an 'anti-popular' policy. The Tudeh Party is certainly open to criticisms of various kinds, but the terms in which the criticisms have been conventionally made by its critics on the left in Iran are inadequate. For this reason the important and difficult questions posed by the Tudeh's history and its present programme have not been properly discussed; rather one set of schematic answers has been substituted for another, and the Iranian left has made little progress towards generating an analysis and practice that really does measure up to the issues it faces. Instead of a slavish loyalty to Moscow, characteristic of Tudeh, the large body of Iranian militants influenced by China have equally slavishly followed the policies of Peking, even after Peking began to support the policies of the Shah. Similarly, many who rejected the excessively cautious practice of the Tudeh after 1963 then veered towards an unfounded optimism about the possibilities of armed struggle and the political effects of small military actions in Iran. Moreover, many of those who denounced the Tudeh Party for its compromises were themselves willing to form alliances with religious leaders like Khomeini, whose policies were in some respects as conservative as those of the Shah himself.

The Tudeh's record is a tragic one, of sectarianism and missed opportunities. And its current attempts to rectify this are themselves flawed. The most extreme instance of this is Tudeh's expectations from progressive sections within the armed forces – an illusion fostered, to its tragic cost, by the Chilean Communist Party prior to the military coup of September 1973, and, in a different way, by the Palestinian Resistance in Jordan, prior to King Hussein's successful attack on it in September 1970. Such elements may exist, but they are in no position to alter the army's political direction. However, the underlying problem with the Fourth Plenum revisions, and Kianuri's analysis of 1976, is that these leave untouched the problem of the Tudeh's relations with the Soviet Union. It is this which has hamstrung the Tudeh Party since its foundation – forcing it to endorse Soviet demands for an oil concession in 1944, or to condone Soviet arms shipments to the Shah in 1967. All pro-Moscow communist parties face this problem, but it is an especially acute one in a country such as Iran which has experienced Russian military occupation and pressures in the past. In addition, Tudeh has been weakened by the destructive effects of following current Russian policies at a time when these did not accord with the situation in Iran: this was true during the left sectarian phase up to the latter part of 1952, when the Tudeh would not cooperate with Mossadeq, and with the rightist policies pursued since the mid-1960s, which have alienated the younger generation and thereby fostered the militarist illusions of the period.

In anti-communist eyes, the Tudeh benefits from operating in a country which shares a common border with the Soviet Union: but this is a dubious asset. For the Soviet Union only aids such a party directly, i.e. sends support of any kind across the border, in conditions of global conflict, such as obtained during the First and Second World Wars. Otherwise, the existence of a common border is of no practical use, and indeed has, as we have seen (see p. 36), certain negative consequences. In numerous countries bordering the Soviet Union it is evident how Soviet policies have been of a more or less blundering kind and have indeed increased the opposition to the Soviet Union – Finland in 1940, Iran in 1946, Czechoslovakia in 1968 and China in 1960. In the future, any revolutionary movement in Iran will need solidarity from outside and good relations with the Soviet Union; but servile loyalty of the kind practised by the Tudeh, in common (be it said) with most other Middle Eastern communist parties, has been and remains a serious obstacle to its making headway in Iran.

The criticisms made of the Tudeh by groups elsewhere on the left are, however, usually of an inaccurate kind. The most common accusation is that the Tudeh leadership are 'traitors' because they have left Iran: this is in itself a completely invalid argument, since many of the most important revolutionary leaders of this century have left their own countries when repression has been severe and when the only base for political work has been abroad. This was true of Lenin, Ho Chi Minh and Fidel Castro, to name but a few. Nor is the fact that the Tudeh leadership is loyal to the Soviet Union a reason for calling them 'traitors', even though this policy is in error. Use of such a term betrays an unresolved nationalist residue in the critique. The revulsion which the younger generation have felt against the Tudeh Party since 1963 has led them to refuse to cooperate with it in any kind of united front work. But this too is a sectarian response, one that fails to take account of the real situation in Iran and the forms of political practice this requires. The Tudeh Party is a very weak party, and one which fosters a number of illusions about the régime. Its record is also a disastrous one. But it remains a constituent of the left in Iran (which taken all together is very weak) and it is the only one that has avoided the temptations of optimistic rhetoric as a way of surmounting the objective problems which the opposition faces. It is, as we shall now see, this latter pitfall into which the post-1963 generation of militants has stumbled, in its attempt to break through the barriers that contained older organizations.

Organizations 3: The Guerrillas

The younger generation of militants active in the mid-1960s could see that the Iranian opposition had been through three separate defeats since the fall of Reza Khan: in 1946, 1953 and 1963. It was not therefore surprising that they should have turned away from the National Front and Tudeh, and from the non-violent methods these espoused. Instead they turned for inspiration to models of combat pioneered elsewhere in the third world, and in particular to the theories of guerrilla war prevalent in the late 1960s: in Vietnam, China, Cuba and Palestine. The works of Mao, Ho, Debray and Guevara were translated and different attempts made to apply them, in theory and deed, to Iran.

The climate of this period was one of considerable frustration among Iranian students. The defeat of 1963 had given way to a period of inactivity on the part of the urban opposition and the interlude of relaxation after 1965 had taken a predominantly literary form. Armed resistance had taken place in the countryside, but these attempts had been confined to specific nationalities and were defeated (the Qashqai tribe in Fars province, 1962–3; the Arabs in Khuzestan, 1964–5; the Kurds, 1967–8). Out of this period there emerged a number of different groups, each planning to undertake some armed opposition to the régime.

There seem to have been between half a dozen and a dozen such groups in the late 1960s,[25] but only two were able to initiate and sustain armed opposition to the régime: the Mojahidin of the People, and the Fedayin of the People. The former originated amongst followers of the National Front who in the mid-1960s formed a political organization, the Liberation Movement of Iran (*Nezhat-i Azadi-yi Iran*).[26] In 1966, a group affiliated to the Liberation Movement established a guerrilla organization, the Organization of the People's Combatants (*Sazman-i Mojahidin-i Khalq*), usually known as the Mojahidin. After five years of preparation it began armed actions in 1971.

While it is hard to be precise about the ideology of this group, its main concepts seem to have been drawn from Islamic thinking; it was fighting against 'tyranny' and 'falsehood', and for some general kind of freedom. An indication of Mojahidin thinking can be gained from the speech made at his trial in 1972 by one of the leaders of the group, Said Mohsin. He began by justifying his actions on the basis of a quote from the Koran; this called on those who believe 'to do battle for the cause of Allah' and to 'fight the minions of the devil' since 'the devil's strategy is ever weak'.[27] In 1975 there occurred a division within the Mojahidin. They declared that they now rejected their previous Islamic orientation; they were not only a secular party, but had decided to attack the Islamic religion in their publications. They also criticized their previous policies for excessive reliance on purely military actions, and for failing to unite with other opposition forces. They claimed that half of the membership had been expelled from the group for opposing this change, and that their ideology was now 'Marxist-Leninist'. But despite this abrupt and rather surprising change of position there can be no doubt that some Mojahidin still use religion for opposing the régime. Despite the nature of the *ulema* and the bazaar, appeals couched in this language may therefore continue for a long time to come to provide a basis for armed actions against the state.

The other main group originated in the Tudeh Party and has always claimed that it espouses Marxism. It was founded by half a dozen or so members of the Tudeh Party who left that organization in 1963; their leader was Bijan Jazani, born in 1937, who had been imprisoned in the aftermath of the 1953 coup. Jazani and six other members of his group were arrested in 1968 (denounced, it is claimed, by Shahriyari, the SAVAK agent in the Tudeh), but five members remained free: two, Ali Akbar Safayi Farahani and Mohammad Ashtiani, escaped from Iran and went for two years to work with the Palestinian resistance whilst three others remained underground in Iran; the leader of this latter group was Hamid Ashraf, born in 1946, a former gymnastics and mountaineering champion at Tehran University.[28] In 1970 the two members of the group who had been with the Palestinians returned to Iran – by which time 22 others had joined in – and in early 1971 they prepared their first action, an attack on a gendarmerie post at Siahkal, in the mountains north of Tehran. The attack on Siahkal occurred on 8 February 1971 and was the first incident in the guerrilla campaign; in strictly military terms the attack was a failure, since the group was repulsed by the security forces, and within a few days fifteen guerrillas had been killed or captured. But in political terms it symbolized the end of over seven years of passivity in the face of the state apparatus and, at least within the student milieu where the groups recruited, it had a certain resonance.

Around this time, another group of similar ideology, led by Masaoud Ahmadzadeh, the son of a prominent Mossadeq supporter, was also planning to start armed action, and in the spring of 1971 it attacked a police station in the Qolhaq district of Tehran. The Hamid Ashraf group, despite its setback, was able to assassinate the chief military prosecutor, General Farsiu, around the same time. Following these three incidents the two groups combined to form the Organization of the Iranian People's Fedayin Guerrillas (*Sazman-i Cherikhaye Fedayin-i Khalq*), usually known in English as the Fedayin.[29]

The main features of the Mojahidin and Fedayin's activities in the six years between 1971 and 1977 can be listed as follows. Both groups have been confined to specific, sudden, clandestine operations: bomb explosions, bank raids, attacks on police stations, assassinations. In the latter category, the Fedayin, after killing General Farsiu in April 1971, killed a number of other supporters of the régime: Mostafa Fateh, an industrialist some of whose workers had been shot during a strike in 1971, was shot in August 1974; in March 1975 they killed the head of the police guard attached to Aryamehr University in Tehran, and Shahriyari, the man accused of being a SAVAK agent within the Tudeh. The Mojahidin killed a SAVAK official, General Taheri, in August 1972, and also a number of Americans working in Iran: in June 1973, Colonel Lewis Hawkins, an officer attached to the US Embassy in Tehran; in May 1975, two colonels in the US Air Force; and in August 1976, three US civilians working on the secret Ibex spy system.

There is no record of the number of operations carried out, nor of the number of clashes in which the initiative lay with the régime's forces; it seems that the number of incidents was considerable in 1971 and 1972, that it increased again in 1976, but that after each increase the régime was able to capture or kill a significant number of those involved. Government sources state that between February 1971 and August 1976 55 of its officials died in clashes with the guerrillas, and that at least 300 people were executed for guerrilla actions in the same period, while a further 300 are estimated to have been killed in clashes with the forces of the régime. Beyond these details, a number of more general features of the guerrilla movement can be noted. First, nearly all of those involved have been in some sense intellectuals – people with a university education, and who, even if they came from poor backgrounds, have derived their political outlook from their period in higher education. Few of those reported as killed or arrested have been workers; none have been from the rural poor. This relates to a second feature, namely that, after the initial incident at Siahkal, virtually all the operations have taken place in large towns, in particular Tehran, and to a lesser extent Mashad, Isfahan and Tabriz. Some of the first writings on guerrilla struggle in Iran, borrowing from Mao and Guevara, or inspired by the history of tribal resistance in Iran, thought it was possible to launch a guerrilla struggle in the countryside; but conditions in Iran were not favourable to such a form of resistance. It is, indeed, believed that some of those involved in the Siahkal operation were betrayed to the police by the local peasantry, whilst the guerrilla campaign of Dr Hushang Azami in Luristan in 1974 was a local affair, on a tribal basis, and seems to have had no connection with the guerrilla organizations.

The most important characteristic of the movement is that it has operated under conditions of extreme clandestineness and difficulty. Neither organization had any ties to existing mass political organizations when they began, and it has not proved possible for them to build any such organizations in the period since. While each of the organizations survived the first six years in some form or another, all of the leaders of the first operations were killed. The last of the original group that carried out the Siahkal incident, Hamid Ashraf, was shot dead in a clash in Tehran in August 1976. It is probably true that these groups have continued to recruit from their original support area, the student milieu, and that this can continue indefinitely; they may too be able to sustain a minimal level of armed actions against the Iranian state. But this very fact of survival is of limited significance, and quite apart from the high cost in human lives involved does not amount to a political success. For the whole purpose of such groups is not just to sustain a degree of armed combat, in itself a technical operation of no political import, but rather to carry out actions which will have certain political effects – either demoralizing government forces, or weakening them in some other way, or encouraging the oppressed to organize themselves and take initiatives of a political kind. On the basis of seven years of guerrilla struggle, the signs are that neither of these two things has occurred, and that the guerrillas have remained virtually isolated from the population in whose name they claim to be acting. It may be that the events of 1978 have created a more favourable climate, but they also showed the limits of the guerrilla groups, who played no significant part in generating the mass mobilizations.

Guerrilla Strategy

The problems raised here are of two kinds: first, what forms of politically significant action are possible under régimes like that which exists in Iran? Secondly, how does such urban guerrilla activity contribute to the growth of an opposition? In order to discuss these in the context of Iran it is not enough merely to point to the objective limitations of the guerrilla movement, since it will be argued that these can be overcome in time, or to say that the views of outsiders on this are misconceived in that they are unaware of the profound popular effect of military actions. The root of the problem can be located with more certainty elsewhere, in the theoretical works of the guerrillas, for it is here that the shortcomings of their strategy are most evident.

There are four main texts which have served as the basis for the guerrilla strategy in Iran. Although the latest was written in 1973, the ideas contained in them have continued to guide the guerrilla opposition. All four are by authors who were leaders of the Fedayin group, and it can safely be assumed that for this reason they will contain a more coherent analysis than the rhetorical appeals of the first generation of Mojahidin. These four texts are:

1. *On the Necessity of Armed Struggle and a Refutation of the Theory of 'Survival'*, by Amir Parviz Pouyan, written in the spring of 1970.
2. *Armed Struggle: a Strategy and a Tactic*, by Masaoud Ahmadzadeh, written in the summer of 1970.
3. *What a Revolutionary Must Know*, by Ali Akbar Safayi Farahani, written in 1970.
4. *Armed Struggle: the Road to the Mobilization of the Masses*, by Bijan Jazani, written in 1973.[30]

There are certain differences between these texts. Ahmadzadeh and Jazani seem to lay more stress on the possibilities of armed struggle in the countryside than do the other two. Ahmadzadeh for his part sees armed action as a strategy for the whole liberation movement, whereas the others, to varying extents, see it more as an initial tactic which will set in motion other political movements of a mass character. Yet, when it comes to the underlying themes of guerrilla struggle, these four texts share common assumptions and weaknesses of analysis. Since these texts were written, all four of the authors have died at the hands of the régime. Farahani took part in the attack on Siahkal, was captured, and died in captivity in March 1971; Pouyan was killed in a gun battle in the Niruyehavai district of Tehran in May 1971; Ahmadzadeh was arrested later in 1971, tortured (see p. 87), and executed in February 1972; and Jazani was murdered with his comrades in captivity some time in early 1975. Yet, although these four therefore represent a generation of thinkers and activists that has now been destroyed, the ideas they upheld remain those which guide the guerrilla movement. In this sense it is possible to assess the theories of the guerrillas by reference to these works .

The arguments of these writers can be summarized as follows:

1. *the bankruptcy of the old organizations*: Farahani, for example, reviews the previous thirty years of activity by the National Front and the Tudeh and concludes they are no longer capable of playing a political role. Pouyan condemns those who, like the Tudeh, are intent only on 'survival' and who are against taking the offensive against the régime. Ahmadzadeh, for his part, calls the Tudeh 'a caricature of a Marxist-Leninist party' and condemns both groups for their 'paralysing tactics' in 1960–63.[31]

2. *the passivity of the workers and peasants*: Jazani writes that 'the great majority of the working class lacks a minimal political and class consciousness'. Ahmadzadeh contrasts the situation in Iran, where repression is so severe that a workers' opposition is impossible, to that in Tsarist Russia where it was possible. Farahani argues that 'under present conditions, any idea of an actual rising by the peasantry, and of rural guerrilla war by the peasantry, is unfounded'.[32]

3. *the necessity for armed actions by a vanguard group as the only way to challenge the régime*: Farahani writes: 'We have no doubt that political confrontation with a régime which is essentially a military dictatorship is not possible except

through armed struggle ... An organization that spends a considerable time politicizing and which defers military operations until a later stage will never succeed.' Pouyan lays great stress on the need to win support amongst the population by challenging the enemy's apparently absolute power with what he calls 'revolutionary power'. Ahmadzadeh, stressing the role of the vanguard, states: 'It is only through the most acute form of revolutionary action, that is, through armed struggle, and the shaking of the colossal barrier, that the vanguard can show the masses the struggle which finds its course in history.'[33]

The influence of other writings on guerrilla warfare is evident enough in these writings, in particular the influence of Latin American theories of guerrilla war which claim that organizations can be built through struggle, and theories which claim that armed actions by small underground political groups can lead to wider political actions by the oppressed.[34] However, the Iranian writings also reproduce the weaknesses of these Latin American writings, with the added problem that in Iran the guerrilla movements have operated in objective conditions as unfavourable as those in most Latin American countries, or even more so: not only have these groups begun without any links to other, pre-existing mass political formations (in contrast to Uruguay, Argentina or Chile) but they have also had to face repressive apparatus as well equipped and confident as any in Latin America. If it is borne in mind that every Latin American guerrilla group has been defeated, then the prospects for this form of stuggle in Iran can only be bleak.

There are three underlying theoretical weaknesses in these writings: first, voluntarism – i.e. a failure to see what the conditions for the growth of a mass movement of any kind are, and a fixation on the acts of a small group; secondly, an overestimation of the potentialities of armed action as propaganda and a belief in the potential explosiveness of the population; thirdly, an underlying moralism.

1. Throughout these writings there is a tendency to minimize the importance of political preparation and of the need to ensure that the minimal conditions for a military campaign

are satisfied. All four texts are marked by a simplification of what is involved in military activities, and by an impatience which, however justified, is in contradiction with the difficulties facing the Iranian left. Ahmadzadeh, for example, claims: 'By a study of the objective conditions in our country, we have demonstrated that any recourse to "lack of preparedness of the objective conditions for revolution" reflects opportunism, compromise and reformism. It reveals a lack of political courage and is a rationalization for inaction ... The absence of spontaneous movements results not from the insufficient development of contradictions, but from persistent police suppression and the inactivity of the vanguard.' He continues: 'The real vanguard must itself come to the fore in the course of the armed struggle and through politico-military action. Must we wait until the Communist Party is formed, and then initiate the revolutionary war on a large scale, for example with an army? No. The politico-military nucleus itself can, by initiating guerrilla warfare and in the process of its development, create the party, the people's true vanguard politico-military organization, and the people's army.' In Farahani's work, this voluntarism takes an equally acute form since he seems to scorn any political preparation: 'To set up a revolutionary cell, no special political background or credentials are necessary. Revolutionary individuals themselves can organize such groups. They do not derive their respect and credentials from their political background or past titles, but rather from their programme of action and struggle ahead of them ...' And again: 'The would-be organizers of such centres need not carry any old (political) credentials or titles. Their faith, perseverance, and revolutionary programmes are the stepping stones to the build-up of these centres.'[35] While all four texts claim they have made an analysis of the objective situation in Iran following the Shah's transformations, none of them has done so in any adequate way: all underestimate the degree to which the repression and the post-1963 boom have placed new weapons in the hands of the régime. This leads directly to the second shortcoming.

2. All four texts overestimate the degree to which armed

actions will in themselves have political effects, and all fall back on abstractions and simplifications when facing up to this, *the* crucial question when assessing a policy of the kind they advocate. None establish any plausible link between their actions and a mass response. Pouyan's text was the first to be distributed among the Tehran student body in 1970, and enjoyed a wide popularity because it appeared to offer a way out of the impasse of the Iranian left; yet, on closer examination, Pouyan has no real answer to this question. In his words:

In order to liberate the proletariat from the dominant culture, to cleanse its mind and its life of petty-bourgeois poisonous thoughts, to terminate its alienation from its special outlook and equip it with ideological ammunition, it is necessary again to shatter its illusion that it is powerless to destroy the enemy. Revolutionary power is used to deal with this matter. The application of this power ... makes the proletariat conscious of a source of power which belongs to it ... Neither terror nor suppression can hinder the march of the workers towards the source of their vanguard's power ... The spell breaks and the enemy looks like a defeated magician. What makes his defeat is precisely our victory in establishing a most intimate and direct relationship with the proletariat, which is no longer confronted with the hindrances by the workers themselves in order to turn into organizational ties.[36]

Farahani, for his part, holds the dangerous idea that popular resistance to the régime will increase because of the increase in repression following on the guerrillas' activities. He writes: 'Undoubtedly the régime will increasingly veer towards even more harshness and mete out severe punishment; but let us not forget that this same trend will fan the flame of true struggle and will pull the régime reluctantly into an arena that is not to its liking. Urban struggle has the advantage of being nearer to a mass of people who can easily offer their cooperation ...'[37] Ahmadzadeh has nothing except rhetorical hopes to offer on this matter: 'It must be shown in practice that counter-revolutionary violence can be conquered and that stability and security are a farce. It is in the course of this action that the masses' historical stamina, accumulated and dormant behind the colossal barrier of the repressive power, is gradually released; and it is in this same course that the masses gradually and in the heart of the armed struggle become conscious of themselves, their historical mission, and their undefeatable strength'.[38]

Jazani's work is of a different character in this respect: writing three years later, with hindsight and from the relative distance of prison, he adopts a much more cautious approach. He stresses the dangers of adventurism in political practice and his very first sentence recognizes that 'One of the most important problems facing the fighters and the armed movement is the transition from the present limited armed struggle to a mass armed movement.' He goes into a much more detailed analysis of the problem. But he too provides an evasive answer, for he concentrates on the technical problems within the groups rather than on the links between the groups and the population. He proposes a scheme by which armed struggle expands, but this too remains abstract, and when it comes to the central issue he resorts to generalities: 'The armed struggle will, on the one hand, neutralize counter-revolutionary force with revolutionary forces; and, on the other hand, reveal, in the best possible manner, to the people and the world in general, the true colour of the ruling groups. This will cause the masses to rise up after every blow, and at the same time stop the régime's oppressive rule over society.'[39] But, one wants to ask, what if the people are terrorized and lack organization? And what if the coercive resources of the régime are so much greater than those of the guerrilla groups that the latter will not be able to 'neutralize' the former? Neither Jazani, nor his comrades, have provided an answer to this, in theory or in practice.

3. The moralism of these writers comes, it would appear, from two distinct sources. One is a general leftist impatience with the political situation and the failure of the old organizations, which leads these militants into an exaggerated sense of their own capabilities; inevitably, given their reluctance to produce a sober objective analysis of Iranian society, and indeed their contempt for any such work, their enemies are seen to be corrupt, cowardly, and so on, whilst the solution to political problems is seen to lie in moral qualities – in heroism, sincerity,

a spirit of sacrifice. Certainly, the hundreds of militants who have died since February 1971 have been possessed of these qualities in abundance. But just as in Latin America the heroism of a Carlos Marighela or a Che Guevara was not able to substitute for or surmount objective conditions, so too in Iran such attributes are not on their own an answer to the problems faced by the left. There is a further factor which it may be unwelcome to identify but which seems to play a certain role here, namely an unresolved legacy of Muslim ideology; in particular one can note the conception of the individual believer whose purity of spirit stands against the evil of the world and, through sacrifices, reverses it. The cult of 'martyrs' and of 'martyrdom' has a similar resonance. There are undeniable, if superficial, similarities between the ideology of earlier Islamic underground groups, active in the 1950s, and the ideas of the guerrillas of the 1970s; the latter, unable to demonstrate any real link between their actions and the mass movement, have fallen back on optimistic abstractions and a moralistic conception of struggle.

The mobilization of popular opposition to the Pahlavi régime, and its eventual overthrow, will require much more than individual heroism, a generic invocation of the 'masses', and mere survival as an armed group. Yet it is not possible for an outside observer to provide any clear answer as to what the best alternative strategy might be. Such an answer can only come from those directly and actively involved in political work in Iran itself. What can be stated from outside are *some* of the preconditions for such work, preconditions that do not, unfortunately, emerge from the very process of active involvement itself, but have to be created through conscious political choices, often of a difficult kind.

In the first place, the Iranian opposition will have to develop an analysis of Iranian society that goes beyond the simplification characteristic of most of what has so far been produced, either by the earlier generation of Marxists, influenced by Soviet theories, or by the more heterogeneous post-1963 generation. In contrast to Turkey and the Asian subcontinent, areas in some other respects comparable to Iran, there has been no substantial development of a Marxist culture within the Iranian intelligentsia which could find a wider resonance in future situations. Unless the Iranian opposition can show that it has accurately and in detail comprehended the nature of Iranian society today, there is little possibility of any socialist movement being able to act in the future, except on the margin of politics. Secondly, it will require the unification of all those on the left who are opposed to the régime, and an end to the compulsive feuding that plagues the Iranian opposition at home and abroad. This kind of sectarianism is a product of defeat, clandestineness and exile, and in no sense peculiar to the Iranian opposition; but unless it is deliberately overcome, it will be even harder for the defeat to be reversed. Thirdly, and most importantly, the opposition will have to develop forms of struggle that go beyond the military and can reach as wide a section of the population as possible. There are opportunities within the Iranian situation for such political activities – protesting at government policies, working with students, workers and other groups conscious of their situation. To deny the importance of such work in the name of a military purism, even to deny the significance of divisions within the ruling group itself, is a retreat from a revolutionary political practice into utopianism. If it is to regain any active relationsip with the oppressed classes in Iran, the left opposition must study the variety of openings facing it, and be able to use the changes that emerge in the political climate.

The situation in which the opposition found itself in 1977 illustrated both the constraints and the possibilities of resistance to the Pahlavi régime. On the one hand, it appeared that both the guerrilla groups had lost ground, that most of their top cadres had been killed and that their capacity for armed actions had been reduced or even eliminated. Moreover, in exile, a new frenzy of division and sectarian dispute was sweeping Iranian groups, in the Middle East, in Europe and in the U S A. Talks on cooperation between the Mojahidin and the Fedayin broke down, with accusations from both sides of bad faith. On the other hand, the emergence inside Iran, especially among religious, professional and student circles, of new opposition currents showed that beneath the surface hostility and criticism were prevalent. From what emerged in this period – among students, writers, lawyers, as well as in the mass protests – it was evident that the Shah had neither cowed the older generation nor successfully recruited the new. He was, by using the army, able temporarily to contain his foes, but the conditions for the régime's success will not last for ever and, as the economic problems increase in the future, the state's room for manoeuvre, in repression and in ensuring a continued boom, will contract. In such a situation there will exist greater mass awareness of the limitations of the régime, and a greater opportunity for an opposition movement to develop that is neither limited by constitutional means nor misled by militarism and simplification. We shall return to this perspective and its implications in the final chapter.

9 Foreign Relations

Since the middle 1960s the régime has pursued a foreign policy designed to make Iran the strategically dominant power in western Asia. This is an aim it has been encouraged to pursue by the U S A, and which has, at the same time, been made possible by the internal transformation of the country – the suppression of internal opposition, and the availability of the necessary economic recources. Iran is indisputably the most prominent example of what is known as the Nixon Doctrine: this can be described as the theory that selected third-world capitalist states should play an active military and political role, relying in the first instance on their own resources, and that they should in this way help to spread the load of maintaining capitalist stability which the U S A had borne almost alone since the Second World War.[1]

Five factors explain why Iran is one of the countries that has come to play such a role. In the first place, Iran has, since the end of the Second World War, been a close ally of the U S A. This does not, as we shall see, mean that the relationship with Washington has been static, nor that Iran is in any simple sense of the word an instrument of U S foreign policy. Nor does it mean that there have not been, and will not be, disagreements between Iran and the U S A. What it does mean is that the U S A has guaranteed the Iranian régime since 1945 and has, since the late 1960s, been willing to back Iran in its drive for regional dominance by providing most of the diplomatic and military support that Iran has requested. Without U S support Iranian foreign policy would not be conceivable in its present form: indeed, it would be impossible. Secondly, Iran occupies an important strategic position in Asia, since it is in military and economic terms one of the strongest capitalist countries between western Europe and Japan. Saudi Arabia, which is much richer, has neither the population nor the military potential of Iran. The only comparable countries in the Middle East in population terms are Egypt and Turkey, but neither of these has the economic resources derived from oil that Iran can, for the moment, deploy. Further east, India has a stronger army and is potentially a greater capitalist power, but it, like Egypt, is constrained by its internal problems, and has not so far developed comparable relations with the U S A.

However, Iran is not only in a strategic position because of its relationship to the Gulf and to other capitalist countries, but also because it lies to the south of the Soviet Union, and since the Second World War has received U S aid that is primarily justified in terms of a Soviet threat. Although this is a spurious claim, since the Soviet Union would only have invaded Iran in the event of a global conflagration in which Iran could not have resisted the Red Army, the supposed red threat served as explicit legitimation for Iranian foreign policy and military posture until the mid-1960s. Since the mid-1960s, on the other hand, the cold war has receded and Iran has improved its relations with the Soviet Union; hence, whilst Russia has supposedly remained the greatest long-term concern of the Iranian régime, the latter has been able to concentrate on more immediate concerns, and to redeploy its forces in order to deal with other, regional, foes.

Two further factors underlie Iranian foreign policy, this time of an internal character. Iran's present policy initiatives are only possible because of the consolidation of the state at home. Prior to the 1960s Iran, though never a colony, was exposed to foreign influences which, because of the domestic divisions in the country, were able to act upon different factions in Iranian politics. Although the degree of such interaction was overstated by Iranians, there is no doubt that this internal disunity did provide the occasion for external manipulations of various kinds – during the Constitutional Revolution, in the 1941–53 period, and again in the early 1960s. Moreover, the overriding concern of the state was internal, survival and repression, and there was little room for a coherent, active, foreign policy. Since the early 1960s, and especially since the crushing of the June 1963 uprising, foreign influence, especially that of the U S A, has continued; but it has been directed through the government itself, rather than through factions in a political milieu outside it. The state itself has had full political control and this has enabled it to develop an active foreign policy.

Furthermore, this process has been closely associated with the consolidation of the monarch's own rule. As two writers sympathetic to the régime put it: '... the Shah has made every foreign policy decision of any moment since the late 1950s'.[2] This is not just a matter of who takes decisions, but indicates a factor in the Shah's consolidation of his own position, since he has presented the growth of Iranian power abroad as confirmation of the legitimacy of the Iranian monarch. He has done this by drawing historical parallels with other kings who fought Iran's enemies, and he has used the growth of Iranian influence to cloak his régime in the garb of national pride. Consequently, if the domestic consolidation of the régime is in one way a precondition for Iran's current foreign policy, the latter for its part helps to confirm the domestic allocation of power and reinforce the political image which the Shah tries to foster. At this point the themes of nationalism, monarchy and military power intersect.

Finally, Iran's attempt to dominate western Asia is not taking place in a constant environment but in the context of the decomposition of the colonial system built up in the decades prior to the First World War. The most obvious feature of this is the British departure from the Arabian peninsula: this began with the independence of Kuwait in 1961, and was followed by withdrawals from South Yemen in 1967, the United Arab Emirates, Bahrain and Qatar in 1971, and Oman in 1977. Iran has, quite simply, tried to replace Britain as the dominant military power and guarantor of the existing local régimes, whilst the latter have a political independence that they did not have under the British. There is, moreover, a further side to the regional context, namely the rise in various forms of a national liberation movement. As long as the states bordering Iran and in the periphery of Iranian influence were safe in the hands of conservative régimes there was little room for Iranian interventions. What has given Iran its opening has been the overthrow of these régimes and the emergence of threats to others. The monarchies have been overthrown in Iraq in 1958, North Yemen in 1962 and Afghanistan in 1973; guerrilla forces have operated in Oman after 1965 and in Pakistan after 1973; Iran has also tried to play a role in counter-revolutionary activities elsewhere – in Ethiopia, South Vietnam and Zaire (see p. 272). In all such cases it has assumed the role of restabilizing a situation that has become unstable in the aftermath of colonialism.

One can summarize this argument by saying that from 1945 until 1963 the central concern of Iranian foreign policy was internal repression: the elimination of threats to the monarchy and the capitalist régime from inside the country. Until that time Iran had no foreign policy worth speaking of, beyond its alliance with the U S A. Domestic repression remains a major concern but it has not been an issue of sustained, immediate urgency. The new focus has therefore become one of external repression, a policy that serves the interests of the Iranian state and those of the U S A and its other capitalist allies.

Relations with the U S A

The tie with the U S A was formed during the Second World War when U S military missions were directed to Iran to set up the rudiments of a repressive apparatus. Through this aid, the Iranian state weathered the crises of 1945–6 and 1951–3, and, following the overthrow of Mossadeq, Iran became part of what is called 'The Northern Tier', the line of pro-western states along the southern borders of the Soviet Union, from Turkey through to Pakistan. In 1955 Iran joined the Baghdad Pact (later C E N T O) and this enabled the U S A to provide Iran with the arms it needed for internal repression whilst justifying these in terms of the needs of the anti-Soviet alliance; at the same time the U S A acquired an extremely convenient base area from which to menace the Soviet Union.

At the end of the 1950s the internal repression had been more or less completed, and developments in missile technology were reducing the military importance of countries like Iran. In this context, U S–Iranian relations entered upon a difficult period. On the one hand, the overthrow of the monarch in neighbouring Iraq in July 1958 alarmed the Shah and he asked the U S A for more aid. As a result a new defence treaty was signed in March 1959. On the other hand, the U S Congress had begun to investigate corruption and the misuse of U S aid in Iran, and when Kennedy came to power in January 1961 he made it clear that there had to be internal reform in Iran if the Shah's régime was to survive. This was a policy similar to that being urged in Latin America, and in the Iranian case Kennedy was especially alarmed by Soviet prognoses that the Shah's régime would soon fall.[3] The response to U S pressure was the White Revolution, launched in 1962, and although pro-U S prime minister Amini was sacked in July 1962 U S approval of the régime's internal policies was won, and was retained throughout the subsequent decade and a half (see pp. 26–7).

Iran's relations with the U S A since the early 1960s have, therefore, been close and there has been a multiple expansion in military cooperation between the two states. The closest relations of all were with the administration of Richard Nixon (1969–74) during which Iran emerged as the dominant regional power with full U S support. As a token of this alliance's importance, Nixon sent to Iran as ambassador Richard Helms, the former head of the C I A, and a fellow schoolmate of the Shah's in Switzerland.[4] Between 1971 and 1981 it is estimated that U S military sales to Iran will have reached $20 billions (see p. 95). Throughout this period, Iran's growth as a regional power has gone hand in hand with the growth of its cooperation with the U S A.

The U S A has therefore been the key external factor in Iranian foreign policy since the Second World War, but there are many changes in the way this relationship has worked. First of all, Iranian economic development has made the country much less directly dependent on the U S A in simple economic terms (U S military *aid* ended in 1969). Moreover, the nature of the U S interest has also shifted. Up to the 1960s the main interest was strategic – to prevent the emergence of a revolutionary threat in Iran. As the oil boom has developed, the U S has acquired greater economic interests in Iran: Iran is now a major importer of U S goods, for a time at least the largest importer of U S arms in the world, and a major power in O P E C. Not only does this represent a shift in the kind of interest which the U S has, but it has also accounted for clashes between Iran and the U S A. After the 1973 price rises, the latter was intent on keeping the price of oil stable, whilst Iran, needing all the oil revenues it could acquire, remained intent on expanding its revenues. In the light of these developments, it is misleading to claim that Iran is simply under some kind of colonial domination by the U S A, since this ignores the changes in the relationship and the fact that Iran has some room for manoeuvre when its interests and those of the U S A diverge. The reality of Iranian–U S relations lies somewhere in between the official rhetoric about Iran being a fully independent country, ready to stand up to the U S A if necessary, and the claims of the opposition that the Shah is some kind of 'agent' of Washington's. He is not independent in that his freedom of action is circumscribed by what the U S A allows, and he could not use his military forces in any sustained campaign without direct U S assistance. He is not an 'agent', however, (a) because he has challenged the U S A and (b) because many of his actions are explicable in terms of the interests of the Iranian state, as much as in the interests of the U S state. The alliance is an unequal one, but one of converging interests, that has changed over the past three decades, and will no doubt do so again in the future.

A central specific aspect of this relationship is policy towards the Shah. He knows that the U S A supports him not out of any special loyalty to the Pahlavi monarchy but because he appears best able to safeguard U S interests, in the broadest sense. He has no doubt studied the fate of South Vietnamese dictator Ngo Dinh Diem and Cuban dictator Fulgencio Batista, and knows that, if the U S government favours another candidate, he could be abandoned as they were. He has on a number of occasions stressed the unreliability of U S aid, and has laid especial stress on the dangers involved in relying on U S support during a war: U S failure to aid Pakistan in the 1965 war with India (despite Pakistan's membership of C E N T O), and Israeli dependence on U S re-supplying in the 1973 Arab–Israeli war have both led to reassessments in Tehran. There is not much he could do in such circumstances, but such events do underline his crucial dependence on Iran's major patron.

A further complication is that there are significant divisions within the overall policy of U S imperialism towards Iran. The U S Congress has on occasion criticized the U S military programme in Iran (1959, 1976) and there has also been conflict between the C I A and the State Department (e.g. over C I A aid to the Kurds) and between the State Department and the Department of Defence (as over the Ibex espionage system – see p. 101). Furthermore, there have been conflicts between the U S state, as a whole, and U S business interests. The former has a more long-term view of the problems and policies in Iran; the latter operate on a much more partial and short-term basis. It is therefore a simplification to talk about 'U S policy in Iran' as if this represented a single approach. There is of course an overall coherence in U S policy towards Iran, but the variety within it needs to be kept in mind in order to explain some of the conflicts and shifts that are observable.

The Shah for his part tries to play up his disagreements with the U S A in order to pose as an independent ruler. He uses his stand on oil prices and on arms sales, and even, preposterously, his rejection of accusations of torture, to harp on nationalist themes. Much of this is, and always has been, of limited significance, since the Shah knows that without the cooperation of the U S state and U S capital his régime would not be viable. For without the guarantees given by the U S A to the Iranian state the present foreign and domestic policies would be impossible, and the areas for conflict that do exist are limited by the character of these guarantees.

The Advanced Capitalist Countries: Trade and Investment

In the first half of this century, inter-imperialist rivalries played an important role in Iranian politics, with Britain, Tsarist Russia, Germany and later the U S A trying to increase their influence at the expense of others. Since the emergence of the U S A as the undisputed leader of world capitalism, and since the consolidation of the Iranian state itself, rivalries of *this* kind have ceased to occur; but, whilst the U S A has played the leading political and military role in Iran since the early 1950s, Iran's integration into the international system of capitalist relations has enabled it to form a much more diverse pattern of economic ties.

Prior to the establishment of U S dominance, Britain was the strongest power in Iran, and because of historic links, and because of the continued British presence in the Gulf, a degree of political and military cooperation continued. Britain has supplied some of the Iranian army's main military equipment (tanks, hovercraft) and small British training teams have worked with the Iranian navy and army. As part of the secret military cooperation covered by C E N T O, planes of the British Royal Air Force have also used airfields in northern Iran for espionage flights over the Caspian Sea, where the Soviet Union has missile practice ranges.[5]

The greatest diversity has been in the economic rather than in the political or military spheres, and it is here that inter-capitalist rivalries remain strong. In oil production, the dominant countries have, since 1954, been Britain and the U S A; whilst companies from other nations have been granted concessions (French, Italian, German, Japanese), output by these firms has remained very low – only 4 per cent of total output in the mid-1970s. In investment outside oil, U S firms have also been strong: between 1956 and 1974, 43 of the 183 foreign firms investing in Iran were U S, the largest from any single country, and they accounted for a third of all the capital invested. At the end of 1972 the U S A had assets valued at $570 millions in Iran – a large amount, but less than it had in Israel ($600 millions), Libya ($1,145 millions) or Saudi Arabia

($2,000 millions).[6] But other countries also have a strong presence – the Japanese in petrochemicals, the British and the Germans in automobile production, and the Germans in cement and steel.

The greatest diversity is in trade, and here West Germany has contested the leading position with the U S A. There has been a long history of cooperation between Iran and Germany, since Berlin and now Bonn have been regarded as a counter to London, Moscow and Washington. Reza Khan developed economic links with the Nazis, and it was more than accident that Mossadeq hired Hitler's former adviser Dr Schacht to run his economic policy. The largest Iranian community in western Europe is to be found in West Germany. In 1970–71 West Germany accounted for 20·75 per cent of Iran's non-military imports, compared with 13 per cent from the U S A; but following the oil boom the U S A overtook West Germany and in 1975 the U S A accounted for 21·6 per cent of Iran's imports ($486 millions) whilst West Germany's share fell to 18 per cent ($404 millions). However, following a visit to Tehran by Chancellor Brandt in 1972, a long-term plan for economic cooperation between the two countries was worked out and this guarantees a continued and major West German role in Iran's development. West Germany will get Iranian oil and gas, whilst West German firms, appreciative of Iran's putative stability, know that they can obtain a good return on their investment. For its part, Iran needs the technology and training which German firms can offer, and in 1974 Iran purchased a 25·04 per cent share in the West German steel firm of Krupp. While this endowed the German firm with needed funds, it provided a basis for German aid in expanding steel production in Iran itself.

The picture is therefore one of a shift in the character of Iran's relation to the major capitalist powers. Prior to the 1960s the economic interests of the imperialist countries, apart from oil, were comparatively small, whilst the political and strategic interest was high. With the domination of the U S A and a stabilized Iranian state there is now little room for the older kind of political and strategic rivalry. Where there is conflict it is in trade and investment; and disputes could arise over arms sales if Iran tried to turn to France or Britain after a dispute with the U S A. In these fields, given Iran's increased economic importance the stakes are now much higher than they ever were. Competition is consequently more restricted, but at the same time and in its own way as intense.

The Soviet Union: Caution and Coexistence

Iranian official statements frequently claim or imply that the Soviet Union poses a threat to Iran; the justification of Iran's arms purchases is usually phrased by reference to past Soviet threats to Iran, and by the possibility of such threats in the future. This argument is often taken to its limits: for example, an Iranian official whom I interviewed at the Embassy in Washington in 1976 began his defence of Iran's current arms purchases on the grounds that 'in the early nineteenth century the Russians conquered twenty-eight cities and three provinces of ours in the Caucasus'.

This is not the place to present an overall account of Soviet foreign policy, nor is it my intention to defend the Soviet Union's foreign policy as a whole. Russia has behaved in a brutal and repressive manner in Eastern Europe (as, for example, in the invasion of Czechoslovakia) and has since the 1920s treated foreign communist parties as instruments of its own foreign policy. But whilst there are many aspects of Soviet foreign policy that are indefensible, there is little basis for alleging that the Soviet Union is either an expansionist or an aggressive power. Indeed all the indications are that the Soviet Union is a rather cautious state; its last offensive action, in a situation where it itself had not first been attacked, was in the summer of 1920 when the Red Army advanced on Warsaw. In some more recent situations Russia has been able to consolidate its position in third-world countries, but this has been where the course of the local class struggle has already paved the way (Vietnam, Cuba, Angola).[7]

The record of Soviet relations with Iran follows this pattern, and it is a weakness of most discussion of Russian policy in

Iran that this policy towards one country is abstracted from the global orientation from which this specific policy derives. However, far from indicating aggression, Russian policy towards Iran highlights what, from a socialist perspective, is probably the most significant criticism of the Soviet Union's foreign policy, namely its extreme timidity, and the subordination of local communists to this overall line. Indeed, rather than asking how Iran has tried to resist a largely imagined Soviet threat, one can ask an alternative question: how has the Soviet Union helped the Iranian revolutionary movement? The answer to this helps to indicate the underlying character, and weaknesses, of Soviet policy in Iran.

On three occasions since 1917 the Soviet Union has had the opportunity to play an active and interventionist role on behalf of the revolutionary forces in Iran. The first was immediately after the First World War, when a coalition of Iranian communists and nationalist guerrillas in the northern province of Gilan was able to form a socialist republic. The Bolsheviks at first supported this movement, and in 1920 some Bolshevik troops landed in Gilan, partly in pursuit of White Russian forces and partly to bolster the Gilanis. But in March 1921, after Reza Khan had seized power, the Soviet Union exchanged diplomatic relations with Tehran. Some months later Russian forces left and the Gilan Republic, the first revolutionary state in the Middle East, was then crushed.[8]

The second opportunity came in 1944–7, when northern Iran was occupied by Russian troops and U S and British forces were present in the rest of the country. A mass movement, led by the Tudeh Party, had emerged after the removal of Reza Khan in 1941. Even some U S reports of the time agree that the communists enjoyed widespread popularity and could have won in an election.[9] In such a situation Soviet aid to the communists would not have been, as it undoubtedly was in certain Eastern European countries at that time, a case of the Russians forcing a small pro-Moscow party into the government. Yet, with all these advantages, and despite initial Soviet support for the antonomous republics in Azerbaijan and Kurdistan, Russian policy was extremely cautious and in the first half of 1946 Soviet troops withdrew from Iran under pressure from Washington. Within nine months the two regional republics had been crushed, and the mass movement led by the Tudeh Party had been forced onto the defensive.

The third opportunity came in the Mossadeq period. Here again a real opportunity presented itself, but was thrown away. Because Mossadeq was not a communist, and was hostile to communism, the Tudeh Party at first refused to support him; it only altered its approach in the latter part of 1952, by which time the initiative had slipped from Mossadeq's grasp. The communists were unable to resist the tide of counter-revolution in 1953, and like most of Mossadeq's own supporters the Tudeh put up no serious resistance when the coup came. This initially sectarian policy was itself a reflection of Soviet policy; for, had the Soviet Union supported Mossadeq from the start with military and economic aid, and had the Tudeh rallied all its forces in Iran behind Mossadeq from the beginning, a different outcome might well have eventuated.

A number of factors account for this record, and it is these that continue to shape Soviet policy in Iran. In the first place, Soviet policy in Iran is dictated primarily by global considerations: in 1921 and again in 1945 the Soviet Union was trying to guarantee international peace, and was not prepared to take initiatives in Iran that would have contradicted this policy. Stalin's retreat in Iran resulted from a more general attempt to reach an accommodation with the West – part of the same policy that led him to abandon the guerrillas in Greece, and to discourage communist parties in France and Italy, China and Vietnam. An additional factor that is often misinterpreted is geographic – the fact that Iran is on the borders of the Soviet Union; far from this acting as an advantage for the Russians, or Iranian revolutionaries, it has turned out to be a disadvantage. Any action by local groups can immediately be presented by the régime as part of a Soviet threat, and rapid suppression is therefore all the more justified in anti-communist terms. This simple conflation of strategic and local conditions has operated against Iranian revolutionaries ever since the days of the Gilan Republic.

On top of these considerations, there is also the fact that the Soviet Union has often acted in a manner calculated to antagonize Iranian nationalist feeling, and to confirm the régime's claim that Russian policy, Tsarist and Bolshevik, is a continuum. A flagrant case of this was at the end of the Second World War when for no justified reason the Soviet Union demanded an oil concession in the north and forced the Tudeh Party into backing this demand. The reaction to this in Iran was, obviously, to arouse anti-Russian and anti-communist feeling. Equally damaging has been the manner in which the Soviet Union has manipulated Tudeh's policies on more general issues – forcing it into an ultra-left policy as in the first years of Mossadeq's rule, and abandoning it after initial encouragement, as in 1921 and again in 1946. The enforcement of such loyalty to the Soviet Union has therefore continually damaged the Tudeh Party and undermined the credibility of any communist opposition; and, whereas such an orientation is always damaging to communists, even in countries as far from Russia as Portugal, it is especially so in a country that borders the Soviet Union and where internal and strategic issues are so closely interwoven.

Since 1953 Soviet relations with Iran have been relatively tranquil, with the exception of the years 1959–62. In that period the Soviet Union was extremely critical of Iran's military links with the U S A, and of the 1959 treaty between Washington and Tehran. It appears that the Russians expected the Shah to be overthrown and were also concerned lest this should provoke a crisis in U S–Soviet relations.[10] But in September 1962, as the Cuba missile crisis was building up, the Shah gave the Soviet Union an undertaking that Iran would not allow the U S A to station missiles on its soil, and a year later Brezhnev was in Tehran to confirm the new understanding between the two countries.

The main focus of Soviet–Iranian relations since then has been economic. In 1967 Iran bought $110 millions worth of 'non-sensitive' Soviet military equipment, and this was followed by a $280 millions economic treaty. Fifteen hundred Russian experts came to Iran to participate in joint projects, the most important being the Isfahan steel mill, and the gas pipeline to the Soviet Union. The Soviet Union then became a major trading partner, accounting for 15 per cent of Iran's exports in 1973. In 1976 a five-year trade agreement was signed, worth $3,000 millions. Under it Iran will export gas, textiles, shoes, cotton, mineral ores and dried fruit to the Soviet Union, whilst the Soviet Union will export machinery, iron, steel, chemicals, wood, cement and trucks to Iran. The gas link with the Soviet Union is significant in that it could, in the 1980s, be extended to western Europe and thereby give Iran access to West German and other markets in a manner much cheaper than the alternative means, liquefaction and transport by tanker (see p. 146). But the cost of this will be that the Soviet Union acquires a potentially lethal grip on Iran's export earnings. On the other hand, the Soviet Union itself provides a market for the manufactured goods that continue to make up a part of Iran's non-oil exports. In its belated attempt to expand this sector, Iran is finding that the non-competitive markets of the communist world are more accessible to it than those of the capitalist countries, with the result that Iran may be forced to link its economic future more closely to its cooperation with the country that is supposed to be its greatest foe.

Real issues of disagreement do, however, remain. Whilst relations with the U S A are no longer so much at issue, given the end of the cold war, Iranian and Russian statements occasionally attack each other's policies; in Dhofar, the Soviet Union armed a guerrilla force that was directly engaged with the Iranian army, and the Soviet Union continues to support Iran's other major potential rival, Iraq. In 1975, in a move generally held to be a veiled criticism of the Russians, Iran broke off diplomatic relations with Cuba, after Fidel Castro had held a meeting in Moscow with the Tudeh Party's secretary-general. There is, therefore, considerable room for conflict between Iran and the Soviet Union in the future, as long as Iran sees itself as playing a regional counter-revolutionary role. But both states are likely to maintain economic ties, independently of these other disagreements.

A major crisis in Iranian–Soviet relations is likely in only two situations: either in the event of a major U S–Soviet clash in which, as in previous international conflicts, Iran finds itself inevitably involved; or in the event of the two assisting different sides in a third country where there exists a strong revolutionary movement that Russia supports. Direct intervention by the Soviet Union in Iran, politically or militarily, in the absence of a wider international conflict, is much less likely.

The People's Republic of China

China's policy towards Iran is, like that of the Soviet Union, very much a derivative of its overall international approach, but given the distance between the two countries, and China's limited economic potential, relations between the two are, for both sides, much less significant. Iran, like other pro-western states, refused to recognize the People's Republic after the triumph of the Chinese Revolution in 1949 and diplomatic relations were established only in 1971. Since then, however, relations between the two states have flourished and China has gone to great lengths to praise the Shah's policies.

China supports Iran, in the first place, because of Iran's hostility to the Soviet Union, and this has led Peking explicitly to endorse Iran's economic and military policies. This has involved compliance with Iran's counter-revolutionary role. In 1972, for example, when Iran sent Phantom jets to South Vietnam at the height of the Vietnamese war, the Chinese press criticized other states that had done this (South Korea, Taiwan) but refrained from criticizing Iran.[11] China also altered its position on the guerrilla movement in Dhofar: whereas between 1968 and 1971 China helped the Omani guerrillas and publicized their struggle, this aid ceased after the establishment of relations between Tehran and Peking, and China then began to condemn what it called 'Soviet-backed subversion' in the Gulf.

Chinese statements on Iran follow conventional lines. Great play is made of the historic ties between the two countries (the ancient caravan route 'Silk Road'), and of the greatness of the two Asian civilizations. But the central themes are those expressed by Chi Peng-fei, the then Chinese Foreign Minister, during his visit to Tehran in May 1973. His arguments have been repeated many times in subsequent editorials and speeches:

Everyone's attention is now drawn to the situation in the Persian Gulf. Intensified expansionist activity, unwarranted use of influence and the struggle of some of the big powers have severely jeopardized the peace and security in this region. Iran is one of the important littoral states of the Persian Gulf. Your concern over the situation is natural and logical. We have consistently held that the affairs of one country must be managed by that country ... Iran and a number of other littoral states of the Persian Gulf believe that Persian Gulf affairs should be managed by the littoral states. They oppose outside interference. This is an equitable demand. We strongly support this. As the Shahanshah has said, the situation on the eastern and western sides of Iran is a very serious warning to Iran. Bearing in mind the situation created in this region, this country must strengthen its defence forces.[12]

Statements like this, and similar ones praising the Shah's economic policies, present, of course, only a small part of the truth. The Chinese omit to point out that the Shah's military power is being strengthened with the aid and encouragement of one of the two major powers in question, the U S A, or that it is being used to crush national liberation movements in the area. Chinese press reports pass over in silence any resistance to the Shah inside Iran, and exceed in vacuity and collusion anything that the Russians have ever said about Iran.

What the Iranian and Chinese governments are saying about each other in the 1970s is, needless to say, in total and almost comic contrast to what each was saying about the other in the two decades previously. In his autobiography, published in 1961, the Shah expressed the hope that the Russians would in time ally with Iran to curb what he called 'the new sprawling, fast-breeding Giant of the Far East, lying at its back door'.[13] As we have seen, the Shah refused, for twenty-two years, to recognize People's China. The Chinese, for their part, adopted an equally pugnacious view of the Shah. China was, for example, quick to denounce the 1953 coup. An official statement declared that 'A government totally subservient to the American ruling clique has been formed' and added: 'The U S A is utilizing the Royalists of Iran to realize its goal. The Royalists have become ardent American running-dogs.' The 19 August coup was, it added, 'instigated by American special agents'.[14]

In the early 1960s, the Tudeh Party was divided by the Sino-Soviet dispute (see p. 231) and the Chinese at that time attacked the Russians, not for menacing Iran, but for the opposite, their cooperation with the Shah. A statement issued in Peking in 1966, on what was termed 'the puppet Shah régime', provided the following analysis of events in Iran: 'The Iranian régime is using every means – threats, intimidation, imprisonment, tortures and death sentence – to suppress the workers, peasants and revolutionary intellectuals, and bans all organizations ... The régime in Iran is one which is meekly subservient to the U S imperialists, even though it talks about reforms and the preservation of national independence and though the splittists [i.e. the Russians] have close relations with the Iranian reactionary régime and carry out propaganda favourable to the régime.' The statement concluded by expressing the belief that 'the toiling people of Iran, who are subjected to colonial domination, will certainly destroy in good speed the reactionary régime and win victory in their struggle.'[15]

Then, six years later, the 'sprawling, fast-breeding Giant of the Far East' and the 'puppet Shah régime' had buried their differences; the Iranians were now allying with the Chinese against the Russians whilst the Chinese, quick to score points against the Soviet 'splittists', were now outdoing Moscow in heaping praise upon the Shah. In May 1975 the Shah's sister Princess Ashraf, who had personally helped the C I A to organize the 1953 coup, was received by Mao Tse-tung. Yet the Shah was still suppressing his people, as he had been a decade before, torture and intimidation continued and Iran was still, as much as it ever had been, 'meekly subservient to the U S imperialists'.

Both régimes look rather foolish in the way they have gone from abuse to flattery, but there is an underlying continuity beneath these zigzags in policy. For Iran it is hostility to the Soviet Union. The Shah's autobiography contains an attack on what he calls 'the new imperialism' of the Soviet Union and when the Chinese began to denounce 'Soviet social-imperialism' in the late 1960s the underlying congruence of the two states' strategic thinking became clearer. Once Iran agreed to recognize Peking, China was able to switch its characterization of the Shah's régime accordingly. But there is a further continuity, evident on the Chinese side. Both the statements of 1966 and those of the 1970s are extremely superficial; in neither case is any serious attempt made to grasp the class character of the Iranian state, or to evaluate in any precise way how Iran relates to the U S A. In both places, generality, itself directed by current diplomatic concerns, is the norm. In 1966 the Shah's reforms were *not*, as Peking claimed, merely talk, and Iran was not under 'colonial domination' in any serious sense of the term, any more than it was in 1976. On the other hand the Shah was not independent of imperialism in the 1970s any more than he was a decade before. In this way, the clichés of both phases reflected an underlying Chinese ignorance, and disinterest, and for this reason they were all the more replaceable by those of another. 'Puppets' and 'running-dogs' gave way to 'just struggles' in defence of the Iranian people's interest. But in neither case was Peking able to produce an analysis of Iran that went beyond banalities or to present a picture of development that took account of the class forces involved.

Regional Policy

The central concern of Iranian foreign policy has, since the mid-1960s, been the situation in western Asia – in the Gulf to the south, in the Arab countries to the west, and in Afghanistan, Pakistan and the Indian Ocean to the east and south-east. Iran justifies its policies on the grounds, first, that it has its own national security interests to protect, and secondly that it alone can assume responsibility for maintaining the stability of the existing states. It points to such issues as the security of tankers exporting oil through the Gulf, revolutionary movements in

Arab states, and instability in the South Asian continent as reasons why Iran must be a strong military force in the area.

Official Iranian View of Threats

	'High Intensity' Threats	*'Low Intensity' Threats*
Present	U S S R Iraq	Oman Separatism Terrorism
Future	U S S R Iraq India	Arab Gulf Separatism Terrorism

Source: *U S Military Sales to Iran, Staff Report to the Subcommittee on Foreign Assistance of the Committee on Foreign Relations, United States Senate*, July 1976, p. 8.

However, this presentation of Iran's policy begs a number of questions. It is also a reflection of conditions inside Iran – of the pressure of the army for more weapons, and the desire of the Shah's to mobilize nationalist feelings. Above all else, there is the knowledge that a successful revolutionary movement in any of the neighbouring states would have unsettling repercussions on the position of the Pahlavi régime: the alarmed response of the Shah to the nationalist military régimes in Iraq and to Nasserism during the 1960s, none of which ever posed a major threat, is indicative in this respect. The Shah knows too that any concessions won by the suppressed nationalities in neighbouring countries (Iraq, Pakistan) will only be liable to encourage similar movements inside Iran.

There are certainly real issues of security that any Iranian régime would have to take account of: the freedom of navigation for oil tankers is one such obvious case. But these irreducible security interests are not in themselves sufficient to explain the dynamics of Iran's present foreign policy. The latter is a combination of legitimate security concerns with a further, aggressive, component that results from the character of the régime. The question therefore poses itself of what the nature of this further component is.

The simplest epithet to apply to Iran is to say that it is an 'expansionist' power: some Arab politicians characterize it in this way, and draw a parallel between the actions of Iran, in the east, and Israel, in the west. But while it is certainly true that Iran is 'expansionist' in some vague sense, the real question is to determine *in what way* Iran is and is not expansionist. There are at least three senses in which the term is not an apposite one. In the first place, Iran is not now intent on annexing any part of its neighbours' territory. The last border disputes (with Iraq and Afghanistan) have been settled; in 1970 the Shah abandoned Iran's claim to Bahrain, and in 1971 the Iranians seized three disputed islands in the Gulf, the last outstanding claim. This may seem an obvious point, but it is important, if only to counter the more exaggerated notions current in the Middle East that the Shah is trying to 'recreate the Persian Empire'. There is a need to draw a distinction, which the régime in Iran itself does not always draw, between the manner in which Iran will achieve influence in the latter part of the twentieth century and that in which it did so in previous ages – either in the eighteenth century, or in the fifth century B.C. The latter involved territorial aggrandisement of some kind, but the boundaries of formal Iranian power in this century have apparently been more or less definitely fixed. Secondly, there is no reason to believe that Iran is interested in expanding its influence through the establishment of Iranian communities outside its boundaries. There are up to a million Iranians, or people of Iranian descent, in the Arab countries of the Gulf; but these are not, and could not be, instruments of Iranian foreign policy. They are in no sense colonizers, in the way Jewish settlers in Palestine were. They are people who have migrated, not at the behest of their government, but in response to market forces, seeking employment and trading opportunities. In the event of a military clash between Iran and the Arab states in which these communities live it would be an invading Iranian army, not the local Iranian merchants and workers, who would act as instruments of Tehran's policy. Under peacetime conditions, Iran's policies are effected through influencing the rulers of these states, who are *Arabs*, rather than through directing the Iranian communities.

Thirdly, whilst Iran has shown itself to be capable of aggression, and while it is certainly determined to achieve military superiority in the Gulf, it is misleading to assume that for these reasons alone Iran will try to take over some of the neighbouring territories, once its power is assured. To take an obvious analogy: Iran has not been arming itself in the 1970s, as Germany and Japan did in the 1930s, in deliberate preparation for an offensive against its neighbours. Iran will become militarily involved with states in the region, but only as a consequence of certain developments in those countries or after other unsettling developments in Iran: in the meantime it will try to ensure domination through political, rather than in the first place military, power. For those three reasons, the simple model of 'expansionism' is a misleading one.

On the other hand, there are several factors that do encourage Iran to intervene in other countries, and which may well become stronger in the future. In the first place, the glory won by foreign military actions helps to bolster the régime's image, and the position of the army in Iranian society. The Shah's many references to the 'heroic' actions of the Iranian army in Dhofar are indicative of this. In the future the Shah or a military régime that takes his place may be tempted to strengthen their hand domestically by exploiting an opportunity to launch a war abroad. This possibility is increased by the role of the military and of militarism inside Iran, and by the country's overwhelming superiority in the region. Secondly, Iran's economic interests may impel it to dominate other countries, and in extreme cases to seize the assets of neighbouring states. Iran is already investing in Pakistan and India to ensure supplies of materials needed by the Iranian economy. From the mid-1980s onwards, as Iran's oil output falls, the temptation will be strong for Iran to make up for the fall in its domestic output by using its armed forces to seize the wells of neighbouring states, which still have considerable reserves and an income in excess of their requirements: Kuwait, Qatar and Saudi Arabia all fall into this category. Economic pressures of this kind have, of course, accounted for much of the aggressive policies of other states in the twentieth century. They account, for example, for Japan's expansionist policies in the Far East. Whilst international conditions – i.e. the end of formal colonialism – now make such a policy less likely, there is no doubt that Iran's interests, as a capitalist country bent on rapid growth, will encourage it to intervene outside its boundaries in order to compensate for economic shortcomings at home.

The most important factor is, however, directly political, in that the Iranian régime is concerned to prevent any movement or state from emerging in the region which could weaken Iran's own strategic position. This means, simply, that Iran will intervene to crush any nationalist or revolutionary forces outside its boundaries which it regards as a threat to it, and which it believes it has a reasonable chance of suppressing. The Shah has on more than one occasion declared that he will not tolerate 'subversion', i.e. any democratic or nationalist movement, in the region, and the record of his foreign policy since the mid-1960s bears this out.

This outlook provides the basis for an extremely ambitious policy of intervention, one that has already provided legitimization for a number of aggressive actions, and which could do so again in the future. Iranian military activity abroad since the mid-1960s has been widespread, and has taken two main forms: direct intervention by Iranian military forces, and indirect intervention, via the provision of aid – bases, weapons, equipment, training – to forces which Iran supports. The most prominent instances are the following:

1. *North Yemen*: during the civil war between Yemeni royalists and the republicans (1962–70) Iran intervened to support the royalists. Whilst most of the latter's aid came from Saudi Arabia, with additional help from Britain and Israel, Iran also provided arms to the royalists and trained an unknown number in Iran itself. The Shah, like the Saudis, saw this as a means of countering the influence of Nasser, whose troops were aiding the republic.

2. *United Arab Emirates*: in November 1971, a day before Britain handed over sovereignty to the seven Emirates of the

U A E, Iranian forces seized three islands in the Gulf: one, Abu Musa, belonged to the Emirate of Sharjah, whose ruler had agreed to allow Iran to take it over, whilst the other two belonged to the ruler of Ras al-Khaima, who opposed the Iranian action. Some Arab soldiers were killed in the action, and the small Arab population of the islands was later driven off.

3. *Oman*: Iran began to help the Sultan of Oman in 1971, in his campaign against the guerrillas of the Popular Front fighting in the southern, Dhofar, province of the Sultanate. In 1972 Iranian naval detachments were stationed on the Omani island of Umm al-Ghanem, to guard the entrance to the Gulf, while some helicopter gunships were sent to Dhofar. From December 1973 until the end of 1976, several thousand Iranian troops were deployed in Dhofar against the guerrillas, and were only withdrawn after the main forces had been defeated. No overall casualty figures have been given, but officially announced military losses in 1975–6 came to 25 officers and 186 other ranks killed; presumably most of these died in Dhofar. This was the largest military operation in which Iranian forces were involved, and the Iranian role in Oman continued, despite the virtual end of fighting. Iran undertook responsibility for air and sea patrolling of Oman's frontiers, and it retained units in some Omani bases – in the air base of Thamrit, in Dhofar, less than 100 miles from the South Yemeni border, and in naval positions on the Omani side of the Straits of Hormuz. Given the short distance between the two countries, and given the fact that base facilities are already present, Iran could deploy its forces in Oman again at a few hours' notice.

4. *Pakistan*: after the Indo-Pakistani war of 1971 Iran made it clear that it was opposed to any further weakening of Pakistan, from without or within. In 1973, when guerrillas in the Pakistani province of Baluchistan, which borders Iran, started operating on a considerable scale against the Pakistani army, Iran sent around thirty Chinook helicopter gunships to assist the Pakistani armed forces. The guerrillas, of the Baluchi People's Liberation Front, report that three of these were shot

down in 1973–4. Iran has also provided economic aid in support of the Pakistani army's military campaign and civil action programme in the province.

5. *Iraq*: between 1972 and 1975 Iran helped the Kurdish forces led by Mostafa Barzani in northern Iraq to conduct a war against the Baghdad government. Iran sent arms across its common border with the Kurdish areas of Iraq, and up to 1,000 Iranian troops operated inside Iraqi Kurdistan, manning anti-aircraft guns.[16] Iranian artillery positions inside Iran were at the same time used to fire on Iraqi planes. SAVAK also played a role in this campaign: it was responsible for ferrying foreign journalists to and from the Iraqi border, and inside Kurdistan it operated its own secret police force, the *Parastin*, a unit responsible only to itself and to Barzani. This aid was abruptly terminated in March 1975, when the Iranian and Iraqi governments reached an agreement on the issues in dispute between them.

In addition to these five direct interventions, Iran has played a role in a number of other conflicts over the past decade, by sending arms or financial aid to forces it supported. In 1972 it sent Phantom jets to help President Thieu in South Vietnam. Earlier, prior to the first ceasefire between the Iraqi government and the Kurds in 1970, it had supplied the Kurds with Russian equipment sold off by Israel, after the Israelis had themselves captured it from Egypt in the 1967 Arab-Israeli war. Iran has also supplied planes to Morocco, Jordan, and Oman and in the spring of 1977 it sent aid of an unspecified kind to the government of General Mobutu in Zaire, when the latter was facing an uprising in Shaba province.[17] In the second part of the year it began to send arms to Somalia to aid it in its dispute with Ethiopia, following substantial Soviet aid to the latter.

No third-world state has a record of intervention outside its frontiers comparable with Iran's in the period since the mid-1960s. South Korea, Indonesia, Zaire, Israel, Brazil and Saudi Arabia have all intervened, directly or indirectly, in support of counter-revolutionary forces beyond their frontiers, but none have done so on the scale of Iran, and on closer examination Tehran's policy can be seen to go far beyond the mere defence of Iran's security interests, as these can legitimately be presented. In the case of the three Gulf islands, the historic and military justifications were of a flimsy kind: in particular, Iran had no need to control them, given its overall dominance of the waters of the Gulf. The real reason appears to have been political – a desire to boost the Shah's image at home, and to compensate for the apparent weakness of surrendering the claim to Bahrain. In the words of one British official: 'Advisors to the Iranian government told us that the Shah did not want the islands for military or strategic reasons, despite his statement and much official propaganda to that effect. Rather, he needed to take them in order to enhance his image as a forceful and decisive monarch.'[18]

In Oman too, the Shah's motivation was more than defensive. The Shah claimed that he had sent troops to Oman at the 'invitation' of the Sultan; but even if one accepts the contentious point that the Sultan was in any sense a legitimate ruler, given his reliance on foreign (British) support, it is doubtful if the Shah would have refrained from going in without an invitation, since on several occasions he made it clear that he would not, under any circumstances, permit a revolutionary nationalist movement to gain power in Oman. Moreover, the Shah had two further reasons for the Omani engagement. One was to train as many troops as possible in realistic combat conditions: troops were rotated every four months in order to spread combat experience over as wide a number of soldiers as possible. The other reason for the Omani action was the desire to menace the most radical state in the region, South Yemen, a state which supported the guerillas in Dhofar and had a common boundary with it. Once Iranian jets were established at Thamrit, and Iran had formally taken over responsibility for Omani air space, the Iranian air force began to overfly South Yemeni territory. The Iranians made no secret of their activities, and for a long time the South Yemenis let them continue. Then, in November 1976 South Yemen shot down an Iranian Phantom over its territory; this coincided with a meeting of Gulf foreign ministers in Muscat, at which

Iran was trying to persuade the Gulf states to enter a new alliance, the Gulf Security Pact. Iranian embarrassment was considerable, and Tehran, which had but a few weeks before been happy to admit to its activities on the South Yemen–Oman border, now claimed that the plane had been on a training mission.[19] Such was the hostile reaction of Arab states to the Iranian position, however, that Iran was unable to use this incident to launch an attack on South Yemen, and the Gulf Security Pact was, for the time being, shelved.

The clearest case of Iranian aggression has been towards its neighbour Iraq, were since 1958 there have been a number of military régimes espousing one or other form of radical nationalism. Iran has had a number of specific disputes with Iraq – over borders, and over some small Iraqi support for some Iranian dissidents. Prior to the 1975 agreement, the Baghdad government provoked Tehran by expelling tens of thousands of Iranians resident in Iraq, in a brutal and unjustified manner. But a more important reason for Iranian hostility has been Iraq's ties with the Soviet Union, and Iraqi propaganda in favour of underground political groups in the Arabian peninsula. The two states also disputed shipping rights on the Shatt al-Arab river. Iran has used the supposed threat of Iraq as a reason for an Iranian military build-up, even though Iran has in fact long had considerable military superiority over its neighbour.[20]

The full history of Iranian involvement in Iraq is unknown. In July 1969 Iran was implicated in an unsuccessful coup attempt against the ruling Ba'ath régime, and in 1971 the head of the Iraqi intelligence forces, Nazim Kazzar, was captured while fleeing towards the Iranian frontier, after another failed coup. It is possible, though not definite, that Kazzar also had links with Iran. Iran's most direct form of pressure on Baghdad has, however, been through the Kurds. Iran gave a small amount of arms to the Kurds in the 1960s, and after a ceasefire between the government and the rebels in 1970, Iran began two years later to encourage the Kurds to restart the war, as a means of pressuring Iraq.

Details of this episode were made known in 1976 through the

revelations of the U S House of Representatives Select Committee on Intelligence. This report makes clear that, while the Kurds had their own reasons for wanting to fight, the Iranians had been manipulating the Kurds: 'The C I A had early information which suggested that our ally would abandon the ethnic group the minute he came to an agreement with his enemy over border disputes.' Two months after initiating the project a C I A memo of 17 October 1972 states: 'Our ally has apparently used another government's Foreign Minister to pass the word to his enemy that he would be willing to allow peace to prevail in the area if his enemy would publicly agree to abrogate a previous treaty concerning their respective borders.'[21] It also emerges from the report that had the Shah not misled the Kurds as he did, it might have been possible for them to have reached a more advantageous agreement with the Baghdad government: 'It appears that, had the U S not reinforced our ally's prodding, the insurgents may have reached an accommodation with the central government, thus gaining at least a measure of autonomy while avoiding further bloodshed. Instead, our clients fought on, sustaining thousands of casualties and 200,000 refugees.' On the other hand, the U S and Iran prevented the Kurds from launching an all-out offensive, when they were in a position to do so: '. . . the apparent "no win" policy of the U S and its ally deeply disturbed this Committee. Documents in the Committee's possession clearly show that the President, Dr Kissinger and the foreign head of state hoped that our clients would not prevail. They preferred instead that the insurgents simply continue a level of hostilities sufficient to sap the resources of our ally's neighbouring country. This policy was not imparted to our clients, who were encouraged to continue fighting.' A C I A memo of 22 March 1974 emphasized: 'We would think that our ally would not look with favour on the establishment of a formalized autonomous government. Our ally like ourselves has seen benefit in a stalemate situation . . . Neither our ally nor ourselves wish to see the matter resolved one way or the other.'

In 1975, after three years of covert action in Iraq, the Shah was able to reach agreement with the Baghdad government.

The border dispute was settled. The Iraqis also undertook not to give any more support to Iranian dissidents in Iraq: their access to radio facilities was terminated and those in Baghdad had to flee the country, or take refuge in friendly embassies. Iraq soon afterwards exchanged diplomatic relations with Oman, another issue in dispute. Iranian aid to the Kurds ended immediately. On the other hand, on 5 March, a representative of SAVAK visited the Kurds' headquarters and in the words of a CIA telegram, 'told them in bluntest terms that (a) the border was being closed to all repeat all movement, (b) ... could expect no more assistance from our ally, (c) ... should settle with our ally's enemy on whatever terms he could get, and (d) his military units would be allowed to take refuge in our ally's country only in small groups and only if they surrendered their arms to our ally's army.'

Certain aspects of the March 1975 agreement were reasonable, particularly that concerning the Shatt al-Arab river in the south: prior to the agreement Iraq had had a predominant position on the river (under a previous treaty with Iran) and the new agreement divided the river in a more equitable manner. Protests by Arab nationalists about *this* aspect of the agreement were therefore unjustified. But the agreement did result in a terrible tragedy for the Kurds, who had been manoeuvred by the Shah into a situation where they had become totally dependent on him and where he could abandon them at will. The picture of Iranian foreign policy that emerges from this episode, as with that illustrated by military operations against the UAE and in Oman, is that of a country prepared to commit aggression and engage in duplicity on a massive scale in order to achieve its ends. The Kurdish episode shows that such manipulations are an integral part of Iranian foreign policy, as they are of some other states, and there is no reason to believe that as its military power increases Iran will refrain from acting in a similar manner agan, if the occasion arises.

Not surprisingly the scope of Iranian activities has continued to widen as its strength has grown. After the military overthrow of the monarchy in Afghanistan in 1973 Iran played an active role there, supporting a pro-western group of officers and giving aid in order to tie the Afghan economy and communications system more closely to the Iranian. In Pakistan the Shah has also used his aid to win influence in the country's economics and politics, and has declared his intention to intervene if there is a chance of Pakistan breaking up. Further afield, Iran has developed its economic ties, at a state-to-state level, with India, Bangladesh, South Korea, Taiwan and Indonesia. A new arena of potential Iranian activity has been the Indian Ocean, although it is not yet clear how far Iran, whose navy faces serious problems, will be able to play a truly significant role there in the 1980s. As part of its Indian Ocean strategy Iran has developed its economic and military cooperation with South Africa, from whom it receives uranium, and acquired naval facilities on the island of Mauritius. Its aid to Zaire in 1977 also illustrates the scope of the Shah's current concerns. And, nearer home, there remains the Arabian peninsula: the Iranians have already intervened here, in North Yemen, Oman and the Emirates, and they could easily do so again, if there was a threat to Kuwait by Iraq, or if popular unrest grew in Bahrain. One can reasonably doubt that the 1975 pact with Iraq will stand the test of time. Finally, there remains Iran's north-western neighbour, the country with probably the most militant working class in the Middle East, Turkey. At the moment, the Turkish army appears well able to cope with domestic dissent; but, if the situation deteriorated there, there is little doubt that Iran would be quick to come to the aid of any Turkish régime that could claim it had 'requested' such assistance.

Regional Partners: Saudi Arabia, Israel, Egypt

Saudi Arabia, Israel and Egypt are the three countries in the Middle East with which Iran has tried to develop a special relationship, involving cooperation of various kinds. Saudi Arabia has, like Iran, only come to have a significant foreign policy since the mid-1960s, and whilst it does not have any armed forces to speak of, it has acquired considerable influence in the Arab world because of its financial power. Since the

1967 Arab–Israeli war Saudi Arabia has become the dominant country throughout the Arab world – supporting Egypt, Sudan, Syria, Jordan, North Yemen and Morocco financially and acting as the main source of guidance in the Arab–Israeli dispute.

The Saudis are certainly suspicious of the Iranian role in the Gulf, both because of long-standing hostilities between Iran and Arab countries, and because of Iran's arrogance and desire to preserve an eminently superior military position. Many Saudis have a vague foreboding about Iranian policy, almost as if they expect Iran to take their country over at some time in the future. Some Saudi irritation at the Iranian role in Oman was also reported. But the extent of this hostility should not be exaggerated. American policy in the Gulf has been explicitly directed at fostering the growth of a kind of low-level alliance between the two – the 'twin pillar' policy; and the U S A would certainly take great pains to prevent any serious disagreement between them. Nor, in the current situation, is there any major issue in dispute between them, nothing that could serve as a cause for war. Mutual suspicion and the arms build-up certainly make a conflict more likely, but there are also strong countervailing pressures which will at least tend to channel Iranian–Saudi rivalry into other, political, forms.

Iran has had a close relationship with Israel that began when Iran extended *de facto* recognition to the state in 1950. As long as Iran was at odds with Egypt and the Arab world generally the alliance with Israel was especially close, as the two states faced a common enemy. Since the 1967 war, and especially since the 1973 war, a shift in Iranian attitudes can be seen. Iran has criticized Israel for holding on to the West Bank and Gaza, and has voiced some support for the Palestinian cause, whilst opposing the idea of a Palestinian state for fear it would be Soviet-dominated.[22] Iran has also been able to develop its relations with Egypt since the death of Nasser, and this too has removed a factor in the friendship with Israel. Iran's post-1973 position is very much a two-sided one, designed to encourage a settlement of the Arab–Israeli question that will be of a durable kind and guarantee both Israel and the Egyptian régime.

However, despite the shift in Iranian policy, it retains a close relationship with Israel, which is evident in a number of fields:[23]

1. *Military Training*: an unknown number of Iranian officers have been trained in Israel. According to one author, basing his information on discussions with the Shah, 'virtually every general officer in the Shah's army has visited Israel, and hundreds of junior officers have undergone some aspects of Israeli training.'[24] It is believed that Israeli advisers took part in operations against the southern tribes of Iran, during the 1963 revolt.

2. *Military Supplies*: though both states are supplied mainly by the U S A, Israel has provided Iran with Soviet equipment it captured in 1967, whilst Iran has acquired arms for Israel that the latter has not been able to get for itself because of embargoes (particularly from France). Israel could also supply Iran with some of the technicians it needs to service its new material.

3. *Intelligence*: Israel's Mossad and SAVAK have co-operated since the 1950s.[25] In addition to the exchange of information, it is also believed that a number of SAVAK officials have been trained in Israel.

4. *Oil*: Iran is the main supplier of oil to Israel, and this is the most important single item in cooperation between the two countries. After the 1967 war, Israel built a 162-mile pipeline from Eilat on the Red Sea to Ashkelon on the Mediterranean; this was financed by Iran and used to transfer Iranian oil to markets in Europe, particularly Romania and Italy. After 1975, when Israel surrendered the Abu Rudeis oilfield in Sinai to the Egyptians, Iran undertook to meet all Israel's future needs, and this guarantee formed part of the secret clauses in the Sinai disengagement treaty negotiated by American Secretary of State Kissinger at that time.[26]

5. *Agricultural Development*: Israeli experts have participated in at least two agricultural development projects in Iran;

one of these is at Qazvin, covering an area of 125,000 acres.

6. *Trade*: Israeli exports to Iran reached $22 millions in 1970, $33 millions in 1971, rising to $63 millions in 1974. These goods are shipped either through Turkey (which also has relations with Israel) or on the empty tankers making the return run to the Gulf. El Al also flies to Iran – although Iran Air does not fly to Israel.

Iran has therefore a continuing relationship with Israel that goes beyond any merely diplomatic convenience. Iran could become embroiled in an Arab–Israeli conflict on the side of Israel if the Arab states chose to stop or fire on tankers ferrying Iranian oil to Eilat: the ships sail along the southern coast of the Arabian peninsula, and up the Red Sea, so that they could easily be attacked if Arab countries wanted to do so. On the other hand, in the 1973 Arab–Israeli war, Iran provided some logistical support to the Arabs, ferrying Saudi troops to the front line in Syria, and the general tendency of its policy has been one of developing ties with the Arab world.

This is clearest of all in the growth of Iran's ties with Egypt, a country with which it was in open dispute between 1960, when Nasser broke off diplomatic relations, and 1967, when Egypt withdrew from North Yemen. Since the 1973 Arab–Israeli war, Iran has made a special effort to develop links with Egypt. Iran has provided a $1 billion economic aid loan, and it has been suggested that if Egypt acquires new weapons from the U S A, Iranian instructors will help with the training programme. Egypt has a population of around the same size as Iran and Iran sees a close Tehran–Cairo axis as a means, first, of circumventing Saudi domination, and secondly, of playing an influential role in Arab politics. By developing ties with both Israel and Egypt, Iran no doubt hopes that it will be able to exert more pressure on the principal protagonists in the Arab–Israeli dispute.

Iran: Imperialist? Sub-Imperialist?

An active Iranian foreign policy, in the sense of a dynamic relation with other countries beyond the great powers, is little more than a decade old. Yet it should already be possible to draw some conclusions about the character of this policy, and how it compares with that of other similar capitalist states. One country that suggests a comparison is Japan. The Shah himself has frequently claimed that Iran will follow the path of the only Asian state to have carried out a successful capitalist industrialization, and, whilst he does not make this further point, it is well known that the process of economic growth in Japan, from the 1890s to the 1940s, was accompanied by widespread attacks on neighbouring states in an attempt to subjugate the markets and gain access to the raw materials of these countries.[27] Japan wanted to acquire an empire, comparable to that of the other imperialist powers.

In narrow political terms there is some similarity between the Iran of the 1970s and the Japan of some decades previously. In both countries the ideology of empire, and the figure of the Emperor, is central to political life – the latter even more so in Iran than in Japan. Iran is certainly trying to dominate its neighbours and catch up with the advanced capitalist countries. But here the similarity stops, for Japan was an imperialist power in a way that Iran could never be. First of all, Japan was becoming a major industrial power as it began to expand: its military power rested on its own domestic productive capacities, and it was able to export manufactured goods itself. Iran's arms are purchased from abroad, by the sale of a raw material, and do not reflect the internal technical and productive capabilities of the Iranian economy. Secondly, although the search for markets and raw materials plays some part in Iran's foreign policy, and could increasingly do so in the future, it would be a mistake to exaggerate the significance of this factor which was far more important in Japan's case. Finally, there is no sense in which Iran can become a rival to the most advanced capitalist countries, in the way that Japan did. The era of empires is over, and Iran is in economic terms a far weaker country compared with the more advanced one that Japan was from the 1890s onwards. The formal similarity between the two Asian imperial régimes of the twentieth century is therefore one that highlights Iran's relative weakness.

Another model that suggests itself for the analysis of Iran is that of 'sub-imperialism', one that has been applied to Iran by a number of writers.[28] The concept of sub-imperialism was originally developed in the context of Brazilian development since the coup of 1964 and was an attempt to explain why Brazil had become a major exporter of manufactured goods to other parts of the third world. According to the theory, this reflected: (a) the flow of capital from the advanced capitalist countries into Brazil; (b) the restriction of the domestic market within Brazil, which was such that, in order for capital to be reproduced, manufactured goods had to be exported; (c) the growth of monopoly and finance capital within Brazil itself. Such a process, it was argued, reflected a new international division of labour, in which a few of the eighty or so third-world countries were being transformed into intermediate manufacturing entities of the Brazilian kind. In addition, this economic change was being accompanied by political and military developments: while Brazil became to some extent more autonomous of the U S A, it was also carrying out political and military activities that were in the interests of the advanced capitalist countries; as well as facilitating the reproduction of capital on an international scale, it was at the same time building a sphere of influence in the South Atlantic, and assisting the military régimes in a number of neighbouring state (Chile, Uruguay, Bolivia and Argentina).

The political and strategic similarities between Iran and Brazil are striking enough. Both countries are in terms of population and the size of their armed forces the dominant ones in their respective regions, and both are to some extent set apart by linguistic and cultural factors from their neighbours. If Iran's military build-up and foreign campaigns have far exceeded Brazil's, the character of their policies is in this respect certainly similar. Moreover, both are countries where military régimes, initially installed with the assistance of the CIA, were for a time able to crush dissent by the use of a secret police and torture, and where such a political consolidation has paved the way for faster economic growth and an active counter-revolutionary role in the region.

However, in economic terms, there is very little similarity between the two and the application of the concept 'sub-imperialist' as defined in the Brazilian case to Iran is an inaccurate one which, as with the Japanese analogy, underlines Iran's weakness. In the Brazilian case the basis of the phenomenon is the limitation of the domestic market, and the consequent need to export manufactured goods; in Iran's case, manufactured goods form a tiny part of total (oil and non-oil) exports – probably 1 per cent; the major export is, obviously, oil. This is a consequence of the fact that Iranian industry is far less developed than that of Brazil; at the same time the considerable expansion of the domestic market resulting from the oil boom has outstripped the supply capacities of Iranian industry. Foreign capital is investing in Iran under conditions that are, in the long run, less favourable than in Brazil, since it is only the temporary boom given by oil that sustains domestic demand and provides an overall investment climate that is so congenial. It is the state with its oil revenues, rather than financial and monopoly capital in the proper sense, that dominates Iran. In strict economic terms, particularly in connection with the import of capital and the export of goods, Brazil has more in common with certain Asian countries such as Singapore, Hong Kong and South Korea than with Iran.

However, the concept of 'sub-imperialism' as developed in the case of Brazil is itself open to criticisms since it posits a relationship between the economic and the politico-military spheres that is probably invalid. There is little reason to believe that Brazil's strategic role in Latin America has a dependent connection to its economic role; its exports, for example, are not, in the main, sent to those countries where its support for right-wing military forces has been exercised. Once this is clear, the room is open for a much looser concept of 'sub-imperialism', one that concentrates on the strategic dimension; without denying the fundamental weight of the interests that underline imperialism, this looser concept of sub-imperialism denotes (a) a continuing if partial strategic subordination to US imperialism on the one hand and (b) an autonomous regional role on the other. Such a concept is certainly applicable both to Brazil and to Iran. For Iran is pursuing policies that Washington supports and which the USA appears unwilling now to carry out itself, and at the same time these policies are in the interests of the dominant class in Iran itself. This class, having developed through the expansion of the past two decades, is now in a position to play such a role and, on certain issues, to defy the USA: oil is the most evident example of this. In the end it is the importance to the advanced capitalist countries not of Iran's economic resources but of the whole region's wealth that gives to Iran its special importance; it appears that only Iran can fulfil the counter-revolutionary role that it believes some state must perform and which the advanced capitalist countries no longer wish to perform in a direct manner themselves.

10 Conclusions

The preceding analysis has described the growth of the contemporary Iranian state. It has also examined some of the other main economic and political constituents of Iran, as well as the limitations of the recent years of capitalist development. A central theme of this previous discussion has been that the political success of the Shah in the decade and a half after 1963 was, to a considerable extent, made possible by the economic advantages which the government enjoyed; it follows from this that, as the economic difficulties of Iran increase in the years to come, so its political room for manoeuvre and for containing dissent will also be reduced. It has been argued that behind the appearance of a prosperous economy and official predictions of a 'Great Civilization', many serious problems have remained unsolved, whilst other new ones have been generated. Hence, in the longer run, and particularly through the 1980s and early 1990s, the margin of freedom enjoyed by the Iranian state will necessarily contract.

The Economic Constraints

Since the limitations of Iranian economic development have been discussed above it is only necessary here to provide a résumé of the main features:

1. a protracted crisis in agriculture, necessitating massive food imports and/or food controls, combined with continued deprivation for at least half of the rural population.

2. growing inequality in incomes, within the urban areas, between Tehran and the provinces, and between urban and rural populations.

3. a decline in oil revenues by the second half of the 1980s, with little prospect of finding alternative sources of foreign exchange on a comparable scale.

4. continued low productivity in industry, rendering Iranian

manufactured goods non-competitive on international markets, and the continued reliance of the industrial sector (public and private) on supplies of government funds.

5. an inefficient state machine, without a proper planning apparatus, marked by widespread corruption and an inability to implement social and economic reforms.

6. continued need to spend on military purchases in order to sustain existing military forces and Iran's foreign policy.

These are the factors which now exert increasing pressures on the Pahlavi régime; and, as these problems combine, the régime's room for manoeuvre will contract. For example, it has been able to win temporary support or at least acquiescence because of its disposal of oil revenues, the increased consumption available to much of the population, and the hopes these have aroused. But it will no longer be able to do this as the 1980s wear on. The loyalty of the middle class to the Pahlavi régime is at best a trade-off – resentful and querulous, this sector has agreed to surrender political power because of the Shah's ability to deliver the economic goods. But this acceptance will certainly evaporate if the positive contribution which the régime makes, the economic bonus, is reduced. Moreover, the inevitable increase in economic uncertainty will further unsettle a middle class that has always shown itself extremely nervous about trusting the state and investing in long-term projects.

At the popular level similar developments appear likely. No doubt, in the Iran of the late 1960s and early 1970s there was considerable and widespread expectation of an improvement in material conditions. Some improvement did indeed occur, but by the middle 1970s the tide had already begun to turn, and the capacity of the régime to meet popular demands whilst satisfying its priorities as a capitalist state had decreased. Some examples of how the régime's room for manoeuvre has declined may make this clearer. In 1975, in order to boost output, a law was passed threatening those farmers who did not sell their lands to state farms with expropriation: this, naturally, provoked increased uncertainty amongst small farmers and further decreased their willingness to invest in and exert themselves for higher output. In the same year the régime introduced the workers' share programme which was designed to increase output in the industrial sector; leaving aside the fact that it only applied to a minority of workers (see pp. 193ff.), the measure also had negative effects in that it provoked a sharp loss of confidence amongst both Iranian and foreign businessmen – it thereby prejudiced future industrial growth. In the realm of food supplies the régime has, up to 1977, been able to meet shortfalls in supplies by (a) importing food and (b) subsidizing market prices: hence the possibly negative political impact of the food crisis has been reduced. But the cost of doing this in the future will impose increased strains at a time when available funds are less, and when, with the revival in Iranian international borrowing, foreign bankers may be unwilling to allow such a policy to continue. Just as, in 1976 and 1977, prolonged power cuts in Tehran made it clear to everyone that all was not well, so a sharp and continued inflation in food prices will telegraph the message to every home in Iran that the oil-based boom is coming to an end.

It is via this economic deterioration that the political dissensions in Iran have already been brought into the open. It is manifest that there exists a growing level of popular resentment, both at the cutbacks and shortages that are bound to occur, and at the continuing inequalities in Iranian society. As early as 1971 a cautious observer of Iran remarked that, on walking through the streets of the southern, poorer part of Tehran, he encountered 'more expressed hatred than I have ever heard before' from 'people who watch the cars of those people who are doing well'. The wealth in Iran was being distributed in a manner that was 'ostentatious' and 'grotesque'.[1] This small, but convincing, insight suggests that, even before the worst excesses of the 1973–5 boom, the inequalities we have mentioned (see p. 166) were finding some echo in the attitudes of the majority of Iranians who are, to a greater or lesser extent, excluded from these benefits. As economic problems grew, it was impossible for the passivity of the urban poor to continue, and Tehran and other big cities have seen a return to the kinds of popular unrest that occurred in the 1940s and

1950s. But this time, in contrast to this earlier period, the régime has neither political credibility nor such future oil resources to fall back upon.

The Sixth Crisis

Iran has not had to wait for the full impact of the economic crisis to take effect, for in 1978 the régime was shaken by a nationwide protest, the first since 1963. It revealed the depth of popular anger at the régime's policies and the continuing failure of the Pahlavi monarchy to consolidate a political base. After all the years of rhetoric and censorship, of make-believe and popular silence, there occurred a vast mass upsurge that was inchoate in form but of unexpected tenacity and diffusion. The imperial régime may well survive this challenge as it did in 1946, 1953, and 1963, but whatever the short-term outcome the crisis of 1978 is comparable to these earlier ones. It is, in the series enumerated in Chapter 1, the *sixth crisis* of the Iranian state in this century. The régime is in some ways stronger than it was in previous crises, and its foreign support is, as we shall see, confirmed. Moreover, the opposition has been devoid of coherent organization, even more so than in any previous crisis. But, on the other hand, the popular protests of 1978 are more deeply rooted in Iran's socio-economic structure than any previous ones: they have mobilized a much larger proportion of the population than any before and, in contrast to all the others, have been provoked almost entirely by internal rather than international developments. A summary discussion of this crisis, its course and causes, is therefore important, both in its own right and for what it tells us about the capacities of the Pahlavi régime. Whatever the outcome, it serves notice that Iran faces turbulent years ahead and that the breathing space which the Pahlavi régime brought with its combination of repression and oil revenues is coming rather sharply to an end.

The first signs of a change in the political climate came in the earlier half of 1977, when a number of Tehran-based politicians and intellectuals began to voice criticisms of the régime; they requested a return to constitutional freedoms and warned of the economic problems Iran was facing. One letter, sent to the Shah, was signed by three former National Front politicians – Karim Sanjabi, Shahpour Bakhtiar and Dariush Foruhar. Other open letters came from Ibrahim Khajenouri, an establishment historian, and Hajj Sayyid Javadi, a former editor of *Kayhan* newspaper. Other protests came from fifty-six members of the regrouped Writers' Guild, another from fifty-four judges, and another from 144 lawyers, the latter objecting to the ineffectual nature of the proposed changes in procedures for trying political offences (p. 90). In December 1977 three former constituents of the National Front, the Iranian Nationalist Party, the Iran Party and the Society of Iranian Socialists, announced that the Front had been reconstituted, and in the same month thirty opposition personalities announced the creation of the Iranian Committee for the Defence of Freedoms and the Rights of Man.

Whilst in the first part of 1977 the opposition was confined to intellectuals and former politicians, it took on a wider dimension in the latter part of the year. In October and November there was a new wave of student protests, particularly at Tehran and Aryamehr Universities, and some of these meetings were attacked by plain-clothes SAVAK personnel. On 22 November twelve bus-loads of SAVAK agents assaulted a gathering of Islamic opposition members at Karaj, north of Tehran, and for a few weeks after mid-November it seemed that the Shah had forced the opposition underground again. But protests soon re-emerged, this time in a wider and more explosive form involving the religious leaders, the *ayatollahs*, and the mosque officials, the *mollahs*.

This link between the intellectuals and students on one side and the wider opposition on the other seems to have been made by two incidents. First, the son of Ayatollah Khomeini was killed in a car accident and the Iranian government was suspected of responsibility. Then an article appeared in an official paper which criticized the religious leaders, including Khomeini. As a result, there was a clash in Qom on 8 January 1978 in which several people were killed, and a chain of protests was then established, with mourning ceremonies every forty days, as is the Iranian custom, leading to further clashes and hence further mourning.

As a result of the Qom clashes there were widespread demonstrations in the northern city of Tabriz on 18–19 February when an estimated 40,000 people came onto the streets. Cinemas, banks and other buildings were attacked and troops were brought in from outside the city in the first direct urban clash between the army and the population since June 1963. Protests followed in other places and by May mass demonstrations were reported in over thirty cities. At first centred in provincial towns, the protests soon spread to Tehran, where merchants in the bazaar went on strike and troops occupied the bazaar area.

The régime's response to these developments was erratic, veering between promises of change and outright repression. It seems that the Shah had decided in early 1977 to allow some changes in the political system. He felt confident that the security threat to his régime had been crushed. He realized that with mounting economic and social problems it was necessary to provide some safety valves for criticism and protest. And he was probably in some measure disconcerted by the 'human rights' policy of the new Carter administration in Washington. The Iranian opposition was certainly encouraged by Carter's emphasis on human rights – the precedent of the Kennedy administration was in many people's minds – and the subsequent failure of Carter to sustain his campaign and his indulgent approach to the Shah has certainly reinforced the strong nationalist and anti-American current within the opposition movement.

In the early part of 1978 the government switched uneasily from one policy to another. The press was loosened slightly and began, albeit in official terms, to report on social problems and some opposition activities. But no press other than the official one was tolerated. The Shah also made a point of redistributing some of the personnel in his security apparatus. The responsible SAVAK officials in Tabriz were dismissed after the February riots, and in June two leading SAVAK members were sent abroad as ambassadors. General Nassiri, head of SAVAK since 1965, was sent to be ambassador in

Pakistan, and General Motazed, the Assistant Director, was despatched to Syria. These changes were, however, of less significance than was claimed. General Nassiri's new position was an extremely important one, given joint Pakistan–Iranian concern about the new revolutionary government in Afghanistan and the danger this posed to the military régime in Pakistan, whilst the new head of S A V A K, General Nasser Moqaddem, was a veteran intelligence officer (see p. 80), and no proponent of liberal reforms. Nor did S A V A K cease its intermittent attacks on opposition leaders: in March the homes of several National Front politicians were bombed, and a prominent opposition lawyer, Karim Laheji, was beaten up by plainclothesmen.

Matters came to a head in August. On 6 August the Shah suddenly announced that he was pushing ahead with his liberalization programme, and that elections for the June 1979 Majlis would be 'one hundred per cent free'. Other parties would be permitted to stand and, although the Tudeh Party was not allowed, within days fourteen new political groupings had announced their existence. However, the Shah did not say if he would allow this newly elected Majlis to play any part in government, and his commitment to a multi-party system was open to suspicion: he had spent the past three years trying to build up the single Rastakhiz Party, and had only the previous May declared that the multi-party system was quite unsuited to Iran.[2]

Whatever the Shah's intentions, this announcement came too late to stem the tide of popular protest. Soon afterwards demonstrations broke out in Isfahan, where martial law was declared, and on 19 August there occurred a terrible fire in a cinema in Abadan in which nearly four hundred people were burnt to death. The Shah blamed the opposition, some of whom had made cinemas targets of attack as symbols of 'atheism'; the opposition claimed the fire was a provocation by S A V A K. Amidst the recrimination and continuing demonstrations, the government of Jamshid Amuzegar, who had replaced Hoveida as premier in June 1977, resigned.

The new cabinet was headed by Jaafar Sharif Emami, who had been premier in 1961 and subsequently President of the

Senate. Himself the grandson of a religious leader, he declared his intention of bridging the gap between the opposition and the régime. In cosmetic moves, he abandoned the imperial calendar foisted on Iran by the Shah three years before and reintroduced the Muslim one; casinos were to be closed and some films controlled. In response, the leader of the more cautious *mollahs*, Ayatollah Sharriat Madari in Qom, called for a breathing space for the new government. But popular pressure was not quelled by the appointment of Sharif Emami, and on 4 September several hundred thousand people demonstrated in Tehran at the end of the Muslim month of Ramadan. This was a peaceful demonstration in which the crowds, many of them women, appealed to the armed forces not to oppose them. Some called for the restoration of the constitution, and some for a republic. Others shouted '*Marg ber Shah*' ('Death to the Shah').

This demonstration, the largest in the capital at least since the days of Mossadeq, must have caused alarm in government circles by its scale, its discipline and its appeal to the armed forces. A ban on further marches was then imposed, but on 7 September, the following Thursday, a similar demonstration took place in which an estimated 300,000 people took part. They defied the *mollahs*' appeals to stay at home and marched through central Tehran from morning to night. Again, appeals were made to the army. This proved too much for the régime, and on the morning of Friday, 8 September, martial law was declared in Tehran and eleven other cities. Troops clashed with demonstrators in Tehran's Jaleh Square, and in a gruesome replay of June 1963 up to three thousand people were killed. The 'Iranian spring' had been brought to an abrupt end, as hundreds were arrested and many more tried to hide from SAVAK.

It is, at the time of writing, too early to say what the longer-term consequences of these dramatic events will be, but certain provisional judgements are possible on the basis of what has occurred.

1. The major conclusion to be drawn from the events of

1978 is that it has revealed in a stark form just how isolated the Shah and his entourage are in political terms. The depth of hatred and rejection shown by the Iranian population after fifteen years of apparent passivity must have startled everyone, and the Shah, veering from one policy to the other, has been unable to stem the rising tide of anger. His belated and half-hearted reforms were dismissed by a people impatient for substantial changes and no longer impressed by high-sounding promises. The Rastakhiz Party was demonstrated to be an empty shell with no legitimacy, no appeal. No new politicians had emerged to bolster the imperial régime and it was an index of the Shah's weakness that he had to fall back on Sharif Emami, a loyal supporter from a previous epoch. Nor was this rejection confined to the poorer sections of the urban population: the new political formations and professional groups that emerged testified to the anger and panic that have spread through the Iranian middle classes as the political rigidity and economic mismanagement of the régime have become clearer.

2. The only institution upon which the Shah has been able to fall back is the army, and it must have been, in part, the fear of dissent spreading within it that impelled the Shah to declare martial law in twelve cities after the mass demonstrations of 4 and 7 September in Tehran. There were reportedly a few cases of soldiers refusing to obey orders and shooting their officers, and two mutinies in garrisons around Tehran allegedly occurred in early September. But these were, at the most, isolated cases and the armed forces as a whole remained loyal to the imperial régime. Presumably those sent into the streets to shoot unarmed demonstrators have been drawn from the 90,000-strong professional core of the army, and are not conscripts; if anything, the overall position of the armed forces within Iranian society has been strengthened by the role allotted to them in the crisis and by the absence of any credible civilian forces around the Shah. General Gholam Ali Oveissi, a former colleague of the Shah's at Tehran Military Academy and a former commander of the First Army Corps and of the Gendarmerie, was appointed Military Governor of Tehran and

was believed to be a potential prime minister in the event of the Shah appointing a military cabinet. At the same time the Shah's programme of arms purchases was continuing unabated: during his visit to the U S A in November 1977 he presented a new list of weapons he wished to purchase totalling between $9 and $10 billions and the military budget rose 25 per cent in 1978–9. Whatever other cutbacks the Shah was contemplating in government expenditure, the military was apparently immune to the retrenchment being imposed on the Iranian state by its economic difficulties.

3. One factor that was given widespread emphasis in the popular protests was corruption, and former prime minister Ali Amini claimed that the Shah had for fifteen years been surrounded by a group of three or four thousand people who had profited by their connections to the court. 'If matters are not dealt with in a rapid and radical manner,' he warned, 'communism will in the end triumph in this country. The Shah is in great danger, but he can still be saved by disassociating himself from his entourage (brothers, sisters and other hangers-on). This authoritarian, oppressive and rigid régime was bound to disintegrate sooner or later, because its foundations are rotten.'[3] As had occurred in the early 1960s, during Amini's own premiership, the régime began to prosecute officials, including former ministers. Several were arrested, including Mansur Rouhani, the former Minister of Agriculture, and Fereidun Mahdavi, a former Minister of Finance. But many of those closest to the Shah, including his relatives, were untouched, and there was some scepticism about the determination of Sharif Emami to end corruption, since he had at one time been a Director of the Pahlavi Foundation, a government fund where considerable corruption was known to have occurred.[4] Moreover, in the case of a man like Mahdavi, there was some suspicion that as on previous occasions anti-corruption drives were being used more to remove dissident elements than to put an end to speculation. As in the changes at the top of S A V A K, little more than window-dressing was involved.

4. The Shah's difficulties did reveal one area from which he

could expect support, and from a wider spectrum than in any previous crisis, namely from Iran's foreign allies. The Carter Administration did not take long to make its peace with the Shah: following the latter's visit to Washington in November 1977 Carter paid a brief visit to Tehran in the following month. He announced that the Shah and he had identical views on human rights, and that there was no leader in the world for whom he felt such 'deep gratitude and personal friendship' as the Shah. In the days following the Jaleh Square massacre Carter telephoned the Shah to reassure him of U S support, while regretting the loss of life, and U S diplomats underlined the vital importance of the Shah to their strategy. Other western leaders did the same, but the Shah also received a visit in the midst of the August crisis from another friend, Chairman Hua Kuo-feng of China. Hua repeated conventional Chinese views about the importance of Iran to the security of the Gulf, and when the Shah's troops shot at the Iranian population a few days later the Chinese press attacked the demonstrators for being 'financed and organized from abroad'.[5] Nearer home, the Saudi Arabians and Israelis both expressed concern about the Shah's difficulties, whilst the Iraqis obliged by expelling Khomeini and forcing him to flee to France. For its part, the Soviet press confined itself to factual reports, and to repeating the conventional criticisms of the Shah's alliance with the U S A. Washington and London, Riyadh and Tel Aviv, Peking, and, with qualifications, Moscow, all appeared concerned about the Shah's fate in the face of his manifest rejection by the population over which he ruled.

5. The crisis of 1978 appears to have left the régime in an even more exposed position than it was before the cautious relaxation begun eighteen months before. The Shah promised that after six months martial law would be lifted and the 'liberalization' could continue, but it is difficult to see how this could occur except in the most superficial way. What, above all, the events of 1978 showed was that the Pahlavi régime is incapable of democratizing in any real sense. Through years of oppression it has generated such a degree

of popular rage in the urban population than any controlled release of the pressure will be extremely difficult and has been made more difficult by the Shah's handling of the 1978 protests.

The Opposition Reborn

The 1978 crisis was also revealing about the Iranian opposition, as it emerged from the shadows for the first time since 1963. Again, it is too early to draw an accurate picture of the forces and organizations involved, yet certain features can be noted and there is enough evidence to identify some of the strengths and weaknesses of this movement.

1. The Tehran-based politicians who emerged in 1977 and who were prominent through 1978 were in many cases men who had played a prominent role under Mossadeq or in 1960–63. Some, like Foruhar and Sanjabi, had been in opposition for many years. Foruhar had been a right-wing nationalist, imprisoned for opposing the abandonment of Iran's claim to Bahrain in 1971, Sanjabi had represented the Iranian case to the International Court of Justice at the Hague during the oil crisis. Some other Tehran-based politicians emerged from a split amidst the Rastakhiz deputies in parliament: these included Mohsen Pezeshkpour, deputy for Ahvaz, who re-established the Pan-Iranist Party, and Ahmad Bani Ahmad, deputy for Tabriz, who tried to found another party. Like the writers and lawyers, they focused their demands on the restoration of civil and constitutional liberties. A twelve-point programme issued by the National Front in August 1978 included a demand for the dissolution of SAVAK and of the military tribunals, the release of political prisoners and the right of political exiles to return, and the rights to freedom of expression and to the formation of trades unions.

2. The religious leaders who were in the forefront of the movement from December 1977 onwards represented a variety of viewpoints. Khomeini and his supporters demanded the removal of the Shah and the creation of an 'Islamic state'.

Sharriat Madari, in Qom, adopted a more cautious position, demanding, like the Tehran-based politicians, a return to constitutional rule. The Shah accused these *ayatollahs* and *mollahs* of being 'black reactionaries' or 'Islamic Marxists', but these were misleading descriptions for a number of reasons. First, both Khomeini and Sharriat Madari made explicitly anti-communist statements, and Khomeini in particular forbad his followers to work with any Marxists, even in a united front.[6] Moreover, the demands of these religious leaders were a mixture of conservative and progressive. There was no evidence at all to confirm, as the Shah claimed, that these officials wanted to reverse the land reform. Khomeini himself explicitly denied this. There was, however, more truth in the accusation that they were opposed to the emancipation of women and statements by them to the effect that Islam treated men and women equally were evasions. The form which some of the popular protests took – attacks on banks and cinemas – reflected an ill-defined anger phrased in Islamic terms and within which the conservative view on the position of women was one undeniable element. But religious leaders also wanted an end to the Shah's system of autocracy – something that *was* progressive and which the régime tried to obscure with its characterizations.

3. The left organizations as such played a very small role in these demonstrations, yet they did participate as far as they could. The Tudeh Party, long accused by its opponents on the left of having disappeared, distributed a newsheet entitled *Navid* (Good News) in Tehran, although it had lost what could have been its greatest asset, its radio station, two years before. The guerrilla groups, Fedayin and Mojahidin, were also able to distribute material in the popular upsurge, and a new wave of guerrilla actions was reported, though it was not clear by which group. It is probable that the guerrillas will be able to recruit from a new generation of angered and disillusioned students after the régime's clampdown.

4. The most important question concerns the character of the hundreds of thousands of people who demonstrated in

Tehran and other cities. These were the urban poor, the people who had come to the cities and had experienced the rough face of the oil boom, enduring food shortages and inflation and paying up to 70 per cent of their income on rent. It was their anger that exploded in Tabriz in February and which spread throughout the country. They were joined in their protests by the merchants of the bazaar, who were traditionally close to the mosque and who had felt their position threatened by the pattern of capitalist development in Iran. This movement incorporated members of more than one class – proletarians, and petty bourgeois. It was not in any proper sense of the word 'religious'. Its complaints and demands were eminently materialist. But it did follow the religious leaders and phrase some of its demands in an Islamic form for want of any other alternative. Fifteen years of repression had divided the opposition organizations from the mass of the population, many of whom were newcomers to the town or too young to remember earlier crises. The mosque was the one place where an independent voice was heard, the *mollahs* the one group who could articulate their protests. And this is why, as had happened in many other countries in different stages of their history, the enraged population turned to religion as the means through which to voice their protest. These people, many of whom paid with their lives for their hostility to the Shah's government, were not organized from abroad, or Marxists, or reactionaries. They were people who could no longer tolerate the stifling political atmosphere and the gross inequalities of Iranian urban life.

5. The depth and nation-wide character of this protest movement are beyond doubt, but it was at the same time marked by certain substantial weaknesses that prevented it from realizing its full potential. First, it involved, so far as is known, neither the rural poor nor the organized urban working class: prior to the proclamation of martial law there were no reports of protests in the countryside, nor of increased strike activity in workplaces. The movement took the form of spontaneous actions on the streets and whilst most of those protesting must

also have been workers it was not as *organized* proletarians that they acted. There were several major strikes – in the oil refinery and in the public services of Tehran – in the weeks following the proclamation of martial law, and this form of protest may become much more significant in the future. Secondly, there was an undeniable strand of obscurantist and even reactionary ideology in the movement. The conservative position on women was one such element. So too was the hostility directed against the Bahai, a sect that broke away from Shi'a Islam in the nineteenth century and which has been the target of persecution in many Muslim countries. Thirdly, the movement was so rapidly pushed along by the anger of the people, and so isolated from any political leadership, that it very soon adopted perspectives that were bound to lead it into a lethal clash with the régime. The slogans calling for 'Death to the Shah' and Khomeini's intransigent proclamations from his place of exile in Iraq were inappropriate since the régime could reply to them only with repression. However understandable, these maximalist positions gave the régime the excuse it needed to counter-attack.

The *ayatollahs* and *mollahs* on their own can probably not sustain or channel the popular upsurge, and the greatest problem which the movement had in 1978 was that of organization. Without it, the movement could both rush into head-on clashes with the régime such as occurred, and could disintegrate over a period of time. It was an ironic success of the Shah's policies that whilst he had been unable to remove or contain popular anger he *was* able to prevent it from acquiring any political form, and it is here that the greatest challenge to the opposition parties, left, centre and right, can be located. As long as the movement lacks organizational form it will be unable to marshall the challenge to the Shah's government that the protest movement of 1978 showed was possible.

The Future of the Pahlavi Régime

The crisis of the Pahlavi régime could take several forms. A number of capitalist dictatorships were overthrown in the early 1970s – Portugal, Greece and Spain – but it is noteworthy that in all these three cases the popular opposition played a secondary role in the actual replacement of the dictatorship by more democratic forms and that capitalism itself was not replaced. It is essential to bear this in mind, lest it be assumed that the main agents of the overthrow of the Pahlavi monarchy will necessarily be the urban and rural oppressed or that socialism will necessarily follow. In fact, there are a number of ways in which capitalist rule could continue in Iran, and it would be premature to assume either that the removal of the Pahlavis will of itself introduce the possibility of socialism, or that the Iranian bourgeoisie and its advanced capitalist allies have only one strategy. At least four capitalist options are available:

1. continued dictatorship by the Pahlavi monarch – by the present Shah and his successors.
2. modification of the present régime to allow for a degree of political freedom and some participation in government by civilian politicians – a return to the situation in 1961–2, and in the period up to 1953.
3. military dictatorship, after the complete removal or political neutralization of the Shah and his family.
4. a bourgeois democracy, under a republican régime, or with a monarchy that is of a purely constitutional kind.

The Shah himself is, however limited by the role of the individual in history, a factor in these calculations. He was born in 1919: in 1980 he will therefore be 61 years old, in 1990 71, in 2000 81. It is conceivable that it will be he who will preside over the Iranian state as it traverses this turbulent period. On the other hand, he has said on a number of occasions that at some stage in the 1980s he might abdicate and hand power over to his son. The latter, Prince Reza, was born in 1960, and will therefore be 25 in 1985; and the Shah has a further son, Prince Ali Reza, born in 1966, who could step in if anything happened to Prince Reza. His two daughters are unlikely to be allowed to play a central role, but there are two other women who play a role already and could fulfil executive functions in any transition period – the Shah's twin sister,

Princess Ashraf, and his wife, Queen Farah (born 1938). Apart from abdication and natural death, there is a third possibility, namely assassination. The Shah has decreed that if this occurs his wife will take over as Regent until Reza reaches the age of 21 (1981), but if such an act reflected a more widespread conspiracy, and not some individual action, then it could make a transition and restabilization difficult. Certainly, the disappearance of the Shah is the one thing that could, by removing the vital cog in the machinery, produce a rapid deterioration in the overall capacity of the Iranian state.

If the Shah does not die, then it is hard to see him surrendering power voluntarily, whether he abdicates formally or not. Like Franz Josef of Austria he may be fated to preside, as he ages, over the decomposition of his empire; and it is a reasonable psychological possibility to suggest that as Mohammad Reza Pahlavi gets older his long-standing political weaknesses may increase: his intolerance of criticism, his *folie de grandeur*, and above all his incapacity to realize the economic limitations of his own state. It is evident that such a combination of personal and national conditions is completely unsuited to coping with the kinds of problems that Iran will in all likelihood face. No doubt he, or his successors, will blame the problems Iran has on others – on 'greedy' businessmen, on foreign investors, and foreign governments. A retreat into nationalism is the easiest way out. But the indications are that, as the Pahlavi state enters the critical period when oil has ceased to provide prosperity, it will be even less capable than it was in the 1970s to implement policies that are really able to solve the difficulties Iran faces.

There are, nevertheless, ways in which the Pahlavi régime could remain intact and some changes be introduced (i.e. by remaining within option 1 above). Control of freedom of the press and political activity is an essential feature of the dictatorship; but there are other features that are not and could probably be relaxed. This applies, for example, to the more brutal forms of repressive activity: torture, maltreatment of those in prison, harassment of prisoners' relatives. Similarly, the relaxation of the terms under which political offenders are held is not in itself going to weaken the power of the dictatorship. (Such changes can, when necessary, be reversed.) It is hard to see how the permitting of a degree of linguistic diversity in Iran (in cultural matters) whilst retaining Persian as the one official language would be impossible. No doubt too, changes in economic policy and in military purchases could be introduced. From the early 1970s onwards a number of liberal critics of the régime urged it to carry out some changes in these areas and these options were consistent with the continuation of the system of political dictatorship. There are definite boundaries to what the Pahlavi régime can do, but within these boundaries certain policies can be altered or modified.

Despite this room for manoeuvre, the factors militating against a continued retention of full political power by the Pahlavi dynasty are going to increase, as the economic conditions that have enabled it to survive deteriorate. In such conditions, one can expect to see situations similar to those in Portugal, Greece and Spain – ones in which considerable *direct* pressure on the dictatorship comes from within the ranks of the state and the bourgeoisie, with the encouragement of some more developed capitalist countries, whilst popular mobilizations continue to apply pressure from outside. Those who since 1963 have, however grudgingly, accepted the Shah's monopoly of power will do so the more reluctantly as (a) he fails to provide the economic *quid pro quo* and (b) his policies themselves seem to be leading to greater economic and political difficulties. It is through pressure from such quarters that options 2 (a return to the 1961–3 situation), 3 (military dictatorship) and 4 (bourgeois democracy) will become possibilities. As a popular opposition develops it may as in these other countries provoke elements within the state into pre-emptive changes.

Options 2 and 4 appear less likely than military dictatorship. Certainly, the Shah's first instinct, if he really is under pressure, will be to bring in some civilian politicians, possibly veterans of the 1960–63 period: there are many such individuals and they are still waiting. But his purpose in this will be the better to conserve the monarchy's position, and as window-dressing vis-à-vis Washington, and it will therefore be an inherently unstable system, as were its predecessors. It is improbable that such a partial democracy can last: either the king must go (as he did in 1953, and as he did, under somewhat analogous situations, in Greece), or else the monarch will re-establish full control (as the Shah did in 1953 and in 1963, and as King Hassan II of Morocco was able to do in the 1970s). On the other hand, the prospects for a system of bourgeois democracy are not good in Iran, even though, when it has been possible, this has proved the most stable means of consolidating capitalist rule. In the first place, there exists no history of bourgeois democracy in Iran – as there had existed, however buried, in Greece, Spain and Portugal. Indeed the Iranian bourgeoisie has, as we have seen, shown itself remarkably reluctant to challenge the Shah, and has hidden comfortably behind the economic power of the state since the oil-based growth began.

There are additional factors which make it less likely that such a system of bourgeois rule could be maintained. There is the pressure of the urban and rural poor, who may threaten the capacity of the bourgeoisie to retain power under democratic conditions. The challenge of the oppressed accounts, in part, for the establishment of the Pahlavi dictatorship and its maintenance, and is the greatest argument which the Shah has to justify the form of régime he has built. Probably the only way in which capitalism can be preserved in the future will also be through a form of dictatorship.

A further factor that must be remembered is the regional one, for here the differences are great between Iran on the one side, and Greece, Portugal and Spain on the other. The bourgeois forces in these latter three countries were aided by European and American allies who were themselves bourgeois democrats and who made clear that the economic future of all three countries lay in closer integration with the EEC. Such an integration was possible only under conditions of democracy, and the ruling classes in the three southern European countries knew this. There was a general agreement that for political reasons bourgeois democracy *had* to be established, and could only be abandoned in extreme conditions.

The regional situation in which Iran finds itself is rather different. There are no proper democracies in the region, and the two countries which have had intermittent experiences of democracy – Turkey and Pakistan – are two with very little capacity to influence Iran. The states that will be influential and which could well play a counter-revolutionary role in Iran in response to pleas for help will be Saudi Arabia and Kuwait. No one imagines that they will make it a condition of their aid to the bourgeois forces in Iran that democratic norms be respected. What could make a difference would be a substantial radicalization in either Turkey or Pakistan and the advent to power in one of these of genuinely socialist government: under these conditions a regional pressure *for* democracy could emerge.

For all of these reasons, it appears more likely that capitalism in Iran will in the end fall back on a military dictatorship, if and as the Pahlavi monarchy relaxes its grip. Although as politically authoritarian as the monarchical system, it could provide a greater degree of freedom in economic terms and enable civilians to be integrated into the government as influential ministers and advisers without this, in itself, being seen as a threat to the régime. The conditions for such a takeover are, to some extent, already there. Provided the army acts with a minimal cohesion there is no force in Iranian society that could stop it. So far, this is a distant possibility, and the last coup attempts that are known about were those of Generals Gharani (1958) and Bakhtiar (1961–2). Since then, the armed forces have been controlled carefully by the Shah, and there have been no reports of political dissent. A U S State Department official put it to me in this way: 'The U S Embassy has no direct contact with junior levels of the Iranian officer corps. But of the twenty people we consider most supportive of the Shah many are military, and our day to day contacts suggest the army supports the Shah.'

The limitation is that these generals, like private businessmen, and, for that matter, the government of the United States, have a *conditional* loyalty to the Shah, which will continue as long as he and his family remain the best candidates for guaranteeing the army's position and the capitalist system in Iran. But if this ceases to be the case – if economic and political problems mount, and the Shah seems unable to cope with them – then a coup will become more likely. The purely technical problem of organizing it will remain, given the Shah's careful surveillance of top officers, but his capacity to be sure that he knows what is going on may decline as he himself gets older and the loyalty of those who serve him will be eroded by the developing crisis of the régime. No doubt, any serious conspiratorial group will make sure that it wins at least tacit approval from the U S Embassy before going into action.

The assumption of this argument so far has been that such a military coup will be led by officers of a conservative and pro-western orientation, motivated by a desire to prevent the growth in Iran of popular or socialist forces likely to pose a threat to Iranian capitalism. It would seem likely that the top ranks of the Iranian army share the world-view of their confrères in Indonesia and Chile, where a similar orientation has been evident. But, it may be suggested, there is another possibility, namely that of a more nationalist current emerging within the officer corps, one that might espouse the kind of vaguely socialist ideology found in Nasserite Egypt or Baathist Iraq. In so far as some of the officer corps are recruited from petty-bourgeois backgrounds, and as the conflicts between the Iranian state and the more advanced capitalist countries regain in the 1980s the vivacity they had in the early 1950s, some of the conditions for such a development may come into existence. But there are other factors at work which suggest that a development of this kind is not as likely as that of continued dominance by right-wing generals of a more conventionally conservative mould. First, the Iranian officer corps is not a newly formed one, of the kind that in other developing countries was impressed by nationalist ideologies. Moreover, the controlling group in the army, whether the Shah or his successors, possesses a pervasive intelligence system designed to root out any such tendency. There may well be Iranian officers with the ideology of a Qaddafi or a Nasser, or with ideas such as those that triumphed in the Ethiopian and Portuguese armies in 1974. They could emerge on top, but Iran is a very different context and there are strong forces at work making this a less likely eventuality than it was in these other countries.

A Socialist Alternative?

There exists, of course, another possibility for Iran, namely the overthrow of capitalism through revolution and the establishment of a socialist society. Such an eventuality is conceivable, and there appears to be a possibility that as crisis and discontent grow in the last two decades of the century the régime will not be able to buy loyalty and quiet with its promises. By the late 1980s, there exists a very real possibility of hunger and unemployment on a massive scale in Iran, with an ailing Shah or inexperienced successor, or perhaps a junta of generals in power. Their capacity to suppress the demands of the majority of, by then, 45 million Iranians will be very limited.

However it would be foolish to simplify the problems involved in such a venture and to ignore the problems which the Iranian left, as presently constituted, faces if it is to achieve this end. In the first place, the state will still be capable of mobilizing formidable repressive capacities, and will continue to be able to draw on the support of its developed allies; if necessary, Saudi Arabia, which will be enjoying massive oil revenues well into the next century, can give financial assistance. The capitalist state in Iran will not fade away in any automatic manner. Secondly, the Iranian opposition will have to organize a mass following almost from zero, since however much popular hostility there now is to the régime, the left organizations are extremely weak. Moreover, the opposition will have to develop a programme that mobilizes as wide a support as possible – combining the demands of the oppressed classes with those of the oppressed nationalities, in a way that previous opposition organizations have failed to do. The economic crisis in itself will never bring down the Pahlavi régime or its capitalist replacements: this can only be done by a mass movement led and organized by a revolutionary organization. Unless such an organization is able to develop, the present state will continue through the decades after oil.

There are other features of the contemporary Iranian left which give cause for disquiet once these organizations are measured against the opportunities and, at the same time, the tasks they may face. The Tudeh Party remains loyal to the Soviet Union, and it is quite conceivable that, if the Soviet Union felt an overthrow of capitalism was undesirable in Iran for international reasons (e.g. it threatened détente with the U S A), the Tudeh would be commanded not to take revolutionary initiatives. The groups who declare their loyalty to China present an even more forlorn perspective, given Peking's devotion to the Iranian régime. On the other hand, the guerrilla groups that have pursued militarist tactics have relied in their work on rhetorical analyses, and have shown too little interest in concrete problems of political practice and programme. All these groups share an as yet restricted theoretical culture – a tendency to apply borrowed ideas in an impatient and secondhand manner – and all have practised a highly factional kind of politics in which mutual abuse takes priority over the more difficult tasks of building a united front of all those opposed to the Shah's dictatorship.

These failings cannot be passed over in silence since they are matters of central relevance to the capacity of the opposition to take advantage of the opportunities presented to it; nor do they represent a temporary distortion, the product of isolation and defeat, for, without explicit attempts to remedy these forms of political analysis and practice, they will continue and flourish in the perhaps more open contexts that will arise in the future. One has indeed to present this problem in its starkest form, since unless it is confronted, the Iranian left will suffer further defeats: if the left opposition continues its present course, divided, rhetorical, and in many cases subservient to one or other communist country, then it will be extremely unlikely that a coherent mass challenge to capitalism in Iran, led by a political organization uniting the widest possible support, will emerge.

The Iranian left may, in the past, have erred on the side of caution, but this is not the only temptation it may face in the future. The history of the past half century of socialist struggles is eloquent on how opportunities for socialism can be thrown away in the aftermath of a dictatorship's defeat, not only through excessive caution on the part of the left (the reason conventionally adduced by revolutionary critics), but also through sectarianism and an exaggerated sense of confidence. In Germany, parts of the communist movement isolated themselves through ultra-left policies in the years immediately after the overthrow of the Wilhelmine régime in 1918, and again, in the years leading up to 1933, the Communist Party pursued a suicidal and sectarian course that ended in the most bloody defeat. In Portugal after the overthrow of the fascist régime in 1974, sections of the left, enamoured of adventurist slogans, and exaggerating their own strength, were isolated over time and defeated by a regrouped right. These and other examples show how the advantages of a rupture in the dictatorship and the rise of a mass movement sympathetic to socialism can be thrown away through factionalism and infatuation with rhetoric. The left in Iran must present itself as a strong and unifying force to overcome these dangers. If, therefore, one rejects the optimism of the régime, and its illusions about the 'Great Civilization', one should also reject any facile revolutionary optimism about the ease with which capitalism will be overthrown in Iran or about the capacity of the Iranian opposition forces to attain and administer power.

The problems involved in any such venture are enormous. In addition to the whole question which has just been discussed, of tactics and strategy, there is the further problem of the kind of political system which a revolutionary movement creates. This is an acute political issue for two reasons: because the Iranian opposition has developed in conditions of clandestineness and exile, and because the most influential states in the international communist movement have failed to produce convincing systems of socialist democracy. Hence it is extremely difficult for a movement such as the Iranian one to develop and sustain forms of democratic activity during and after a revolutionary process. Yet it is here that the greatest test, and the greatest opportunity, must lie. For it is in the superiority of socialism over capitalism that the argument for a revolution and for a new social system in Iran must lie: in economic terms, in the capacity of a socialist régime to use Iran's wealth for the benefit of the working class and its allies and to distribute the wealth and services to these forces, and politically, in the capacity of socialism to provide the context for establishing a genuinely democratic system in Iran, of a kind never seen before in that country. The legacy of the failure of the international communist movement to resolve this question hangs over the Iranian left, as it does over the left everywhere, and it is a failure that can only be reversed by conscious and far-sighted political practice and analysis. If the left can evolve a practice and a programme that guarantees political freedom after the end of capitalism in Iran, then it may be able to rally a wide and ultimately victorious popular movement against the Pahlavi régime or its capitalist successors.

If I have here stressed the problems involved it is precisely because a socialist revolution is a possibility in Iran and because the many-sided problems that such a revolution will face should be stated quite clearly now. Nothing is to be served by a rhetorical and naive catastrophism which assumes that history will automatically sweep the Shah and his group away, or that if this does occur the régime that succeeds it will automatically be in every respect better. The prospects for liberating the Iranian people and building a truly just and democratic society in that country, in which the working class and its allies will play the leading role, are realistic enough. It is quite possible that before too long the Iranian people will chase the Pahlavi dictator and his associates from power, will surmount the obstacles in its way, and build a prosperous and socialist Iran.

Notes

Notes

Chapter 1: Iranian Society: An Overview

1. Statistics prior to 1976 are drawn from Julian Bharier, *Economic Development in Iran 1900–1970*, London, 1971, Chapter 2, 'Human Resources'; figures for 1976 from *Iran Almanac 1977*.

2. A source of confusion in accounts of this issue is the use of the word 'tribe' to denote the non-Persian elements in Iran, with the related assumption that these tribes are nomadic. The majority of those groups which retain some form of tribal system are settled people, not nomads, and the most important non-Persian group of all, the Azerbaijani, is not organized along tribal lines. The three categories of nomad, tribe, and linguistic non-Persian group are not therefore coextensive.

3. *Iran, Oil Money and the Ambitions of a Nation*, Hudson Institute Special Report, Paris, 1975, p. 11.

4. Ehsan Yar-Shater, *Iran Faces the Seventies*, New York, 1971, p. 220.

5. An incisive critique of Iranian male attitudes to women is found in Reza Baraheni, *The Crowned Cannibals*, New York, 1977, pp. 45–63.

Chapter 2: The State: Historical Background

1. It is one of the common assumptions of the Iranian opposition that Reza Khan was in some sense a 'British agent'. He was certainly encouraged by the British authorities in Iran to seize power, and insofar as he was seen to be blocking the spread of communism into Asia his consolidation of a new state was welcomed by the British. However, the latter were not able in any real sense to control Reza's actions after he seized power. For an account of Reza Khan's régime see Amin Banani, *The Modernization of Iran, 1921–1941*, Stanford, 1961.

2. Among several available accounts of the CIA's role now available see Andrew Tully, *CIA – The Inside Story*, London, 1962,

Chapter 7 and David Wise and Thomas B. Ross, *The Invisible Government*, London, 1964, pp. 108–12.

3. See Rodolfo Stavenhagen, ed., *Agrarian Problems and Peasant Movements in Latin America*, New York, 1970, pp. 96ff., for U S encouragement of land reform in Latin America.

4. Marvin Zonis, *The Political Élite of Iran*, Princeton, 1971, p. 63, n. 45.

5. On the theory of the post-colonial state, see Hamza Alavi, 'The Post-Colonial State', *New Left Review*, no. 74, July–August 1972.

6. J. D. Barrington-Moore, *The Social Origins of Dictatorship and Democracy*, London, 1966.

7. *New York Times*, 15 June 1946, as quoted in Ervand Abrahamian, 'The Social Bases of Iranian Politics', Ph.D. thesis, Columbia.

Chapter 3: The State: General Characteristics

1. A common claim by pro-régime academics and writers is that Iran cannot be analysed in terms of 'imported' or 'western' analytic concepts, and in particular in terms of class concepts. Apologists of virtually every régime in the world claim this for their own countries, and with equally little justification: each society does have specific features, but this does not mean that general theoretical categories are inapplicable in these countries, any more than are the concepts of medicine or engineering.

2. Marvin Zonis, *The Political Élite of Iran*, Princeton, 1971; James Alban Bill. *The Politics of Iran*, Columbia, Ohio, 1972; Leonard Binder, *Iran, Political Development in a Changing Society*, Berkeley and Los Angeles, 1962. It would take us beyond the limits of this work to go into the general theoretical assumptions of each of these three works which, despite their definite differences in approach, are within a common school. Nor is this discussion intended to deny that each of these works reflects informed observation of the Iranian scene and contains a considerable amount of original analysis. However, certain critical points can be made in brief. Zonis, p. 5, explicitly states that it is his purpose to study 'the attitudes and behavior of powerful individuals' without analysing what this power consists of and what its relation to property and income is. He also reports, p. 11, that 'access to active duty military officers was denied the author by the Shah', a serious limitation on any such study. Bill, for his part, claims to be applying

the concept of class, but it is not at all clear what his concept of class is. He considers the 'professional middle class' to be a 'new' class (p. 7), but does not identify any distinct industrial or financial middle class, and he also seems to assume that classes existing in one pre-capitalist society can simply continue to exist under capitalism. Binder's work was written before the White Revolution, and while devoting twenty pages to the analysis of 'cabinet government' in Iran (hardly a serious topic) and many more to various governmental 'processes' he is also uninterested in the socio-economic context of Iranian government.

3. Lenin in *The Development of Capitalism in Russia* makes this point very clearly in opposition to the romantic nostalgia of the *narodniks*: similar points could be made about some Iranian opposition literature today.

4. For example, Thomas Ricks, 'Contemporary Iranian Political Economy and History: an Overview', in *The Review of Iranian Political Economy and History*, December 1976, vol. 1, no. 1.

5. *Le Monde*, 6 October 1976.

6. A general account of the changing investment policies of the advanced capitalist countries in Latin America can be found in the work of Fernando Enrique Cardoso, for example 'The Contradictions of Dependent Development', *New Left Review*, no. 74. The difference between Iran and countries such as Argentina and Brazil is that the Iranian state has much larger resources of capital to invest in joint ventures, and also that, whereas in these more developed Latin American countries foreign investment is partly designed to produce goods for export to third markets, production in Iran is at this stage almost totally for the domestic market.

7. Zonis, op. cit., p. 18.

8. Binder, op. cit., pp. 221–2.

9. Mohammad Reza Pahlavi, *Mission for my Country*, London, 1961, p. 173.

10. *The Times*, 16 October 1972; *Financial Times*, 3 January 1975.

11. The Shah, speech of 2 March 1975, Ministry of Information and Tourism pamphlet, pp. 11–13.

12. See the works of Paul Vieille on the land reform, summarized in *Le Monde*, 27 January 1973. See also p. 319, n. 18.

13. On repression in Brazil, see Amnesty International, 'Report on Allegations of Torture in Brazil', London, 1973.

14. Nicos Poulantzas, *Fascism and Dictatorship*, London, 1974,

provides a theorization of the workings of what he calls the 'exceptional' capitalist state, although he does not discuss the different forms such an exceptional state can take.

15. Nicos Poulantzas, *Political Power and Social Classes*, London, 1973, contains a discussion of Marx's theory of Bonapartism.

16. Marx and Engels, *Selected Correspondence*, Moscow, 1965, p. 214.

17. Karl Marx, 'The 18th Brumaire', in Marx and Engels, *Selected Works*, Moscow, 1968, p. 170.

18. R. K. Karanjia, *The Mind of a Monarch*, London, 1977, p. 236, reports the Shah as hoping for a 'revival of the great Aryan civilization' as seen in the days of the Emperor Cyrus. Under the Third Reich, Iranians resident in Germany were officially classed as 'Aryans' and permitted to marry German citizens.

19. See Poulantzas, *Fascism and Dictatorship*, op. cit., for an account of this.

20. Zonis, op. cit., pp. 329–30.

21. Interview with Oriana Fallaci, *New Republic*, 1 December 1973, p. 16.

22. For example, E. A. Bayne, *Persian Kingship in Transition*, New York, 1968, pp. 29ff. 'The protocol of the meeting is strict. The monarch speaks *ex cathedra*, his use of the royal "we" is consistent, and his ministers *salaam* with courtly formality and address the monarch in a convoluted, respectual Farsi.'

Chapter 4: The Armed Forces and S A V AK

1. On the early history and general character of the armed forces, see J. C. Hurewitz, *Middle East Politics: the Military Dimension*, London, 1969, Chapter 15; Ahmad Salamatian, *Historique du Rôle Politique de l'Armée en Iran*, University of Paris, thesis, 1970; Marvin Zonis, *The Political Élite of Iran*, op. cit., pp. 102–16.

2. Zonis, op. cit., p. 66.

3. Richard Cottam, in *New Perspectives on the Persian Gulf*, Washington, 1973, p. 135.

4. *Newsweek*, 21 May 1973.

5. *Financial Times*, 28 July 1975.

6. Quoted in David Horowitz, *From Yalta to Vietnam*, London, 1966, p. 190.

7. This list draws on that in James Alban Bill, *The Politics of Iran*, op. cit., pp. 42–3.

8. The full text is published in *Human Rights and the Legal*

System in Iran, International Commission of Jurists, Geneva, 1976, pp. 32–3.

9. *Newsweek*, 14 October 1974.

10. *Iran News and Documents*, Ministry of Information, Tehran, 12 April 1971.

11. *Newsweek*, 14 October 1974.

12. *Washington Post*, 26 October 1976.

13. The Shah in the *New York Times*, 22 October 1976, Sabeti in the same, 29 May 1976.

14. Amnesty International, *Annual Report 1974–1975*, p. 8.

15. I C J report, see note 8 above; Amnesty International Briefing, *Iran*, November 1976.

16. Amnesty, op. cit. (note 15), p. 7.

17. *The Times*, 9 June 1977.

18. Amnesty, op. cit. (note 15), p. 6.

19. ibid., p. 8.

20. *Sunday Times*, 19 January 1975.

21. Ashraf Dehqani, *Torture and Resistance in Iran*, Iran Committee publication, London, 1977.

22. Reza Baraheni, *God's Shadow*, Bloomington, Indiana, 1976.

23. Amnesty, op. cit. (note 15), p. 9.

24. *New York Times*, 29 May 1976.

25. Alfred Atherton, Assistant Secretary for Near Eastern and South Asian Affairs, in Department of State News Release, 8 September 1976.

26. Theodore Sorensen, *Kennedy*, New York, 1965, p. 628.

27. *Guardian*, 20 October 1976, 4 January 1977.

28. For details of the internal problems relating to the US arms programme see the most informative *US Military Sales to Iran*, Staff Report to the Subcommittee on Foreign Assistance of the Committee on Foreign Relations, United States Senate, July 1976.

29. *Washington Post*, 13 May 1977.

30. For details see *Multinational Corporations and United States Foreign Policy*, Hearings before the Subcommittee on Multinational Corporations of the Committee on Foreign Relations, United States Senate, 1975. For a summary of the charges against Khatami and Shahram see Anthony Sampson, *The Arms Bazaar*, London, 1977, pp. 241ff.

31. Details on Ibex in the *Guardian*, 4 January 1977.

Chapter 5: Agricultural Development

1. More has probably been written about the land reform than about any other aspect of recent Iranian socio-economic development apart from oil. For a very selective list of sources see the bibliography, below.

2. V. Lenin, *The Development of Capitalism in Russia*, Moscow, 1956.

3. *Employment and Income Policies for Iran*, I L O, Geneva, 1973, p. 40.

4. Nikki Keddie, 'The Iranian Village Before and After Land Reform', in H. Bernstein, *Development and Underdevelopment*, Harmondsworth, 1973.

5. *Khosh-neshin*, literally 'good-sitter', is a vague term applying both to those who are casual labourers and to the minority of those in the village, such as shopkeepers and artisans, who do not work on the land. But the great majority are in the former, poor, category. See 'The *Khwushnishin* population of Iran' by Eric Hoogland, *Iranian Studies*, vol. vi, no. 4, Autumn, 1973.

6. Keddie, op. cit., pp. 157ff.

7. Eric Hobsbawm, 'Peasants and Politics', *Journal of Peasant Studies*, vol. 1. no. 1, October 1973.

8. See the paper by Farhad Kazemi and Ervand Abrahamian, 'The Non-Revolutionary Peasantry of Modern Iran'. They write (p. 4, note 3): 'During the turbulent periods of 1946 and 1963, the Iranian press reported only 22 incidents of peasant protests. Of these 22, 8 consisted of peaceful demonstrations in mosques, 4 involved rival villages, and only 10 directly challenged landowners.'

9. The background to the reform is given in Anne Lambton, *The Persian Land Reform*, London, 1966.

10. Keddie, op. cit., p. 165 n.

11. Details from D. R. Denman, *The King's Vista*, London, 1973.

12. *Middle East Report and Information Project*, no. 43, 'Land Reform and Agri-business in Iran', by Helmut Richards.

13. *Financial Times*, 28 July 1975.

14. M E R I P, op. cit., and *Financial Times*, 21 October 1976.

15, Keddie. op. cit., p. 162.

16. Denman, op. cit., p. 165.

17. Imperial Organization of Social Services, 'Report of the Commission on the Study of Health and Medical Problems', second edition, 1975, p. 1.

18. Paul Vieille, 'Les paysans, la petite bourgeoisie et l'état après la reforme agraire en Iran', *Annales*, no. 2. p. 27.

19. On Arsanjani see Lambton, op. cit., and Marvin Zonis, *The Political Élite of Iran*, op. cit., pp. 53–60. Denman manages to write his book on the land reform without once mentioning Arsanjani, an omission indicative of the author's generally uncritical approach to the Iranian government's policies.

20. Peter Dorner, *Land Reform and Economic Development*, Harmondsworth, 1972, pp. 16–17.

21. *Financial Times*, 28 July 1975.

22. *Economist*, 'A survey of Iran', 28 August 1976, pp. 40, 43.

23. Iran's future reliance on food imports will constitute an important part of its foreign economic relations, and may contribute to its interfering in neighbouring countries (Pakistan, Afghanistan, perhaps Oman), in order to ensure that their economies are directed to meeting the needs of the Iranian one.

24. Vieille, op. cit., contains a detailed discussion of credit distribution.

25. Dorner, op. cit., pp. 92–3. The U N has estimated that between 1970 and 2000 the urban population of the less developed countries will increase by 242 per cent.

26. Information on the widening gap in incomes in one specific village after land reform is given by Nico Kielstra in his *Ecology and Community in Iran*, Amsterdam, 1975. Before land reform the 3 leading village families earned 25 per cent of the total income, the 42 small cultivators 48 per cent and the 56 landless families 27 per cent. After land reform, and the introduction of opium as a cash crop, the corresponding figures were 42, 47 and 11 per cent (p. 250).

27. Robert Looney, *The Economic Development of Iran*, London, 1973, p. 9.

28. Denman, op. cit., p. 171.

29. ibid., p. 159.

30. Samuel P. Huntingdon quoted in Al McCoy, 'Land Reform as Counter-revolution', *Bulletin of Concerned Asian Scholars*, vol. 3, no. 1, Winter–Spring 1971, p. 115.

31. On Japan, McCoy, ibid.; on Egypt, Robert Mabro, *The Egyptian Economy 1952–1972*, Oxford, 1974, Chapter 4, 'Land Reform'.

32. Terry Byers, 'Land reform, industrialisation and the marketed surplus in India', in David Lehman (ed.), *Agrarian Reform and Agrarian Reformism*, London, 1974, p. 248.

33. Hossein Mahdavy quoted in Keddie, op. cit., pp. 162–3.

34. Vieille, op. cit.

Chapter 6: Oil and Industrialization

1. See 'Patterns and Problems of Economic Development in Rentier States: the Case of Iran' by Hossein Mahdavy, in *Studies in the Economic History of the Middle East*, M. A. Cook, ed., London, 1970, and 'The Impact of the Oil Industry on the Economy of Iran', by William H. Bartsch in *Foreign Investment in the Petroleum and Mineral Industries*, Raymond Mikesell, ed., London, 1971.

2. I have avoided going into the long and contentious history of the Iranian oil industry. A detailed study can be found in Fereidun Fesharaki, *The Development of the Iranian Oil Industry*, New York, 1976.

3. The history of the oil dispute is given in L. P. Elwell-Sutton, *Persian Oil: a study in Power Politics*, London, 1955.

4. Iran's role in OPEC up to 1974 is discussed in Joe Stork, *Middle East Oil and the Energy Crisis*, New York, 1975.

5. *Petroleum Economist*, July 1976.

6. *Iran: Past, Present and Future*, published by the Aspen Institute, New York, 1976, p. 100.

7. Robert E. Looney, *The Economic Development of Iran*, London, 1973, p. 9.

8. Bharier, op. cit., p. 184. There are obvious analogies here with the growth of industry in Latin America during the depression and the Second World War, when previous foreign trade and investment links were also disrupted, and local industry thereby stimulated.

9. Banks and banking shares dominate the Tehran stock exchange: of the 24 member brokers in 1976 19 represent banks whilst of the total shares traded between March and October 4,461,071 were banking shares and only 377,459 industrials (*Kayhan International Weekly*, 16 October 1976).

10. For the background see Ahmad Ashraf, 'Historical Obstacles to the Development of a Bourgeoisie in Iran', in Cook, op. cit.

11. An example of an organization originating in the bazaar is the Behshahr group. Beginning as a trading company in 1944 it consisted in 1976 of 22 distinct companies and 9 partnerships, with interests in textiles, consumer products, trade and banking. However, this, one of the most prominent industrial groups, was still concentrated in the light industrial field and financial services and employed only 9,000 people.

12. In 1974 CAPFI was renamed the Iran Investment and Economic Technical Assistance Organization, and attached to the Ministry of Economic Affairs and Finance.

13. For example, see 'State a Barrier to Investment', *Financial Times*, 25 July 1977.

14. B. T. Goodrich tyre company, operating in Iran since 1959, sold off its 46 per cent share in 1976 after two consecutive years of losses: among its complaints were payroll costs rising 73 per cent, raw materials 30 per cent with government control on prices, disputes over the workers' share programme and transportation problems (*Economist*, 26 June 1976).

15. Looney, op. cit., p. 88.

16. *Investitionen in Iran*, Bundesstelle für Aussenhandelsinformation, Cologne, 1974, p. 3, quoted in *Rüstung und Unterentwicklung*, by U. Albrecht, D. Ernst, P. Lock and H. Wulf, Hamburg 1976, p. 97.

17. *Financial Times*, 21 October 1976.

18. Eric Rouleau in *Le Monde*, 3–4 October 1976. In 1977 an ordinary four-bedroom Tehran flat cost £300–500 per month (*The Times*, 6 May 1977).

19. *International Herald Tribune*, 5 June 1975.

20. Looney, op. cit., p. 30, and Rouleau, ibid.

21. *Iran: Past, Present and Future*, op. cit., pp. 90–91.

22. *Iran, Oil Money and the Ambitions of a Nation*, Hudson Institute, Paris, 1974.

23. *The Times*, 24 March 1976. Venezuela shares with Iran a combined surplus of unskilled and a shortage of skilled workers, as well as excessive centralization, and other characteristics of oil-based development.

24. *Iran, Oil Money and the Ambitions of a Nation*, op. cit., p. 7.

25. Bill Warren, 'Imperialism and Capitalist Industrialization', *New Left Review*, no. 81, September–October 1973.

26. ibid., p. 42.

Chapter 7: The Working Class

1. Bharier, op. cit., Chapter 2, 'Human Resources'; International Labour Office, *Employment and Income Policies for Iran*, Geneva, 1973, Chapter 2, 'Employment Situation'.

2. For a general discussion with many implications for Iran, see David Turnham, *The Employment Problem in Less Developed Countries*, OECD, Paris, 1974.

3. Nicos Poulantzas in his *Classes in Contemporary Capitalism* (London, 1975) has explored the implications of this problem for analysis and socialist strategy in the advanced capitalist countries: his emphasis on the need for class alliances that do not at the same time involve a confusion of the distinction between the proletariat and its allies applies equally to the developing capitalist countries. On the other hand, the thesis associated with Fanon, that the industrial working class in the third world is not a revolutionary class, is without foundation.

4. The fragmented ethnic situation in Iran (see p. 12) obviously adds a further dimension to this question of divisions internal to the proletariat. One classic example of this was in the oilfields in 1945–6 when the A I O C tried to mobilize Arab employees against the other workers.

5. Figures given here are for total numbers employed in these branches of economic activity: hence not all will be workers. We do not have the information to separate wage-earners from salaried and self-employed, but clearly the great majority will fall into the former category.

6. Charles Issawi, *The Economic History of Iran 1800–1914*, London, 1971, pp. 48–9.

7. Iranpour Djazani, *Wirtschaft und Bevölkerung in Khuzistan und ihr Wandel unter dem Einfluss des Erdöls*, Tübingen, 1963, pp. 94ff.

8. An introduction to the internal life and policies of the oil company is L. P. Elwell-Sutton, *Persian Oil: a Study in Power Politics*, op. cit. Chapter 8 discusses working conditions and includes a critique of the rather indulgent I L O report *Labour Conditions in the Oil Industry in Iran*, Geneva, 1950.

9. I have explored this problem further in 'Labour Migration and the Formation of the Working Class in the Oil Producing States of the Middle East', published in M E R I P Report no. 59, August 1977.

10. I L O, *Employment and Income Policies for Iran*, op. cit., and William Bartsch, 'The Industrial Labour Force of Iran: Problems of Recruitment, Training and Productivity', *Middle East Journal*, Winter 1971.

11. The government hopes to have produced 200,000 new technicians, and 600,000 new skilled and semi-skilled workers by the end of the Fifth Plan, i.e. 1977. This is an improbable target, but there is considerable disagreement amongst labour experts about how far Iran does lack the labour it needs. Bartsch, op. cit.,

presents a 'pessimistic' view that is contested by Walter Elkan, 'Employment, Education, Training and Skilled Labour in Iran', *Middle East Journal*, Spring 1977.

12. *Le Monde*, 6 October 1976.

13. Bartsch, op. cit., p. 27, n. 48.

14. I L O, *Employment and Income Policies for Iran*, p. 46.

15. Mohammad Hemmasi, *Migration in Iran*, Shiraz, 1974, p. 63.

16. John Connell, 'Tehran: Urbanisation and Development', Institute of Development Studies Discussion Paper, no. 32, September 1973, p. 17.

17. I L O, *Employment and Income Policies for Iran*, op. cit., and Mission Working Paper No. 1, 'The Problem of Employment and Unemployment in Iran', by P. Sen Gupta, the latter being an unpublished paper on which the former draws.

18. *Le Monde Diplomatique*, May 1975, p. 22. This is taken from an unpublished study carried out by the Plan and Budget Organization, with the assistance of the Maclin Institute and Stanford University.

19. Data for this section drawn from 'The Role of Women in Iranian Development' by M. Sedghi and Ahmad Ashraf, in *Iran: Past, Present, Future*, New York, 1976, and I L O, *Employment and Income Policies for Iran*, op. cit.

20. *Le Monde Diplomatique*, op. cit. I am also extremely grateful to Professor Fereidun Firoozi for allowing me to consult his unpublished article 'Profit-Sharing in Iran'.

21. *Financial Times*, 28 July 1975.

22. *US Military Sales to Iran*, U S Senate Subcommittee on Foreign Assistance of the Committee on Foreign Relations, July 1976, p. 33.

23. According to one estimate, there were 400 South Koreans working in the Gulf area in 1974; there will be 240,000 by 1980. Many work for Japanese or Japanese-owned construction firms who bring in labour as part of their arrangement with the local governments. This had already occurred in South Vietnam, where a substantial number of U S bases were built in this way by Korean contract labour.

24. On this early period, see Ervand Abrahamian, 'The Crowd in Iranian Politics', *Past and Present*, December 1968.

25. Schapour Ravasani, *Sowjetrepublik Gilan*, Berlin, n.d., pp. 221ff.

26. The most detailed discussion of the trades union movement in this period is that of Ervand Abrahamian in 'The Social Bases

of Iranian Politics: The Tudeh Party, 1941–1953', Ph. D. Columbia, 1969. The information used here is drawn mainly from Abrahamian's detailed investigations, Chapter 8. I have also drawn on Fereidun Firoozi, 'Labour and Trades Unions in Iran', unpublished paper.

27. Reza Rusta was born the son of peasants in an Azari-speaking village in Gilan. He went to school in Rasht, and helped to organize local unions for shoemakers, blacksmiths and construction workers. After studying in the Soviet Union between 1923 and 1925, he returned home and worked underground until imprisonment in 1931. When union activity became possible again in 1941 he was ideally suited to head the new movement. Abrahamian, op. cit. He died in exile in 1966.

28. Elwell-Sutton, op. cit., describes the workers' movement in the oil-fields up to 1953.

29. Nicos Poulantzas, in *Fascism and Dictatorship*, London, 1974, Part Four, has analysed the policy of the German and Italian fascist states towards the working class. In particular he brings out the policy of increasing the differentials between skilled and unskilled workers, the use of a spurious anti-capitalist rhetoric, and the mobilization of workers in such organizations as the *Arbeiterfront* in Germany and the corporatist unions in Italy. He also brings out the specific role of the S S in working through the unions to win support for the régime (p. 195), in a manner analogous to S A V A K's role in Iran.

30. I L O Mission Paper no. IX, 'Labour Legislation, Practice and Policy' by J. de Givry and J. Scoville, p. 20.

31. The role of S A V A K is emphasized in the U S Department of Labor Report *Labour Law and Practice in Iran*, B L S Report no. 276, 1964, p. 28.

32. T. Jalil, *Workers of Iran: Repression and the Fight for Democratic Trades Unions*, London, 1976, p. 39. For the more skilled workers, the cash benefits and non-cash bonuses may account for up to 40 per cent or even 50 per cent of the total remuneration. Cash bonuses and profits have been known to reach 30 per cent of the workers' total income; but this applies to only a small percentage of the total workforce.

33. Zonis, op. cit., pp. 93–4. Zonis also details the role of the teachers' union during the turmoil of the early 1960s.

34. The general *fact* of an increase in strike activity is attested to in a number of reports in the western press (e.g. *Le Monde*, 5 October 1976). The details here are taken from a number of

opposition publications, including Jalil, op. cit., and Tudeh Party publications.

35. *Tehran Economist*, 22 May 1976.

Chapter 8: The Opposition

1. There are the nine political prisoners who were officially 'shot while trying to escape' in early 1975. They were almost certainly killed under torture. But there are others where persistent doubts exist and where no clear answer is available. Samad Behrangi was a well-known writer of children's books who was reported to have drowned while swimming in the Aras rivers in 1968. Yet Behrangi was a good swimmer; and he was known to be an advocate of linguistic and cultural rights for the Turkish people of Iran. The noted writer Jalal Al-i Ahmad, the scourge of vulgarized western culture and of the *nouveaux riches* in Iran, is reported to have died suddenly at his country cottage near the Caspian in 1974. Yet he was only 46 and was believed by friends to have been in the best of health a few days beforehand. Moreover, funeral arrangements made by his family were cancelled by SAVAK who ordered immediate burial (this information from Reza Baraheni). Another case is that of the wrestling champion Gholamreza Takhti, who was a popular personality and a supporter of the National Front, whose movements were restricted by the police in 1966 and who died a short while afterwards. Although it was officially stated he had had a heart attack, thousands of people attended his funeral in the belief that he had been murdered. Doubt also surrounds the sudden deaths of people higher up in the régime. Dr Hassan Arsanjani, the Minister of Agriculture sacked by the Shah in 1963 and later exiled as Ambassador to Rome, died of a heart attack in 1969 or so it was said; Arsanjani may indeed have died of this, but it is also known that despite his dismissal he had remained critical of the régime and enjoyed a wide audience. Or take the case of Nasser Amiri, the head of the Mardom party sacked by the Shah in late 1974 for criticizing the régime: a few months later he died, apparently in a car crash. In all these cases as in many others an element of doubt persists.

2. *Iran Research*, Bulletin no. 8, London, January 1975.

3. *Iran People's Struggle*, vol. 1, no. 3, New York, July 1975.

4. Eric Hoogland, 'The *Khwushnishin* Population of Iran', *Iranian Studies*, Autumn 1973.

5. 'The Non-Revolutionary Peasantry of Iran'. unpublished paper by Farhad Kazemi and Ervand Abrahamian, 1976.

6. *Iran People's Struggle*, vol. 2, no. 3, New York, October 1976.

7. I have drawn here on Javid Sadiq, 'Nationalities and Revolution in Iran', English typescript, New York, 1976.

8. Zonis, op. cit., pp. 179–80.

9. See Sadiq, op. cit., and Ervand Abrahamian, 'Communism and communalism in Iran: the *Tudah* and the *Fidqah-i Dimukrat*', *International Journal of Middle Eastern Studies*, vol. 1, 1970.

10. *Iran: Chronique de la repression 1963–1974*, Paris, 1975, p. 90

11. James Bill, *The Politics of Iran*, Columbus, Ohio, 1973, p. 90. *Kayhan International Weekly Edition*, 2 July 1977.

12. Bill, op. cit., pp. 78ff. provides an interesting illustration of this. The number of university students in Iran has risen from 10,000 in 1953–54, to 67,000 in 1970, to 170,000 in 1976–77.

13. Bill, op. cit., p. 76.

14. Sadegh Hedayat, *The Blind Owl*, London, 1957, p. 1.

15. *Al Horria*, Beirut, no. 411, 6 May 1968.

16. *Documents of the Third Congress of the Kurdistan Democratic Party – Iran*, Stockholm, 1974.

17. See, for example, *Al-Dhikri al-Thamana wa al-Arbaun l' Ihtilal al-Ahvaz*, published by Al-Jabha al-Sha'abia l-Tahrir al-Ahvaz, Baghdad, 1974.

18. Sepehr Zabih, *The Communist Movement in Iran*, Berkeley and Los Angeles, 1966, p. 239.

19. *Yearbook of International Communist Affairs*, Hoover Institution, Stanford.

20. Statement by Alfred Atherton, Assistant Secretary for Near Eastern and South Asian Affairs, before the Sub-committee on International Organizations of the House International Relations Committee, 8 September 1976.

21. See note 9.

22. Zabih, op. cit., pp. 220–21.

23. Nureddin Kianuri, 'Alignment of Class Forces at the Democratic Stage of the Revolution', *World Marxist Review*, February 1976.

24. Zabih, op. cit., pp. 240ff.

25. As well as the two pro-Chinese groups mentioned already (p. 231), there were: the 'Palestine' group of activists led by Shokrallah Paknejad, who were arrested in 1970 whilst trying to cross the border into Iraq and enlist with the Palestinian guerrillas; the thirty-four people arrested in February 1970 and accused of belonging to a group called the Muslim Nation of Iran; and the Cause of the

People (*Arman-i Khalq*) group, all of whose members seem to have been arrested in 1971 prior to their starting military activities. There were almost certainly others.

26. *Iran Research*, no. 1, June 1972.

27. *Biography of Said Mohsin*, published by the Liberation Movement of Iran, Abroad, January 1976, p. 5.

28. *The Life of Hamid Ashraf*, London, 1977.

29. Details of guerrilla activities are taken from *Iran Research*, *Iran People's Struggle*, and other exile publications.

30. Pouyan issued as 'Iran: the struggle within', by Support Committee for the Iranian People's Struggle, New York, 1975; Ahmadzadeh issued 1976 by the same group; Farahani by the Iran Research group, London, 1973; Jazani by the Iran Committee, London, 1976.

31. Farahani, op. cit., pp. 55–61; Pouyan, op. cit., p. 28; Ahmadzadeh, op. cit., p. 2.

32. Jazani, op. cit., p. 39; Ahmadzadeh, op. cit., pp. 28–9; Farahani, op. cit., p. 47.

33. Farahani, op. cit., pp. 62–3; Pouyan, op. cit., p. 24; Ahmadzadeh, op. cit., p. 34.

34. An excellent critique of these theories is given by Joao Quartim in his 'Régis Debray and the Brazilian Revolution', *New Left Review*, no. 59, January-February 1970, and *Dictatorship and Armed Struggle in Brazil*, London, 1971, especially pp. 168–76. I have drawn on his arguments here.

35. Ahmadzadeh, op. cit., pp. 30–31, 40; Farahani, p. 64.

36. Pouyan, op. cit., p. 25.

37. Farahani, op. cit., p. 69.

38. Ahmadzadeh, op. cit., pp. 34–5.

39. Jazani, op. cit., p. 63.

Chapter 9: Foreign Relations

1. This policy was first enunciated in a speech by President Nixon on the Pacific Island of Guam, in July 1969. In the words of the then Defence Secretary the policy involves the following: 'Each partner does its share and contributes what it best can to the common effort. In the majority of cases, this means indigenous manpower organized into properly equipped and well-trained armed forces with the help of matériel, training, technology and specialized skills furnished by the United States' (as quoted in *Open Secret: The Kissinger–Nixon Doctrine in Asia*, ed. Virginia Brodine and Mark Selden, New York, 1972, p. 103.)

2. Shahram Chubin and Sepehr Zabih, *The Foreign Relations of Iran*, Berkeley and Los Angeles, 1974, p. 10.

3. ibid., p. 101.

4. The novel by John Ehrlichman, Nixon's former adviser, entitled *The Company*, London, 1976 (later televised as *Washington: Behind Closed Doors*), contains a fictionalized account of relations between Nixon, the Shah and Helms.

5. I am grateful to Winslow Peck, a former employee of the U S National Security Agency, for this information.

6. *The Persian Gulf, 1974: Money, Politics, Arms, and Power*, House of Representatives, Hearing before the Sub-committee on the Near East and South Asia, Washington, 1975, p. 122.

7. For an analysis of Soviet policy that avoids the pitfalls of cold war alarmism see the study by a British Foreign Office official, *Soviet Foreign Policy, 1962–1973*, by John Edmonds, Oxford, 1975.

8. On the Gilan Republic see *The Communist Movement in Iran* (op. cit.), by Sepehr Zabih, and *Sowjetrepublik Gilan*, by Schapour Ravasani, Berlin, n.d.

9. *New York Times*, 15 June 1946.

10. See note 3.

11. *Le Monde*, 8 November 1972.

12. B B C Summary of World Broadcasts, Part 4, 18 June 1973.

13. Pahlavi, op. cit., p. 316.

14. B B C Summary of World Broadcasts, Part 5, 3 September 1953.

15. *Peking Review*, 15 July 1966.

16. *The Kurds*, Minority Rights Group Report no. 23, London, 1975, p. 21.

17. On supplies of Russian equipment, via Israel and Iran, see *New Perspectives on the Persian Gulf*, House of Representatives, Hearings before the Sub-committee on the Near East and South Asia, Washington, 1973, p. 205.

18. John Duke Anthony, *Arab States of the Lower Gulf*, Washington, 1975, p. 28.

19. *The Times*, 9 December 1975, and the *Observer*, 15 May 1977, report on operational Iranian flights along the Oman–South Yemen border.

20. On the Iran–Iraq military balance, see Dale R. Tahtinen, *Arms in the Persian Gulf*, Washington, 1975.

21. All quotations in this section are from the House of Representatives, Select Committee on Intelligence report, dated 19 January 1976, published as a special supplement by the *Village Voice* mag-

azine in February 1976. The report was later issued in book form by Russell Press, Nottingham.

22. In 1975 there were reports that Iran would allow the Palestine Liberation Organization to open an office in Tehran, and Yasir Arafat gave an interview to Iranian TV in which he praised the Shah's role in the Middle East. But, as a result of continuing Iranian government suspicions about contacts between Iranian guerrillas and some sections of the Palestinian movement, the permission for the office to be opened was not given.

23. Details of Iran's relations with Israel are taken from Robert Reppa, *Iran and Israel*, New York, 1974.

24. E. A. Bayne, *Persian Kingship in Transition*, New York, 1968, p. 212.

25. *Newsweek*, 14 October 1974.

26. On Iran's oil links with Israel, see the *Sunday Times*, 13 December 1970; on the commitment to Israel in 1975 see the *Guardian*, 10 October 1975.

27. Japanese foreign policy and economic relations with the rest of the Far East are analysed in Gavan McCormack and Jon Halliday, *Japanese Imperialism Today*, London, 1972.

28. Among others, by Feroz Ahmed in *Pakistan Forum*, March-April 1973, and myself in *Arabia without Sultans*, London, 1974, Chapter 14. The theory of 'sub-imperialism' is presented in Ruy Mauro Marini, 'Brazilian Sub-Imperialism', *Monthly Review*, February 1972, and in greater detail in the same author's *Subdesarrollo y Revolucion*, fifth edition, Mexico City, 1974, Chapters 1 and 2.

Chapter 10: Conclusions

1. *New Perspectives on the Persian Gulf*, p. 137, from the testimony of Richard Cottam.

2. *Kayhan International Weekly*, 21 May 1978.

3. *Le Monde*, 12 September 1978.

4. *New York Times*, 26 September 1976; MERIP Reports no. 40, September 1975.

5. *Afrique-Asie*, no. 170, 18 September 1978.

6. Interview with Khomeini in *Le Monde*, 6 May 1978, abbreviated version in MERIP Reports no. 69, July–August 1978; interview with Sharriat Madari in *Libération* (Paris), 12 May 1978.

Maps

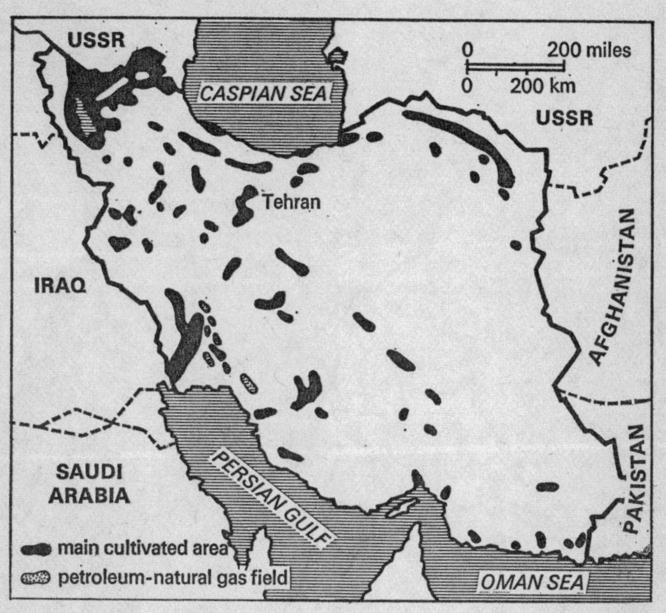

1. Main cultivated areas

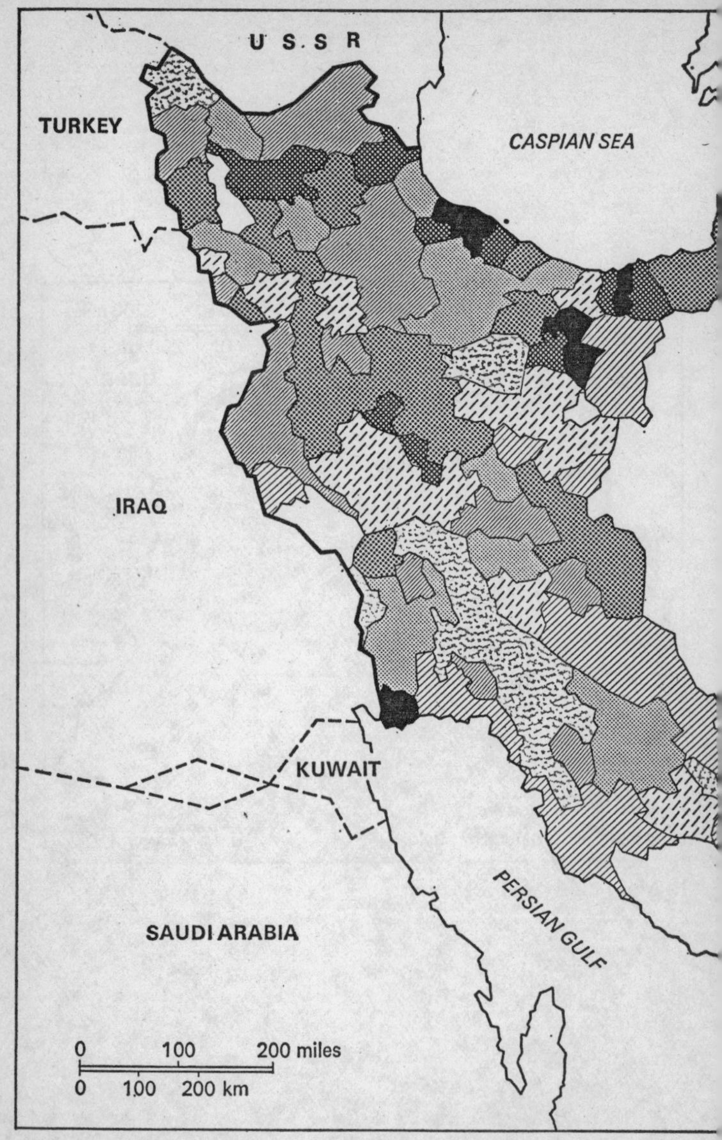

2. Population density 1966

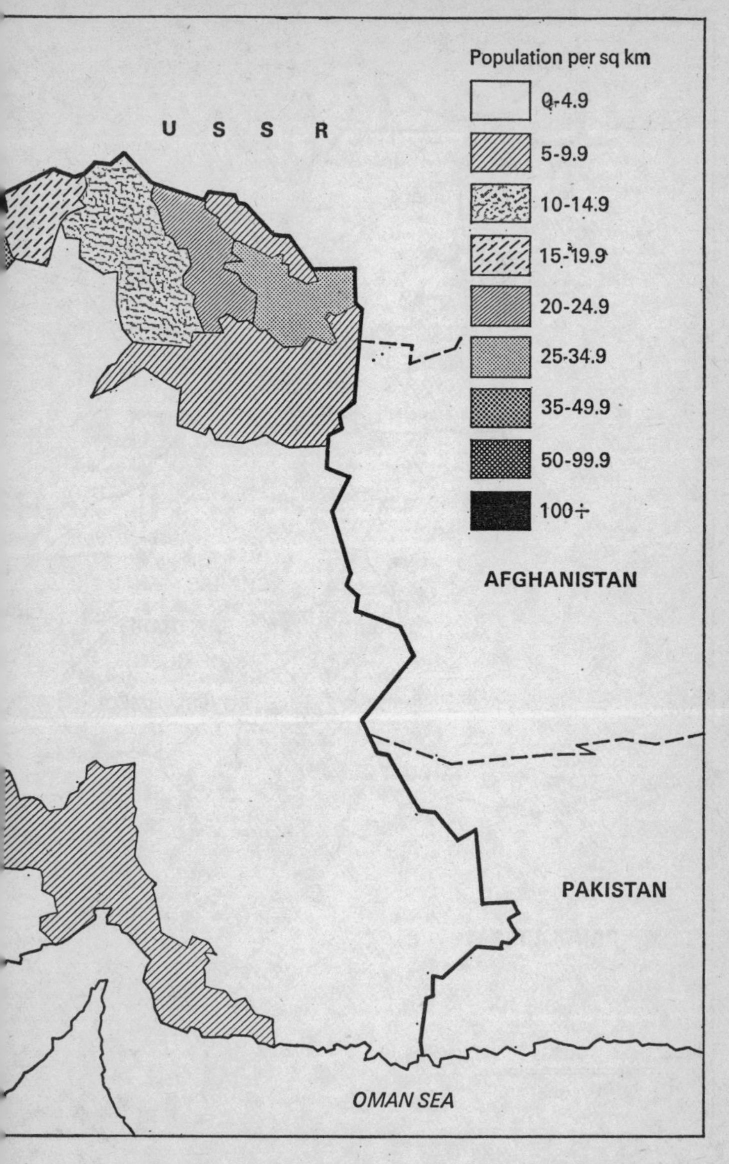

Population per sq km
0-4.9
5-9.9
10-14.9
15-19.9
20-24.9
25-34.9
35-49.9
50-99.9
100+
U S S R
AFGHANISTAN
PAKISTAN
OMAN SEA

3. Provinces and cities

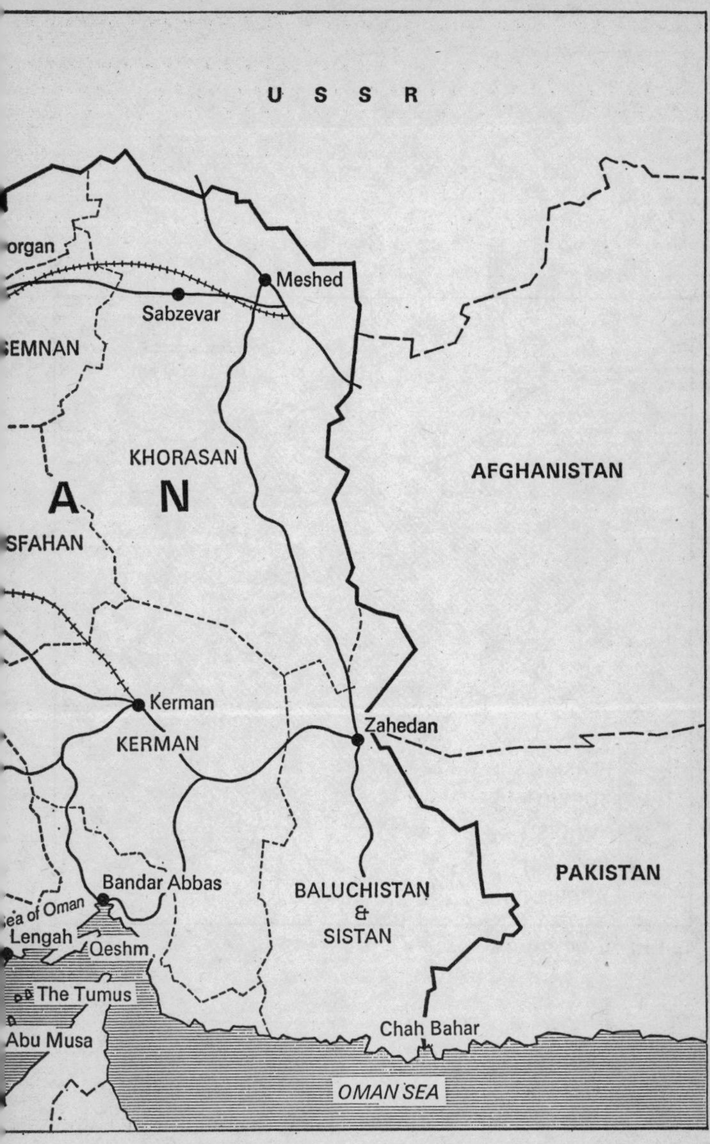

U S S R

organ

Meshed

Sabzevar

EMNAN

KHORASAN

AFGHANISTAN

A N

SFAHAN

Kerman

KERMAN

Zahedan

PAKISTAN

Bandar Abbas

BALUCHISTAN & SISTAN

Sea of Oman

Lengah

Qeshm

The Tumus

Abu Musa

Chah Bahar

OMAN SEA

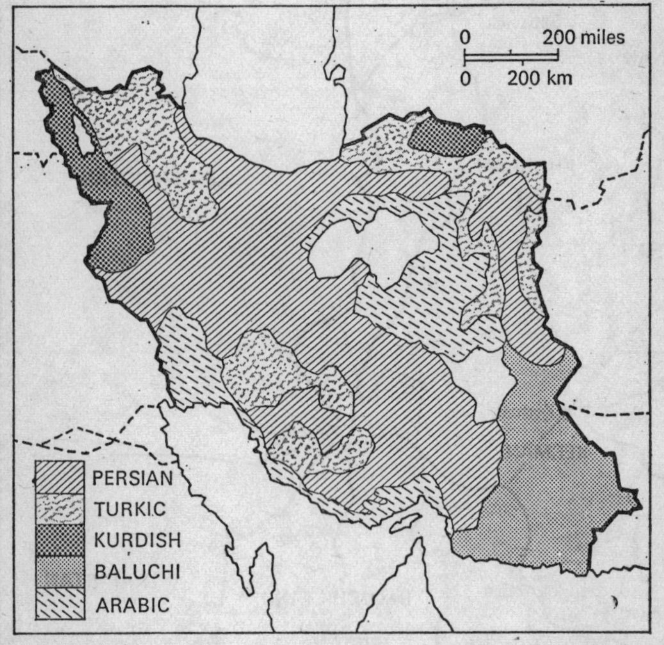

4. Linguistic groups

Bibliography

Bibliography

The following list of books and articles covers the main sources on contemporary Iran that I have used. It is in no sense a comprehensive reading list, nor have I included those works not specifically related to Iran to which I have referred. Some of the books below include substantial bibliographies: those by Peter Avery and Marvin Zonis cover history and politics; Julian Bharier's covers economics; and Shahram Chubin and Sepehr Zabih's deals with foreign policy. Much of the more recent material has not yet been recorded in books and articles, and can only be followed from the press. The U S papers *Washington Post* and *New York Times* are most informative on foreign policy and military matters; the *Financial Times* covers economic developments well, and the best political information, such as is available, can be found in *Le Monde*. Items of special interest are marked with an asterisk.

General: History and Background

American University, Washington D C, *Area Handbook for Iran*, Washington, 1971.

Arasteh, Reza, *Man and Society in Iran*, Leiden, 1964.

Avery, Peter, *Modern Iran*, London, 1965.

* Barang, Marcel, 'L'Iran: Renaissance d'un empire', *Le Monde Diplomatique*, May 1975.

Browne, Edward, *A Year Among the Persians*, London, 1893.

* Cottam, Richard, *Nationalism in Iran*, Pittsburgh, 1964.

Nirumand, Bahman, *Iran: the New Imperialism in Action*, New York, 1969.

* Rey, Lucien, 'Persia in Perspective', *New Left Review*, no. 19, March–April 1963; no. 20, May–June 1963.

* Rouleau, Eric, 'L'Iran dix ans après Mosadeq', *Le Monde*, 14–16 October 1963; 'L'Iran à l'heure de l'embourgeoisement', *Le Monde*, 3–7 October 1973; 'Iran: mythes et réalités', *Le Monde*, 3–6 October 1976.

* Upton, Joseph, *The History of Modern Iran: An Interpretation*, Cambridge, Mass., 1960.

Yar-Shater, Ehsan, *Iran Faces the Seventies*, London, 1971.

The State

Abrahamian, Ervand, 'Oriental Despotism: The Case of Qajar Iran', *International Journal of Middle East Studies*, vol. 5, 1974.

Banani, Amin, *The Modernization of Iran*, Stanford, 1961.

Bayne, E. A., *Persian Kingship in Transition*, New York, 1968.

* Bill, James, *The Politics of Iran*, Columbus, Ohio, 1972.

Bill, James, 'Class Analysis and the Dialectics of Modernization in the Middle East', *International Journal of Middle East Studies*, vol. 3, 1972.

Bill, James, 'The Patterns of Elite Politics in Iran', in *Political Élites in the Middle East*, ed. George Lenczowski, Washington, 1975.

Binder, Leonard, *Iran: Political Development in a Changing Society*, Berkeley and Los Angeles, 1972.

Fallaci, Oriana, 'Interview with the Shah', *New Republic*, December 1973.

Fitzgerald, Frances, 'Giving the Shah Everything He Wants', *Harpers Magazine*, November 1974.

* Keddie, Nikki, 'The Iranian Power Structure and Social Change 1800–1969: an Overview', *International Journal of Middle East Studies*, vol. 2, 1971.

Mohammadi-Nejad Hassan, 'The Iranian Parliamentary Elections of 1975', International Journal of Middle East Studies, vol. 8, 1977.

Pahlavi, Mohammad Reza, *Mission for my Country*, London, 1961.

Vieille, Paul, *La féodalité et l'état en Iran*, Paris, 1975.

Wilber, Donald, *Reza Shah Pahlavi*, New York, 1975.

*Zonis, Marvin, *The Political Élite of Iran*, Princeton, 1971.

The Armed Forces and S A V A K

(a) The Armed Forces

Albrecht, Ulrich; Ernst, Dieter; Lock, Peter; Wulf, Herbert, *Rüstung und Unterentwicklung*, Reinbek bei Hamburg, 1976, Chapter 3, 'Militarisierter Subimperialismus: der Fall Iran'.

Arfa, Hassan, *Under Five Shahs*, London, 1964.

Croizat, Victor, 'Imperial Iranian Gendarmerie', *Marine Corps Gazette*, October 1975.

Haddad, George, *Revolutions and Military Rule in the Middle East: the Northern Tier*, New York, 1965, Chapter 4, 'Military Coups d'Etat and the Reform Movement in Iran'.

Hurewitz, J. C., *Middle East Politics: the Military Dimension*, London, 1969, Chapter 13, 'An American Client: Iran'.

Institute for Strategic Studies, London, *The Military Balance*, annual.

Klare, Michael, 'Hoist on Your Own Pahlavi', *The Nation*, 31 January 1976.

Klare, Michael, 'Arms, Oil and Petrodollars: U S Strategy in the Persian Gulf', unpublished manuscript, 1976.

Lenczowski, George, *Russia and the West in Iran 1918–1948*, London, 1949.

Rumney, Mason, 'The View from Iran', *Military Review*, vol. 52, no. 1, January 1972.

Salmatian, Ahmad, *Historique du Rôle Politique de l' Armée en Iran*, thesis for the Faculté de Droit et des Sciences Politiques, University of Paris, 1970.

Sampson, Anthony, *The Arms Bazaar*, London, 1977, Chapter 14, 'The Arming of the Shah'.

Tahtinen, Dale, *Arms in the Persian Gulf*, American Enterprise Institute for Public Policy Research, Washington, 1974.

* United State Senate, Staff Report to the Subcommittee on Foreign Assistance of the Committee on Foreign Relations, *U S Military Sales to Iran*, Washington, 1976, and see also works by American University, Zonis.

(b) S A V A K

*Amnesty International Briefing, *Iran*, London, 1976

International Commission of Jurists, *Human Rights and the Legal System in Iran*, Geneva, 1976.

*Jacobson, Philip, 'Torture in Iran', *Sunday Times*, 19 January 1975.

Tudeh Party of Iran, *S A V A K: the Shah's Secret Police*, n.d.

Unitarian Universalist Service Commission of Enquiry, *Political Prisoners in Iran*, 1976.

Young, Gavin, 'The Shah's Police State', *Observer*, 23 November 1975; see also under The Opposition.

Agriculture

Denman, D. R., *The King's Vista*, London, 1973.

*Abrahamian, Ervand, and Kasemi, Farhad, 'The Non-Revolutionary Peasantry of Modern Iran', unpublished manuscript, 1976.

Gharatchehdaghi, Cyrus, *The Distribution of Land in Varamin*, Opladen, 1967.

*Hoogland, Eric, 'The Khwushnishin Population of Iran', *Iranian Studies*, vol. vi, no. 4, Autumn 1973.

Imperial Organization of Social Services, *Report of the Commission on the Study of Health and Medical Problems*, Tehran, 1975.

Kaneda, H., 'Agriculture', I L O Employment and Incomes Mission Working Paper, no. 3, Geneva, 1973.

*Keddie, Nikki, 'The Iranian Village Before and After Land Reform', *Journal of Contemporary History*, July 1968, reprinted in Henry Bernstein, ed., *Development and Underdevelopment*, Harmondsworth, 1973.

Kielstra, Nico, *Ecology and Community in Iran*, Amsterdam, 1975.

Lambton, Anne, *The Persian Land Reform*, London, 1966.

McLachlan, Kenneth, 'Land Reform in Iran', Chapter 21, *Cambridge History of Iran*, Cambridge, 1968.

Mahdavy, Hossein, 'The Coming Crisis in Iran', *Foreign Affairs*, October 1965.

Richards, Helmut, 'Land Reform and Agribusiness in Iran', *Middle East Research and Information Project*, no. 43.

Rudulph, C., *The Land Reform Program in Iran and its Political Implications*, American University, Ph.D., 1971.

United States Department of Agriculture, Economic Research Service, *Iran: Agricultural Production and Trade*, Washington, 1974.

Vieille, Paul, 'Les Paysans, La Petite Bourgeoisie et l'État après la Reforme Agraire en Iran', *Annales*, vol. 27, no. 2.

Oil and Industrialization

Amuzegar, Jahangir, and Fekrat, M. Ali, *Iran: Economic Development under Dualistic Conditions*, Chicago, 1971.

Ashraf, Ahmad, 'Historical Obstacles to the Development of a Bourgeoisie in Iran', in Michael Cook, ed., *Studies in the Economic History of the Middle East*, London, 1970.

Baldwin, George, *Planning and Development in Iran*, Baltimore, 1967.

Bartsch, William, 'The Impact of the Oil Industry on the Economy of Iran', in Raymond Mikesell, ed., *Foreign Investment in the Petroleum and Mineral Industries*, Baltimore, 1971.

Benedick, Richard, *Industrial Finance in Iran*, Boston, 1964.

*Bharier, Julian, *Economic Development in Iran 1900–1970*, London, 1971.

Clark Carey, J. C., and Carey, A. G., 'Industrial Growth and Development Planning in Iran', *Middle East Journal*, Winter 1975.

Fesharaki, Fereidun, *The Development of the Iranian Oil Industry*, New York, 1976.

Financial Times, Annual Supplements on Iran, 28 July 1975, 21 June 1976, 25 July 1977.

Flick, F. C., *Auslandsinvestitionen in einem Entwicklungsland. Ein Darstellung am Beispiel des Iran*, Hamburg, 1972.

*Housego, David, 'A Survey of Iran', *Economist*, 28 August 1976.

*Hudson Institute, *Iran, Oil Money and the Ambitions of a Nation*, Paris, 1974.

Looney, Robert, *The Economic Development of Iran*, London, 1973.

Looney, Robert, *Iran: Economic Projections to 2000*, London, 1977.

Mahdavy, Hossein, 'Patterns and Problems of Economic Development in Rentier States: the Case of Iran', in M. A. Cook, ed., *Studies in the Economic History of the Middle East*, London, 1970.

Melamid, A., 'Industrial Activities', Chapter 16 of *The Cambridge History of Iran*, Cambridge, 1968.

Najmabadi, N., 'Strategies of Industrial Development in Iran', in *Iran: Past, Present, Future*, Aspen Institute, New York, 1976.

Preston, Roger, 'Iran: economy on the run', *Arabia and the Gulf*, 27 June 1977.

Sampson, Anthony, *The Seven Sisters*, London, 1976.

*Stork, Joe, *Middle East Oil and the Energy Crisis*, New York, 1975.

*Vakil, F., 'Iran's Basic Macroeconomic Problems', in *Iran: Past, Present, Future*, Aspen Institute, New York, 1976.

The Working Class

*Abrahamian, Ervand, 'The Crowd in Iranian Politics', *Past and Present*, December 1968.

Bartsch, William H., 'The Industrial Labour Force of Iran: Problems of Recruitment, Training and Productivity', *Middle East Journal*, Winter 1971.

Bartsch, William H., 'Unemployment in Less Developed Countries:

a Case Study of a poor district of Tehran', *International Development Review*, vol. 13, no. 1, 1971.

Committee Against Repression in Iran, *The Iranian Working Class*, London, 1977.

Connell, John, *Tehran: Urbanization and Development*, Institute of Development Studies Discussion Paper no. 32, Brighton, 1973.

Djazani, Iranpour, *Wirtschaft und Bevölkerung in Khuzistan*, Tübingen, 1963.

Elkan, Walter, 'Employment, Education, Training and Skilled Labour in Iran', *Middle East Journal*, Spring 1977.

Elwell-Sutton, L. P., *Persian Oil: a study in power politics*, London, 1955, Chapter 8.

Firoozi, Fereidun, 'Labour and Trades Unions in Iran', unpublished paper, 1974.

Firoozi, Fereidun, 'Profitsharing in Iran', unpublished paper, 1976.

Givry, J. D., and Scoville, J., 'Labour Legislation, Practice and Policy', I L O Employment and Incomes Mission Working Paper no. 9, Geneva, 1973.

Hemmasi, Mohammad, *Migration in Iran*, Shiraz, 1974.

International Labour Office, *Labour Conditions in the Oil Industry in Iran*, Geneva, 1950.

International Labour Office, *Employment and Income Policies for Iran*, Geneva, 1973.

Institute for Social Studies and Research, University of Tehran, 'Survey of Squatter Settlements in Iran: Preliminary Results for Tehran', Tehran, 1972.

Jalil, T., *Workers of Iran: Repression and the Fight for Democratic Trades Unions*, Committee for the Restoration of Trades Union Rights in Iran, London, 1976.

Jalil, T., *Workers Say No to the Shah: Labour Law and Strikes in Iran*, Committee for the Restoration of Trades Union Rights in Iran, London, 1977.

Pessaran, H., 'The Growth of Income Inequality in Iran', in *Iran: Past, Present, Future*, Aspen Institute, New York, 1976.

Tudeh Party of Iran, *La Classe Ouvrière en Iran et les grèves*, n.p., 1976.

United States Department of Labor, *Labor Law and Practice in Iran*, B L S Report no. 276, 1964.

Vieille, Paul, 'Abadan: Tissu urbain, attitudes et valeurs, in *Revue Géographique de l'est*, 1969, nos 3–4.

The Opposition

Abrahamian, Ervand, 'Kasravi: the Integrative Nationalist of Iran', *Middle East Studies,* vol. 9, October 1973.

Abrahamian, Ervand, 'Communism and communalism in Iran: the *Tudah* and *Firqah-i Dimukrat*', *International Journal of Middle East Studies*, vol. 1, 1970.

Ahmadzadeh, Masaoud, *Armed Struggle: both a strategy and a tactic*, New York, 1976.

Alavi, Bozorg, *Kampfendes Iran*, Berlin, 1955.

Baraheni, Reza, *The Crowned Cannibals*, New York, 1977.

Dehqani, Ashraf, *Torture and Resistance in Iran*, London, 1976.

Farahani, Ali-Akbar Safayi, *What a Revolutionary Must Know*, London, 1973.

Ghassemlou, A. R., *Iranian Kurdistan*, n.p., n.d.

Jazani, Bijan, *Armed Struggle in Iran*, London, 1975.

National Front of Iran (III), *Iran: Chronique de la repression 1963–1974*, Paris, 1975.

Nirumand, Bahman, ed., *Feuer unterm Pfauenthron*, Berlin, 1974.

Pouyan, Amir Parviz, *On the Necessity of Armed Struggle and a Refutation of the Theory of 'Survival'*, New York, 1975.

Ravasani, Schapour, *Sowjetrepublik Gilan*, Berlin, n.d.

Sadiq, Javid, *Nationalities and Revolution in Iran*, unpublished manuscript, 1976.

Zabih, Sepehr, *The Communist Movement in Iran*, Berkeley and Los Angeles, 1966.

I have also made use of the periodical publications of the Iranian opposition in exile, including: *Iran Research* (London), *Iran People's Struggle* (New York), *Resistance* (Chicago), *Iran Free Press* (Washington), *C A I F I Newsletter* (New York), *Iran Report* (Frankfurt), *Bulletin d'Information du Front National de l'Iran, III* (Paris), *Iranform* (Rome). See also the works by Richard Cottam and Marvin Zonis listed above.

Foreign Relations

Ahmed, Feroz, 'Iran: Subimperialism in Action', *Pakistan Forum*, March–April 1973.

Chubin, Shahram and Zabih, Sepehr, *The Foreign Relations of Iran*, London, 1974.

Duke, Anthony John, *Arab States of the Lower Gulf*, Washington, 1975.

Ramazani, R. K., *Iran's Foreign Policy: 1941–1973*, Charlottesville, 1975.

Ramazani, R. K., 'Iran's Search for Regional Co-operation', *Middle East Journal*, Spring 1976.

Reppa, Robert, *Israel and Iran*, New York, 1973.

United States House of Representatives, Subcommittee on the Near East and South Asia of the Committee on Foreign Affairs, *New Perspectives on the Persian Gulf*, Washington, 1973.

United States House of Representatives, Subcommittee on the Near East and South Asia of the Committee on Foreign Affairs, *The Persian Gulf 1974: Money, Politics, Arms and Power*, Washington, 1975.

See also references to the armed forces.

Current Developments

The following is a list of some of the publications carrying information on developments in Iran:

1. Annual:

Bank Markazi of Iran, *Annual Report and Balance-Sheet*, Tehran.
Financial Times, annual supplement on Iran, London.
Echo of Iran, *Iran Almanac and Book of Facts*, Tehran.
Europa Publications, *The Middle East and North Africa*, London.

2. Periodicals:

C A I F I Newsletter, New York.
Economist Intelligence Unit, *Iran*, Quarterly Economic Report and Annual Supplement, London.
Iran People's Struggle, New York.
Iranian Studies, New York.
International Journal of Middle East Studies, Cambridge.
Middle East Journal, Washington.
Middle East Research and Information Project, Washington.
Middle East Studies, London.
Review of Iranian Political Economy and History, Washington.

3. Weeklies:

Kayhan International Weekly, Tehran.
Middle East Economic Digest, London.

RAVES FOR ABIGAIL PADGETT AND *STRAWGIRL*

◆ ◆ ◆

"A page turner . . . a worthy second outing, and this is one reviewer looking forward to No. 3."

—*Washington Sunday Times*

◆

"A daring and obviously gifted writer."

—*Chicago Tribune*

◆

"A tense, subtle plot with several striking characters . . . the mystery is a devilish riddle. Its solution remains hidden until the final moments."

—*St. Louis Post-Dispatch*

◆

"Bo's back in an equally impressive second novel. . . . We guarantee it will remain in your thoughts and dreams for a long time."

—*Sunday Denver Post*

◆

more . . .

◆

"An engrossing work . . . sensitive, colorfully populated, and carrying the authority of an author who knows the territory."

—Charles Champlin,
Los Angeles Times Book Review

◆

"Readers should enjoy Padgett's unique take on mystery, as embodied by her sympathetic, compelling detective."

—***Newsday***

◆

"She is a strong, skillful writer, not afraid to tackle difficult topics—altogether a welcome new voice in the mystery genre."

—***Murder & Mayhem***

◆

"Resonant . . . a tale worth reading."

—***Knoxville News-Sentinel***

◆

"A skillful storyteller with a deft and literate style." —***San Diego Union-Tribune***

◆

◆

"Padgett has written an intense, involving book. . . . Don't miss *Strawgirl*."

—***Mystery News***

◆

"Stirring and insightful."

—***Hackensack Sunday Record*** (NJ)

◆

"Featuring a captivating, witty, soul-searching investigator . . . *Strawgirl* is exciting, thought provoking and original."

—***The Page Turner***

◆

"With its complex plot and snappy dialogue, this is very enjoyable reading."

—***Toronto Star***

◆

"Painful, powerful, and wholly original. Even more radical than in her striking debut, Bo's gutsy work redefines the role of the detective in a darkly contemporary society."

—***Kirkus Reviews***

◆

Novels by Abigail Padgett

Turtle Baby
Strawgirl
Child of Silence

ABIGAIL PADGETT

STRANGIRL

THE MYSTERIOUS PRESS

Published by Warner Books

A Time Warner Company

Grateful acknowledgment is given for permission to quote from "In Response to Those Who Say The Mad Are Like Prophets," by Pamela Spiro Wagner, © 1993, from *CAMI*, the Journal of the California Alliance for the Mentally Ill. Permission granted by Dan E. Weisburd, editor and publisher.

MYSTERIOUS PRESS EDITION

Cover design and illustration by Wendell Minor

The Mysterious Press name and logo are registered trademarks of Warner Books, Inc.

Mysterious Press books are published by
Warner Books, Inc.
1271 Avenue of the Americas
New York, NY 10020

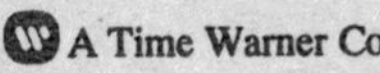
A Time Warner Company

Printed in the United States of America

Originally published in hardcover by The Mysterious Press
First Printed in Paperback: February, 1995

10 9 8 7 6 5 4 3 2 1

In Memory of a Friendship
Joan Garfinkel Glantz and Dassia Porper

Acknowledgments

To Adirondack poets Adelaide Crapsey and Jeanne Robert Foster, and Hudson River painter Charlotte Buell Coman, for the inspiration of their work.

To the Iroquois Indian Museum of Schoharie, New York, for research assistance.

To Mary Schifferli of the Albany Institute of History and Art, Albany, New York, for discovering women artists of the Hudson River School.

To Robert Pell Dechame and Fort Ticonderoga Director Nicholas Westbrook for their gracious permission to view privately held work of artist Ella Ferris Pell.

To Professor Marilyn J. Ireland of San Diego's California Western School of Law, for technical legal advice.

Note: Shadow Mountain and its Seekers exist only in my imagination. The lodge, however, is really there in the guise of Hemlock Hall, near the town of Blue Mountain Lake, New York.

" . . . and in the bloodshed
of a yawning barn there is
only straw, all there is,
and she grasps for it."

Pamela Spiro Wagner

Chapter 1

Bo Bradley watched the day unfold with the wary eye of a Cornish hen touring a fox farm. Days were never this benign; something was peculiar. She had been leery of the day since it started. An ordinary Wednesday, stolidly constructing itself of midweek events so unremarkable they seemed fake. Early-morning San Diego traffic drifting inland too smoothly. Coffee in the chilly Department of Social Services cafeteria too aromatic. The outdated rotary phones too quiet, the footsteps of other investigators in the hall too unhurried.

It wasn't the lithium, couldn't be. The medication she took when necessary to control symptoms of a manic-depressive disorder could do that. It could blur the razor-sharp edges of reality, slow the frenzied input of detail to a manageable, waltzy tempo. It could make everything seem sluggishly *nice*. Except she'd stopped taking the lithium eighteen days ago. So far so good. But this dreamy, dull Wednesday was hiding something. Bo acknowledged the prescient feeling, blunted for the last six months by medication, as a familiar if unpredictable friend.

The feeling had brought a grin to her face when at 8:15

supervisor Madge Aldenhoven burst into the office Bo shared with one other child abuse investigator, flapping an interdepartmental memo in one hand.

"Bo, you're third on today's rotation for new cases. You won't get one until this afternoon, and I know your paperwork is caught up. Please don't waste my time and yours trying to weasel out of what I'm about to ask you."

Aldenhoven had tucked a stray wisp of floury hair into an otherwise impeccable chignon and smiled beatifically. Bo recognized the look as one turn-of-the-century artists would have lavished on the faces of dewy-eyed mothers surrounded by hordes of children in formal attire. The supervisor's gaze was directed at the neat row of orange-banded case files between plastic, county-issue bookends on Bo's desk. A painting of Madge Aldenhoven in biblical robes sweetly cradling a copy of the Department of Social Services procedures manual took shape in Bo's mind. The painting would be done in thick oils, with an ornate gold-leafed frame. Bo sighed and experienced the bone-deep antipathy that characterized her relationship with her supervisor. The daily jousting of bureaucrat and iconoclast without which the job might just be tolerable.

"You know the department is sponsoring a workshop today on Satanic cults and child abuse," Madge went on, waving the memo as if it were a command from the White House. "Estrella was going to represent our unit, but we got another toddler trapped on the freeway median last night . . ."

"And the mother?" Bo asked with genuine concern. Mexican families illegally crossing the border from Tijuana to San Diego's southernmost community often made a run for it across the eight lanes of Interstate 5 to the scrubby, unpopulated safety of the flatlands on the other side. Some didn't make it.

"Hit by a bakery truck in the northbound lane," the supervisor answered briskly. "Fortunately not fatal, just broken bones. The two-year-old was thrown clear, made it to the median. Estrella's over at St. Mary's with him now."

Bo's officemate, Estrella Benedict, was the Spanish-speaking investigator in Madge Aldenhoven's unit, and Bo's best friend.

"Sure," Bo said, brushing an imaginary bit of lint from the arm of her chair, "I'll go sit through your devil worship seminar for Es. Do I get extra points if I bring back a bloody ceremonial dagger or cloven hoof still reeking of sulfur?"

It had been impossible to keep the cynical edge from her answer, and Aldenhoven's renowned insubordination sensors hadn't failed to go off the scale in response.

"Don't take that attitude, Bo," Madge warned from the door. "The department's brought an expert on the subject down from Los Angeles at great expense. Representatives of the police department will be there as well. It's a serious topic. Bound, printed guidelines for recognizing Satanic abuse will be distributed. I want to be sure our unit has its own copy." Bo could see one of Madge's contact lenses drifting precariously off center against the hyacinth-colored iris. Tracking the lens's progress precluded proper attention to the woman's words, which continued. "You've been doing so well these last six months. I'd like to keep it that way."

Bo folded the workshop memo into an origami swan and left it dead center on the gray Formica surface of her desk.

The workshop itself had been ludicrous. A rented hotel conference room with Berber carpet on the walls and what appeared to be woven steel wool on the floor. Lukewarm coffee, several dozen cops and social workers with preformed personal ideas about the devil, and a presentation that in Bo's opinion had not changed since the thirteenth century.

"Some of you will find this hard to believe," a very blonde psychologist named Dr. Cynthia Ganage told the group, "but right now, today, right here in the United States . . . there is a growing and powerful Satanic conspiracy." The psychologist was so fashionably dressed and made up, her expression so glowing, it occurred to Bo that she might be picking up a little money on the side doing bathroom cleanser commercials.

"I don't find this hard to believe," Bo whispered to a social worker from the probation department seated beside her, "I find it impossible to believe!"

"Shh," the woman replied, writing "Satanic conspiracy" in purple ink on a lavender legal pad. "That's how they operate. They *know* people won't believe it."

". . . even at the highest levels of society," Ganage continued, "and the principal Satanic ritual invariably involves sexual defilement, torture, and sometimes murder . . . of innocent children."

"Oh, God," Bo sighed.

"Praise God," said the social worker from probation.

"You're not going to believe this!" Bo told Estrella when she returned at noon. "I've seen a lot of nuts in my day. I've *been* a nut in my day. But nothing can touch this overdressed psychologist the department imported from la-la land. The woman's either delusional or she's found the best moneymaker since junk bonds. According to her, every school, church, day-care center, even 'the United States government,' is crawling with secret Satanists panting to torture children. Not to mention rock stars, pop bands, and everybody connected to the entertainment industry!"

"Does that include TV evangelists?" Estrella grinned over a steaming cup of instant noodle soup on her desk. The sun streaming through miniblinds over their single window sliced Estrella's braceleted arm with wavy black and white lines.

"I think it includes the Pope," Bo sighed. "But what really bugs me is that this woman is billing enormous consulting fees to stand around in a five-hundred-dollar suit showing pictures of rock bands whose lyrics, if played backward on the wrong speed underwater, may or may not contain messages urging people to sacrifice babies."

"Wanna know what bugs *me*?" Estrella queried vaguely, examining in a thin band of sunlight the chipped polish on a manicured nail.

"What?" Bo answered, distracted by her own reflection in the mirrored office door. Her appearance had not altered appreciably since she'd checked it that morning. Silver-red shoulder-length curls in typical disarray. Changeable green eyes that today had adopted a shade Bo ruefully identified as "cucumber." Less-than-flat midriff and thighs that, if not stopped, would soon resemble Dickensian sausages. Even the loosely cut hip-length jacket she wore nearly every day could not re-create her prelithium lankiness.

"What bugs me," Estrella told the cup of Ramen noodles,

"is when manic-depressive friends of mine stop taking their medication and don't tell me."

Bo turned slowly from the mirror and tossed a xeroxed pamphlet entitled *Casework Intervention in Ritual Abuse* onto her desk. The pamphlet's jacket, of folded legal-size yellow card stock, was decorated with a clip-art head of a little boy in a sailor cap, circa 1939, facing the head of a horned devil with an obscenely protuberant tongue. "How did you know I stopped the lithium?" she whispered.

"When I'm not dancing in cantinas, feeding my faithful burro, or strewing rose petals in dusty religious processions," Estrella sang in an accent as broad as it was phony, "I have been known to see what is in front of my face!" The dark eyes looked straight at Bo. "So why didn't you tell me?"

Bo studied the back of one freckled hand as if the answer were written there. "I knew you'd worry?" What was it about psychiatric problems, she pondered, that caused people with no medical training whatever to dispense pharmacological opinions so freely?

"You knew I'd worry," Estrella repeated as if translating a difficult phrase from High German. "Why should I worry? You almost got yourself killed in a mine shaft last year, crazy as a tumbleweed on that case with the deaf boy. You almost blew it permanently, but why should I worry?"

Bo sat in her desk chair and spun to face an exquisitely dressed woman of Hispanic parentage who was about to assault her with a Styrofoam cup of lukewarm Ramen noodles. "I'm sorry, Es," Bo said through the tumble of hair shielding her penitently bowed head. "I should have told you."

The act, which wasn't entirely an act, worked. Head-ducking, a simple primate conciliatory gesture learned from watching *Gorillas in the Mist*, had proven useful to Bo more than once in defusing aggressive humans.

"So how come you stopped the lithium?" Estrella inquired with slightly less feeling. "You've been doing okay."

"Some people with mood disorders have to take medications all the time," Bo explained. "I just have to take it some of the time, and the side effects aren't exactly fun."

Estrella adjusted a mother-of-pearl comb in her sleek coif and narrowed her eyes. "What side effects?"

Bo saw no civilized way to avoid answering the question. "Weight gain, for one. On lithium I tend to feel like a jumbo marshmallow with the personality of a road kill. I long to pick up small objects in less than two minutes and react to cataclysmic world events in under a week. It's sort of like snorkeling in potato soup."

"And it doesn't help your love life either, right?"

"Es . . . !"

"Well, I knew it was something."

"Es, I keep telling you I don't want a love life, as you so quaintly put it. Too many complications. I want to paint, that's all. Did I tell you two of the Indian primitives sold last week? I'm thinking of spending the money on a weekend at an elegant spa like the movie stars go to. You know, where they feed you grapes and pack you in warm mud?"

"You can do that in my backyard for free," Estrella suggested. "So tell me why you're so antsy about that cult workshop this morning."

The ordinariness of the day was wearing on Bo. The endless, nonsensical details juggled in elaborate patterns behind which, she sensed, other things hid.

"It was just so stupid . . ." she began as Madge Aldenhoven knocked, opened the door and swept into the small office in one efficient gesture.

"I think you're going to be glad you attended the workshop on Satanism, Bo," the supervisor announced in tones resonant with vindication.

"Why is that, Madge?" Bo queried, scanning the ceiling for cobwebs.

"Your new case is a molest. The little girl was just brought to St. Mary's in an ambulance, badly injured. We have reason to believe this case may involve ritual abuse because some sort of bizarre symbol was painted on the child's abdomen. There's an older sister. What little information we have suggests that the most likely perpetrator is the mother's live-in boyfriend, known to be a member of a cult. I want you to go to St. Mary's immediately and assess the situation. It will probably be necessary to pick up the sister from school while the family is still at the hospital. Do your best. This is going to be a messy one."

Bo admired a pearl and lapis ring on Aldenhoven's hand as it slid a new case file onto the desktop. The ring went well with a Chinese-blue linen mantua the supervisor wore over a simple knit sheath dress the color of alabaster. Madge, who never went out of the building, never confronted the reality documented in reports she merely read, could cultivate the illusion that this was a desirable line of work. Madge could dress as though she were the ladies' wear buyer for a conservative department store. It was, Bo acknowledged, a healthy self-deception. Across the manila folder's orange band the words "FRANER, SAMANTHA, 3 YEARS 6 MONTHS/ HANNAH, 8 YEARS 1 MONTH" had been penned in heavy black marker. A chemical scent drifted from the fresh ink, dissolving the day's facade like rain on a dusty window. It wasn't an ordinary Wednesday after all. Bo had known it all along.

"I don't want this case," she told Estrella when Madge had closed the door behind her. An odd feeling, similar to panic but full of sadness, rose in her throat. Another unthinkable set of horrors to sort through. Against the deceptive vapidity of the day the new case loomed like a signpost to hell, offering no hope in any direction. "I don't even want to *work* here," she groused with a petulance that seemed to have come from nowhere. "I can't face another molest case, with or without Satanic conspiracies. I just want to stay home and paint pictures."

Bo listened to herself and heard the whiny voice of a spoiled brat. Still, the words were true. The case file on her desk shimmered poisonously.

"I knew it!" Estrella pounced on the moment. "You're off your medication and you're getting weird. You never let work get to you before. You need the lithium, Bo. You can't handle this job without it."

"Maybe," Bo pondered, stuffing the unread case file into a battered briefcase and grabbing her keys, "and then maybe there's just something peculiar about today . . ."

"May first," Estrella pointed sharply to a wall calendar. "We don't celebrate the Russian Revolution here, and Cinco de Mayo is still four days off. Nothing noteworthy about today."

Bo's lips curled upward in a knowing grin. May first? Beltane! The day Caillech Bera ceased her wintry wailing and turned to stone until the following All Hallow's. Bo could almost hear her Irish grandmother telling the tale.

"Aye, an' old Cally's a-turned to stone some lonely place tonight, her staff a-lost i' the gorse. We'll not see 'er for all the bright summer, we won't, not hear 'er, neither!"

A comforting revelation, Bo smiled broadly. With the ancient symbol of madness put out of commission by a warming sun, people might safely walk the land without lithium. People might just quit whining and hang on to whatever jobs were paying their rent.

"Thanks, Es," Bo waved at the door. "You're more help than you know."

Chapter 2

During a recently completed renovation St. Mary's Hospital for Children had retained the services of an image consultant. Bo, swiftly assessing that the hospital's parking lot was full, eased her dowdy blue BMW into the only remaining parking spot—one marked RESERVED FOR CLERGY. Then she stuck out her tongue at the smiling magenta wooly mammoth whose painted fiberboard figure adorned every light pole. "Mabel," as the logo had been named by the image consultants, held strings to multicolored balloons in its long-extinct trunk, and wore a stethoscope around its neck. Bo found the creature aesthetically atrocious.

"Why," she'd asked Dr. Andrew LaMarche, director of the hospital's child abuse unit, "would a children's hospital in southern California use a logo depicting an extinct elephant that never set foot south of Schenectady, New York?"

LaMarche had, uncharacteristically, laughed aloud over his roasted Anaheim chili at a five-star steak house on the one occasion in six months on which Bo had agreed to dinner with him.

"The idea," he explained, "was that children would see

a prehistoric, long-haired elephant as strange, like being in the hospital is strange. And that the smile and bright colors would make the strangeness friendly. Of course the thing is hideous, but the concept's sound. Young children, basically, are able to identify familiar/unfamiliar and friendly/unfriendly constructs. It's helpful to adorn the hospital with repetitions of a figure that's at once unfamiliar and friendly. Hence, Mabel!"

Bo sneered dramatically at the Mabel smiling into her windshield and pulled the Franer case file from her briefcase. Samantha Alice Franer, it told her, was a three-and-a-half-year-old Caucasian female who had been brought to St. Mary's Hospital after her mother, Bonnie Corman Franer, had taken her to a local pediatrician. The pediatrician, Susan Ling, M.D., had phoned the police after arranging for an ambulance to transport Samantha from her office to St. Mary's. According to Susan Ling's report, Samantha Franer had suffered internal injuries consistent with a sexual assault perpetrated sometime the previous day. According to Susan Ling, those injuries were serious.

Stuffing the case file back into a saddle-stitched cowhide briefcase whose brass clasp was the Mayan snake-head glyph for rain, Bo tugged down the cuffs of her black knit slacks and headed toward the hospital's lobby. A sound truck from local TV station KTUV was parked in front of the hospital's sliding glass doors.

"Uh-oh . . ." Bo breathed uneasily, and grabbed for the case file again. No TV news team worth its journalism credentials would sink to invading a hospital where children lay sick and in pain. Not unless the story were irresistible. And TV station "K-TOUGH," as it chose to be known, had built a reputation on scooping San Diego's most bizarre, or bloodthirsty, events.

"A symbol of some sort has been painted on the child's lower abdomen in what appears to be yellow Magic Marker," Dr. Ling's report went on. "It is a strange face surrounded by spikes. This may or may not have any bearing on the child's injuries, which I do not hesitate to define as having resulted from rape."

"Shit," Bo said flatly as the automatic doors opened with a whoosh. Dr. Ling, obviously new to San Diego County and its procedures for reporting child abuse, had phoned her report directly to the police instead of to the Child Abuse Hotline. In the systemic relay of the report to an assignment desk and then back out to detectives in the field, the information might have been carried on one of the standard police radio bands. Accessible to anyone with a short-wave radio who happened to be listening. And somebody *had* been listening. The sound truck made that evident.

"It's somebody from Child Protective Services!" a voice noted from a cluster of people surrounding the lobby information desk. Bo watched a woman approaching her from the group. She was followed by an unshaven boy with stringy blond hair wearing a Grateful Dead T-shirt and carrying a Minicam. The woman was still wearing the oversized ecru silk jacket she'd chosen for the morning workshop. Bo had hoped never to see the matching bleached lizard three-inch heels again. It was Dr. Devil, the sensationalist psychologist from L.A. who could find Satan-worshippers at any convenience store but clearly couldn't grasp the concept of cruelty-free footwear. A sound bite of the woman being gummed to death by geckos flashed across Bo's brain.

"I'm afraid I've forgotten your name," Bo said, cheerfully jerking her elbow out of the woman's well-manicured grasp. "What on earth are you doing here at St. Mary's?"

Besides skating on a child's pain right into your own personal spotlight?

"Cynthia Ganage. *Doctor* Cynthia Ganage," the woman announced urgently. At close range Bo could see lipstick in two shades, skillfully applied with a brush, a dusting of blush over flawlessly creamy cheekbones, smallish hazel eyes set too close together but widened by artful application of gray eyeliner. The hammered hoop earrings were not brass, but gold. "As you know from my workshop this morning," Ganage went on, "I'm a psychologist specializing in the cult-related ritual abuse of children."

Ganage's voice, Bo realized with renewed contempt, was just loud enough to be heard by two newspaper reporters hurrying through a side door from the ambulance bay. The lobby of St. Mary's was gradually assuming the frenzied atmosphere of a shark tank at feeding time.

"I'd love to chat, but duty calls," Bo smiled with patent insincerity, handing her identification badge to a security guard at the elevators.

Cynthia Ganage raised her voice another two notches. "Are you here to investigate the Franer case? From available information I'm certain that Satanism is involved. I'm here to volunteer my professional services, free of charge—"

As the elevator doors smothered the blonde woman's words, Bo took deliberately deep breaths and reminded herself that sensationalism was not really a criminal offense, even though it should be. In publicly revealing the child's name and details of the case, Cynthia Ganage had just violated every protocol observed by police and Child Protective Services personnel alike. Staring at the Mayan snake-face clasp on her briefcase, Bo decided that compared to Ganage the snake was actually cute.

"I'm here on the Franer case," she said at the fifth-floor nurses' station. "Is the child still being examined? I need to speak with the mother, too. I assume she's with Samantha?"

"The child's still in surgery," a heavyset black nurse with whom Bo had worked on previous cases answered quietly. A look in the hooded eyes issued a warning. Bo had seen the look before. The silent language of medical personnel.

"Put the walls up," it said. "Get ready to face the intolerable."

"You can go on down to the observation deck," the nurse suggested. "See how much longer it'll be. The mother's in the surgical waiting room."

Every nuance of the softly spoken words told Bo things were not going well. Nodding, she forced herself to walk through the unmarked door at the back of an office behind the nurses' station. The door opened into a short corridor that led to a small observation cage through which activities in the operating room could be observed. The observation chamber, always dark, held a row of chairs bolted to the floor for silence, and a speaker projecting voices from the brightly lit operating arena below. It was, Bo thought, like entering the interior of a Christmas tree ornament.

". . . unable to effect substantive prophylactic measures already described . . ." the familiar voice of Dr. Andrew LaMarche pronounced slowly as Bo made herself focus on the scene seven feet beneath her. Something wasn't right. The green-clad surgical team was too quiet, moving too slowly. The surgical nurse empty-handed. The anesthesiologist failing to monitor his bank of screens, which appeared to be blank. One surgeon walking away, another closing a wide incision across the child's abdomen with unusually large stitches. The little girl's skin was as pale as the cap of short blonde curls above her closed eyes. She seemed more representational than real, a chunky Raphaelesque cherub on an unfinished canvas. In the intense operating room lights the tousled blonde curls seemed crystalline. Like spun glass. Bo fought a realization that blurred her vision. The realization that the child's body was merely an empty and fading husk from which the personality of someone named Samantha Alice Franer had already fled.

"The cause of death . . ." Andrew LaMarche pronounced into a microphone suspended above the operating table, "is internal hemorrhage secondary to . . ."

Bo turned back into the small corridor and pressed her forehead against its cool tile wall. What was it like to be three years old? She searched her memory and found very little. A favorite green plaid sunsuit with white eyelet ruffles on the straps. Her grandmother had embroidered the first three bars of "Kitty of Coleraine" on the sunsuit's bib and taught Bo to pick out the melody with one finger on the piano. And a Cairn terrier named McDermott who howled when her mother practiced the violin and slept every night with his head on Bo's pillow. Vague, innocent memories devoid of the complexity only possible after the brain has completed its circuitry between five and six years of age. "The age of reason" defined by the ancients. The age when it is possible to learn to read, to manipulate symbols, to frame ideas of right and wrong. Samantha Franer would never be six years old now. She would remain forever three, just a memory of a flaxen-curled toddler frozen in the minds of those who loved her. Like Bo's sister, Laurie, who twelve years after her death was still twenty. Who would always be twenty.

Bo squeezed her eyes shut and felt tears spill and run down her flushed cheeks. But was she crying for the dead child on the operating table or for her own sister whose suicide twelve years ago had triggered in Bo a depression so profound she'd been hospitalized for three months? It was hard to tell. But she was going to have to get control of herself.

"So what will it take?" the imagined voice of her best-loved psychiatrist, the sprightly Dr. Lois Bittner, echoed from the past. "A piano has to drop on your head out of the sky before you see you're in trouble?"

"I'm not in trouble," Bo told the gray ceramic wall. "I'm okay without the lithium. I've just never seen a child dead on an operating table before. I mean anybody might *decompensate* a little . . ." she exaggerated the psychiatric term, ". . . seeing that."

"You're not anybody," the memory pointed out with dogged good cheer. "You have manic depression. You have to protect yourself."

Bo considered the savage arrogance necessary for the act of rape, and realized that she would never comprehend it, only hate it. An act somehow generated in the chemistry of the male, where apelike charades of dominance could go wrong and become brutal defilement. But to defile a thing with no defenses, no hope of resistance or self-protection? Even though her job required near-daily brushes with its not uncommon reality, the rape of children continued to shock Bo. A sickening horror endured by millions of children every day. And this one was magnified by its deadly outcome—the pale, still body below.

Bo wished Lois Bittner were still alive. Wished she could talk about what she'd just seen. Wished she could climb the wooden stairs to the shrink's comfortable loft office in a seasoned downtown St. Louis building that had been new when Teddy Roosevelt took office, kick off her shoes, and talk. Bittner had been a complete fluke, a coincidence, a mistake. And the best thing that had happened in Bo's train wreck of a life.

Turning to hunker on her heels with her back to the wall, Bo massaged her skull to erase the scene in the operating room and let herself remember Lois Bittner. A reassuring memory in spite of its beginning. A mental earthwork buffering the shadowless image of the dead child below.

A depression, the worst ever, had crept like an iron fog into Bo's brain after Laurie's funeral. In the beginning she'd thought she could handle it. Driving the new BMW Mark had bequeathed her as compensation for annulling their marriage of three years, she'd left Boston a week after the funeral and begun the cross-country trek. The long drive back to Los Alamos where she'd continued to work on the Navajo reservation after her husband left to find a wife who would bear his children. A wife with no history of psychiatric problems. The BMW had held up well, but by St. Louis the same could not be said of Bo. Everything had turned dark, colorless, without hope.

Waking in a Holiday Inn overlooking the Mississippi River, Bo had looked out the window and understood that to go outside was to succumb. To go outside was to walk over the roughly cobbled bank and into mud-brown water that would swiftly cover her, swiftly drag her downward to an utter, final silence. There was no question about it; something in her brain had signaled that it was time to die. The neurochemical pathway for dissolution, hardwired into every brain for an inevitable future when it would be needed, could be activated prematurely. It could happen in an acute depression. It had happened.

But something else said "No!" Something in the very cells of her body screamed that death made no sense. It was an intelligence even more primitive than the most ancient segment of her brain, the pons, nestled at the base of her skull. An intelligence of a billion mere cells that pulled her from the window and locked her body in a fetal curl on the floor of a hotel room closet. It would not let her go outside to the cold, swift water. It would hide her in the preconscious darkness of the unborn until something came to derail the brain's grim command.

Twelve hours later the hotel manager, alerted by complaints of a guttural moaning heard in the next room, had unlocked the door with a passkey, and phoned the police. In the emergency room of a state mental hospital Bo was asked to select a psychiatrist from a typed list. Unable to talk, she had barely succeeded in organizing her thoughts sufficiently to identify the first letter of each name. Somehow the letter B seemed familiar, and Bo pointed to one of the B names.

"Lois Bittner?" The emergency room physician chuckled. "She's a little unorthodox. You sure you want Bittner?"

Bo was sure of nothing but the battle raging between her own life and the urge to drown in a strange midcontinental river whose name she couldn't at the moment pronounce, much less spell. "Uh," she'd answered, nodding. A pain like dull acid filled her, outlining her body darkly against the white room. She felt like a demon, a cartoon figure filled with black ink. When the admitting psychiatrist muttered, "This is thorazine; it'll pinch a little," and eased a sparkling hypodermic needle into her left hip, she couldn't feel it.

They'd taken her to a musty, high-ceilinged room and fastened leather cuffs to her wrists. At some point the door opened and a pastrami-scented woman who looked like a miniature schnauzer in a batik dashiki, long skirt, and Frye boots, burst in. "I'm Lois Bittner," the woman said as if her name were the answer to some amusing conundrum. "So why are you here?" The accent was clearly German, the aging dark eyes full of mirth. Bo felt a smile struggle through the darkness inside her and twitch at the corners of her mouth. The smile had felt like a lifeline, a hint of a way out.

That night Lois Bittner sat by Bo's bedside and regaled her with tales of St. Louis eateries—the fried ravioli at Garivelli's, floating in butter, the Steak'n'Shake French fry, perfect in its crispness, the Caesar salad at Al Baker's, mouthwatering. "Good food here," the diminutive doctor had grinned, "not a place for death."

Not a place for death.

Bo shook her head and forced herself back to the present. San Diego was not a place for death, either. Just a sun-washed desert city with a beach. A pastel city of nursery colors where three-year-olds in ruffled sunsuits would build things in sand, not be buried in it. "I've got to find another way to make a living,'' she told the empty corridor as she struggled to her feet. ''My psychiatrist recommends something involving fried foods.''

In the office behind the nurses' station Bo recognized the oxlike frame of Dar Reinert, the San Diego Police Department's most experienced child abuse detective. A former tackle at Notre Dame, the hulking cop had yet to find a suit that didn't make him look like one of Rembrandt's syndics.

''She didn't make it,'' Bo answered the question in Reinert's gentle, delft blue eyes. ''She's dead.''

''Sonofabitch,'' Reinert huffed softly. ''You'd better grab the sister now! We figure the perp's this wacko boyfriend of mom's—guy named Paul Massieu—lives with 'em. Better get the eight-year-old outta the loop. I'll send a coupla uniforms out to the kid's school, back you up. You meet 'em there. What's the older one's name?''

''Hannah,'' Bo remembered from the case file. ''Hannah Franer. Why do you think the boyfriend's the perp?''

The small room was airless, dim.

''Nine times outta ten it is, isn't it?'' Reinert sighed, jabbing numbers into the phone. ''You look like spoiled milk, Bradley. Go out in the hall. Get a drink of water or something. Besides,'' he said into a blue and gold striped tie askew over a blue oxford cloth shirt unbuttoned at its size eighteen collar, ''this Massieu's known to be involved with a cult.''

Bo noted the small stainless-steel Ruger revolver tucked in the waistband of Dar Reinert's wash-and-wear dress pants, and grimaced. This was the job. It often felt like an old episode of *Dragnet*.

Over a water fountain in the hall she breathed the flat chemical scent of San Diego's multiply recycled water, and assessed her future. How many more months, years of this could she take? How many more tortured children? And how many more officious remarks from Madge Aldenhoven, who would undoubtedly die on the job at ninety-three? In the living room of Bo's beach apartment a newly stretched canvas waited on its easel. Two coats of gesso applied over the weekend would be thoroughly dry. Time to paint, but paint what? No inspiration twitched before her eyes. Only the lifeless image of a chubby blonde girl.

Get a grip, Bradley. Let it go. Just go pick up the sister and then do something fun tonight, something distracting.

Bo tried to imagine what fun, distracting thing she could do that wouldn't involve sugar or saturated fats, and drew a blank.

At the end of the hall she could see Andrew LaMarche, elegant even in green surgical scrubs, somberly closing the door of the waiting room. His head was bowed. In seconds Samantha Franer's mother would be told as compassionately as possible that her younger daughter had ceased to exist. Bo considered the reality behind the closed door and shuddered.

"Bradley!" Dar Reinert's scratchy tenor voice bawled from the nurses' station, "you're going with me. Come on!"

"Going where?" Bo asked, joining the burly detective at a near-run toward the elevators.

"Franer place," came the reply. "Seems this Paul Massieu character showed up at the sister's school forty-five minutes ago, told the staff Samantha was in the hospital, and took Hannah. There's an outside chance they're still at home."

In the elevator Reinert shrugged on a navy blazer that effectively hid the gun in his belt. Bo could taste his fear like a metallic film in her own mouth. They both knew that if the older child had been victimized as well, the perpetrator might kill her to ensure her silence.

"Any news?" Cynthia Ganage asked in the lobby.

"Rats live on no evil star," Bo said, her eyes wide with apparent meaning.

"What was *that* all about?" Reinert scowled.

"The woman's a snake," Bo answered as Ganage made a note of the remark. "Do you really think we'll find Hannah with this Paul Massieu at home?" she asked once they were out of earshot.

Dar Reinert glared at the horizon beyond the hospital parking lot as if it had just maligned his mother's virtue. "Ganage may be a snake, but she may also be right," he said. "And no, I don't think we're going to find Hannah Franer at all."

Chapter 3

By 4:30 in the afternoon the windows of the five-sided tower atop the Victorian lodge gleamed amber in the setting sun. The tower had been added to the sprawling camp when the original owner's young wife contracted tuberculosis. Local Adirondack legend maintained that the desperate man confined his beloved in the tower, imploring her to breathe the famous, healing air. But before the renowned mountain cure could return the blush to her cheeks, the frail consumptive had tumbled mysteriously from one of the tower's windows. In the three-story fall her neck snapped cleanly as a twig, killing her in a second that, had her death not filled it, would surely have escaped the notice of history. A cascade of flowers, century-wild descendants of those the young wife had planted, still spilled beside the lawn. Her ghost was said to roam among them, weeping.

Eva Broussard sat motionless in one of the hickory rockers on the broad porch below the tower. The story of the consumptive bride was to her a soothing mantra, a mental chant possessing infinite avenues for inquiry. Had the Victorian lady jumped, or fallen? Was she pushed? And why a tower of five sides, crafted with such obvious architectural difficulty, buttressed between second-story casement windows? Had the tower been, really, a prison? Had death been the only possible escape?

Eva pondered a similar, if evolutionarily recent, human hunger for a way out of biological bondage. The hunger for something beyond the demands, and then decay, of flesh. That hunger had produced religions. And it had undoubtedly produced the experience that brought her here to document its influence on a hundred people. A hundred people who had in the Adirondack night seen beings who seemed not of this planet. A hundred people frightened and exalted, forever altered, longing for a return of the strange visitors who might, just might, know a way out other than death.

A tall, ropelike woman of mixed French-Canadian and Iroquois blood, Eva exhibited the tensionless grace of a high-wire artist even when still. But her otter-brown eyes were pure French, a Gallic amalgam of passion and rationality. Tugging a creamy knit turban from her head, she ran bronzed fingers through two inches of stubby, chalk-white hair. The chemotherapy that had caused her ebony mane to fall out in clumps was a necessary hedge against a cancer that might or might not abridge a life already sixty years in the making. But it had drained the color from her hair forever. Not that it mattered.

A uniquely beautiful woman by any standard, Eva had cherished only that part of her body which lay behind her eyes. Her mind—superbly trained, boundlessly curious, always rational. She had observed no evidence that her mind would survive her bodily death, however desirable that hope might seem. And after the sharp warning implicit in cancer, the realization had brought her to this odd locale in the mountains of New York State, where she watched and documented a particular groping of the human soul toward understanding. The endeavor would be the last work of her life; its significance was paramount to her. She wanted to leave behind a record, something useful to future generations. The study would be her legacy.

Eva Broussard did not believe that actual spacecraft had brought extraterrestrial beings to earth. The near-impossibility of transporting anything with physical mass across cosmic distances precluded that occurrence, and probably always would. Neither did she dismiss all claims of sightings as error or delusion. Hadn't the pioneering psychologist Carl Jung suggested that the first sightings in the 1940s might herald a change in the human brain? Perhaps that change, occurring for unknown reasons in some people but not in others, enabled certain individuals under certain circumstances to perceive weightless images beamed from elsewhere in the universe. And perhaps these images, routinely described as "silvery" and only visible at night, had been here all along, their creators waiting millennia in the past for the brain of a race of apes to mature. To "see." Eva's curiosity about those who "saw" and about how that experience would reorder their behavior was the thrumming pulse of her life. The only thing she cared about. Until now. Before today's phone call from California. Before the incomprehensible death of Samantha Franer.

Eva searched her mind for a link to the child, some particular memory that would define the personality now vanished. But there was nothing. A healthy, attractive little girl, toddling energetically behind the other children last summer when members of the group with school-age children were present. Eva remembered chubby exuberance, platinum curls, an obvious contrast with the older sister, Hannah, who was shy and reclusive. But nothing more. Samantha had still been a baby, and Eva did not share the traditional womanly fascination with barely verbal people. The sadness, she realized as conflicting winds raised angled ripples on the lake below, lay in the fact that whatever Samantha Franer might have become was now an impossibility. In the face of that, Eva wondered if her own intellectual pursuits might not seem ludicrous.

She had purchased the lodge for its proximity to areas of the Adirondacks in which sightings were reported. Paul Massieu and others who'd seen lights, saucer-shaped vehicles, and frail, shimmering humanoid figures while alone on some mountain escarpment spent as much time as possible at the compound, assessing their similar experiences. The expenses of utilities, food, and a kitchen staff from nearby Night Heron Village were shared on a monthly basis by everyone present. And in exchange for accommodations the Seekers willingly signed releases and underwent exhaustive interviews with Dr. Eva Blindhawk Broussard, who had never seen one of the silver people, but who took their stories seriously. Each Seeker provided a social and family history as well as medical and psychiatric records, and agreed to update all information twice yearly for the next decade. A comprehensive database. An intriguing longitudinal study that promised to provide clues to the psychosocial bedrock of an important shift in human awareness. A paradigm shift that as yet made no sense, although one day it would. The same could not be said of Samantha Franer, whose future had been canceled. Eva pondered a suprahuman ethic that permitted immortality for computerized data, but allowed an innocent life to be snuffed by another's depravity. The model brought her to her feet in rage at its cruelty.

Skating barefoot across a lawn only faintly green with spring grass, Eva Broussard stopped beside the woody spill of Madagascar periwinkle, legacy of a woman whose death, like Samantha's, remained a mystery. Amid the million pale green leaves not a single bud had emerged. It was too early.

It was, she admitted, gazing over the lake her own Iroquois ancestors had named, probably too early for many things. Too early to comprehend a human behavior that could result in the death of a child. Certainly too early to comprehend the human endeavor to find a link with the universe. The purpose for which she'd bought Night Heron Lodge, nestled beneath Shadow Mountain. The purpose for which a hundred people came there to stare into the sky and wait for visitors who might come again. Who might have answers to questions about life and death. Who might show the way out.

That it was too early had been made clear by the unconscionable death of a little girl. That death would destroy the group. It would curtail the intent of Eva Broussard's carefully framed research. It would confuse the mystery that had by whatever means created an experience that several rational people interpreted as visitation by nonearthly beings.

Now outsiders would come, asking questions for which there would be no solid answers. The Seekers on Shadow Mountain would be dragged into a very earthly, and very ugly, reality. They would be ridiculed, labeled. The bond of their common experience would be eroded. Worse, they would be accused of complicity in one of the most loathsome crimes possible—the sexual violation and murder of an innocent child. Beside that reality the hope of an end to cosmic loneliness seemed pitifully premature.

Eva Broussard pulled a blade of grass and held it to the waxy, dimming sun. What possible set of facts, she thought, could explain the senseless horror of Samantha Franer's death?

From the darkening lake a chill breeze wrapped her skirts about her legs. There was no answer.

Chapter 4

According to a check run by police on the address given St. Mary's Hospital, Bonnie Franer had signed a six-month lease on the three-bedroom house in a quiet central San Diego neighborhood shortly after Christmas. Dar Reinert shared the information with Bo as he drove and wolfed a Mounds bar. The candy's sweetish coconut smell gave the interior of the car a sickly tropical flavor.

"Why would Franer have signed the lease rather than Massieu?" Bo said from the passenger's seat, trying to ignore the odor. She felt oddly uninvolved with the case, and yet pulled toward some dimension of it that seemed peripheral. Something distant, almost cerebral. If she really decided to quit her job, she realized, this would be her last case. Maybe the nagging tug toward irrelevant facts was just a way of making the break. At least it wasn't manicky. She felt none of the dramatic emotional response that would signal a need for lithium.

"We ran a check. Massieu's Canadian, not a U.S. citizen," Reinert replied, easing his eight-cylinder Olds diagonally across the driveway of the house. "Some people will only rent to legal citizens. Cuts down on the problem of a bunch of illegal Mexicans renting a place and tearing it apart."

Bo considered launching an argument that "illegal Mexicans" were no more likely to tear a house apart than, say, "legal Norwegians," but abandoned the idea. What Reinert suggested was often true. A cultural dilemma created when agrarian people from villages as yet unblessed by electricity or modern plumbing walked hundreds of miles to work north of an invisible line called "U.S.–Mexico Border." Unsophisticated people, who might keep chickens in the laundry room of a rental house or cook them over Sterno in the living room. Reinert's expansive maroon car, she noticed, effectively blocked any possible exit from the closed, two-car garage.

"Nobody's here," she said. The beige stucco ranch with its fading brown shutters and bare, weedy lawn provided a wealth of information. Keenly aware of nuance, Bo missed none of it. "They haven't lived here long, and they don't intend to stay." A network of cracks in the unwatered lawn created a miniature badland. "There aren't any bikes or toys in the yard, which means they haven't bought any. And no personal touches. The house looks exactly as it did when they rented it."

"Whaddaya mean?" Reinert sniffed, watching the living room picture window for movement. "Place looks okay to me."

"That's the point," Bo went on. "People invariably mark their living spaces, personalize them. A butterfly decal on the mailbox, plaster St. Francis in the yard. Maybe a plant or a lamp visible in a window. Something that changes the physical structure into a habitation. This place is just a structure. The people haven't created any identity here. Their hearts are someplace else."

"So?" Reinert opened his door.

"So they're not going to stay. It's temporary, like a motel room. Nobody feels compelled to personalize a motel room; there's no point."

"Women pick up stuff like that." The detective nodded fondly as Bo followed him toward the slightly warped front door. She kept to herself the fact that any man with a diagnosis of manic depression would probably exhibit the same sensibilities. It came with the territory.

The house seeped a sort of breathy grayness, the hallmark of places where no one is. There would, Bo sensed as Reinert removed the Ruger from beneath his blazer, also be no dog or cat. The grayness lacked even an animal presence.

Dar Reinert's fist thumped on the hollow-core door as he bellowed, "Massieu? Open up. Police."

Beside the drab rental the adjoining property seemed to have been groomed as a set for a country-and-western video. A picket fence banked with waist-high scarlet geraniums bordered a verdant lawn punctuated by an artistically placed birdbath, a small gazebo of white lath, and an unidentifiable piece of antique farm equipment. From a bed of Charlotte Armstrong roses between the geraniums a salty male voice roared, "There's nobody home over there! They've been gone since 7:00. You won't need that gun!" The man, about seventy and dressed in painter's pants and a pajama shirt, grinned sheepishly from his position flat on the ground amid the roses. "Been skittish around guns since the war," he explained. "Lost an eye at Pearl."

Bo wondered for the millionth time in her life just how she was able to know, without even *caring*, that the old codger was lying. He had a glass eye, all right. But he hadn't lost the real one defending Pearl Harbor.

"It's an acute sensitivity to tone and presentation," Lois Bittner had tried to explain years ago. "You're a walking litmus test for imperceptible clues that anyone else would miss. Have you given any thought," the wiry psychiatrist lapsed into her characteristic accent, "to a chob as a chypsy?"

Bo smiled to herself as Reinert made easy work of unlocking the flimsy door with the edge of his tie clasp.

"Isn't this illegal?" she said.

"Door was unlocked," the detective recited. "I feared that the older child might be alone in the house, injured and unable to call out. On that cause I entered the premises accompanied by a representative of Child Protective Services, Ms. Bradley."

Reinert's written report of the entry would say precisely that. But they couldn't stay beyond a few minutes or remove any evidence.

The living room, carpeted in a threadbare chartreuse shag, was completely empty. A dining ell to the left contained a

Formica table and four mismatched chairs that could have been purchased in any thrift store in North America. Four plastic placemats in a sunny yellow showed evidence of regular cleaning, and matched a basket of silk daisies in the table's center. The kitchen was equally tidy, if devoid of personality. There was nothing about the place to suggest that anybody really lived there. There was also nothing to suggest diabolical secrets.

"I don't get a sense of anything unwholesome going on here," Bo said tentatively. Houses sometimes seemed to whisper of events they had sheltered. This one merely yawned. "What makes you think this Massieu's involved in a cult?"

Reinert was checking the contents of the refrigerator. "The mother told the admitting clerk at St. Mary's that they were in San Diego so Massieu could buy some land out in the desert for this New York group she called the Seekers."

"So? California's full of people *seeking* something different. It's the primary pastime. Crystals, channeling, past lives, Eastern mysticism, Zen dentistry—it's just openness, curiosity. What's wrong with that?"

"People get a little *too* curious, you ask me," Reinert answered enigmatically from a cabinet beneath the sink. "Makes 'em crazy."

Marveling at the non sequitur, Bo chose not to respond to it and congratulated herself. There would be no point in explaining to Dar Reinert what "crazy" really meant or that it could not be the result of curiosity, a quality already erroneously damned for its ability to kill cats. Moving into a hall accessible from both kitchen and living room, Bo inspected a bathroom situated between two bedrooms. On a shelf was a half-used pack of pink bathroom tissue and a large bottle of baby shampoo. Bo remembered pale curls and shivered. The baby shampoo would have been for Samantha. On the toilet seat and on the floor bright red stains were already drying.

"Dar," she whispered, "better see this."

"Mother said she was bleeding this morning," he said gruffly behind her. "Bastard must've torn her up last night. She goes to bed. The blood pools in her abdominal cavity while she's sleeping. Then when she gets up . . ."

Bo touched the door frame in an attempt to curb a wave of nausea. What had been done to Samantha Franer did not bear close scrutiny. Not without throwing up, at least.

You've seen this before, Bradley. Remember your job is to protect the sister. Let the police worry about the perp.

"Well, well, looka here . . ." Reinert singsonged from one of the bedrooms. The tone made it clear that he'd found something he was looking for.

Bo smoothed her forehead with the heels of both hands. "What is it?" she asked, entering the room Samantha and Hannah Franer had obviously shared. Red, white, and blue Raggedy Ann sheets adorned a double-bed mattress on the floor. Above a red-enameled bureau whose half-open drawers revealed children's socks, T-shirts, pajamas, hung a face. Or a head. A thing woven of straw with protuberant, empty eye sockets, a sharp nose, and an oval mouth that appeared to be blowing. Bo recognized the mouth as similar to one in an Irish children's book her sister, Laurie, had loved. The north wind's mouth in a cloud, gusting winter over Lough Derg. The memory of Laurie was, as usual, unsettling.

"I dunno what the hell it is," the detective snarled at the hollow eyes, "but didn't the pediatrician's report say somebody painted a spiked face on the poor kid's belly before he raped her? This looks like a spiked face to me, made of straw or something. So what does that say?"

"I don't know what it says," Bo answered. The straw face seemed to tell some story far removed from the terrible stains in the bathroom. A story Bo sensed in the same way she could tell, even in windowless rooms, when clouds covered the sun. But a closer story was that Hannah Franer, if she were still alive, had just entered a world Bo knew very well. A world in which there only used to be a little sister.

"It says these people are into some weird stuff that may involve sex with children. Ritual abuse stuff. That psychologist, Ganage, says they do it because destroying innocence pleases Satan, or something like that. And with this devil mask right here in the kids' room, it's safe to guess Mom might just have gone along with it. Time for a warrant—at least accessory to felony child sexual assault. I'm gonna call it in . . ."

Bo watched the straw mask. It stared wildly at nothing, howling soundlessly. Things were moving too fast, assumptions being made with senseless velocity. Accustomed to occasional manic episodes in which her own perceptions accelerated beyond the boundaries of reality, Bo now felt like an inert stump rooted in a hurricane. Something was off, wrong, skewed. Why was everybody in such a hurry to jump on the devil worship thing? The situation, Bo gauged uneasily, was assuming the framework of mania. Too fast. Out of control. But recognizing it didn't mean there was anything she could do about it.

"I want you to interview the mother as soon as we get back to the hospital," Reinert said from the kitchen where he was on the phone arranging a warrant for the arrest of Bonnie Franer. "I hear you're magic getting the truth outta people. I want you to break her. Now. Before she gets a lawyer."

It was perfectly legal. The cops and CPS workers did it whenever necessary. A suspect could not be interrogated by police without counsel. But a social worker could interview the suspect in order to secure information that might affect the welfare of that suspect's children. Whatever was said in that interview would be submitted to juvenile court in a confidential report prepared to document recommendations for the child's placement and protection. In theory, that report could be seen by no one outside juvenile court. In practice, the report or even the social worker could be subpoenaed to other courts, and the CPS worker could simply tell the cops anything she or he thought they needed to know. In actuality, if Bonnie Franer chose to tell Bo Bradley that her live-in boyfriend, Paul Massieu, raped her three-year-old daughter, Samantha, in a Satanic ritual involving bug-eyed masks, she might as well have told KTUV's evening news.

Bo experienced the weight of her own role in the mercurial sequence of events, and sighed. A hundred-pound raven perched on her head would have been more comfortable.

"Mind if I smoke in your car?" she asked Reinert, lighting a Gauloise and exhaling thoughtfully.

"Hang it out the window," Reinert replied.

Bo bit her lip and did not produce any of the twenty-seven possible comebacks crossing her mind.

Chapter 5

Andrew LaMarche clasped long, bony fingers atop a desk calendar advertising soy-based infant formula. On a bookcase to his right a Seth Thomas clock informed Bo in gilded Roman numerals that it was 2:15 and that time, in fact, possessed wings.

"Why do you have to interview the poor woman right now, Bo?" he asked quietly. The edge of a French accent never lost from his New Orleans upbringing betrayed emotion otherwise scrupulously contained. The death of Samantha Franer seemed to have upset him inordinately. Bo wondered why. As director of the hospital's child abuse unit, the world-famous expert on brutalized children had undoubtedly seen more than one small cadaver.

"The suspected perp has taken off with the older sister," Bo explained. "The mother may know where he's taken her." On the physician's desk was a rough potter's clay sculpture of a human baby in the arms of a Barbary ape. "Where did you find that piece?" she asked, intrigued. The ape's eyes were wide with fear.

"I made it," he replied without interest. "Bo, Bonnie

Franer had nothing to do with the death of her daughter. Neither did Paul Massieu. They're both innocent. I'm sure of it."

Bo raised her eyes from the sculpture to gaze levelly at Andrew LaMarche. "The police think differently."

"The police think *obviously*," he said from beneath a graying mustache. "I had expected better from you. I simply can't allow you to interrogate Bonnie Franer right now, Bo." His voice dropped to a husky whisper. "She's just lost a child."

Bo examined her patience and found it worn to translucent thinness. Every minute ticking by might increase the danger to Hannah. "I know she's just lost a child! And I'm not here to discuss it with you. I'm here to get information that might just save the sister from a similar fate. Now where's Bonnie Franer?"

The baritone voice rasped with anger. "Do you think I don't know what you and Reinert are up to? The woman's in shock. She could say anything. You'll concoct enough evidence to hang her by tomorrow. I won't permit it!"

His hands, Bo noticed as he stood and wrenched a mole-gray pinstriped jacket from the back of his desk chair, seemed wooden. Beneath close-cropped hair the color of loam his eyes swept the room as if searching for hidden assassins. Bo would not have been surprised if he'd grabbed the odd little sculpture and smashed it against the wall of diplomas at her back. The framed documents proclaimed Andrew Jacques LaMarche a doctor of pediatrics, a fellow at three universities, and a legal expert on criminal pediatric trauma. None of them mentioned that the dashing baby doctor had the temperament of a coloratura soprano opening *La Traviata* at the Met. But the peculiar thing was the direction of his anger. Long a defender of the rights of children, Andrew LaMarche had never before evinced any interest in the feelings of parents.

Puzzled, Bo showed her ace. "I think Bonnie Franer has told you what happened to Samantha, and I think she's told you where Paul Massieu has taken Hannah."

"She told me Samantha seemed strange last night, refusing to eat her dinner. She said that Paul Massieu returned from the property their group is purchasing out in the desert near

Jamul at about 7:00, when he and the mother checked on Samantha, who was asleep, and decided not to call a doctor because she wasn't feverish. After that, she said she, Paul, and the older sister, Hannah, watched television until Hannah went to bed at 9:00. Apparently there was some muted talking and activity in the girls' room at that time, indicating that Samantha had awakened when her sister came to bed. But since neither girl came back out to say anything was wrong, Bonnie and Paul didn't check further. Bonnie said that Paul was not alone with Samantha at any time last night, and so couldn't have been the one who raped her, even if he'd been capable of such a thing. The couple went to bed at 10:00 and heard nothing from the girl's room during the night. Paul rose at 5:00 to breakfast with an earthmoving contractor they've apparently hired to clear a road into the desert property. He was gone when Bonnie heard Samantha's cries from the bathroom and then saw that the child was pale and bleeding from the pelvic region. She told me she phoned a local pediatrician's service then, at about 6:30, and made arrangements to meet in the doctor's office after dropping the older sister at her school." There was a pause. "And that's it, Bo. Anything else she may have said is privileged."

"Another child's life is at risk," Bo told him. "Against that fact your privilege means nothing. If Hannah is harmed because you kept me from interviewing the mother, you're accountable."

They'd both known it all along. Bo couldn't imagine what lay behind the verbal grandstanding. His eyes were the color of wet slate.

"She's in the surgical social worker's office with a priest," he muttered, tugging French cuffs to a point precisely a half inch below his jacket sleeves. "But you're wasting your time."

Bo had scraped knuckles on the renowned LaMarche pomposity before. "Oh, thank you, massa," she bowed, shuffling across what she realized was an Aubusson carpet. "I's jus' doin' my job."

"Don't push me, Bo." The deep voice held an unaccountable dagger edge.

Bo merely pulled the office door closed behind her and wondered why everyone seemed mad as hatters. The thought found form on an imaginary canvas in her head. LaMarche in a top hat and cutaway coat, pouring tea for a March Hare who was Madge Aldenhoven, while a burly dormouse with a Ruger revolver in its belt snored with its head in a plate of crumpets. The day was not going well, despite its bland beginning. Bo found a measure of comfort in the accuracy of her earlier foreboding. And in her decision to explore the possibility of quitting this torturous job. In the surgical social worker's office that comfort evaporated like water on a heated stone.

"Hannah is fine," Bonnie Franer pronounced with wrenching effort after Bo explained her own function in the nightmare. "Please, dear God please, just leave me alone!" The gaunt woman had doubled over in a series of shallow, racking gulps that would only later become sobs. The gulping and breathing created a rocking motion. Bo watched with growing alarm as Bonnie Franer's tattered fingers roamed aimlessly over the suede surface of a purse. Most of her fingernails were bitten to the quick. A glance at the woman's skeletal forearms revealed long, fine scratches threading the pallid skin. Similar marks raked the sides of her face and neck. Some were fresh, trickling spidery filaments of blood. More were dried and healing. Bo had seen it before. Even with her gnawed fingernails, Bonnie Franer made a habit of scratching herself. A bad sign.

The priest, who in Bo's estimation couldn't have been a day over fourteen, sat boyishly on the social worker's desk and reeked concern. "I'm Frank Goodman," he curbed a naturally wide smile tugging at the corners of his mouth, "from St. Theresa's."

"Hi, Father," Bo replied and ran a freckled hand through her hair, then tapped a Bic pen against her teeth. Bonnie Franer presented a textbook picture that screamed "victim." Had Paul Massieu done this as well? Stripped the mother of her very personality while using her daughters as sexual toys? Maybe this *was* one of those tabloid cases beloved of talk show hosts, cases in which secretly monstrous men held thrall over helpless women and their children. In three years with Child Protective Services, Bo had never seen such a case. They were never that simple. But this might be a first.

Bonnie Franer's agitated, crablike hands seemed to be searching for something. Bo recognized the behavior. A pair of scissors, a drapery cord, even a ballpoint pen might become a weapon in those hands. A weapon turned against the woman holding it. Bonnie Franer, Bo noted glumly, was a Class A candidate for suicide.

"Did Paul Massieu ever molest or sexually assault your daughter Samantha?" Bo forced herself to address the pathetic figure.

What do you do for an encore, Bradley? Bite the heads off kittens?

As the woman continued to rock from the waist, hanks of fine, dust-blonde hair pulled loose from a hastily brushed bun at the nape of her neck. In the artificial light of the social worker's office, the floating tendrils might have been the hair of a swimmer. Underwater. Riding currents no words could penetrate.

The tiny office seemed to be shrinking. There was no air. Bo wished the priest would go out into the hall rather than witness the spectacular barbarism indigenous to her job. But he merely sat gazing with kind, basset-brown eyes at the grieving mother.

"Paul loves the girls," Bonnie Franer whispered in a final attempt at coherence. Then her eyes rolled back and she began to rock harder. "It's my fault, my fault, always all my fault." The last words emerged as a moan, continued as a mindless chant. The rocking and moaning would go on, Bo realized, until the woman was medicated. There would be no more communication. Gently Bo placed a hand on the woman's frail wrist, but there was no response.

"Let me." Father Frank Goodman jumped off the desk and slid a muscular arm around the woman's shoulders. Inexplicably, he began to sing something that sounded remarkably like "Send in the Clowns" in a soft tenor. His singing actually seemed to relax the frenzied rocking.

Bo wondered what had happened to the Catholic church since she left it twenty years ago.

"Had enough?"

It was Andrew LaMarche, glacially present at the door.

"Reinert's issued a warrant," she said in tones designed to encourage a professional response. "But this woman won't survive a night in jail. She'll . . ." her voice began to crack, "she'll find a way to . . ." The words were cardboard stuck in her throat. The same words required in describing Laurie's death. "She's got to have a suicide watch."

"I've called for a psychiatric consult." LaMarche conceded the point while ignoring Bo's discomfiture. "Mrs. Franer will be taken to County Psychiatric. I hope this will end the involvement of Child Protective Services with this unfortunate woman."

Bo regarded the man who'd sent long-stemmed roses to her office and phoned every week since saving her life in an unusual case the previous fall. A tin statue would have produced more warmth.

"Nothing would please me more, Doctor," she emphasized the title, "but a child has been killed. The district attorney will order the immediate filing of a sibling petition. Fifteen minutes after I leave here, Hannah Franer will legally be in the custody of San Diego County's Juvenile Court for her own protection. It's my case until she's found and her safety is protected."

"You're destroying innocent people. Can't you see that?"

"At least one innocent person has already been destroyed," Bo said as she pushed past him. "Or had you forgotten?"

In the parking lot Bo found a small picture of St. Theresa under her driver's-side windshield wiper. On the back a large hand had penned, "This is *clergy* parking, bozo! Fr. F. Goodman"

Climbing on the hood of her car, Bo tucked the prayer card onto the left foot of Mabel Mammoth, clambered down and lit a cigarette.

"I have the most noxious job on the planet," she told the creature, "involving not only malignant acts and vile individuals, but pompous pediatricians and priests who should still be playing video games after school. Someone has slaughtered a child, and I have a sense that everyone connected to the case is locked into dead-end viewpoints that are obscuring the truth. I don't know why I feel that way, Mabel, but I do. Is it because I stopped the lithium? Am I getting too imaginative here? And is there any chance I can find a job somewhere that doesn't surpass Dante's Inferno in wretchedness?''

The magenta mammoth said nothing but continued to smile at an oleander blooming profusely at its feet. Bo sighed and scrounged through the jumble of tape cassettes in her glove compartment until she found the one she was looking for. *Carmina Burana*. Its ''O Fortuna'' had been the anthem of her adolescent rebellion, wholly approved by her violinist mother.

''If you've got to lurk about in excessive eye makeup,'' Margot O'Reilly had said one long-past Boston morning, ''then I suppose it's best you lurk to some enduring music.''

Bo drove the few blocks back to her office with a dog-Latin chorus to spring and fate blasting from her car. Its invocation of rebellion created a focus for her discomfort with everything so far connected to the Franer case. A child brutally dead, her mother plunging into a hellish depression, her sister vanished with the only suspect, and the odd coincidence of a Satanic workshop the same day a purportedly Satanic case turned up. None of the pieces really fit. But then they never did. Not at first. Bo decided to start eliminating pieces, narrow the field. And she knew just where to start.

Back in her office she nudged the door closed and picked up the phone. ''Information for Quantico, Virginia, please. I'd like the number for the Federal Bureau of Investigation's task force on ritual crime.''

It was after 5:00 in Virginia, but somebody answered his phone anyway. And in ten minutes provided Bo with enough information to tar and feather Cynthia Ganage. Not that anybody would listen.

Bo mentally filed what she'd heard and then stared into her own green eyes in the mirror on the office door. Those eyes didn't always see exactly what everybody else saw. The brain behind them was different, its neural pathways prone to the odd bypass, the occasional derailment. But that brain, her brain, her *self*, would never cling to an insubstantial fantasy to avoid facing a truth. The realization was centering, like opening the door to a personal integrity she'd known was there but couldn't name. She was pretty tough, she acknowledged, to be able to face a world in which human behavior could not be blamed on a Satan. One tough crazy lady. She wished everyone else involved in the Franer case could say the same.

Chapter 6

An early ground fog already drifted luminously in the stand of paper birch east of the lake path. Towering behind her, Eva Broussard felt more than saw the thick, crumbled silhouette of Shadow Mountain. Its vastness had taken form countless millions of years in some unknowable past. Webbed at its base by veins of glassy quartz and pink feldspar, its highest peak was of a rare stone found also in lunar rock samples—anorthosite. In a leap of near-mindless concatenation Eva had at one point allowed herself to wonder if the moon rock itself might somehow figure in the curious experience related by Paul Massieu and the others. The Adirondack peaks consisted of some fifteen hundred square miles of erosion-resistant, metamorphosed anorthosite. A huge expanse. Did it in its massiveness create a magnetic field capable of producing realistic hallucinations? The theory made as much sense as any. Which wasn't saying much. After three years Eva Broussard had yet to frame a coherent theory of why a number of demonstrably rational people insisted they'd had contact with extraterrestrials on or near Shadow Mountain.

Padding across the porch to the inlaid maple floor in fringed moccasins pulled on against the evening chill, the graceful woman knelt to lay a fire in the largest of three fireplaces. There would be a community meeting after dinner to deal with the grim news of Samantha Franer's death. Later she would drive to Albany to pick up Paul Massieu and Hannah at the airport. After settling Hannah, Paul would flee to Canada. The decision had not been an easy one to make. Yet everyone was certain Paul was innocent, and that by the time he could be extradited from Canada, Samantha's real murderer would have been apprehended. The level of confidence exhibited by the group in California's law enforcement agencies reflected nothing so much as a familiarity with American television. Eva found herself staring into the stacked wood.

Could she be wrong about Paul? Could her fondness for the quiet, lonely man have obscured her judgment? *Could* Paul Massieu be a pederast, a child-molester, the rapist and murderer of a little girl?

As she lit a match to the kindling she stripped herself of the layered identities that might blind her to a distasteful truth. Like barely perceptible cloaks, she removed the personae of psychiatrist, Bolduc Chair in Social Psychology at the Séminaire de Sainte Jeanne d'Arc, and author of the popular self-help series, *The Meaning of Your Life*, as well as a highly praised biography of the Christian mystic Hildegard of Bingen. When the intellectual trappings of forty years had fallen away, Eva addressed her core being—a mature Iroquois woman. The fire caught and flared, its dancing light a filigree on her broad hands.

"What do I want?" she thought inwardly to a gallery of masks floating near her subconscious. "Do I need to believe in the normalcy of this man's personality so much for the sake of my own research that I've overlooked a terrible inadequacy? Have I wanted the project more than the truth?"

The Iroquois mask Eva named "Pride," an elongated visage woven of age-darkened willow with mere slits for eyes and a clown's wide smile, did not drift into view behind her closed eyes. She'd more than half expected it, the quality called pride having been a continual stumbling block in her adult life. But it wasn't there. Nothing was there. Just a reversed-out image of flames, black on a gray background. If Eva Broussard had failed to perceive a disturbing sickness in Paul Massieu, there was nothing in her mind to account for it. Still, she acknowledged, there was always the minuscule margin for error. The margin in which wholly inexplicable events could occur. This might be one of them, but Eva was prepared to contend that it wasn't. Eva was comfortable with a ninety-eight percent certainty that Paul Massieu was innocent.

Rising from the stone hearth, she stretched bronze, muscular arms toward Night Heron Lake, now gray marble beneath a patchy scarf of fog, and thought about the other victims of Samantha's killer. The child's death would destroy the mother. That realization scarcely required the plethora of professional sensitivities possessed by Dr. Eva Blindhawk Broussard.

Bonnie Franer had been beaten by a drunken sod of a father on a bleak farm outside Syracuse, New York, until marrying at nineteen an arcade games salesman she'd met at the truck stop where she worked as a cashier. Eight years later and three months into the pregnancy that would produce Samantha, Seth Franer had taken the remaining two hundred dollars in their bank account and vanished. A postcard from Niagara Falls informed Bonnie that he was sorry, but he guessed he was just a rolling stone. He wouldn't be back. The day the postcard came Bonnie Franer had taken her daughter Hannah to kindergarten, returned home, and swallowed a hundred and thirty-six over-the-counter sleeping pills. A neighbor found her vomiting on the rickety wooden porch of the Franers' rented duplex in Troy, New York. After her stomach was pumped, the defeated woman's only fear was that she had harmed the child growing within her. Now that child was dead.

Eva Broussard shivered slightly and hugged herself against the flimsy substance of Bonnie Franer's life. Nothing had been given the woman to uphold her during difficulty. No family or cultural ties, no education, no financial resources. No substance of any kind. The woman was prey to every vagary of emotion, every whim in the shifting winds of her time. When Paul Massieu met Bonnie Franer working the food concession at one of Eva's lucrative self-help lectures in Buffalo, he'd fallen in love with his own need to protect something. A cultural anthropologist specializing in the nineteenth-century United States, he'd seemed to grieve for everything lost in time. Suffrage banners, quart-sized beer bottles, the Elizabethan dialect still spoken on the Outer Banks of North Carolina before a causeway to the mainland was built. Everything lost filled him with a helpless urgency to protect it, save it from an annihilation already accomplished. Bonnie Franer and her daughters had represented a fragility he *could* protect. Until now.

Over the mantel a small oil painting reflected the flames below. A gloomy local New York State landscape painted on cardboard in 1874 by an artist named Ella Pell who would later achieve renown in the great salons of Europe. Eva had discovered the painting among rubbish stored in the tower when she bought the lodge. Probably, she thought, a gift of the artist to the lodge's first owners. Perhaps a gift to the woman who'd died falling from the tower itself. Paul Massieu had insisted that the painting be framed and hung.

In its lower left corner dim figures occupied a small boat, dwarfed by looming, mist-covered mountains and the lampblack surface of the lake. But the seated figure, a woman in a black hat, wore at her neck a scarlet kerchief. The minuscule banner, barely visible in its dark field, was to Eva a symbol for the very striving she'd come here to document. A frail emblem of hope in a tumult of darkness. But there would be no hope for Bonnie Franer now. Too much had hurt that defenseless soul for too long. And Paul Massieu could no longer protect her.

The little picture with its single thread of color was for the inquisitive Broussard an apt standard for their whole endeavor. An unusual, perhaps irrational endeavor. Now doomed. Idly she adjusted the painting on the stone wall and remembered her first meeting with the somber anthropologist.

He'd come unannounced to her office in Montreal three years ago.

"I want you to tell me if I'm insane," he'd explained in the familiar Canadian French. "I'll pay whatever the standard rate is for such things."

A soft-spoken man of about thirty-five, dressed in rumpled corduroys, a forest green turtleneck sweater, and the predictable professor's tweed jacket. Strong, clean-shaven jaw. Shaggy black hair showing inherited evidence of male pattern baldness. Raven-dark eyes with thick, curling lashes. Black French, Eva decided. Or part Indian, like herself. Whatever his genetic heritage, it, and a mutilated right hand injured, he said, on an archaeological dig, gave him a sinister quality that was misleading. Paul Massieu would prove himself to be one of the gentlest men Eva had ever met. He'd hunched his wide shoulders and clasped stocky hands, the right of which was missing the little finger, in his lap as she outlined the reasons his request couldn't be met.

There was in actuality no measurable quality named "sanity." The term could be defined only by its absence or impairment, and even that was subject to wide fluctuations based on social and cultural expectations. Certain patterns of behavior had been given certain names, and certain medications were known to control certain symptoms. But literally no one could define sanity, much less measure it.

"But you're a psychiatrist, aren't you?" he'd insisted.

"Among other things," Broussard answered. "Tell me why you've come to me."

Paul Massieu had leaned forward nervously, his elbows on his knees. "I remembered something that happened a year ago. Something that *couldn't* have happened, and yet the memory is there . . . details, feelings, everything. So either it *did* happen, or I'm somehow making up this whole memory, and I'm crazy."

"And you want me to . . . ?"

"I read one of your books. You sound, well, practical. I want somebody objective. Somebody who's not connected to any of this weird stuff . . ."

"Connected to what weird stuff?" Broussard had inquired, curious.

Massieu straightened his shoulders. "To any of these people running around saying they've seen flying saucers and creatures from other planets."

"I'm afraid you've come to the wrong place," Broussard began professionally. "I really can't—"

"Please," his appeal had been direct and unflinching. "You've got to help me."

She had agreed. And after polygraphs, hypnosis, batteries of tests, and analysis, Paul Massieu, an adjunct professor of anthropology at McGill University who loved camping in the Adirondacks, was revealed to be a marginally introverted personality with no evidence whatever of thought or affective disorder. Either he had been abducted by wraithlike humanoid figures in metallic clothing, and examined by them, or he had hallucinated the experience in whole or in part for reasons completely inconsistent with the entire history and practice of psychiatry. Eva Broussard didn't dismiss that possibility.

But then, when word of her work with Massieu got out in Montreal's psychiatric community, others began to show up at her office. Most were so impaired that their narratives of extraterrestrial contacts were specious, either attention-seeking or delusional. Still, for every ten of them, one believable witness would appear. A fifty-four-year-old grocer from Malone, New York. A young computer skills teacher from Quebec City who wanted to be a fashion designer. A Roman Catholic grandmother of ten from Mishawawka, Indiana, who'd been on a tour of religious shrines when she, too, saw the strange beings.

Eva Broussard had gone into seclusion for two months at a Carmelite convent on the St. Lawrence River near Cap-de-la-Madeleine. In silence and barefoot on the old limestone floors she'd considered the nature of cancer, which had claimed her left breast and might eventually claim her life. She had watched her dreams in the Iroquois way for the masked faces who would reveal her deepest need. "To know," the masks had murmured. "Your great need is simply to know." Then she'd pondered the motley collection of frightened people who told of a near-identical experience—contact with beings unlike any known human form.

An orig'nal text of F. H. Bradley's *Appearance and Reality* arrived from Oxford and was carefully read. Experience, the Victorian philosopher told Eva, is what matters. Thinking about experience is a maze of misleading relational complexity. The experience is what it is; interpretations of it are flawed by attempts to describe it as like something else. Paul Massieu and the others had known an experience. Describing it in relational terms was just the way of the human mind. It might be like science-fiction fantasies familiar to Massieu and the others from novels and movies, but it was not, in reality, any kind of fiction at all. Something had happened in the experience of these people. Eva Broussard decided to spend the remaining years of her life trying to identify what that something was. At sixty she felt that her very life, her experience and training, her travel and writing, had groomed her, prepared her, for precisely this. She regarded her decision to pursue the research as the most exciting moment of her life.

Within another month she had closed her office and liquidated enough assets to purchase the old Adirondack camp beneath a mountain where Paul Massieu was examined in a silver craft by papery beings with huge, glassy-black eyes. The creatures smelled, he said, like the aromatic spice called mace.

For Eva it had been a homecoming. Born on the Onondaga Reservation near Nedrow, New York, young Eva Blindhawk had only been taken in by relatives of her father in Montreal at seven, when her mother died of the same cancer Eva herself now fought. In the critical first five years of life she'd been an Iroquois Indian, an Onondaga from whose ranks the chief of the six Iroquois nations must, by ancient tradition, be chosen. She'd been the daughter of Naomi Blindhawk and granddaughter of a dream-woman who ordered the midwinter rituals. Tracing her lineage to one of the oldest longhouses, she knew herself a member of the Heron Clan. One of her great-great-grandmothers had named the very lake now hidden in mist below the lodge. Eva Broussard was home. But trouble was winging its desperate way from California. A fugitive man and frightened child, and all that would follow them.

As members of the community gathered from adjacent cottages and climbed the maple tower stairs for the evening chant, Eva sighed and relaxed. Some of the Seekers, as they called themselves, believed that a technically perfect plainsong in human voice, beamed regularly into space from a transmitter atop Shadow Mountain, would entice a return of the frail, terrifying visitors. The chants, performed at sunrise and at sunset from the five-sided tower, were the most lovely, plaintive sound Eva had ever heard.

Chapter 7

Bo had delivered the paperwork on Hannah Franer to the district attorney's office at 3:00 P.M. His signature scrawled across the petition at 3:10 ensured that the eight-year-old girl was legally under the jurisdiction of San Diego County's Juvenile Court. A formality under the circumstances, the legal documents would ensure that police could seize the child without hindrance in the event that she were found. A "sibling petition," no more than a handful of paper in which a county assumed the duties of a parent when the real parent had "failed to protect."

For the rest of the afternoon Bo worked another case, and brooded. The case involved an abandoned ten-year-old found by police in the closet of a fleabag hotel room where his mother lay dead on the floor, having freebased her way into the next world. The boy, now waiting at the county receiving home for whatever would happen next, said he had no relatives except a father named Lee John who'd "killed some dude" in Iowa, or maybe it was Idaho. When twenty-seven phone calls to corrections agencies in states beginning with *I* turned up no information whatever on a Lee John or John Lee

Crowley, Bo wrote up a court report recommending that the boy be released for adoption. Then she stood outside the window of Madge Aldenhoven's office, smoking.

No one would adopt Jonas Lee Crowley. That was a joke. In fact, hell would freeze before the hypothetical nice couple would welcome into their hypothetical loving home a skinny, snarling boy with hate in his ice-blue eyes, lice in his hair, and a hobby of peeing on shoppers from the top of department store escalators. Jonas would spend the next eight years in foster homes and correctional schools. After that he would be released to the streets where he would unquestionably sire another generation of misery. If there were a way to stop the cycle of ruin she saw every day, Bo couldn't imagine what it might be.

Her own childhood home in Boston had seemed perfectly awful at the time. A little sister who was deaf, everybody having to use sign language. Her mother, a violinist with the Boston Symphony, constantly practicing in the dining room. The scent of imported tobacco drifting from her father's meerschaum in a living room converted to library for his endless and highly paid research into antiquated patents and copyrights. And a paternal grandmother whose annual summer visits from Ireland wreaked havoc. In retrospect Bo knew her childhood to have been a well-managed haven, despite the problems her family faced. This job had forced her to see what hell life could be for children, and the hell those children would later create for *their* children, ad infinitum. She wished her parents had lived long enough for her to thank them.

"You look like your best friend *es morte*." Estrella butchered the common remark while struggling through the parched bushes outside their supervisor's office. "You just smoke out here to irritate her, don't you?"

"No, I like the view," Bo answered, gazing through a chain-link fence at four lanes of traffic on Genesee Avenue. "It's the best part of this job."

Estrella grabbed a limb of a relatively healthy bottlebrush tree for balance and stood squarely on two-inch heels. "I hate it when you get nasty," she said. "I think—"

"I know. You think I should go back on the lithium." Bo ground the cigarette under a shoe and retrieved the smashed filter. "But it's not that. I *know* when I need medication, and right now I don't. I'm just tired of pretending it's normal to spend my days chatting about things that would gag most convicted felons. I mean, how many people do you know in the real world who schmooze over lunch about how to get evidence of oral copulation on infants? Or show each other pictures of roach-infested diapers, not to mention tire marks on—"

Estrella grimaced and held up a hand. "Spare me. I work here, too. You just don't think about it, is all. You just do the job and then go home and *forget* it, which reminds me—"

"The kid on the case I got this morning," Bo interrupted, tossing the filter into a trash can by the door, "died on the operating table. She looked like a cherub, a Rubens maybe, and she's dead. The mother creates a whole new meaning for the term 'self-hatred,' the boyfriend's run off with the older sister, and that publicity shark of a psychologist is getting miles of exposure screaming 'The devil did it!' Reinert seems to believe there's ritual abuse involved simply because the boyfriend's in some cult, even though we don't know what kind of cult. LaMarche has gone off the deep end defending the suspected perp and the mother . . ." Bo paused for a breath, "and even though I've eaten nothing but one Granny Smith apple and a half pint of skim milk all day, I'm still fat. I think it's time to find another job."

"You're not fat, but hunger can make people mean," said Estrella, unaccountably beaming. "You don't need another job. I think we've found the answer."

"What was the question?" Bo asked suspiciously. Estrella looked like a cat with the keys to the parakeet sanctuary.

"Will you promise me something?"

"No promises on Wednesday. Old Irish superstition."

Back in the office Estrella fussed over a tube of lipstick found in the bottom of her purse. "Not even for an *amiga* who may or may not take care of your dog while you run off to a fat farm this weekend?"

"You win," Bo conceded. She wouldn't entrust Mildred, her crotchety old fox terrier, to anyone else. "What do I have to promise?"

Estrella appeared to inspect the glazing of their office window. "That you'll go out with LaMarche the next time he asks you. Just go out and relax and have a good time."

"Deal." After the day's encounter Bo was sure his interest had waned, perhaps perished entirely. Just as well.

Later at home in her Ocean Beach apartment, Bo retrieved Mildred from day care with an elderly neighbor, slipped on faded jeans that had, in another life, belonged to her ex-husband, and headed for Dog Beach. The expanse of sand designated for San Diego's canine population had cinched Bo's decision to relocate to the coastal city after federal money for social service programs on New Mexico's reservations dried up. Where else would they set aside a whole beach for dogs? And just up the street was a fashionable dogwash designed specifically for Dog Beach patrons. She'd bought Mildred a vinyl-coated foam life vest at the dogwash boutique, signed a contract with Child Protective Services, and found a nearby apartment with an ocean view the same day.

Mildred dug in the sand as if hundreds of prime filets lay just beneath the surface, and barked greetings at a neighboring basset. Bo sat and threw a ratty tennis ball for Mildred until it was appropriated by a show-off Doberman puppy whose owner also owned the local pizza parlor.

"You owe me one slab with garlic and anchovies," she yelled at the man. "That tennis ball's an antique!"

"So are my anchovies," he yelled back.

Offshore a fuzzy gray band hovered at the horizon, moving toward land. The marine layer. Perennial bane of tourists who believed the myth of southern California's endless sun. In fact, until late June San Diego would be awash in weak, salty haze until 11:00 every morning when it burned off, only to return at dusk. It was coming in again. Bo relished the fog's predictability. Found its slow approach comforting as Mildred flung arcs of sand in all directions, including into Bo's hair. Without interest she noticed a pair of denimed legs bisecting the horizon. Ragged cowboy boots that might have been new at the siege of the Alamo. When they didn't move she glanced upward, straight into a shadowed face she associated mainly with windsor knots and antiseptic.

"I'm sorry I've been a beast today," said Andrew LaMarche.

"If you'll permit . . ." The word came out "*pear*-mit." "I'd like to repair the damage."

How? By rounding up a few stray longhorns before the lariat tricks?

"Don't tell me. Let me guess." Bo sighed. "Estrella has asked you to rescue me from madness by doing John Wayne imitations, right?" Under a mound of sand between her hands Bo imagined she was burying Estrella Benedict slowly, alive.

"I'd like to take you to dinner," LaMarche suggested in businesslike tones, "and explain my behavior about the Franer case."

The pediatrician looked, Bo thought, like an ad for designer prisonwear. His blue workshirt lacked only a number stenciled over its pocket.

"I've been set up," she told Mildred.

"So it would seem," Andrew LaMarche agreed happily.

Chapter 8

"Where are we going?" Bo inquired through cool, road-scented air whipping her hair into tangles a forklift couldn't separate. LaMarche had removed the Jaguar's roof in what she assumed was an attempt at savoir faire.

"Santa Ysabel," he replied as the last, muted bars of Respighi's *Pines of Rome* faded from the car's speakers. Bo found the music an uncomfortable reminder. Her ex-husband, Mark, an aspiring choreographer of radio drama, had as a graduate student read the athletic final chapter of John Updike's *Rabbit Run* over the climactic music so many times Bo couldn't hear it without gasping. Later Mark Bradley had produced an award-winning series of Navajo children's stories, recorded over tracks of Indian flute, wind, and an occasional howling coyote. Bo knew the recordings were inspired by Nicholas and Jaana, his children of a second and happy marriage to a hearty nutritionist from Minnesota whom Bo never ceased envisioning in a Wagnerian chorus. Mark's wife's name had been Ingrid Soderblom. Impossible not to think of metal bras and the entire Wagnerian Ring Cycle. With a smile, Bo forced her attention to the present.

"Santa Ysabel? We're having dinner at a mission?"

Andrew LaMarche's gray eyes glowed with a pewterlike patina, signaling his enjoyment of the moment as well as his knowledge of a pleasant answer to her question. The answer would, she knew, not be given without some tangential discourse. It was his style. Bo wondered if the discomfort with straightforward speech, the maddening verbal perambulations, had something to do with his French-speaking childhood. Or maybe he was nervous. Or maybe he just liked to talk.

"The church was built as an *asistencia*, or sub-mission in 1818," he said as if Bo had asked for a detailed history of California missions instead of the location of her next meal. The glow in his eyes became a twinkle. "Fascinating, really. They say pirated gold is buried among the old graves, although no one has ever—"

"Andy," Bo employed the familiar name out of desperation, "we've been driving for thirty-five minutes, I have enough dirt in my teeth to plant geraniums and my hair's something mice would kill to nest in. Why are we going to Santa Ysabel?"

"Duhon Robicheaux's in town with his Cajun band. There's a *fais-do-do*," the baritone voice explained with excitement. "I hope you like *andouille*!"

The setting sun created pastoral landscapes in shades of gold as the car sped up the slow grade from the San Diego suburb of Ramona into shadow-mottled foothills. Chinese coolies had labored, Bo remembered, beside Irish immigrants to wrest tourmaline, garnet, topaz, and gold from these hills. Hungry, she wondered how the two groups had managed to combine menus at mining camp chuckwagons. Sweet-and-sour finnan haddie? Steamed soda-bread rolls stuffed with thousand-year egg paste? In her side mirror she could see the Palomar Observatory looming whitely in the distance behind the car. Its two-hundred-inch Hale reflector telescope nightly scanned the heavens for things not visible to the naked eye. The facility's pale dome looked like a huge soup bowl inverted in the hills. Bo decided to ignore it.

"What in God's name is a fay-doe-doe and how would I know if I liked an-dewey? Is it edible?" Hunger had become a nagging irritant.

"The best food north of Ponchatoula," LaMarche replied as he navigated a turn onto a dusty mountain road that quickly lost itself in rolling meadows. "I'm scheduled to keynote a conference in New York this weekend. Supposed to be there today, in fact, to revise the agenda or something. But I rescheduled the flight for tomorrow just so I wouldn't miss this!" At a barnlike structure beside a dilapidated general store whose rusting gas pumps still wore the round glass heads popular during the Depression, he parked the maroon Jag among at least a hundred pickup trucks. "And a *fais-do-do* is just a big get-together. Food, dancing, a little wine . . ."

Bo remembered her own admonition to spend the evening in revelry in order to forget the cherubic corpse on an operating table. She'd followed her own advice, and yet it seemed wrong.

LaMarche noticed her downcast gaze and nodded. "We'll talk about it later. Right now we'll eat, enjoy. It isn't over, you know. It won't be over until Samantha's killer is imprisoned. The others," his thin lips were ashen beneath his mustache, "will see to an appropriate punishment."

Both sets of eyes stared at nothing as physician and social worker allowed themselves the unprofessional fantasy of revenge. Even the most hardened criminals sometimes felt revulsion at the rape of a child. And lacking a restraint characteristic of the general population, they wouldn't hesitate to mete out a biblical punishment. It was likely that Samantha's killer, released to a general prison population, would relive his victim's torment a thousand times.

The satisfaction of the fantasy made Bo half sick.

"Enough," LaMarche said with finality as an accordion wheezed to life inside the building followed by the scratchy tuning of violins. "Duhon's going to cheer you up!"

Having made a conscious decision to forget Samantha Franer for at least an hour, Bo cocked an eyebrow at the dustbowl parking lot with its army of trucks and grinned. The interior of the huge shed, which had from its pervasive scent been used to store apples from nearby orchards, was lit by a series of emergency lights whose extension cords all snaked to a single generator. Long tables covered in newspaper lined the walls, and a flatbed farm wagon served as a bandstand.

Over the sweet apple smell Bo noticed a pervasive odor of hot, buttery flour.

"What's that smell?" she sniffed appreciatively.

"*Roux.*" He was steering her toward two empty folding chairs at one of the long tables.

"Roo? Kanga's baby in *Winnie the Pooh*? They're cooking baby kangaroos here? I'm calling the animal cruelty people—"

"It means . . . it's a dark, sticky sauce made of butter and flour," he answered her jibe seriously. "How about some shrimp *étouffée*?"

"Does it have roo in it?"

The answering smile was warm. Almost, Bo realized, seductive.

"No, *ma cherie*, no *roux*."

You've always been a sucker for an accent, Bradley. Remember that Portuguese environmentalist who played pan pipes and got you to donate a month's salary for the protection of freshwater clams from a dam proposal? Try not to forget that.

"Shrimp sounds fine," she agreed. "And after dinner you'll provide the promised explanations about the Franer case?"

"Dinner, a little wine, maybe a two-step. Then . . ." He was busy acknowledging greetings from some of those present who seemed to know him, but greeted him as Jacques.

"I come around sometimes when there's a Cajun band," he explained. "It reminds me of summers I'd spend down in the bayous with my uncle. His name was Pierre Auguste, but everybody just called him Oncle Gus. He could catch snakes right out of the water with his bare hands, and my aunt would make a mouth-watering jambalaya out of them . . ."

"Snake jambalaya—my all-time favorite," Bo said with a wide-eyed smile. "And I'm really Princess Anastasia, heir to the vanquished Russian throne. *We* used to catch beluga caviar, barehanded of course, right out of the Volga. What a coincidence!"

"*Mais non,*" came the amused reply. "I'm serious."

His gray eyes wore a pleasant, faraway look. A look not related to the unremarkable red wine they were drinking from jelly glasses. Andrew LaMarche was plainly enjoying himself.

"You come out here to get away from it all, don't you?" Bo asked. On the dance floor people from three to ninety waltzed and two-stepped energetically. "It's a different world. Away from what you see at the hospital . . . like today?"

"Yes." His look shifted to one of concern. "And what do you do, Bo Bradley? How do you get away?"

Bo jabbed a *boudin* sausage on her plate with a plastic fork. "I jog," she informed the sausage. "Mostly I paint. Usually things like this . . . things from other worlds."

"Maybe you'll paint a Cajun sausage?" he joked.

Bo looked straight ahead and sifted the remark for unpleasant innuendo. There was none. A silly comment, not a crude come-on. She wondered if she'd been out of circulation so long she was anticipating trouble that didn't exist. Or else the absence of lithium was allowing a manicky hypersexuality to surface, coloring every innocuous encounter with a brush of eroticism. Bo hoped not. The guy was just being nice in his courtly, old-fashioned way.

Several lively two-steps later, she began to wonder if her politically correct, non-animal-tested deodorant would withstand the exertion. Her hair was soaked at the neck and curling ferociously.

"Let's go outside," LaMarche suggested with flawless timing. "I do want to talk seriously about what happened today."

In the moonlit parking lot a cool breeze ruffled the taffy-colored homespun shirt Bo had hurriedly tucked into her old jeans. Lighting a cigarette, she watched its smoke dissipate beneath a towering cottonwood beside the still-raucous building. "So why did you go off half-cocked over the Franer case today?" she asked. "And why did you do that curious sculpture of the ape carrying the baby?"

LaMarche leaned thoughtfully against the cottonwood as Bo sat on a truck bumper the size of a church pew.

"I have no children," he began, looking at a point above her head. "And the ape is a sort of metaphor, I guess, for what we do. The attempt to rescue children from the *côte noir*, the dark side of human nature, or ourselves. It's always there. And we often fail. We failed today."

Bo chose to ignore the enigmatic first statement in favor of the one she deeply understood. "We didn't fail," she said. "*You* didn't fail. There was nothing you could have done. Dr. Ling's report clearly stated that Samantha's injuries were life-threatening long before she got to the hospital. Don't blame yourself for her death."

"I don't," he went on, watching the sky as if it were making gestures he couldn't decipher. "The failure doesn't lie in the child's death. That shouldn't have happened, but it did. I'm not sure anything could have prevented it. Certainly no medical intervention could have saved her. But the failure I'm talking about is something different." He lowered his gaze to Bo's face. "The failure that resulted in my behavior today is in the way we look at things. We're blind. We only see what we expect to see, even if it's not really there. I saw that in myself today. It made me angry."

"What are you talking about?"

The suddenly moody doctor was lapsing into abstraction.

"I had a child once, Bo," he muttered abruptly. "I never saw her. Her name was Sylvie. She drowned in a bathtub in New Orleans while I was still with the Corps in Vietnam. Her mother, who was not my wife, left her alone only a little while. Apparently she'd been trying to bathe her toys. She was two."

Bo listened to dust settling on cottonwood leaves and did not move. After a while she said simply, "I'm sorry, Andy."

"Whoever violated Samantha blew apart the entire world for everyone connected to her," he continued through clenched teeth. "Her whole family and everyone close to her. The murdering bastard raped and killed more than just one little girl. He raped and killed the world for those people!"

His hands, Bo noticed, were knotted into fists.

"That's how you felt when your daughter died, isn't it?"

"I don't deny that her death propelled me into pediatrics, and then into the field of child abuse. It was a way of holding the world together, of trying to make sense of the senseless. Until you . . . until recently, it's been my whole life . . ." His voice trailed off.

Bo shifted uneasily on the truck's bumper. There was no denying the intensity of his words, but there was something else. Something very personal in the narrative, and it was directed at her. An appeal? More like a declaration. So powerful in its vulnerability and candor it felt like a threat, abrading a boundary she hadn't realized was there, but now wanted to keep intact.

"You've identified with the parent in this case," she stated the obvious, creating a palpable wall between them. A wall behind which she could play social worker all night if necessary. A wall that would blunt the intimacy he offered. "I can understand that. But why does that lead you to believe this Paul Massieu isn't the perp? Why else would he run?"

The change of subject wasn't lost on LaMarche, who crossed his arms over his chest and shook his head as if reprimanding himself. After a lengthy examination of the cottonwood's higher limbs, he turned again to Bo. "In French it's called *le monde*," he began softly. "That means 'the world,' but no one's world is the same. The assumption that we share an identical world is at the root of most problems, especially the serious ones."

"What has this to do with the Franer case?" Bo asked, lost.

"Everything. Please hear me out, Bo. It's important."

The decision to listen had to be made consciously. With a brain always scanning the external environment and its own stores of imagery for constant stimulation, even in periods of relative calm such as this one, it was too easy to grasp subtlety after subtlety and nothing more. Too easy to catch merely a mood and then move on. Not easy at all to open the mind in slow silence while another spoke. Bo looked at the man who'd saved her life and that of a deaf little boy six months in the past, and decided she owed him that much, if not the deeper bond he'd reached for only minutes earlier. With a deep breath she exerted the Herculean effort necessary to mute the sweep of her mind. "All right," she said quietly.

He had been watching. "Estrella told me you've stopped taking the lithium, Bo. Do you think—"

"We're not here to talk about lithium. What was it that you wanted to say about the world and Samantha Franer?"

It was difficult to arrest the lecture framing itself for delivery to Estrella Benedict first thing in the morning, but Bo managed.

"As a young man I lived in a world where men accepted no responsibility for pregnancies in women to whom they were not married. This same world included a corollary mythology that held that all female people, simply by virtue of certain bodily organs, were magically able to provide years of tedious daily care for children. Had I moved one inch outside that world, my daughter might still be alive."

"You're still blaming yourself—" Bo began.

"Let me make my point. *You're* now in another world—the world of child abuse investigation, its legality. That world makes assumptions based on previous cases. That's the way law works. In your world it's assumed that the perpetrator in a molest is the mother's live-in boyfriend because very often it is. But what if somebody from another world falls into yours? Will you bother to try looking through his eyes before deciding what's real?"

"You seem to have forgotten that I have a rather special relationship with this issue," Bo bristled. "I have a psychiatric disorder, a passport to more worlds than most people see on a three-continent tour. In addition to that, my undergraduate degree is in art history. Sophomoric lectures on cultural perspective are scarcely necessary. I've already considered the possibility that this case isn't typical. But how do you explain the fact that Paul Massieu *ran*?"

"What about *his* world, Bo? What if he ran because something in his reality, and that of Bonnie and Samantha and Hannah, demanded that he return Hannah to it?"

Bo's ears flattened against her skull as a strand of awareness spun out ahead of her. She couldn't keep up with it, but its message was clear. "What did Bonnie Franer tell you?" she asked, watching him now as closely as he had watched her.

"The woman loves her children, Bo. She's weak, a longtime victim. That love is her only strength. She has literally nothing else. She allowed Paul Massieu into her life precisely *because* he would never hurt the girls. He offered them love and protection. She didn't care what else he did, or what he believed in—"

"How can you . . . ?" Bo interrupted. "Bonnie Franer is an extremely fragile personality, prone to depression, probably self-destructive at times. You can't have had time to interview her in any depth, anyway. How can you trust her assessment . . . ?"

LaMarche kicked an exposed root of the cottonwood. "What if Paul Massieu has simply returned Hannah to a world, the only world he knows where she'll be safe?"

The knowledge racing ahead had taken on form. Bo felt her eyes widen in the dark at what he was telling her.

"You know where Massieu is! Bonnie Franer told you, and you're withholding the information!"

There was no denial.

"Think about what I've said, Bo. Just think about it. Looking at things differently may just make it possible for you to stay in this line of work. You're good. But without a broader view the pain and disgust will break you. I don't want that to happen."

"Andy," Bo said as the senselessness of a child's death took on even more sinister ramifications, "if you're right and Paul Massieu really isn't the perp, then who is? Who destroyed that little girl? What world does he live in?"

Andrew LaMarche stretched his angular hands at his sides and turned the palms slowly skyward. "I don't know," he answered.

From the door of the sprawling shed a sonorous waltz drifted liquidly on violin strings. Bo hated the warm flush that crept up her cheeks at his earlier compliment, and the dismay that accompanied any possibility of Paul Massieu's innocence. Domestic child sexual abuse was nothing unusual; it was her turf. But the notion of a "stranger molest" opened doors on a bewildering darkness. She wondered why the idea of a child eviscerated by the sexual demands of a trusted, familiar adult seemed less horrific than the same crime perpetrated by a stranger. The answer lay in LaMarche's words. The familiar, however repugnant, constituted her world. But what if this crime had its origins in a different one?

"That's the last dance." LaMarche gestured toward the spilling light. "Would you do me the honor?"

In his arms Bo felt an odd sense of kinship, as if they were compatriots in some film noir struggle involving World War II resistance fighters. Dim lighting. Frenchmen in berets and baggy shirts. Edith Piaf singing "Non, Je Ne Regrette Rien" from a cabaret stage. The feeling was smoky, warm . . .

Snap out of it, Bradley. You're tired and your brain's turning to oatmeal. That really is Piaf. What happened to the band?

"Duhon always ends with that recording," Andrew LaMarche said, leading her toward the door with his right arm firmly around her waist. "It's his trademark."

"Mine too," Bo nodded sleepily, aware that he was kissing the top of her head occasionally as they walked to the car, and too tired to break the mood.

On the way home Bo heard the Jaguar's motor murmuring "*le monde*" repetitively. Something about the notion, the insistent syllables of it, kept breaking and spreading in her mind like an egg. The man beside her was harboring a secret. Why? Because there were different worlds? It made little sense, but then what did? A broad view, then. Blurry, gentle. Maybe wise. Lois Bittner, Bo smiled to herself, would probably approve. Madge Aldenhoven would vaporize with rage.

"Thanks for the evening," she nodded as LaMarche saw her to her door. "I'll think about what you said."

He left with a polite nod. No future dates set. No promises to call or be called. It was good. And, Bo reminded herself, it was over. Andrew LaMarche just didn't fit into her world. Nobody did.

Inside, the answering machine on the tiled counter between her living room and lilliputian kitchen was blinking.

"Bo?" Madge Aldenhoven's voice announced, "you're going to have to fly to New York tomorrow. The police have captured the perp in the Franer case at some cult hideout in the Adirondacks. We're sending you to retrieve the sister. Your plane leaves at 6:19 A.M. for Albany. I'll meet you at the office at 5:00 with the tickets."

In the neon glare of her bathroom Bo stared at a pharmacist's brown plastic bottle half full of pinkish tablets. Lithium. A surefire way to remain uninvolved, to stop the French "*le monde*" thumping in her brain. But did it need to be stopped?

Maybe LaMarche was right. Maybe there was another way

to view the broken lives that fell across her desk in orange-banded case files. Maybe more to it than disgust and helplessness. The possibility felt like new canvas, stretched and beckoning.

Bo tossed the pills in her carry-on bag for the journey, just in case. Then she fell in bed humming a French song about having no regrets, and fell asleep wondering what life would be like without them.

Chapter 9

Eva Broussard lay sleepless upon a large bent-twig bed that had belonged to one of the lodge's Prohibition-era owners. A Pittsburgh glove manufacturer with stern views on temperance, the man had given his ideas immortality in the property's deed. No alcohol could be served within the lodge walls while the government of the United States remained intact. The troubled woman turned softly, imagining a bloodless coup at that very moment in Washington, D.C. A large cognac, she thought, might muffle the incessant mating whistles of the thousand spring peeper frogs calling, bog to bog, through the Adirondack night. Hannah Franer lay asleep on a cot beside the antique bed.

In shadow the child seemed merely a younger version of the mother. The same fine blonde hair drifting across the pillowcase. The same wide-set hazel eyes, full lips, and overlarge nose that reddened at the slightest emotion. Eva wondered if the similarity between mother and daughter extended to what lay inside—that core being some might name "soul." If so, extreme caution must be exercised now. For Hannah Franer's future would lie squarely in the ways she learned to deal with the pain of the present. And even that wasn't complete. Eva was certain there would be at least one more devastating blow for the child to absorb. Grimly certain.

Soundlessly she slipped to an open casement window. Below the lodge Night Heron Lake appeared to hold floating beneath its surface scattered sparks of light identical to those in the sky above. At the water's edge a pale glacial boulder left there twelve thousand years ago by a retreating wall of ice seemed a small, abandoned moon.

"I know nothing," the rangy woman whispered in French to the stone sphere. "We don't live long enough to know anything. Our little jelly brain is just a chemical flash, like heat lightning. But you," she addressed the stone intently, "have had time to observe a great deal. And you aren't talking." On the night wind a whiff of hemlock drifted into the room. Beavers at work, damming some upper tributary of Shadow Creek. The little mammals' engineering feats seemed elegant and full of meaning compared to the chaos that lay before Eva Broussard.

The New York State Police had burst into the lodge only minutes before Paul Massieu would have made his escape across the glassy darkness of Night Heron Lake. A lightweight canoe was prepared and waiting. The anthropologist had, as was a sort of ritual among the Canadian Seekers, canoed the chain of lakes from Montreal to this wilderness outpost where he'd first seen "Them." A covert return to Canada by the same watery route seemed the safest. It would never have occurred to New York lawmen routinely checking I-87 as a courtesy to the state of California that their prey was paddling a handmade canvas canoe beneath silent miles of red spruce.

But Paul Massieu was no wizard of stealth. He'd left a paper trail as wide as the Hudson River connecting him to an organization incorporated as "Shadow Mountain Interests" with an Adirondack mailing address. When a ticket agent at San Diego International Airport told Dar Reinert, "Sure. The French guy and the little girl? Bought tickets to Albany, New York, ETA 6:27 P.M. Albany time," it had taken only two phone calls to get an address and a New York warrant.

"You should not have run, Paul," Eva insisted through

pursed lips at Albany's homey airport terminal. "It can only be interpreted as evidence of guilt."

"Bonnie begged me to get Hannah back here when she called from the hospital. That was before Sammi . . . before we knew . . ." His voice broke with emotion. "The doctor who tried to save Sammi, this doctor had already told Bonnie they'd take Hannah away, put her in a foster home. I'm not Hannah's real father; this doctor told Bonnie they'd never let me get Hannah back, even if . . . He told Bonnie the police are certain I'm the one who . . ." His eyes rolled upward as a shudder rippled across his bulky shoulders. ". . . who raped a three-year-old baby that I loved as if she were my own. . . . They'd never let me have Hannah, and they won't let Bonnie have her, either, now. Bonnie's going to crack under this. I know it."

People at the airport were beginning to stare at the weeping man with a terrified little girl clinging to his hand.

"We'll talk later," Eva suggested quickly. "We need to take Hannah home now."

"They know about us," he sighed in despair. "They know we're Seekers and they think we're crazy. It's one of the reasons they think I'm crazy enough to . . ."

"Yes." The older woman nodded.

It had been something of a risk, establishing a community of people devoted to the exploration of an experience that couldn't have happened. But the rugged moors of upstate New York had cradled unconventional notions before. In a rocky field near Palmyra Joseph Smith talked to an angel named Moroni, and the Mormon Church was conceived. In Victorian Arcadia, Brockport, Ithaca, Syracuse, and Buffalo the first American mediums communed with spirits and initiated an idea that would spellbind the Western world. There was something in the land, Eva sensed, and in the ominous cloud paths forever drifting across the river valleys. Something "otherly" her own people had seen fit to honor with rituals against madness, especially at the darkest time of the year. That something had turned up again, she was sure, on the ever-receptive screen of the human mind in the form of frail but magnetically powerful beings who seemed to have come from space.

But Eva Broussard could trace social patterns in history as well as she could follow pheasant tracks in the hedgerows of her childhood. Ideas spawned in the shadow-mists of New York State never stayed there. Those that did, died. There had been no further sightings. It was time to go elsewhere, and the group had selected California for the state's renowned openness to unorthodox ideas. A desert location for privacy and an ascetic wildness that might free the group to shape whatever philosophy it would make of its joint experience. A desert location within driving distance of the Goldstone Tracking Station in Barstow, where NASA scientists watched as a computer program sifted a million radio bands of celestial static for the telltale, nonrandom blips that would prove we are not alone in the universe. Blips that could only be created by nonearthly intelligence. Eva Broussard wanted to interview those scientists, include that perspective in her research. Wanted it deeply.

Paul Massieu had been sent to purchase the land. Eva felt concern when he announced that Bonnie and the children would go with him, but they preferred to remain together. Bonnie was sure she could get a part-time secretarial job to pay for trips to Disneyland and the thousand things she wanted the girls to see. And as a lifelong resident of New York State, Bonnie Franer had hated to be cold. The prospect of a winter in sunshine was too attractive to forestall. Now her younger daughter lay dead while the other clung to the man accused of the crime. Eva Broussard had driven them away from Albany and into the Adirondack deeps, weighted with apprehension. The act that robbed Samantha Franer of her life had also slammed like a fist through Eva's fascination with a collection of strangers and their encounters with tin men in the woods. A psychological inquiry that had seemed sufficient to occupy the rest of her life paled before the anguish of the man and child now huddled in her car. Eva felt a cold, murderous resentment for the man who had shattered their lives, whoever he was. He had shattered hers as well.

Later Eva took Hannah alone to the five-sided tower and gave her, one by one, the strings of Iroquois grieving beads she'd woven for the child after the news of Samantha's death.

In candlelight reflected from two hundred panes of hand-blown glass in the tower's windows, she gently recited the words in Iroquois and in English. The words Hayenwatha had given to a people who lived in cloud-shadows and sometimes perished of a terrible grieving that would only later be named depression.

"Samantha is gone and cannot return," she began the soft, chanting ritual. "Samantha has died. And you hurt so much the tears blind your eyes. With these words I wipe the tears from your eyes so you can see. These beads are my words for your eyes, Hannah."

The child took the woven rush with its irregular purple beads carved from the shells of the quahog clam. Wrapping dry, tremulous fingers about the small strip, she buried her head against Eva Broussard's ribs and sobbed. Eva sank to the floor, rocking the child against her and humming a song her own grandmother had sung in the dark. A story of the Huron prophet Deganawida in his canoe of white stone. Deganawida with a speech impediment so profound he must carry his voice with him in the person of Hayenwatha, the translator mystic. The story gave form to an Iroquois reverence for sensitive communication and human interdependence. It was also, Eva had realized years ago, an excellent therapeutic model.

After a while she said again, "Samantha is gone and cannot return. Samantha has died. And you hurt so much there's a roaring in your ears that drowns out everything else. With these words I silence the roaring so you can hear. These beads are my words for your ears, Hannah."

When the third strip of beaded rush had been given to the child, so that her throat choked by pain might be opened for speech, Eva Broussard breathed deeply and contemplated the words she would next pronounce. They were truly necessary, she concluded. And she was prepared to undertake the responsibility.

"As the oldest woman of this tribe," she recited, stretching the definition of tribe to fit the emergency, "I adopt you and make you one with us. I adopt you. You are now a child of the longhouse people, member of the Heron Clan, great-granddaughter of Naomi Blindhawk, granddaughter of Eva Blindhawk. You belong to us now. I am your grandmother. You have a home forever."

When the New York State Police arrived to take Paul Massieu away in handcuffs, they demanded to take Hannah Franer as well.

"The child is my granddaughter, an Iroquois of the Onondaga Reservation," Eva Broussard had said, her black eyes fierce beneath a leather-banded scarf. "She cannot be taken without permission of the tribal council. And she is safe here."

A veteran of clashes with radical Mohawks near the Canadian border, the trooper was not without experience in dealing with the state's original citizens. And there were recent federal laws ensuring that the children of native peoples could not be removed from the jurisdiction of their tribes. A century-late acknowledgment that to strip a human being of his or her language, culture, and mythology is a kind of death. He glared at the blonde child snuffling in the Indian woman's skirts. She didn't look like an Indian, but then neither did a lot of the people he'd seen sitting on tribal councils. Each tribe had its own rules for determining who was one of them and who wasn't. The kid had straw grieving beads pinned to her Minnie Mouse sweatshirt. He'd seen the Iroquois beads before; it was enough. California wouldn't like it, but he wasn't about to stir up another confrontation between Indians and New York State's government.

"Okay," he rumbled, "but you're responsible for her safety. And they'll come after her from California, anyway. You'll have to turn her over then."

By 4:00 A.M. the lake and sky were merely graying patterns without identity. Nothing moved among the shaded tracings that in daylight would be trees, lake, sky. Shaking the thick stubble framing her head Eva strode purposefully back to the twig bed. The steps she had taken were meant to protect Hannah's fragile being from irreversible harm. Eva was confident that her decisions were correct, but now what? Her thinking had run down like bog water, reedy and thick with odd skitterings. No point in seining it anymore tonight. There was too much turbulence to see what might come next.

Chapter 10

Descending over the Hudson River on its approach to the Albany airport, the Boeing 767 provided a spectacular view. Sleepily Bo eyed the streams of hazy, gilded light bathing the valley below. She'd been dozing since the plane change in Chicago, and was unprepared.

"I'll be damned!" she breathed in amazement. "So *this* is what they were doing!"

Her companion in the aisle seat pulled a brimmed Red Sox cap further over an already low forehead and grimaced. The off-center set of his shoulders beneath a brown nylon jacket made clear his intent to create distance between himself and this redhead who talked to herself.

"I mean the Hudson River School," Bo explained, pulling her hair from her face with both hands. "This light! This is what they painted! You know . . . Thomas Cole, Asher Durand, Charlotte Coman . . . ?"

The man shifted his weight further into the aisle and sighed miserably. It was clear to Bo that whatever interest he might have in the renowned artists of the region was eclipsed by a deeper fascination with his own shoes.

"And even *they* never got to see the light from up here," she concluded, "since there were no planes in the nineteenth century."

The man appeared to be painfully at prayer.

Beyond the scratched window rivers of light, cream-colored, pinkish, sometimes deepening to pale honey or muted flax, poured through clouds and spilled on the rising ground below. The effect was stunning. Bo thought of sending Madge Aldenhoven a thank-you note quoting something from Washington Irving. The light was astonishing, and a little eerie. No wonder so many had tried to capture it in paint. Bo wondered if the shape-shifting quality of the sky had anything to do with whatever Paul Massieu's cult was up to. Aldenhoven had provided an address, but no other information about the activities of the group.

Debarking into moist spring air, Bo reminded herself to rein in some of the elation buoying her steps. The day was, in fact, a bit too wondrous. The sky entirely too awe-inspiring with its washes of golden light. Too much goodness sloshing around, and it could only be coming from one source—her own brain.

You're here to pick up an eight-year-old with a dead sister, not to rejoice in spring, Bradley.

In the airport's parking lot Bo did a series of stretches beside the beige rental car, and thought about neurochemistry. Her near-religious awe at the sky could be a trained artist's response to unusually brilliant light patterns, or it could be something else. It could be that first heady surge of euphoria that would later become a torrent of racing impressions and feeling. Mania.

"It's too bad, but the truth is, you must always be suspicious of feeling too good," Lois Bittner stated flatly years ago. "Most manic-depressives like the euphoria so much they don't want it to stop. The problem is, it won't stop, like a carousel spinning faster and faster. You must always stop and dissect your euphoria, Bo. It's the minefield between you and a battle you can never win. Sometimes it will be safe, just a little surge of glee like other people experience. And sometimes it will be your last warning. Learn to tell the difference."

Bo slid behind the wheel of the nondescript Ford and admitted that twenty years after her first skirmish with manic depression, she still couldn't tell the difference. Moreover, she was sick of worrying about it. If things got worse, she'd deal with it. In the meantime it was sheer joy to be herself again, free of the numbing medication that, however necessary, made her feel like a senile otter swimming in glue.

A map provided by the rental car agency provided easy access to a six-lane freeway unimaginatively named 90 West. Bo admired the lush greenery bordering the road and adorning its median. Southern California, more desert than its chambers of commerce would like known, could not in its dampest moment produce such fervent, undulating greens. She wondered why Massieu's group, whatever they were, had decided to relocate. And how they would respond when she took from their midst the child Massieu had broken every law to return to them.

Bo plumbed her memory for information on religious cults and utopian communities. Terms such as "wide-eyed idealists" and "vegetarian mystics" readily came to mind. Could a child-rapist arise from within such a context? Of course. Pedophiles might be anywhere. But was Paul Massieu the rapist whose violence destroyed Samantha Franer? Maybe. But if he weren't, then who was?

A shadow fell sleekly over the road, turning the emerald trees to moss. What if Andrew LaMarche were right? What if Massieu had abducted Hannah for reasons other than guilt? Then Samantha's killer was free to rape, perhaps kill, again. Might, in fact, be doing so at this very moment.

To her right Bo noticed a red barn in a field beside the road. On its side were painted three huge shamrocks, outlined in white. In spite of herself Bo reacted exactly as her grandmother would have done.

"*Dia's muir dhuit,*" she pronounced the traditional "Mother of God be with you" salutation. "Even though ye've forgot the true sign!"

Bridget Mairead O'Reilly had told her granddaughters a hundred times that no true child of Eire would display any symbol but the harp. Still, the popular American symbol for all things Irish reminded Bo of her heritage. A heritage in which intuition had value. And her intuition was suggesting a picture in which a sexual pervert was free to select his next victim from a population of children in training pants.

The appalling notion did not diminish as Bo directed the little car to the right on Route 30, across the Mohawk River and through the town of Amsterdam. Miles later the thought had become an unprovable certainty. A sign announcing the manufacture of "Havlick Snowshoes" in a village provided the final straw. Bo had forgotten the reality of snow. Webbed contraptions for walking on it seemed, at best, apocryphal. Could there *really* be a company with employees at this very moment constructing snowshoes? Shepherd's crooks? How about butter churns? Everything was relative.

"*Le monde*," Andrew LaMarche's phrase rumbled pointedly in the wind from the open car window. The world. A world. One of many. This one contained snowshoes, an unknown cult, and a bereaved child who must be returned to the jurisdiction of the California court that had assumed the burden of protecting her from her sister's fate. Except that if Paul Massieu were innocent, then Hannah Franer was in no peril. And the swift action of police in two states and Bo's own hurried journey were exercises in futility. Like snowshoes in San Diego.

An informative marker placed by the state of New York informed Bo that the damming of the Sacandaga River had permanently immersed several small towns. She glanced at the steel-gray water and wondered what worlds were lost beneath it. Comparisons to the system for which she worked were inescapable. As Andrew LaMarche had pointed out, no one had bothered to ask about the world in which Samantha Franer lived. They merely obliterated it with their own. And their own was one in which the perpetrator in a molest was usually the mother's boyfriend, especially if he were odd in some way. And especially if he then kidnapped the victim's older sibling and fled across state lines. That was the world of the juvenile court, the police, the agencies of child protection. It was, Bo conceded as Shadow Mountain rose bluely in the distance, only one world.

"Ye *ken* things," her grandmother had explained. "It's in the family. Be sure to heed what ye ken."

"He's still out there," Bo thought with distaste. "I'm running all over the country, Reinert's probably on another case already, LaMarche is in a tux somewhere giving lectures over chicken-in-aspic, and this sick slimebag is going scot-free!"

An hour later she found the "cult hideout" Madge Aldenhoven had described. It was a sprawling Victorian camp with two boathouses and ten smaller cottages nestled between the looming mountain and a lake strewn with little islands. To her dismay, none of the people lounging on the wide porch of the main building seemed to speak English.

"I need to speak with the person in charge," she informed a grandmotherly woman in a hickory rocker. "I know Hannah Franer is here. I have to return her to California."

The woman's clothes were American, and she involuntarily pursed her lips at the mention of Hannah's name.

"No, no," she fumbled to hide an issue of *People* magazine she'd been reading. "No English." The second word was pronounced "Ing-glish." The Midwest, Bo guessed. Not rural.

An immense bearded man clad in a monk's robe covered by an Indian blanket rose from a small table where he was either taking apart or assembling a vegetable steamer.

"Je m'appelle Napoléon Pigeon," he announced, his French accent unmistakably native. *"Et vous?"*

"Mr. Pigeon," Bo spluttered, marveling at the name, "I'm Bo Bradley from San Diego's Child Protective Services. I'm here to escort Hannah Franer back to San Diego where she is in the legal custody of the juvenile court. Could you take me to her?"

"Je ne parle pas Anglais," he answered, revealing tobacco-stained teeth. One upper incisor had been set with a gold quarter moon that caught and reflected the setting sun. Beneath bushy eyebrows the man's aquamarine eyes glowed with a wild, undirected kindness.

Uh-oh. Basic fanatic here, Bradley. Probably hasn't eaten meat since his pet canary died in 1953 and spends his days trying to communicate with lichen. Harmless, but you're wasting your breath.

"Thanks anyway." She smiled and moved toward a

screened door festooned with millwork. Inside, groups of people read or played cards in a large L-shaped living room boasting no fewer than three stone fireplaces. The floor and ceiling bore designs of elaborate inlaid maple. The walls appeared to have been papered in canvas. Everyone smiled and nodded politely as Bo entered. Everyone who spoke, spoke in French. Flustered, Bo remembered that the lodge was only about an hour's drive from the French-speaking Canadian province of Quebec. Unfortunately there was no eight-year-old girl in sight.

"I'll be back," Bo announced irritably. She was certain that at least half the fifty people present understood her perfectly.

A scent of ginger and garlic drifted from a kitchen behind the spacious dining room. It reminded Bo that, diet or not, she was starving.

"I'll bring the police if necessary."

Nobody batted an eye. They weren't afraid of her, and merely murmured among themselves phrases she couldn't understand.

Defeated, Bo stomped back to her car and considered her options. She could involve the local police. They would have to accompany her to the lodge if she requested their help. They could kick in the door, seize the child, arrest anyone who obstructed the process. Madge Aldenhoven, in fact, would insist on it. Bo Bradley would prefer to avoid it.

Back in the village named Night Heron for the lake below, Bo rented a room in a motel called the Iroquois Inn. Then she deliberately placed a call to San Diego's Child Abuse Hotline rather than to Madge Aldenhoven's office number.

"Just tell Madge I've run into a snag, but nothing big, and I'll call her tomorrow," she reported briskly. Then she hung up before the hotline worker could ask for her phone number.

A photograph of a buck whitetailed deer in snow stared from above the motel's bed. Bo stared back and wondered what to do next. How to get inside the group without causing further trauma to the child. LaMarche had said he'd be in New York City today, addressing a conference on child abuse. By now he'd be at the speaker's table of a banquet crawling with experts on matters not normally discussed at banquets. With an abandon she chose not to dissect, Bo placed a call to LaMarche's service in San Diego and left the address and phone number of the Iroquois Inn.

"I need a French translator on the Franer case," she said. "Please ask Dr. LaMarche to phone me."

In the pine-paneled coffee shop of the inn she enjoyed an enormous hamburger and four cups of decaf while penning a postcard to Madge Aldenhoven. The postcard featured a yellow-rumped warbler eating a caterpillar.

"It's a different world here," she noted. "Love, Bo."

Chapter 11

At 7:00 social worker Rombo Perry placed his office phone neatly atop a midnight blue corduroy throw pillow stuffed in the bottom drawer of his desk. Then he placed a matching pillow over the offending instrument and kicked the drawer shut. On his desk was a steaming thermos of hazelnut coffee Martin had left for him at the admitting desk only an hour ago.

Other staff on the 3:00 to 11:00 shift at San Diego County's grimly underfunded psychiatric facility usually went out for their union-mandated half-hour dinner break. Sometimes Rombo went along, more for the sake of goodwill than desire to eat greasy burritos in somebody's car. But usually he barricaded himself in the immaculate cubicle of his office, read the paper, relaxed. He and Martin would have a light snack when he got home at 11:30. Maybe a Parmesan omelette or a small salad tossed in rice vinegar. They'd worked it out years ago. A sensible schedule for a couple in which one ran a catering business from home and the other was bound by the strictures of hospital work.

Rombo was proud of the fact that in five years he'd never

missed a day of work. His clients could count on him, just as Martin could. An ordinary, decent, hardworking man was all Rombo had ever wanted to be. And now, after years in which an addiction to alcohol made that goal impossible, Rombo had it all. For a near-sighted thirty-eight-year-old gay man who'd never top a hundred and sixty pounds no matter how much iron he pumped, it was a pretty good life. Especially, Rombo grinned to himself, for a gay man burdened with a name you'd only give to a St. Bernard. Sober for seven years now. With Martin for five. A meaningful job that he liked. Rombo Perry was content.

Unfolding the afternoon edition of San Diego's only daily, he nudged his new black wire-frame glasses upward on a boxer's crooked nose. The front page carried the story he was looking for. The story about the new patient, Bonnie Franer.

Somebody named Dr. Cynthia Ganage was quoted repeatedly as believing Bonnie Franer's three-year-old daughter had been the victim of a "sexual Satanist." Ganage insinuated that a large Satanic cult might be operating in San Diego. For that reason, she told reporters, she would immediately relocate her professional offices from Los Angeles to San Diego. She had, in fact, already leased office space in an unfinished downtown office building. Until she could move in she would continue her practice from a suite at the elegant U.S. Grant Hotel.

"As a specialist in the ritual abuse of children," Cynthia Ganage said, "I've pledged full cooperation with police and Child Protective Services."

Rombo shook his head. As a psychiatric social worker he was familiar with the interface of myth and mind. During psychosis people sometimes said they actually were popular religious figures, or had been singled out for special responsibilities or for persecution by such figures. Once stabilized, Rombo's clients were uniformly puzzled by the clarity of their experiences. "I know there aren't any devils," one had told him years ago, "but that doesn't change the fact that every third person on the bus *is* one. Don't ask me how, but I can *tell*. I know it's crazy, but it doesn't feel crazy; it feels like the most real thing I've ever known!" The human brain, Rombo acknowledged, was wired for terrors so deep and joys so exultant that names must be given to cap the sanity-threatening experiences. Devil—God. And whole cultures would react like Pavlov's dogs when one of the names was mentioned.

Disclaimers by the police department's public relations liaison did little to buffer the impact of the newspaper story. Neither did a sidebar on page four featuring the president of the San Diego Ecumenical Council warning against sensationalism in spiritual matters. The paper had handled it with kid gloves, but nothing could diminish the tabloid aura of the story. No mention was made of the fact that the mother, Bonnie Franer, was in a locked psychiatric facility under suicide watch. Rombo was sure the omission reflected nothing more than Cynthia Ganage's ignorance of the situation. Had she known, she would have used the fact to advantage, as she was using the primitive facts of human psychology. Ganage was, Rombo assessed with distaste, a real pterodactyl. A media harpy of the most repugnant stripe. The knowledge only reinforced his sense of protectiveness toward Bonnie Franer.

He'd done the intake interview himself, not that it was actually an interview. The poor creature had merely hunched on a chair in his office, rocking and clawing at herself with pale, trembling fingers. She'd said nothing. Later he'd sat with her until the sedative took effect and she collapsed on her bed in a drugged sleep.

They could only keep her for seventy-two hours. Then the law required her release. It would be Rombo Perry's job to discharge Bonnie Franer to some intermediate setting where she could receive support and care. Except there wasn't any such place. Rombo knew he'd discharge this client to the street with an antidepressant prescription in her pocket, just like all the others. There wouldn't even be money for cab fare. There wasn't really enough to keep the understaffed crisis unit open. The county had been juggling funds for years, and psychiatric services were invariably the first on everybody's cutback list.

To say that nobody cared about people with psychiatric problems, Rombo acknowledged for perhaps the ten thousandth time in his career, was to put it kindly. What people really wanted, he suspected, was for the neurobiologically ill simply to vanish. Get out of sight. Go away. Die. They were just too unpleasant. They raised too many questions, demolished too many myths.

As a young man Rombo Perry had thought the stigma attached to homosexuality was about as virulent as hate could get. He'd learned to fight because of it. Been a promising welterweight in college and later, working the Chicago boxing scene, before the booze dragged him down. But being gay, he realized later, was a picnic compared to being labeled mentally ill.

Snapping the paper shut he decided to check on Bonnie Franer and warn the psych techs to keep the *Union-Tribune* out of sight. It would only upset the tormented mother to see it.

In the lounge a few people were watching a TV movie featuring singing pirates. A man in jeans and a cowboy hat, admitted yesterday with a tentative diagnosis of obsessive-compulsive disorder, spoke animatedly on the wall phone by the water fountain. He seemed to be negotiating the sale of a tractor.

"How is Mrs. Franer doing?" Rombo asked the tech heading out of the nurses' station with a clipboard, battery-powered thermometer, and a portable blood pressure cuff.

"Fine twenty minutes ago," the woman answered. "Groggy, but calm. I'm about to go around again."

On orders from the admitting physician, Bonnie Franer would be monitored every twenty minutes. Her vital signs and mental status would be noted, and the information filed in her chart. If she became agitated she would receive additional medication. Straitjackets hadn't been used for a quarter century.

"I'll check on her," Rombo volunteered. "You go ahead and do the others."

The door was slightly ajar and the room dimly lit by a fifteen-watt night-light that could not be turned off. Gently Rombo pushed the door open and whispered, "Mrs. Franer? It's Mr. Perry, your social worker. How are you doing?"

The rumpled bed was empty, and Rombo's first assumption was that the woman had wakened and left the room in search of a bathroom or the water fountain. But then, even though his graduate training had included thorough analysis of this possibility and he'd been to countless workshops on its prevention, he gasped and froze at the reality.

Bonnie Franer's body hung unnaturally still across the wire-webbed window, framed by a yellow sodium light on the street outside. A hospital bedsheet straining at her neck was snagged by its selvage edge to the top of one of the window bars. From the sharp angle at which her head lolled against her gaunt chest, Rombo knew her neck was broken. Instinctively he ran to gather up her weight, anyway, and ripped the sheet loose from its mooring on the vertical bar.

"Nurse!" he yelled over his shoulder. Running feet answered immediately. And pointlessly.

Bonnie Franer, sedated and stripped of belts, shoelaces, all pointed or sharp objects, confined in a space containing no breakable glass, mirrors, accessible electrical circuits, lamp cords, or weight-bearing objects more than three feet off the floor, had succeeded in taking her own life. Rombo lay the lifeless body on the bed and felt a chill spread in patches over his skin. The frail woman who'd sat rocking in his office wasn't there anymore. Whoever she was, whatever her life had been, was gone. The chill circled his right calf and then reproduced itself on both of his ears. The word "suicide" framed itself again and again in his mind, and wasn't enough. The word couldn't begin to encompass the complexity that lay before him.

As two nurses, a psych tech, and the patient in cowboy boots hovered over the bed, Rombo tried to make sense of what had happened. She'd climbed up on the seldom-used radiator, apparently, and pushed out the screen at the top of the window. Then she'd tried to tie the sheet around one of the vertical bars covering the window from the outside, but the knot hadn't held. At the lurch of her weight the knot had pulled loose, but a fold of the fabric over the top of the bar had caught and ripped through to the tightly woven selvage edge. That had been sufficient to support her hundred and two pounds. The patient in cowboy boots was beginning to wring his hands and pace in a precise diamond pattern beside the bed.

"Come on," Rombo said, wrapping an arm about the man's shoulders, "let's go get some juice and try to calm down, okay? This has nothing to do with you. Nothing at all." Shivering, the man acquiesced.

"Martin, I feel really strange," Rombo stammered into his office phone an hour later, after Bonnie Franer was pronounced dead and swiftly wheeled away on a sheet-draped gurney. "I can't seem to get it, why this woman would do that . . ."

"You work in a psychiatric hospital," the familiar voice said. "These things happen."

"I know that." Rombo felt another amoebic chill under his left arm. "But Martin, I told one of the patients this had nothing to do with him. I think I was really talking to myself, Martin, and I don't understand. I've survived being called 'fag' my whole life, my father hating me until he died, and the booze . . . I've stayed alive and it's okay now, Martin. I made it through. And this woman's daughter was murdered, but she might have made it, too. Why did I make it, and she didn't?"

There was a brief silence. "I don't know," came the final reply. "Nobody knows. But I'm going to make a shrimp bisque and chill you a bottle of that sparkling herb stuff you like. We'll talk about it when you get home."

Chapter 12

President Lincoln lilacs enjoyed an unprecedented popularity in the well-kept yards of Night Heron Village. Their heady aroma filled Bo's tiny motel room when she awoke to a knock at the door at 5:00 A.M. Never rhapsodic about morning, she managed to utter only one syllable in the general direction of the sound.

"Whaaa?" she said blearily.

"Your translator," a deep voice replied. The speaker bore telltale signs of being awake. Bo sighed.

"I don't believe this!" she yelled at the door. "It's five o'clock in the morning!"

"Got your message," Andrew LaMarche explained with grating enthusiasm. "Grabbed a red-eye out of JFK into Albany and rented a car. But not before I picked up some fresh bagels and a thermos of coffee. Thought we'd have a picnic . . ."

Bo was already pulling on the slightly rumpled navy designer slacks she'd worn the day before. They'd cost as much as a place setting of sterling, but their attractive cut made her feel thin. With the fresh cream-colored turtleneck in her carry-on bag she'd look like a Campfire Girl on her way to earning a badge in sailboat maintenance. Bo wished she had a little silk teddy or at least something more lascivious than a turtleneck in which to open the motel room door. The thought spun out lazily, even sneakily, but Bo caught it before it drifted into unconsciousness. A silk teddy? She didn't even *own* a silk teddy!

"I'll be dressed in a minute," she mentioned tersely.

"Of course." LaMarche's tone suggested that he had nothing else in mind.

In the bathroom Bo grimaced at herself through toothpaste foam. Seductiveness at 5:00 A.M. wasn't her métier. The pea green eyes looking back from an ill-lit mirror didn't seem manicky. They merely looked asleep. But who knew? An inappropriate sexuality could creep up unnoticed at any time. And the lithium would just about have worn off completely by now. A friendly Edwardian doctor might be transformed, if only briefly, into an object of epic desire.

Deftly outlining her eyes in a color identified by its manufacturer as "Persian Smoke," Bo forced herself to address the issue of why she'd called Andrew LaMarche in the first place. Pulled him away from his conference in New York with a plea for help to which she knew perfectly well he'd respond. She didn't really need his help. One call to the local authorities would bring all the backup she needed to retrieve Hannah Franer from a nest of French-speaking weirdos. Except she hadn't wanted to do it that way. She'd wanted to break through the barrier surrounding the cult, find out something about it. She'd wanted to test whether her own grasp of the situation might be useful in determining the fate of Hannah Franer, rather than subjecting the child without thought to a set of rules already in place. Madge Aldenhoven would not approve of such pointless curiosity. But Andrew LaMarche would. He was a colleague on the case, conveniently in the neighborhood. Since he spoke French it made sense to enlist his involvement. Perfect sense.

The ghost of a silk teddy, Bo decided, was just a mental remnant. Maybe something she'd been dreaming. Quite likely some best-forgotten vignette from a past in which every manic episode involved at least one fascinating and quickly discarded new lover. It could have nothing to do with Andrew LaMarche. Bo was almost certain she wasn't getting manic again, and besides, she actually liked the man. And a cardinal rule of survival involved separating the likable ones from the merely desirable ones. A comfortable, tidy boundary.

"I'm glad you called, Bo," he said when she stepped outside. "I do have an unusual interest in this case, and the conference was really quite boring. Now, tell me what's going on."

In khakis and a thickly handknit Aran sweater over a dress shirt, Andrew LaMarche looked somewhat out of place in the chilly Adirondack dawn. A little beamish, like a city kid on a camp-out. Bo couldn't help laughing when he helped her into a Lincoln town car with plush seats and tinted glass.

"The only thing the rental agency had left," he sighed.

"I want you to see this place, this cult hideout as Madge put it," Bo began. "Everybody speaks French, or at least pretends not to speak English. It's not far, and did you mention coffee?"

She knew she'd be incoherent until molecules of caffeine joined the sluggish red soup in her veins. Conversation prior to 10:00 A.M. without that chemical boost had traditionally proven futile.

In minutes LaMarche had guided the enormous car out of town and over the dirt road to a spot at the edge of Night Heron Lake. The lodge boathouses hugged the shore ten yards from the car.

"Look," LaMarche urged, pointing.

Bo saw nothing but a red eft salamander strolling thoughtfully over a licheny log. The creature seemed almost human in an orange, lizardy sort of way. Bo had been introduced to the diaries of Samuel Pepys by an English professor with the same neckless body and pencil-thin arms.

"I'm going to lecture you on Charles the Second if you don't produce that coffee," she threatened. "Look at what?"

LaMarche pointed to a row of canoes nuzzling the shore. Bo could not remember seeing the man smile this broadly. He must, she realized with a sinking certainty of what would come next, be remembering those childhood summers with Uncle Gus in Louisiana's bayous.

"An English king not known for his love of nature? How about breakfast on the water?" He fulfilled her premonition, already out of the car. "Your Quebecers won't be up for another hour, anyway."

Bo could not bring herself to explain the extent to which the idea of coffee in a canoe at dawn sounded like hell on earth. "Sure," she muttered as the salamander vanished behind a budding silver maple. It was the least she could do, after dragging him away from New York City.

Settled backward in the canoe's forward seat, Bo breathed coffee-scented steam from the thermos top handed her by Andrew LaMarche. The coffee was excellent. She might actually live.

"I have no idea yet what this cult does, what it's about," she began as LaMarche expertly paddled the aluminum craft over glassine water. In the weak light, drifting mists turned briefly gold and then disappeared. Bo noticed that she was whispering. "But they all speak French, or pretend to," she continued. "I got nowhere."

LaMarche, making no sound as he arced the dripping paddle back and forth across the canoe, watched her with an attitude at once ambivalent and bemused. The look had nothing to do with cults. "You're cold," he observed.

Allowing the canoe to drift near the shore of a small island still shrouded in mist, he placed the paddle on the floorboards and pulled off his sweater. Leaning forward on his knees he handed the sweater to Bo, and then leaned back. The sun gilding the eastern shoreline revealed a thoughtful smile beneath his trim mustache. He appeared to have made a decision. Bo was ninety-seven percent certain she knew what that decision was.

"Thanks," she responded, holding the coffee between her feet while struggling into the sweater. Oh well, why not? Their friendship would, of course, be lost. But so what? He was quite attractive in a starchy sort of way. He was going to make a pass at her. She was going to respond as any healthy, experienced woman who hadn't had a lover in two years would respond. Bo eyed the rough floorboards of the canoe and considered logistics. From a paper bag beneath his seat Andrew LaMarche extracted a sesame bagel.

"This probably isn't an appropriate moment, Bo," he began, "but there's something I want to say."

He was, she realized, going to hand her the bagel. She remembered his kindness last year when she'd been really manic, before the lithium kicked in. He'd been there for her as no one else had ever been. It wasn't good to think about that. It would be lost, that memory, after their relationship became merely sexual. It occurred to Bo that she might want to keep that memory more than she wanted a sexual fling.

"This isn't how I imagined it would be," he said, extending the bagel to her, "but, Bo, I want to marry you."

The words were spoken softly, with a hint of self-conscious laughter visible in the gray eyes.

"You what?" Bo made a grab for the bagel as if the crusty circle of dough would explain everything. The movement threw her off center and he instinctively reached to help. In the half second as the canoe tipped irredeemably to its port side, Bo looked straight into his eyes and saw that he wasn't really joking. After that it was hard to see at all. She was swimming in ice water wearing a drenched Aran sweater that seemed to weigh three hundred pounds. Fortunately they were only about fifteen feet from the island.

"I've got the canoe," LaMarche yelled. "Just wade to shore and I'll pull it in."

Bo let her feet fall numbly through the water and discovered the lake's bottom. Her eyes and teeth flamed with cold as a dripping and slightly blue Andrew LaMarche jerked the inverted vessel onto land and turned it over.

"You're crazy," Bo panted, jumping up and down on the rocky shore to maintain what remained of her circulation, "and I don't use that term lightly."

"No, I've just found the woman I love madly and want to marry." Andrew LaMarche grinned with lavender lips. "But right now I want to avoid death from exposure." Stripping off his shirt and pants he put his wet shoes back on and did a series of jumping jacks on the rocks. Bo was amazed to see lowcut jockey shorts in revealing black silk. The garment seemed completely out of character and suggested a side to Andrew LaMarche for which the sacrifice of their friendship might fade by comparison.

"Quit staring and wring out that sweater," he laughed. "Then put it back on and keep jumping. The wool will insulate your body heat even when it's wet. As soon as I dry out we'll head back to the lodge. It's not far."

Bo wrung out his clothes and then the sweater, put it back on and kept jumping. In a few moments her torso beneath the wool actually felt warm, and she buried her aching knuckles against her stomach. An immense confusion seemed to convulse there, making her heart lurch uncomfortably.

"I did have something just short of marriage in mind," Bo said through chattering teeth as LaMarche, clothed again, paddled strenuously back to shore.

"You can see how impossible that would be in a canoe," he replied with a straight face. "Life-threatening. Comparatively, marriage is a most attractive option."

"Not an option for me. I've already done that." The words were leaden, weighted with too much history and the surprising eruption of desire. She felt as though she were suddenly in a drama for which the script had not been written. Andrew LaMarche was not playing by the rules.

"We'll see," he mused, aiming the canoe for its berth beside the others. "I intend to court you relentlessly."

Bo wondered if the term "court" had been used in this context since the Spanish-American War. "Just get me out of this damn lake before my feet have to be amputated," she suggested. The abrasive tone, she hoped, would mask the welter of confusion disturbing her composure.

In minutes the canoe scraped shore.

Napoleon Pigeon was filling a bird feeder on the lawn as they parked the car and damply got out.

"Monsieur Pigeon," Bo introduced the men, "this is Dr. LaMarche."

After what seemed to be an uproarious conversation in French, the berobed giant led them to the lodge, threw new logs on a smoldering fire, and then left them there as he hurried up the staircase. Astonishingly light on his feet, he held his homespun robe like a girl. In minutes he returned accompanied by a lean Indian woman with cropped white hair and black eyes that could, Bo thought, hypnotize snakes. Ever the gentleman, LaMarche rose to meet her, leaving a damp spot on the hearth where he'd been warming himself next to Bo. The Indian woman stifled a smile with visible effort.

After fifteen minutes of animated French conversation in which Bo heard Hannah Franer's name mentioned several times, LaMarche turned and pulled her to her feet.

"I'd like to introduce Ms. Bradley of San Diego's Child Protective Services," he intoned. "Bo, this is Dr. Eva Blindhawk Broussard, founder and director of the Shadow Mountain Seekers, a group whose members either have seen or expect to see visitors from another dimension."

Bo extended her hand to a firm, welcoming grip, and waited.

"Will you help us?" the woman asked directly, and in English. Her eyes bored into Bo's as if searching for something.

Bo knew exactly what the look meant, and returned it. A look of baseline assessment that would miss nothing. A searching out of the little twitches that hide lies, mask deception. Bo could do it naturally. Eva Broussard had learned. The two women stared, blue eyes to black, as a log tumbled in the fire and sent up a spray of sparks. Bo had expected the leader of this odd assemblage to be a marginal character, a little innocent, a little delusional. Instead she found fierce intelligence and a surprising openness.

"I don't know if I can help you; my job is to help Hannah Franer. But I'd like to know about her life, her world"—she glanced briefly at LaMarche—"before I make decisions that will affect her. Will you take me to her?"

The answer was an affirmation of their mutual assessment. "Yes," Eva Broussard replied. "Come with me."

A second unusual happening in one day, Bo mused. The woman had trusted her immediately. Now if Andrew LaMarche would just come to terms with a dawning twenty-first century . . .

"I'm going to phone my service," LaMarche said. "You go on and check on Hannah."

Following Eva Broussard up the maple stairs, Bo was not surprised at the woman's next remark.

"You thought I'd be insane, didn't you?"

"Yes," Bo answered, "but you're not."

"And you'd know, wouldn't you?"

"Yes. I have a bipolar disorder, and—"

"And so you don't miss much." Eva Broussard turned and smiled. "A remarkable quality, enviable in many ways. Unusual in a social worker. How did you fall into this job, Bo Bradley?"

"It's a long story," Bo said as they entered a large bedroom in which the little girl still slept on a cot beside a twig bed.

Eva Broussard's black eyes twinkled. "I'd love to hear it later." She laughed softly. "And here's your quarry."

Bo felt as if she'd known the woman for a lifetime, as if she'd found a friend.

For a while both of them gazed at the sleeping child whose straight blonde hair fanned across the pillow. A dusting of freckles punctuated her cheeks flushed with sleep, and her perfectly arched eyebrows were the color of dust. A huge nightgown fell off one shoulder, revealing a bony frame like the mother's. Pinned to the gown's bodice were three odd strips of woven straw with purple beads attached. Bo made a note to ask about them as Eva grabbed some dry clothes for Bo from a bureau.

"Just change in there," she gestured to a hall bathroom. "Then come downstairs and we'll fill you with hot coffee while we talk."

Minutes later Bo descended the stairs in a warm caftan and wool slipper socks, only to confront LaMarche and the Indian woman looking somberly upward, waiting for her.

"What is it?" she asked from the landing.

LaMarche held out his hand. "Bonnie Franer committed suicide last night, Bo. The bastard has killed two people now."

From above a small voice rose, panicky and shrill. "Eva! Where are you, Eva? I'm scaaared!"

"These people have come from California," Eva explained to Hannah Franer, who was huddled cross-legged on the twig bed. "This is Dr. LaMarche, who tried to help Samantha, and this is Ms. Bradley, who wants to help you."

The child's wide-set hazel eyes watched as if from a great

distance. The burden of pain lay in them, and a defeated disinterest.

"Oh, Hannah," Bo sighed, joining the child on the bed, "it won't stay this way! Things will get better, they really will . . ."

Eva Broussard shot Bo a look. "This is a terrible time for you, Hannah," she began, "and I'm afraid another terrible thing has happened."

Hannah traced patterns with her knuckles on the sheet. "Where's Paul?" she asked softly. "I want Paul and mama. I want to go home." The round, pale eyes glared at Bo accusingly. "Where's Paul and my mom?"

The pleasant, old-fashioned room seemed suddenly cut off from the rest of the lodge, the rest of the world. Bo could almost smell the child's rage and despair. A musty, metallic odor warning of danger. Bo glanced at Eva Broussard for confirmation, and saw the grim nod. Hannah Franer had inherited her mother's fragility. Merely quiet and somber under normal stress loads, the child might break completely now. Bo felt a desperate sense of time running out.

"Paul is okay, but he's been taken back to California," she told the child very slowly. "The police think he's the one who hurt Samantha . . ."

"Nooo!" Hannah breathed, trembling. "Paul didn't hurt Sammi. It was Goody. Goody hurt her. She said Goody hurt her," she pointed toward her crotch beneath the baggy nightgown, "down there."

Bo felt her own pulse quickening. "Hannah, who is Goody?"

"Sammi said mama would die if she told. That Goody would kill mama." The hazel eyes were dry and widening in fear. "Where's mama? Sammi told me! He got Sammi dead because she told! Did he get mama? Is mama dead, too? Where's my mama?" The child sat upright among the bedcovers, a tense, narrow sculpture.

"Your mother is in California," Eva Broussard hedged, her bronze eyelids lowered as if she were deep in thought.

"She'd dead, isn't she?" Hannah addressed the question to Eva with a directness that made Bo wince. "She's in

California, but she's dead. Goody got her and he killed her!"

"Goody didn't kill your mother," Eva said slowly and clearly. And then, because everything that might happen later would hinge on Hannah's trust of her, Eva Broussard did not lie. "But yes, your mother, too, has died."

Bo, sitting on the bed only inches from Hannah, felt the girl's spirit turn away. Turn inward toward some flat, cool landscape where nothing moved, where there was no sound, where nothing hurt. Like a puppet slack on its strings the child curled upon herself and toppled sideways on the bed. A dark stain spread beneath her hips as she lost control of her bladder. The hazel eyes fell vacant even as Bo watched, as if the person inside simply slid down, and away.

"*Mon Dieu,*" Andrew LaMarche uttered raggedly from the doorway. "She's gone into shock!"

"Something like that," the Indian woman replied, gathering the girl in her arms and striding toward the hall bathroom. "Bo, I'll need your help."

Deftly placing Hannah in the deep old bathtub, Eva turned on the water and adjusted its temperature to a tepid level that would cool the child's skin and gently induce a faster heart rate.

"Hold her up while I get the gown off," Broussard directed.

Bo could feel muscle tone over the small bones. Hannah was still with them.

"Bo and I are going to massage you with these washcloths," Eva Broussard explained. "It will help you get some of the hurt out. Let some of the hurt out, Hannah. The water is here to take it away."

Bo watched as Eva kneaded Hannah's pale flesh with a rough cloth, and did the same. Gradually the child's skin turned pink, but the hazel eyes remained empty.

"I am your grandmother now, Hannah," Eva went on. A note of authority rang in her voice. "And this is our way. Samantha and your mother are gone, and your hurt is terrible. You must let some of the hurt out, or you will be very sick. The water is here to take your hurt away . . . now."

Bo watched as Hannah turned her head to face the Indian woman. Slowly the small hands formed fists, extended, and curled tightly again. The child's face contorted as tears sprang up and a rasping hiss escaped her bared teeth.

"Hold her," Eva told Bo. "Don't let her hurt herself."

Hannah began to pound the water with her fists, and then to kick. In seconds she was thrashing violently, flinging gallons of water like liquid groundfire from the tub.

"Fine, that's just right," Eva encouraged until the girl relaxed in exhaustion, sobbing quietly.

Only then did Bo notice the crowd of people standing silently in the hall.

"We were afraid the chanting would disturb her," a young woman in a SUNY Albany sweatshirt addressed Eva Broussard, "so we haven't done the morning chant yet. Is she going to be all right?"

"She's much better," Eva answered, taking a stack of clean clothes from the grandmotherly woman Bo had seen on the porch yesterday afternoon. "Aren't you, Hannah?"

It was in the set of the child's shoulders. Bo saw it before the ramifications became obvious. Hannah allowed Bo to help her into clean white panties and her Minnie Mouse shirt, and pointed to the beads still pinned to the nightgown on the floor. Bo retrieved the amulet and fastened it to the sweatshirt as the child watched, but said nothing.

"Hannah?" Eva repeated.

Hannah's wide lips clamped over her teeth for a moment, and then went slack. In her eyes a deep fear struggled with her need to remain attached. Eva and Bo exchanged a glance of troubled acceptance. To push the little girl right now would be disastrous.

"It's okay if you don't want to talk." Bo smiled, hiding her dismay. "We know how scared you are. You don't have to talk until you aren't so scared."

The only person who might lead them to Samantha's killer had just been pulled from the shock of grief only to stop talking. Hannah Franer had elected to become mute, not out of rational thinking but out of a stark terror operating in the deepest channels of her mind. Somebody named Goody had told Samantha her mama would die if she revealed what he'd done to her. But Samantha had told her big sister, Hannah. Bo could almost see the two, tucked in their Raggedy Ann sheets, one of them bleeding internally, sick, frightened. Sammi had told her big sister what the man had done, and then Sammi had died. Next Bonnie Franer had crumbled under the intolerable weight of her distorted grief and taken her own life. And that left Hannah with irrefutable proof that to talk is to die.

"We're going downstairs for a little while," Eva told her after settling her in a clean bed and assigning one of the group to read aloud from a book of poems by Robert Louis Stevenson. Hannah didn't seem to hear.

"Repetitive rhyme and meter are comforting to children," the Indian woman said as she led Bo and LaMarche to an alcove beside one of the fireplaces. "The brain of a child is not like an adult's. Somehow we've lost sight of that." Bo noticed that the woman's hands were trembling as Napoleon Pigeon laid a glazed pottery tea service on an end table, and padded away.

LaMarche noticed as well, and poured the tea with deliberate indolence. The ploy gave Eva time to regain her composure, and gave Bo an opportunity to contemplate what the term "gentleman" must have meant when it still meant anything. Her grandmother, she thought while admiring the twig chair Eva occupied, would have joined Andrew LaMarche at the altar within minutes of his proposal. Any altar. But Bridget O'Reilly's fondness for "the laddies" had been legendary. Bo monitored a similar proclivity in herself like a radioactive isotope. Dangerous when not properly contained.

"Elective mutism in children is fairly rare these days," he mentioned conversationally. "Understandable in Hannah's case, but she will need to be seen by a child psychiatrist as quickly as possible. Bo, I don't see that you have any choice but to—"

"I am a psychiatrist," Eva Broussard interjected. "I don't specialize in children, but I'm the last available adult this child knows and trusts. She must stay with me. The next days and weeks will be critical. Surely you can see that."

LaMarche smoothed his mustache with a thumb and stared into his tea. "Dr. Broussard, could you explain exactly what these people, including Paul Massieu, are doing here? And could you outline your reasons for choosing to believe that Massieu is innocent of Samantha's injuries and death?"

"Andy!" Bo slammed her cup into its saucer, creating a ripple of clove-scented air in the alcove. "You believed he was innocent from the beginning. Has the mother's suicide changed your mind? And have you forgotten that this is *my* investigation?"

Eva Broussard stood and breathed the steam from her tea. "Dr. LaMarche is asking the obvious questions. Here are the answers. In two years of close professional association with Paul Massieu, I have seen nothing to suggest that he's capable of sexual assault of any kind, particularly sexual assault on a child. His relationship with Bonnie was a healthy one, despite differences in their backgrounds and education. Paul is an unusual man, especially by American standards. More like a European. He does not feel any need to conform to some model he cannot fit. An academic, he teaches cultural anthropology at McGill, devotes his leisure time to camping and the pursuit of numerous interests that center on salvaging cultural artifacts . . ."

"What cultural artifacts?" Bo asked, recognizing that kiddie porn might just fall in that category.

Eva Broussard leaned against the fieldstone wall, one moccasinned foot propped behind her. "Adirondack guideboats, old Huguenot cookbooks in French, and eighteenth-century Roman Catholic ghost stories involving Montreal's numerous convents and monasteries. Paul collects original wine label artwork, belongs to an international organization determined to preserve the oldest known names of streets and roads, and actually lost a finger attempting to rescue a millwheel destined for extinction in Vermont. In addition to that—"

"We see your point," Andrew LaMarche admitted from deep within an overstuffed plaid love seat facing Eva. "And none of Paul's interests, insofar as you know, have involved the usual pastimes of pedophiles?"

"No. Paul has no interests that could be used to attract children. No video games, sports or soda fountain equipment, toys or pets. With the exceptions of Hannah and Samantha,

I feel safe in saying that Paul has a minimal awareness of children."

Bo couldn't restrain herself. "What was he going to do with a *millwheel*?" she asked.

"I don't know," Eva answered. "It was years ago. Before he came to me for help with the experience that has created this community."

"The San Diego police say Paul's a member of a cult." Bo took the cue. "*Is* this some kind of cult?" She couldn't shake a sense that the whole interrogation was pointless. That they might as well have been whistling at each other through straws while something terrible grew worse, unchecked.

"Paul and several of the others here report having seen silvery, humanoid figures at night in these mountains. Paul and three others recall being medically examined by these figures. Those with this experience generally attribute it to contact with extraterrestrial life-forms. The experience was intense and transforming for them. They and others who believe in this experience gather here. That's all. Scarcely a cult, as the term is properly used."

"And Paul isn't delusional?" Bo croaked in disbelief.

"My question as well," echoed Andrew LaMarche.

"And Paul's," Eva continued, sitting to pour more tea. "He came to me fearing that he was going mad. You'll have to trust my assessment that he shows no evidence of any psychiatric disorder. I can't explain what happened to him. But my purpose in establishing this community is to study that experience."

The sound of padding feet alerted them to the presence of Hannah, a leggy wraith in her sweatshirt and underpants. Glaring at LaMarche, the child looked questioningly at Bo and then flung herself against Eva. The dark flesh around her eyes made her look made-up, like a classic Oriental dancer. The effect was eerie.

"I'm right here, Hannah," Eva reassured the child. "And I'm glad to see you. Why don't you get your jeans and shoes now, and then you and I will see what's in the refrigerator to drink."

As Hannah scuttled away, Eva turned to face Bo. "I will

come to California," she said. "I will see to it that Hannah is in the jurisdiction of your agency. It will be better for her to see that Paul is alive, in any event. But she must stay with me."

"What are you going to do?" Andrew LaMarche asked after Eva had coaxed some orange juice into Hannah and taken her out to walk near the lake.

"There are options." Bo sighed. "California may not be the best one. Eva could take Hannah up to Canada for a while. It would take weeks, even months for the paperwork to extradite them back to California. Hannah must stay with Eva if she's to come out of this at all intact. She's like the mother . . ."

"I can see that." LaMarche nodded, buttoning the cuff of his shirt recently returned from the lodge's dryer. "She's a nervous, delicate child . . ."

Bo shook her hair, now a mat of damp tangles. "She's not delicate, for God's sake, Andy, it's more serious than that. If anything she's tough as nails to have made it this far. When will people stop embroidering these cute little terms for life-threatening situations?"

His puzzled look alerted Bo to the intensity of her own words.

"I'm on a soapbox, right? I'm overreacting. She's just a kid with a lot of losses. But Andy," Bo slapped the table where the tea service sat cooling, "it's more than that. The mother's a suicide. That doesn't happen in regular people no matter what the stress. It takes a certain . . . imbalance. Hannah's got the problem, too. I've seen it. My sister . . ."

Bo stopped herself and toyed with the hem of the caftan she was wearing.

"I'd forgotten," LaMarche said softly. "Didn't she . . . ?"

Bo looked up from the wool fabric. "Not an easy word, is it? As manic depression goes, I was lucky. I got the mania, mostly. Laurie got the depression. And yes, she commited suicide when she was twenty."

The gray eyes showed pain. "I'm sorry, Bo. No wonder you're upset."

Bo stood and walked to a window overlooking a small

creek. Its splashing filled the silence. "Just trust me on this, Andy. I'm going to have to do something a little irregular."

"Irregular? What are you talking about?"

"Eva wants to take Hannah back to California, to be near Paul. She's right when she says it will improve Hannah's sense of security. The child has lost her sister and her mother within twenty-four hours. Paul Massieu has been a father to her. He's all she has left."

"But Paul's in jail."

"There'll be a bond. Surely Eva will pay it. Paul will be free until his trial, if the real perp isn't caught first."

"So what's the problem?"

Bo pushed up the sleeves of the woven caftan, and then pulled them back down. Her hands were still cold. "The problem is the system. My system. The one that sent me here to bring Hannah back."

LaMarche leaned back in his chair and crossed his arms across his chest. The body language of mistrust. Bo had expected it.

"I can certify Eva Broussard as a temporary foster parent, and she's already established a relational claim to Hannah by adopting her into her tribe as an Iroquois. That relationship will stand. It's legal. Or at least I think it is. The problem is that even though I can certify Eva, and even though she's technically Hannah's grandmother now, CPS will never allow Hannah to stay with Eva."

LaMarche shook his head. "Why not?"

"Because it's not the way the system works. In particular it's not the way my supervisor works. Madge goes by the book. Temporary foster care certifications are only used in emergency situations when a close relative or family friend steps in to save a child from going to strangers. And while I think Eva matches that profile, Madge won't. If I take Hannah back as Eva's grandchild, Hannah will have to go to an Indian foster home for weeks, maybe months, while Eva establishes residency and jumps through hoops for foster care licensing. Hannah's mental state is too fragile for that, or for any foster home. It would destroy her."

"You may be projecting, Bo. Kids are resilient. They snap back more easily than—"

Bo grabbed a copy of *Adirondack* magazine and threw it against the twig chair. "Why did I know I could count on you to remain stone deaf to what I'm saying? Hannah isn't just a kid, she's a special kid who's just lost her *world*, to quote a pediatrician I once knew. She has to remain under the care of the one person with whom she feels secure. If she's torn away and sent to strangers, we could lose her."

"You're not suggesting," his tone was distant, professional, "that Hannah may try to . . . harm herself, are you?"

"Eight-year-olds, even troubled eight-year-olds, rarely attempt suicide," Bo said through clenched teeth. "But they do learn to live in fantasy, fail to cope. If Hannah is ripped from the last person she has on earth and forced to live among strangers right now, she may very well vanish into a world of her own making. Some dim world inside her own head. That cannot be allowed to happen."

"This little girl isn't you, Bo. More to the point, she's not your sister. You've lost your objectivity." LaMarche's voice bore an impersonal sympathy. "Maybe you should rethink your decision to stop the lithium. You're getting too involved."

Bo felt the flush racing up her cheeks, her hair rising imperceptibly from her throbbing scalp. "Here is what we're going to do," she said in a deliberate monotone. "I'm going back alone today. I will say that Eva has fled to Canada with Hannah. The two of them will secretly fly out later, and rent a place. We'll secure Paul Massieu's release, and Hannah will be able to spend time with him. I'm convinced this plan is in Hannah's best interests. I ask only that you keep your mouth shut. Will you do that?"

His bushy eyebrows became one bristled rope above his eyes. "You're asking me to jeopardize my entire career by withholding information from the police and Child Protective Services, and all on the word of a . . ." He bit his lip and looked at the floor.

"Of a crazy woman? That's what you were going to say, wasn't it? Overlooking, of course, the fact that you've *already* withheld information from the police . . ." Bo stood straight and felt an astonishing calm in spite of her outrage. Why had she not expected this from him? She'd certainly expected it from everybody else. Tears swam in her eyes but she blinked them away. "Yes, I'm asking you to bend the rules on the word of a crazy woman. On the word of a woman who's been in psychiatric hospitals, in restraints, even. A woman who has to take psychiatric medication at times, and who isn't taking any at the moment. Are we abundantly clear about what I'm asking?"

Andrew LaMarche didn't return her direct gaze, but instead rose and walked to the door. "I'll keep quiet if you'll agree to let me check on Hannah at least weekly. That's the only way I can go along with this. But Bo," he turned to glance at the stairs from which a Gregorian chant drifted, "nobody's going to believe you."

"Oh, yes they will," Bo whispered as the door closed behind him.

On a low table near the plaid love seat was a phone. After dialing 619 and the information number, Bo took a deep breath. "Could I have a new San Diego listing for a psychologist named Cynthia Ganage?" she asked, and wrote the number on a matchbook advertising snowshoes.

Chapter 13

In his small office with its view of bamboo plants screening the boy's club dumpsters, John D. Litten signed a name carefully to each of a stack of documents. The quality-control response form for a supplier of volleyball nets. A work order for the June groundskeeping contract service, identical to the May work order. Copy for a classifieds ad that would notify job-seekers that the Bayview Boy's Club needed one bus driver, weekends, and a short-order cook, weekdays four to six. The name he signed was "James Brenner," a halfback who died at fifteen of an undiagnosed heart valve deformity during a high school football game in Dalton, Georgia, fourteen years ago. John Litten's signature, an efficient scrawl practiced to resemble that of a doctor, gave no clue that its writer had once been Jonny Dale Litten of Estherville, South Carolina. Jonny Dale had lived with Gramma in a trailer on "Poot Hill," right over the dump. John D. lived in a downtown loft apartment overlooking San Diego Bay. A loft apartment in a building gutted and refurbished with exposed beams and brushed-chrome doors to attract architects, photographers, designers. Half the units in the building were used as offices, empty at night. No one around to hear anything. And John D. Litten was very, very careful.

At the slightest hint of trouble he moved on, followed the wind to the next big city where he could be invisible and do exactly what he wanted. And it was time to move again. The memory of yesterday began to throb in his cock. The delicious child, pink as a rosebud as she giggled and squirmed in his lap. He'd lost control, but it was so good! Too bad the kid had died. He hadn't meant to go that far, but it was just too good to stop. And the videotape, showing a masked clown named Goody at erotic play with a naked cherub, would be worth some bucks later. Big bucks.

Beneath the Formica-topped desk John Litten felt his penis stiffen inside the gray tropical worsteds he always wore with the navy blazer. A navy blazer identical to one worn by the director of United Way. And the chief of the club's advisory council. And the Methodist minister from a wealthy suburban church who came two Wednesday nights a month to teach a Bible class. John Litten knew exactly how to blend in, to look like what people wanted to see. Except his blazer had a Pierre Cardin label and his gray tie with pinpoint navy polka dots was pure silk, from Saks. Underneath, he wasn't identical at all; he was better. Classier. And smarter.

The hallmark Litten jug ears had been surgically trimmed and contoured to lie attractively flat against his head. The baby-fine mouse-colored hair was razor-cut and given volume by an imported thickener. His crooked, rotting teeth had been capped by the United States Navy, which had also taught him how to order and distribute supplies. John Litten could get a job just about anywhere.

Stepping across the office to lock the door, he unzipped his pants and masturbated quickly into a flyer advertising tumbling mats. The flyer showed a girl in leotards, doing a cartwheel. He came almost as soon as he grabbed himself, thinking about yesterday. Then he zipped his pants, stuffed the flyer to the bottom of his wastebasket, and unlocked the door. The kid was the best he'd ever done, better than anything in his whole life. He felt like superman, like a king. He wondered if part of that was because he'd rammed himself through the very core, some barrier there, and into death.

He'd never killed by mistake before. John Litten didn't make mistakes. He wondered if killing with your cock was like some kind of key to another world. Or maybe it was just killing, period.

Word was all over the papers that some psychologist was blaming devil-worshipers for what happened to the kid. A devil-worshiper who lived with the kid's mother and a sister. John Litten thought about that as he examined the shine on his black hand-sewn loafers. The psychologist wasn't stupid. People loved to hear pooky like that. People could face anything but the truth. He'd known that since he was four and Gramma saw what he did to her one-eyed old cat named Scoot. She just dug a hole in the sunflowers along the front fence, and buried Scoot with the rope still around his scrawny neck. And said, "I know it was an accident, Jonny. I know you didn't mean to hurt Scoot. You was just playin', up in that tree."

Everybody in Estherville said Jonny Dale was a liar just like his no-good whore of a mother. They said she just dropped her bastard like some little, screaming turd and took off. Jonny knew he was the bastard. And after a while he figured out that bastard meant smart.

Two years later they found Dewey Ray Clyde, the shell-shocked Korean war vet, burned up in the rusting truck cab down at the dump where he liked to drink till he passed out. They said he'd blown himself to kingdom come down there by dropping a cigarette into his jar of hundred-proof. Gramma had believed that, too, even when Jonny didn't try to hide the gasoline can. From then on Jonny Dale knew exactly how stupid people could be. How much people only wanted to see what they wanted to see. It was always easy to figure out. Usually, they'd just tell you.

"Jonny, I expect you to come to school on time, and do your lessons."

That was Mrs. Myer, who had a rubber stamp in the shape of a clown's head and ink pads in different colors. Jonny Dale liked the clown head stamped on his second-grade spelling papers when he got all the words right.

"Goody," Mrs. Myer would say, walking up and down the rows with her ink pad, "Goody for you."

Jonny didn't usually get all the words right, just most of them.

Later he heard, "Litten! Your test scores qualify you for Naval Procurement Training. Report to training at 0800 hours Monday. If you rank in the top ten percent, it's an upgrade for you."

You just did whatever they said, and then when they weren't looking you could do whatever you wanted.

But the psychologist had given him an idea. Maybe he wouldn't leave right away. San Diego was big enough to hide in for a while before moving on. It might be fun to stay around and set the stupid town on its ear before heading to Seattle or Tucson or wherever it would be. It might be fun to show them, just this once, how really, really stupid they were.

John Litten straightened his tie over the white pima cotton of his shirt and headed for the club's employee lounge. The clerk he'd been pretending to pursue for months always ate at 1:00. He'd flirt with her again today, enhancing the cultivated image of randy recently divorced young accountant, just out for a lay like all the other guys. The women who worked at the club's three-block-long facility thought he was harmless, a little cute with his pale blue eyes and Southern drawl. That was what he wanted them to think, in case anybody ever asked. He wanted them to think John Litten, known here as James Brenner, was just a short, skinny Southern boy who wouldn't hurt a fly.

"Hey, Brenner! How's it goin'?" It was Ben Skiff, a co-worker who'd invited John Litten to dinner at his home several times. Lisa, Ben's wife, was always trying to fix John up with her divorced friends.

"So-so," John grinned good-naturedly, falling in step with Skiff. "I'm gonna see an old squeeze up in Phoenix this weekend. Who knows? Maybe light an old flame."

The plan was falling easily into place. And it was going to be fun.

Chapter 14

Bo drove back toward Albany through Adirondack shadows, plagued by doubt and a metallic ache behind her nose. Finally she pulled off the narrow road into a picnic area beside the Saranac River. Wide and shallow, the river produced flutelike mutterings as it coursed over its bed of rounded stones. Miles of Boston ferns framed the water in a double band of green. In Bo's mind the ferns were associated with funerals. They'd banked Laurie's casket at Sullivan's Mortuary twelve years ago. And Grandma Bridget's casket, and then both her parents' after a faulty wall furnace claimed their lives in Mexico. Bo watched the postcard scene blur, and realized she was crying. It had been sneaking up for hours and it had nothing to do with ferns.

"I'm too old for this!" she yelled over the broad river. "Mature women do not blubber into scenery."

In the rushing water Bo heard the Bavarian accents of Lois Bittner, chortling. "Who said life was easy? Just take care of yourself, Bo. Be careful."

Bo inhaled what she was sure was almost pure oxygen, given the number of plants in the vicinity, and sighed. "I'm sick of people telling me I'm crazy when I'm not,'' she sniffled at the water. ''The minute anybody knows about the manic depression, they feel compelled to watch me like a mutating virus and provide unsolicited opinions about medication on the hour. No matter what I do, it's suspect. I hate it!''

The river continued to mutter and chirp in a language that seemed almost comprehensible. Bo threw in excess of twenty pebbles at a midstream boulder. The last twelve hit.

Are you finished with your nauseating foray into self-pity, Bradley? Good. Now, forget Dr. Centerfold, remember that you've dealt with this for two decades, go home, and figure out who really murdered Samantha Franer.

Bo grinned at her own unspoken lecture and flung herself back into the rental car. Andrew LaMarche had already flown back to New York City and his conference. For the rest of the trip to Albany, she enjoyed a fantasy of him in his underwear in the lobby of the Ritz Carlton, struggling to remove a sesame bagel impossibly baked around his neck.

Marriage! Couldn't he see how inappropriate that concept was? How antiquated? Marriage was for people like Estrella and her husband, Henry. Younger people. Mainstream people who would buy matching lawn furniture, talk about mutual funds investment, maybe have babies. Marriage was not for free-spirited, manicky artists with jobs requiring lots of overtime. Still, he was attractive. So why couldn't he just settle for a nice, invigorating affair like every other man on the planet?

The answer nagged at Bo throughout her flight back to San Diego. Andrew LaMarche wasn't like every other man on the planet. Not at all.

Madge Aldenhoven was a pillar of bureaucratic indignation when, after crossing the continent, Bo straggled into the office at 3:15.

''How could you let this happen?'' Madge seethed, pointing to a newspaper on Bo's desk. ''All you had to do was get the local police, go in there, and seize the child. Instead, you let them escape.''

Bo glanced at the article's header. ''Cult-Related Kidnapping in New York—Leader Evades San Diego Child Abuse Professional.'' It would not be necessary to read the article. She knew perfectly well what it would say. It would say that Dr. Cynthia Ganage, through a confidential source, had learned of a further development in the shocking Franer case. It would say that a mysterious dark woman, head of the cult in which accused rapist and murderer Paul Massieu held membership, had fled with the slaughtered child's sister to an unknown destination in Canada.

''I'm exhausted, Madge,'' Bo said, slumping into her desk chair. ''There's a three-hour time difference and I haven't had much sleep . . .''

''I've placed you on probation, Bo,'' Aldenhoven snapped. ''Your incompetence has made a laughingstock of the department and fueled an already dangerous public hysteria. If you'd bothered to read the department's directive on handling Satanic cases . . .''

Bo felt an absence of patience that demanded a voice. ''There *are* no Satanic cases,'' she began, allowing her green eyes to widen. ''I checked with the FBI's task force on cult-related crime. There has not been a single documentable case of ritualized child torture or murder anywhere in the United States. It's all media hype, Madge, nothing more. Some people rape, torture, and murder women and children. Sometimes they dress up in devil suits, clerical robes, or uniforms of the Confederate Army. Some of them get off on costumes, which conveniently serve the purpose of hindering identification by their victims. But it has nothing to do with Satanism or any other ism, and anybody who buys that crap is more interested in checkout line reading at the grocery store than in protecting children. If anybody's making a laughingstock of the Department of Social Services, it's you and whoever paid that entrepreneurial shark Ganage to peddle her pamphlets in San Diego.''

Aldenhoven's face, pale under normal circumstances, had turned a greenish white that reminded Bo of kohlrabi. A throbbing vein in the woman's neck provided a dash of color. Bo wondered if her supervisor were going to hit her. She hadn't been in a real fight since bloodying Mary Margaret Fagin's nose during Mass in the third grade after Mary Margaret said dogs couldn't go to heaven. The present conflict, Bo realized, had its origins in the same muddy conceptual pool. The need to impose rational order on irrational pain. For many, a storybook Satan provided comfort when unspeakable human behavior crept out of hiding.

"You're fired," Aldenhoven said through thin, long teeth.

"You can't fire me without going through procedures, hearings, appeals," Bo countered tiredly. "I belong to the union, remember? It'll take months and you know it. By then maybe we'll have found whoever raped and killed Samantha Franer. That's all I care about."

"Your job was to protect Samantha's sister," Madge said and stormed out in a billow of Estée Lauder Youth Dew perfume and dry-cleaned polyester.

"Precisely!" Bo hissed back at her slamming office door. What would Madge Aldenhoven do, she wondered, if she ever actually saw one of the small, frightened lives CPS purported to protect? The question was moot. Madge would do whatever the procedures manual dictated, even if it dictated dropping the child off a cliff.

Sighing, Bo glanced at the newspaper article while placing a call to a rental agent in the coastal San Diego suburb of Del Mar. The agent had the perfect place—a quiet studio apartment on the beach. The summer season wouldn't begin until late June. Not too many people around. And the early-season tourists who were there—retired academics, writers, and artists—kept to themselves and wouldn't take any particular notice of an Iroquois woman and blonde, silent child. But something was wrong with the article in the paper. More there than Bo had expected.

"Police deny any connection between the victimized Franer children and last night's desecration of statuary and a grave at the city's historic Mission San Diego de Alcala," a staff writer reported. It seemed that someone had broken into the mother church of California's fabled chain of twenty-one Franciscan missions and spray-painted crude genitalia and the words "Satan rules" on floors, walls, and priceless antique statues. Since an oil-based enamel had been used, the damage was estimated at over a million dollars. The grave of Padre Luis Jayme, California's first Christian martyr, who had been killed in 1775 when local Indians burned the original mission, was also desecrated. The article concluded with a lukewarm denial by a representative of the San Diego/Imperial County Intertribal Council that local Indian activists had anything to do with the desecrations. Bo was left with a sense that he wished they had.

The article bothered her. Something new and appalling seemed to have taken form in the newsprint. Something unusual, even in her unusual line of work. What if the police were wrong and Samantha's killer really had vandalized the mission? A proud symbol of the city's history, its desecration was bound to feed the hysteria orchestrated by Cynthia Ganage. But why would the killer want further attention? Child-molesters were invariably furtive, preferring to enjoy their activities in secret. Bo had encountered many, and not one would have courted publicity, even to mislead a criminal investigation. If Samantha's killer had spray-painted penises on religious statues just for kicks, then he was a different bird entirely from the pedophiles documented in CPS case files.

"You're tired; you're getting paranoid," she told herself. But the gnawing suspicion didn't go away.

A phone call to Dar Reinert helped.

"Probably just some kids," he grumbled. "Town's full of garage bands dreaming of heavy metal big-time. My bet is it's one of them, hoping for some spin-off publicity. They love the Satanic stuff. It frightens their parents."

His gruff assessment was reassuring.

"But what if wasn't kids, Dar, just for the sake of argument. What if it *was* the same guy that killed Samantha?"

"Then Ganage would be right, and we've got a Satanist," Reinert replied, yawning. "Except the Satanist we've got is already in jail, so he couldn't have vandalized the mission last night, so it was kids. What's bothering you, Bradley? Jet lag?"

"Dar, this ritual Satanic abuse stuff is a crock and you know it! The FBI's done a huge investigation and found absolutely nothing. How can you—"

"How long you been at CPS?" the detective interrupted. "Two, three years, right? And when you can't take it anymore you'll get a transfer over to County Employment Services, or you'll get a job with the Red Cross or a church or the human services department of some company. You're a social worker. I'm a cop."

Bo wondered what can of worms she'd opened. "So?"

There was a long silence.

"So cops can't go be cops out there in the real world. Cops can only make it down in the puddle of day-old jizz that stays alive by preying on the rest of humanity. Did you know that yesterday I just happened to bust a guy who kept his retarded sister chained in a closet while he collected her Social Security disability? Thing is, the sister died at least four years ago, but he left her chained in the closet and kept cashing those checks. Bought himself a plastic lady with real cat-fur pussy and the biggest collection of hard porn on his block. Somebody called when he started inviting the neighborhood boys in to look. I think it was the mother of the five-year-old. I only stumbled on the body by accident when one of the kids said he'd heard there was a *real* plastic lady in the closet. Do I need to tell you there was about a pound of dried semen in—"

"Dar!" Bo interrupted, tasting bile, "I was talking about the FBI's report on Satanism."

"Cops see this stuff for a lifetime, like trying to dam a river of shit that just keeps coming. A lotta cops don't mind it when evil seems to have a name. Someplace it comes from. Makes it easier to understand. Lotta people out there just like cops . . . and Satan's as good a name as any."

"So, is there anything else new on the case?" Bo asked in a fervent attempt to change the subject. In three years of professional association she'd never known Dar Reinert to talk this much.

"Only that you screwed up getting the sister back here," the detective said glumly, "and the damn ACLU's crawled in bed with Massieu, which we need like a case of jock itch."

"The American Civil Liberties Union? Why?" Bo ran her left hand through her hair and considered one of the fashionable new crew cuts. She felt weighted with unfriendly, cartoon hair.

"They're claiming he's being persecuted because of his religious beliefs, because he's in this cult. Yammering, in fact, for his immediate release based on lack of evidence. A handful of New Age types in crystals are picketing for him in front of the jail right now, opposed by a larger handful of right-wing Bible whackers with signs demanding the death penalty for Satan's disciple. I've put in for vacation time. This thing's turning into a circus."

Bo listened to her stomach growling and tried not to remember the ice-cold poultry by-product sandwich provided by the airline for lunch. It had been accompanied by one miniature chocolate mint, frozen solid. "What's this lawyer's name?" she asked.

"Gentzler. Solon Gentzler. Has a practice in L.A. but spends most of his time running up and down the state filing amicus briefs for the ACLU in religious freedom cases. He's the one that handled the Freeway Witch two years ago, remember?"

Bo grimaced. The Freeway Witch had been nothing more than a women's studies graduate student who at Christmas spelled "Mary Was Used" in twinkling lights along the chain-link fence bordering a rental property she shared with three other graduate students. The fence was visible for a mile and a half in both directions along I-805, and had so incensed members of a nearby fundamentalist group that they'd petitioned the city council for removal of the lights as a violation of community standards of decency. Gentzler had gotten miles of publicity for the concept of free speech by leaking to the press elaborate defenses that would, in fact, never be needed since the student would graduate and take a job in South America within months, the petition forgotten. A radical lawyer on the case could prove to be a threat, Bo realized. Could confuse the real issue, which was simply the preservation of Hannah Franer's sanity.

"I'll need to see Gentzler," she told the detective. "What's his number here?"

Reinert provided the number, puzzled. "What do you need to see him for?"

"Oh, just to get a sense of what he thinks of Massieu," she answered vaguely. "Technically, I'll have to hang on to this case until Hannah Franer is located. It can't be transferred or closed until then. I have to document everything I can about the suspected perp so that if Hannah is found and returned—''

''Yeah, yeah,'' Reinert interrupted. ''Except thanks to you the poor kid's been ripped off to Canada with some loony. Great work, Bradley.''

''Thanks, Dar. It's so good to know I can count on your support.''

Gentzler would be sure to foul up the plan worked out with Eva Broussard. He'd operate from an agenda featuring the rights of an accused man, not the uncodified rights of a vulnerable, hurt child to heal. Bo lay her head on her desk and groaned. At this rate she might well find herself waiting tables at some desert truck stop by the end of the month, and for nothing. But maybe she could convince Solon Gentzler to back off, diminish the focus of media attention on Paul Massieu, wait for the police to wise up and find the real killer. Maybe.

''You're back!'' Estrella exclaimed, lurching through the door burdened with case files, a briefcase, and a white paper bag from which rose the odor of the forbidden.

''French fries.'' Bo replied. ''I'll pay anything. I'll wash your car with imported shampoo, train Mildred to howl 'Cielito Lindo' under your window, paint a brooding portrait of Henry for your mantel . . .''

''My car's clean, I despise 'Cielito Lindo' and so does Mildred, and Henry doesn't brood.'' Estrella grinned. ''You've forgotten that French fries are fattening. So what happened in New York? Madge got so upset when she heard you blew it that she publicly threatened to wire your desk with plastic explosives. She mentioned fire ants, too. And something about a sheet metal box in the blazing sun.''

''Madge watches too many old movies on TV.'' Bo nodded. ''And what she's really done is to put me on probation and threaten to terminate my employment. But I'll tell you what really happened for everything in that bag.''

''Deal.''

As the story progressed Bo noticed Estrella's expression run the gamut from mere interest to near-Presbyterian disapproval. The latter was so incongruous Bo had to laugh.

''See?'' Estrella shook a pencil at the space between her

desk and Bo's. "You're laughing. This isn't funny. You're a party to evasion of a court order. You've gone too far this time, Bo, and if you're not crazy you'll meet this Broussard woman and Hannah when their plane lands tonight and take Hannah straight to the county receiving home. You filed the petition yourself. You can't just turn around and decide you don't think she should be in the system. She's already in the system and you're already in trouble! This is dangerous, Bo. You wouldn't be doing this if you were—"

"If I were what? Still taking lithium?" Bo experienced a bitterness that by now felt dusty, historical. How many times in one day would she have to defend a decision that, while unorthodox, was obviously right?

"Let's get something straight," she began, standing to lean backward against her desk, her arms crossed over a stomach already protesting the greasy food she'd just wolfed. "There's no question that even the best foster home would be damaging for Hannah right now. Madge would chew off her own right hand before bending the rules enough to let Hannah stay with Eva. The job here is, ostensibly, to protect children. And lithium or not, the only way to protect this child is to break the rules. I'm sick of hearing how I should be on medication every time I exercise what amounts to simple common sense. It's not my fault this system's a factory, and it's not your job to measure every decision I make for symptoms of madness. Either you're my friend and you trust me, or you're not and you don't. Which is it?"

"Wow!" Estrella breathed beneath raised eyebrows. "Okay, okay. We're friends. I trust you. And from what you've said, you're right about Hannah. But Bo, if this gets out you're not only out of a job, you could go to jail for contempt of court!"

Bo felt her lips curl in an impish grin. "I've got an ace in the hole. No problem."

"What ace?"

"A proposal of marriage. Fairly wealthy guy but a bit stuffy for my taste. Still, it's a backup if prison looms."

Estrella looked as if she'd swallowed a Ping-Pong ball. "LaMarche? You're kidding!"

"Tell you about it later when I pick up Mildred from your

place. Right now I have to call a lawyer, go see Massieu in jail, and meet Eva and Hannah on a 5:56 flight.''

After Solon Gentzler agreed to a Saturday breakfast meeting and seven phone calls finally isolated the fact that Paul Massieu had accidentally been taken to the county jail rather than the city jail where he should have been, Bo scanned her desk for anything that couldn't wait until Monday. In the pile of pink phone memos were six more denying the existence of Jonas Lee Crowley's father, eleven that could wait, and one with no call-back number.

''Satan called,'' the last message told her. ''Will phone again.''

Probably a prank, she told herself. Maybe just a joke by somebody in the message center. Some joke. Crumpling the pink slip to a tight ball, she banked it off the wall and into the wastebasket.

''Nice shot,'' Estrella observed.

''I hope so,'' Bo answered. Outside the office window a eucalyptus tree shuddered as the afternoon began its descent toward darkness.

Chapter 15

John D. Litten left the boy's club at 5:10, near the end of the business staff's Friday afternoon exit. Most people left early on Friday. Litten made it a point to be seen keeping precisely the hours demanded in his job description. Always.

He would have liked to hang around awhile, maybe watched some kids in one of the playrooms. But he'd done that last week under the guise of inspecting a sand table for possible replacement. A little boy in nylon shorts had repeatedly brushed Litten's thigh as the child pushed a plastic alligator through the sand. Leaving, Litten had pulled off his suit jacket and carried it casually over the bouncing bulge in his pants. He'd barely made it to the men's room. Too dangerous right now to play around like that. Probably too dangerous to stay in town.

In the hospital's parking lot he waved to Ben Skiff and considered closing the whole San Diego operation. It had been easy to set up, no big deal to let go of it. In these border towns it was a joke how easy it was to find just the right woman, desperate for money and more than willing to look the other way for enough of it. Some woman as stupid and hungry as Gramma. All you had to do was set up the place, hire the woman, let her handle it, and drop in from time to time for a little noontime delight. If things got hot, you just walked. No way to trace a property rented in the name of some dead guy from another state.

He'd learned to do that in the navy, too. When John Litten discovered that close to ten thousand dollars' worth of equipment was missing and traced the paper to a career noncom named Verlen Piva, Piva made a deal. In exchange for learning how Piva was saving up a nice nest egg for his retirement from the navy at thirty-five, Litten would ignore what he'd discovered. It was, Piva told him, the simplest thing in the world to walk into any town, check the old newspaper obits for the name of some guy near your age who'd bought the farm when he was a kid. Then you could get copies of the dead guy's birth certificate. With this you could get a Social Security card, driver's license, open bank accounts in Mexico where the IRS couldn't touch you. Instant identity. Untraceable.

The rest of Piva's lesson, about fencing off military equipment to surplus stores and a hundred organizations like the Ku Klux Klan, fell on deaf ears. John Litten had a better idea and a different need entirely. As soon as he got out of the navy he tried it. And it worked.

There'd been one foul-up in Gulfport, Mississippi, when they'd nearly nailed him. But he'd put on his old uniform, murmured something at the bus terminal about trying to get home to Montgomery, Alabama, before his mama died of cancer there in the hospital, and beat it out of town. In Mobile he'd got off the bus and hitchhiked to Miami, where it had been easy to start all over. It was always easy. John Litten sometimes wondered who his father was, because his mother's family put together didn't have the brains he had in his little finger. Still, he always kept a couple of military uniforms pressed and ready. People loved to believe a man in uniform was honest. And he didn't settle in any more small towns. Only big cities where nobody knew anybody's business. Or cared.

Back in his apartment John Litten nuked a frozen dinner and knocked it back with a line of cocaine and two ice-cold cans of Yoo-Hoo. The milky drink tasted just like the stuff called Chocolate Soldier when he was a kid. Jonny Dale couldn't have Chocolate Soldier very often. Just watery powdered milk Gramma got in big boxes from the county. Now John D. could have as much as he liked. And anything else he liked.

Selecting a Scandinavian video from his collection hidden beneath a false floor in a kitchen cabinet, he watched a skinny blond boy suck off a fat man wearing nothing but a feather boa and a Viking helmet. The video was an old one. Boring. He'd only bought it for the scene where the naked children throw cake batter on one another in a kitchen. That was classic. But the fat man was a downer. Litten didn't even bother to jerk off. He had something else on his mind. Something different and more exciting than any video. And what it felt like was revenge.

Last night had been risky, breaking into that church. And then when he'd stumbled against a podium or something up there on the left side of the altar and all of a sudden that church song called the doxology was blaring, echoing in the emptiness, and he'd dropped the spray paint and run like hell out into the night, that was scary. The music had followed him out into the dark where he'd crouched inside a huge bougainvillea and watched as a guard and two nuns scuttled through the open church door and turned on the lights. The music had stopped then, but he knew it was the doxology. Gramma took him to a Baptist church in Estherville sometimes. They sang it there, too. He wondered if the music was a message from Gramma that she liked the way he was getting even with the stupidity. Except Gramma had been stupid, too. So maybe it was just nothing.

But today wasn't nothing. Today at work, when the papers came and everybody was reading them with their coffee and talking about Satanists painting the church, John Litten felt something even better than he felt with the kids. He felt control. An immense control that reached out over a whole city like an invisible hand. His hand. He had them all in his hand. All the stupid assholes who thought they knew something. The police, the newspapers, the churches. And that woman named Ganage who'd started the whole thing with her stupid crap about Satan. They wanted a Satan? He'd give them one. And squeeze their nuts until they saw themselves for what they were. Stupid. Inferior.

He'd started today. Just made a few phone calls. To the police detective named Reinert, to the stupid social worker or whatever she was who messed up getting the dead kid's sister, to the psychologist, Cynthia Ganage. They were all stupid. The messages were all the same.

Padding into the kitchen in Gold-Toe socks, John Litten replaced the videotape in its hiding place, made sure he had enough coke for a couple of lines later tonight, and shoved the two Yoo-Hoo cans and the frozen dinner tray into the trash compactor. He felt like Superman, like a king, like somebody who can tell Superman and every king in the world exactly what to do. Like somebody who can *kill* Superman and all the kings if he wants to. And he does. They're all so stupid he wants to kill them, but there are too many.

Changing to a Hawaiian shirt and Bermuda shorts to look like a tourist, Litten headed out for the strip where the youngest hookers hung out. He'd bring one back for a while maybe. Dress her up in the angel costume. But the prospect held little excitement.

What was exciting was the game he was playing with a whole city of morons. And the fact that when the time came, he was going to kill one of them just for being stupid. He wondered which one it would be.

Chapter 16

It hadn't been easy to get into San Diego County's deteriorating jail to see Paul Massieu. Bo was glad the deputies enlisted to bring him back from New York had mistakenly left him in the same jail as the other man they'd picked up on the trip, whose alleged crime had taken place outside the city limits. In the mix-up she'd been able to fast-talk her way into a technically unauthorized visit, which was also technically a felony, if anybody noticed. But nobody would.

Behind the chipped black-enameled grille in the jail's barren waiting area only one woman sat amid piles of greasy manila folders. An open bottle of nail polish remover atop an inverted romance novel revealed that Bo had interrupted meditative pursuits best enjoyed in solitude. The other staff were gone for the day. From a dusty radio Willie Nelson's voice, if not his words, was recognizable.

"Yeah, whaddaya want?" the woman said with a lack of bon vivance born, Bo was sure, of innumerable unpleasant conversations with previous visitors to the jail.

Bo unclipped the Child Protective Services ID badge from her blouse and slipped it under the grille.

"I have permission to visit a prisoner named Paul Massieu," she said.

"This isn't visiting hours."

"I know. But there are mitigating circumstances that I've already discussed with the desk sergeant. I've agreed to speak with Mr. Massieu in the regular visitors' area to save trouble. You should have an order to that effect."

"Oh, yeah. Just wait."

There was no place to sit. Bo paced the bare corridor, reading and rereading a sign explaining in both English and Spanish that to bring drugs or alcohol into the jail was a felony. The sign matched the one outside the building, which had told her unauthorized conversations with prisoners were also felonious. Felonies seemed popular. Finally the woman bawled "Bradley?" in the empty hallway as if trying to be heard over a crowd. A deputy appeared from a battered metal door and wordlessly indicated another battered metal door, which he unlocked and motioned Bo to enter.

Inside, ten stools bolted to both the cement floor and the wall faced ten small, metal-paned windows. Beneath each window on the left was a wall phone, matched by one in an identical room on the other side of the wall. Well, not quite identical, Bo noticed. The walls of the visitors' side had recently been painted. Baby blue and dirty white. The prisoners-side walls were bare concrete. As Bo stood breathing the rotting grapefruit smell of enamel paint, a door opened on the other side and a prisoner in jail blues approached one of the tiny windows, sat and picked up the phone. Bo sat opposite, and picked up hers.

"Allo?" he said softly. "Oo are you?"

The accent was like Eva Broussard's, only magnified. The voice held a tremolo of fear.

"My name is Bo Bradley. I work for San Diego County's Child Protective Services, and Hannah Franer is one of my cases," she said into the phone, watching his face through the window. "You are the sole suspect in the rape-murder of Hannah's sister, Samantha. Serious charges, Mr. Massieu. Are you guilty of them?"

The frontal approach. Most likely to produce a telling response, if not a forthright answer. Bo watched as his right hand tightened around the plastic phone receiver held against an impressive upper jaw. The hand wore a patchwork of scar tissue and was missing its little finger. A bulky man, Paul Massieu might have looked simian except for a sort of intellectual refinement that seemed to cloak him like filtered light. He returned her interrogative stare with deep-set black eyes. Outrage, pain, confusion. But no menace. Not a hint of the disguised contempt Bo had seen in the eyes of many men who preyed upon women and children.

"When I met Bonnie," he began, struggling for precision in an uncomfortable language, "Sammi was very little. She did not know her real father. Hannah could remember him, but Sammi could not. I became like a father to Sammi." He breathed deeply and went on. "To have the trust of children is . . . is honor, *oui*?"

Bo had to nod in agreement.

"I would never break that honor. You will either believe or not . . . I could never hurt a little child. Not in any way."

Behind the riveted playhouse-sized window he exhaled. He'd answered the question. And Bo believed him.

San Diego's downtown airport was conveniently only blocks from the county jail, and Bo left Paul Massieu in plenty of time to meet Eva and Hannah's plane from Albany. Eating a bag of sourdough chips near the arrival gate she wondered why a man like Massieu—apparently healthy, intelligent, educated—would think he saw space aliens on a New York mountainside. Bo knew about delusions, about things seeming to have meaning that wasn't ordinarily there. The decaying body of an opossum on a freeway shoulder highlighted and terrible—a symbol of mindless human sprawl and its slaughter of nature. In an Italian restaurant a cheap candle flickering in a red glass had once brought Bo to tears with its message of the frailty of life, and the valor in not giving up. Emotional images. The stock-in-trade of manic depression. Always there.

But Paul Massieu had not seen just a rock or shrub that *felt* like a message from the universe; he'd actually observed something physical that shouldn't have been there. A hallucination, then. Except that Eva had said Paul didn't use drugs and had no brain injury or disorder that might produce hallucinations. So what had happened to Paul Massieu on that mountain? And for that matter why was it that unusual things always seemed to happen to people hanging around on mountains alone at night? Especially, according to Bo's grandmother, in Ireland.

Bo remembered the story of a now-dead kinsman named Paddy Danaher who threw a loaf-sized stone down a Pouleduve, or fairy-hole, on a mountain called Knockfierna late one night, only to have it thrown back in his face. Paddy Danaher's nose, Bo's grandmother had smiled, was crooked for the rest of his life. The wages of disbelief in shining creatures on mountains. Bo rubbed the bridge of her nose as the plane pulled into its gate.

"Could the silver people on the mountain just be fairies?" she greeted Eva Broussard and the tired, silent Hannah.

"You 'ave 'ad a long day, Bo. No?" Eva answered, her accent as thick as Paul's from exhaustion. "And your maiden name will be something like O'Rourke, am I right?"

"O'Reilly." Bo blushed. "And yes, it's been an interminable day. Let's get out of here before somebody recognizes us. Let's take our young lady safely to her castle on the beach where you both can get some rest. I just came from a visit with Paul," she said, leaning down to make eye contact with Hannah. "He's doing fine. And he can't wait to see you."

The child turned her freckled face abruptly from Bo's, but a nervous smile struggled at the corners of her mouth. Bo dropped to one knee and pulled Hannah gently toward her.

"Look at me, Hannah. I know you're mad at me and that's okay. You're just eight years old and you're tired and hurt and scared. Your mother and sister are gone, you've flown across the country twice in two days, and you feel like everything's just awful. I'd be angry, too. So if you look at me and I see the mad in your eyes, it won't make me get mad back because I understand why it's there. Later maybe we can be friends. Right now it's really okay to show how you feel."

Hannah wrapped a hand tightly about the beads pinned to her denim jacket and let her lower lip protrude in a childish pout. Then she turned to glare directly at Bo, her eyes tight and narrow.

"That's all right," Bo said, nodding. "It's all right to be mad. Maybe tomorrow you could walk on the beach and throw some rocks really hard into the water. I do that sometimes, when I feel like you do. What do you think?"

A relaxation of the muscles around Hannah's eyes revealed that she was considering it.

"Good," Bo concluded, rising.

Eva Broussard removed the calf-length swirl of her lined wool coat and smiled. "You've had excellent training," she told Bo as they followed the crowd through the terminal. "Not everyone could show such sensitivity . . ."

"Not everyone's been told to stop feeling," Bo replied.

"Ah. The manic depression?"

"Yeah." Bo sighed. "It tends to give one a different view."

"Your view is a lifeline for Hannah," Eva Broussard said thoughtfully. "Without you—"

"Without me she'd be in a San Diego County foster home by now, with strangers. As it is, she's a fugitive from the legal system and in the sole care of someone I don't really know. I've trusted you intuitively, Dr. Broussard, but—"

"I know you're taking enormous risks in protecting Hannah this way. I'll do everything I can to prove your intuitions valid." As if expecting this line of conversation, Eva Broussard reached into a black leather attaché case suspended from a matching shoulder strap and withdrew a large envelope. "Recognizing the legal difficulties you may face if things don't go as planned, I have provided for you documentation of my academic credentials, a complete professional history, and the names, addresses, and phone numbers of some thirty personal references. These include an archbishop, authorities in child psychiatry from the United States, Canada, and three European countries, as well as the current chief of the Iroquois Nation and a former U.S. president who has long admired my popular-psychology series. Each will support your decision to entrust Hannah to my care, in writing or in person if it comes to that." She smiled. "And please stop calling me Dr. Broussard. You know perfectly well that sounds like the villain in a French thriller involving unethical nuclear physicists."

Bo took the envelope, grinning. "And here we all thought the next messiah would be another *man*."

At the laughter of the two women beside her, Hannah looked up wide-eyed, and then yawned. Just like an ordinary, tired kid. Bo decided that yawn was the most beautiful thing she'd seen in years.

After settling Eva and Hannah in Del Mar, Bo made the long drive back to Estrella's house on the urban peninsula of Point Loma to pick up Mildred. At the curb she reminded herself not to say anything if the fox terrier had gained weight during her two days with the Benedicts. Estrella and Henry had been known to bake homemade dog biscuits for Mildred. Bo secretly cherished the notion that it was about time for Estrella and Henry to begin a family. An event that would eventually increase the likelihood of chocolate chip cookies as over dog biscuits.

Estrella opened the door before Bo had a chance to ring the bell.

"I was afraid you'd miss it," she said, "but you're just in time. Mildred! Mom's here. Bo, come on in the family room. You won't believe this."

Bo gathered up an elderly dog who behaved as though her mistress had just returned from years as a prisoner of war. "I won't believe *what*?" Bo asked through heartfelt canine kisses.

"KTUV's doing one of those special talk shows. And guess what the topic is."

"Pregnant teenage gang members talking about the impact of international trade on long-term budget reform? Republican nudists supporting greater restrictions on the booming snail industry? I'm too tired to watch TV, Es. I'm just going to take Mildred home and crash."

"No, you're not. Look."

As television station KTUV's logo faded over a cozy talk show set, Bo recognized one of the participants, dressed in a power-red tailored suit beside which the three other guests and the set itself seemed uniformly colorless. Cynthia Ganage. Her lipstick matched her outfit precisely. Bo sank into an overstuffed couch as Estrella placed a tray of vegetables and dip on the coffee table.

"Ganage?" Bo said, reaching for a celery stalk.

"*Sí, amiga*. And she's not there to talk about split ends."

"Our guests tonight," the host told the camera in an anchorman's bass, "are Dr. Cynthia Ganage, a psychologist specializing in Satanic child abuse, the Reverend Clyde T. Cleveland of the San Diego Whole Faith Tabernacle, Mrs. Brenda Hines-Gilroy, who has quite a story to tell us, and the Reverend Dr. Sandra Rae Harvey of San Diego's First Unitarian Church. Our topic tonight . . ." the camera moved in close, "Satan in San Diego. We'll be right back."

"Told you you weren't going anywhere," Estrella said, flinging herself beside Bo and pushing a button on the remote control. "I'm taping this for Henry. He had a meeting at the base. Wonder why they invited two preachers."

"The Unitarian's there for the rational approach, not renowned for its success in dealing with irrational issues. Watch. They'll eat her for lunch."

"A recent and rather sensational child abuse case has San Diegans thinking about an ancient symbol of evil," the host intoned after four commercials. "But does one isolated case, in which there apparently *is* a cult connection, although one involving space aliens rather than Satan, mean that America's Finest City is riddled with Satanists? Dr. Ganage?"

"It's all the same. Where there's smoke, there's fire," Cynthia Ganage said, gazing intently into the camera. "But it's bigger than that."

Bo could not think of a term to cover the muddle of non sequitur, mixed metaphor, and outright gibberish Ganage was using in lieu of coherent speech. Reverend Cleveland and Brenda whatever her name was, however, nodded as if Cynthia Ganage had actually said something.

"One of our own child abuse workers, a woman named Bo Bradley, was outwitted by these people at their hideout in upstate New York only yesterday. There can be no question that this is a conspiracy, a *nationwide* conspiracy," Ganage went on, tossing her shining hair. "And the sister of the child sacrificed here in San Diego has now been kidnapped to Canada. If this isn't a Satanic network, what is it?''

''A great way to make money?'' Bo answered.

The Reverend Clyde Cleveland, sweating under the studio lights, mopped his narrow pink brow with a wadded handkerchief and spoke in a fearful whisper. The Bible, he said, told of a time when Satan would rule the earth. In his view the escalating reports of Satanic activity around the country suggested that the time was near. He didn't think it unlikely that Satanic headquarters would be in San Diego. That's why, he explained, the mission had been desecrated. Wasn't it one of the oldest churches in the country?

Ganage and the woman named Brenda nodded as if this, too, made sense.

''And what do *you* think, Reverend Harvey?'' the host smiled genially. ''Is there anything to all this?''

A diminutive black woman with a streak of silver hair and enormous round glasses, Sandra Harvey clasped her hands and cocked her head at the camera. ''Of course there's something to this,'' she answered. ''Take the 'd' off 'devil' and you've got evil, right?''

Everybody was nodding. Bo nodded, too. ''Now make your move,'' she told the figure on Estrella's TV screen. ''You've got their attention.''

''And the highly publicized rape-murder of a little girl makes us all think about evil, where it comes from, how to stop it,'' Sandra Harvey continued, her words bearing the cadence of some Southern state. ''Maybe it's just a little easier to think about if we give it a name like Satan, and convince ourselves that it comes from outside us, outside our social systems, our books and ideas, our collective history as a species. But to externalize—''

''People worship Satan,'' the woman named Brenda interrupted, her voice shrill. ''They worship Satan in rituals where they make you drink blood and other . . . things. They did it to me when I was little. Then they make you forget it. You're crazy if you think there's no Satan!''

A wild, lost look in Brenda's blue eyes made Bo wince.

''We have been warned . . .'' Reverend Cleveland rasped

as Cynthia Ganage held a copy of her book on ritual child abuse before the camera.

"We'll be right back after these important messages," the host insisted as the scene cut to a commercial for cat litter.

"So what do you think?" Estrella asked, stretching sleepily inside a purple sweatshirt Bo had handpainted for her in gold Aztec symbols.

"I think purple's definitely your color, and I think I'm going home."

"And miss the exciting conclusion?"

"There won't be a conclusion," Bo said, struggling to lift a sleeping Mildred out of the couch. "There never is. But that clam-onion dip is fantastic, and I appreciate your taking care of Mildred. G'night, Es."

On the short drive home to her Ocean Beach apartment Bo tried to imagine a painting that would embody all the reactions spinning from Samantha Franer's death. Metallic paper dolls in murky darkness fleeing wrathful Puritan clerics in frock coats above a dusty, abandoned hell where nothing moved except the ghost of Dante Alighieri spending an eternity admiring his creation. A hanged woman on a Tarot card, the background sky raining tears. A little corpse with crystal hair. A painted quilt of a thousand random black rectangles, some glossy, some flat, some opaque, reflecting light in patterns that could make no sense. That painting would be the truth, Bo nodded to herself. A painting of evil. Inscrutable and ineradicable. It felt right.

Chapter 17

"Where can you get decent lox in this town?" Solon Gentzler bellowed through Bo's bedside phone at 6:45 A.M. With that voice, Bo thought as she struggled to hold her head off the pillow, he should have been an orator. But then as a lawyer maybe he already was. He sounded seven feet tall and deplorably alert.

"This must mean it's Saturday morning," she managed to pronounce. The words defined a sad, nearly tragic reality. She was going to have to wake up. "And there are two places for lox. One in La Jolla and one in the college area. Where are you staying?"

Lois Bittner had introduced Bo to the salty smoked salmon years ago in St. Louis. The orange fish had been folded wetly atop a bagel slathered with cream cheese. One encounter had been enough.

"Travelodge in Hotel Circle," Gentzler roared amicably. "Where I'm starving."

"I'll pick you up in an hour," Bo said into a pillowcase featuring opera-pink cabbage roses against which her hair looked like a neon wig. The linens had been purchased at a swap meet during a manic episode two years ago for their astonishingly reasonable price. Bo hated them and used them regularly, hoping they'd fade or come loose at the seams, either of which would justify donating them to a worthwhile charity. Fifty washings later they continued to look brand-new.

After replacing the phone in its cradle she removed the sheets and replaced them with a beige and cream pinstriped set. Then she folded those back into the linen closet in favor of a dramatic Southwestern design that looked like desert mountains in a hazy sunset. Sand brown, lavender, smoky purple. The message was clear.

"Do other women get these feelings as randomly as I do, or is it just women with manic depression?" she asked Mildred, still pretending to be asleep in her basket beside Bo's bed. The fox terrier raised one graying brown eyebrow.

"I mean *you* even managed an inappropriate liaison with that unwholesome miniature poodle up the street. He had *fleas*, Mil. And an insufferable attitude. What made you do it?"

The dog stretched long white legs and yawned. Then she pushed a chartreuse tennis ball from her basket onto the carpet and looked at Bo expectantly. A confusion initiated by Andrew LaMarche, whose Victorian intentions seemed at odds with his underwear, faded but did not vanish entirely.

"I'll take you out after I shower," Bo told the dog.

Fifteen minutes later, dressed in white cotton slacks and a white sweatshirt on which she'd stenciled "Aardvark Power" in teal blue acrylic, Bo let the sea breeze dry her hair as she walked Mildred. Yesterday's visit with Paul Massieu in San Diego County's crowded old jail had reinforced Eva Broussard's opinion of the man. He was innocent. Bo was sure of it, even if she couldn't say why. He just seemed so beaten and lost, sobbing in broken English across the plastic barrier between prisoner and guest, his twisted right hand with its missing finger white around the phone that enabled them to talk through the shield. A French Canadian lost in an American nightmare whose origins, Bo knew from a college research paper, lay in seventeenth-century Boston and a power-mad governor named John Winthrop.

"Why can they think I raped a child because I believe what I have seen? Because I saw those people like *papier d'argent*, like silver-paper people, on the mountain? Why does this mean that I could kill a child with sex? *C'est fou*, insane!"

"Yes," Bo agreed without argument, and then didn't know what else to say. That somebody drew a yellow face on Samantha Franer's abdomen? That five years after the landing of the *Mayflower* a woman named Anne Hutchinson was exiled to predictable Indian slaughter because she was smarter, more charismatic, a kinder leader, and another gender than the governor of the Boston Colony? That in her absence a culture deeply suspicious of yellow drawings and silver people had come into being?

"There are no silver-paper people in the Bible," Bo told Paul Massieu, "so your belief in them puts you outside the regular religious system in this country. To a lot of people that automatically makes you evil, and so it makes sense to them that you'd do evil things, like rape children. Do you understand?"

"No," Massieu had answered, wide-eyed. "I don't."

"Neither does the ACLU," Bo told him. "Don't worry, they'll help you. In the meantime," she'd lowered her voice so the supervising guard couldn't hear, "let me tell you that Eva and Hannah are here, in hiding, so that as soon as you get out of jail, Hannah can be near you. You can't mention this to anyone. She needs you desperately, Paul. You're all she has now. We're not sure she's going to make it through without permanent damage. She's stopped talking, and . . ."

He'd straightened his huge shoulders and calmed himself at the words. "She's like Bonnie. I know that. She must have gentleness and strength around her. She's like her mother . . . like her mother was. I won't fail. I'll protect Hannah."

When the aging dog tired of chasing her tennis ball Bo picked her up and carried her back to the apartment.

"You're too old for such exertion," she told the fox terrier ensconced on the freshly made bed, "and so am I. If a pediatrician with a French accent calls, tell him I've taken a vow of chastity that precludes everything, including marriage."

On the drive inland to pick up Gentzler Bo congratulated herself on Hannah's care. The child and Eva Broussard had settled quietly into the cozy little beach studio last night, and Hannah had fallen asleep to the sound of surf almost immediately. Bo and Eva had talked softly on a patio overlooking the watery curve of the planet.

"What is this place?" Eva Broussard questioned, laughing. "Where are we?"

"At the edge of a continent," Bo replied. "And in big trouble."

"You don't really mean that, do you? You don't feel overwhelmed and incapable. You know you can help this child, that you can do what makes sense."

"I run on hypomania all of the time," Bo admitted, nodding. "Even when I'm fine, I'm not like other people. Too much energy, too much arrogance. The lithium takes that away, slows me down. I'm not on it right now. And yes, I'm sure that what we're doing is the right thing for Hannah even though I'm breaking rules and could lose my job. I don't care. This makes sense. But there's something else . . ."

"Yes?" Eva Broussard questioned from a chaise lounge where she sipped cognac from a cup embossed with a conch shell design. She exuded openness, interest. "What else?"

Bo tossed back her hair, lit a cigarette and regarded the other woman. A stranger, but already a friend. It occurred to Bo that beyond Estrella, she had no friends. No husband or lover, no children, no family left alive. She'd been a loner for years, and that was okay. Mildred was good company. But it would be nice to have someone to talk to again, like Lois Bittner. Someone wise and different. Someone who could see beyond psychiatric symptoms to what lay beneath. "I'm a little slow right now," she began, "not manicky at all, so I can't put it together. But nothing about this case has felt right from the beginning. Everybody's jumped to conclusions. This woman named Cynthia Ganage is building a professional reputation as a devil-hunter, the police think anything they don't agree with must be criminal, all of a sudden somebody decides to desecrate a church, and the ACLU sees 'landmark case' written all over Paul Massieu, who's really in jail because he thinks he saw little men from outer space in upstate New York. It's a mishmash. Did he really see something up there, Eva? Did you?''

Gracefully Eva Broussard unfolded her body from the chaise, stood and stretched. ''Yes, he did,'' she answered, ''and no, I didn't. What I have seen is my own mortality reflected in the hunger of people for something to bring new ideas, to bring a way out. But their real experience eludes me. I only document it and quite possibly will never understand it. What else about the case bothers you, Bo?''

In the moonlight the woman's cropped white hair looked like a helmet. Over the Pacific Ocean Orion stood belted with stars.

''Lots,'' Bo went on. ''Little pieces. The fact that somebody's getting away with murder and nobody cares. The parts that don't fit anywhere, like the face drawn on Samantha's stomach and—'' From the screen door to the left of the patio a small, sharp intake of breath was audible beneath a canopy of coral vine.

''You may come out and join us, Hannah,'' Eva said quietly. ''We aren't keeping secrets. We were only speaking softly because we thought you were asleep and didn't want to wake you.''

The child stumbled into Eva's arms, weeping. Bo noticed the three strands of beads pinned now to a maroon sweater with cream-colored piping. Hannah clutched at the beads with nervous fingers.

''Do you know about this yellow drawing on Samantha's stomach?'' Eva asked as if the topic were not fraught with horror.

The straw-blonde head nodded. Bo exhaled smoke and forced herself to become very still.

''You saw this drawing on Samantha?'' Eva Broussard's voice was like a silken rope, pulling.

A nod.

''Did Goody draw it?''

A snuffle, a shake of the head.

"Do you know who drew a yellow face on Samantha, Hannah?"

The round face turned up toward Eva, convulsing with something Bo recognized as guilt.

"Oh, Hannah," the Indian woman's eyes registered a sudden understanding, "*you* painted the mask on Samantha to make her feel better where it hurt, didn't you?"

A shuddering nod, then sobs.

Eva gathered up the shaking girl and sat on a deck chair stroking the child's hair. After a while she explained to Bo.

"It is an Iroquois tradition, rather complex. The girls have seen a midwinter celebration. I took them myself. The masks, the 'false faces,' represent things seen in dreams. At midwinter, if someone is ill with unhappiness, they search their dreams for these spirit faces, which are the things they must have in order to survive. When they know, they tell the tribe and the tribe will provide what is needed. A companion or a skill, or something like forgiveness for a wrongdoing. At all the festivals people appear in the crowd wearing these husk masks. They are for insight, for healing. Hannah was trying to heal her sister by drawing a healing mask over her pain."

Bo imagined the scene. The two little girls in their Raggedy Ann sheets, the younger one in pain and terrified that Goody would kill her mother if she told. The older one trying to manage the situation. The older one, burdened always with knowing just enough more to feel responsible.

Softly Bo had knelt beside Hannah and looked straight into the child's eyes. A clear, unveiled look in which there was no pretense. "I had a little sister, too," she said. "Her name was Laurie and she died, just like your sister Samantha did. And then my mother died, just like your mother did. And I was *so* scared and sick. But pretty soon I could start feeling better. You're going to feel better, too, Hannah. I promise."

The wide-set eyes looked back, a brittle smile spasming in the lips. Then Hannah fumbled with the safety pin holding three strips of beaded straw to her sweater. Slowly she took one of the strips off the pin and handed it to Bo.

"They're grieving beads," Eva whispered. "They represent a gift of words for one whose senses are blunted by sadness. Hannah is offering her words to help your sadness."

Beneath the bowl-shaped Pacific darkness Bo felt perfectly isolated, locked in an extended moment that embodied truths too large for her grasp. "Thank you, Hannah," she answered softly, taking the beads from a hand at once childlike and ancient. "Thank you for your words."

At the Travelodge Bo scanned the lobby for an immense attorney whose voice could be heard as far as Tijuana. Somebody who looked like a sumo wrestler, or maybe a lumberjack. No dice. The only figure obviously waiting was a short, barrel-chested guy in an alligator polo shirt that had once been white, before it was washed with something blue. Probably the same jeans he had on, which were too long and frayed where they scuffed the ground at the heel.

"Take me to your lox!" he boomed genially. "That is, if your name's Bo Bradley."

"I was expecting Demosthenes," Bo told him on the way to the restaurant.

"My folks wanted me to be a cantor," Solon Gentzler explained. "Big disappointment when I couldn't carry a tune in a washtub. There was nothing for it but to accept defeat and go to law school. Let me show you."

Throwing his head back he belted out the chorus of "Sunrise, Sunset" from *Fiddler on the Roof*. Mildred, Bo thought privately, could more accurately reproduce the tune.

"The Met's loss is the bar's gain," she agreed. "So what are you doing with Paul Massieu?"

Over a breakfast impressive for its lavish display of calories he outlined strategy.

"The guy's innocent of the charge, but that's not our point. Our thing is, the evidence for the arrest includes references to cult aspects of the case such as a symbol drawn on the victim and Massieu's admitted membership in some group that sees spaceships and metal people. Even if the guy was guilty, the arrest is no good. He's got a constitutionally protected right to exercise whatever beliefs he wants to. You can't arrest people based on their beliefs. Not in this country."

"So what will happen? When can you get him out of jail?"

Bo decided to withhold what she knew about the curious drawing on Samantha Franer's abdomen until she assessed the extent to which she might trust Solon Gentzler. So far, he seemed okay.

"They can't hold him longer than Monday. That's the law. I've signed on as co-counsel with his appointed attorney. I'll be at the preliminary hearing on Monday. We'll get him out of jail then, but of course he'll have to stay around if there's a trial. So what's your part in all this?"

Bo checked her watch and wondered why she felt so restless. Like there were forty things she should be doing instead of nursing a third cup of coffee over the ruin of an epic breakfast. Restlessness wasn't good. It could mean trouble. She made a mental note to watch it.

"I have to document the progress of the case for juvenile court," she said casually. "The status of the alleged perp in the criminal system will be crucial to Hannah's placement, when she's located."

That last bit either sounded crisply professional or hopelessly phony. Bo wasn't sure which.

"You're bullshitting me," Gentzler said, grinning. His teeth showed evidence of successful orthodontia. "What are you really up to? Anything I need to know?"

Hopelessly phony.

"I'm not sure yet," Bo replied. "I'll know more later, I think."

"Great. You'll tell me over dinner. Seafood. I don't eat shellfish, but I love that mahi mahi. Meanwhile I'll give you a copy of everything I've got on Massieu, just to help you know more. Do you think there's any connection between this case and that church desecration?"

"Yes," Bo answered. "But not anything obvious. Do you have any kids, Solon?"

Two could play this game.

"I'm not married," he replied. "Haven't found a woman who wants what I want out of life. Somebody Jewish, traditional, smarter than I am. The usual. She's out there, though. In the meantime I'm free for dinner."

Bo wasn't going to let go of it.

"Do you care about children, about what happens to them when adults get caught in the legal system?"

Solon Gentzler gazed levelly at the parking lot outside the restaurant window. "I care about keeping this country from becoming a police state," he said. "That my life's work."

Bo grabbed her keys and stood. "That's what I thought."

Chapter 18

Bo dropped Solon Gentzler at his hotel and slipped a tape of Handel's Second Concerto for Two Choruses into the BMW's tape deck. The introduction, she mused, might make a provocative sound-back for a pantyhose promo. It would feature a lissome mother of three who just loves her job as a molecular engineer but can still toss off her lab coat in time to drink champagne with a tuxedoed husband in the spray of an Italianate fountain. The husband has chosen this moment to present her with a rope of pearls because her eyes remind him of infinity. In the final frame her reasonably priced pantyhose have not yet run. "May the king live forever!" sang two choruses as Bo miraculously located a parking space on Narragansett only doors from her apartment building. She wondered if she could find a job in advertising if Madge succeeded in getting her fired over this case. Dog food commercials might be fun. Or those ads for 900 services where you could find true love or have your palm read over the phone. Bizarre, but no more so than this case, which seemed to be tapping a vein of primitive tribalism in the community. Everybody in guarded camps of opinion, each one of which seemed to be missing something. But what?

The sudden accumulation of men in her life aside, Bo was free of distractions and able to think clearly. No mania, not a hint of depression. Everything she'd done so far regarding Hannah Franer was, rationally speaking, perfectly sane. The child was safe in Eva Broussard's care, seeming to have begun already her journey out of grief. That Madge Aldenhoven would never acknowledge the wisdom of what Bo had done was irrelevant. So was the fact that Madge had put Bo on probation and was no doubt plotting at this very moment a future in which Bo Bradley would be merely an unpleasant memory. What wasn't irrelevant was a universal lack of insight into what was actually going on.

"So what *is* actually going on?" Bo asked the musicians of the London Symphony. In the final chords there was only music.

In her apartment Bo ignored both the blank canvas beckoning from its easel in the sunny living room and her blinking answering machine. Instead she took Mildred to a grassy park and pored over a folder of information Gentzler had given her. A clinical description of the injuries that had resulted in Samantha Franer's death, signed by Andrew J. LaMarche, M.D. Copies of warrants for the arrests of Paul Luc Massieu, thirty-six, a Canadian citizen, and Bonnie Corman Franer, twenty-nine. Bonnie Franer's warrant was stamped "Deceased." Legal documents setting forth the opinion of the American Civil Liberties Union that a San Diego County Criminal Court had screwed up royally. Cases in which the United States had opposed people named Seeger and Ballard were cited as precedents, as well as a California case in which an unspecified "People" had opposed somebody named Woody. Bo tried not to envision a woodpecker in the dock, and failed. There were also newspaper clippings.

As Mildred rolled in the grass Bo read the most recent clippings. Cynthia Ganage had suggested that Paul Massieu might be issuing orders from jail to escalate Satanic activity in San Diego as a protest against his incarceration. She suggested that San Diegans purchase her recently self-published book, *Protecting Your Children from Satanic Abuse*, available by mail order. Dar Reinert was quoted as hoping public overreaction would subside, and asked that citizens not call 911 to report Satanic graffiti in public places, which was in his opinion the work of bored teenagers seeking attention. A memorial service for Bonnie and Samantha was mentioned, to be held tomorrow afternoon at St. Theresa's Church. Father Frank Goodman would officiate.

Bo scratched the fox terrier's white chest and thought about taping the service so that Hannah could hear it later. She hoped Frank Goodman would chant something. The guy had a great voice. Like an Irish tenor, except with a name like Goodman he probably wasn't Irish.

Goodman.

The realization hit Bo at the back of her tongue. The gag reflex.

"No," she said to Mildred. It can't be. Not him. Not a priest."

But her thoughts ran on. Bonnie had taken the girls to his church. That's why he came to the hospital. Would a three-year-old call somebody named Goodman "Goody"? It wasn't unlikely.

Twenty minutes later Bo, accompanied by one exuberant fox terrier, knocked at the door of St. Theresa's rectory. "I'd like to see Father Goodman," she told the housekeeper.

He was in back, shooting baskets with an older priest wearing a cassock. In T-shirt and sweatpants, Frank Goodman looked even younger than he had at St. Mary's Hospital. "Hello." He grinned, tossing the ball expertly to the older priest and jogging toward Bo. "Aren't you the CPS investigator on the Franer case? You were at the hospital."

"Yes," Bo answered. She kept her gaze open and neutral despite the grisly suspicion that had brought her. This had to be done quickly. Mildred, sensing Bo's edginess, began to growl. "And you're Goody," Bo pronounced.

Her timing was perfect, even with a sour-tasting nausea lurking in her throat. A snake's timing. Quick and clean. He hadn't had time to prepare for the assault, and would inadvertently display some minuscule acknowledgment if he recognized the damning sobriquet. Just a second of darkness in the eyes, or a twitch in the muscle connecting jaw to skull. And Bo wouldn't miss it. She'd know. But there was nothing.

"Huh?" he said, and cocked his head at Mildred. "Dogs usually like me. What's her name?"

Bo slumped to a sitting position in the grass. "Mildred." She sighed. "And sorry, I was just running a check on your potential as an arch-deviant. You flunked."

Frank Goodman sat cross-legged beside Bo and scratched Mildred's head. From his dark curls floated the unmistakable odor of incense. Realizing that her choice of seating would inevitably produce grass stains on her white slacks, Bo decided it was divine retribution. A small price to pay.

"You thought I was the one who hurt Samantha," Frank Goodman said as though he'd solved a puzzle. "The police already checked that out. I was at a diocesan meeting the entire day she was . . . injured. Then I drove back here with Father Karolak." He nodded toward the elderly priest who continued to perform impressive slam dunks, showing off. "I read the Office in the garden in full view of two priests and the cook, ate dinner with the same two priests and a businessman from the parish who's going to pay for restuccoing the educational buildings, and watched an Agatha Christie rerun on PBS, again with Father Karolak, who is quite verbal about his preference for Dorothy Sayers. Then I went to bed. Didn't the police tell you?"

For a man who'd just been accused of one of the most repugnant behaviors imaginable, he seemed remarkably unruffled.

"No," Bo said into her knees, "but then I didn't ask. It hadn't occurred to me yet. Not until I thought you might be an Irish tenor, except you're not Irish." Her grandmother, Bo mused miserably, would have done twenty novenas and made a pilgrimage to Muiredach's Cross, just to atone for her granddaughter's nasty mind. "Look, I'm really sorry, but—"

"Don't be," Frank Goodman said. "It happens. Priests have been known to molest children. The church is finally admitting it, and keeping these guys away from kids. So why did you call me Goody?"

"Hannah Franer, before she stopped talking altogether

when she heard of her mother's death, told me and a woman named Eva Broussard that Samantha said Goody hurt her."

The priest grimaced and shook his head. "That poor kid. It makes sense that you suspected me, with the name and all. I wish I could do something for Hannah. I read in the paper that you were unsuccessful . . ."

Bo pulled Mildred into her arms and turned to Frank Goodman. "Can you keep a secret?" she asked.

"Part of the job. Want to make a confession?"

Bo considered the possibility that trusting Frank Goodman with too much information might be dangerous. "Yeah," she nodded. "But only if it's real, as in privileged communication. Do we need to go into a confessional for that?"

"Nah," he replied, "but I do need a stole to make it official. Wait right here."

In minutes he was back, with the traditional length of purple satin flapping over his T-shirt. "So?"

"I confess that I set Cynthia Ganage up with that story to keep Hannah out of the very system I got her into. To keep her out of foster care. I knew Ganage would blow it all over the papers within ten minutes and give us a cover. Hannah's here, Father Goodman. She's in very, very fragile shape, but she's with Eva, who's adopted her as an Iroquois, like a granddaughter, and since Eva's also a shrink I know she can take care of Hannah. It'll help when Paul gets out of jail and Hannah can see him. Until then, they're laying low in a beach place up in Del Mar. Waiting."

"I can go to visit Hannah at any time, if it'll help," Goodman offered. "She knows me. The mother brought the girls to church here occasionally. Hannah was the quiet one, always looked a little sad. This has got to be hell for her."

"She's like the proverbial house of cards," Bo said, throwing twigs for Mildred. "One more shock, even the smallest break in what's left of her sense of security, and we may lose her to a world inside her head. It's a tightrope right now. Dangerous. But I'll ask Eva if she thinks a visit from you would help."

Bo allowed the youthful priest to pull her to her feet. "The best thing that can happen would be the arrest of the creep who really did this." She sighed. "But there don't seem to be any good leads."

"What about the day-care center?" Goodman asked. "I told the police Samantha stayed at a center while Bonnie worked at a part-time job and Hannah was in school. Paul was gone a lot of the time, scouting for property out in the desert. Bonnie found a place for Samantha to stay. Don't you have that information in your reports?"

Her file on the Franer case, Bo realized as Mildred dropped a soggy twig on Frank Goodman's foot, had not been updated since her return from New York. But all new information would have gone through Madge Aldenhoven. And stayed there. Madge was covering her own tail, making sure Bo couldn't botch the case more than she already had. For once, Bo didn't blame her.

"Do you have an address for this day-care center?" she asked the priest.

"Sure. It's on Kramer, where it dead-ends in a cul-de-sac. But the police have already been there, I'm sure."

"Just curiosity," Bo said as she headed for her car. "I'll see you at the memorial service tomorrow. And thanks."

"Hey!" he yelled from the curb. "I forgot your penance."

Bo pretended not to hear.

A professionally lettered sign above the door identified the residence as KRAMER CHILD CARE CENTER. Gray security bars covered every window of the white-shingled house. The place looked, Bo thought, like Beaver Cleaver's suburban home converted to a jail. The house was long and rectangular and set squarely in the middle of the cul-de-sac. Behind it one of San Diego's innumerable small canyons sloped down through two hundred feet of scrub and sage to the usual seam of eucalyptus and sycamore bordering the canyon's drainage stream. Beside the driveway to the left several mature bougainvilleas created a mass of blazing magenta bracts and murderous thorns over a six-foot chain-link fence. To the right closely set white oleanders, equally mature, formed a dense, attractive wall between the day-care center and the adjoining property. An older house like thousands built in

San Diego during the 1960s well maintained. And private. Very private. Bo carried Mildred, squirming, to the door and rang the bell.

"*Sí?*" a woman answered. In her arms a wet, naked baby boy of about a year struggled to be put down. Behind her a dark-haired girl holding an overweight orange cat stared at Bo with shy curiosity. The cat also stared, its orange tail sweeping laconically beneath the girl's arms.

"I'm Bo Bradley, from Child Protective Services," Bo began, clutching the trembling fox terrier firmly. "And although I know the police have already been here—"

But Mildred, propelled by centuries of canine honor, chose to ignore the message in Bo's grip. A series of imperious barks was accompanied by much thrashing of terrier legs and a resultant small rip in the sleeve of Bo's sweatshirt. The orange cat climbed over the girl's head, causing the child to giggle and stumble against the leg of the baby, who howled in indignation. The woman narrowed her eyes and looked at Bo as if she were there to sell something unpleasant.

"I'll just put the dog in the car and get my identification," Bo said. It occurred to her that this might be the worst interview she'd ever done. A fiasco. The woman obviously spoke Spanish, which Bo did not. And their introduction could only be described as "not conducive to confidence." Bo wondered if her own lighthearted approach might be construed as harebrained. Maybe she was getting a little silly, exuberant, overconfident. A little manic. What was she doing on a Saturday, on her own time, checking out leads with grass stains on her rump and a dog in her arms? A bad sign. Or was it?

Maybe she'd just fallen into the situation through a series of conversations and was exhibiting praiseworthy devotion to her job.

When hell freezes, Bradley. Your devotion to this job is precisely as deep as your checking account. What are you really here for?

The image of a little girl with wide-set eyes handing Bo a strip of beaded rush materialized and then vanished. Hannah had been able to reach out from the papery shell of her own threatened survival. To reach out and offer comfort to another whose pain she understood. In that act, Bo realized as she shoved Mildred into the fading BMW, the child had secured a human bond that demanded Bo's best. Nothing crazy about that. But she'd keep an eye on her thoughts, just to be sure. The minute she started feeling grandiose or dispatched by mystical forces, she'd back off. At the door the little girl hopped from one foot to the other while explaining that her mama had been giving her brother, Jesus, a bath and was now "putting pants on him."

Bo checked her own response to this news for any hint of seeping religiosity. There was none. Latin people routinely named baby boys Jesus. The girl, Bo mentally bet the BMW and a year's rent on her apartment, would be named María.

"I will be there soon," the woman's voice called from inside the house. "Luisa, take Papa Cat to the yard."

Bo cursed herself as an ethnic bigot while Papa Cat eluded Luisa by leaping atop a television and overturning a backlit representation of the Sacred Heart in a frame of starched red lace.

"What do you want?" the woman asked as she emerged from a hall to the right of the living room, still carrying the baby. Jesus, now clad in a disposable diaper and tiny white dress shirt, smiled and offered Bo the remainder of his bottle. From the scent wafting through the door, it was grape juice. Bo sighed and reminded herself that symbolism exists entirely in the mind of its observer.

"I'm from Child Protective Services," she repeated, showing her ID badge. "I'd like to talk to you about Samantha Franer."

The woman grimaced. "The police, they already be here," she said. "I tell them all the children do good here. I take care of them. And I have a helper. This bad thing did not happen to the child here." The dark eyes dropped to a point below the handle of the security door. "No man work here," she whispered, glancing at Luisa, now rolling on a flowered couch with the cat. "No man."

"But could you just tell me," Bo began, "is this your house? Are you a licensed day-care center? How are children referred—?"

"I don't want talk," the woman said, turning from the door. "I already talk to police." In the woman's back, the tense set of the wide shoulders under a thin blue sweater, Bo recognized controlled emotion. But what emotion? Grief? Fear? Whatever it was, a fierce determination held it in check. It was curious, unaccountable. And impenetrable.

Bo headed back to her car and noticed Luisa, opening the heavy security door to wave. At her open car door, Bo waved in return as something orange streaked from the house and across the yard toward the oleanders. Mildred, aroused from a nap by Bo's return, was standing on the front seat, her forelegs braced against the dash. Mildred did not fail to see the streak. With a look of delight, the dog catapulted out the open car door, around the BMW's dented rear bumper, and into the oleander. A trail of barking led downward, into the canyon.

"What next?" Bo asked a cloudless sky as she struggled past twenty yards of dense, white-flowered shrubbery. "You're too old for this," she yelled at the echoing barks. "Remember your arthritis, and you're going to get burrs." There was a predictable absence of response.

The fenced backyard of the day-care center boasted a swing set, large sand box, and several small play tables. At the back of the yard a gate in the chain-link fence opened to a narrow trail leading down into the canyon. Bo edged her way around the perimeter of the fence and began a dusty descent toward the now-stationary cacophony of barks. Mildred had, apparently, treed Papa Cat.

Except the noise had its origin off to the left of the path, halfway up the canyon's side where there were no trees. Only fragrant sage bushes, prickly pale green tumbleweeds, scrub, and rocks. Beyond the trail the canyon wall was treacherous. A terrain of loosening concretized sandstone spall, compacted under tons of seawater when San Diego had been an ocean bed. Bo slipped as a football-sized clump of dirt broke raggedly under her weight and tumbled to rest against what looked like a giant mayonnaise jar full of brown water. It *was* a giant mayonnaise jar full of brown water. Bo stared at the object as comprehension rose sluggishly in her brain. Tea. Somebody was making sun tea in a jar where there should be no people or jars, much less tea. Mildred's barks, tiring now, were only a few yards ahead. Rounding a particularly unstable outcropping, Bo found the dog yipping upward at something on a ledge behind which a crude cave had been dug. The something was not an orange cat. It was a gargoyle, a hunkering figure Bosch might have painted if Bosch had painted urban hermits.

"Oh, my God no." Bo gasped as a sunburned face stared wildly from beneath a thatch of filthy reddish hair. The huge eyes under bleached-out lashes were more frightened than her own. But she'd seen eyes like that before. She knew what to do.

Chapter 19

At eight o'clock Bo found herself seated across from Solon Gentzler on the balcony of a La Jolla seafood restaurant whose chef, if rumors were to be believed, knew not only the secret of perfect sole *blanchaille*, but also the more intimate secrets of several San Diego society matrons. From the distracting flash of moonlight on diamonds about the area, Bo guessed that a few matrons were hanging around for another glimpse of his culinary style.

"I love haddock," Gentzler said with enthusiasm, shrugging off a rumpled suit jacket bearing a Beverly Hills label, "but I'm going to have the shark bisque and then just a simple poached flounder with capers. How's the wine?"

Bo gazed down the length of her own freckled arm to a crystal balloon glass in whose depths a pale golden liquid said poetic things about sun and rain in California's northern valleys. Her hair, she acknowledged, was reflecting candlelight in precisely the way her shampoo intended. And the merest dab of imported scent, strategically placed, was perhaps not the only reason Gentzler's animated gaze kept drifting to the V of a casual little green silk blouse that cost a fortune and gave her eyes a sealike depth. While she knew perfectly well where this evening would lead if she opted for that direction, Bo chose not to analyze her presence in a candlelit restaurant with a lawyer too young to remember where he was when Kennedy was assassinated. Whatever happened, Solon Gentzler would not burden it with cumbersome considerations. Like marriage.

"The wine's lovely," she answered. "But I'm having trouble with the concept of a tuna salad that costs $27.50. Do you realize how much tuna you could buy for $27.50? People are starving, Sol, and we—"

"It's because it's fresh bluefin," he apologized for the restaurant's politically incorrect extravagance, blushing slightly. "And it's on Gentzler, Brubaker, Harris and Gentzler, the family law firm. Brubaker's my sister, incidentally. A CPA as well as an attorney. She'd tell you this dinner is a business expense."

"Who's Harris?" Bo grinned. "And I thought you worked for the ACLU."

"Harris is my dear old mother, who graduated law school four years before I did. We call her Harry. And the ACLU work is pro bono. We all do it. It's sort of a family hobby." He leaned back and stared at the darkening Pacific Ocean beyond the balcony. "My *zayde*, my paternal grandfather, made it out of the death camps. His first wife and baby son didn't. The baby's name was Solon, which explains my old-fashioned name, and why we believe so strongly in what the ACLU does . . ." he turned to smile at Bo, "among which is to make sure people like your Paul Massieu don't get hanged as rapists just because they believe in little green men."

"Silver," Bo sighed. "Little silver men. I think I'll have the broiled snapper."

The contrast was still dizzying. The afternoon's terrifying discovery with a man who called himself Zolar and lived in a canyon because a huge network of people in San Diego were trying to control his mind with radio waves. The radio waves, he said, couldn't reach him there. From Zolar to the sort of eatery weekending movie stars were known to patronize. A shift of epic proportions. Bo thought of Andrew LaMarche's *le monde* and sighed again. There were too many worlds. And Zolar had shown her the grimmest yet. She watched as Solon Gentzler reverently attacked a bowl of bisque the size of a hubcap. Could she tell him about what Zolar had shown her in the canyon? About what she was sure it meant? Would Solon Gentzler believe *anything* she said after she told him just why she was not uncomfortable chatting with madmen? Too risky. Reluctantly she conceded that she should have returned one of LaMarche's six phone calls, as Estrella advised. It was, after all, his words that had made sense of the bizarre scene Zolar showed her.

The man in the canyon behind the Kramer Child Care Center was suffering from schizophrenia, no question. Bo knew the symptoms from others met on her own psychiatric sojourns, and he'd told her as much when he named the litany of neuroleptic drugs he'd been given at a "crazy bin." Thorazine, Haldol, and Cogentin to curb the thick tongue, tremors, tics, and muscular convulsions caused by the first two. Zolar knew his way through a psychiatric pharmacy and was having no more of it. Bo wondered what his real name was. And how long it had been since he'd tried to get help for the illness. The drugs he mentioned were the old standbys, used for decades, lousy with side effects that felt worse than the symptoms they were supposed to curb. But the guy was still young and his elaborate paranoia was a good sign that he could respond well to the right medications. Bo's bet was he couldn't be much over twenty-five. He probably wouldn't have been sick longer than seven or eight years. And there were some impressively helpful new medications for schizophrenia now, if only he'd try again.

"So what is the dog here for?" Zolar had whispered from his cave after Bo defused his anxiety by sitting on the ground and performing her head-ducking act. No threatening eye contact. No aggressive bodily movement. No invasion of his brittle and hard-won psychic sanctuary. Simple courtesy, primate-style. "They don't usually send dogs. Dogs are nicer." At six feet and well muscled, he looked like a healthy if somewhat soiled young giant, lost from myth and unaccountably stuffed into a California hillside. Bo was certain he'd played football in high school, before the pitiless chemistry in his brain made a normal life impossible.

"Dogs *are* nicer," she agreed wholeheartedly, looking at the ground. "And this is my dog, Mildred. We're not here to see you. We were at a house up there to . . . to try to help a little girl who got hurt." Bo could not have said why she chose to explain her presence in that way. It was simply the truth. A spill of dusty gravel from Zolar's ledge indicated sudden movement. Then a sharp intake of breath.

"Goody," he intoned raggedly, beginning to rock from the waist. "Goody, Goody, Goody . . ."

Bo gasped and glanced up through the scrim of her own red hair. He was crying. Incredible. How did he know that name? Either he *was* Goody, or he knew something *about* Goody. But she'd have to act fast or he'd rock and chant himself into a trance. Another world where no one could reach him. Rising slowly and away from the swaying figure, Bo grasped Mildred to her side and said, "Show us where you saw Goody. We need to know about Goody." The words, pronounced clearly and with agonizing slowness, would either have an effect or they wouldn't. He continued to rock.

But he knew something. He knew the name by which a murdered child identified her killer. How could he know? Was he that killer? The stock lunatic of countless horror stories, lurking in shadows like a half-remembered nightmare? Bo felt her abdominal muscles tighten at the thought. She didn't want it to be so. But he lived here, close to the day-care center's yard. Had Samantha somehow wandered off into the canyon and then been raped by this disoriented man?

Just because you don't want it to be so doesn't mean it isn't. Be very careful here, Bradley. Be rational.

Fat chance.

Bo summoned her wits and a vast resource of something she couldn't name, and bent them toward the ragged man. She had to know. Now. "Hear me!" she thought ferociously into the air between them. "I'll try to help you. But right now you've got to hear me." Hard to do it without eye contact. Hard to solidify any connection at all with a young man whose sole desire was to avoid a world in which people existed only to plot against him. "Show us something about Goody," she said again.

The chanting stopped as he clambered down from the ledge and stood ten feet from Bo. "Hi, Mildred," he whispered, holding out his hand toward the fox terrier. "Come on, I'll take you."

Bo felt a stab of fear. The identical fear, she realized, that others had at times felt for her. The fear of someone who does not share the same, widely agreed-upon reality as everyone else. What did he mean by "I'll take you"? What if he took Mildred? Bo hated herself for her reaction and with an inadvertent appeal to St. Francis, the protector of animals, she set the aging dog on the ground. From the side of her right eye Bo watched the man hunker, pull something from his shirt pocket. Mildred advanced, her docked tail wagging. Bo could hear the booming pulse in her own arteries as if the volume had been turned up. But it was jerky. The guy was just giving Mildred a piece of beef jerky.

As relief and a bitterly personal remorse washed over Bo, she found herself wondering where he got jerky. And tea bags for his sun tea. A glance at the little shelter revealed a sleeping bag, empty cardboard juice cartons, several bags of puffed rice cakes, a jar of chewable vitamins, and an economy-sized tub of premoistened towelettes, unopened. Not the typical clutter of the homeless mentally ill. It dawned on Bo that somebody must be providing things for him, trying to help. Another in the web of secrets lacing this innocuous urban canyon.

Seconds later he stood and struck out to the left and downhill from his cave. Bo had expected him to lead them up, to the day-care center, if anything.

"I'm Zolar," he announced as if the name were a state secret. "But they won't get me."

"No, they won't," Bo agreed calmly as she struggled to keep up. He was moving swiftly through the rough canyon, his eyes sweeping the terrain as if every shadow might hide untold danger. Bo scooped up the exhausted dog and plunged ahead, wondering if this might turn out to be the ultimate wild-goose chase.

"There!" he stopped suddenly and pointed. His grubby hand was trembling.

Bo looked where he indicated and saw nothing. Just more

dusty plants, sage, countless rocks, lots of beige dirt. A basic San Diego canyon. Home to owls, rabbits, the random coyote, and people who have nowhere else to go. "Where?" she asked.

Zolar grabbed a rock and pitched it into a spreading, blue-flowered shrub. "There."

The shrub was about four feet high at its center, and about six yards beneath where they stood. Odd mounds of rubble, Bo noticed on closer inspection, peeked from beneath its spreading branches. A faint path led toward its western side from the canyon floor where a medium-sized eucalyptus dropped its bark beside the drainage stream. Bo noticed shreds of the peeling bark littering the path. How would the bark get uphill, twenty yards from its source? Unless somebody put it there, to disguise the path.

Curious, Bo had clambered down to the shrub and found a three-foot opening shored with two-by-fours, concealed behind the spreading branches. Still holding the panting dog, she'd pushed the branches aside.

"Bo? Are you on the planet?"

It was Solon Gentzler, offering a basket of sourdough rolls, piping hot. They weren't microwaved, he was sure. He could tell just by touching one.

"Sorry, I was thinking," Bo belabored the obvious. At an adjacent table a woman in enough tasteful gold jewelry to finance a small emergent nation informed her male companion that she'd had to fire her gardener because he kept sneaking off to visit his wife and children in Mexico. The woman hoped he wouldn't return and salt her lawn in revenge. Bo eyed the salt shaker on the table she shared with Gentzler and toyed with the idea of removing its lid, turning and dumping its contents into the woman's hair.

"I'm getting irritable," she told the sourdough roll on her bread plate.

"This case is getting to you." Gentzler nodded. "Have some more wine. We'll take a walk on the beach after dinner. We'll take off our shoes and talk about baseball."

"I'd like that," Bo replied as a waiter placed a pound and a half of enticing aroma before her. She didn't mention that she'd never been to a baseball game in her life. But Zolar would have. He was the type. Tailgate parties with pretty girls. A Padres baseball cap that he probably wore backward when he was younger. When he still had a life. Bo sighed and cut into the snapper with a pistol-handled knife.

What she'd seen in the canyon was appalling, and at first indecipherable. A rough cave, hand-hewn like Zolar's, but bigger. Carefully shored with boards. And pink. Somebody had spray-painted the walls and ceiling in a bright pink, and lit the dim space with at least three hundred twinkling white Christmas tree lights. Bo easily found the battery pack that powered the lights, hidden under a big pink rock with a happy face on it. When she switched it on a cheap tape recorder began to play the theme from *Sesame Street*. Candy wrappers and empty cans of a children's drink called Yoo-Hoo littered the floor beside a rolled-up futon mattress. The mattress was red with white piping, and beside it on an Astroturf mat covering the dirt floor was the cover of a magazine called *Naughty Nymphets*. Kiddie porn. For a few seconds Bo couldn't make sense of the scene. And then she remembered Andrew LaMarche's explanation of the hospital logo, Mabel Mammoth: "Bright colors make strangeness friendly."

The psychology that would help children accept the unfamiliar in a hospital could do the same in a canyon. Except a child made comfortable here would be primed not for the strangeness of surgery or medical tests, but for the grotesque strangeness of adult sex. Zolar hadn't done this, she was sure. This was the work of a mind capable of complex planning and execution. But Zolar had witnessed something, and had wept at the memory of it. Bo kicked the battery pack to pieces before ducking back through the low door, tears blurring her vision.

This, she was certain, was where somebody had raped a little girl whose hair became spun crystal under operating room lights. Somebody who called himself Goody had created this place for that reason. A place to delight children into acceptance of the intolerable. Children from the day-care center. Little ones, too young to verbalize well. Small, inarticulate people too immature to distinguish cheap paint and sparkling lights from love and safety. In her worst moments

Bo had not imagined anything this diseased. She wanted to scream and tear the canyon apart, rock by rock. Above, Zolar paced and muttered.

"Oh, shit." Bo breathed against Mildred's furry side. "What will happen to him if I tell the police about this?"

The answer was a dead certainty. Paul Massieu might be off the hook, but the young man who'd led Bo to the truth would be crucified. She could see the headlines—"Canyon Crazy Arrested in Child Rape After Cult Member Goes Free." Absolutely no one would believe that Zolar hadn't built the pink hellhole, in spite of his obvious incapacity. Wasn't it similar to his own "home"? And everybody would recall that mentally ill people are universally prone to unspeakable crimes, overlooking the fact that mentally ill people are almost invariably victims, not perpetrators. Bo felt the pressure of an ethical dilemma. An Olympic headache. A desire to leave town and surface in New Zealand with a phony passport.

"You're going to love Auckland," she told Mildred. But the fantasy wouldn't take the place of the tears she'd seen in the young man's eyes when he remembered Goody. When he remembered things he must have witnessed. Zolar had wept for the horror in that canyon, a horror even worse than his own. Bo felt a kinship with the young hermit, and a need to protect him. Dar Reinert, she guessed, would produce a half-baked theory that Zolar might be Goody and not know it. That he was one of the "multiple personalities" now in vogue despite their statistical rarity. Everybody would like that theory; in a matter of days it would be regarded as hard fact. People in diverse bureaucracies would close their cases on Samantha Franer and her sister, Hannah, and an innocent man suffering from one of the most terrifying disorders in the medical annals of the human race would vanish into a prison for criminals who are also insane. There would be widespread relief. And a clever, resourceful rapist would destroy more children.

Bo gave Zolar five dollars, tried to talk to him briefly about new medications, and ascended the canyon wall. After a few yards she looked back and saw nothing. As if Zolar, the pink chamber, none of it were really there.

"And we'll leave it that way," she told Mildred. "At least until I figure out what to do."

The Kramer Child Care Center was dark when Bo left. Her banging on the security bars produced no response from inside. The nameless woman, the children, and even the orange cat were simply gone.

At home she'd phoned Dar Reinert and left a message requesting information on the owner of the Kramer Child Care Center. Then she'd phoned Estrella and begged her to go by the facility before the memorial service tomorrow. If the woman were there, Es could talk to her in Spanish. After a bubble bath shared by Mildred, she'd dressed and driven to pick up a waiting Solon Gentzler, who seemed not to notice the gray cloud nesting on the bridge of her nose as they drove toward La Jolla and its seafood.

"You're exhausted," the radical attorney mentioned much later as Bo stumbled against him on the beach. They'd gone back to her apartment after dinner so Bo could change before their walk. And he was right. She was so tired the familiar beach stretching north of her apartment seemed alien. Its piles of ropy kelp could have been somnolent, feathery eels. And a lone tourist in a Hawaiian shirt just sitting on the seawall appeared to be watching her and Gentzler as if he knew them.

"You're right. I'm so tired I don't think I can drive you back to your motel," she agreed. Something about the tourist made her think of pinball machines. A mechanical carnival of simple gravity. A steel sphere rolling down a maze. The image was cold, inexorable. And crazy.

Are you trying *to bring on another manic episode? Get some sleep!*

"I'll take a cab," Gentzler said. "Don't worry about it."

The sense of implacable cold seemed to roar, bouncing off the young lawyer's words. Bo stared at her sandy feet and listened to the roar. "Sol," she said after several seconds, "this will sound strange, but I don't feel like staying alone tonight. This isn't an invitation to carnal bliss, although I admit to toying with the idea earlier. I'm just a little shaky. I'd like it if you stayed over, if you can handle sleeping on my couch. Does that sound as crazy to you as it does to me?"

"Not crazy at all," he replied, yawning. "I'm tired, too,

and the couch will be fine. Which is not to say,'' he grinned, ''that carnal bliss holds no appeal. Rain check?''

The space on the seawall occupied by the tourist in the Hawaiian shirt was now vacant.

''Who knows?'' Bo answered, although the words were really directed at herself.

After helping Gentzler make up the couch in the tan pinstriped sheets, Bo collapsed into bed and a sleep undisturbed when her answering machine on the kitchen counter clicked on several times, silently recording messages she would not, under normal circumstances, have heard until morning. But a sleep very much disturbed when something tried to beat her door down at 2:00 A.M.

''What the hell . . . ?'' Solon Gentzler growled, stumbling in the darkened living room toward the door as Mildred ran between his feet, barking.

Bo pulled on a luxuriant yellow terry robe with white satin starfish appliqués on the pockets. She hated the starfish, but the robe had been a steal at a bedroom boutique sale. An unclaimed custom order. Not surprising.

Gentzler was booming, ''Who is it?'' in decibels usually reserved for unamplified auctioneers, and struggling with Bo's several locks.

''Dr. LaMarche,'' the familiar voice answered as Bo opened the door.

In the greenish exterior lights of her apartment building Andrew LaMarche's face registered dismay and then something like nausea.

''Oh, God,'' Bo said, turning on the interior lights and then turning them off again when she realized how she and Solon Gentzler must . . . did . . . look. ''Andy . . .''

''I was terribly worried about you, Bo,'' he explained in a voice that struggled to remain impersonal and failed. ''I've phoned several times, as has Detective Reinert and Madge Aldenhoven. You may be in danger.'' He noted the rumpled attorney with something like a sneer. ''How reassuring to see that you're not alone.'' With that he turned and stalked toward the stairs, a lean figure in khakis and a wrinkled blue dress shirt with a white collar. Running after him, Bo noticed that he had on only one sock. For a second she thought she might burst into tears, but then rejected the idea. What was the point?

"Andy, what *is* it?" she called from the top of the stairs.

He stopped and turned to face her. "Cynthia Ganage, that conniving psychologist who created this whole Satanic frenzy, was murdered tonight, Bo. I didn't like her, couldn't abide what she was doing, but she didn't deserve this." He leaned against the stair railing and looked out to sea. "Reinert phoned me an hour ago, asking questions about Satanic killing as if there were such a thing. He said Ganage's body was found in the bathtub of her hotel suite, fully clothed and floating in her own blood. The killer apparently knocked her unconscious, placed her body in the tub, and then opened her left large jugular with a kitchen knife. Then he collected blood in a hotel ashtray, carried it into the sitting area of the suite, and used it to write 'Satan claims a stupid pig' on the wall. According to Reinert 'claims' was misspelled 'clams,' although it may be construed to mean 'silences.' But the reason I'm here . . ." he took a deep breath, "is that Ganage received an anonymous message earlier today saying, 'Satan called.' Reinert got an identical message and so, according to Madge Aldenhoven, did you."

"My God." Bo shuddered. "Everybody connected to the Franer case. And Andy," she remembered the man on the seawall, "there was a guy on the beach tonight watching us walk. He looked like a tourist, but there was something weird about the way he seemed to know who we were."

Andrew LaMarche's tanned face grew ashen. "Perhaps he did, Bo. Am I safe in assuming that your guest will remain with you for the rest of the night?"

"Yes," she answered. "But Andy, it's not what it looks like. He's sleeping on the *couch* . . ."

"You don't need to explain," he muttered. "As long as you're not alone. I've already phoned Eva. She did not receive one of the Satan calls, so she and Hannah may not be at risk. I'm going there now in any event. I'll be with them if you need me."

With no further discourse Andrew LaMarche bolted down the stairs and was gone. Bo gripped a weathered support holding the roof over the walkway of her apartment building, and bumped her forehead softly against the wood.

You've done it now, Bradley. You've ruined his sugary little fantasy. There will be no more Cajun dancing.

"No big deal," Bo said aloud, and recognized a lie when she heard it. Nobody as decent as Andrew LaMarche deserved to be hurt, even if it was his own damned fault. Or if it was nobody's damned fault. Bo decided to file the entire incident for some future moment when she might redeem a personal reputation about which she had never cared one whit. But now, for some reason, did.

The news of Cynthia Ganage's grisly death only confirmed what she'd sensed all along. Paul Massieu was innocent, and Samantha Franer's unknown rapist was uncharacteristically responding to media attention by escalating his activity to church desecration and now cold-blooded murder. Not a run-of-the-mill child-molester at all. Not the ill-developed male personality she'd seen a hundred times in her work, afraid of or repulsed by adult sex, aroused by the powerless innocence of children. There had always been such men. They were noteworthy for nothing so much as their unshakable devotion to a particularly repugnant lust, no matter what therapy tried to reshape them. But beyond their clandestine sexual practices, they were usually indistinguishable from anyone else. Mail-carriers, preachers, bankers, computer repairmen. Socially adept men, often active and popular in church and community work. Not prone to criminal activity. They never regarded their torment of children as criminal, merely as their right. But this man was different. This man was playing a high-stakes game that didn't fit the profile of a common child-molester. This man, Bo conceded, was a mystery.

From the beach beyond her apartment's balcony a scent of iodine, of sea chemicals and drying kelp floated against her nose. Hannah Franer was safe. Bo inhaled sea air and congratulated herself on that much. But she was going to have to tell the police about Zolar and the pink horror in the canyon. They would have to inspect the hidden cave for fingerprints, fibers, traces of Samantha's killer. And then what would happen to Zolar? The picture made her sick.

Exactly where is your loyalty, Bradley? You're as sane as it gets, for the moment. But when the time comes to draw the line between us and them, you identify with a depressed child and a lost soul whose hospital chart would undoubtedly read "Paranoid Schizophrenia." Is this what you want?

Through a tear in the fog a patch of blue-black sky sparkled with stars. There was nothing else. No hidden meaning, no subtle, multifaceted message. No unaccountable feeling adrift anywhere. No wailing of Caillech Bera, that old Celtic barker for the sideshow called madness. Those things were not gone permanently, Bo knew. They'd be back. They were part of her. But right now they were absent, leaving a window through which stars and clear thinking were possible. Bo memorized the moment, photographed it mentally against an inevitable future when she would doubt the decision she was about to make.

"Yes," she answered her own question. "This is what I want. Being me is just fine. I knew how to protect Hannah and talk to Zolar. I didn't learn those skills being somebody else, and I'm sick of pretending to be somebody else. And there's a pederast-turned-killer out there who's going to be sorry Samantha Franer wound up on my caseload."

Back in her apartment Bo found Solon Gentzler standing gloomily before her open refrigerator. "Three pounds of carrots?" he asked. "A bag of raw broccoli, two six-packs of salt-free tomato juice, and a picture of some gorgeous broad who looks like the head of an island protectorate where art thieves vacation. Bo, why do you have no food and this picture taped to your butter bin?"

"That's Frances Lear," Bo grinned, "role-model for ladies-on-lithium who aspire to wardrobes without polyester. I'm trying to lose weight because I've been taking lithium for nine months."

The cat, out of the bag, merely sat there.

"Isn't that the stuff they make batteries out of?" Gentzler queried, still searching for edible objects.

"I haven't been eating batteries for the better part of a year, Sol. Why don't we get dressed and find an all-night diner for coffee? There's something I want to tell you. And I've got an idea I need your help with."

Chapter 20

Rombo Perry set the front elevation of the NordicTrak Pro to eight degrees and slid the videotape of Vermont scenery Martin had given him for his thirty-eighth birthday into the VCR. But no New Age Indian flutes today. Selecting his *Best of the Supremes* CD, he turned up the volume, began the hour-long acceleration of his workout, and grinned. Diana Ross had not completed the impassioned story of her decision to avoid conceiving a "Love Child" when Martin St. John, dramatically patient beneath a film of whole wheat flour, approached from the kitchen.

"I know you've been upset," Martin began, "but can this sort of adolescent regression really help?"

Martin St. John's whole wheat Parker House rolls were the flagship of St. John Catering, in demand by the thousands every weekend for the endless buffets, cocktail trays, and dinner-party fund-raisers of San Diego's upscale liberal community. Special wiring had been required for the huge vertical freezer in the spare bedroom where the partially baked delicacies were stored on wire racks. A characteristic odor of bakery yeast invariably caused passers-by in the apartment's hall to salivate, and completely defeated the hi-tech decorating scheme Rombo and Martin had chosen five years ago. Before the rolls caught on. When Martin was still carving radish roses for vegetable trays and Rombo was job hunting between twice-daily AA meetings. The cozy smell wafted from the kitchen now.

"Motown has been demonstrated to help eliminate free radicals from the bloodstream," Rombo lectured as footage of Green County, Vermont, under snow crossed the television screen. "And if I listen to one more Celtic harp and flute combo over running water, I'm going to shave my head and start wearing an orange sarong."

"The sarong has possibilities." Martin beamed, his brown eyes fudge-dark in a floury face. "But this music reminds me of the Nixon administration. Bad karma. The rolls won't rise. And you're still a wreck. The woman died two days ago, Rom. You didn't even know her, really. You've got to let go of it."

A film of sweat on his forearms reassured Rombo of his cardiovascular system's ongoing efficiency. "Let's go check on Leonor after we deliver the rolls, before the memorial service. Okay? Maybe take her a rawhide bone or something."

Leonor was the very pregnant golden retriever who would soon present Rombo and Martin with a puppy already named Watson in honor of their collection of Sherlockiana. Rombo had given Martin a traditional Holmesian deerstalker cap to celebrate the news of Leonor's successful weekend idyll with a champion retriever stud named Gothard's Brendan, brought to San Diego from Palm Springs for the occasion in a vintage Mercedes. Leonor's owner, a rotund freelance window dresser, had bartered the expected puppy for a three-year supply of whole wheat rolls. And the best part, Rombo thought, was that Watson would have a yard. A real yard, with a view.

"Sure," Martin agreed, abandoning hope of an end to the music. "Probably be good for you. Take your mind off things, huh?"

Rombo watched Martin pad, barefooted, back into the

kitchen, and thought about the house as he exercised. Between his salary and Martin's burgeoning business they'd been able to save enough for a sizable down payment on a house in North Park with a canyon view. The loan had included funds for renovation of the kitchen, to be used by Martin for his money-making little rolls. There would be no more chrome furniture with black basketball-rubber upholstery. They'd even picked out a couch at Ethan Allen, incurring from friends a shower of exquisitely awful grapevine wreaths and refrigerator magnets featuring geese in bow ties pushing wheelbarrows. The house would be ready in less than a month.

Increasing the tension on the ski flywheel, Rombo breathed evenly and wondered why he wasn't dead. More than a decade of booze, poppers every night in Chicago bars, fucking around, trying to be the hot'n'hung young top everybody'd get down on their knees for. The one everybody'd want when some bartender in tit-clips and a leather jock under unbuttoned Levi's yelled "Last call, Mary!" through the smoke. It hadn't occurred to Rombo to ask himself what *he* wanted. Not until it was almost too late and he was working out of Manpower every other day, cleaning warehouses and portable toilets to pay for a room and watery shots of bar whiskey at 6:30 in the morning.

One of the derelicts in the phlegmy hotel where Rombo slept had died on the lobby's curling linoleum floor. Nobody cared. Rombo thought he'd probably stepped over the body himself that night, maybe. And then the ratlike little man in his ashtray of a cage where you paid for your room told Rombo the pile of stinking rags on the floor had once been a teacher. A high school math teacher, according to the sister whose name and phone number the cops found in the guy's room. In the acidic haze of his own breath Rombo saw the future, panicked, and did the one thing for which his father would have spit in his face. At thirty, he called his mother.

A social worker in Gary, Indiana, she drove over to Chicago, picked him up, and dumped him at the best detox program she could pay for.

"Your father's love and approval are never going to happen," she told him at the admitting desk. "You've always had mine, for what it's worth. But the important thing is to earn your own. Go for it!"

He'd slipped a couple of times after that, but picked himself up and climbed back on. When his AA sponsor in Gary offered him the chance to drive a U-HAUL truck full of furniture to San Diego for a niece in the navy, Rombo grabbed it. And loved San Diego. The airy, sunlit city seemed to promise a new life. Clean and sober. And free. Within the year Rombo had moved. Within another year he'd met Martin St. John, at whose good-natured devotion Rombo marveled. It was the life he'd always wanted. Calm. Orderly.

And an even greater miracle was that neither of them had AIDS. Tested twice in two years, they'd both been negative. Rombo hadn't been able to think about that, about how he'd been spared that and the other deaths he'd courted while dancing with his father's hatred. Now he couldn't think about anything else. The image of a frail woman hanging by the neck from a bedsheet kept asking questions he knew it was time to answer.

By 11:00 Martin had delivered the last of the rolls to a beachfront restaurant where a hundred and fifty people would gather at dusk to raise funds for a women's shelter.

"Ready to visit mama dog?" he asked Rombo. "Or ready to tell me what it is about this woman's suicide that's got you reciting Hamlet's soliloquy in the shower?"

"I didn't know you heard." Rombo cringed. "And I don't know why this thing's hit a nerve. It just rips it, you know? We have everything, the best life there is, and that pitiful, *little* woman had nothing. Absolutely nothing. Some walking pustule with his brain in his dong guts her kid, and she's gone. They're both just gone. It's over. And that's not right, Martin. It's too unfair."

Twenty minutes later they were sitting on Maxwell Grasic's enclosed rear deck, watching a golden retriever shred the *L.A. Times* in a wooden box with six-inch-high slats over its entry. The slats and box had been sanded smooth.

"She's gonna blow tonight. I just know it," their friend announced the obvious, pacing. "I've called the vet three times today already. She told me to stop calling until something happens. I've got everything ready—towels, weak tea with sugar, sterilized scissors, a Brahms tape so they'll feel relaxed. Kevin and Barry sent flowers already—yellow roses and baby's breath in a Wedgewood dog dish. The suspense is killing me."

When the dog rested briefly from nesting, Rombo sat beside her on the gray tweed outdoor carpeting and stroked her swollen sides. Tiny movements were palpable beneath the long fur. Little kicks and nudges, and something that felt like hiccups. Leonor panted and resumed her work in the box.

"I really feel that I haven't done enough, Martin," he said when Max went inside to answer the phone. "I've spent so much time hauling myself out of the sewer that I've forgotten to live in the world. This wad of worm snot rapes little girls and all I care about is us and our house and our dog and our life. I want to *do* something. Something to help."

"Got any ideas?" Martin smiled.

"Yeah." Rombo smiled back. "I do."

Chapter 21

By 8:00 Sunday morning John D. Litten had completed the careful packing necessary for his camera equipment, TV, VCR, and sound system. Those things and his clothes would fit in the car, registered to Craig Alan Sanford, a boy who had died in a Florida water-skiing accident when he was eight. Everything else would be left behind.

Outside his ninth-story window sailboats rode the gray-blue swells of the bay beneath overcast skies as tourists queued up for cruises. The sun struggling through a weak haze both warmed him and hurt his eyes. He'd been up most of the night. And he felt strange, as though parts of him were missing. One minute the back of his head, then his left shoulder, then the muscle and connective tissue inside his right hand. His right hand was hollow. And then it was just a hand again, and his dick was gone. But when he touched it, it was there and his nasal passages seemed to evaporate in his skull. A creepy parade of empty spaces probably caused, he judged, by the two lines of coke he'd blown last night. The coke and what had happened. The way he'd felt killing that woman, even though he'd meant to do the other one. Like glass. He'd felt like a man made of frozen glass. Like a light you'd see through a telescope, blazing with cold. His dick had stayed hard all night.

Everything was different now, that was for sure. Everything changed. Like finding out a secret that's been there all along, waiting. Out of habit John Litten had prepared to leave quickly. Just leave town before there was the slightest chance of getting caught. The old, regular part of him said that was the thing to do. But something else said to wait before starting on the trip that would take him away from San Diego, away from the amazing thing he'd learned. That to become Superman, all he had to do was kill.

Dressed in jeans and a black T-shirt adorned with a printed portrait of somebody named Wittgenstein, he looked like a student at any university in the country. Nobody would remember seeing some college student walking around in downtown San Diego. And even if they did, so what? Nobody was looking for him. They didn't know what to look for. They were too stupid. Locking his apartment door carefully behind him, John D. Litten bounded down eight flights of stairs and headed into the street.

In the haze things looked strange, shimmery. Like the city, knowing who he was, had polished itself for him. Beneath his feet a brick sidewalk, its basketweave mortared lines clean and new, led toward a future John Litten could scarcely imagine. A future in which he alone knew the secret of transformation. A future in which he would play with them, all the stupid ones who knew nothing, and then kill them. He didn't know why he hadn't seen it before. It had been there, all along.

In an orange, recessed doorway something moved on the ground. Litten looked at it and for several seconds could not identify it. Something long and foul-smelling, stirring beneath damp slabs of cardboard torn from a large box. One of the slabs had the name of a San Francisco importer printed on it. And the thing under it was a man. Litten looked at the sign over the orange doorway—DICK'S LAST RESORT. It was just a darkened restaurant with a wino sleeping in its doorway. Across the street a Cost Plus dumpster revealed the source of the cardboard slab. Litten wondered why it had taken him so long to piece together the ordinary scene. And then he knew why. He'd crossed over, finally, become something completely different from the creature on the ground. So different that at first he hadn't recognized it as human. That was because he was superhuman now. A superhuman walking, almost invisibly, on the misty streets of a sleeping city. It was like something he'd read in a comic book, years ago.

On Island Avenue he crossed to an old brick hotel refurbished in a downtown development project. The Horton Grand, a plaque told him, had been built in 1886. The date meant nothing. Why would anyone care when an old building was built? It was strange. Two men in white shirts and black pants lounged against the hotel's gleaming facade. They would park cars for tips, Litten remembered.

"Pretty good breakfast," one of them mentioned. "Pricey, but good."

"Yeah?" Litten answered. Why had the man told him that? Gradually it made sense. They thought he was a tourist looking for someplace to eat breakfast. In his college-boy clothes he looked their age. The man was operating on assumptions to which John Litten would have to accommodate. He went inside, feeling like a puppet. It would be okay to eat, he guessed. Probably a good idea. But things were so strange. Why would Superman have to do what a parking attendant said?

The hotel lobby had a green tile floor and a bunch of white furniture made out of sticks. And big white birdcages lined with the edges of computer paper. John Litten had torn these edges off miles of paper in the navy. Their presence was familiar and comfortable, but he would never have thought of using them for anything. Why hadn't he thought of birdcage lining? Because there were no birds around in the navy, he decided. If there had been birds he would have thought of it. Anybody as smart as he was would have thought of it. Except nobody was as smart as he was. Not anymore.

"Breakfast, sir?" a tired-looking woman in a ruffled blouse asked. Her smile seemed to go right through his face and stick somewhere behind his head. She couldn't see what he was, couldn't really see him at all. That was good.

The hotel's restaurant was dimly lit and almost empty as

he followed the woman to a wooden booth with some kind of rough, flowered pad to sit on. The same material padded the back of the booth, where your head hit. Litten looked at the fabric, the tens of thousands of little sewing stitches that made flowers and leaves, vines and birds in different colors. It looked hard to do, complicated. Why would anybody bother? Something about the fabric irritated John Litten, but he didn't know what.

A man and woman seated at a round table nearby both ordered coffee with smoked salmon and onion omelettes. Nervous, Litten gave an identical order even though he hated coffee. What was wrong with him? Why didn't he feel good, now that he'd found the secret?

Some kind of music drifted from the restaurant's speakers.

"Mozart would have enjoyed this place," the man at the table told his companion. "It's so Baroque."

"I think Salieri would have liked it better." she answered, and they both laughed.

John Litten stared into his omelette, which smelled like fish. Not spoiled fish like Gramma got sometimes from a grocery in Estherville that gave it away on Saturday nights because they were closed on Sunday. But still fish. He couldn't understand why the man and woman were laughing. What were they talking about? He felt himself frowning at them, but they didn't see. They didn't see *him*. They didn't know he was there.

John Litten wondered if he *was* there. Something wrong. Lots of things he didn't understand, couldn't name. Were the people talking about music? How could you talk about music? Why couldn't he understand what they were saying, if he was Superman? Superman would understand everything, probably even make designs with a million little sewing stitches if he wanted to. But John Litten didn't even know what to call it once it was made.

An impossible realization began to form like a half-circle cloud between his ears. An awareness of difference that had always been there, ever since he could remember. A difference nobody could see, that was now complete. He wasn't like the people at the table, not at all. He couldn't understand them and they couldn't see him. He wasn't like anybody.

He'd learned how to become frozen glass, and he was alone. He would always be alone.

Leaving a twenty-dollar bill on the table he rose and swiftly left the hotel. In the vacant Cost Plus parking lot he vomited behind the dumpster. Sour, fishy coffee spewing from his throat. It felt good to get rid of it. Only stupid people drank coffee, he realized. People, period. He was no longer one of them, if he ever had been.

A somber rage, like a pillar of white granite, filled him as he straightened his torso in the shadows behind the dumpster. He hated them, that was all. And he could kill them, and become glass. A painful erection throbbed behind the button fly of his denim pants. Pulling out his cock he gasped as he ejaculated to a memory of blood, and death. It was so easy. And so good. He would never need anything else.

Chapter 22

By 10:30 Bo was toying with a cup of coffee on the patio from which Eva Broussard studied a particularly inept surfer in an overlarge wetsuit who tumbled off his board with each wave.

"I'm sure nobody was following me," Bo explained, "but I drove way inland and came down through Encinitas, just in case. Sharp turns, hiding in parking lots, backtracking. Nobody could have stayed with me. I had to talk to you."

The older woman kneaded her temples with the fingertips of both hands. "Yes," she nodded, turning from the sea after Bo explained the decision she had made. The alarming risk she would take in court tomorrow. "It's a dangerous but courageous step. If you're really ready, I'm sure it's the right one for you. And the situation has become even more complex. Do you believe there is any danger to Hannah from the man who killed Cynthia Ganage? Do you think there is really any connection at all between these two killings?"

Eva Broussard seemed distant, lost in thought. Bo couldn't read the woman's mental state at all.

"It may be that Ganage was killed by someone unconnected to this case," Bo began. "We don't know anything about Ganage. She was from L.A. The police are checking her contacts there. Maybe she had an enemy, a rejected boyfriend, somebody who wanted her dead and just used the bloody message on her wall to mislead the investigation. But . . ."

"I don't think so," Eva Broussard said, her voice barely audible, "and neither do you." Bo leaned forward in a canvas deck chair, curious. Broussard seemed anxious to complete a troubling train of thought. "There are aspects of this murder that lead me to a different conclusion. A very different conclusion. But first I must hear all that you know." The graceful Iroquois woman pulled a matching chair close to Bo's and sat. Even though the dark eyes were unfocused, Bo felt the woman's concentration like a palpable force. Eva Broussard was taking the murder of Cynthia Ganage very seriously.

"At the day-care center where Samantha stayed while Bonnie worked part-time," Bo said quietly, "I've discovered a sort of cave dug in the wall of the canyon behind the property, carefully shored with two by fours. A cave painted pink and decorated with Christmas tree lights. There's a man suffering from schizophrenia who lives in the canyon. He showed me the cave. He knew that the perp called himself Goody. I think Samantha's killer was connected to the day-care center in some way. I think he went there and took children to this place down in the canyon, and . . . did things to them. There was a battery pack in the cave—"

"A battery pack?" The raven-black eyes widened.

"Yeah. He used it to power the lights and a tape recorder. Children's music . . ."

"And perhaps a video camera as well," Eva Broussard breathed. "Have you told the police?"

Bo glanced through the picture window of the studio apartment across the patio. Hannah Franer lay on the floor playing with a huge assortment of Legos. Now and then she flipped her long hair from her face in a gesture oddly adolescent, as if an older personality were already framing itself in the childlike visage. Flute music drifted from stereo speakers through two screened windows flanking the picture window.

"Only this morning," Bo admitted. "Dar Reinert called.

I'd asked him to check out the registration for the center. He told me the house is rented in the name of somebody who died in Texas eighteen years ago. A phony name, in other words. The property owner lives in Oregon, pays a management service to rent and maintain the house. The management service is actually a bankrupt realtor named Brock Mulvihill who runs his business out of his garage up in San Marcos. Mulvihill says he never saw the guy who rented the Kramer Street property; it was all done over the phone and through the mail. He says the guy's checks were good, and that he paid for a new chain-link fence around the backyard so his wife could run a playschool on the property. Mulvihill drove by the house once, three months ago on a weekend, found it well kept up, and left. No questions. The market's rotten. He was thrilled to have a responsible, solvent tenant. The center isn't licensed by the county. A Hispanic woman who ran the place has vanished, although I've got a co-worker who speaks Spanish checking this morning to see if the woman's come back. It's obvious that the perp set the whole thing up to have access to children, but there's no way to learn more until tomorrow when parents start showing up to drop off kids. I told Reinert about the cave, and about Zolar, the man who took me to it. Reinert's been out there already. Zolar's vanished, but the cave's still there. The police are checking it out now, but they don't expect to find much. Reinert, of course, now thinks Zolar is our perp. Meanwhile the media are 'cautiously exploring' the possibility of a Satanic takeover of San Diego. Ganage was their pet."

Eva Broussard sighed and remained silent for some time.

"I trust your judgment on Zolar," she said. "And even if I didn't, the elaborate preparations you describe—the construction and shoring of the cave, the paint and lights—it's all too calculated and consistent for an individual with untreated schizophrenia. No, from what you've told me, I feel safe in predicting that our killer is scarcely delusional. But more significantly, I think he's an isolate. To do what he does successfully, he can have no real contact with other people. His entire existence is a sequence of performances designed to disguise what he is inside."

"A child-molester?" Bo filled in. "That's what he is inside. I've had a lot of contact with child-molesters. This guy's not your typical—''

"No," Eva Broussard answered, "he isn't typical and that's not what he's hiding. He's hiding the fact that inside, he's nothing."

"Huh?"

"It will be almost impossible for you to comprehend, Bo," Broussard went on, the pace of her speech accelerating slightly. "You are . . . how can I say this? . . . uniquely equipped to understand the experiences of the living—joy and passion, despair and hopelessness. You *are* the masks of drama—comedy and tragedy. But this man is nowhere in that world your brain magnifies. This man is devoid of all emotional capability with the possible exceptions of anger and fear, which are in him one thing. His experience is not accessible to most people, but least of all to you. Don't even try."

Bo made a stab at digesting Eva Broussard's words, and then merely filed them for later. "If you're saying he has a mental disorder, like command voices in schizophrenia or something, that accounts for his behavior, it's like nothing I've ever seen."

"He has none of the major psychiatric disorders, least of all schizophrenia, as I've said," Broussard went on. "If anything, he'd be diagnosed with one of the personality disorders—borderline, narcissistic, one of those. But he's quite sane." She appeared to study a patch of succulent ground cover spilling over the edge of the patio. "Terms like 'personality disorder' are just categories for the inexplicable. Categories that define the ways in which some people simply cannot feel normal concern and interaction with others. But this man is plagued less by disorder than by an absence of personality altogether. He feeds on power, nothing else. His power to manipulate reality. Sexual gratification with children is an almost pure exercise of power. But now he may have found something better . . ."

Bo inhaled slowly, Eva Broussard's train of thought finding completion in her own mind. "Cold-blooded murder," she exhaled. "He's found a source of power in killing." The sun-warmed beach seemed suddenly wintry. "And just as he's certainly molested more than one child, he'll kill more than once as well."

"It's quite possible that what we have here," Broussard completed her assessment carefully, "is the birth of a serial killer."

Overhead a gull dipped and squawked, wheeling out over the sea as if to avoid the grim pronouncement hanging in the air. Bo closed her eyes and shivered.

Inside, Hannah continued to work on an elaborate enclosure made of Legos. In the space of silence as the taped music stopped and reversed, Bo heard the child's voice through the screened windows, humming tunelessly. As Hannah hummed, her lips moved. "There," she pronounced, snapping Lego to Lego. "And there."

"She's talking," Bo whispered.

"Not exactly." Broussard smiled. "She isn't aware that she's forming words as she hums. Her mind is occupied with play. But eventually she'll hear herself, and if no attention is brought to the fact that she's speaking, if it's treated as perfectly normal and unremarkable, I think she'll abandon her mutism. And then even more care must be exercised as she begins to verbalize her pain and loss. Hannah will need professional care for some time."

Bo smiled. "And love, Eva. Look what your love has done for her already."

The Indian woman's face was pensive. "Like many Americans you tend to romanticize everything, Bo. This wasn't included in my plans. After surgery for a breast cancer that may or may not have been caught in time, I determined to devote the remainder of my life to researching a particular human experience. I was content with my decision, excited about the project. Then Samantha Franer was killed, her mother a suicide, Paul in jail. These people weren't especially close to me, Bo. I'm essentially an intellectual, not what you Americans would call a people person. I would have avoided this love if there had been any way to do so, but there wasn't." She looked curiously into Bo's eyes. "I think most of us will avoid the responsibilities of love in favor of less troubling attachments, don't you?" A twinkle visible in the dark eyes was a dead giveaway.

"I understand Dr. LaMarche stayed with you and Hannah last night after Ganage's murder." Bo accepted the challenge. "Can it be that he mentioned his harebrained intentions regarding me?"

Eva Broussard's smile became a grin. "He brought Hannah the Legos but said little about you," she answered, "although his discomfiture at your not being alone last night was rather too obvious. The male ego is perhaps the most fragile construct on the planet, you know. And hopelessly transparent."

"Precisely why I don't want—"

"You owe me no explanation, Bo. That debt is to yourself, no one else. I assume you're clear on your reasons for spurning his advances?"

"The problem is, he doesn't *make* advances." Bo sighed. "He's like something out of *Godey's Ladies Book*—the perfect gentleman. Besides, I like him. I'd rather keep that. And this case is a bit distracting . . ."

"Of course," Eva Broussard agreed, rising. "So what is the next move?"

Bo stretched and checked her watch. "I'm meeting my co-worker, Estrella Benedict, at the day-care center in forty-five minutes. If the woman who runs the place has returned, Estrella can interview her in Spanish. Then we're going to the memorial service for Samantha and Bonnie. Reinert thinks there's an off chance our killer will attend, if it's not Zolar. Reinert's got cops scouring San Diego for him, too. I hate it that I involved him in this."

"Your Zolar is unmedicated and miserable," Broussard noted crisply. "If he's found and gets help, it may be his salvation."

"Spoken like a true shrink." Bo laughed. "It's clear that you've never been tied down and shot full of Haldol. But maybe you're right. And Eva . . . ?" Bo couldn't resist asking. "You seem to know quite a bit about the killer, the way his mind works. But I've checked out your credentials. All your work has involved social interaction, religious mysticism, stuff like that. Nothing published on pederasts or serial killers. How do you know so much?"

"One becomes, in a sense, what one researches," Broussard answered. "A long time ago I chose to avoid research into the dark side of human behavior. I chose to avoid it precisely because it fascinates me. Too dangerous. For one who lives by choice outside the usual interpersonal frameworks of marriage and family, intense research in psychopathology can create a distorted view of the human condition. Surely you've seen that among some of your co-workers who've come to view the world as nothing but a cesspool. Nonetheless, I keep up on others' work. Sometimes it's impossible to understand the up side without some comprehension of the depths."

"Oh," Bo replied. It was the answer she had expected. Sort of.

Forty minutes later she nosed her ratty old BMW into the curb behind Estrella Benedict's immaculate silver coupé. Estrella herself paced in the driveway of the Kramer Day Care Center, her high heels popping like BB shots. Estrella pacing was not a good sign.

"What's happened?" Bo asked, hurrying from her car to the driveway. "Was she here? Was the woman here?"

"*Sí,*" Estrella answered, singing the monosyllable in two notes. Her cheeks twitched with something like anger. "She was here."

"So? What happened? Where is she?"

Estrella curled her lips inward over her teeth and looked at the sky. Bo could see white oleanders reflected in her friend's sunglasses. "She's gone," Estrella announced.

"Gone? You mean you talked to her and then just let her walk away? She's our only witness. She's the only person who can identify this pervert. I asked you to try talking with her, in Spanish. I didn't really think she'd be here, but—"

"She didn't think I'd be here, either," Estrella went on. "And I wish I wasn't. Bo, I hate it when you get me involved in these crazy schemes of yours. Why can't you just do your job like everybody else and then go home? You always have to go too far, know too much. You get too involved."

Estrella appeared to be on the verge of tears.

"Es, tell me what happened," Bo said, leading her co-worker to lean on the BMW. "What's going on?"

Estrella smoothed a black linen skirt obviously selected for the memorial service they were about to attend, and crossed her arms over a white silk blouse pinstriped also in black. "I told her I just got a job as a secretary to a Latino lawyer, and needed day care right away for my two little girls. I said the lawyer wanted me to start next week and wouldn't wait. I said I was desperate. And you know what she told me? You know what this illiterate peasant woman from some village in Chihuahua told me?"

"What?" Bo asked. Estrella had bowed her head, Bo realized, to avoid smearing her eye makeup with tears.

"She told me to take my babies back to wherever I came from, to get out of the U.S. no matter how bad things were at home. She told me the devil had bought her soul here for a thousand dollars a month. That's what he paid her, Bo, to run this place and look the other way. She said he let her live here with her two kids for free, and paid her a thousand a month, cash. And sometimes he'd come by at noon and take one of the children, usually a girl but not always, for walks in the canyon. She thought it was strange, but Bo, she didn't know until Samantha's death what he was doing to the kids. She said they'd act funny, sometimes vomit later, at snack time. But no evidence of injury. He was probably . . ."

"Oh, God," Bo breathed through her nose to fight the familiar nausea, "how can something like that just walk around?"

Over Estrella's shoulder the gray house seemed to be watching from behind its white bars.

"So where is she now?" Bo went on. "Why did you let her go?"

"She told me she took her kids to Tijuana yesterday and left them overnight in an orphanage with some nuns. Then she just walked around, tried to think what to do. She's been supporting about fifteen family members back in her village with that money, Bo. Their situation is desperate. She decided to leave her children in T.J. for a week, come back and try to get more money out of the creep before taking off for home."

"My god. You mean even after she knew . . . ?"

Estrella squared her shoulders and looked at Bo over the top of her sunglasses. "Yes," she replied. "And I have to tell you that *I* advised her to leave before you got here, to get over that border and home with her kids before she wound up in jail. I told her who I really am and I told her what would happen when the police finally put this picture together. She's gone, Bo. She's safe."

"Well, well," Bo said. "The voice of doom who thinks *I'm* crazy even when I'm not has just joined the ranks. And for what it's worth, you did the right thing. The woman could have lost her kids, spent years in a California prison as an accessory to crimes she didn't know were being committed. More innocent lives ruined pointlessly. I would have done the same thing, Es."

"I know," Estrella grimaced, kicking the tire of Bo's car. "That's what's so upsetting."

Chapter 23

St. Theresa's Church, a 1950s A-frame featuring a rose window Bo suspected had been pieced from old wine bottles, given the preponderance of green, was barely visible behind four TV sound trucks lining the curb. One of the trucks bore an L.A. logo. The story was, unfortunately, gaining momentum. On the residential sidewalk across the street from the church, twenty people dressed in black held aloft hand-lettered posters. "Satan Is Loosed out of His Prison," one poster announced. "And Whosoever Is Not Found Written in the Book of Life Will Be Cast into the Lake of Fire," another picked up the refrain. From the looks on the demonstrators' faces, Bo would have bet they'd *invest* in a lake of fire if they could just throw into it everybody who didn't agree with their view of the world. She was sure she'd be among the first to be flung.

"Comforting, aren't they?" she muttered to Estrella after finding her co-worker in the milling crowd outside the church. More than half of those milling had that white-sock aura Bo associated with cops.

"Revelation," the familiar voice of Madge Aldenhoven

mentioned behind them. "Written by the Apostle John while in exile on Patmos."

"There's every reason to believe the book of Revelation was actually written by an ancestor of *mine.*" Bo smiled at her supervisor. "It's so nice to see you, Madge. But what a sad occasion."

"*Madre de dios.*" Estrella said under her breath.

"Don't forget that you're on probation, Bo," Madge murmured, narrowing her eyes. "I can tell from your attitude that you're up to something. I have to stress that I think you'd be more comfortable in another line of work. Surely you agree."

Bo saw Dar Reinert beckoning from the church steps.

"I had almost come to that conclusion on my own, but now I don't think so." Bo slid out of the conversation. "We'll know tomorrow. Right now I hope you'll excuse me while I chat with Detective Reinert."

"What did she mean by 'we'll know tomorrow'?" Madge asked Estrella.

"I have no idea," Estrella answered, shaking her head.

Dar Reinert, commandeering the church steps by sheer bulk, could not have looked more obviously official if he'd been in uniform. "You're gonna like hearing this," he grumbled into Bo's ear. "We found your nut-case Zolar last night, sleeping in a tree in Balboa Park. And here's the weird part. When we got him out of County Psychiatric and took him down to the canyon this morning, just to see if he'd say anything, this seventy-year-old retired schoolteacher who looks like she pumps iron comes crashing through the shrubbery. Says she has a house on the other side, hikes in the canyon a lot. Says she knew this psycho was there, that she gave him vitamins or something."

Bo swallowed an erupting lecture on the meaningless term "psycho" and remembered Zolar's cache of wholesome supplies. So that's where he got them. But the schoolteacher had bombed with the premoistened towelettes. They wouldn't have helped much anyway.

"Here's the part you're gonna love," Reinert went on as a small pipe organ began the Guardian Angels' Song from Humperdinck's *Hansel and Gretel*. "This schoolteacher says your nut was in her backyard sleeping on a picnic table Tuesday afternoon from 1:30 to about 6:00. Bonnie Franer said she picked up Samantha from the day-care center at about 5:15. Your guy's got an alibi for the whole afternoon the day of the rape."

Bo couldn't tell if the news or the sentimental music were responsible for the tears in her eyes. Probably both, she decided. There had been a guardian angel for Zolar. She made a mental note to take the old schoolteacher a fifth of good Irish whiskey.

"Bradley, I didn't know you were gonna *cry* for chrissakes," Reinert spluttered. He seemed amazed when the handkerchief he pulled from the breast pocket of his jacket turned out to be a small fan of paisley stapled to a piece of cardboard. Grimacing, he wadded the object into a ball and dropped it behind one of the Hollywood junipers bending over St. Theresa's steps.

People were filing in to take seats in the little church as Bo became aware of something covered in fawn-colored cashmere, nudging her side. It was an arm, attached to the shoulder of Dr. Andrew LaMarche.

"May I?" he offered in a calm baritone.

Behind him Estrella and Madge Aldenhoven formed a smiling wall.

Bo nodded demurely, placed her left hand through the doctor's arm, and wished she were in Dixie, wherever that was. At the holy water font inside the door she dipped her fingers and touched her forehead out of childhood programming before recalling that she hadn't been attached to Roman Catholicism in any meaningful way since her first bra. The holy water ran over her left eyebrow and into her eye. Never fond of funerals, Bo measured the possibility that this might be the worst yet. In less than a minute the merely possible became hard fact.

In a quiet frenzy of courtesy LaMarche stood aside as Madge and then Estrella entered a pew followed by Bo and finally the elegant doctor. Estrella quickly dropped to the kneeler, pulling Bo with her as if for comfort.

"Don't freak," Estrella whispered into clasped hands, "but isn't that the ACLU guy sitting in front of LaMarche?"

"Oh, God," Bo breathed. A heartfelt prayer. The unkempt

mop of sandy curls in the next pew belonged to Solon Gentzler. It was going to be the funeral from hell.

"In the name of the Father and the Son and the Holy Ghost," Father Frank Goodman pronounced as everyone settled into blond and oddly Scandinavian pews. Sunlight filtering through the predominantly green rose window created an aquarium-like atmosphere. The effect was not diminished by a robed figure of Christ ascendant above the altar. In sparkling green light, the statue seemed to be drifting upward from the depths of a pale sea. Behind her Bo heard Dar Reinert's gruff whisper.

"Keep your eyes open, Bradley. See if anything looks fishy to you."

Only an invitation from Frank Goodman to join in singing "We Shall Overcome" saved Bo from an inappropriate grin tormenting the corners of her mouth. Too much watery imagery. And now the anthem of the civil rights movement? What next?

Solon Gentzler's enthusiastic and off-key rendering of the familiar song, audible above everyone else, only made matters worse. Bo was glad to cover her face with her right hand as Frank Goodman began his homily, which had to do with overcoming an evil that had destroyed a little girl and her mother. When she was certain of her composure, Bo placed her hand properly in her lap and scanned the assemblage. Lots of cops. Some of the staff from St. Mary's surgical floor. Lots of media types. A number of nuns.

Bo scanned the nuns closely for any who might not be what they seemed. If Samantha's killer were stupid enough to attend the service, an old-fashioned religious habit might make an interesting disguise. Of the twenty-seven nuns in the church, representing Benedictine, Carmelite, and Sacred Heart orders, not one could conceivably have been a man.

Frank Goodman was doing something with two roses—one creamy white, the other a tiny pink bud. He was tying the roses together with a broad silver ribbon. Estrella dabbed at running mascara with a handkerchief; LaMarche looked waxen. Bo didn't want to hear the priest's words. Didn't want to think about the lost mother and child the flowers were meant to represent.

"Humph," Dar Reinert snorted behind her.

Turning to see what had caused the detective's reaction, Bo noticed two men taking seats at the rear of the church. One was short, well muscled, and had obviously suffered a broken and badly set nose in the past. His eyes behind black wire-frame glasses were somber. His companion was taller, blond, and wore a Hollywood-style silk Armani jacket with more grace than most talk show hosts. On the jacket's lapel was a tiny gold and enamel rainbow flag.

"You know those guys?" Reinert whispered over the back of Bo's pew.

"No," she answered, turning to face the detective. "Neither one of them's from CPS. And I haven't seen them at St. Mary's, either."

"Shh," Madge admonished as everyone dropped to the kneelers while Frank Goodman led them in prayer.

Bo grabbed a program from St. Theresa's morning services out of the hymnal rack on the pew behind Solon Gentzler and carefully read announcements for a youth group car wash, a marriage encounter group for seniors, and the sung rosary group's need for an alto and a bass. As an MTV video, she mused, the sung rosary might be an unexpected hit. Anything was better than attending to Frank Goodman's words, which were about a child Bo had seen in the transitional moments just after death. Between the medical ritual and those that would follow—the closing of the eyes, the covering of the face. Rituals incongruous and horrible when performed for a tiny child.

In the pocket of her long khaki skirt Bo felt the grieving beads Hannah had given her, and allowed herself to remember her own sister. Her own hopelessness in the face of suicide. Hannah would have to face that, too, when she came to terms with her mother's death. A difficult reality to face. Pulling the strip of beads from her pocket she held them in clasped hands as Frank Goodman finished an appeal for the repose of both daughter and mother. In the front row the elderly Father Karolak succumbed to a sudden fit of coughing clearly designed to obscure Frank Goodman's words. Goodman could, Bo pondered, find himself in deep trouble for that prayer, assuming anybody heard it over Father Karolak's staged hacking. Deep trouble for including a suicide in his kindly intentions. The Roman Catholic church was not renowned for its sympathetic understanding of clinical depression's worst-case scenario. It was apparent that Father Frank Goodman didn't care.

"The man has courage," Andrew LaMarche noted quietly as they stood. "And so do you, Bo. I'm sorry that I questioned your judgment. Your decision regarding Hannah was the right one." He glanced at Madge Aldenhoven, ramrod straight in a navy linen suit beside Estrella. "I admire what you've done."

Frank Goodman, accompanied by pipe organ, was singing Gounod's Ave Maria in his fine, almost Irish, tenor. Bo fought down a resurgence of the confusion Andrew LaMarche seemed determined to promote. "Thanks, Andy," she whispered, and stuffed the grieving beads back into her pocket. When he took her hand briefly she felt ridiculous and comfortable simultaneously, but didn't pull away. Not until Solon Gentzler, in unfamiliar territory and checking the crowd for clues as to what to do next, turned to glance over his shoulder. His big smile faded to a flush of chagrin when he saw LaMarche leaning in what could only be described as a husbandly attitude against Bo. Bo jerked her right hand from the pediatrician's left one and looked at the church's beamed ceiling. It provided, as she had known it would, no exit.

"Oh, boy . . ." Estrella pronounced through a clenched smile.

"Thank you all for coming," Frank Goodman concluded as the organist began to play an obscure but upbeat medieval gavotte. Rivulets of sweat gathered momentum and dribbled down her back as Bo stood gratefully to leave. The memorial service had possessed, she decided, all the better-known qualities of the Spanish Inquisition.

Once outside she made a dash for the shade of a well-leafed liquid amber tree at the edge of St. Theresa's property, ducked behind its trunk, and lit a cigarette. Madge Aldenhoven materialized within minutes.

"I hope you're prepared for tomorrow's hearing," the

supervisor reminded her. "You will represent the department and you will say that in your professional opinion Paul Massieu is the person responsible for Samantha's death. You will recommend, on behalf of the Department of Social Services, that he be held over for prosecution. You will note in your testimony that he represents a threat not only to Samantha's kidnapped sister, but to all children. I've prepared a statement outlining the department's position on this case. All you have to do is read it."

Bo exhaled smoke at the envelope Madge was handing her, and stared at one of the tree's star-shaped leaves. "And if I don't?" she asked.

"This is a directive from the department," Aldenhoven answered as if the words were a creed. "Failure to represent an official position is grounds for immediate dismissal."

"Ah." Bo nodded, rolling the envelope into a tube and looking through it at the leaf. "I assume you have a copy of this statement against which to match my testimony."

"Yes. But of course it doesn't need to be word-for-word."

"Refreshing," Bo told the leaf. "So refreshing."

"I'll see you tomorrow, Bo." Madge smiled without authenticity, and left.

Bo stubbed out the cigarette and dropped the butt in her best purse, which would now reek of rancid filter. She never left cigarettes lying around, and also never remembered to retrieve the butts from purses and pockets. It seemed a minor problem compared to those lining up behind tomorrow's showdown. But she'd made her decision. Gentzler had it choreographed down to the last nuance. All she had to do was follow through.

"Are you Bo Bradley?" the man with the broken nose inquired, making his way across St. Theresa's robust lawn.

"Yes," Bo answered. "Why?" His attitude was businesslike, but tinged with a sort of planned determination.

"I'm Rombo Perry," he explained. "I was the social worker for Mrs. Franer. I was there when she . . . when she died."

"It was nice of you to come," Bo said, puzzled. Rombo Perry's handsome, unusual face seemed haggard. The look was inconsistent with the man's remarkable fitness. She would not have been surprised if he'd attempted to sell her a health club membership.

"I've been a little upset since it happened . . ." he explained.

"A little?" his companion in the Armani jacket interrupted, approaching from the sidewalk with obvious concern for possible damage to the grass. "It's been a dark night of the soul, let me tell you. I'm Martin St. John, by the way. We've been following the case in the papers, of course. And we're concerned about you."

Bo was relieved that St. John did not pronounce his surname "Sinjin" in the British way. The lack of affectation boded well for whatever it was they wanted to say. "Yes?" she prodded. The sky was beginning to glower in a way that whispered of early tropical storms. Bo tried to remember if one were predicted.

"I don't think Mrs. Franer's boyfriend, the one they've got in jail, hurt the little girl," Rombo Perry continued hurriedly. "It just doesn't make any sense. I think the guy that killed the child is the same guy that trashed the mission and killed that obnoxious psychologist last night."

"This Satanic nonsense is a smokescreen behind which somebody's getting away with murder," St. John added, frowning at the sky. "Is it supposed to rain?"

Bo pondered the intense interest with which people in arid regions regard precipitation, and waited for a point to be made. Any point.

"This may sound a little dramatic," Rombo Perry went on, "but have you considered the possibility that this guy may come after you next? I mean, he may have a list . . ."

It occurred to Bo that the two men standing before her were total strangers. Rombo Perry might not be a social worker at all. And what kind of name was Rombo? Jamming her hands in her skirt pockets, she strolled toward Dar Reinert, conferring with a reporter near the curb. The two followed. "I've thought of it," she admitted. "But what has it got to do with you?"

"I see you've met Mr. Perry and Mr. St. John," Reinert boomed after Bo shot him a concerned look. "I've already checked 'em out, Bo. They're who they say they are. In fact, everybody here is who they say they are. The mystery man, if there is one, didn't show."

"But he *will* show," Rombo Perry insisted. "He can't just get away with what he's done."

"We don't even know who he is," Reinert sighed, swinging his arms as if the activity would make something happen. "Massieu may have raped the little girl, and some other fruitcake may have vandalized the mission, and yet *another* nut may have taken Ganage out. This Satan crap has every loony in town sharpening knives and jumping at shadows. My take on the whole mess is, we'll never solve this case."

Bo was confident that she'd never heard so many casually inaccurate terms used at the same time. "But what if your nut/fruitcake is Samantha's killer and he isn't loony at all?" she asked. "What if he decides to kill again?"

"If he does," Rombo Perry took a deep breath, "doesn't Ms. Bradley seem the most likely victim? Of the three people whose names have been publicly linked to the Franer case—you, Detective Reinert, Cynthia Ganage, and Ms. Bradley—she is the remaining woman."

"What's being a woman got to do with it?" Reinert asked.

"He won't go after a man, a cop," St. John interjected as Bo felt a chill unrelated to the darkening sky. "He'll only go for somebody weaker than he is. If you don't have enough extra patrolmen to give Ms. Bradley a guard, at least at night, Rombo and I have decided to volunteer. Would that be all right with you?"

The question was directed to Bo.

"Uh, no, really, I'll be fine. I'm staying at a friend's tonight. But thanks," she replied. The offer was disturbing.

Martin St. John extracted a business card from his jacket and handed it to Bo. "St. John Catering" was embossed in script above a quirky pen-and-ink drawing of a place setting featuring seven forks, the last of which seemed to be falling off the side of the card.

"Just call us if you need help," Rombo added. "I'm serious."

Nodding, Bo left to find Estrella and make arrangements to spend the night in safety.

"You're finally showing some sense," Estrella agreed. "We'll expect you for dinner."

The black-clad demonstrators were gone as Bo eased her car from the curb, but something of their spirit hung over the windswept street. A sense of judgment, of irrational and relentless retribution.

Chapter 24

The streets had become a lavender web of jacaranda blossoms as the wind blew them in storms from curbside trees. Bo watched the purple carpet ripple and tear where the BMW's tires disturbed it, and then settle again when she had passed. The little flowers created a fairy-tale atmosphere in which thoughts of bloody murder seemed merely unpleasant. The leaves of a silver-dollar gum tree bristled in the wind and turned from gray-green to silver in a tremulous wave.

"Rattling silver, rattling sorrow," her grandmother's voice murmured the Irish warning out of nowhere.

"The referent there is money, not leaves, Grandma Bridget," Bo said aloud and then frowned at her own reflection in the car's side mirror.

Uh-oh. The proverbs are back. Better get some rest.

At first the residential neighborhoods she traversed en route to the freeway appeared to be making a statement about what Sunday afternoons were meant to be. Green ivy. Nice fences. A white dog and teenage boy, playing Frisbee. Then an elderly woman in a red muumuu and cat's-eye sunglasses throwing soapy water on a rose bush. Strange. Followed by two potbellied men, one black and the other white, trying to wrestle what looked like a wire sculpture of a giant amoeba off the bed of an old pickup truck with Oklahoma plates. Stranger. A cluster of children staring murderously at a utility meter . . .

Oh, right. Check it out, Bradley. Whether you like it or not, you're edging into the Twilight Zone. Quit pretending that anything's normal. Go to Estrella's and get some sleep.

Norman Rockwell had given way to David Mamet. Just as well, Bo decided. Rockwell painted a fantasy of Stockbridge, Massachusetts, as it was before Alice's Restaurant. Mamet would be more comfortable with freeze-frames of southern California collapsing on a Sunday afternoon into naked scraps of inexplicable human behavior. Weird vignettes that might be terrible and might be meaningless. Grainy snapshots lacking the narrative that would impose on them an illusion of sense. Bo turned a corner and nearly hit a longhorn chicken drifting from between two parked Nissan Pathfinders, both blue and immaculately clean. The longhorn turned out to be a wadded newspaper, caught in the wind. Or else it really was a chicken, blown in from a Depression-era newsreel, lost in time. Bo pulled the car to a stop in front of a mustard yellow bungalow with brown trim, and tried not to see the plaster elf peeking over the porch railing. An elf with pitiless, painted eyes.

This could happen sometimes, without the lithium. As if a veil of imposed coherence, of mundane ordinariness were lifted away and the raw truth made visible. The raw truth that things were stranger than they seemed to be. The first hint had been on Wednesday, when the veil began to unravel. That was to be expected, just the usual manic-depressive drift. Bo was used to it. It might happen, Lois Bittner said, when Bo was under stress. Or when she was premenstrual, or postmenstrual, or when she had the flu. It might happen with a sudden drop in atmospheric pressure, or with a poignant memory, or with indigestion. Nobody knew when it might happen, in other words. But it was happening now. Bo closed her eyes and listened to the engine's idle.

"I'm scared," she said aloud and lit a cigarette.

"So?" Lois Bittner's voice echoed in her head. "What is it that's scaring you?"

"Somebody might try to kill me, for one," Bo exhaled. "But that's not really it. It's what I'm going to do tomorrow. I'm terrified."

"This thing you're going to do tomorrow scares you more than somebody trying to kill you?" the familiar voice asked.

"A lot more," Bo answered, shivering. "Should I go through with it?"

There was no answer, only the sound of wind rustling the fronds of a palm tree in the bungalow's yard. In her mind Bo could see a picture of Lois Bittner, the wise old eyes bright and fond. The Frye boots, the long skirts, the Indian jewelry. Clothes from another era. Pastrami lunches in St. Louis restaurants that probably weren't even there anymore. The shrink's warm office in a building now leveled for a mall parking garage. The truth, unvarnished.

Bo had stayed in St. Louis for over a year after her collapse at the Holiday Inn, just to work with Lois Bittner against the shifting chemistry in her skull. They'd perused the medical literature, tried varying medications, read the famous mood-disordered writers—Keats, Poe, Virginia Woolf, Hemingway, Robert Lowell, Sylvia Plath, Anne Sexton—until Bo knew their lives and symbols, their depressions and manias, better than they had. Bittner discouraged Bo's interest in van Gogh and the other affected painters, suggesting that Bo's similar talent might forge too great an identity. In defiance Bo had freelanced an article on "Van Gogh's Use of Black" for an art journal and dyed half her wardrobe to match the artist's indigo irises. A job as volunteer coordinator for a Jewish community center of whose board Lois Bittner was a member provided a living. The position had preserved a vocational integrity useful in getting her old job back at the reservation, and then in getting this one. But a year after Bo returned to New Mexico Lois Bittner had traveled to Germany for a conference, and died of a massive cerebral hemorrhage in a Bremen *bierstube*. Friends had arranged for her burial there. Bo was saving for the day when she would lay a pastrami sandwich on that grave.

"You're gone, aren't you?" she addressed the picture of Lois Bittner in her mind. "You're not there anymore. You're dead." The picture didn't change. But a message gleamed in the familiar eyes. "I'm not dead as long as some part of me lives in you," Bo answered for the best friend she'd ever had. "Don't blow it."

Grinning, she gunned the car to the nearest 7-Eleven and dropped a quarter in its pay phone. "This is Bo Bradley from County Social Services," she abridged her place of employment to a more serviceable label for the floor nurse at County Psychiatric. "The police have informed me that a client I know as Zolar was taken there yesterday night. Is he still there?"

The news was that Zolar, aka Patrick Darren Preble, had been taken by a family overjoyed that he was alive to a private psychiatric hospital called, like fully half of San Diego's schools, streets, and office buildings, Mesa Vista. Bo knew right where it was, only a few miles from her office. In fifteen minutes she was there.

"So Patrick," she smiled, propping her feet on the edge of the bed where he lay clean and frozen in a darkness Bo recognized as a cousin to her own so long ago, "why are you here? Ignore the voices for a minute and let me tell you about this great little Mexican restaurant up the street. Fabulous carne asada and the best chicken chimichangas north of the border. Sound good? We'll go there in a few days, and that's a promise."

A pulse of light deep in the teal blue eyes, a barely perceptible spasm near the corner of the mouth under the trimmed red beard were sufficient evidence of success. And then there was more. The blazing finale for any remaining reticence Bo might have regarding tomorrow's dive off an outgrown cliff.

"How's Mildred?" Patrick Preble inquired thickly.

Bo could only imagine the effort necessary to frame the polite and wondrously appropriate question through both the illness and the muddying medications that had given the young man back his name.

"Mildred's fine," she answered. "And she remembers the jerky you gave her."

Driving west on I-8 a half hour later, Bo turned on the radio for an explanation of the purple-gray clouds roiling above San Diego. One of them, she decided as the announcer explained that a freak tropical storm named Annabelle was swirling offshore, looked like a Kodiak bear stretching to eat a file cabinet.

It was exhaustion, she admitted. And the monumental stress of this case. There was no medication that could take away the disturbing imagery, the sense that odd and potentially horrifying realities lurked everywhere, their disguises simply gone. It was a perception Bo accepted simply as a truth few others could see. A perception to which she could give form in her paintings. Not quite delusional. Sometimes fascinating. Always unnerving.

She'd run home, pick up Mildred and a change of clothes, and get to Estrella's before the storm hit. She'd be safe at Estrella's. She could rest and calm the odd sensibility, prepare for tomorrow. It was going to be okay.

Chapter 25

Eva Broussard walked barefoot along the beach, nearly deserted as Sunday afternoon picnickers and the perennial bands of surfers fled the oncoming storm. Hannah Franer ran before her, chasing flotsam thrown on the dull golden sand by frothing waves. In the dim light the child looked magical, like one of the Jo-Ge-Oh, the Iroquois Little People said to live in the lost ravines of the Adirondack and Catskill wildernesses.

Eva watched the child and considered the reasons why all the nations of the world told stories of "little people" with magical power whose homes were hidden in natural places. Perhaps the tales were a way of honoring childhood itself, lost in each individual forever with the grim surge of reproductive chemistry at puberty. Lost, but remembered and reified in myth. The preservation of childhood, she nodded at her own thoughts, might be the telling variable in a human equation now dangerously skewed toward destruction.

The man who destroyed Samantha Franer had violated that necessity. The man who raped a three-year-old child was removed from the human community and all its future. But he wasn't the only one. Thousands of others like him, perhaps millions, walked on the earth, self-absorbed and forever alone. A terrible power lay in their ability to damage the very foundation on which human happiness must be built. A power to poison the little people, and thereby tear apart the web of life. Most of them, Eva thought as cream-colored spume bubbled and then vanished in the sand at her feet, had no awareness of the cruel distortion they threw into the future. But this one, the one who eviscerated Samantha Franer with the weapon of his own body, had somehow glimpsed it. And embraced it. He knew what he was now. And his rage at the knowledge would propel him to kill and kill until something stopped him.

Hannah seized a broken shell from the littoral and held it up for Eva to see. A penknife clam shell, purplish and similar in color to the quahog beads pinned on the child's shirt. The clams were related, their shared history documented under ancient seas. Like the two people on this Pacific beach, Eva smiled, with their shared history of stories. "Let's go sit up there," she gestured to a small amphitheater in the worn cliffs where a sandstone layer had collapsed in piles of rubble beneath a stripe of white quartz.

Hannah scrambled ahead, her golden hair streaming in the odd light. "Up there, up there," she sang into the whipping wind, ozone-scented and laden with salty chill. "Let's go sit up there."

It was a mark of the child's strong spirit, Eva conceded, that she'd been able to speak again so quickly after the horrors that locked her in silence. But her speech wasn't self-generated, not spontaneous. Not yet. Since early in the afternoon she'd repeated phrases Eva said to her in a peculiar singsong voice, as if words were audible toys to be played with, not symbols that could define Hannah Franer and her experience to the world outside her head. That experience was too terrible to define, Eva knew. But the experience also *was* Hannah Franer. If the child could not be brought to define it, that fierce, boundaried core of being called self would never wholly return.

Purple-gray clouds fringed in shifting yellow glare jostled over the windswept water as Eva gathered her skirts and climbed into the small amphitheater beside Hannah. Cupped in the western edge of the North American continent, a dim silence seeped from the curved stone walls. Eva Broussard listened to the silence and heard the pulse of ten thousand stories, told so that people might know what they were.

Hannah sat cross-legged in jeans wet to the knee, and drew lines in the sand with her broken clam shell. The jeans, Eva noted as if from a great distance, were already snug, a little too short. The child's body was growing. Could her mind be brought in step? Far at sea filaments of lightning threaded toward an invisible horizon. In the flickering surge of light Eva saw a woman's face beneath the child's. A face like Bonnie Franer's, but also different. A firmer set to the wide jaw. A smoothness over the sandy eyebrows that in the mother had seemed a landscape of crimped cloth. The face of the woman Hannah Franer might become, if she were given tools with which to survive.

"Look how your California clam shell is purple," Eva began in the storyteller's voice she had heard in childhood, "just like your clam shell grieving beads from New York are purple. The California clam shells are *like* the New York clam shells."

"Like New York," Hannah sang in the quiet shelter, watching Eva from the sides of wide-set eyes.

"And I'm going to tell you a special story," Eva went on, almost chanting. "It is the story of Otadenon, whose name means 'The Last One Left.' "

"Last, last," Hannah sang, rocking slightly to the sound of Eva's voice.

"Otadenon was the last one left of his family," Eva continued softly. "His family had been taken away forever by something *otgont*, something very bad."

"Bad," Hannah repeated in a quavering falsetto. Her left hand reached for the grieving beads over her heart.

Eva let herself rock beside the child as she told the story, of how Otadenon, to save the life of the man who cared for him, traversed a trail guarded by two snakes, two bears, and two panthers on the way to the terrible chestnut grove where the flayed skin of a woman hung in the trees, singing a warning if anyone came near.

"Skin Woman," Hannah repeated, but did not sing. *"Otgont."*

"Yes," Eva replied, taking no apparent notice of the emerging conceptual connection. "And Otadenon was very, very afraid. But he tricked Skin Woman by giving her a worthless wampum belt, and got plenty of chestnuts to feed everyone, and went home. Otadenon was very afraid, but he didn't give Skin Woman his life. Otadenon was the Last One Left, and he went on being Otadenon, Hannah. He won. Can you guess who Otadenon, the Last One Left, is like?"

Hannah drew a tightening spiral in the sand with the penknife clam shell, rocking hard. "Clams like . . . New York," she pronounced, gasping. "Otadenon is like . . . me. Because I'm the Last One Left."

"Yes, Hannah," Eva whispered as the wind gusted a shower of sand up from the beach and the child's face broke in sobs. "Otadenon's story is your story, too." From deep in her heart Eva Blindhawk sent a prayer of thanks to the chain of Iroquois storytellers who had preserved through time a story that would teach Hannah Franer who she was.

After Hannah wept for a long time within the circle of Eva's arms, she looked up through matted eyelashes, her head cocked to one side. "Can there be two Last One Lefts?" she asked.

Eva was puzzled. "What do you mean, Hannah?"

"There's two Last One Lefts. Like Otadenon. I'm one, and there's another one." She smoothed her windblown hair with both hands in a businesslike gesture that made Eva smile. "I think you're not really the Last One Left when there's two. And Bo's the Last One Left, too. She said so. So me and Bo, we're the last *two* left. Kind of like sisters. See?"

In the keening of the sea wind Eva imagined she heard an ancient wooden flute, its music sent from the midwinter fire of a vanished Iroquois longhouse. Sent into the future through the mind of a child on a California beach. The gamble had succeeded; the story had given coherence to mere fragments of pain. When Hannah plumbed its depths and molded it to fit her own need, the story became a bridge to a future unimagined when the tale was first told.

"I do see, Hannah," Eva answered. "And you're very,

very smart to have figured out how you and Bo are both like Otadenon, how you and Bo are both the Last One Left. You have a good mind like a *Hageota*, a storyteller. I am proud to be your grandmother."

The child's eyes glowed as a smile lit her wide, freckled face.

"I'm hungry," she mentioned, standing and stretching her arms toward the sea. "Can we get a hamburger? Can we call Bo? I want to tell her about Otadenon. Skin Woman won't get *us*!"

In a flurry of sand and pebbles Hannah scrambled from the little enclosure and dashed across the gray-lit beach, her face exultant. Eva followed, smiling. The story of Otadenon, created in a time when sickness and cold might leave anyone the sole survivor of a family, had leaped three thousand miles and probably as many years.

"Nyah-weh," Eva pronounced into the wind. "Thank you."

Chapter 26

Mildred, bored with her long day alone in the apartment, had overturned Bo's kitchen wastebasket and strewed pizza crusts, cigarette ashes, coffee grounds, and half a microwave tray of moldering macaroni-and-cheese onto the dining area carpet. The little dog's breath bore a telltale hint of Italian spices.

"I see you didn't eat the crusts again." Bo sighed. She'd forgotten to put the wastebasket on the counter, a necessary precaution when going out for extended lengths of time. "And I've got to take you out now, before the rain starts."

Mildred wagged her stubby tail in anticipation as Bo grabbed the red leather collar and leash from an easel in the dining area. Beyond her second-story deck the Pacific Ocean pounded the empty beach and gray cliffs with tons of murky saltwater. Bo could almost see the Flying Dutchman, crewed by skeletons in ragged pantaloons, floundering in the storm-driven surf. St. Elmo's fire flashing from the tattered riggings. The mainmast groaning and then breaking with a sound like blasted rock.

"Yark!" Mildred said at the door. A reminder to curb the

enjoyable rush of imagination. Stay with the program. Take the dog out.

"Hurry up," Bo told the dog as they hurried toward a grassy area abutting the seawall. Beneath the Ocean Beach pier, walls of water surged upward and split in white flumes of spray against the pier's underside. Ahead, palm trees dropped fronds on the balconies of a pink motel facing south from Newport Street. The motel seemed deserted, its sets of glass doors dark. Except there was someone on one of the balconies. A man. Short and nondescript in a black T-shirt and jeans, he appeared to be watching the storm. But Bo thought she could feel his attention shift to her and Mildred when they stopped beside a trash can on the grass. Mildred sniffed the receptacle with scholarly ardor as Bo tried not to look upward again. Had the man in the Hawaiian shirt on the beach been short? She couldn't remember. The man on the beach had been sitting on the seawall. Hard to tell if a seated figure is short. When she glanced at the balcony again, he'd gone inside. She could see the drape move slightly behind the sliding glass door, but no light. Why would he be sitting around in the dark? A lamp in the motel's street-level office indicated the presence of electricity in the building. Maybe he was watching them, unseen. Maybe he was the one who carved a hole in a canyon and painted it pink. Maybe he was the one who preserved hotel carpeting by exsanguinating people in bathtubs.

"And maybe my imagination is running at full-tilt boogie," Bo told Mildred. "Let's get to Estrella's."

Back in the apartment Bo regarded the mess on the floor and then picked up the phone.

"Es . . . Mildred's dumped the trash on the carpet. I don't want to face this when I get home tomorrow. I'll clean it up and then come right over, okay?"

Estrella mentioned several matters more pressing than tidy carpets, principally storms and blood-filled bathtubs.

"Just as soon as I can . . ." Bo promised, and hung up.

The vacuum cleaner was wedged in a broom closet among four outdated editions of *The Physicians' Desk Reference*, a striped beach umbrella, and a collapsible snow shovel Bo had kept after St. Louis for the simple elegance of its design. The storm broke just as she disentangled the vacuum's cord from a nest of dust-filmed Christmas tree lights on the closet floor. Gusting wind slammed sheets of black rain against the deck doors, making the glass wobble. In the watery design Bo imagined she saw Irish beasts from her grandmother's tales—the Dun Cow, the "slim, spry deer," a Selky seal with woeful eyes who'd once been human for a while—their mouths all wide and warning. Mildred stood growling under an easel, her ears cocked.

"It's just the storm," Bo said, suddenly edgy. Patches of orange cheese sauce had dried, flecked with coffee grounds, to the carpet's nap. Bo scrubbed the offending islands of color with a soapy sponge, rinsed and blotted the area until the carpet was spotless.

"Aye 'n' they found yer Aunt Mary Duffy," Bo's grandmother had reminded Bo's father every summer during her visits from Ireland, "dead as a stone, her rooms like a pigsty they said. 'Twas a crime 'n' a shame, such a thing." The idea had been to induce neatness in the perennially messy library of Michael O'Reilly, whose elder daughter, if now found dead, would at least not be found dead in a pigsty. Bo wondered if her father's Aunt Mary Duffy had possessed a dog with a fondness for trash. And how the negligent housekeeper had died. Outside a tree limb cracked in the wind, and fell to the street with a whoosh.

Bo abandoned the vacuum cleaner where it stood, and hurried to her bedroom closet.

"And what shall I wear to the court, tomorrow?" she sang to an Irish tune, and then finished the song. "You haven't an arm and you haven't a leg. You're an eyeless, noseless, chickenless egg. And you'll have to be put in a bowl to beg. Och, Bradley, I hardly knew ye."

The forest green bijou jacket, she decided. Matching skirt if she could still button the waist, and cream silk blouse with a Mandarin collar. The emerald drop earrings her mother had worn onstage with the Boston Symphony. No rings. Gold watch. Don't forget the damn green shoes. New pantyhose, still in the package. It was important to look conservatively smashing for the event in which she would reveal to a hostile world just how "different" it was possible to be. As the lights flickered and then regained their normal luminosity, Bo considered how she might appear in this outfit, pushing a wire grocery cart through alleys. Pausing to glean handfuls of brown-edged lettuce from dumpsters behind restaurants. Exactly how did one hold the second glove, while grubbing through pre-used food?

But Solon Gentzler had said it couldn't happen. Not after the Disabilities Act. Madge Aldenhoven and all her demonic bureaucracy couldn't touch Bo, he'd said. And it would be a landmark step for those who would come after, like Hannah Franer. Bo remembered the child's trembling hand, the gift of grieving beads. Zolar weeping in the canyon. Her people. A lost family.

Folding the clothes neatly, Bo placed them in a waterproof duffel bag, zipped it shut, and turned off the lights. Something made a thumping noise on the deck. An overturned plant, Bo decided, clipping her car keys to the edge of her skirt pocket. Not worth dealing with in the rain. Mildred was whining near the door, her terrier eyes wolflike from fear.

"I can't believe you're losing it over a simple storm," Bo told the dog as the phone rang on the shadowy counter defining the kitchen. Bo tripped over the vacuum cleaner in a dash to answer.

"I'm leaving now, Es," she said into the phone.

"Leaving?" the voice of Rombo Perry replied. "Martin and I were thinking you might like a catered dinner and some company tonight. How about it? Breast of chicken in an orange brandy sauce over wild rice, steamed Japanese eggplant, rolls, of course, and a milk chocolate mousse. Martin's version of meals-on-wheels."

Bo leaned over to rub her ankle where it collided with the vacuum. "Sounds like heaven," she answered as she stood again, "but . . ." Something was wrong. Something moving in the dark outside. Not a potted plant. A man. "Oh shit, it's him."

Accustomed now to the dark, her eyes had been able to discern the dripping figure standing on the redwood deck. A figure in a black T-shirt with a white face on it. A bearded, old-fashioned face on a T-shirt. Distorted and ghostly on its black background. The figure wearing the T-shirt was holding something above its head in both hands. Something big. A deck chair. He was standing in the rain on her deck holding a chair over his head. As if in slow motion she saw the chair begin its descent in an arc toward the glass doors.

Bo heard the bell inside the phone jangle as it fell from the counter and hit the vacuum cleaner. Then a splintering of glass as she grabbed Mildred and ran from the apartment, leaving the door open to the wind-driven spray that blinded her as she stumbled on slick stairs, caught herself, and made it to the deserted street.

Her car was half a block away, wedged between a pickup truck and an illegally parked motorcycle with a faded surfboard chained to its gas tank. In the streetlight the hard rain made little inverted cups, brief and glasslike, as it hit the surfboard. Bo ran toward the car, imagining splashing footsteps in pursuit, the reach of a wet, pale arm. Her legs felt numb; the contraction and then expansion of large muscles necessary for running had to be thought about. The BMW seemed a receding mirage until Bo finally touched its metal surface. Grabbing her keys, she unlocked the car door and dived inside, pulling the door closed behind her and locking it. Through her rain-blurred rear window she saw the soaked figure jump the last three steps from her apartment stairs to the street, and look straight at her car. Mildred, cowering on the front seat, glanced nervously at Bo.

"We're outta here!" Bo bellowed, starting the car and pushing the motorcycle over the curb and into a streetlight pole. The surfboard cracked and split lengthwise, its two pieces making a twisted white fiberglass X over the crumpled bike. The BMW's rear wheels sent clouds of spray over the running figure whose hands grabbed and slipped on Bo's right fender as she spun out on Narragansett, away from the beach.

As he began to sprint after her, Bo thought he was going to try to catch her on foot.

"You imbecile," Bo yelled out the window, "you can't chase a car on foot!" The wind gripped her words and carried them away as the running man veered across the street and was lost between a darkened bungalow and an apartment complex whose backlit stained-glass lobby door featured dolphins rising through watery bubbles. Bo thought she felt his soul behind her like a globe of frozen ammonia. Not like dolphin bubbles. Caustic. Poisonous. She accelerated and then jammed on the brakes at Sunset Cliffs Boulevard where a fallen eucalyptus limb bisected the intersection diagonally. There was no option but to turn right, but so what? He must have gone to get his car. He'd never catch up. Bo turned onto Sunset Cliffs Boulevard where it snaked along the continent's edge. Something about his running unnerved her. An assurance, a businesslike determination that made no sense. Bo pushed down on the accelerator and within three blocks could no longer see the intersection where he'd vanished.

Six blocks later Bo took her foot off the accelerator to slow the car as the road curved left above the famous Sunset Cliffs, a sea-torn granite shelf from which the sunrise in Honshu, Japan, could easily be foreseen in North American twilight. The car was heading into the curve too fast. Bo pressed the brake pedal gently. Nothing. Pushed it to the floor. Still nothing.

Shit, it's the brakes! He's cut the brakeline and you just pumped the last of the fluid out at the intersection. He's back there, not far, and you have no brakes!

The BMW sheared a guardrail on the right as it careened around the curve, out of control. Heavily traveled, the boulevard wore a chemical skin of oil seldom cleaned off by the pressure of a thousand rubber tires scrubbing in rainwater. San Diego's yearly rainfall could be measured with kitchen utensils. The road was an oil slick.

Bo knew the point, only one long block away, at which the sea cut a notch to within feet of the road. Another curve to the left there. A curve she could never make. The car would fishtail, flip backward into the sea. Ramming the gearshift into reverse, Bo heard the scream of warring metal as she clutched Mildred tightly to her right side and scraped the guardrail for fifty feet before plowing through it into a pile of boulders. The boulders, she remembered as the steering wheel bent under her weight, had been hauled there from the desert. Dumped there to buffer the sea where it chewed into million-dollar property. Dumped there, maybe, to stop a runaway car headed for a watery burial. As her head cleared Bo thought of the runaway truck ramps all over New England. She'd seen them as a child. Off-ramps leading to hills of gravel that could catch and stop an eighteen-wheeler with no brakes. Boulders, she smiled dizzily, were just big gravel. The BMW hissed a smell of burnt metal, but was stationary. Its front end had crumpled like a stiff blanket thrown against the rocks.

Bo tried the driver's side door. Jammed. Most of the homes fronting the sea along the boulevard were lit and gleaming yellow in the black rain. But none of the doors was open. No one coming to see what had happened. In the roar of the surf, Bo realized, the headlong crash of a car into a rockpile might not be heard. Quickly she scooted to the passenger's side, tucked Mildred under her left arm, and tried the door. It opened into a cold torrent of rain and salt spray from the tumultuous waves lashing the cliffs twenty feet from the car. The man in his car might round the first curve any moment now. But there was still time to make a dash across the boulevard to one of the houses.

As Bo struggled out of the car an enormous wave rose, serpentine from the darkness below the cliffs, and broke in a blast of spray that stung her eyes. Rivulets of seawater ran down the back of her nose, leaving a bitter taste. Mildred sneezed and lurched out of Bo's grasp, landing clumsily on the wet stone. In a second the little dog had vanished into the rocks ahead, down toward the sea.

"Mildred!" Bo yelled pointlessly. Her voice was lost in the wind. As she clambered down the rocks after the dog, Bo saw a car's lights slicing the rain in wide, misty cones.

Chapter 27

Estrella Benedict watched as Henry threaded chunks of tequila-marinated turkey on metal skewers. The turkey alternated with ripe tomatillos and ruffled black mushrooms out of a jar. After a minute Estrella noticed that she'd torn a flour tortilla into four pie-shaped wedges and arranged them in an overlapping fan design in the sink.

"Bo should have been here by now," she said, mashing the wedges into the garbage disposal. "I'm worried."

"So am I," Henry Benedict agreed. "Maybe the storm's held her up."

In a red polo shirt and baggy white cotton pants he managed to look even more like a blond Abraham Lincoln than he did in his naval officer's uniform. Estrella noted the ridge of muscle wrinkling his forehead above the brow line. The last time she'd seen the furrow that deep they'd been camping in the desert and found a nest of newborn Western rattlers writhing in a shady wash. He'd stomped them with a Tony Lama boot and then thrown up behind an ocotillo cactus. Henry Benedict, Estrella had learned in four years of marriage, didn't say much and considered the implications of everything as if those implications mattered.

"I think I'll call LaMarche and see if he's heard from her," Estrella told the front of her toaster oven.

"Already called him five minutes ago," Henry replied into a hardwood cutting board hanging from a leather loop on the wall. "He says the Indian woman called him, saying the little girl's all upset, thinks something bad's happening to Bo."

"Hannah said that? Bo said she wasn't talking, that she's been mute since they told her her mother was dead."

"Well, I guess she's talking now," Henry concluded. "LaMarche said he was going over there, to Bo's place. Nothing to do but wait."

Estrella wrapped her arms around her husband's waist and listened to his heart beating slowly, its thump echoing through his back. "Bo's special," she said into his shirt. "Things never happen for her like they do for other people. She always goes deeper or something. It's scary."

"Maybe it's just what she has to deal with," he answered. "The manic-depressive thing. Maybe she just sees deeper. But we're here for her, Strell, and she knows that."

"Yeah." Estrella sighed and stared at a bright blue wall clock with hands shaped like crayons. Bo Bradley had given them the clock for Christmas last year, with numerous hints that the godchild she was expecting as soon as they were ready would undoubtedly learn to tell time within months of birth. "But this guy that raped Hannah's sister and killed the psychologist may be smarter than we think. He's really smart, Henry. What if he's gone after Bo?"

Henry Benedict aligned the skewers evenly on a foil-covered tray and glanced at the rainy kitchen window. "What makes you think he's so smart? Do you know something about this creep I haven't read in the papers?" he asked.

And then he listened as Estrella told him about a woman from a village in Chihuahua who would probably be heading there at this moment on a fumey second-class bus strung with Christmas tree lights, her children asleep on her lap. Somebody on the bus would have chickens in a cage, Estrella told her husband, crying. Somebody would be drunk. And somebody would be singing.

"You did the right thing, hon," he whispered as Estrella wept into his chest. "You really did."

"That's what Bo said," Estrella cried harder.

Chapter 28

Mildred, her pink skin visible under wet white fur, had wedged herself beneath a jagged rock at the edge of a drop into foaming black water that seemed alive. Bo found the white dog easily and then realized why. Her sodden blouse with its peasant sleeves and seven-button cuffs was white, too. If her pursuer were looking, he'd see her instantly.

No time left to cross the narrow road, find safety in a lighted house where people would open the door, phone the police. Nothing to do but crawl further into the rocks and hide. Nothing to do but hope the man would assume she'd made it to one of the houses, and leave. Bo pictured the house on the corner across from her ruined car. A mansion. Painted unaccountably pink. A historical landmark, in fact, with a lighted American flag in the yard. Once the home of a sporting goods magnate who'd been a lover of the mystical Theosophist Madame Tingley. Maybe the man chasing her would think Bo was in that house, safe, phoning the police. She grabbed Mildred, huddled beside a black rock, and conjured an image of the long-dead mystic. Maybe Madame Tingley's ghost would stay the hand of the killer.

As a flash of lightning tore the sky Bo looked across the vertical tube of angry water below to a flat ledge extending out to sea from behind another pile of boulders. Below the ledge was a tiny inlet, now swollen with surf.

That pink house is the Spaulding Mansion, Bradley. The cave is there, remember?

Holding Mildred in a viselike grip, Bo climbed down through ragged darkness to the surging trough of seawater she now remembered was usually a pleasant tidal estuary, full of hermit crabs and anemones. But how deep was it now? And how strong the pull as a thousand gallons of churning water receded through its channel after every wave? In the sea at the base of the five-foot-wide trough a jumble of sharp-edged rocks disappeared under the next surge of water. Barnacle-encrusted, they would shred the flesh of anything thrown against them by the outgoing torrent. Bo shifted Mildred to her right arm, waited for the thundering influx of water to peak and begin its rush back to the sea, and stepped into the trough.

The receding water, ice-cold, only came to a point two inches above her knees. On her numb feet a pair of button-sided pumps, purchased to complete a costume that suggested Katharine Hepburn in *The African Queen*, proved themselves worthy of the role and did not disintegrate. Bo made a mental note to send Nordstrom's shoe department a thank-you card, if she survived.

In the next step her left foot found a fissure, pulled back and balanced the combined weight of woman and dog on the edge of a fin-shaped rock. The next wave was rolling in, its shape like a truck-sized snake beneath the water. In a second it would arc against the rocks, higher than Bo's head, and then pull them both back down a frothing cataract to the sea. Bo pushed off, landed crookedly on her right foot, which seemed to bend, and in another step achieved the pile of rocks beyond the trough. The incoming wave plowed against her back with a force that pushed the air from her lungs and left her drenched in foam, but did not succeed in dragging her down the maelstrom of its backwash. Mildred shook her head violently against Bo's side, and struggled to be set free.

"Forget it, Mil," Bo told the dog. "You got us into this. Just ride it out."

After three more minutes of agonizing rock-crawling, Bo reached the cave. Not much as sea caves go, it looked like Atlantis to Bo. Just a hole in the continental shelf where the sea had dissolved a sandstone accretion when there was still a land bridge over the Bering Strait. Bo flung herself on the rocky floor and looked around. She'd been there before. The cave was a favorite local spot for picnics, esoteric rituals, romantic trysts. Also for the homeless, who had left mounds of trash and a stained orange blanket beside the sodden remains of a fire. Bo eyed the blanket with gratitude. It might introduce her to exotic skin diseases, but it would also forestall the effects of hypothermia. Edging toward the blanket, Bo realized there was something wrong with her right ankle. A throbbing pain. An odd limpness. Pulling off her shoe she tried to arch her toes, and watched as they responded with random, guppylike movements.

The storm was diminishing. On the fissured granite shelf that sloped downward thirty feet from the cave's mouth to a wave-lashed precipice, the rain fell now in steady, vertical strings. Bo wrung out her hair and the heavy folds of her khaki skirt. Then she dragged herself and Mildred to the fetid blanket and wrapped it around them, covering her own head so that anyone looking into the cave would see a dirty blanket thrown over a rock. Not a helpless woman with a badly sprained, possibly broken, ankle.

There was no way out of the cave except through its mouth facing the sea. Behind her left arm Bo felt the rough surface of a cement patch in the cave wall, five feet high and wider than her shoulders. Spaulding had made his fortune in more than pigskin footballs. During prohibition, Bo knew from an article she'd read in a local paper, the millionaire had dug a tunnel from a closet in the mansion and under Sunset Cliffs Boulevard to the cave. Mexican rum-runners, anchoring in the tiny cove below, would haul wooden cases of *ron negro* up the cliffs and through the tunnel to luxuriant safety. The tunnel was still there, under the street, but sealed over at both ends. Bo tried not to think of the historic crawlspace as a last, dashed hope. Mildred, snug against Bo's side under the odorous blanket, appeared to have fallen asleep. Bo hated herself for the warm tears she felt running over her cheeks.

Quit sniveling, Bradley. If it's time to die, do it so as not to disgrace your ancestors.

The words, straight from the mouth of Bridget Mairead O'Reilly, made Bo smile. Her grandmother, it seemed, never shut up. Under her breath Bo sang the Irish national anthem.

"Tonight we man the bearna baoghal," she crooned to Mildred. "In Erin's cause, come woe or weal . . ."

Beyond the cave mouth, waves crashed repeatedly over the jutting granite apron. Rain fell through winds that moaned eerily among the rocks. Mildred snored. Bo sang softly. And nothing happened. No drenched figure in black leapt to the cave's door. Nothing moved at all except the thundering surf and an occasional pebble shaken loose from the chamber's walls, probably by a car on the street above.

But if there were cars, wouldn't somebody have seen the smashed BMW and stopped to investigate? Bo glanced at the stone ceiling above her. Of course. The police would have been called by now. Might even be eight feet over her head at this very minute, asking door-to-door of the beachfront residents if anyone had seen the driver of the wrecked car. Bo focused on the churning foam beyond the cave's long, flat lip. Were there flashing red lights reflected from above? Once she thought she saw a shard of red bounce off the water, but maybe not. What if she were just sitting down here while a dozen rescuers walked above? Eventually they'd abandon their search, tow her car away, and leave. And the tide was turning.

The realization felt like a slab of ice laid over her chest. The waves beyond the cliffs loomed larger, their spray splattering closer to the ragged opening of the cave. Bo scanned the walls for a high-water line and found it two feet above her head. There was a high shelf to her left at the cave's rear. If it came to that, she could climb up there and simply wait out the storm. She probably wouldn't drown. It wasn't the threat of drowning that froze her heart. It was the Celtic belief that souls leave bodies at the turning of the tide. The time of wrenching, final transition. But whose?

In the rain-sliced dark at the cave's mouth something

moved. A lump of shadow indistinguishable from a hundred others shrouded in mist became a human figure, rising from a crouch before the ragged cave opening. In his right hand an open pocketknife gleamed as raindrops slid off its four-inch blade. A short, pale man whose sodden visage was oddly reptilian, the eyes unblinking.

Bo knew he couldn't quite see her in the gloom, yet his gaze was locked to hers in a psychic connection more damning than a spotlight. He knew where she was. In that connection Bo felt the force of something alien, something savagely empty. The man was not a man, but merely a form whose hatred of what he was not seethed like invisible spume around him. Something sick and deformed from the moment of its conception. A damned soul.

"You're *nothing*." Bo thought into his eyes, her heartbeat throbbing in her fingertips.

"Don't think this Irish girl can't see straight through you. You may kill me, but it won't make you human."

As he began to advance toward her, Bo threw off the filthy blanket and stood. In her head a thousand ancestral bones clamored in brogue. On the cave floor Mildred bristled and barked.

And then another figure filled the cave opening, spun the man in the black T-shirt around by his left shoulder, and sent him sprawling on the wet rock with an uppercut to the jaw. Bo watched the knife slide sideways into a puddle of foam. The second man wore black wire-frame glasses and had a crooked nose.

"It's okay, Bo!" Rombo Perry shouted into the cave as he pulled the black-clad reptile to his feet and flattened him again with a murderous punch to the nose. "We knew he was down here, but we weren't sure you were until your dog barked."

Bo thought she could smell the blood bubbling from the face of the man scuttling away from Rombo toward the edge of the cliff. A smell like peat, swampy and burnt.

"Fight, you son of a bitch!" Rombo screamed, moving toward the cowering form. "You fucking creep, you wanna rape a few more babies? Then fight for it! Give me the chance to kill you."

Bo saw the knotted muscles beneath Rombo's wet gray

dress shirt. And saw through the weakening rain what was coming.

"Don't do it, Rom!" another voice called from the rocks beside the shelf. "Let the police have him!"

Martin St. John, covered in mud, jumped down from the rubble. After him a fourth man, familiar and pale, rounded the cave entry and ran to Bo. She could only point as a huge swell, pitch black and silent, reached the southwestern edge of North America.

"Oh my God," Andrew LaMarche breathed as Martin St. John grabbed Rombo's shirt, Mildred barked, and a wave weighing more than the average two-bedroom house broke against the edge of the granite precipice. The splash knocked Martin and Rombo flat, surged up into the cave, and receded. Nothing lay at the cliff's edge now. The man in the black shirt was simply gone. Ten yards below in rocks like shrapnel something bobbed in the violent surf, and then vanished. But it wasn't a man, Bo knew. It never had been.

Chapter 29

Bo awoke wearing a U.S. Navy T-shirt in a room she recognized as Henry and Estrella Benedict's guest room. She had helped Es pick out the white-on-white striped wallpaper herself. A chaste fashion statement with the white wainscoting Henry created from strips of wood floor edging. On a bed table stood a vase containing two dozen long-stemmed American beauty roses. Beside Bo in the bed were Mildred—and Dr. Andrew LaMarche, unshaven and grinning in a matching T-shirt and Navy-issue denim bell-bottoms that obviously belonged to Henry.

"I have not compromised your virtue," he explained, shielding his eyes from the sun streaming through uncurtained windows. "You were so adamant about not remaining at the hospital that I brought you here, still sedated from the minor surgery necessary to set a few bones. Estrella didn't think you should be alone."

"My virtue is unassailable," Bo replied, "except under certain circumstances. You might just *try*, Andy."

"Very well." He flung himself to one knee beside the bed. "Will you marry me, Bo?"

"Oh God, do I have a broken leg? And I've told you—I've already been married. Can't we just be . . . something other than married? And why does my right foot smell like mouthwash?" Bo dragged herself up on her elbows and glanced at a porcelain clock beneath the roses. "It's 6:30. Plenty of time to get to court by 9:00. I would kill for a cigarette. And did all of that really happen last night, or am I delusional?"

"I take it that the issuing of banns may be premature." LaMarche shook his head, standing. "And I'd already sent my morning coat out to be pressed."

"Andy!" Bo replied with bemused irritation. "What happened after we went to the hospital? Did the police fish that guy out of the water? Who is . . . was he? Have they released Paul, now that the real perp's turned up? Did Rombo and Martin go over to my place and board up the deck doors like they said? Have you called Eva? And what about my car?"

"You have sustained rather bad displacement of the tarsal ligaments and fractures in the tibia, two metatarsals, and the great toe," Andrew LaMarche began as Bo glared at her right leg, encased in what looked like pieces of beach furniture fastened together with Velcro. "Your car has been towed to a facility that specializes in the sale of spare parts. The frame was bent. You totaled it, Bo." His face paled at the words. "You could easily have been killed."

"I think that was the idea," Bo muttered. "So who *was* that creep?"

LaMarche walked to the window and clasped his hands behind his head, stretching. "There was no identification on the body," he said. "It could be anybody. The police are trying to establish his identity through fingerprints, but there's nothing to prove that man had anything to do with the deaths of Samantha Franer or Cynthia Ganage. What it looks like," he turned to face Bo but fastened his gaze on the roses instead, "is just some guy with a personal vendetta against you. A 'fatal attraction' is the term Detective Reinert used. You live in a rather bohemian area, Bo." He looked up warily. "Without knowing it you may have engaged the warped attention of—"

"Oh, come *on*!" Bo snapped, incredulous. "Out of the

blue a total stranger smashes into my home *after* cutting my brake lines, chases me through a tropical storm and comes after me with a knife in a sea cave because I live in a bohemian neighborhood? That's a plot straight out of a right-wing guide-book for women. I suppose Cynthia Ganage asked for it, too. She had the gall to make a lot of money and lease her own suite of rooms in a posh hotel. And Samantha, of course, would still be alive if only her mother had known her place and stayed at home instead of getting a part-time job. No matter what brutal, vicious thing happens, it's really some woman's fault. Is that it?"

Andrew LaMarche sat in a wicker wing-chair that squeaked under his weight. "I only said the police have hypothesized—"

"The police can't *spell* 'hypothesized,' " Bo yelled, lurching to stand and then sitting back on the bed as a sharp pain exploded in her right leg. A picture formed briefly in her brain. The stranger, his wet, wispy hair the color of chewing gum under a school desk. His eyes barely blue, almost clear. Vacant as glass. "That *thing* out there on the cliffs was Samantha's killer. Eva said he might have . . . changed, after knowing he killed Samantha."

"Changed?" LaMarche rubbed the stubble on his chin. "Changed how?"

"He might have been transforming into a . . . a serial killer. It has something to do with power. First, sexual power over little children. And then murder."

"Ganage, and then you, right? I'm not disagreeing with Dr. Broussard's train of thought, Bo. I suspect she's on to something. But there's not a shred of evidence to support such a contention. Moreover, Dr. Broussard cannot be called to advance her theory in court because the court doesn't know she's here. And even if she did, there's really nothing in her theory that exonerates Paul Massieu. The whole city's on a witchhunt, edgy over the Satanism thing. Paul is demonstrably a member of a group whose beliefs are not routinely taught from pulpits. The human race is only an eyelash away from a past framed in barbarous superstition, Bo. When they're scared they want a scapegoat. No judge is going to release Paul Massieu today. It's just not going to happen."

"Why can't they scapegoat the creep with the knife?" Bo argued. "He looked demonic to me."

"Because nobody knows about him. Massieu's visible, different, barely speaks English. Add to that the fact that he was living without benefit of marriage with a woman who committed suicide the same day her daughter's rape was made public. What would you think, Bo?"

"What I wouldn't think," Bo said while gingerly edging to her feet, "is that any set of facts, in any situation, suggests the existence of a horned mastermind on little goat feet."

"It's not the mythological details so much as a projection of otherness," LaMarche continued, wincing in sympathy as Bo stood. "It's the Other that matters. People are prone to persecute anybody who can be identified as Other. Paul has been identified. Getting him out of that isn't going to be easy."

"I intend to give it my best shot," Bo told a space just above the doctor's head. "Will you drive me to my apartment? I need to get ready for the hearing."

"Martin found a packed bag," LaMarche said, "and brought it to you, along with two dozen whole wheat rolls. Estrella and Henry are preparing breakfast. Shall we?" He stood, held his arm to her, and bowed slightly in a display of courtesy so genuine Bo felt like crying.

"Andy," she grinned, "have I told you that I'm growing fond of the way you talk?"

"I'm honored," he answered.

Downtown San Diego's steeply pitched streets gleamed in post-storm sunlight as Henry Benedict found a parking lot close to the criminal courts building. Urban jacarandas, planted in cement tubs and elegantly fenced, appeared to be lavender balloons lining the street.

"Do I look okay?" Bo asked Estrella from the back seat where her right leg sprawled and throbbed in its canvas splint.

"You look great, and the crutches are an interesting accessory," Estrella replied. "I don't understand what you're so nervous about. Everything's under control, even if Paul isn't released today. Hannah's safe and doing well with Eva. She's talking again. It may take a while longer to free Paul. Quit worrying."

As Bo hopped around the corner from the parking lot, sweating from the exertion required by the crutches, she saw them. The black-clad crew from the street in front of St. Theresa's Church, their number quadrupled. Their placards less literary.

"San Diego Says No to Satan," one declared. The woman carrying it, sixtyish in theatrical makeup and red high-top sneakers, seemed to take personal pride in her poster. Her eyes sparkled like a child's.

Bo's favorite was one that botched a traditional exorcism. "Get Thee Behind Me, Satan," it commanded, "the Lion of Judy Casts Thee Out!"

"What in hell is the Lion of Judy?" Henry Benedict whispered as they ran the gauntlet of demonstrators.

"It's supposed to be Judah." Bo grinned. The carrier of the errant sign glowered beneath a cap advertising beer brewed in Colorado. Bo was grateful for the moment. It would be a while, she thought, before she was likely to smile again.

Solon Gentzler paced inside the lobby door in a rumpled three-piece suit. He looked like a teddy bear in a mortician's costume.

"LaMarche phoned and told me what happened last night," he said, furthering the cause for canonization of the ever-proper pediatrician. "I'm glad you're all right. But right now I need to speak with you privately."

Estrella and Henry nodded and moved toward the building's smudged brass elevator doors. In the lobby of a criminal court building, Bo realized as Gentzler pulled her behind a dusty silk ficus tree bent over a row of newspaper machines, the scent of floor wax could not overcome a mustier scent of despair. In the crowd a prostitute wearing revealingly torn shorts conferred with a woman attorney in Brooks Brothers gray. A Mexican couple struggled to read the English building directory, and then bowed their heads when the man's blunt finger found the courtroom they were looking for.

"Cuatro," he pronounced sadly, "numero cuatro." The woman began to cry.

A thousand stories. All terrible.

Oh, no. Not now, Bradley. Ignore everything but the reason you're here.

"Eva Broussard also phoned me this morning," Solon Gentzler explained quickly. "She says that Hannah has begun to speak again and wanted to know if there were any way for Hannah to testify in Paul's behalf without falling into the hands of the Department of Social Services."

"No!" Bo exclaimed. "There's a petition in place. I filed it myself. She'd be seized by the bailiff and taken away the minute her identity became known."

"I told Broussard as much," Gentzler went on. "Hannah's testimony that Samantha told her somebody named Goody raped her would only be hearsay, anyway. Not admissible. Nothing can be gained by exposing Hannah to the court. I just wanted to get your feel for the idea. I *could* stall this thing, ask for a later date based on new evidence. Are you sure you want to go through with this, Bo? With public interest as high as it is, the best we can hope for is manageable bail and a quick trial date. It can't help Paul."

"I want to go through with it," Bo answered. "It's for me now. And Hannah. And a guy named Patrick who just might need a job in a few months. Let's do it!"

Criminal Court Number Seven was oak-paneled and brightly lit as Bo hobbled to the long table facing the bench. A metal sign on the broad, high desk said JUDGE ALBERT GOSSELIN.

"Who's Gosselin?" Bo asked Solon Gentzler as she sat and pushed her crutches under the table.

"Antioch Law School, graduated in '76. A Quaker, sits on the National Prison Reform Board, collects quilts as a hobby. He's a dream-come-true, but I'm afraid it won't help us today."

Bo glanced at the tiered seats behind her. Estrella and Henry, smiling. Reporters with notepads. Rombo Perry and Martin St. John in dark suits, looking like 1950s jazzmen. Andrew LaMarche, resplendent in pinstripes and vest, a gold collar pin gleaming under the most conservative tie Bo had seen west of Tulsa. Madge Aldenhoven entering through the double doors at the back of the courtroom, accompanied by a bleak man in tan gabardine whom Bo recognized from his picture in the reception area of her office building. The director of San Diego County's Department of Social Services. Bo felt a tissue-thin glacier spread beneath her skin. Madge had brought in the big dog for the kill.

Solon Gentzler grinned at a group following Madge. An older couple and a woman with masses of sandy curls identical to his own.

"My folks, my sister," he told Bo. "I told them what you were going to do; they came down to lend support. There's some pressing business to attend back in L.A. this afternoon, so I'll be leaving as soon as the hearing's over. But no matter what happens, Bo, the ACLU is behind you. Nationally, if necessary."

Paul Massieu, handcuffed and in the blue polyester uniform of the jailed, was brought in, followed by the black-robed judge.

"All rise," the bailiff roared. "The Honorable Judge Albert Gosselin presiding."

Bo smoothed her green skirt with sweaty palms as the prosecuting attorney called Dr. Andrew Jacques LaMarche, attending physician to Samantha Franer at the time of her death, to testify. From the stand LaMarche listed his credentials without looking at Bo, and then quietly described the injuries that had killed a little girl.

A representative of the San Diego Police Department outlined its case against Paul Massieu, mentioning at one point its official discomfort with the accused man's membership in a group known to hold unusual beliefs.

"Objection!" Solon Gentzler boomed. "The man's personal beliefs are not at issue . . ."

Bo was certain his voice could be heard in Denver, and equally certain that an impassioned speech had been planned for precisely this moment.

"Sustained," the judge replied briskly, dashing all hope of oratory.

Solon Gentzler took his seat, sighing.

"I call Barbara J. Bradley," the prosecuting attorney announced, and Bo summoned a picture of Lois Bittner in Frye boots, smiling. It was time to do this. Others were doing it—movie stars, novelists, publishers, and TV personalities—all throwing off secrecy and demonstrating to a misanthropic public that people with psychiatric disorders had been right there all along. That people with psychiatric disorders differed from people with diabetes only in the body part affected. Bo wanted to join them. *Would* join them, now.

"You may testify from your seat if reaching the stand presents a problem," Judge Albert Gosselin noted as Bo pulled her crutches from under the table and stood awkwardly.

"No, I'll take the stand," Bo answered. The only way. Would Bernadette Devlin do this with her back to a crowd? Never.

Madge Aldenhoven's gaze, benign and phony, followed Bo like a tracking device. The DSS director seemed to be asleep.

"It is the opinion of San Diego County's Child Protective Services," Bo pronounced after describing herself and her credentials, "that Paul Massieu represents a danger to children."

Remember to breathe, Bradley. Here it comes.

"His release into the community at this point would constitute warrantless endangerment of our own children."

Bo had said what she was ordered to say. Madge Aldenhoven's smile was small and perfect.

"You may cross-examine," Albert Gosselin told the defense attorney.

"I defer to co-counsel of record, Solon Gentzler," the defense attorney said as Gentzler stood and strolled toward Bo. At the last-minute question in his eyes Bo merely nodded.

"Ms. Bradley," he began, "is it not true that you suffer from a psychiatric disorder known as manic-depressive illness, and that you have in fact been hospitalized for your own protection due to this illness, which can distort your perceptions of reality?"

"That is true," Bo said.

"And is it not also true that you are not currently taking any of the medications routinely prescribed for the control of symptoms connected to this illness?"

"Yes."

"Your Honor," Solon Gentzler turned toward the judge. "I have no further questions, and ask that the testimony of this witness be stricken from the record on the basis of the witness's history of mental illness."

Bo's eyelids felt metallic, her lungs flattened by the weight of her blouse. She'd wanted to do this. It was her choice. Facts that did nothing toward the restoration of normal breathing. A silence in the room collapsed upon itself like a soundless gasp, and then began to expand.

"Ms. Bradley appears perfectly competent to me," Albert Gosselin answered. "Denied. Unless there's any redirect, you may step down, Ms. Bradley."

None of the lawyers had further questions.

Bo inhaled deeply and heard the rush of air like a choir in her ears. Twenty years of shame and fear, a legacy of vicious superstition extending back to prehistory, had fallen away at her words. Out of the ancient closet, she'd joined the others, the pioneers who would make a world free of psychiatric stigma. And whatever the consequences, it felt like triumph. Her words hadn't helped Paul Massieu, given Gosselin's denial. But they had defeated a bureaucracy at its own game and released their speaker from an invisible constraint worse than any straitjacket. In the front row of seats Andrew LaMarche's eyes glowed with a fierce pride. In the back, Madge Aldenhoven pursed her lips and leaned to whisper something to her companion. Bo heard Bach's Toccata and Fugue in D in her head as she regained her seat at the table. Pipe organ. All stops out.

"If there is no further testimony . . ." the judge began as Dar Reinert appeared at the rear doors, carrying something in an evidence bag. Quickly he approached the prosecuting attorney.

"Detective Reinert has produced unexpected evidence critical to these proceedings," the prosecuting attorney noted, standing. "May we approach the bench?"

"It's a videotape of somebody in a clown suit with Samantha in the cave," Reinert whispered in Bo's ear as the attorneys flocked before the judge. "We found it in the creep's car right behind where you tossed yours. Could be Massieu, if there's anything to this Satanist conspiracy thing. You don't wanna see what's on that tape."

Five minutes later a puzzled assemblage watched as the

bailiff put the tape into a VCR brought into the courtroom. On the television screen above the VCR someone in a polka-dot clown costume and smiling mask fondled a living Samantha Franer. Bo gasped at the scene. The child beneath the crystalline curls was alive, moving, smiling. The same child Bo had seen motionless and cold on an operating table. In the taped scene the little girl's unease at the man's groping hands was overcome by her delight at the sparkling lights, the candy he offered her, the balloons and trinkets. There was no sound on the tape, but Bo could almost hear the tinnily reproduced theme from *Sesame Street*. As the pale hands began to pull at Samantha Franer's blue corduroy shorts, Albert Gosselin directed the bailiff to freeze the action. Paul Massieu, his handcuffed hands held tightly against his broad chest, was sobbing.

"If the man's features are never discernible throughout this event," the judge growled at Reinert, "there is no point in subjecting ourselves to this horror. Is the face ever visible?"

"No," Reinert answered.

"But the man is obviously not Paul Massieu," Solon Gentzler began. "He's three inches shorter and—"

"A distortion caused by the camera angle," the prosecuting attorney interjected. "There's no way . . ."

Bo's head felt buoyant, her eyes full of light. The creature in the clown suit had died last night, his brain smashed to inactivity by thundering surf. The tide had turned. That leprous soul was gone. And now she would free the man who would be Hannah Franer's father, who would stand between Hannah and this nightmare.

"Your Honor," Bo grinned broadly, ignoring courtroom protocol, "did you get a look at Paul Massieu's right hand?"

Expectation filled the silent room as every eye memorized the scene before them. A pervert in a clown's costume, pulling with hungry hands at the clothing of a blond little girl. Each hand below the costume sleeves bearing five fingers, clearly visible on the screen. Then every head turning to Paul Massieu, his black eyes still wet with tears. Slowly he spread his clenched hands for all to see the right one, scarred and bent. Missing its little finger.

Thirty minutes later Bo led Paul Massieu to a wall phone

in the hall outside Criminal Court Number Seven, and gave him the number of a studio cottage in Del Mar. A cottage where he could go freely as soon as he'd gotten his clothes and effects from the jail, signed innumerable forms, and returned his blue uniform.

"Eva!" she heard him begin, *"je suis libre."*

And you're free, too, Bradley. About time.

As her friends waited in a cluster, Bo approached Madge Aldenhoven and her guest. Solon Gentzler, his parents and sister, followed.

"Well, Madge?" Bo broke the ice. "What now?"

Aldenhoven's fake smile had died. "I've known all along there was something wrong with you, Bo. Your unfortunate grandstanding here has only—"

"I scarcely see anything wrong with the courage and dedication Ms. Bradley has brought to the performance of her duties in this case," a voice boomed. "I'm Barry Gentzler, by the way." The elder Gentzler directed his remarks to the man in tan gabardine. "The Americans with Disabilities Act precludes any government agency from discharging an employee on the basis of medical disability. I feel safe in assuring you that the American Civil Liberties Union will take deep interest in any punitive action directed at Ms. Bradley as a result of her courageous disclosure here today. Our interests, as you undoubtedly know, have been known to reach the Supreme Court."

The DSS director inspected his knuckles. "There will be no punitive action." He smiled. "Ms. Bradley is one of our most valued employees."

Bo had never seen Madge Aldenhoven turn quite this unbecoming a shade of green.

"All right!" Rombo Perry whooped from the clustered group, clasping his hands over his head like the winner of the fight. "We won!"

Chapter 30

Bo lounged comfortably on a sand chair beneath a robust palo verde whose spidery limbs still boasted yellow spring blooms. In the setting Anza-Borrego Desert sun, the little flowers seemed constructed of buttery paper. She divided her time between admiration of the desert's flora and perusal of a book on the Hudson River artists. The California desert light, she decided, was simply not on a par with that of the Hudson Valley. No moisture from which those rainbow refractions might spin. Still, the desert had its own magic. Accessible only in closeup. A verity well documented by one of Bo's favorite artists, Georgia O'Keeffe. Grabbing her sketchbook and pastels, Bo concentrated fiercely on the creation of a single palo verde blossom, borne on shaded, dancing winds.

"Petals on a wet, black bough?" Andrew LaMarche quoted Ezra Pound interrogatively, flinging himself on the ground beside her after an hour of strenuous Frisbee-chasing with Paul and Hannah. Mildred lay on a blanket in the sparse shade at Bo's head, eyeing the numerous surrounding cholla cactus plants with enmity. The pediatrician had earlier extracted over thirty of the barbed cholla spines from the pads of her right front paw.

"Something like that," Bo agreed. "Pound spent thirteen years in a psychiatric facility, you know. Privately I think of him as an uncle."

"My favorite poet," LaMarche insisted. "Are we really going to roast Hershey Bars over a campfire?"

"Of course! This camping trip is Hannah's party. No camping party is complete without S'mores. Except you roast the marshmallows. The Hershey Bars melt by themselves from the heat of the marshmallows, squashed between graham crackers. It's ambrosia; trust me."

Andrew LaMarche continued to exude skepticism as he rose to help Estrella and Martin St. John unload firewood from Henry's truck, parked beside the rented jeep that had brought the rest of them through trackless dry washes. The little canyon selected by Paul for their campsite provided shelter from the wind and a spectacular eastern exposure. Already a vanishing sun gilded the layered, rubble-strewn hills with coppery light that quickly spread to lavender, gray-brown, black. Eva Broussard, in a plaid flannel shirt, jeans, and moccasins, stood at the canyon's mouth, looking east. In the shifting light the Indian woman seemed to have sprung up from what lay beneath her feet, like one of the chollas, or catclaws, or silvery smoke trees whose eerie metallic sound in the night wind always reminded Bo of tinsel. Struggling to her feet, Bo hobbled on crutches through the sand to Eva's side.

"It's only been ten days since Samantha's death," Eva said. "And yet it seems a very long time."

"The desert does that," Bo responded, watching a particularly purple rock cloak itself in a color like ashes. "Out here things rearrange themselves somehow. It's hard to describe—like a place where the truth is free to walk in your mind. It scares some people."

"I love it!" Eva smiled and turned to face Bo. "And of course you would put it so aptly." Her gaze grew somber. "You have risked your livelihood and, finally, your life in order to help Hannah. Why did you risk so much, Bo? What makes you do what you do?"

Bo balanced on one leg and stretched her crutches toward the color-washed hills. "Who knows?" she grinned. "I have risk built into my chemistry. Any day," she braced herself again, "may bring fears beyond anything real life can produce. It provides a somewhat larger perspective, maybe. Or it may merely be a pitiably adolescent need to defy authority."

"*Merde*," Eva said with conviction. "You're an exceptional person, 'with a mind that nobleness made simple as a fire.' "

Bo felt every freckle on her face resist the furious blush raging there. "Yeats," she acknowledged the compliment, "describing Maud Gonne." It occurred to her that her friends must have spent the last week holed up at a seminar on poetic imagery.

"Yes," Eva Broussard said with finality. "An Irish heroine."

As they strolled toward the ring of stones that would contain the campfire, Bo changed the subject. "I still don't get what made this John Litten the monster he was," she mentioned, making sure that Hannah was out of earshot. "When the police finally identified him through navy records using his fingerprints, his IQ scores turned out to be above average. He excelled in navy training programs. Even though he came from some impoverished South Carolina backwater, he had every chance to make something of himself. Instead he used his mind to destroy the most beautiful—"

"You've answered your question," Eva interrupted, watching Hannah as the child listened to Rombo Perry tell for the fourth time the story of a wonderful new puppy named Watson who would soon come to live with Rombo and Martin, and who would certainly play Frisbee. "It's difficult for many, especially Americans, to accept, but not every person is born with identical potential. In John Litten's case, something absolutely essential was missing. Not intelligence, but a sense of his own beauty. That inner self that is capable of seeing its own beauty reflected in other living things. Something so basic it defies description, but without it we get John Litten."

"But isn't there treatment, some training or medication . . . ?"

Eva Broussard sighed as the desert valley was lost in darkness. "It's not a psychiatric problem, Bo. It's beyond that. Maybe a century from now we'll know what it is—a mutant chromosome, or specific brain inadequacy. For now such creatures fall by default to the analysis of philosophy. They're simply evil."

The whispered word drifted and then vanished in desert darkness as Estrella helped Hannah to light the fire with a torch of dried sage. Its pungent odor filled the air like incense.

"I'm starving!" Paul Massieu bellowed happily. "Do we eat now?"

As Bo pulled her sand chair close to the fire, Paul grabbed Hannah and held her laughing over his head. From a new gray sweatshirt her grieving beads hung, gleaming in the firelight. The third of the set was pinned to Bo's jacket. As Rombo and Henry Benedict showed Andrew LaMarche how properly to load hot dogs on green oak sticks gleaned from the mountains before them, Hannah ran from Paul to Bo's side. A falling star arced faintly across the darkening sky.

"Did you see that, Bo?" Hannah asked, wide-eyed. "Do you think it's the silver people? Do you think they'll come here? What do you think they are, Bo? Paul says people have seen them here before."

"I've heard that, too," Bo answered, hugging the little girl. "And what I think they are is something like shadows we see in our mind. They're not real, but then they're not *not* real. And that's what I think, Hannah, besides thinking you're about the bravest, prettiest, smartest kid in the whole, entire desert!"

Hannah giggled and glanced at Bo's sketchbook on the ground.

"Can I see your picture, Bo?" she asked. "What is it? It looks like a flower, but it looks like a straw mask, too, all by itself in the wind. Can I have it, Bo? What is it?"

"You may have it, Hannah." Bo grinned and ruffled the golden hair. "Because it's us. It's the Last One Left."

money
postage
sterCard.
only the
p. Date
Zip
tax.
632